THE TRIAS OF MAIMONIDES /
DIE TRIAS DES MAIMONIDES

STUDIA JUDAICA

FORSCHUNGEN ZUR WISSENSCHAFT
DES JUDENTUMS

HERAUSGEGEBEN VON
E. L. EHRLICH UND G. STEMBERGER

BAND XXX

WALTER DE GRUYTER · BERLIN · NEW YORK

THE TRIAS OF MAIMONIDES /
DIE TRIAS DES MAIMONIDES

JEWISH, ARABIC, AND ANCIENT CULTURE
OF KNOWLEDGE /

JÜDISCHE, ARABISCHE UND ANTIKE WISSENSKULTUR

EDITED BY
GEORGES TAMER

WALTER DE GRUYTER · BERLIN · NEW YORK

♾ Printed on acid-free paper which falls within the guidelines of the ANSI to ensure permanence and durability.

ISBN-13: 978-3-11-018399-3
ISBN-10: 3-11-018399-4

Bibliographic information published by Die Deutsche Bibliothek

Die Deutsche Bibliothek lists this publication in the Deutsche Nationalbibliografie; detailed bibliographic data is available in the Internet at <http://dnb.ddb.de>.

Printed in Germany
Cover Design: Christopher Schneider

Table of Contents / Inhaltsverzeichnis

Der arabische Kontext / Arabische Kultur

Einleitung

von

Georges Tamer
Universität Erlangen-Nürnberg

Der vorliegende Band versammelt die Beiträge eines internationalen Kongresses, der vom 7. bis zum 11. Juli 2004 an der Universität Erlangen-Nürnberg stattfand. Der 800. Todestag von Maimonides war weltweit Anlass für zahlreiche Veranstaltungen, auf denen er gewürdigt wurde. Unser Interesse richtete sich besonders darauf, sein Werk als Paradigma für einen fruchtbaren Kulturaustausch im Mittelalter zu präsentieren. Diesem Vorhaben entspricht auch, wie sich die einzelnen Beiträge unterschiedlichen Aspekten des maimonidischen Werkes nähern.

Mūsā Ibn Maimūn erblickt zwischen 1135 und 1138 – die Forschung ist sich über sein Geburtsdatum nicht einig – als Sohn eines jüdischen Richters im andalusischen Córdoba das Licht der Welt. Seine jüdische Identität stellt sich zweifelsohne als maßgeblicher Faktor seines Lebens dar. Die jüdische Umgebung, in der Maimonides aufwächst und wirkt, ist jedoch auch Teil eines weiteren politischen und geistigen Kontexts, der vom Islam geprägt ist. Sein Leben lang steht er zu diesem Kontext in einem engen Verhältnis produktiver Spannung. Religiös-politisch motivierte Repressionen der Almohaden (*al-muwaḥḥidūn*, das heißt die Bekenner der Einheit Gottes) gegen Nichtmuslime zwingen 1148 die Familie des Maimonides, Córdoba zu verlassen und erst 1158/1159 nach Jahren, die in der Forschung als „dunkel" gelten, nach Fez im heutigen Marokko überzusiedeln. Es wird berichtet, dass Maimonides dort zum Schein zum Islam konvertierte. Zur selben Zeit dürfte der ungefähr zwanzig Jahre alte Moses seine erste längere Schrift verfasst haben, eine Abhandlung über die Logik, die er, wie seine meisten Bücher, auf arabisch schrieb.[1] Vermutlich im Frühjahr 1165 begibt sich die Familie ins Heilige Land, um ein halbes Jahr später nach Ägypten zu ziehen. Nach einem kurzen Aufenthalt in Alexandria kann sich Maimonides 1167–1168 in al-Fusṭāṭ (Alt-Kairo) niederlassen. Er bleibt dort bis zu seinem Tode am 13. Dezember 1204 / 20. Tevet 4965.

1 Herbert Davidson, *Moses Maimonides. The Man and his Works* (Oxford: Oxford University Press, 2005), S. 313–322, äußert seinen Zweifel daran, dass Maimonides diese Schrift verfasst haben könnte.

Vor rigider muslimischer Herrschaft in seiner Heimat geflüchtet, findet Maimonides also letztlich Aufnahme in einem anderen, von einer toleranteren muslimischen Dynastie beherrschten Land. Er verlässt die arabischsprachige Welt nicht. Arabisch ist die Sprache, in der ihm Wissenschaften der Antike vermittelt werden. Durch eine in der vorhergehenden Geschichte beispiellose Übersetzungsbewegung, die sich hauptsächlich vom achten bis zum zehnten Jahrhundert abspielte, wurden besonders durch christliche Gelehrte zahlreiche Schriften verschiedener Wissensgebiete wie Philosophie, Medizin, Mathematik, Astronomie, Astrologie, Musik, Agrikultur und Geheimwissenschaften aus dem Griechischen – in vielen Fällen über das Syrische – ins Arabische übertragen. Da die weitreichende Übersetzungsbewegung nicht nur durch das Engagement der Vermittler zustande kam, sondern auch von breiten Gesellschaftsschichten über alle religiösen, konfessionellen, ethnischen und sozialen Grenzen hinweg getragen wurde, dürfte sie tief verwurzelte Bedürfnisse und Tendenzen in der abbasidischen Gesellschaft reflektieren. Eine Vielfalt von antiken wissenschaftlichen Schriften trug maßgeblich zur Entstehung eines islamischen Kulturkreises bei, an dessen Gestaltung Muslime, Juden und Christen beteiligt waren. Mit der Übertragung antiker und spätantiker Schriften in jenen Kulturraum ging ein Schaffensprozess einher, der es dem mittelalterlichen Arabisch durch die Entwicklung von neuen Begriffen erlaubte, die eingeführten Ideen und Fragestellungen aufzunehmen und ihnen einen wiederum spezifisch arabischen Ausdruck zu verleihen.

Maimonides gehört zu der vornehmlich von Aristoteles und Platon geprägten Epoche mittelalterlicher arabischer Philosophie, die mit ihren Hauptgestalten al-Fārābī, Avicenna und Averroes durch die Bemühung um die Harmonisierung von Religion und Philosophie gekennzeichnet ist. Das bedeutet natürlich nicht, dass diese Philosophen ausschließlich religiöse Themen behandelten. Ihre Schriften sind vielmehr größtenteils den klassischen Gebieten der Philosophie wie der Logik, Ethik und Metaphysik gewidmet, die keinen unmittelbaren Bezug zur Religion haben. Im Mittelpunkt ihres Philosophierens steht jedoch die Berücksichtigung der Lehren ihrer Religion. Die islamische Theologie (*ʿilm al-kalām*) konnte in ihre Bestrebungen, die religiösen Lehren des Islams überzeugend darzustellen und gegen Angriffe von Andersgläubigen und Atheisten zu verteidigen, logische Argumente und philosophische Inhalte schon derart integrieren, dass solche Inhalte die Entwicklung der Theologie fördern konnten. Vor eine ganz andere Herausforderung sahen sich indes die großen muslimischen Philosophen gestellt. Sie sollten im Hinblick auf die Vormachtstellung des religiösen Denkens in ihrer Gesellschaft eine Symbiose von Philosophie und Religion bewirken, die es der Philosophie erlaubte, dem neuen Kontext inhaltlich angepasst zu werden, ohne dass sie von der Religion vereinnahmt würde. Ein besonderes Merkmal der arabischen Philosophie im Mittelalter ist es daher, dass sie sich in einem produktiven Spannungsverhältnis zur Religion befindet.

Maimonides' Beschäftigung mit den philosophischen und medizinischen Schriften der Antike steht keineswegs im Widerspruch zu seinem intellektuellen und religiösen Engagement für die Religion seiner Väter. In Ägypten wird er als Arzt berühmt; er kümmert sich jedoch auch verstärkt um religiöse und rechtliche Fragen seiner Glaubensgenossen. Ob Maimonides zum Oberhaupt aller Juden Ägyptens aufgestiegen ist, kann laut jüngster Maimonides-Forschung nicht mit Sicherheit entschieden werden.[2] 1180 beendet er sein einziges großes Werk auf hebräisch, die *Wiederholung der Torah (Mišneh Torah)*. Es umfasst 14 Bücher, in denen der Autor die gesamte mündliche Überlieferung des Gesetzes in einer neuen Anordnung darstellt.

Die erste Schrift, die Maimonides in Ägypten beenden kann, ist sein großer *Kommentar zur Mischna* (*Kitāb as-Sirāǧ*), in dem er dreizehn Grundlehren des Judentums (*Ikkarīm*) formuliert. Der Kommentar enthält auch eine aus acht Kapiteln bestehende ethische Abhandlung, die sich stark an der besonders von al-Fārābī vertretenen aristotelischen Ethik orientiert. Noch vor 1170 schreibt er das *Buch der Gesetze*, in dem er die 613 jüdischen Ge- und Verbote kommentiert. Sein philosophisches Hauptwerk, *Führer der Unschlüssigen (Dalālat al-ḥā'irīn)*, ist spätestens 1191 entstanden. Es ist, bis auf wenige kurze Briefe und Rechtsprechungen, die letzte und wohl wichtigste Schrift des Maimonides. Auch sie wurde auf arabisch geschrieben.

Das dreiteilige Werk vereinigt Elemente der hebräischen Bibel und der griechischen Philosophie, wie diese in der arabischen Epoche der Philosophie rezipiert wurde. Der *Führer der Unschlüssigen* ist ein jüdisches Buch, das einem arabisch-islamischen Kontext entstammt und davon strukturell und inhaltlich maßgeblich beeinflusst ist. Seinen großen muslimischen Vorgängern folgend bezweckt Maimonides darin, die wesenhafte Einheit von Philosophie und Religion zu demonstrieren. Daher weist er die beobachteten Unterschiede zwischen philosophischen Überzeugungen und biblischen Aussagen dem Bereich der Deutungen zu. In diesem Sinne legt er die biblischen Ausdrücke, die auf Körpereigenschaften Gottes hindeuten, aristotelisch aus, bietet eine naturwissenschaftliche Interpretation der Schöpfungsgeschichte und interpretiert die Vision Ezechiels vom Thron Gottes metaphysisch. Maimonides verneint allerdings die Möglichkeit, dass man positive Aussagen über Gott machen könne. Die Metaphysik wird somit zu einer negativen Theologie, die angesichts der Unbeschreiblichkeit und Eigenschaftslosigkeit Gottes in mystisches Schweigen mündet. Maimonides' Anerkennung der Notwendigkeit negativer Theologie in Bezug auf die Natur Gottes ist eine konsequente Folge seines gläubigen Rationalismus. Dieser manifestiert sich auch in seiner kritischen Haltung gegenüber der bei muslimischen und jüdischen Theologen des Mittelalters geläufigen Art und Weise, in der Existenz der Schöpfung eine Begründung für die Existenz

2 Davidson, ibid., S. 54–57 passim.

des Schöpfers zu sehen. Maimonides' Gegenargument beruht auf der grundlegenden Überzeugung vom radikalen Unterschied zwischen Schöpfer und Geschöpf. Dementsprechend vertritt er die Ansicht, dass die Welt vergehen könne, ohne dass dadurch Gottes ewige Existenz beeinträchtigt würde. Deshalb könne die Existenz der Welt kein Beweis sein für die Existenz Gottes. Diese Auffassung führt in letzter Konsequenz zu einem zweifachen Befreiungsakt: Zum einen wird der Glaube an Gottes Existenz von Zwängen der wissenschaftlichen Beweisführung, die dem Glauben dienen sollte, befreit; zum anderen wird die Erforschung der Natur von der Instrumentalisierung losgelöst, letztendlich nur der Gottesverehrung zu dienen. Der methodische Grundsatz, der den gläubigen Rationalisten Maimonides dabei leitet, könnte folgendermaßen formuliert werden: Wissenschaft treibt man nicht, um Beweise für den Glauben zu finden. Wenn aber ein Gläubiger Wissenschaft treibt, wird diese für ihn zu einer Art Gottesdienst.

In der Nachfolge Aristoteles' bestimmt Maimonides die in der Philosophie angestrebte intellektuelle Vollkommenheit als das höchste Ziel menschlichen Lebens. Aus seiner Sicht gewähren die Torah und die rabbinische Tradition dem Menschen die notwendige Leitung, um dieses Ziel zu erreichen und auch die geeigneten sozialen Bedingungen zu schaffen, die ihm dies ermöglichen. Die muslimischen Philosophen, allen voran Maimonides' verehrter al-Fārābī, betrachten die Philosophie als den Weg zur intellektuellen Perfektion, die auch eine ethisch-religiöse Lebensführung umfasst und vorzüglich in einer Idealgemeinschaft erlangt werden kann. Maimonides folgt ihnen dabei und hält Torah und Philosophie für wesenhaft einig. Deshalb unternimmt er eine rationale Lesart der hebräischen Bibel. Dass er vielleicht mehr Zeit und Energie in rabbinische als in philosophische Studien investierte, stärkte ihn bei der Harmonisierung von Religion und Philosophie. Vermutlich ist ihm gerade dadurch deutlicher geworden, dass beide im Wesen eine homogene Einheit bilden.[3]

* * *

Im Werk des Maimonides verschmelzen drei geistige, voneinander nicht zu trennende Welten: die antike, die arabische und die jüdische. Alle drei werden meisterhaft zu einer Synthese vereinigt, die in derselben Person den Arzt, Philosophen und Rabbiner ausmacht. Seine Auseinandersetzung mit den muslimischen Theologen zeigt außerdem, dass er auch die islamische Theologie gut kennt. Hingegen weiß er offensichtlich über das Christentum nicht viel; von den christlichen Logikern wie Yaḥyā Ibn ʿAdī im Bagdad des zehnten Jahrhunderts hält er wenig. Die geistige Epoche, zu deren großen Gestalten Maimonides gehört, weist ohnehin pluralistische Züge auf. Aus der Begegnung zwischen Antike und Islam hervorgegangen, umfasste sie drei Kulturräume, die jeweils

3 Ebenfalls Davidson, ibid., S. 544–545 und 555.

von einer der drei monotheistischen Religionen geprägt waren. Neben dem umfangreicheren islamischen existierte ein arabisch-christlicher und ein arabisch-jüdischer Kulturraum, wobei alle drei relativ offen füreinander waren und sich gegenseitig beeinflussten.

Die triadische Struktur des Werkes von Maimonides zeigt unmissverständlich, dass religiöse Zugehörigkeit kein Hindernis auf dem Wege von produktiven Kulturbegegnungen zwischen Angehörigen unterschiedlicher Religionen sein muss. Maimonides, der griechische Philosophie und Medizin auf arabisch studiert, verweigert sich diesen Schriften nicht, etwa weil sie von Heiden stammen oder von Andersgläubigen übertragen und kommentiert wurden. Nein, er betrachtet sich selbst als Teil einer Kultur, die verschiedene Religionen und Literaturen umfasst, und beteiligt sich aktiv an ihrer weiteren Gestaltung. Wie bereits erwähnt, verfasst Maimonides die überwiegende Zahl seiner Schriften auf arabisch, in denen er auch Beispiele aus der arabisch-islamischen Literatur verwendet. Meiner Auffassung nach tut er dies nicht nur, weil Arabisch die *lingua franca* jener Zeit war. Vielmehr dürfen wir annehmen, dass er sich seinem arabischsprachigen Umfeld verpflichtet fühlte. Er war ein Gelehrter, der nicht nur konsumierte, was ihm auf arabisch zugänglich war, sondern der auch arabische Schriften jüdischer Prägung schuf. An seinem Werk zeigt sich somit eine hebräisch-arabische Identität, deren Komponenten sich nicht widersprechen, sondern einander ergänzen: Für ihn ist Hebräisch die Sprache des Glaubens, Arabisch die Sprache des Wissens. Die intellektuelle Elite ist im Hinblick auf Maimonides' arabische Schriften insofern doppelt eingeschränkt, als diese im Judäo-Arabischen, das heißt in arabischer Sprache mit hebräischen Lettern, geschrieben sind und damit sowohl Arabern, die die hebräische Schrift nicht lesen können, als auch Juden, die das Arabische nicht beherrschen, verschlossen bleiben müssen. Sollte diese Tatsache im Umkehrschluss nicht etwa eine Aufforderung bedeuten, dass diejenigen, die sich mit Maimonides beschäftigen wollen, beide Sprachen erlernen müssen?

* * *

Der vorliegende Band enthält sechs Teile, deren Einzelbeiträge verschiedene Facetten von Leben und Werk des Maimonides beleuchten. Der erste Teil ist historisch orientiert und behandelt die sozialen und politischen Räume, in denen Maimonides lebte. So geht KLAUS HERBERS auf die historischen Bedingungen, die das jüdische Leben auf der iberischen Halbinsel des 12. Jahrhunderts nachhaltig prägten, ein und stellt sie in einen Zusammenhang mit den religiös-politischen Entwicklungen im Maghreb. NIKOLAS JASPERT beschreibt eine während der Kreuzzüge von politischen Unruhen und Herrschaftswechsel gekennzeichnete Epoche des Heiligen Landes, in dem sich Maimonides zwar nur kurz aufhielt, das für ihn aber aufgrund seiner jüdischen Identität immer von großer Bedeutung war. In der Studie von MARK COHEN wird ein Bild gezeichnet, in dem sich Maimonides' soziales Engagement und intellektuelles Leben zu einem harmonischen Ganzen fügen. Dabei eröffnet die Studie auf der Grundlage von bisher in Teilen unveröffentlichten Quellen aus der Kairoer Geniza nicht nur den Blick auf die Vorgaben im Talmud, sondern auch auf die tatsächliche Praxis in den jüdischen Gemeinden vor Ort.

Der darauf folgende philologisch orientierte Teil hat einen doppelten Charakter. SIMON HOPKINS führt dem Leser eine kritische Sicht auf die Sprachen des Maimonides vor und hebt dabei besondere Merkmale seines arabischen Sprachgebrauchs hervor. Der Beitrag von AHMAD CHAHLANE geht über Maimonides hinaus. Am Beispiel der hebräischen Übersetzung von Averroes' mittlerem Kommentar zur aristotelischen *Rhetorik* präsentiert er Probleme der arabisch-hebräischen Übertragung im Mittelalter, die zu falschen Urteilen führte und die moderne Forschung vor die Aufgabe stellt, hier korrigierend einzugreifen.

Der der jüdischen Welt gewidmete dritte Teil beginnt mit LENN E. GOODMANS Aufsatz, in dem die Zentralstellung der Idee Gottes in der auf moralische und intellektuelle Vollkommenheit ausgerichteten Lebensführung des Gläubigen diskutiert wird. Daran knüpft der Beitrag von GAD FREUDENTHAL an, der das Thema der intellektuellen Vollkommenheit aus dem Blickwinkel der Beschränktheit der menschlichen Natur erörtert und zu dem Ergebnis kommt, dass der Indeterminist Maimonides gute leibliche und geistige Verfassung als Gottes Geschenk betrachtet. Von der Frage geleitet, wie sich die negative Theologie der *Moreh Nevukhim* mit der expliziten Kodifizierung des jüdischen Gesetzes in der *Mišneh Torah* vereinbaren lässt, arbeitet ARYEH BOTWINICK skeptische Motive bei Maimonides heraus, die zwischen beiden Werken eine intertextuelle Brücke schlagen. ALFRED IVRY stellt die Rezeption von Maimonides im Deutschland des 20. Jahrhunderts dar, in dem eine Wissenschaft des Judentums hauptsächlich als Fortschreibung der arabisch-jüdischen Tradition mittelalterlicher Philosophie angestrebt wurde.

Im vierten Teil wird die arabische Welt des Maimonides von zwei Seiten beleuchtet. Zum einen werden einige seiner philosophischen Leistungen in Beziehung zu den Leistungen seiner muslimischen Vorgänger gesetzt. Damit werden die Hauptzüge einer im Mittelalter existierenden islamisch-jüdischen Denkbewegung nachgezeichnet. In diesem Sinne demonstriert OLIVER LEAMAN am Beispiel von Maimonides' *Mišneh Torah* die Entwicklung jüdischen Denkens innerhalb von islamischen Denkstrukturen. HANS DAIBER setzt sich mit Leo Strauss' These von der uneingeschränkten Abhängigkeit Maimonides' von al-Fārābī auseinander und vertritt dabei die differenzierte Ansicht, dass Maimonides al-Fārābī zwar in vielen Punkten folgt, aber sich auch von ihm zu distanzieren weiß. MAURO ZONTA diskutiert die Frage, ob und inwieweit Maimonides Avicennas philosophische und medizinische Schriften unmittelbar oder nur durch die kritische Wiedergabe derselben durch al-Ġazālī und andere Gelehrte kannte. In den Beiträgen von RALPH LERNER und GEORGES TAMER wird die Beziehung zwischen den andalusischen Zeitgenossen Maimonides und Averroes thematisiert. Während Lerner diskutiert, wie jeder der beiden Philosophen in seinem eigenen religiösen Kontext die Philosophie vor der Religion verteidigt, erörtert Tamer die hermeneutischen Prinzipien, denen beide Philosophen bei der Behandlung der heiligen Schriften folgen. Maimonides' großes halakhisches Werk, *Mišneh Torah*, wird von SARAH STROUMSA als Teil eines von der Ideologie der Almohaden geprägten religiös-politischen Umfelds betrachtet. HASAN HANAFI beschreibt Maimonides' Kritik an den muslimischen Theologen in *Dalālat al-ḥā'irīn* als Teil eines von Juden, Christen und Muslimen geteilten andalusischen Modells, das auf der Identität von Offenbarung, Vernunft und Natur basiert.

In den drei nachfolgenden Beiträgen wird ein weniger positiver Aspekt der Auseinandersetzung Maimonides' mit dem Islam dargestellt. Ging die Forschung bisher wie selbstverständlich nur von jüdischen Einflüssen auf die Entstehung des Islam und die Entwicklung seiner Theologie aus, fragen die beiden folgenden Beiträge umgekehrt nach Entwicklungen im jüdischen Denken des Mittelalters, die als Reaktion auf islamische Lehren in einer islamischen Umwelt zustande gekommen sind. Im Beitrag von HARTMUT BOBZIN wird die koranische Auffassung von Muhammads Prophetentum mit Maimonides' Prophetenlehre kontrastiert, in der talmudische Konzeptionen auf islamisch-philosophischer Grundlage interpretiert werden. FRIEDRICH NIEWÖHNER spitzt den Vergleich zu, indem er biblisch fundierte Stellungnahmen von Maimonides und anderen jüdischen Gelehrten zur Prophetie Muhammads präsentiert. Einen weiteren religionsgeschichtlichen Rahmen steckt STEFAN SCHREINERS Darstellung der maimonidischen Kritik an Jesus ab, die weniger an der historischen Person Jesu interessiert als vielmehr von innerjüdischen Debatten bestimmt zu sein scheint.

Im fünften Teil kommt die antike Welt des Arztes Maimonides zum Vorschein. SAMUEL KOTTEK untersucht Maimonides' Kommentar zum ersten Aphorismus des Hippokrates und mithin die theoretischen Grundlagen seines ärztlichen Wirkens. Im Beitrag von GOTTHARD STROHMAIER wird der Galen-Leser Maimonides als ein herausragender Vertreter der arabisch-islamischen Rezeption antiker Wissenschaft vorgestellt.

Zu den Lesern von Maimonides' Schriften gehören schließlich auch christliche Gelehrte. Ihnen ist der sechste und abschließende Teil des vorliegenden Bandes gewidmet. Die vergleichende Studie von MAXIMILIAN FORSCHNER zeigt, wie Thomas von Aquin sich auf den jüdischen Denker bezieht, dabei jedoch das Verhältnis zwischen dem Menschlichen und dem Göttlichen anders auffasst. GÖRGE HASSELHOFF gibt in seinem Aufsatz einen Überblick über die lateinischen Übersetzungen von medizinischen Schriften des Maimonides im 14. und 15. Jahrhundert, um im zweiten Schritt anhand von ausgewählten Beispielen zu zeigen, wie diese Übersetzungen verwendet wurden. Im Beitrag von REIMUND LEICHT wird Johannes Reuchlins Interpretation von *Moreh Nevukhim* diskutiert, die den christlichen Kabbalisten zur Entdeckung einer eigenständigen jüdischen Philosophie brachte.

* * *

Die Konzeption dieses Buches beruht auf der festen Überzeugung von der internen Vielfalt einzelner Bestandteile und Erscheinungen der arabischen, zwar vom Islam geprägten, dennoch bedeutende Komponenten der Antike sowie des Judentums und des Christentums enthaltenden Kultur im Mittelalter, die im Osten begann und sich in Andalusien fortsetzte. Der Orient ist vielgestaltig, ebenso wie seine Religionen und Kulturen. Keine von ihnen kann behaupten, frei von der Wechselwirkung mit den anderen Nachbargrößen zu sein. Diese These darf keineswegs darüber hinwegtäuschen, dass die Beziehungen zwischen den Anhängern der verschiedenen Religionen dort nicht immer friedlich verliefen und seit Jahrzehnten sogar die Form eines folgenreichen politischen und militärischen Konflikts annehmen. Neben den politischen und religiösen Spannungen spielen sich jedoch fast immer Bewegungen aus unterschiedlichen Richtungen ab, die einen regen Kulturaustausch zustande bringen und zur gegenseitigen kulturellen Befruchtung führen. Dies gilt für die Zeit des Maimonides genauso wie für die Gegenwart. Nicht nur die mittelalterliche Epoche der arabischen Kultur als ein Ganzes, sondern auch ihre herausragenden Figuren verdienen daher, jeweils von einer Forschergemeinschaft aus Vertretern der Philosophie, Historie, Islamwissenschaft und Judaistik sowie Kennern des Christlichen Orients untersucht zu werden. Eine angemessene Beschäftigung mit Denkern wie Maimonides kann nur interdisziplinär erfolgen, denn sein Werk reflektiert das „Goldene Zeitalter" der arabischen Kultur, die schon während ihrer Genese durchaus offen stand für geistige Strömungen aus älteren Religionen und Kulturen, deren verschiedene Komponenten sich hier zu einer reichhaltigen Kultursynthese zusammenfügen. Der synthetische Charakter der arabischen Kultur im Mittelalter vermindert keineswegs ihren Wert im Ensemble der Weltkulturen. Ganz im Gegenteil. Denn alle Kulturen – gleich ob sie einander folgen oder gleichzeitig existieren – sind miteinander derart verbunden, dass sie sich gegenseitig speisen.

In unserer immer stärker vom gesteigerten Umlauf von Information und Wissen gekennzeichneten Gegenwart darf die Beschäftigung mit einem mittelalterlichen Denker wie Maimonides nicht nur aus rein historischem Interesse herrühren, sondern muss ebenso aktuelle Fragen des interkulturellen und interreligiösen Austauschs berücksichtigen. Ethnischer, religiöser und kultureller Pluralismus sind längst auch in Gesellschaften, die sich einst als einfaches Gefüge darstellten, zur unumgänglichen Realität geworden. Solche Veränderungen in Gesellschaftsstrukturen beanspruchen, wissenschaftlich derart reflektiert zu werden, dass die geistigen Identitäten ihrer Akteure umfassend beleuchtet werden. Identitäten sind keine fertigen Produkte, sondern prozessual entstandene

Strukturen, deren Wurzeln in früheren Zeiten liegen. Sie sind auf Kontinuität angelegt. Damit Identitäten besser verstanden werden können, müssen ihre Wurzeln und historischen Entwicklungen offen gelegt werden. Vergangenen Verhältnissen können deshalb in diesem Zusammenhang Muster entnommen werden, die bei der Entwicklung von Antworten auf gegenwartsbezogene Fragen förderlich sind. Das arabische Mittelalter, das sich geographisch und historisch auf verschiedene Kontexte erstreckt, in seinen mannigfaltigen Wechselwirkungen sowie in seiner Stellung zwischen der Antike einerseits und dem europäischen Mittelalter und der Renaissance andererseits bietet sich als geeigneter Boden an, um den Verlauf von Prozessen gegenseitiger Befruchtung von Kulturen und Religionen in der Vergangenheit sowie die Möglichkeit und Tragweite von ähnlichen Prozessen in der Gegenwart zu untersuchen.

* * *

Dieses Buch wäre ohne die eingangs erwähnte Tagung nicht zustande gekommen. Sie wurde vom Lehrstuhl für Orientalische Philologie und dem Graduiertenkolleg 516 „Kulturtransfer im europäischen Mittelalter" veranstaltet und mit Mitteln der Deutschen Forschungsgemeinschaft großzügig gefördert. Der DFG gebührt an dieser Stelle unser Dank. Prof. Dr. Hartmut Bobzin, Prof. Dr. Hartmut Kugler, Prof. Dr. Otto Jastrow sowie Mitglieder des Graduiertenkollegs gewährten mir Vertrauen und vielseitige Unterstützung, wofür ich ihnen hier herzlichen Dank aussprechen möchte. Mein Dank gilt ebenfalls Prof. Dr. Almut Bruckstein, Prof. Dr. Mohammed Ait El Ferrane, Prof. Dr. Clemens Kauffmann, Prof. Thomas Philipp, Ph.D., Prof. Dr. Renate Wittern-Sterzel und Dr. Florian Steger für ihre freundliche Mitwirkung. An der umfangreichen Vorbereitung und Durchführung der Konferenz beteiligten sich mehrere Mitarbeiter und Mitarbeiterinnen, von denen ich Frau Jasmin Allousch, Frau Anika Conrad und Herrn Thomas Rotter M.A. dankend hervorheben möchte. Für die sorgfältige und verantwortungsvolle Mitarbeit an der Bereitstellung der vorliegenden Publikation danke ich ebenso Frau Annika Kropf. Schließlich gebührt mein Dank dem Verlag Walter de Gruyter, besonders Herrn Dr. Claus-Jürgen Thornton für freundliche und kompetente Betreuung.

Erlangen, im Juni 2005 Georges Tamer

Introduction

by

Georges Tamer
University of Erlangen-Nürnberg

The present volume collects the contributions to an international congress which took place from the 7th until the 11th of July 2004 at the University of Erlangen-Nürnberg. The fact that 800 years have now passed since the death of Maimonides gave an opportunity for many events in appreciation of him. Our aim here is to present his work as a paradigm for fruitful cultural exchange in the Middle Ages. The individual contributions in this volume also correspond to this goal, with articles covering many different aspects of the thought of Maimonides.

Mūsā Ibn Maimūn was born between 1135 and 1138—research is not in agreement about his birth date—the son of a Jewish judge in Andalusian Córdoba. His Jewish identity was undoubtedly to be the decisive factor of his life. The Jewish surroundings in which Maimonides grew up and worked were but a segment of a wider political and intellectual context deeply imprinted by Islam. It was in this context that he spent his entire life, in productive tension between the constraints of these relations. Religio-politically motivated repression by the Almohads (*al-muwaḥḥidūn*, those who profess of the oneness of God) against the non-Muslims forced the Maimonides family to leave Córdoba in 1148, and in 1158/1159, after years referred to in research as "dark," relocated to Fez in present day Morocco. It is reported that while there Maimonides feigned conversion to Islam. Also at this time the approximately twenty-year-old Moses probably composed his first long work, a treatise on logic that he wrote, like most of his works, in Arabic.[1] It is presumed that in early 1165 the family traveled to the Holy Land and moved again half a year later to Egypt. After a short stay in Alexandria, Maimonides established himself 1167–1168 in al-Fusṭāṭ (old Cairo), where he remained until his death on the thirteenth of December 1204 / twentieth of Tevet 4965.

1 Herbert Davidson, *Moses Maimonides: The Man and his Works* (Oxford: Oxford University Press, 2005), pp. 313–322, expresses his doubts that Maimonides could have composed this text.

Having fled from a rigid Muslim authority in his own country, Maimonides found a home in another, one ruled by a tolerant Muslim dynasty. He did not leave the Arabic-speaking world though, as Arabic was the language in which the sciences of the ancient world were transmitted. In a translation movement unparalleled in previous history, which occurred mainly from the eighth to tenth century, numerous works were brought, especially by Christian scholars, into Arabic from Greek, in many cases through Syriac, in various scholarly subjects including philosophy, medicine, mathematics, astronomy, astrology, music, agriculture and the occult. Since the extensive translation movement did not only consist of the activities of the translators, but was also carried across all religious, denominational, ethnic, and social boundaries by a significant part of society, it is likely to reflect deep-rooted needs and tendencies in ʿAbbāsid society. A diversity of scholarly writings from antiquity significantly contributed to an Islamic culture in the formation of which Muslims, Jews and Christians all participated. Along with the transmission of works from antiquity and late antiquity into Islamic culture, a process of shaping occurred that allowed medieval Arabic, accompanying the development of new ideas, to take these ideas and questions and confer specific Arabic expressions upon them.

Maimonides belongs to the era of medieval Arabic philosophy that was influenced primarily by Aristotle and Plato and which, with its main figures al-Fārābī, Avicenna and Averroes, was known for its efforts at harmonizing philosophy and religion. This does not mean, of course, that these philosophers treated exclusively religious topics. Rather, their writings largely cover the classical areas of philosophy, such as logic, ethics, and metaphysics which are not directly related to religion. However, in the center of their philosophical thinking is the consideration of the teachings of their religion. Islamic theology (*ʿilm al-kalām*), in its attempts to present convincingly the religious teachings of Islam and defend against attacks from those of different faiths and atheists, could integrate logical argumentation and philosophical content in order to promote the development of theology. The great Muslim philosophers, meanwhile, saw an entirely different challenge: in view of the supremacy of religious thought in their society, they had to bring about a symbiosis of philosophy and religion that would allow philosophy to adapt its content to its new context, without being usurped by religion. A distinct characteristic of Arabic philosophy in the Middle Ages was precisely its having been in a relationship of productive tension with religion.

Maimonides' involvement with philosophical and medical texts of antiquity was in no way a contradiction to his intellectual and religious commitment to the religion of his forefathers. In Egypt he became famous as a physician; he concerned himself, however, also with the religious and legal questions of his coreligionists. Whether or not Maimonides became the head of all Jews in Egypt cannot, according to the most recent Maimonides research, be decided with any certainty.[2] In 1180 he finished his single greatest work in Hebrew, *The Repetition of the Torah (Mišneh Torah).* It comprises 14 books in which the author presents the entire oral tradition of the law in a new arrangement.

The first text which Maimonides may have finished in Egypt is his great *Commentary on the Mishna* (*Kitāb as-Sirāǧ*), in which he formulates thirteen basic principles of Judaism (*Ikkarīm*). The commentary also contains an ethical treatise consisting of eight chapters, which is strongly oriented toward the Aristotelian ethics advocated especially by al-Fārābī. Before 1170 he wrote the *Book of Commandments,* in which he comments on the 613 Jewish positive and negative commandments. His main philosophical work, the *Guide of the Perplexed* (*Dalālat al-ḥā'irīn*) appears at the latest in 1191, also written in Arabic. It is the last, excepting a few short letters and juridical responses, and certainly the most important text of Maimonides.

The three-part work combines elements of the Hebrew Bible and Greek philosophy as it was adapted in the Arabic philosophical era. The *Guide of the Perplexed* is a Jewish book that comes out of an Arabic-Islamic context, and is significantly influenced by it in its content and structure. Maimonides follows his great Muslim predecessors in attempting to demonstrate the intrinsic unity of philosophy and religion. He therefore puts the evident differences between philosophical beliefs and biblical statements into the realm of interpretation. In this spirit he interprets the biblical expressions that suggest corporeal attributes of God in an Aristotelian manner, offers a scientific interpretation of the creation story, and construes Ezekiel's vision of the throne of God metaphysically. Maimonides rejects, however, the possibility that one can make positive statements about God. This metaphysics is consequently a negative theology that, in view of the indescribability and lack of characteristics of God, meets God in a mystical silence. Maimonides' acknowledgment of the need for a negative theology in relation to the nature of God is a consequence of his believing rationalism. This also manifests itself in his critical stance in relation to the prevalent position of medieval Muslim and Jewish theologians of seeing in the existence of creation a proof for the existence of the Creator. Maimonides' argument against this is based on his fundamental conviction of there being a radical difference between Creator and creation. Accordingly, he held the view that the world could disappear without impairing the eternal existence of God. This view therefore leads to a twofold act of liberation: firstly, the belief in the existence of God would not require a scientific line of argument as its basis; secondly, the investigation of nature would ultimately be freed from only being used to serve the worship of God. The methodological principle which guided the believer and rationalist Maimonides can be summed up in the following manner: one does not force science to find a proof for belief. When,

---

2 Ibid., pp. 54–57 passim.

however, a believer would practice science, it would become for him a form of worship.

Following Aristotle, Maimonides defines the aspiration to intellectual perfection in philosophy as the highest goal of man's life. In his opinion, the Torah and rabbinic tradition afford humans the necessary guidance to reach this goal, as well as shaping the suitable conditions to make it possible for them. The Muslim philosophers, above all Maimonides' revered al-Fārābī, regarded philosophy as the path to intellectual perfection, which also encompassed a religious-ethical way of life and which, ideally, might be achieved in a perfect society. Maimonides went along with them in this, and held Torah and philosophy to be in essence the same thing. He therefore undertook a rational method of reading the Hebrew Bible. That he perhaps invested more time and energy in rabbinical rather than philosophical studies only strengthened him in his harmonization of religion and philosophy. Presumably it was all the more important to him precisely because he believed that the two form, in essence, a "homogenous unity."[3]

* * *

In the work of Maimonides three intellectual worlds are inseparably melded together: the Ancient, the Arabic and the Jewish. All three of these were masterfully unified in the same person, the physician, philosopher and rabbi. His debate with Muslim theologians shows moreover that he knew Islamic theology very well, whereas he apparently did not know much about Christianity, and did not think very much of the Christian logicians like Yaḥyā Ibn ʿAdī in Baghdad in the tenth century. The intellectual era, in which Maimonides ranks as one of the great figures, already showed pluralistic features. Having emerged from the encounter between antiquity and Islam, it embraced three cultures each of which was imprinted by one of the three monotheistic religions. In addition to the extensive Islamic culture, there also existed a Christian-Arabic and a Jewish-Arabic culture; all three were relatively open to each other and mutually influenced each other.

The triadic structure of the works of Maimonides show irrefutably that religious affiliation did not have to be an impediment in the path of productive cultural encounters between members of different religions. Maimonides, who had studied Greek philosophy and medicine in Arabic, did not refuse these texts either because they came from heathens, or because they had been copied and commented upon by those of other faiths. He regarded himself, rather, as a part of a culture which included different religions and literatures, and in which he himself actively participated in their further formation. As was

3 Also Davidson, ibid., pp. 544–545 and 555.

already mentioned, Maimonides composed the preponderance of his writings in Arabic, and also used examples out of Arabic Islamic literature. In my judgment he did not do this simply because Arabic was the *lingua franca* of his time; we should rather assume that he felt himself to be a part of his surroundings. He was a scholar that did not only take what was available to him in Arabic, but also created Arabic texts of Jewish character. In his work, consequently, there appears a Hebrew-Arabic identity, whose individual components do not contradict but rather complement each other. For him the language of faith was Hebrew, the language of science, Arabic. In regards to Maimonides' texts in Arabic, the intellectual elite is actually doubly challenged, as these texts were written in Judeo-Arabic—that is, in the Arabic language with Hebrew letters—and therefore Arabs who could not read the Hebrew script, as well as Jews who were not in command of Arabic remained closed out. Does this not in fact imply a challenge, as those that wanted to involve themselves with Maimonides would have had to learn both languages?

* * *

The present volume is comprised of six sections, whose articles highlight various facets of the life and work of Maimonides. The first section is historically oriented, and addresses the socio-political realm in which Maimonides lived. To do this, KLAUS HERBERS addresses the historical conditions which indelibly stamped Jewish life on the Iberian peninsula in the twelfth century, and connects them with the religious-political development in the Maghreb. NIKOLAS JASPERT describes an era in which the Holy Land during the Crusades was marked by political instability and change of leadership which, although he had only stayed for a short period was of great importance for Maimonides due to his Jewish identity. In the study of MARK COHEN, a picture is painted in which Maimonides' social engagement and intellectual life join together to form a harmonious whole. This article which is based on sources from the Cairo Geniza previously unpublished in part, not only sheds light on the Talmudic teachings but also on the actual practice of the local Jewish communities.

The ensuing philologically-oriented section has a two-fold nature. SIMON HOPKINS shows the reader in a critical way the languages of Maimonides and highlights the particular features of his Arabic linguistic usage. The entry from AHMAD CHAHLANE steps away from Maimonides. Taking as an example the Hebrew translation of Averroes' middle commentary on Aristotle's *Rhetoric*, he presents the problems of Arabic-Hebrew transmission in the Middle Ages, which led to many incorrect judgments—and charges modern research with the task of taking corrective action.

The third section, dedicated to the Jewish world of Maimonides, begins with LENN E. GOODMAN's essay, in which the centrality of the idea of God is discussed in relation to the manner in which believers guided by moral and intellectual perfection led their lives. Tied in to this question is the article by GAD FREUDENTHAL, in which the theme of intellectual perfection is discussed from the perspective of the limitations of human nature. Freudenthal comes to the conclusion that Maimonides, the indeterminist, regarded a good physical and mental constitution as a gift from God. Coming from the question of how the negative theology of the *Moreh Nevukhim* can be in agreement with the explicit codification of Jewish law in the *Mišneh Torah,* ARYEH BOTWINICK points out themes of skepticism in Maimonides, which form an intertextual bridge between the two works. ALFRED IVRY depicts the reception to Maimonides in twentieth-century Germany, in which *Wissenschaft des Judentums* was aimed primarily at continuing the Jewish-Arabic tradition in medieval philosophy.

In the fourth section, the Arabic world of Maimonides is highlighted from two sides. On one side, some of the philosophical achievements of Maimonides are looked at in relation to the achievements of his Muslim predecessors. Using this, the main thread of a movement of Islamic-Jewish thought that existed in the Middle Ages is traced. In this spirit OLIVER LEAMAN demonstrates, using as his example Maimonides' *Mišneh Torah,* the development of Jewish thought within an Islamic structure of thought. HANS DAIBER deals with Leo Strauss' thesis of the unqualified dependence of Maimonides on al-Fārābī, and offers a modified opinion on it: While Maimonides does follow al-Fārābī in many respects, he also distances himself from him. MAURO ZONTA discusses the question of whether and how much Maimonides knew the philosophical and medical writings of Avicenna, directly or through critical rendering of them by al-Ġazālī and others. In the entries from RALPH LERNER and GEORGES TAMER, the connections between the Andalusian contemporaries Maimonides and Averroes are explored. While Lerner discusses how each philosopher defended philosophy from religion in their respective religious contexts, Tamer discusses the hermeneutical principles that each of the philosophers applied to the Holy Scriptures. Maimonides' great halakhic work, the *Mišneh Torah,* is looked at by SARAH STROUMSA as a part of the religious-political environment imprinted by the ideology of the Almohads. HASAN HANAFI describes Maimonides' critique of Muslim theologians in *Dalālat al-ḥā'irīn* as part of a shared Andalusian Jewish, Christian, and Muslim model based on the equivalence of revelation, reason, and nature.

In the three following articles, a less positive aspect of the relationship of Maimonides with Islam will be presented. If up to this point research had regarded it almost a matter of course that Judaism influenced the development of Islam and its theology, the two following contributions conversely ask how Jewish thinking during the Middle Ages developed as a response to Islamic teachings in an Islamic environment. In the article by HARTMUT BOBZIN, the Koranic perception of Mohammed's prophecy is contrasted with Maimonides' teachings on prophets, which were formed using Talmudic conceptions interpreted on an Islamic philosophical basis. FRIEDRICH NIEWÖHNER more closely sharpens the comparison, by presenting scripturally-based opinions of Maimonides and other Jewish scholars on the prophecy of Mohammed. In another religious-historical frame STEFAN SCHREINER depicts Maimonides' criticism of Jesus, one which is less interested in the historical person of Jesus than, as it seems, to have been conditioned by an inner-Jewish debate.

In the fifth section, the ancient world of the physician Maimonides is brought into view. SAMUEL KOTTEK examines Maimonides' commentary on the first aphorism of Hippocrates, and consequently the theoretical basis of his medical practice. In the article from GOTTHARD STROHMAIER Maimonides, the reader of Galen, is presented as a prominent example of the Arabic-Islamic reception of ancient science.

Finally, Christian scholars were also among the readers of Maimonides' texts, and to them the sixth and final section of this volume is dedicated. The comparative study of MAXIMILIAN FORSCHNER shows how Thomas Aquinas related to the Jewish thinker, while at the same time, however, understanding the relationship between the human and the divine differently. In his essay, GÖRGE HASSELHOFF gives an overview of the Latin translations of the medical texts of Maimonides in the fourteenth and fifteenth centuries and, using selected examples, shows how these translations were used. In the entry from REIMUND LEICHT, the discussion is about Johannes Reuchlin's interpretation of the *Moreh Nevukhim,* which brought the Christian Kabbalists to the discovery of an independent Jewish philosophy.

* * *

This book was conceived with the firm conviction that there is internal diversity in the components that make up medieval Arabic culture which began in the East and continued in Andalusia. Although it was strongly shaped by Islam, antiquity and the medieval cultures of Judaism and Christianity played important roles in forming its individual elements and features. The Orient, like its religions and cultures, takes on many shapes and forms. None of them can claim to be free of reciprocal relations with their other great neighbors. This assumption in no way denies that relations between adherents of the various religions did not always go smoothly, and for decades have even taken the form of very consequential political and military conflict. Along with the political and religious tension, however, there are almost always tendencies from different sides that bring about active cultural exchange and lead to cultural cross-fertilization. This applies to the time of Maimonides as much as to the present. Not only the medieval era of Arabic culture as a whole, deserves to be studied therefore, but also their prominent figures respectively, by a community of researchers, as exponents of philosophy, history, Islamic studies, Jewish studies and scholars of Eastern Christianity. An adequate study of a thinker like Maimonides can only be carried out interdisciplinarily, since his work reflects the "Golden Age" of Arabic culture. This culture was during its formation entirely open to streams of thought from older religions and cultures, the various components of which joined to form a rich cultural synthesis. This composite character of medieval Arabic culture in no way diminishes its worth in the cast of world cultures; far from it. All cultures—whether they succeed one another or exist at the same time, are in such a manner connected, that they stimulate one another.

In our present world, characterized by an ever-growing environment of information and knowledge, the study of a medieval thinker like Maimonides should not arise from purely historical interest, but should take into consideration questions of intellectual and interreligious exchange. Whereas society was once simple, ethnic, religious and cultural plurality long ago became an inevitable reality. Such changes in the structure of communities demand an in-depth scholarly reflection of the intellectual identities of those who brought them about. Identities are no finished products, but structures that have developed in a process and whose roots are in the past. They have a tendency towards continuity. To better understand their identities, their roots and historical developments must be laid bare. Therefore, in this context past circumstances can offer patterns that are useful in forming answers to present-day questions. The Arabic Middle Ages which geographically and historically has various contexts in its multifaceted reciprocity and its placement between antiquity on one end and the European renaissance on the other offers itself as an appropriate place for examining the processes of the mutual inspiration of cultures and religions in the past, as well as the possibility and impact of similar processes in the present.

* * *

This book would not have come into being without the previously mentioned conference, which was organized by the Chair for Oriental Philology and the *Graduiertenkolleg 516*, "Cultural Exchange in the European Middle Ages," and generously funded with the help of the *Deutsche Forschungsgemeinschaft*. Our thanks go out here to the DFG. Prof. Dr. Hartmut Bobzin, Prof. Dr. Hartmut Kugler, Prof. Dr. Otto Jastrow and the participants in the *Graduiertenkolleg* afforded me their trust and all-around support, for which I would like to express my heartfelt thanks. My thanks go as well to Prof. Dr. Almut Bruckstein, Prof. Dr. Mohammed Ait El Ferrane, Prof. Dr. Clemens Kauffmann, Prof. Thomas Philipp, Ph.D., Prof. Dr. Renate Wittern-Sterzel and Dr. Florian Steger for their kind involvement. In the extensive preparation and realization of the conference many people contributed, of whom I would like to mention with thanks: Ms. Jasmin Allousch, Ms. Anika Conrad and Mr. Thomas Rotter M.A. For the painstaking and thorough assistance in the preparation of this publication I would also like to thank Ms. Annika Kropf. Finally, the Walter de

Gruyter Verlag has my thanks, especially Dr. Claus-Jürgen Thornton, for his kind and able supervision.

Erlangen, June 2005 Georges Tamer

Historische Räume

Die Iberische Halbinsel im 12. Jahrhundert

Streiflichter auf die politisch-kulturelle Geschichte eines „Grenzraumes"

von

Klaus Herbers

Universität Erlangen-Nürnberg

I. Einleitung

Er hüte lieber Kamele für die Almoraviden als die Schweine von Alfons VI., soll al-Muʿtamid, der Taifenherrscher von Sevilla, gegen Ende des 11. Jahrhunderts angeblich gesagt haben.[1] War es eine Wahl zwischen Scylla und Charybdis, die für zahlreiche Taifenherrscher im muslimischen Spanien des 11./12. Jahrhunderts anstand? Die Geschichte des muslimischen Spanien unterschied sich im 12. Jahrhundert deutlich von der Zeit zuvor. Dieser Umbruch wird eindrücklich dokumentiert durch die Lebensgeschichte des Maimonides, dessen Todesdatum (1204) den Anlass zu einem Kongress und dem vorliegenden Sammelband bot. Er wurde 1135 in Córdoba geboren, seine Familie floh aber – wie es häufig heißt – schon bald, 1148, aus dieser Stadt, um sich später in Fez und ab 1165 in al-Fusṭāṭ niederzulassen. Dort entfaltete Maimonides vor allem seine geistigen Aktivitäten, die jedoch von seiner andalusischen Zeit beeinflusst wurden, denn obwohl er den größten Teil seines Lebens außerhalb der Iberischen Halbinsel verbrachte, scheint ihn seine Herkunft stark geprägt zu haben. Musste die Familie fliehen? Die äußere Geschichte des Maimonides steht anscheinend den geläufigen Vorstellungen von den Zuständen auf der Iberischen Halbinsel entgegen, denkt man an die Schlagworte von Austausch und *convivencia* der verschiedenen religiösen und ethnischen Gruppen. Dieser Austausch und die Bedeutung des Zusammenlebens waren lange Zeit gerade innerhalb Spaniens umstritten,[2] jedoch schien sich in den letzten Jahrzehnten

---

1 Vgl. Joseph F. O'Callaghan, *A History of Medieval Spain* (Ithaca, London: Cornell University Press, 1975 = 1983), S. 208. Der Text folgt im Wesentlichen der Vortragsform, für kritische Hinweise danke ich den Diskussionsteilnehmern, weiterhin besonders Dr. N. Jaspert.

2 Vgl. zur Kontroverse zwischen Américo Castro und Claudio Sánchez Albornoz die zusammenfassenden Bemerkungen bei Ludwig Vones, *Geschichte der Iberischen Halb-*

eine gewisse Beruhigung und nüchterne Einschätzung in dieser Frage anzubahnen. Inzwischen schlagen jedoch die Wellen in den aktuellen Diskussionen wieder höher, nachdem Schriftsteller wie Juan Goytisolo den muslimischen Beitrag zur Genese Spaniens mehrfach hervorgehoben haben, während andere Autoren wie Serafín Fanjul diesen neuerdings schlichtweg leugnen.[3] Unter Geschichtswissenschaftlern scheint sich allerdings ein Konsens dahingehend anzubahnen, dass nur eine Differenzierung verschiedener Phasen und Räume angemessene Einsichten erbringt. Ein Blick auf die Person des Maimonides und die Rahmenbedingungen in seiner Zeit fügt sich auch in diese größeren Diskussionszusammenhänge ein. Wie war die Situation zu seiner Zeit? Welche Voraussetzungen hatten sich vielleicht gegenüber der zuvor liegenden Phase verändert?

Wenn das Lebensschicksal des Maimonides maßgeblich – so eine Ausgangsthese – von den veränderten politischen und geistigen Rahmenbedingungen bestimmt war, so sind diese ohne eine eingehende Berücksichtigung des Werks hier kurz zu umreißen. Mit Blick auf Maimonides ist in spezifischer Weise zu fragen, welche Voraussetzungen das Wirken von Personen wie Maimonides behinderten, erleichterten oder erschwerten. Dafür habe ich das Leitmotiv von Grenzen, Grenzräumen und Grenzüberschreitungen gewählt. Darunter sind die Grenzen im übertragenen Sinne, wie zum Beispiel zwischen den Religionen, ebenso gemeint wie die sich ändernden geographisch-politischen Grenzen.[4] Diese betrafen nicht nur das muslimisch und das christlich beherrschte Spanien, sondern zugleich die Neustrukturierungen unter verschiedenen muslimischen

---

insel im Mittelalter (711–1480). Reiche, Kronen, Regionen (Sigmaringen: Thorbecke, 1993), S. 12–17. Weiterhin Walther L. Bernecker, „Die Vertreibung der Juden aus Spanien. Zur Diskussion über das ‚Dekadenz-Syndrom'", in *Spanien und die Sepharden. Geschichte, Kultur, Literatur*, ed. Norbert Rehrmann und Andreas Koechert (Romania Judaica 3; Tübingen: Niemeyer, 1999), S. 27–42. Vgl. als Überblick Yaacov Ben-Chanan, „Juden im maurischen und christlichen Spanien (711–1492) – Chancen und Scheitern zwischen unterschiedlichen Kulturen", in ibid., S. 7–26; zu den Folgen auch die weiteren Beiträge in diesem Band.

3 Vgl. hierzu zusammenfassend Werner Altmann, „Die beiden Spanien. Eine historische Debatte geht weiter", in *Terror oder Toleranz? Spanien und der Islam*, ed. Raimund Allebrand (Bad Honnef: Horlemann, 2004), S. 181–194 mit Bezug auf die Beiträge von Juan Goytisolo (der behauptete, nicht die arabische Conquista, sondern die christliche Reconquista sei das Grundübel der spanischen Geschichte) (ibid., S. 183–184), sowie die neuerliche Gegenposition von Serafín Fanjul, der die Geschichte von al-Andalus mit seinen politischen und kulturellen Hervorbringungen als einen Mythos entlarven möchte (ibid., S. 185–188; vgl. auch bei Altmann weitere bibliographische Angaben zur aktuellen Diskussion in Spanien).

4 Zu Fragen der Grenzen und des Grenzbegriffs fand im Herbst 2004 eine Tagung in Erlangen statt; die Tagungsakten erscheinen unter dem Titel: *Grenzräume und Grenzüberschreitungen im Vergleich. Osten und Westen im mittelalterlichen Lateineuropa*, ed. Klaus Herbers und Nikolas Jaspert (Europa im Mittelalter. Abhandlungen und Beiträge zur historischen Komparatistik; Berlin: Akademie Verlag [in Vorbereitung]).

Herrschaftsträgern in al-Andalus und Nordafrika. Ich beginne mit einem kurzen Abriss zum frühen Lebensweg des Maimonides (II), skizziere dann die politischen Rahmenbedingungen von den Taifenreichen über die Almoraviden- zur Almohadenherrschaft (III), um schließlich danach zu fragen, wie sich die Stellung nichtislamischer Religionen veränderte und welche Bedeutung vielleicht die in diesem Zusammenhang meist vernachlässigten Interventionen verschiedener christlicher Reiche und Gruppen im Rahmen der so genannten Reconquista für den frühen Lebensweg des Maimonides besessen haben könnten (IV).

II. Biographische Skizze

Handbücher und Nachschlagewerke zu Maimonides stellen meist vor allem dessen Werk und geistige Entwicklung, weniger die äußeren Umstände in den Vordergrund.[5] Beides hängt aber zusammen. Der Vater unseres Protagonisten, Rabbi Maimon, ein Spross der Daviden, gehörte zu einer der bekanntesten und ältesten Familien Córdobas, wo er als oberster Richter eine hohe Stellung einnahm. Sein Sohn Moses ben Maimon, der vor allem seit der Renaissance unter dem Namen „Maimonides" bekannt ist, wurde am 14. Nissan, das heißt am 30. März 1135 oder 1138,[6] in Córdoba geboren. Wo das Haus der Familie stand, ist unbekannt, vermutlich in der so genannten *judería*, dem jüdischen Viertel, wie dies in den meisten multireligiösen Städten in dieser Zeit im muslimischen Spanien üblich war. Jedenfalls hat man ihm hier in jüngerer Zeit auf der Plaza Tiberias ein Denkmal errichtet.[7]

Seine Mutter war wohl die Tochter eines Metzgers, angeblich hatte Rabbi Maimon sie geheiratet, weil er im Traume dazu aufgefordert worden sei. Sie starb jedoch bei der Geburt ihres Sohnes Moses. Der Vater heiratete erneut,

5 Die folgenden Daten basieren vor allem auf den Darstellungen von Abraham Heschel, *Maimonides. Eine Biographie* (Judentum in Geschichte und Gegenwart. Eine Schriftenreihe 1; Berlin: Reiss, 1935; Nachdruck Neukirchen-Vluyn: Neukirchener Verlag, 1992) und Ilil Arbel, *Maimonides. A Spiritual Biography* (New York: Crossroad, 2001), besonders S. 11–42; vgl. weiterhin die einleitenden Bemerkungen von Judit Targarona Borrás (Übersetzerin), *Maimonides. Sobre el Mesías. Carta a los judíos del Yemen. Sobre astrología. Carta a los judíos de Montpellier* (Barcelona: Riopiedras, 1987), S. 13–76. Vgl. zum Werk und zur geistesgeschichtlichen Einordnung die weiteren Beiträge des vorliegenden Sammelbandes. Zu seiner Wirkung im lateinischen Westen vgl. jetzt vor allem Görge K. Hasselhoff, *Dicit Rabbi Moyses: Studien zum Bild von Moses Maimonides im lateinischen Westen vom 13. bis zum 15. Jahrhundert* (Würzburg: Königshausen & Neumann, 2004).

6 Zur Frage des Geburtsjahres siehe Anm. 1 des Beitrages von Stefan Schreiner in diesem Band, S. 323.

7 Vgl. die Abbildung in Ramon Menéndez Pidal, *Historia de España*, Band 8 (Madrid: Espasa-Calpe, 1998), S. 598.

diesmal wohl die Tochter einer bedeutenden jüdischen Familie Córdobas. Aus dieser Verbindung ging ein weiterer Sohn, David, hervor, um den sich der junge Moses intensiv kümmerte. Rabbi Maimon erzog seine Söhne wohl zu Hause. Die Welt- und Religionsvorstellungen seines Vaters, der Gott als ein liebendes Gegenüber, nicht als eine intellektuelle Abstraktion ansah, dürften auch Maimonides geprägt haben. Außerdem geriet Maimonides mit Rabbi Joseph ibn Migash in Kontakt, der ihn stark prägte, so wie er schon seinen Vater beeinflusst hatte. Zu den Lehrgebieten zählten Astrologie, Astronomie, Mathematik, Geometrie, Philosophie, Recht und Rhetorik sowie weitere Fächer. Sprachlich bewegte man sich vor allem im Arabischen und Hebräischen. Damit erhielt Maimonides Zugang zu diversen prägenden Schriften, über die in anderen Beiträgen dieses Bandes noch weiter gehandelt wird. Die große Wissbegier und die frühen Erfolge des jungen Maimonides mögen teilweise aus der Rückschau und der Erinnerung etwas überhöht dargestellt worden sein.

Dann erfolgte 1147/1148 ein Einschnitt: Córdoba wurde von den Almohaden erobert. Änderten sich die Lebensbedingungen so sehr, dass die Familie aus Córdoba floh? Verschiedene Ansichten der Forschung liegen hier im Widerstreit. Während manche Gelehrte eine Flucht aus Córdoba annehmen,[8] wird dies von anderen als unbelegt abgelehnt.[9] Allerdings besteht Einigkeit darin, dass die Familie zunächst wohl in al-Andalus blieb. Sollte die Familie Córdoba verlassen haben, so führte sie das Exil zunächst nach Ansicht einiger Autoren wohl nach Almería, wo sie mindestens vier Jahre lang, bis 1151, geblieben sein soll.[10] In diese Zeit gehört möglicherweise die Begegnung und Freundschaft zwischen Maimonides und Averroes, der einige Jahre älter war und sich hier wohl im Exil befand, weil er mit politischen Instanzen in Konflikt geraten war. 1151 oder später verließ die Familie Almería vielleicht wieder und zog umher. Die zweite Frau des Rabbi Maimon starb, und dieser war nun mit seinen Söhnen und zwei Töchtern allein.[11]

Manches über diese Lebensphase im südlichen Spanien zur Zeit der Almohaden ist erst aus den späteren Werken des Maimonides allgemein erschließbar, denn immer wieder verweist Maimonides auf die „Hispania" als sein Ursprungsland. Zu den Werken, die in dieser Zeit entstanden, gehörten wahrscheinlich die Einführung in die Logik, seine Schriften über den Kalender, seine Untersuchungen zu den *geonim*, den Gelehrten des frühen Mittelalters, sowie der Beginn seiner *Mišneh Torah*, die er erst 1180 in Alt-Kairo abschloss.[12]

---

8 Heschel, *Maimonides* (wie Anm. 5), S. 18; Arbel, *Maimonides* (wie Anm. 5), S. 22–24.

9 Targarona Borrás, *Maimonides* (wie Anm. 5), S. 32–33.

10 So Arbel, *Maimonides* (wie Anm. 5), S. 23.

11 Eine dieser Töchter hieß vielleicht Miriam, wie die Geniza-Dokumente nahe legen, vgl. Arbel, *Maimonides* (wie Anm. 5), S. 24.

12 Vgl. zum Werk zum Beispiel Friedrich Niewöhner, *Maimonides. Aufklärung und Toleranz im Mittelalter* (Kleine Schriften zur Aufklärung 1; Heidelberg: Schneider et al., 1988), besonders S. 10ff. Zum Jubiläumsjahr ist eine Fülle von Literatur erschienen, die auch

Wir wissen nicht, ob der Druck auf die jüdische Bevölkerung weiter zunahm, aber schließlich wurde eine Schiffsüberfahrt in das nördliche Afrika anvisiert. Dies soll 1159 geschehen sein.[13] In Nordafrika lebte die Familie bis etwa 1165/1166. Die Situation der Juden war hier zwar grundsätzlich mit derjenigen in al-Andalus vergleichbar, aber offensichtlich waren die Möglichkeiten besser, als Jude weiterhin seinem Glauben treu zu bleiben, wenn auch mit gewissen Einschränkungen und Kompromissen. Maimonides wurde jedoch 1165 nach dem Zeugnis des Abū l-ʿArab ibn Moisha arrestiert, nach seiner angeblichen kurz zuvor erfolgten Konversion zum Islam. Nach seiner Freilassung ging die Familie daraufhin nach Ceuta, um ein Schiff nach Palästina zu nehmen. Von dort übersiedelte sie wenig später nach Alexandria, dann nach al-Fusṭāṭ. So weit die äußeren Daten der ersten Lebenshälfte des Maimonides. Erst ab 1166 scheint das seit der frühesten Jugend bewegte Leben in ruhigere Bahnen geraten zu sein.

III. Taifenreiche, Almoraviden und Almohaden

Warum diese Unrast, diese Wanderjahre einer eingesessenen jüdischen Familie? Was hatte sich auf der Iberischen Halbinsel oder in Córdoba seit dem 11. Jahrhundert verändert? Waren die neuen politischen Strukturen für Nichtmuslime so problematisch? Blickt man in diverse Lexika zur Geschichte Córdobas, so findet man sich sehr schnell mit einem merkwürdigen Befund konfrontiert: Fast überall endet die Geschichte der Stadt mit dem Kalifat 1031/1035. Auch einer der jüngeren Aufsätze über Córdoba als kulturelles Zentrum behandelt auf nur einer Seite die Zeit nach 1035,[14] und der *Encyclopedia of Islam* genügen wenige Zeilen.[15] Zwar war die große Zeit Córdobas 1031/1035 beendet, jedoch verlor die Stadt nicht vollends an Bedeutung. Nunmehr übernahmen die Familien der Ǧahwariden sowie der ʿAbbādiden in Córdoba die Herrschaft. Zwar verlagerte sich im Tal des Guadalquivir das Schwergewicht deutlich zum Meer hin, nach Sevilla, jedoch ist mit David Wasserstein daran festzu-

---

jeweils Bemerkungen zu Biographie und Werk bietet, hier aber nicht angemessen gewürdigt werden kann, vgl. vor allem jedoch jetzt die Studie von Hasselhoff, *Dicit Rabbi Moyses* (wie Anm. 5), S. 22ff.

13 Vgl. die Werke in Anm. 5.

14 Robert Hillenbrand, „Medieval Córdoba as a cultural centre", in *The Legacy of Muslim Spain*, ed. Salma Khadra Jayyusi, Band 1 (Leiden, New York, Köln: Brill, 1994), S. 112–135, hier S. 127–128. Dort wird irrig die Almohadenherrschaft ab 567/1172 angesetzt. Von den Lexika vgl. man nur den Eintrag des *Lexikon des Mittelalters*, Band 2 (München, Zürich: Artemis, 1986), Sp. 230–234, wo zwei Zeilen die Zeit zwischen dem Ende des Emirates und der Stadt unter christlicher Herrschaft charakterisieren (Sp. 231).

15 *The Encyclopedia of Islam.* New edition, ed. Clifford Edmund Bosworth, Bd. 1–12 (Leiden, New York, Köln: Brill, 1960–2004), s.v. „Ḳurṭuba".

halten, dass die Zeit der *„Party-Kings"* in Spanien zu den Epochen zählt, die in kultureller Hinsicht besonders hervorzuheben sind.[16] Dies gilt prinzipiell auch für das 11. Jahrhundert in Córdoba. Die Situation in den Städten des muslimisch dominierten Spanien und die Veränderung durch den Herrschaftswechsel ist insgesamt differenziert zu sehen.[17]

Die unabhängige Position der einzelnen Taifenreiche wurde jedoch zunehmend kritisch, als die christlichen Reiche des Nordens ihre Reconquista-Bemühungen intensivierten, gegen Ende des 11. Jahrhunderts sehr erfolgreich nach Süden vorstießen und damit auch die Grenzen nachhaltig veränderten. Ein wichtiger Wendepunkt war sicherlich die Eroberung Toledos 1085.[18] Alfons VI. von Kastilien-León bezeichnete sich entsprechend auch als *imperator Toletanus.* Manchmal nannte er sich auch Kaiser der beiden Religionen, weil Muslime in seinem Herrschaftsbereich verblieben waren, oder er machte durch weitere Titel Ansprüche auf die gesamte *Hispania* geltend. Vielleicht plante Alfons VI. sogar, eine Art Schutzherrschaft über den gesamten Süden aufzurichten und durch eigene Amtsträger verwalten zu lassen.[19] Verhindert wurde die Ausfüh-

---

16 David Wasserstein, *The Rise and Fall of the Party-Kings. Politics and Society in Islamic Spain 1002–1086* (Princeton, N.J.: Princeton University Press, 1985), zusammenfassend S. 294–295.

17 Vgl. zu den muslimischen Städten dieser Zeit auch: Leopoldo Torres Balbás, *Ciudades hispanomusulmanas* (2 Bände; Madrid: Instituto Hispano-Árabe de Cultura [1988?]); weiterhin den Sammelband: *Simposio internacional sobre la ciudad islámica. Ponencias y Comunicaciones* (Zaragoza: Institución Fernando el Católico, 1991) (allerdings eher zum Städtebau und weniger zur inneren Organisation); vor allem zur Frühgeschichte nach der westgotischen Zeit vgl. *Genèse de la ville islamique en al-Andalus et au Maghreb occidental. Actes recueillis et préparés par Patrice Cressier et Mercedes García Arenal* (Madrid: Casa de Velázquez, 1998); zur inneren Struktur: Christine Mazzoli-Guintard, *Villes d'al-Andalus. L'Espagne et le Portugal à l'époque musulmane (VIIIe–XVe siècles)* (Rennes: Presses universitaires de Rennes, 1996) (mit Kartengrundrissen der verschiedenen Städte).

18 Vgl. zur Eroberung Toledos und den Folgen: Ludwig Vones, „Reconquista und Convivencia. Die Könige von Kastilien-Leon und die mozarabischen Organisationsstrukturen in den südlichen Grenzzonen im Umkreis der Eroberungen von Coïmbra (1064) und Toledo (1085)", in *Die Begegnung des Westens mit dem Osten. Kongreßakten des 4. Symposiums des Mediävistenverbandes in Köln 1991 aus Anlaß des 1000. Todesjahres der Kaiserin Theophanu,* ed. Odilo Engels und Peter Schreiner (Sigmaringen: Thorbecke, 1993), S. 221–242; zum Zusammenleben: Jean-Pierre Molénat, „Mudéjars et mozarabes à Tolède du XIIe au XVe siècles", in *Revue du Monde Musulman et de la Méditerranée* 63/64 (1992), S. 143–153; idem, „Tolède, fin XIe–début XIIe siècle: le problème de la permanence ou de l'émigration des musulmans", in *De Toledo a Huesca: Sociedades medievales en transición a finales del siglo XI (1080–1100). Congreso celebrado en Huesca, 21 y 22 de noviembre de 1996* (Zaragoza: Institución Fernando el Católico, 1998), S. 101–111.

19 Die genauen Vorstellungen bleiben etwas unklar, weil der Briefwechsel Alfons' mit Muḥammad b. ʿAbbād al-Muʿtamid, dem Taifenherrscher von Sevilla, erst in einer Chronik des 14. Jahrhunderts überliefert ist und die Forschung bis heute nicht weiß, ob diese Briefe echt sind; vgl. Vones, „Reconquista und Convivencia" (wie Anm. 18), S. 225 mit Anm. 14.

rung in jedem Fall durch die Eroberungen der aus Nordafrika kommenden muslimischen Almoraviden, die nach dem zeitweiligen militärischen Druck Kastiliens auf Sevilla schon 1086 in Südspanien landeten und nach dieser Zeit keine weiteren großen militärischen Erfolge Alfons' VI. mehr zuließen.

Damit kam eine neue Kraft im Süden Spaniens ins Spiel. Schon um 1058 hatte Abū Bakr Eroberungszüge in Nordafrika begonnen. Marrakesch wurde 1070 als künftige Hauptstadt der späteren Herrschaft gegründet. Abū Bakrs Vetter, Yūsuf ibn Tašufīn (1061–1106), verdrängte Abū Bakr vom Oberbefehl und überließ diesem nur noch einige saharische Gebiete. Yūsuf gewann zwischen 1071 und 1082 West-Algerien, 1073 nannte er sich schon *amīr al-muslimīn*. Ab 1082 erreichten die Hilferufe einzelner Taifenkönige Spaniens die Almoraviden. Diese erfolgten besonders deshalb, weil der Druck durch König Alfons VI. auf einige wichtige Orte zu groß wurde, so auf Sevilla, Granada oder Badajoz.[20]

Nach diesen Hilferufen setzte der Führer der Almoraviden, Yūsuf ibn Tašufīn, viermal, 1086, 1088, 1090 und 1102/1103 nach Südspanien über. Er schlug Alfons 1086 bei al-Zallāqa, 1091 wurde mehr oder weniger der Rest des muslimischen Spanien erobert, so beispielsweise im Süden die Herrschaften von Málaga und Granada 1090, diejenigen von Sevilla, Córdoba und Almería im Jahre 1091. Nur das Reich von Valencia unter der Herrschaft des Cid und das Reich von Zaragoza blieben von einer Eroberung durch die Almoraviden zunächst verschont.

Die Almoraviden folgten strengen islamischen Reformvorstellungen malikitischer Ausrichtung, die zugleich auch Ansätze zu einer verstärkten Missionierung einschlossen. Es kann nicht Aufgabe eines Historikers sein, die religiösen Vorstellungen der Almoraviden hier im Einzelnen darzustellen. Wichtig erscheint mir jedoch ein Aspekt: Seit den ersten Erfolgen der Almoraviden in Nordafrika wurde zunehmend deutlich, dass bei einer Expansion auf die Iberische Halbinsel der Maghreb und al-Andalus in der Zukunft noch engere Bindungen eingehen würden.

Führte schon die Almoravidenherrschaft im Süden Spaniens dazu, dass bereits jetzt der Druck auf die nichtmuslimischen Bevölkerungsgruppen zunahm?[19] Eine relativ gut dokumentierte Episode scheint dies zu belegen. Mozarabische Christen baten den aragonesischen Herrscher Alfons I. el Batallador (gest. 1134) in einem Brief, in dem sie die Reichtümer Granadas schilderten, zu einer

---

20 Grundlegende Informationen finden sich bei Hans-Rudolf Singer, „Der Maghreb und die Pyrenäenhalbinsel bis zum Ausgang des Mittelalters", in *Geschichte der arabischen Welt*, ed. Ulrich Haarmann (München: Beck, [3]1994), S. 264–322 und 675–682. Vgl. zur allgemeinen Entwicklung und zum Verhältnis von Juden, Christen und Muslimen unter Almoraviden und Almohaden: *El retroceso territorial de Al-Andalus. Almorávides y Almohades. Siglos XI al XIII*, ed. María Jesús Viguera Molíns (Historia de Espana 8/2; Madrid: Espasa Calpe, [2]1998). Darin vor allem Maribel Fierro, „La Religión", ibid., S. 423–546, besonders 523–546.

Befreiungsaktion nach Andalusien aufzubrechen. Alfons zog 1125–1126 mit großer Unterstützung nach Süden, gewann auch mehrere Schlachten,[21] kam aber offensichtlich zu spät. In Granada habe er 1126 dem mozarabischen Führer Ibn al-Qalas vorgeworfen, er habe seine Versprechungen gebrochen. Dieser habe nur geantwortet, ein Überraschungsangriff gegen die Almoraviden sei unmöglich geworden, weil diese inzwischen ihre Truppen gesammelt hätten. Alfons I. kehrte daraufhin zurück, denn die Ausgangslage hatte sich verschlechtert. Schließlich soll Alfons aber 14.000 andalusische Christen aus dieser Gegend im Ebrotal angesiedelt haben. Über die verbliebene Bevölkerung der Mozaraber in al-Andalus wissen wir recht wenig, über Deportationen nach Afrika berichten erst Quellen aus den 1170-er Jahren.[22] Nach den Gutachten (Fatwā) des Großvaters von Averroes, der damals Qāḍī (Richter) in Córdoba war, kann man nur ansatzweise erkennen, dass eine Repression wohl nicht unmittelbar, sondern allenfalls später einsetzte.[23] Durch das Verhalten der andalusischen Mozaraber, das zur Aktion des aragonesischen Herrschers führte, war zwar das Abkommen der *ḏimma*, die gewisse Grundrechte für Anhänger von Buchreligionen vorsah, gebrochen. Andalusien war nach dieser „Befreiungsaktion" jedoch fast nur noch von Muslimen bevölkert, besonders Christen spielten nach Emigrationen oder Konversionen, später auch Deportationen, wohl kaum noch eine Rolle, obwohl alle quantitativen Näherungswerte spekulativ bleiben müssen.[24] Diese Ereignisse und die Widerstände zeigen aber zugleich, dass der Höhepunkt almoravidischer Herrschaft an manchen Orten bereits überschritten war. Offensichtlich war auch das Zusammenleben der Religionen in manchen Gebieten schon in dieser Zeit in eine Krise geraten, ohne dass von einer grundsätzlichen Konfliktsituation die Rede sein sollte.[25]

Schon bald suchte jedoch eine neue Reformbewegung, die der Almohaden, auch auf den südspanischen Raum herrschaftlich auszugreifen. Die Anfänge

21 Allgemein zu den Almoraviden: Vincent Lagardère, *Les Almoravides. Le Djihâd Andalou (1106–1143)* (Montréal, Quebec: L'Harmattan, 1998), S. 81–162, zur Aktion Alfons' I. S. 98–114 mit weiteren Nachweisen und den entsprechenden Quellenangaben.

22 Vgl. unten S. 32 mit Anm. 30 und 31.

23 Vgl. Rainer Oswald, „Spanien unter den Almoraviden. Die Fatāwā des Ibn Rušd als Quellen zur Wirtschafts- und Sozialgeschichte", in *Die Welt des Orients* 24 (1993), S. 127–145, besonders S. 128–131 mit Angabe des Drucks und der quellenkritischen Probleme (S. 128 Anm. 4).

24 Vgl. die verschiedenen Vorschläge der Forschung bei Fierro, „Religión" (wie Anm. 20), S. 524 (mit Nachweisen in Anm. 12–15).

25 Zu den verschiedenen Phasen des Zusammenlebens aus vergleichender Perspektive Richard W. Bulliet, *Conversion to Islam in the Medieval Period. An Essay in Quantitative History* (Cambridge, Mass.: Harvard University Press, 1979), S. 122–125 (mit Schaubildern).

der Almohaden liegen ebenfalls im nördlichen Afrika.[26] Sie propagierten das strikte Bekenntnis der göttlichen Einheit, den Glauben an einen von Gott gesandten Mahdī und forderten einen streng geregelten Islam. Die Gründerfigur, der Berber Ibn Tūmart (gest. 1130), verweist nach Córdoba, denn dort erhielt er eine erste Ausbildung, bevor er nach einer Pilgerfahrt im Irak weiter studierte. Hier wurde er von den Lehren al-Ġazālīs beeinflusst, der die islamische Orthodoxie mit mystischen Strömungen zu vereinen suchte. 1116 kehrte Ibn Tūmart in den Westen zurück, wo er mit Unterstützung seines späteren Nachfolgers ʿAbd al-Muʾmin vor allem gegen die Almoraviden kämpfen wollte. In Marrakesch führte Ibn Tūmart mit malikitischen Rechtsgelehrten ein Streitgespräch, und Ende 1121 proklamierte er sich als Mahdī, als ein von Gott gesandter rechtgeleiteter Herrscher. Die Gefolgschaft nannte sich entsprechend *al-muwaḥḥidūn* oder Almohaden (Unitarier). Nach dem Tod des Ibn Tūmart 1130 folgte ihm ʿAbd al-Muʾmin nach, der durch administrative und militärische Fähigkeiten hervortrat. Die Eroberung Marokkos (1133–1149) und von Marrakesch (1147) führten zum endgültigen Sturz der Almoraviden und zur weiteren Ausbreitung der Almohaden.

Davon war auch al-Andalus betroffen, denn seit der Almoravidenherrschaft waren das muslimische Spanien und der Maghreb äußerst eng aufeinander bezogen. Da die Almoraviden dort in den dreißiger und vierziger Jahren zunehmend Schwierigkeiten gewärtigen mussten, gewann sogar seit den zwanziger Jahren zwischenzeitlich eine neue Generation von Taifenherrschern[27] an Gewicht, so beispielsweise in Córdoba im Januar 1145. Im Mai 1146 erreichten die ersten Kontingente der Almohaden von Nordafrika aus die Iberische Halbinsel und errichteten vor allem im Süden ihre Herrschaft. Zunächst erlangten sie die Macht in Sevilla, Córdoba und anderen wichtigen Städten. Manche Herrschaften leisteten ihnen auch energischen Widerstand, so Stadt und Umland von Murcia. Nach dem Tod des ʿAbd al-Muʾmin (1163), besonders unter Abū Yaʿqūb Yūsuf (1163–1184), verstärkte sich der almohadische Druck, so dass Murcia schließlich 1165 ebenso wie die übrige Levante erobert wurde. 1172 beherrschten die Almohaden alle wichtigen Reiche des noch verbliebenen muslimischen Spanien.[28]

---

26 Singer, „Maghreb" (wie Anm. 20), S. 299–301; María Jesús Viguera Molíns, „Historia Política" in *El retroceso territorial de Al-Andalus* (wie Anm. 19), S. 41–123, hier S. 73–83.

27 Zu dieser zweiten Phase vgl. zusammenfassend Singer, „Maghreb" (wie Anm. 20), besonders S. 298–299 und Viguera Molíns, „Historia Política" (wie Anm. 26), S. 65–72 mit den jeweiligen Nachweisen.

28 Vgl. zum Wirken in Südspanien zusammenfassend Singer, „Maghreb" (wie Anm. 20), S. 302–306 und Viguera Molíns, „Historia Política" (wie Anm. 26), S. 83–111 (mit weiteren Nachweisen) sowie die Karten bei Menéndez Pidal, *Historia de España* (wie Anm. 8), S. 66 und 77.

IV. Religiöser Druck und die Bedeutung des christlichen Spanien?

Lassen sich die Veränderungen im Zusammenleben der drei großen Religionsgruppen noch etwas genauer fassen? Dabei ist es dienlich, das Verhältnis von Muslimen und Christen sowie von Muslimen und Juden zu unterscheiden. Die neuere Forschung bietet zum Zusammenleben von Juden, Christen und Muslimen in der fraglichen Zeit keinen eindeutigen Befund. Der schon erwähnte Zug des Aragonesen Alfons' I. dient oft dazu, die Lebensverhältnisse der mozarabischen Christen in düsteren Farben zu malen, denn manche Deutungen gehen davon aus, dass anschließend die christliche Bevölkerung in al-Andalus weitgehend eliminiert war. Dagegen hat insbesondere Bulliet unterstrichen, dass der rechtliche Status der Christen als *ḏimmīyūns* grundsätzlich nicht angetastet wurde. Christen, die in al-Andalus hätten bleiben wollen, seien nicht vertrieben worden. Die christliche Bevölkerung habe vielleicht sogar zugenommen, weil die Almoraviden christliche Söldnertruppen einsetzten.[29] Wie auch immer man strittige Fragen und rechtliche Bestimmungen beurteilt, Einigkeit besteht darüber, dass unter den Almoraviden insgesamt weniger die Juden als die Christen in die Defensive gerieten. Dies wird zunehmend mit der politischen Konstellation erklärt: Die Almoraviden hätten nur den Druck, den die christlichen Reiche auf sie ausübten, vor allem an die in ihren Herrschaften lebenden Christen weitergegeben. Dennoch habe man den Rechtsstatus der Mitglieder von anderen monotheistischen Religionen grundsätzlich gewahrt, von einem neuen Fanatismus sei keineswegs zu sprechen.

Änderte sich dies unter den Almohaden?[30] Zwar gab es bei der almohadischen Eroberung von Sevilla christliche und jüdische Opfer,[31] aber erste Deportationen – in diesem Fall von Christen – sind erst für 1170 belegt. Wie stand es um die Juden? Von direkten Verfolgungen jüdischer Bevölkerungsanteile zur almoravidischen Zeit ist wenig bekannt. Norman Roth verweist auf eine Aus

29 Vgl. außer Bulliet, *Conversion* (wie Anm. 25), S. 122–125, idem, „Process and Status in Conversion and Continuity", in *Indigenous Christian communities in Islamic lands. Eighth to eighteenth centuries*, ed. Michael Gervers und Ramzi Jibran Bikhazi (Papers in Mediaeval Studies 9; Toronto: Pontifical Institute of Mediaeval Studies, 1990), S. 1–12, hier S. 8; vgl. auch die weiteren Beiträge in diesem Band von Joanne E. McWilliam, „The Context of Spanish Adoptionism: A Review", S. 75–89; Hanna E. Kassis, „Roots of Conflict: Aspects of Christian-Muslim Confrontation in Eleventh-Century Spain", S. 151–161. Ein guter Forschungsüberblick mit neuen eigenen Einschätzungen findet sich in: Fierro, „Religión" (wie Anm. 20), S. 523–546.

30 Zur Beurteilung der almohadischen Religionspolitik vgl. allgemein Fierro, „Religión" (wie Anm. 20), S. 526.

31 Lagardère, *Histoire et société* (wie Anm. 21), S. 194; Fierro, „Religión" (wie Anm. 20), S. 525 mit Anm. 24.

schreitung gegen die Cordobeser Juden im Jahr 1135.[32] Die Situation scheint sich jedoch unter den Almohaden zugespitzt zu haben. Nun standen vor allem die wohl noch vergleichsweise zahlreich verbliebenen Juden stärker unter Druck. Zerstörungen von Synagogen, Verbrennungen hebräischer Bücher, das Verbot, den Sabbat und andere Festtage zu heiligen, sind belegt.[33] Gleichzeitig förderten die Almohaden mögliche Konversionen. Nicht zufällig dürfte Maimonides zu diesem aktuellen Problem in seinem Brief über die Apostasie Stellung beziehen.[34]

Trotzdem bleibt ein Befund auffällig: Auch die Almohaden scheinen das *ḏimma*-System nicht grundsätzlich in Frage gestellt oder abgeschafft zu haben, frühere rechtliche Bestimmungen blieben grundsätzlich erhalten.[35] Die spärlichen Notizen deuten eher darauf hin, dass Verschärfungen in einigen Zonen und zu gewissen Zeiten erfolgten, aber nicht durchgängig implementiert wurden. Der almohadische Druck dürfte jedoch den späteren Angriff Maimonides' auf den Islam im 1172 verfassten Brief an den Jemen erklären.[36]

Waren somit Grenzen zwischen den Religionen in verschiedenen Schüben seit der Almoravidenzeit weiter gewachsen, so führte die sukzessive Eroberung des südspanischen Raumes durch die Almohaden tendenziell auch dazu, dass Juden, Christen oder Muslime mit einer anderen religiösen Ausrichtung sich nach 1147 auch innerhalb des Südens Spaniens dem religiösen Druck durch Auswanderung entziehen konnten. Dies war vor allem deshalb interessant, weil nicht alle Herrschaftsgebiete gleichzeitig unter almohadische Botmäßigkeit gebracht worden waren und damit unterschiedliche Lebensbedingungen existierten.

Der Grenzraum von al-Andalus war jedoch auch – und dies ist mit Blick auf Maimonides bisher meist nicht beachtet worden – von den christlichen Anstrengungen der so genannten Reconquista beeinflusst. Aus dieser Perspektive können auch zur Biographie des Maimonides zumindest einige neue Aspekte und Überlegungen beigetragen werden. Den möglichen Eroberungsplan Alfons' VI. von 1086 hatte ich schon erwähnt, ebenso den Zug von Alfons I.

32 Norman Roth, *Jews, Visigoths and Muslims in Medieval Spain. Cooperation and Conflict* (Medieval Iberian Peninsula 10; Leiden: Brill, 1994), S. 115 mit Anm. 8.

33 Fierro, „Religión" (wie Anm. 20), S. 526 spricht von einer grundsätzlichen Verschärfung zur Almohadenzeit (vgl. auch die weitere reichhaltige Literatur).

34 Ich benutze die spanische Fassung: „Maimonides, Carta sobre la apostasía", in *Cinco epístolas de Maimónides.* Introducción, traducción y notas por María José Cano y Dolores Ferrre (Barcelona: Riopiedras, 1988), S. 9–75.

35 Jedenfalls gibt es keinen Text, der eine Aufhebung der *ḏimma* belegen könnte, vgl. Fierro, „Religión" (wie Anm. 20), S. 526.

36 *Moses Maimonides' Epistle to Yemen. The Arabic Original and the three Hebrew Versions,* ed. Abraham S. Halkin and with an English Translation bei Boaz Cohen (New York: American Academy for Jewish Research, 1952); ich benutze die spanische Übersetzung: Targarona Borrás, *Maimonides* (wie Anm. 5); zur Datierung S. 80–81.

1125–1126 nach Andalusien. Da sich also die Grenzen nicht nur innerhalb von al-Andalus im Zusammenspiel mit dem Maghreb, sondern auch durch die Reconquistazüge der christlichen Reiche ständig verschoben, finden wir in der Folge auch in den so genannten christlichen Reichen eine beachtliche jüdische Bevölkerung, denkt man nur an Toledo.[37]

Für die Familie des Maimonides hat die Forschung bisher rundweg abgelehnt, dass eine Flucht in christliche Reiche überhaupt zur Diskussion gestanden habe. So vermerkt Ilil Arbel: „Rabbi Maimon refused to stay in Córdoba, preferring exile to pseudo conversion. He decided to avoid the Christian lands, where the language and culture were alien to him, and stay as long as possible in Muslim Spain".[38] Und wenig später heißt es: „Rabbi Maimon preferred remaining in Muslim lands, and felt a strong aversion to the Christian lands".[39] Diese apodiktischen Aussagen verkennen jedoch den Wechsel der Herrschaften und der sich stets verändernden Grenzen im so genannten muslimischen Spanien, an dem gerade in der fraglichen Zeit auch die christlichen Herrscher beteiligt waren. Von kastilisch-leonesischer Seite war dies in dieser Zeit vor allem Alfons VII. (1126–1157).[40] Es gab keine religiös homogenen Räume und Reiche. Unter muslimischer Herrschaft lebten Christen, wie Muslime unter christlicher Herrschaft lebten. Und Juden gab es grundsätzlich in allen Reichen.

1146 stieß Alfons VII. über Baeza nach Córdoba, der Heimatstadt des Maimonides, vor, wo damals ein Taifenherrscher regierte, obwohl gleichzeitig ein Almoravide, Ibn Ġāniya, Ansprüche aufrechterhielt. Im Mai 1146 erreichte den christlichen Herrscher ein Hilfegesuch von Abū Ǧa'far b. Hamdīn, der in den lateinischen Quellen Abenhandim oder ähnlich genannt wird.[41] Ende Mai

37 Vgl. den Forschungsbericht zur englischsprachigen Literatur über Parallelgesellschaften bei Robert I. Burns, „Mudejar Parallel Societies: Anglophone Historiography and Spanish Context, 1975–2000", in *Christians, Muslims and Jews in Medieval and Early Modern Spain. Interaction and Cultural Change*, ed. Mark D. Meyerson und Edward D. English (Notre Dame Conferences in Medieval Studies 8; Notre Dame: University of Notre Dame Press, 2000), S. 91–124.

38 Arbel, *Maimonides* (wie Anm. 5), S. 22.

39 Ibid., S. 30.

40 Zu diesem Herrscher und seiner Politik vgl. Bernard F. Reilly, *The Kingdom of León-Castilla under King Alfonso VII (1126–1157)* (Philadelphia: University of Pennsylvania Press, 1998) und zuletzt Manuel Recuero Astray, *Alfonso VII, 1126–1157* (Burgos: Editorial La Olmeda, 2003).

41 „Chronica Adefonsi imperatoris" II cap. 92–108, besonders cap. 105, ed. Antonio Maya Sánchez, in *Chronica Hispana Saeculi XII*, ed. Emma Falque, Juan Gil et Antonio Maya Sánchez (Corpus Christianorum. Continuatio Mediaevalis 71; Turnhout: Brepols, 1990), S. 109–248, hier S. 238–247, besonders S. 246. Vgl. auch die *Anales Toledanos*, ed. Enrique Flórez (España Sagrada 23; Madrid: Sanchez, 1727) und allgemein Recuero Astray, *Alfonso VII* (wie Anm. 40), S. 243; zur schwierigen zeitlichen Rekonstruktion vgl. Reilly, *Kingdom of León-Castilla* (wie Anm. 40), S. 92 Anm. 6 (10.–12. Mai, beziehungsweise 24. Juni).

wurde Ibn Ġāniya von christlichen Truppen besiegt. Alfons VII. zog wenig später triumphal mit seinem Verbündeten Ibn Hamdīn in Córdoba ein, der weiterhin die Stadt beherrschen sollte, nun allerdings als Vasall Alfons' VII. Die Moschee wurde in eine christliche Kirche umgewandelt.

Wichtiger als die nur bis 1148 währende Oberherrschaft Alfons' VII. in Córdoba, die den Alltag in der Stadt wahrscheinlich kaum betraf, ist die von den Maimonides-Biographen meist übersehene Tatsache, dass Almería 1147–1157 unter christlicher Herrschaft stand. Im Zuge des Zweiten Kreuzzugs kam es zugleich zu militärischen Aktivitäten auf der Iberischen Halbinsel, von denen die Eroberung Lissabons 1147[42] und die Einnahme von Tortosa[43] besonders bekannt sind. Neben Tortosa wurde 1147 noch eine weitere Stadt erobert, wohl mit genuesischer Hilfe, wie in einem Bericht von Caffaro *Ystoria captionis Almarie et Tortvose ann. 1147 et 1148* und weiteren Quellen festgehalten ist.[44]

Während der Belagerung von Córdoba 1146 empfing Alfons VII. einige genuesische und pisanische Legaten, die nicht nur aus religiösen Gründen Almería belagern und erobern wollten. Genuesen hatten schon zuvor Razzien gegen Menorca und Almería durchgeführt. Almería gehörte nicht nur zu den ökonomisch wichtigen und prosperierenden Städten am Mittelmeer, sondern

---

42 Vgl. Giles Constable, „The Second Crusade as seen by Contemporaries", in *Traditio* 9 (1953), S. 213–279; idem, „A Note on the Route of the Anglo-Flemish Crusaders of 1147", in *Speculum* 28 (1953), S. 525–526 (Nachdruck in idem, *Religious Life and Thought* [11th–12th centuries], Nr. XI und X [London: Variorum Reprints, 1979]); Ernst-Dieter Hehl, *Kirche und Krieg im 12. Jahrhundert. Studien zu kanonischem Recht und politischer Wirklichkeit* (Monographien zur Geschichte des Mittelalters 19; Stuttgart: Hiersemann, 1980), besonders S. 259–262; Richard A. Fletcher, „Reconquest and Crusade", in *Transactions of the Royal Historical Society* 5th ser. 37 (1987), S. 31–47, besonders S. 43–44; Matthew Bennett, „Military Aspects of the Conquest of Lisbon, 1147", in *The Second Crusade. Scope and Consequences*, ed. Jonathan Phillips and Martin Hoch (Manchester: Manchester University Press, 2001), S. 71–89 (eher zu militär- und technikgeschichtlichen Aspekten); zu Fragen der Legitimation auch Klaus Herbers, „‚Gott will es!' – Christlicher ‚Fundamentalismus' im europäischen Mittelalter?", in *Fundamentalismus. Erscheinungsformen in Vergangenheit und Gegenwart. Atzelsberger Gespräche 2004*, ed. Helmut Neuhaus (Erlanger Forschungen Reihe A Geisteswissenschaften, Band 108; Erlangen: Universitätsbund Erlangen-Nürnberg, 2005), S. 9–40, hier S. 23–27 (mit weiterer Literatur).

43 Vgl. Nikolas Jaspert, „*Capta est Dertosa, clavis Christianorum*: Tortosa and the Crusades", in *The Second Crusade* (wie Anm. 42), S. 90–110, dort S. 93–94 zum Verhältnis von Genua und Katalonien bei den Kämpfen der so genannten Reconquista. Vgl. auch die weiteren Beiträge dieses Sammelbandes, der aber keinen speziellen Beitrag zur Eroberung von Almería enthält.

44 Vgl. Caffaro, *De captione Almerie et Tortuose*, ed. Antonio Ubieto Arteta (Valencia: Anúbar, 1973); *El Cantar de la conquista de Almería por Alfonso VII*, ed. Florentino Castro Guisasola (Almería: Instituto de Estudios Almerienses, 1992) bietet außer der lateinischen Edition eine Übersetzung der auch von Juan Gil (Ed.), „Prefatio de Almeria", in *Chronica Hispana Saeculi XII* (wie Anm. 41), S. 249–267 gedruckten Dichtung. Zu weiteren Quellen vgl. auch oben Anm. 41.

war zugleich ein Zentrum muslimischer Piraten, die den Mittelmeerhandel behinderten. Dies erklärt aus einer weiteren Perspektive, warum sich neben den Genuesen und Pisanern auch Graf Raimund Berenguer IV. von Barcelona am Kriegszug beteiligte. Die Zusammensetzung der Eroberungswilligen zeigt damit gleichzeitig die verschiedenen Interessen am Einfluss im südwestlichen Mittelmeerraum. Dem Katalanen Raimund wurde außerdem genuesische Hilfe für die spätere Eroberung von Tortosa in Aussicht gestellt.[45] Die Eroberung, die ab Mai 1147 vorbereitet wurde, wird in mehreren Quellen, sogar in dichterischer Form, gewürdigt.[46] Demnach dürfte Alfons mit etwa 5000 Kriegern den Angriff begonnen haben. Die Belagerung der Stadt und des Umlandes zog sich durch den Monat September bis Anfang Oktober 1147 hin. Zunächst boten die Bewohner Gelder an, um die Stadt freizukaufen, jedoch verhinderten laut dem Bericht von Caffaro die Genuesen, dass diese Summe akzeptiert wurde. Die Herrschaft übernahmen anschließend Genuesen und Kastilier, obwohl der Genueser Geschichtsschreiber die Akzente etwas anders setzte. Als Vertreter ernannten die Genuesen Otto von Bonovillano und die Kastilier Pons de Cabrera.

Von 1147–1157 stand Almería unter der Herrschaft von Kastilien-León und Genua.[47] Allerdings ist nicht ganz klar, wann die Genuesen ihre Herrschaft aufgaben,[48] und Alfons VII. nannte seine Ansprüche auch *expressis verbis*: „imperante ipso Alfonso Imperatore Toleto, Legione, [...] Almarie", so lautet die Titulatur in einer seiner Urkunden.[49] Die zehnjährige Herrschaft in Almería hatte auch

45 Zu den Interessen an Almería aus den erwähnten übergeordneten, besonders auch wirtschaftlichen Perspektiven, vgl. Blanc Garí, „Why Almería? An Islamic Port in the Compass of Genoa", in *Journal of Medieval History* 18 (1992), S. 211–231; John B. Williams, „The making of Crusade: the Genoese anti-Muslim Attacks in Spain, 1146–1148", in *Journal of Medieval History* 23 (1997), S. 29–53. Vgl. ausführlich zur Vorbereitung und Durchführung José Angel Tapia Garrido, *Historia general de Almería y de su provincia* (3 Bände; Almería: Editorial Cajal, 1981–1986), Band 3: *Almería musulmana I (711/1172)*, 1986, S. 401–433 (mit Verarbeitung lateinischer und arabischer Quellen), sowie weiterhin Reilly, *Kingdom of León-Castilla* (wie Anm. 40), S. 93.

46 „Chronica Adefonsi Imperatoris" (wie Anm. 41), S. 101–106, 244–246. Vgl. ferner „Prefatio de Almeria" (wie Anm. 44), S. 249–267. Vgl. in weiteren Quellen neben Caffaro, *De captione* (wie Anm. 44), die Urkunden Alfons' VII., die bei Reilly, *Kingdom of León-Castilla* (wie Anm. 40), S. 92–97 verarbeitet sind (vgl. auch die Auflistung der Urkunden ibid., S. 323–398).

47 Viguera Molíns, „Historia Política" (wie Anm. 26), S. 69.

48 Vgl. Tapia Garrido, *Historia general de Almería* (wie Anm. 45), Band 3, S. 458, der wahrscheinlich macht, dass die Genuesen sich etwa 1149–1152 zurückzogen.

49 Vgl. zum Beispiel eine Urkunde vom 3. März 1155, zitiert bei Tapia Garrido, *Historia general de Almería* (wie Anm. 45), Band 3, S. 456; vgl. zu den Urkunden Alfons' VII. die Zusammenstellungen von Peter Rassow, „Die Urkunden Kaiser Alfons' VII. von Spanien", in *Archiv für Urkundenforschung* 10 (1928), S. 327–467; 11 (1930), S. 66–137; hierzu die Ergänzungen von Bernard F. Reilly, „The Chancery of Alfonso VII of León-Castilla: The Period 1116–1135 Reconsidered", in *Speculum* 51 (1976), S. 243–261; Manuel Lucas Álvarez, *El reino de León en la Alta Edad Media V: Las Cancillerías Reales (1109–1230)*

deshalb eine andere Qualität als das christliche Zwischenspiel in Córdoba kurz zuvor, weil Alfons VII. die Moschee zur Kathedrale machte und Dominikus, einen Benediktiner, zum Bischof erheben ließ[50]. Wie es scheint, wurden Fragen der kirchlichen Strukturen auch auf dem Konzil von Valladolid 1155 verhandelt, jedenfalls unterzeichnete dort der Bischof von Almería die *Canones*.[51] Allerdings dürften die Almohaden schon ab 1151 versucht haben, Almería ihrer Herrschaft botmäßig zu machen.[52]

Vor dem Hintergrund einer kurzfristigen Herrschaftszeit unter Alfons VII. und anderen christlichen Machthabern am südlichen Mittelmeer wird aber interessant, dass die Familie des Maimonides zumindest von 1148–1151 in Almería geweilt haben soll. Vielleicht war diese christliche Herrschaft dem geistigen Leben und dem Austausch deutlich weniger abträglich und anderen Religionen gegenüber aufgeschlossener als in den neu von den Almohaden eroberten Herrschaften. Andere Städte, die im 11./12. Jahrhundert unter christliche Herrschaft gekommen waren, könnten dies vergleichend belegen. Vielleicht bewirkte auch gerade die genuesische Mitherrschaft, die spätestens 1152 geendet haben dürfte,[53] dieses augrund von Handelsinteressen vergleichsweise tolerante geistige Klima. Jedenfalls lebten Muslime weiterhin in Almería, obwohl die islamischen Geschichtsschreiber Verwüstungen und Zerstörung beklagen.[54] Über das Leben der Juden ist allgemein – soweit ich sehe – nichts überliefert. Ohne die Einzelheiten der Stadtgeschichte Almerías in dieser Zeit weiter zu bemühen, sollte vor dem Hintergrund dieser Beobachtungen betont werden, dass gleichzeitig auch Ibn Rušd (Averroes) – eher aus politischen denn aus ideologischen Gründen[55] – in Almería Zuflucht gesucht hatte.[56] Jedenfalls gehört wohl die er-

(León: Centro de Estudios e Investigación „San Isidoro", 1993) (dort keine Urkunde zu diesem Datum; vgl. weiterhin den Anhang bei Reilly, *Kingdom of León-Castilla* (wie Anm. 40), S. 323–398 (dort nicht aufgenommen).

50 Vgl. J. A. Tapia [Garrido], „Almería", in *Diccionario de Historia Eclesiastica*, Band I (Madrid: Institución Enrique Florez, 1972), S. 42–45, hier S. 42, sowie ausführlicher Tapia Garrido, *Historia general de Almería* (wie Anm. 45), Band 3, S. 460–461 mit Zweifeln an der Glaubwürdigkeit, weil ja allenfalls christliche Soldaten die Stadt bevölkert hätten. Vgl. aber die folgende Anmerkung.

51 Druck: Carl Erdmann, *Das Papsttum und Portugal im ersten Jahrhundert der portugiesischen Geschichte* (Abhandlungen der preußischen Akademie der Wissenschaften und der Literatur 1928/5; Berlin: Verlag der Akademie der Wissenschaften, 1928), S. 1–63, hier S. 55: „[...] et venerabilibus episcopis [...] B. Almariensi ...".

52 Tapia Garrido, *Historia general de Almería* (wie Anm. 45), Band 3, S. 461–465.

53 Vgl. neben Tapia Garrido, *Historia general de Almería* (wie Anm. 45), Band 3, S. 458, auch die Vermutungen von Reilly, *Kingdom of León-Castilla* (wie Anm. 40), S. 120.

54 Vgl. Tapia Garrido, *Historia general de Almería* (wie Anm. 45), Band 3, S. 459–460.

55 Vgl. Emilio Tornero Poveda, „La filosofía", in *El retroceso territorial de Al-Andalus* (wie Anm. 20), S. 587–602, hier S. 595: „cuya motivación real parece se debió más a intrigas palaciegas y políticas que a sus opiniones filosóficas".

56 Ibid.

wähnte Begegnung des Maimonides mit Averroes in diesen Zusammenhang, und es ist nicht ohne Grund von Seiten der Philosophiegeschichte unterstrichen worden, wie sehr das Werk des Maimonides dieser andalusisch-philosophischen Schule nahe stand.[57]

Die These, dass Almería vielleicht in der kurzen Zeit unter leonesisch-kastilisch-genuesischer Herrschaft eine Art Begegnungsraum für die Denker und Kritiker auch aus dem muslimischen Spanien wurde, führt allerdings zur Frage, warum die Familie des Maimonides Almería wieder verließ. Hier sind zunächst nur Spekulationen möglich: Gab es beispielsweise Hoffnungen auf Möglichkeiten, in Nordafrika eher Gleichgesinnte und Juden zu finden? In den hier präsentierten Befund der wichtigen Rolle Almerías in den Jahren 1147–1157 fügt sich ein allerdings nicht ganz sicher zu datierendes Zeugnis ein: Ein junger jüdischer Händler aus Almería schrieb etwa in dieser Zeit in einem Brief, nachdem er aus Handelsgründen nach Nordafrika gereist war, dass in Fez den Juden großer Hass entgegentrete, während Almería ein Ort der Rettung sei.[58] Handelsstädte, die am Meer lagen, atmeten wohl besonders im südlichen Spanien einen vergleichsweise freieren Geist.

V. Bilanz

Aus den kurzen Streiflichtern auf die bewegte Zeit eines Raumes, dessen Grenzen sich oft geändert haben, besonders in kultureller und politischer Hinsicht, möchte ich folgende vier Aspekte thesenhaft hervorheben:

1. Der Niedergang Córdobas nach der Zeit des Kalifates war keinesfalls so einschneidend, dass geistig-kulturelles Leben seit dieser Zeit nur in anderen Städten von al-Andalus anzutreffen gewesen wäre; Córdoba behielt weiterhin großes Gewicht.
2. Seit dem ausgehenden 11. Jahrhundert war al-Andalus besonders eng mit Nordafrika verbunden, wie die Anfänge der Lebensgeschichte von Maimonides unterstreichen. Jedoch dürfte der Druck auf die Juden – anders als im Falle der Christen – im Wesentlichen erst mit der Almohadenherrschaft in unterschiedlicher Intensität eingesetzt haben.
3. Unter den Almohaden kam es zu einer Neudefinition von Grenzen im wörtlichen und übertragenen Sinn. Die religiösen Grenzen wurden teilweise neu gesteckt, wenn auch nicht vollständig mit bisherigen Regelungen des

57 Joel L. Kraemer, „Maimonides and the Spanish Aristotelian School", in *Christians, Muslims and Jews in Medieval and Early Modern Spain* (wie Anm. 37), S. 40–68, besonders S. 45–48.

58 Zitiert nach Fierro, „Religión" (wie Anm. 20), S. 526.

ḏimma-Systems gebrochen wurde. Der Druck betraf besonders die Juden; die regionale Differenzierung und die in Schüben erfolgte almohadische Eroberung des südlichen Spaniens führten zu Wanderungsbewegungen, welche die Unterschiede in den verschiedenen noch abgegrenzten Herrschaften auszunutzen suchten. Dabei ist von Grenzräumen mit stets wechselnden Personengruppen auszugehen.

4. Bisher zu wenig beachtet wurde die Rolle von Genua, der Krone Aragón und Kastilien-León im Süden Spaniens im 12. Jahrhundert, die auch die Fluchtwege der Familie von Rabbi Maimon in ein neues Licht stellen könnte. Religiöse, wirtschaftliche und politische Gründe waren für die Eroberung von Almería 1147 bestimmend. Nicht unbedingt die Herrschaft von Christen, aber dafür die Bedeutung des Ortes für Handel und Austausch könnten in Almería insgesamt ein aufgeschlossenes Klima für das Nebeneinander verschiedener Religionen und Lebensformen begünstigt haben. Wenn es aber nach Jahrhunderten der Vorherrschaft der Muslime im Mittelmeer manchen westlich-lateinischen Eroberern darum ging, mit Almería nun auch den Handel im westlichen Mittelmeer neu zu gestalten, und wenn dies zeitgleich mit den Anstrengungen des Zweiten Kreuzzugs 1147 einherging, dann sind sicherlich auch Vergleiche zwischen West und Ost angebracht, denkt man nur an die Rolle der italienischen Seerepubliken im östlichen Mittelmeer, was auf den zweiten Teil der Biographie des Maimonides verweist.

Jerusalem und die Kreuzfahrerherrschaften im Leben und Denken des Maimonides

von

Nikolas Jaspert

Universität Erlangen-Nürnberg

I. Jerusalem und seine Herrscher zu Lebzeiten des Maimonides

Im Verlauf seines langen Lebens kam der sephardische Arzt und Rechtsgelehrte Mose ben Maimon (1135–1204) an unterschiedlichen Orten mit dem Christentum in Kontakt. Am intensivsten geschah dies im Vorderen Orient, wo er vierzig Jahre in unmittelbarer Berührung mit dem Christentum verbrachte. Teile Syriens, Palästinas und Mesopotamiens befanden sich seit der Zeit des Ersten Kreuzzugs unter christlicher Herrschaft: Zwischen 1097 und 1109 entstanden dort die Grafschaft Edessa, das Fürstentum Antiochia, die Grafschaft Tripolis und als viertes und bedeutendstes Territorium das Königreich Jerusalem. In den Jahrzehnten von 1165 bis 1204 – dem Zeitraum, in dem sich Maimonides in Ägypten aufhielt – erlebten diese Herrschaften dramatische Wandlungen, die sich nicht zuletzt auf die Biographie des Gelehrten auswirkten.[1]

Als Maimonides im Jahre 1165 Ceuta im westlichen Maghreb verließ und in den Vorderen Orient zog, stand das Königreich Jerusalem in hoher Blüte. Unter ihrem König Amalrich hatten die Christen gerade den ersten einer Reihe von Kriegszügen durchgeführt, die das fatimidische Ägypten kurzzeitig zu einer Art Protektorat des Königreichs Jerusalem machen sollten. Doch der Tod des Königs im Jahre 1174 läutete den Niedergang der christlichen Herrschaften Outremers (also jenseits des Mittelmeers) ein. Amalrichs Sohn Balduin IV. war noch minderjährig, und spätestens als er 1176 die Regierungsgeschäfte übernahm, wurde

1 Einführend zu dieser Phase in der Geschichte der Kreuzfahrerstaaten: Reinhold Röhricht, *Geschichte des Königreichs Jerusalem 1100–1291* (Innsbruck: Wagner, 1898; Nachdruck Amsterdam: Hakkert, 1966), S. 309–704; Joshua Prawer, *The Latin kingdom of Jerusalem. European colonialism in the Middle Ages* (London: Weidenfeld & Nicolson, 1972), S. 43–59, 167–212; Jean Richard, *The Crusades: c. 1071 – c. 1291* (Cambridge etc.: Cambridge University Press, 1999), S. 188–269 (französisches Original: *Histoire des croisades* [Paris: Fayard, 1996], S. 177–258); Hans Eberhard Mayer, *Geschichte der Kreuzzüge* (Urban-Taschenbücher 86; Stuttgart: Kohlhammer, [9]2000), S. 107–188; Ralph-Johannes Lilie, *Byzanz und die Kreuzzüge* (Urban-Taschenbücher 595; Stuttgart: Kohlhammer, 2004), S. 114–175.

offenbar, dass er an der Lepra litt und nur noch wenig Zeit zu leben hatte. Im selben Jahr entfiel durch die byzantinische Niederlage gegen die Seldschuken bei Myriokephalon der wichtigste Protektor und Verbündete der Kreuzfahrerstaaten; zeitgleich erwuchs diesen in Saladin ein mächtiger Gegner, dem es zwischen 1174 und 1185 gelang, Ägypten mit den syrischen und mesopotamischen Herrschaften Damaskus, Aleppo und Mosul zu verbinden und damit die Kreuzfahrerstaaten einzukreisen. Am 3./4. Juli 1187 entschied sich das Schicksal des Königreichs von Jerusalem auf dem Schlachtfeld von Ḥaṭṭīn, auf dem fast die gesamte kampffähige Schicht des Reichs tot, verwundet oder gefangen zurückblieb. Die nunmehr ihrer Verteidiger beraubte Heilige Stadt kapitulierte am 2. Oktober. Nur das Eingreifen der christlichen Glaubensbrüder im Kreuzzug von 1189 bis 1192, dem so genannten Dritten Kreuzzug, und der Tod Saladins im Jahre 1193 verhinderten die vollständige Vernichtung des Königreichs, das jedoch auf einen schmalen Landstreifen mit Zentrum in Akkon und Tyrus reduziert wurde. Bis zum Jahre 1204, in dem Maimonides starb und der unglückselige so genannte Vierte Kreuzzug mit der Plünderung Konstantinopels endete, sollte sich die als zweites Königreich Jerusalem bekannte Herrschaft durch die Rückgewinnung einzelner Städte und Gebiete wie Beirut (1197) oder Sidon (1203) zwar stabilisieren, aber nicht wirklich von dem in der Schlacht von Ḥaṭṭīn erlittenen Rückschlag erholen. Dieses anfangs bedrohlich starke, später geschwächte Reich also bildete den östlichen Nachbar Ägyptens, der Wahlheimat des Maimonides.

II. Maimonides und die Christen der Kreuzfahrerstaaten

Der Rechtsgelehrte wohnte über zwanzig Jahre hinweg – bis zur großen Expansion unter Saladin – in relativer Nähe zu den Christen, und auch in den letzten, knapp zwanzig Jahren seines Lebens blieben die Kreuzfahrerherrschaften eine Realität, der er auf verschiedene Weisen begegnet sein dürfte. Doch wie sicher sind derartige Kontakte zu belegen? Wissen wir von direkten Beziehungen zwischen Maimonides und den christlichen Kreuzfahrerstaaten des Vorderen Orients?

Kontakte sind in der Tat von seiner Immigration aus Fes im Jahre 1165 an nachzuweisen. Maimonides scheint anfänglich sogar eine Übersiedlung ins Königreich Jerusalem erwogen zu haben, denn das Schiff, das er am 18. April 1165 in Ceuta bestieg, hatte nicht das muslimische Alexandria mit seiner großen jüdischen Gemeinde, sondern das christlich beherrschte Akkon zum Ziel. Nach den Erfahrungen, die er unter den Christen in Almería und unter den Almohaden in Fes gemacht hatte,[2] scheint Maimonides also erwogen zu haben,

2 Vgl. den Aufsatz von Klaus Herbers in diesem Band (siehe oben S. 23–39).

sich wieder unter christliche Herrschaft zu begeben. Als er nach einer langen Reise und schwerem Seesturm am 16. Mai 1165 dort an Land ging,[3] traf Maimonides Glaubensgenossen an, denn das jüdische Leben war in den Kreuzfahrerherrschaften zwar begrenzt, aber keineswegs verboten. Zur damaligen Zeit besaß Akkon die größte jüdische Gemeinde des Landes.[4] Wir wissen hierüber unter anderem durch einen weiteren sephardischen Reisenden jener Jahre, Benjamin ben Jona aus Tudela in Navarra, der während einer durch Südfrankreich, Italien, Byzanz, Mesopotamien, Syrien, Persien, Ägypten und Sizilien führenden Reise in den Jahren 1166 bis 1168, also zeitgleich mit Maimonides, Palästina aufsuchte und einzigartige Informationen über das Leben der örtlichen jüdischen Gemeinden hinterlassen hat.[5]

---

3 Die Darstellung der Reise und des Aufenthalts in Palästina folgt Abraham Joshua Heschel, *Maimonides. Eine Biographie* (Judentum in Geschichte und Gegenwart 1; Berlin: Reiss, 1935; Nachdruck Neukirchen-Vluyn: Neukirchener Verlag, 1992), S. 52–68; David Yellin und Israel Abrahams, *Maimonides* (Philadelphia: Jewish Publication Society for America, 1936; Nachdruck Ann Arbor, Mich., 1979), S. 51–54; Ilil Arbel, *Maimonides. A spiritual biography* (New York: Crossroad, 2001), S. 47–53. Zum Sturm siehe die bei Arbel (S. 48) abgedruckte Passage des Maimonides.

4 Zu Akkon als jüdischem Zentrum zur Zeit der Kreuzfahrer siehe Joshua Prawer, *The History of the Jews in the Latin Kingdom of Jerusalem* (Oxford: Clarendon Press, 1988), S. 61–62. Allgemein zum Akkon der Kreuzfahrerzeit siehe Bernard Dichter, *The orders and churches of Crusader Acre* (Acre: Municipality of Acre, 1979); Derek Jacoby, „Les Italiens en Egypte aux XIIe et XIIIe siècle: du comptoir à la colonie?", in *Coloniser au Moyen Age*, ed. Michel Balard und Alain Ducellier (Paris: Armand Colin, 1995), S. 76–88; Marie-Luise Favreau-Lilie, *Die Italiener im Heiligen Land. Vom ersten Kreuzzug bis zum Tode Heinrichs von Champagne (1098–1197)* (Amsterdam: Hakkert, 1989); *San Giovanni d'Acri: Akko. Storia e cultura di una città portuale del Mediterraneo*, ed. Luciana Menozzi und Gabriella Ferri Piccaluga (Rom: Graffiti, 1996).

5 Binyamīn Ben-Yōna Tudela, *Syrien und Palästina nach dem Reisebericht des Benjamin von Tudela*, übersetzt und erklärt von Hans Peter Rüger (Abhandlungen des Deutschen Palästinavereins 12; Wiesbaden: Harrassowitz, 1990), der auf S. 26 die Entstehungszeit näher eingrenzt. Weiterhin zu diesem Werk und zu jüdischen Reiseberichten: Aryeh Grabois, „Travels and pilgrimages by Jews in Eretz-Israel in the twelfth and thirteenth centuries", in *Proceedings of the Ninth World Congress of Jewish Studies* (Jerusalem: World Union of Jewish Studies, 1986), Band 2, S. 63–70; Joseph Shatzmiller, „Jews, pilgrimage, and the Christian cult of saints: Benjamin of Tudela and his contemporaries", in *After Rome's Fall. Narrators and Sources of Early Medieval History*, ed. Alexander Callander Murray (Toronto: University of Toronto Press, 1998), S. 337–347. Über das Leben der Juden in den Kreuzfahrerherrschaften siehe: Prawer, *The History of the Jews* (wie Anm. 4); Sylvia Schein, „Jewish settlement in Palestine in the Crusader Period (1099–1291)", in *The Jewish settlement in Palestine 634–1881*, ed. Alex Carmel, Peter Schäfer und Yossi Ben-Artzi (Beihefte zum Tübinger Atlas des Vorderen Orients: Reihe B, Geisteswissenschaften 88; Wiesbaden: Reichert, 1990), S. 22–39; Sylvia Schein, „Between East and West: the Latin kingdom of Jerusalem and its Jewish communities as a communication centre (1099–1291)", in *Communication in the Jewish Diaspora – The Pre-modern world*, ed. Sophia Menache (Brill's Series in Jewish Studies 16; Leiden: Brill,

Zu Akkon berichtet Benjamin Folgendes: „[...] es ist der Anfang des Landes Israel. Und es liegt am großen Meer. Und dort ist der große Hafen für alle Umherirrenden, die auf Schiffen nach Jerusalem ziehen [die christlichen Kreuzfahrer und Pilger]. Und davor fließt der Strom hinab, der Bach Kedumin genannt wird. Und dort sind etwa zweihundert Juden. Und an ihrer Spitze sind Rabbi Zadok und Rabbi Japhet und Rabbi Jona."[6]

Zu einem der genannten Gemeindevorsteher, Japhet ben Eliahu, suchte Maimonides bei seiner Ankunft Kontakt. In seiner Begleitung unternahm er vom 17. bis 19. Oktober 1165 eine Reise nach Jerusalem und Hebron.[7] Zwar war Mitte des 12. Jahrhunderts mittlerweile das nach der christlichen Eroberung von 1099 ausgesprochene Verbot der Wiederansiedlung jüdischer Gemeinden in Jerusalem gelockert worden, und Benjamin von Tudela berichtet von Juden, die an der Westmauer des Tempels ihre Andacht verrichteten,[8] doch lebten zur Zeit seines Besuchs dort lediglich vier Familien: „Und dort gibt es eine Färberei, welche die Juden in jedem Jahr vom König kaufen, damit sonst keiner die Färberei von Jerusalem betreibt als allein die Juden. Und es sind etwa vier Juden. Sie wohnen unter dem Davidsturm am Rande der Stadt."[9]

Die Patriarchengräber von Hebron wiederum waren unter den Kreuzfahrern ein Pilgerzentrum, das Gläubige aller drei Religionen, also Christen, Muslime und Juden, gleichermaßen anzog.[10] Auch hierzu liefert uns der sephardische Reisende eine Beschreibung: „[...] wenn ein Jude dorthin kommt, der dem Türhüter der Höhle eine Belohnung gibt, dann öffnet er die Tür aus Eisen, die als Bau unserer Väter gemacht ist, und der Betreffende kann auf Stufen nach unten steigen. Und ein brennendes Licht ist in seiner Hand. Und er steigt nach unten in die Höhle hinab und dort gibt es nichts, und ebenso in die

1996), S. 141–169; Marie Luise Favreau-Lilie, „‚Multikulturelle Gesellschaft' oder ‚Persecuting Society'? ‚Franken' und ‚Einheimische' im Königreich Jerusalem", in *Jerusalem im Hoch- und Spätmittelalter* (wie Anm. 35), S. 55–93.

6 Binyamīn Ben-Yōna Tudela, *Syrien und Palästina* (wie Anm. 5), S. 34–35.

7 Zur Reise, mit Textpassagen aus einem fälschlicherweise dem Maimonides zugeschriebenen Kommentar zum *Rosh ha-Shanah*: Prawer, *The History of the Jews* (wie Anm. 4), S. 141–143.

8 Binyamīn Ben-Yōna Tudela, *Syrien und Palästina* (wie Anm. 5), S. 44: „Und dorthin kommen alle Juden, um vor der Mauer im Vorhof zu beten".

9 Ibid., S. 41–42. Zur Bedeutung des Färbergewerbes für die palästinensischen Juden der Kreuzfahrerzeit vgl. Prawer, *The History of the Jews* (wie Anm. 4), S. 122; Schein, „Jewish settlement in Palestine" (wie Anm. 5), S. 29.

10 Kaspar Elm, „‚Nec minori celebritate a catholicis cultoribus observatur et colitur'. Zwei Berichte über die 1119/20 in Hebron erfolgte Auffindung und Erhebung der Gebeine der Patriarchen Abraham, Isaak und Jakob", in *Zeitschrift für Religions- und Geistesgeschichte* 49 (1997), S. 318–344. Vgl. auch Prawer, *The History of the Jews* (wie Anm. 4), S. 130–131. Zur Bedeutung Hebrons als Pilgerzentrum im Judentum siehe Josef W. Meri, *The cult of saints among Muslims and Jews in medieval Syria* (Oxford etc.: Oxford University Press, 2002), S. 161–162, 195–196.

zweite, bis er zu der dritten kommt. Und siehe, dort sind sechs Gräber: das Grab Abrahams und das Isaaks und das Jakobs und das Saras und das Rebekkas und das Leas, jeweils eins dem andern gegenüber. [...] und dort sind viele Fässer, die mit den Gebeinen Israels gefüllt sind. Denn dorthin pflegten sie in den Tagen Israels ihre Toten zu bringen, jeder einzelne die Gebeine seiner Väter, um sie dort zu lassen bis auf diesen Tag".[11]

Maimonides verbrachte ungefähr ein Jahr im christlichen Königreich Jerusalem,[12] um sich schließlich doch zur Übersiedlung nach Ägypten zu entschließen. Erleichtert wurde die Entscheidung durch die damalige politische Situation insofern, als das christliche Protektorat über Ägypten den Kontakt und die Mobilität zwischen den beiden Reichen vereinfachte. Über die Gründe für den neuerlichen Umzug kann man nur spekulieren. Die Gemeinden Palästinas waren zahlenmäßig mit den ägyptischen nicht zu vergleichen, wo Benjamin von Tudela allein in Kairo/Al-Fusṭāṭ und Alexandrien 7000 beziehungsweise 3000 Glaubensbrüder zählte.[13] Auch die ehemals autoritative Stellung des Jerusalemer Gemeindevorstehers war längst auf denjenigen Kairos übergegangen.[14] Wahrscheinlich boten sich dem hoch begabten und ehrgeizigen Gelehrten in Palästina einfach nicht die erhofften Entfaltungsmöglichkeiten. In der Tat stieg Maimonides bereits 1171 kurzzeitig sowie 1195 endgültig zum *Ra'īs al-yahūd* beziehungsweise *Nagid*, also zum Oberhaupt aller Juden Ägyptens auf.[15]

11 Binyamīn Ben-Yōna Tudela, *Syrien und Palästina* (wie Anm. 5), S. 49–50.

12 Von Mai 1165 bis Mai 1166: Prawer, *The History of the Jews* (wie Anm. 4), S. 142–143.

13 Binyamīn Ben-Yōna Tudela, *The itinerary of Benjamin of Tudela. Critical text, translation and commentary by Marcus Nathan Adler* (London: Henry Frowde, 1907; Nachdruck Frankfurt am Main: Institute for the History of Arabic-Islamic Science, 1995), S. 56. Allerdings überging Maimonides damit die Halakhah, die den Juden ausdrücklich verbot, sich in Ägypten niederzulassen: Isadore Twersky, „Maimonides and Eretz Yisrael: Halakhic, philosophic, and historical perspectives", in *Perspectives on Maimonides. Philosophical and historical studies*, ed. Joel L. Kraemer (Oxford etc.: Oxford University Press, 1991), S. 257–290, hier S. 257; vgl. dazu seine eigenen Worte unten, Seite 62.

14 Mark R. Cohen, „Administrative Relations between Palestinian and Egyptian Jewry during the Fatimid Period", in *Egypt and Palestine. A millennium of association (868–1948)*, ed. Amnōn Cohen (New York: St. Martin's Press, 1984), S. 113–153, der die Frühgeschichte der Beziehungen beider Gemeinden aufarbeitet. Vgl. auch Prawer, *The History of the Jews* (wie Anm. 4), S. 111–113.

15 Shlomo D. Goitein, „Moses Maimonides, ‚Man of Action'. A Revision of the Master's Biography in Light of the Geniza Documents", in *Hommage à Georges Vajda. Études d'histoire et de pensée juives*, ed. Gérard Nahon und Charles Touati (Collection de la Revue des Études Juives 1; Louvain: Peeters, 1980), S. 155–167, hier S. 160–166, der die Karriere anhand der Dokumente der Kairoer Geniza verfolgen kann. Zum Titel des *Nagid* siehe auch Prawer, *The History of the Jews* (wie Anm. 4), S. 113–116, mit Hinweis auf die Stellung der Nachkommen des Maimonides. Offenbar verlor Maimonides diese Stellung um 1177, um sie nach einigen Jahren – 1187 oder 1195 – wiederzuerlangen: Heschel, *Maimonides* (wie Anm. 3), S. 205–206; Mark R. Cohen, „Maimonides' Egypt", in *Moses Maimonides and his time*, ed. Eric L. Ormsby (Studies in philosophy

Nicht zuletzt aufgrund dieser herausragenden Position trat Maimonides noch verschiedentlich mit den Kreuzfahrerstaaten in Kontakt – auch unfreiwillig, wie die Ereignisse von 1168 belegen. Im Zuge der Ägyptenfeldzüge König Amalrichs stießen im November jenes Jahres christliche Truppen bis nach Al-Fusṭāṭ vor und verwüsteten es. Maimonides wurde zur Flucht nach Kairo gezwungen.[16] Es ist nicht belegt, ob die weiteren vier Ägyptenzüge Amalrichs unmittelbare Auswirkungen auf die Lebensverhältnisse des Gelehrten hatten, doch waren die Jahre bis zum Tode des Königs von Jerusalem 1174 zweifellos die Zeit, in der die Kreuzfahrerherrschaften besonders unmittelbar die Muslime und Juden Ägyptens bedrohten.[17] Nicht nur für die eigene Person, sondern auch für Glaubensbrüder und -schwestern des Maimonides hatten die Kriegshandlungen Folgen. Die Plünderung Al-Fusṭāṭs und vor allem Bilbays, des Zielorts der palästinensisch-ägyptischen Karawanenroute mit einer beträchtlichen jüdischen Gemeinde, führten zur Versklavung vieler Jüdinnen und Juden. Für ihre Freilassung forderten die Christen die horrende Summe von 33 ein Drittel Dinare pro Person.[18] Hier tritt uns Maimonides zum ersten Mal als Autorität seiner Gemeinde entgegen: In verschiedenen Rundschreiben aus dem Sommer 1169 setzte er sich dafür ein, zugunsten der Glaubensbrüder und -schwestern Geld zu sammeln, um sie aus der Sklaverei auszulösen beziehungsweise sie vor diesem Schicksal zu bewahren.[19] Ich lasse offen, ob man dieses Wirken mit Goitein als ein „first rate publicity stunt"[20] bezeichnen möchte oder eher wirkliche Sorge um die Glaubensbrüder dahinter vermuten sollte.

Die kriegerischen Ereignisse unterbanden keineswegs die Kontakte zwischen Maimonides und den Christen der Kreuzfahrerstaaten. Im Gegenteil: Maimonides sandte ausdrücklich zwei hochgeachtete Glaubensbrüder nach Palästina, um – wohl mit König Amalrich – über die Freilassung der gefangenen Juden zu verhandeln.[21] Der ägyptische Autor Ibn al-Qifṭī (gest. 1248) überliefert in seiner Sammlung von Biographien berühmter Ärzte und Philosophen, dass der „König der Franken" von Askalon aus sogar einen Gesandten mit der Bitte

---

and the history of philosophy 19; Washington, D.C.: The Catholic University of America Press, 1989), S. 21–34, hier S. 27. Über die Unsicherheiten in dieser Frage vgl. Prawer, *The History of the Jews* (wie Anm. 4), S. 53. Zur Judenheit Ägyptens jener Zeit vgl. neben den genannten Werken die im Beitrag von Mark Cohen zitierten Werke.

16 Heschel, *Maimonides* (wie Anm. 3), S. 85–88.

17 Noch im Jahre 1204 unternahmen die Christen einen Angriff auf das Nildelta, der zur Plünderung von Fūwwa führte: Röhricht, *Geschichte des Königreichs Jerusalem 1100–1291* (wie Anm. 1), S. 693; vgl., mit Datierung auf 1200: Andrew S. Ehrenkreutz, „Saladin's Egypt and Maimonides", in *Perspectives on Maimonides* (wie Anm. 13), S. 303–308, hier S. 307.

18 Goitein, „Moses Maimonides, ‚Man of Action'" (wie Anm. 15), S. 157.

19 Ibid., S. 156–159 (mit dem Text zweier Briefe). Vgl. auch den Beitrag von Mark Cohen in diesem Band (siehe unten S. 65–81).

20 Goitein, „Moses Maimonides, ‚Man of Action'" (wie Anm. 15), S. 162.

21 Ibid., S. 158–159 mit Würdigung der beiden *qādīs*.

nach Ägypten geschickt habe, Maimonides möge in sein Königreich kommen, um ihm als Leibarzt zu dienen; doch habe dieser die Einladung ausgeschlagen.[22]

Dennoch hatte Maimonides keine vollständig ablehnende Haltung gegenüber den Christen. Zwar sah er in ihnen Götzenanbeter und kritisierte sie häufig, doch im Gegensatz zu den Muslimen, von denen er sagte, sie bestritten den Offenbarungsursprung der Torah und seien folglich unbelehrbar, fänden die Christen „in ihrer Lehre keine Gegensätze zu unserer".[23] Und man sollte auch nicht vergessen, dass der Gelehrte durchaus über seine Familie in Handelsaktivitäten involviert war,[24] die ihn mit den in Ägypten und den Kreuzfahrerstaaten ansässigen italienischen Händlern in Kontakt gebracht haben dürften.[25]

Auch zu den jüdischen Gemeinden der Kreuzfahrerstaaten unterhielt Maimonides Beziehungen, wie seine *Responsa* an die große Gemeinde von Tyrus belegen,[26] und selbst mit der Akkonenser Judengemeinde blieb Maimonides aus der Ferne Ägyptens aufgrund seiner autoritativen Rechtsstellung in lockerer Verbindung.[27] Ein eigenhändiges Schreiben des Meisters ist an den Gemeindevorsteher Japhet ben Eliahu gerichtet, mit dem er seinerzeit nach Jerusalem

---

22 Françoise Micheau, „Médicins orientaux au service des princes latins", in *Occident et Proche-Orient: Contacts scientifiques au temps des Croisades. Actes du colloque de Louvain-la-Neuve, 24 et 25 mars 1997*, ed. Isabelle Draelants, Anne Tihon und Baudouin van den Abeel (Réminiscences 5; Turnhout: Brepols, 2000), S. 95–116, hier S. 100–101. Wahrscheinlich bezieht sich die Anekdote auf Amalrich, Graf von Jaffa-Askalon: Prawer, *The History of the Jews* (wie Anm. 4), S. 108. Diese Episode entwickelte sich aufgrund fehlerhafter Lesungen zu der Legende, Richard Löwenherz habe nach dem jüdischen Gelehrten gerufen: Bernard Lewis, „Maimonides, Lionheart and Saladin", in *Eretz-Israel* 7 (1964), S. 70–75.

23 Zitate des Maimonides nach Heschel, *Maimonides* (wie Anm. 3), S. 63. Grundlegend: Howard Kreisel, „Maimonides on Christianity and Islam", in *Judaism and Christianity. Honoring the memory of Rabbi Arthur Gilbert*, ed. Ronald A. Brauner (Jewish civilization 3; Philadelphia: Reconstructionist Rabbinical College, 1985), S. 153–165. Vgl. den Beitrag von Stefan Schreiner in diesem Band (siehe S. 323–345).

24 Goitein, „Moses Maimonides, ,Man of Action'" (wie Anm. 15), S. 162–163.

25 Zum christlichen Handel mit Ägypten siehe: Wilhelm Heyd, *Geschichte des Levantehandels im Mittelalter* (2 Bände; Stuttgart: Cotta, 1879; Nachdruck Hildesheim: Olms, 1984); Adolf Schaube, *Handelsgeschichte der romanischen Völker des Mittelmeergebiets bis zum Ende der Kreuzzüge* (Handbuch der mittelalterlichen und neueren Geschichte 3,5; München etc.: Oldenburg, 1906; Nachdruck Osnabrück: Zeller, 1973); Subhi Labib, *Handelsgeschichte Ägyptens im Spätmittelalter 1171–1517* (Vierteljahrschrift für Sozial- und Wirtschaftsgeschichte. Beihefte 46; Wiesbaden: Steiner, 1965); Marie-Luise Favreau-Lilie, *Die Italiener im Heiligen Land* (wie Anm. 4); eadem, „Der Fernhandel und die Auswanderung der Italiener ins Heilige Land", in *Venedig und die Weltwirtschaft um 1200*, ed. Wolfgang Stromer von Reichenbach (Centro Tedesco di Studi Veneziani: Studi 7; Sigmaringen: Thorbecke, 1999), S. 203–234.

26 Prawer, *The History of the Jews* (wie Anm. 4), S. 52–53, 106.

27 Ibid., S. 62, 97. Allerdings liegt ein Schreiben des Meisters vor, aus dem seine Zweifel an der Gelehrsamkeit der Weisen Palästinas hervorgeht: ibid., S. 111–113.

und Hebron gereist war.[28] Es wurde im Jahre 1176 aufgesetzt und stellt die Antwort auf einen Brief des Akkonenser Gelehrten dar. Offenbar hatte Maimonides seit seiner Übersiedlung nach Ägypten den Kontakt ruhen lassen; nun beschreibt er die vielfältigen Herausforderungen, derer er sich im persönlichen und öffentlichen Bereich seit seiner Ankunft zu erwehren hatte. Ganz nebenbei jedoch wird auch an die gemeinsame Zeit im Gelobten Land erinnert, in der beide „gemeinsam durch die Wüste und die Wälder wanderten, auf der Suche nach Gott" – eine Erfahrung, die Maimonides nach eigenem Bekunden nie vergessen werde.[29]

Die Einnahme Jerusalems durch Saladin im Oktober 1187 eröffnete den Juden des Vorderen Orients neue Möglichkeiten: Ihnen wurde nun die Heilige Stadt zugänglich, und viele machten von dem Angebot Gebrauch. Besonders nach der Eroberung Askalons durch die Muslime im Jahre 1191 und der anschließenden Zerstörung dieser Stadt siedelten viele Mitglieder der ehemals blühenden Askaloner Gemeinde nach Jerusalem über.[30] Dass diese Entscheidung auf das Wirken des Maimonides zurückging, wie verschiedentlich behauptet oder suggeriert wird,[31] ist nicht zu belegen. Auffällig ist indes, dass sich dieses Ereignis ebenso wenig in den Werken des Maimonides widerspiegelt wie viele andere zeitgenössische Begebenheiten.[32] Trotz aller Kontakte, die er im Laufe seines Lebens auf unterschiedlichste Weise mit den Christen der Kreuzfahrerstaaten machte, bleiben diese, ebenso wie ihre Auseinandersetzung mit den Muslimen, in seinen Schriften merkwürdig abwesend. Was sich zu seinen Lebzeiten in Palästina, aber auch in der muslimischen Welt ereignete, wird im Œuvre des Maimonides kaum greifbar.

Dies bedeutet jedoch keineswegs, dass Palästina und Jerusalem im Denken des Maimonides und seiner Zeitgenossen keine Bedeutung gespielt hätten. In ihrer Hochschätzung Jerusalems treffen sich Judentum, Christentum und Islam, weswegen es sich lohnen dürfte, näher und vergleichend auf die Bedeutung einzugehen, die Palästina und insbesondere Jerusalem für alle drei großen monotheistischen Religionen im Hochmittelalter spielte.

---

28 *Letters of Maimonides,* translated and edited by Leon D. Stitskin (New York: Yeshiva University Press, 1977), S. 70–73. Es handelt sich dabei um das einzige Schreiben des Maimonides an einen Einwohner Palästinas (S. 71).

29 Nach der englischsprachigen Übersetzung: *Letters of Maimonides* (wie Anm. 28), S. 73.

30 Schein, „Jewish settlement in Palestine" (wie Anm. 5), S. 30.

31 So bei Arbel, *Maimonides. A spiritual biography* (wie Anm. 3), S. 148, sowie Yellin und Abrahams, *Maimonides* (wie Anm. 3), S. 156.

32 Joseph Drory, „The Early Decades of Ayyubid Rule", in *Perspectives on Maimonides* (wie Anm. 13), S. 295–302, hier S. 302.

III. Die Bedeutung Jerusalems für Christentum, Islam und Judentum

1. Christentum

Beginnen wir mit den faktischen Herren Jerusalems zur Ankunftszeit des Maimonides in Palästina, also den Christen. Worauf gründete ihre Sicht der Heiligen Stadt, und welche Auswirkungen hatte dies auf die Entstehung der Kreuzfahrerherrschaften und das Selbstverständnis ihrer Bewohner? Dies sind Fragen, die unmittelbar auf die Lebensumstände des Maimonides und seiner Glaubensgenossen einwirkten, denn die Geschichte des Vorderen Orients im 12. Jahrhundert ist ohne Berücksichtigung Jerusalems und seiner Wirkmächtigkeit nicht zu verstehen.

Die Fülle an Deutungen und die Zahl der Assoziationen, die der Name der Stadt bei den Christen hervorrief, war gewaltig.[33] Neben den 656 Nennungen Jerusalems in der Bibel lassen sich eine Vielzahl umschreibender Bezeichnungen festmachen, Grundlage genug für unterschiedliche Deutungen, wobei sich sogar noch Unterschiede zwischen den christlichen Denominationen ergaben. Denn selbstverständlich schufen sich nicht nur die lateinischen und griechischen Christen, sondern ebenso die Angehörigen der verschiedenen orientalischen Kirchen – von den Kopten über die syrisch-orthodoxen Christen bis zu

33 Sibylle Mähl, „Jerusalem in mittelalterlicher Sicht", in *Die Welt als Geschichte* 22 (1962), S. 11–26; Adrian H. Bredero, „Jérusalem dans l'Occident médiéval", in *Mélanges offerts a René Crozet (à l'occasion de son soixante-dixième anniversaire)*, ed. Yves-Jean Riou und Pierre Gallais, Band 2 (Poitiers: Société d'études médiévales, 1966), S. 259–271; Franz Niehoff, „Umbilicus mundi – Der Nabel der Welt. Jerusalem und das Heilige Grab im Spiegel von Pilgerberichten und -karten, Kreuzzügen und Reliquiaren", in *Ornamenta Ecclesiae. Kunst und Künstler der Romanik*, ed. Anton Legner, Band 3 (Köln: Schnütgen-Museum, 1985), S. 53–72; Joshua Prawer, *Crusader Institutions* (Oxford: Clarendon Press, 1980); Kaspar Elm, „Die himmlische und die irdische, die verworfene und die heilige Stadt", in *Die Reise nach Jerusalem – Eine kulturhistorische Exkursion in die Stadt der Städte, 3000 Jahre Davidsstadt*, ed. Hendrik Budde und Andreas Nachama (Berlin: Argon, 1995), S. 12–24; *Le mythe de Jérusalem. Du Moyen Age à la Renaissance*, ed. Evelyne Berriot-Salvadore (Saint-Étienne: Publications de l'Université de Saint-Étienne, 1995); Joshua Prawer, „Jerusalem in the Christian perspective of the early Middle Ages", in *The history of Jerusalem*, Band I: *The early Muslim period, 638–1099*, ed. Joshua Prawer (New York: New York University Press, 1996 [hebräisches Original 1987]), S. 249–282; John France, „Le rôle de Jérusalem dans la piété du XIe siècle", in *Le partage du monde. Échanges et colonisation dans la méditerranée médiévale*, ed. Michel Balard und Alain Ducellier (Série Byzantina Sorbonensia 17; Paris: Publications de la Sorbonne, 1998), S. 151–162; Colin Morris, „Memorials of the holy places and blessings from the East: devotion to Jerusalem before the crusades", in *The Holy Land, Holy Lands, and Christian History*, ed. Robert N. Swanson (Studies in Church History 36; Woodbridge: Boydell Press, 2000), S. 90–109.

den Armeniern – ihre Bilder von der Heiligen Stadt.[34] Um der Vielzahl allein der lateinischen Jerusalembilder größere Übersichtlichkeit zu verleihen, sollen diese im Folgenden in lockerer zeitlicher Abfolge – nach alttestamentlichen, neutestamentlichen und späteren Deutungen geschieden – vorgestellt werden. Doch gilt es zu bedenken, dass sich unterschiedliche und sogar widersprüchliche Vorstellungen im mittelalterlichen Denken durchaus überlagerten und ergänzten.

Das Gelobte Land als geographischer Bezugspunkt erlangte durch die Heilige Schrift und ihre Auslegung vielfältige Sinngehalte, die im Verbund auf die hochmittelalterlichen Christen wirkten. Dies lässt sich in besonders eindrücklicher Weise an den Kreuzfahrern und Pilgern des 12. Jahrhunderts illustrieren. Die am Alten Testament orientierten Wurzeln ihres Handelns sind gerade in der neueren Kreuzzugsforschung stärker betont worden, denn für die Kreuzfahrer und Pilger dürfte ein ganz wesentliches Movens darin bestanden haben, dass ihr Zug in das Gelobte Land des Alten Testamentes führte.[35] Die *terra promissionis* oder deren Schutz zum Ziel zu haben verlieh den Expeditionen einen eigenen, höheren Stellenwert. Auch in diesem Kontext kam Jerusalem eine überragende Stellung zu. Nur vor diesem Hintergrund wird verständlich, dass sich die ersten Kreuzfahrer in direkte Parallele zum Volke Israel setzten und vom päpstlichen Legaten Adhemar von Le Puy als dem „neuen Moses" sprachen. Im Kreuzzug wiederholte sich der Aufbruch des Volkes Israel aus Ägypten in das Land der Verheißung und zur Stadt Jahwes. Die Kreuzfahrerinnen und Kreuzfahrer waren die neuen Makkabäer, die den

---

34 Siehe, mit weiterer Literatur: Robert L. Wilken, „Loving the Jerusalem below: The monks of Palestine", in *Jerusalem. Its sanctity and centrality to Judaism, Christianity and Islam*, ed. Lee I. Levine (New York: Continuum, 1999), S. 240–250; Abullif Wadi, „The Centrality of Jerusalem in the Arabic-Christian Literature", in *Jerusalem. House of prayer for all peoples in the three monotheistic religions*, ed. Alviero Niccacci (Studium Biblicum Franciscanum: Analecta 52; Jerusalem: Franciscan Printing Press, 2001), S. 102–112; Johannes Pahlitzsch, *Graeci und Suriani im Palästina der Kreuzfahrerzeit. Beiträge und Quellen zur Geschichte des griechisch-orthodoxen Patriarchats von Jerusalem* (Berliner historische Studien 33 = Ordensstudien 15; Berlin: Duncker & Humblot, 2001); Hubert Kaufhold, „Die Bedeutung Jerusalems für die syrisch-orthodoxe Kirche", in *L'idea di Gerusalemme nella spiritualità cristiana del Medioevo: atti del Convegno internazionale in collaborazione con l'Istituto della Görres-Gesellschaft di Gerusalemme. Gerusalemme, Notre Dame of Jerusalem Center, 31 agosto – 6 settembre 1999* (Atti e documenti 12; Città del Vaticano: Libreria Editrice Vaticana, 2003), S. 132–163, der Pisenzius, Samuel von Kalamon und andere Kopten behandelt.

35 Zum Folgenden siehe Kaspar Elm, *Die Kreuzzüge. Kriege im Namen Gottes?* (Kirche und Gesellschaft 231; Köln: Bachem, 1996) sowie idem, „Die Eroberung Jerusalems im Jahre 1099. Ihre Darstellung, Beurteilung und Deutung in den Quellen zur Geschichte des Ersten Kreuzzugs", in *Jerusalem im Hoch- und Spätmittelalter. Konflikte und Konfliktbewältigung – Vorstellungen und Vergegenwärtigungen*, ed. Dieter Bauer, Klaus Herbers und Nikolas Jaspert (Campus Historische Studien 29; Frankfurt am Main: Campus-Verlag, 2001), S. 31–54.

Tempel befreiten, den wahren Kult erneuerten und sich für die Gemeinschaft opferten – ein Bild, das gerade im 12. Jahrhundert immer wieder von Päpsten, Kreuzzugspredigern und Theologen bemüht wurde.[36]

Noch vielfältiger waren die Bezüge zum Neuen Testament. Immer wieder betonen die Quellen, dass die Kreuzfahrer und Pilger das Land betraten, wo Christus gewandelt sei – oder „wo seine Füße einst standen". Das Wissen um den Ort, wo Jesus unter anderem mit den Schriftgelehrten disputierte, die Geldwechsler vertrieb und später das Kreuz trug, war den Christen vollkommen präsent. In diesem Zusammenhang entfaltete der „Christozentrismus" des Hochmittelalters seine größte Wirkung. Vor allem die Orte des Leidens und Sterbens Christi – Jerusalem und die Grabeskirche – erlangten vor diesem Hintergrund gesteigerte Bedeutung. Aber auch nach Kreuzigung, Tod und Auferstehung des Erlösers blieb die christliche Heilsgeschichte bekanntlich aufs engste mit Jerusalem verbunden: Hier versammelte sich um Maria die Urgemeinde, entstand die *ecclesia primitiva,* wirkten die Christus nachfolgenden Apostel und Jünger.[37]

Die hier umrissenen, auf das Alte und Neue Testament zurückgehenden Bilder und Vorstellungen Jerusalems wurden durch die historischen Ereignisse im spätantiken und frühmittelalterlichen Palästina, aber auch durch das frühe Christentum und die Schriften der Kirchenväter erweitert. Doch waren diese nachbiblischen Interpretamente nicht nur positiver Natur, denn das Verhältnis der frühchristlichen Theologie zu Jerusalem war durchaus ambivalent.[38]

---

36 Paul Alphandéry, „Les citations bibliques chez les historiens de la Première Croisade", in *Revue de l'Histoire des Religions* 99 (1929), S. 137–157; Yael Katzir, „The Conquest of Jerusalem, 1099 and 1187. Historical Memory and Religious Typology", in *The Meeting of Two Worlds. Cultural Exchange between East and West during the Period of the Crusades,* ed. Vladimir P. Goss und Charles V. Bornstein (Studies in Medieval Culture 21; Kalamazoo, Mich.: Medieval Institute Publications, 1986), S. 103–112.

37 Alphonse Dupront, „La spiritualité des croisés et des pèlerins d'après les sources de la première croisade", in *Convegni del centro di studi sulla spiritualità medioevale 4* (Spoleto 1963), S. 72–86; Bernard McGinn, „Iter Sancti Sepulcri. The Piety of the First Crusaders", in *Essays on Medieval Civilization,* ed. Bede Karl Lackner und Kenneth Roy Philip (The Walter Prescott Webb Memorial Lectures 12; Austin, London: University of Texas Press, 1978), S. 33–71; Norbert Brox, „Das ‚irdische Jerusalem' in der altchristlichen Theologie", in *Kairos* 28 (1986), S. 152–173, hier S. 162–168; Helmut Merklein, „Jerusalem – bleibendes Zentrum der Christenheit? Der neutestamentliche Befund", in *Zion – Ort der Begegnung. Festschrift für Laurentius Klein zur Vollendung des 65. Lebensjahres,* ed. Ferdinand Hahn (Bonner biblische Beiträge 90; Bodenheim: Athenäum, 1993), S. 47–61.

38 Peter W. L. Walker, *Holy city, holy places? Christian attitudes to Jerusalem and the Holy Land in the fourth century* (Oxford: Clarendon Press, 1990); Robert L. Wilken, *The Land called Holy. Palestine in Christian History and Thought* (New Haven, London: Yale University Press, 1992); Elm, „Die himmlische und die irdische" (wie Anm. 33); Lorenzo Perrone, „‚The mystery of Judaea' (Jerome, Ep. 46): the Holy City of Jerusalem between history and symbol in early Christian thought", in *Jerusalem. Its sanctity and*

Einerseits war die Heilige Stadt der Ort des Wirkens und der Auferstehung Christi. Andererseits war der Erlöser dort gepeinigt und getötet worden. Daher erlangte Jerusalem in den Schriften der frühen christlichen Theologen das doppelte Antlitz einer sowohl geheiligten als auch verworfenen Stadt. Bereits nach Ansicht einiger Kirchenväter hatten Titus und Vespasian als Werkzeuge Gottes Rache für den Kreuzestod Christi genommen, als sie Jerusalem zerstörten.[39] Diejenigen, die der Stadt Davids reserviert gegenüberstanden, konnten sich sogar auf Worte Christi berufen, der im Dialog mit einer Samariterin angekündigt hatte, es werde der Tag kommen, an dem sie den Vater „weder auf diesem Berg noch in Jerusalem" verehren werde (Johannes 4:21), oder auf Paulus, der im Galaterbrief die Stadt als „versklavt" herabsetzte (Galater 4:25).[40]

Jerusalem galt nach Ausweis der Evangelien aber auch nach dem Kreuzestod Jesu als heilig (Matthäus 4:5; 27:53[41]), und von hier ging der neue Glaube in die Welt hinaus;[42] der Sieg des Christentums zur Zeit der so genannten „konstantinischen Wende" trug weiter zur Aufwertung der Stadt bei. Nach ihrer Inbesitznahme durch die Muslime im 7. Jahrhundert mehrten Erzählungen und Legenden die Kenntnis über das historische Jerusalem: Man wusste im Westen von Karl dem Großen, dem angeblichen Jerusalempilger und Kreuz-

---

centrality (wie Anm. 34), S. 221–239; Mieczyslaw Celestyn Paczkowski, „The Centrality of Jerusalem in the Reflections of the Fathers of the Church", in *Jerusalem. House of prayer* (wie Anm. 34), S. 115–134; Georg Hentschel, „Jerusalem aus der Sicht des Christentums", in *Jerusalem im Widerstreit politischer und religiöser Interessen. Die Heilige Stadt aus interdisziplinärer Sicht*, ed. Helmut Hubel und Tilman Seidensticker (Frankfurt am Main etc.: lang, 2004), S. 73–97.

39 Origenes, *Contra Celsum* IV,22 (*Contre Celse*, edité et traduit par Marcel Borret [Sources chrétiennes 136; Paris: Cerf, 1968], S. 235–239); Eusebius von Caesarea, *Vita Constantini* 33.1–3 (Eusebius von Caesarea, *Über das Leben des Kaisers Konstantin*, ed. Friedhelm Winkelmann [Die Griechischen Christlichen Schriftsteller der ersten Jahrhunderte 7; Berlin: Akademie Verlag, [2]1991], S. 99; Eusebius, *Life of Constantine*, translated by Averil Cameron und Stuart G. Hall [Oxford: Clarendon, 1999], S. 135). – Dazu: Paczkowski, „The Centrality of Jerusalem" (wie Anm. 38), S. 116–121.

40 Die ambivalente, doch insgesamt eher negative Bewertung Jerusalems im Neuen Testament zeigt Peter W. L. Walker, *Jesus and the Holy City. New Testament perspectives on Jerusalem* (Grand Rapids, Mich. etc.: Eerdmans, 1996) auf. Demnach hätten sich die Jerusalem betreffenden Weissagungen des Alten Testaments durch das Wirken Christi erfüllt; vgl. auch Ed P. Sanders, „Jerusalem and its Temple in Early Christian Thought and Practice", in *Jerusalem. Its sanctity and centrality* (wie Anm. 34), S. 90–103, hier S. 93–100.

41 Worauf schon Hieronymus hinwies: Hieronymus, Epistula 46,6 (*Sancti Eusebii Hieronymi Epistulae 1*, ed. Isidorius Hilberg [Corpus Scriptorum Ecclesiasticorum Latinorum 54; Wien: Verlag der Österreichischen Akademie der Wissenschaften, 1996], S. 334–336).

42 Was schon Justin und Irenäus betonten: Brox, „Das ‚irdische Jerusalem'" (wie Anm. 37), S. 152–154.

fahrer, oder von Kaiser Heraklios, der 630 das von den Persern verschleppte Heilige Kreuz auf den Golgathafelsen zurückbrachte. Die im 4. Jahrhundert auftretende, gerade seit dem 9. Jahrhundert anwachsende Heiligkreuzfrömmigkeit dürfte ihren Teil zur Aufwertung des irdischen Jerusalem beigetragen haben.[43] Die historische Dimension der Stadt reichte also vom Beginn der Zeiten mit Adam über die Perioden des Alten und Neuen Testaments, des Frühchristentums und der islamischen Herrschaftszeit bis in die Zukunft. Denn in Zion wird sich nach christlichem Glauben am Ende der Zeiten die Parusie und das Endgericht ereignen. Damit wiesen auch die chiliastischen und eschatologischen Vorstellungen, die im Hochmittelalter neuerlichen Auftrieb erfuhren, einen konkreten Bezug zu den Gegebenheiten Palästinas auf.

Neben diesen aus der Vergangenheit beziehungsweise der Gegenwart gespeisten Jerusalembildern besaß die Stadt zudem eine zweite, spirituelle Dimension. Schon im Neuen Testament lässt sich das Bestreben beobachten, die Deutungen Jerusalems von der historischen in die symbolische Sphäre zu rücken. In den ersten drei Jahrhunderten des Christentums verstärkte sich diese Tendenz: Jerusalem wurde nun einerseits als Wiege der neuen Religion und andererseits als Versinnbildlichung des kommenden Reiches Gottes verstanden. Entscheidende Bedeutung für diesen Wandel kam hierbei der Offenbarung des Johannes zu, die zum einen das ältere, vorchristliche und von Paulus im Galaterbrief tradierte Bild der kreisrunden, von zwölf Toren umgebenen Himmelsstadt aufgriff (Offenbarung 21:9–27 und Galater 4:26–27), zum anderen aber um die eschatologische Vorstellung des in Jerusalem herabkommenden tausendjährigen Friedensreiches erweiterte (Offenbarung 20:1–7).[44] Die Stadt

43 Joseph Szövérffy, „Crux fidelis. Prologomena to a History of the Holy Cross Hymns", in *Traditio* 22 (1966), S. 1–41; Dominique Iogna-Prat, „La croix, le moine et l'empereur: dévotion à la croix et théologie politique à Cluny autour de l'an mil", in *Haut Moyen-Âge: culture, éducation et société. Études offertes à Pierre Riché*, ed. Michel Sot (Nanterre: Publidix, 1990), S. 449–475; Ewald Volgger, „Die Feier von Kreuzauffindung und Kreuzerhöhung. Ursprung, Verbreitung und Bedeutung unter besonderer Berücksichtigung als Hochfeste des Deutschen Ordens", in *Beiträge zur Geschichte des Deutschen Ordens*, ed. Udo Arnold (Quellen und Studien zur Geschichte des Deutschen Ordens 49; Marburg: Elwert, 1993), S. 1–50; Guy G. Stroumsa, „Mystical Jerusalems", in *Jerusalem. Its sanctity and centrality* (wie Anm. 34), S. 349–370; Holger A. Klein, *Byzanz, der Westen und das ‚wahre' Kreuz: die Geschichte einer Reliquie und ihrer künstlerischen Fassung in Byzanz und im Abendland* (Spätantike – frühes Christentum – Byzanz: Reihe B 17; Wiesbaden: Reichert, 2004), S. 19–91.

44. Konrad Robert, „Das himmlische und das irdische Jerusalem im mittelalterlichen Denken. Mystische Vorstellung und geschichtliche Wirkung", in *Speculum historiale. Geschichte im Spiegel von Geschichtsschreibung und Geschichtsdeutung*, ed. Clemens Bauer, Laetitia Böhm und Max Müller (Freiburg, München: Alber, 1965), S. 523–540; *La dimora di Dio con gli uomini*. Ausstellungskatalog, Milano, Università Catolica del S. Cuore, 20 maggio – 5 giugno 1983, ed. Maria Luisa Gatti Perer (Milano: Vita e Pensiero, 1983); Georg Kretschmar, *Die Offenbarung des Johannes. Die Geschichte ihrer*

behielt auch im Hochmittelalter ihre Stellung als eschatologische Erinnerungslandschaft, und apokalyptische Vorstellungen lassen sich – vor allem in Krisenzeiten – immer wieder beobachten.[45]

Beide Traditionen – sowohl die historische als auch die spirituelle – wurden im 3. bis 5. Jahrhundert wesentlich im Zuge der christlichen Jerusalemallegorese geprägt, wobei die anfangs stärkere Tendenz zum spirituellen Verständnis Jerusalems bei gleichzeitiger Distanz zur realen Stadt nach der konstantinischen Wende einer positiveren Lesart wich. Kirchenlehrer und andere Theologen wie Origenes (gest. 253/254),[46] Eusebius von Caesarea (gest. 339),[47] Kyrill von Jerusalem (gest. ca. 386),[48] Hieronymus (gest. 420),[49] Augustinus (gest. 430)[50] und

---

Auslegung im 1. Jahrtausend (Calwer Theologische Monographien B 9; Stuttgart: Calwer Verlag, 1985); Bianca Kühnel, *From the earthly to the heavenly Jerusalem. Representations of the Holy City in Christian art of the first millennium* (Römische Quartalschrift für christliche Altertumskunde und Kirchengeschichte. Supplementheft 42; Rom etc.: Herder, 1987); Jan Pieper, *Das Labyrinthische. Über die Idee des Verborgenen, Rätselhaften, Schwierigen in der Geschichte der Architektur* (Braunschweig etc.: Vieweg, 1987); Avraham Grossman, „Jerusalem in Jewish Apocalyptic Literature", in *The history of Jerusalem*, Band I (wie Anm. 33), S. 295–310; *The real and ideal Jerusalem* (wie Anm. 59). Sanders, „Jerusalem and its Temple" (wie Anm. 40), S. 93–100; Peter Söllner, *Jerusalem, die hochgebaute Stadt. Eschatologisches und himmlisches Jerusalem im Frühjudentum und im frühen Christentum* (Texte und Arbeiten zum neutestamentlichen Zeitalter 25; Tübingen etc.: Francke, 1998); vgl. unter anderem Tobias 13:17 zu älteren Bildern Jerusalems als edelsteinbesetzter Stadt der Herrlichkeit.

45 Norman Housley, „The eschatological imperative: Messianism and holy war in Europe, 1260–1556", in *Toward the Millennium: Messianic expectations from the Bible to Waco*, ed. Peter Schäfer und Mark Cohen (Studies in the History of Religions 77; Leiden: Brill, 1998), S. 123–150; Christoph Auffarth, *Irdische Wege und himmlischer Lohn. Kreuzzug, Jerusalem und Fegefeuer in religionswissenschaftlicher Perspektive* (Veröffentlichungen des Max-Planck-Instituts für Geschichte 144; Göttingen: Vandenhoeck & Ruprecht, 2002), weist darauf hin, dass die Bedeutung dieser apokalyptischen und eschatologischen Vorstellungen nicht überschätzt werden darf.

46 *Commentarii in Evangelium Ioannis* 10:18 und *Homilien zu Jeremia* 5:13 (*Homélies sur Jérémie*, ed. Pierre Husson und Pierre Nautin [Sources chrétiennes 232; Paris: Cerf, 1976], S. 311–315).

47 *Vita Constantini* 3.33 (wie Anm. 39).

48 Kyrill von Jerusalem, *Katechese* 4.10; 10.19 (*The Works of Saint Cyril of Jerusalem 1*, trans. Leo P. McCaulay und Anthony A. Stephenson [The Fathers of the Church 61; Washington: The Catholic University of America Press, 1969], S. 124, 207–210).

49 Hieronymus, *Epistula* 46 (ed. Hilberg, Band 1 [wie Anm. 41], S. 329–345) – den auffälligen Wandel in der Bewertung Jerusalems durch Hieronymus (Ep. 58, 129 – ibid., S. 527–241; Band 3, S. 163–175) beschreiben Perrone, „„The mystery of Judaea'" (wie Anm. 38), S. 234–236 und Paczkowski, „The Centrality of Jerusalem" (wie Anm. 38), S. 129–132.

50 Augustinus, *Enarrationes in Psalmos* 64:1 (*Sancti Aurelii Augustini Enarrationes in Psalmos* LI–C, ed. Eligius Dekkers und Iohannes Fraipont [Corpus Christianorum, Series Latina 39; Turnhout: Brepols 1990], S. 822–824); idem, *Confessiones* IX,13 und XII,16 (*Sancti Augustini confessionum libri XIII*, ed. Lucas Verjeijen [Corpus Christianorum,

vor allem Cassian (gest. 435)[51] erkannten Jerusalem in Anwendung der Lehre vom mehrfachen Schriftsinn nunmehr verschiedene Auslegungen zu: Fortan verstand man Jerusalem im historischen Sinn (Buchstabensinn) als die Stadt in Palästina, im allegorischen Sinne als die Kirche und Christus, im tropologischen Sinn als die Seele des einzelnen Gläubigen und im anagogischen Sinn als das himmlische Jerusalem und unser aller Mutter.[52] Das klarste Anzeichen für die christliche Aneignung Jerusalems im Verlauf des 4. Jahrhunderts ist die zu jener Zeit aufblühende Jerusalempilgerfahrt.[53] Doch blieb diese nicht unumstritten,[54] und erst im Zuge des allgemeinen Aufschwungs des Pilgerwesens im 11. Jahrhundert, gekoppelt mit dem Christozentrismus und der Jerusalemfrömmigkeit jener Zeit, erlangte sie herausragende Bedeutung.[55]

Auch für die nun errichteten Kreuzfahrerstaaten hatten das Heilige Land und Jerusalem fundierende Bedeutung. Die Bewohner entwickelten eine eigene „Siedleridentität", die nur entstehen konnte, weil in Palästina verschiedene identitätsstiftende Elemente zur Verfügung standen, zu denen neben einer eigenen Sprache vor allem zentrale Orte und wirksame Symbole gehörten.

Series Latina 27; Turnhout: Brepols, 1990], S. 152–154, 227–228). Dazu: Brouria Bitton-Ashkelony, „The attitudes of Church Fathers toward pilgrimage to Jerusalem in the fourth and fifth centuries", in *Jerusalem. Its sanctity and centrality* (wie Anm. 34), S. 188–203, hier S. 189–194 und Paczkowski, „The Centrality of Jerusalem" (wie Anm. 38), S. 132.

51 Cassian, *Collationes* XIV,8 (*Jean Cassien, Conferences*, ed. Eugène Pichery [Sources chrétiennes 54; Paris: Cerf, 1958], S. 189–192).

52 Walker, *Holy city, holy places* (wie Anm. 38); Wilken, *The Land called Holy* (wie Anm. 38); Elm, „Die himmlische und die irdische" (wie Anm. 33); Perrone, „‚The mystery of Judaea'" (wie Anm. 38); Stroumsa, „Mystical Jerusalems" (wie Anm. 43), S. 358–360; Oded Irshai, „The Jerusalem Bishopric and the Jews in the Fourth Century", in *Jerusalem. Its sanctity and centrality* (wie Anm. 34), S. 204–220, hier S. 207–214, der zu Recht auf den lokalen Kontext mancher Äußerungen Kyrills von Jerusalem hinweist.

53 John Wilkinson, *Jerusalem Pilgrims Before the Crusades* (Warminster: Aris Phillips, 1977); Herbert Donner, *Pilgerfahrt ins Heilige Land. Die ältesten Berichte christlicher Palästinapilger (4.–7. Jahrhundert)* (Stuttgart: Verlag Katholisches Bibelwerk, 1979, [2]2002); Bernhard Kötting, *Peregrinatio religiosa. Wallfahrten in der Antike und das Pilgerwesen in der Alten Kirche* (Forschungen zur Volkskunde 35; Münster: Stenderhoff, [2]1980); Edward D. Hunt, *Holy Land Pilgrimage in the Later Roman Empire AD 312–460* (Oxford: Clarendon Press, 1982); Heribert Busse und Georg Kretschmar, *Jerusalemer Heiligtumstraditionen in altkirchlicher und frühislamischer Zeit* (Abhandlungen des Deutschen Palästinavereins 8; Wiesbaden: Harrassowitz, 1987); Josef Engelmann, „Das Jerusalem der Pilger. Kreuzauffindung und Wallfahrt", *Jahrbuch für Antike und Christentum*, Ergänzungsband 20/1 (1995), S. 24–36.

54 Giles Constable, „Opposition to Pilgrimage in the Middle Ages", in *Studia Gratiana* 19 (1976), S. 123–146; Bitton-Ashkelony, *The attitudes of church fathers toward pilgrimage* (wie Anm. 50); Walker, *Holy city, holy places* (wie Anm. 38).

55 John Wilkinson, Joyce Hill und W. F. Ryan, *Jerusalem Pilgrimage 1099–1185* (Works issued by the Hakluyt Society II,167; London: Hakluyt Society, 1988); Giles Constable, „The Place of the Crusader in Medieval Society", in *Viator* 29 (1998), S. 377–403.

Unter den herausragenden, identitätsstiftenden Orten ist besonders die Heilige Stadt und hier insbesondere die Grabeskirche mit dem Heiligen Grab herauszuheben. Hier residierte die höchste geistliche Autorität des Königreichs – der Patriarch –, hier wurden die Monarchen seit 1118 gekrönt und bestattet. Zusammen mit anderen berühmten Bauten Jerusalems wie dem Davidsturm und dem Felsendom wurde die Grabeskirche auf offiziellen „Bedeutungsträgern" des Königreichs abgebildet: Man fand sie unter anderem auf Siegeln und auf Münzen. Schließlich die Symbole: Für alle vier Kreuzfahrerherrschaften gleichermaßen war dies das Kreuz, in dessen Namen sie erobert und gegründet worden waren.[56] Im Königreich Jerusalem traten außerdem die Grabeskirche und die wichtigste Reliquie des Reiches hinzu: die Heiligkreuzreliquie. Diese wurde bei den wichtigeren Prozessionen vorangetragen und mehr als dreißigmal als Kriegszeichen in die Schlacht geführt.[57]

Resümierend kann man feststellen, dass zur Zeit des Maimonides nicht nur die Kreuzzüge, sondern auch die aus ihnen hervorgegangenen Kreuzfahrerstaaten ältere christliche Deutungen Jerusalems um weitere Auslegungen erweiterten.

2. Islam

Zu Lebzeiten des Maimonides herrschten jedoch nicht allein die Christen über Jerusalem. Seit der Übergabe der Stadt an Saladin im Oktober 1187 war diese muslimisch, was aus der Sicht des Sultans und seiner Kämpfer einer Rückkehr zu einem als gottgegebenen und gerecht empfundenen Zustand gleichkam. Denn auch für den Islam ist Jerusalem einer der heiligsten Orte.[58] Dies drückt

---

56 Giles Constable, „Jerusalem and the sign of the Cross (with particular reference to the cross of pilgrimage and crusading in the twelfth century)", in *Jerusalem. Its sanctity and centrality* (wie Anm. 34), S. 371–381. Rudolf Hiestand, „‚Nam qui fuimus Occidentales, nunc facti sumus Orientales' – Siedlung und Siedleridentität in den Kreuzfahrerstaaten", in *Siedler-Identität: neun Fallstudien von der Antike bis zur Gegenwart*, ed. Christof Dipper und Rudolf Hiestand (Frankfurt am Main etc.: Lang, 1995), S. 61–80.

57 Deborah Gerish, „The True Cross and the Kings of Jerusalem", in *The Haskins Society Journal* 8 (1996), S. 137–155; Alan V. Murray, „Mighty Against the Enemies of Christ: The Relic of the True Cross in the Armies of the Kingdom of Jerusalem", in *The Crusades and Their Sources: Essays Presented to Bernard Hamilton*, ed. John France und William Zajac (Aldershot: Ashgate, 1998), S. 217–238; Nikolas Jaspert, „Vergegenwärtigungen Jerusalems in Architektur und Reliquienkult", in *Jerusalem im Hoch- und Spätmittelalter* (wie Anm. 35), S. 219–270.

58 Francis E. Peters, *Jerusalem and Mecca. The typology of the Holy City* (New York University Studies in Near Eastern Civilization 11; New York etc.: New York University Press, 1986); Hadia Dajani-Shakeel, „Al-Quds: Jerusalem in the consciousness of the counter-crusader", in *The Meeting of Two Worlds* (wie Anm. 36), S. 201–222; Angelika Neuwirth, „Erste Qibla – Fernstes Masjid? Jerusalem im Horizont des historischen

sich schon im Namen aus, unter dem die Stadt seit dem 10. Jahrhundert im Islam vor allem bekannt ist: *al-quds* (Heiligtum). Ihre besondere Bedeutung für die Muslime rührt aus verschiedenen Wurzeln: zum einen daraus, dass in ihr Christus starb, der im Islam als bedeutender Prophet gilt. Zum anderen und vor allem aber ist *al-quds* der Zielpunkt der so genannten „Nachtreise" (arabisch *isrā'*) Muḥammads. In einer Nacht sei der Prophet nach Jerusalem und zurück nach Mekka entrückt worden, ein Beleg für seine Übernatürlichkeit und für seine Gottgefälligkeit. Außerdem soll er nach einem bis heute populären Stoff der volkstümlichen Muḥammadvita von Jerusalem aus auf der so genannten „Himmelsleiter" (arabisch *mi'rāǧ*) in den Himmel und von dort mit der Auflage zum fünfmaligen täglichen Gebet zur Erde zurückgekehrt sein. Schließlich gilt Jerusalem auch im Islam als der Ort, an dem sich das Jüngste Gericht ereignen werde. Es erstaunt also nicht, dass diese Heilige Stadt für Muslime einen besonderen religiösen Nimbus besitzt und nach Mekka und Medina das drittwichtigste Pilgerzentrum darstellt.[59] Dies wird auch an den Bauten des Tempelplatzes (arabisch *al-ḥaram aš-šarīf)* ersichtlich: Nach der Eroberung um die Jahre 636–638, welche die Muslime als eine Befreiung aus der Herrschaft der Polytheisten ansahen, wurde um den von Muḥammad bei seinem Aufstieg zurückgelassenen Fußabdruck im Jahre 691/692 der Felsendom vollendet – ob als Konkurrenzbau zur Kaaba in Mekka oder zur benachbarten Grabeskirche in Jerusalem, ist in der Forschung umstritten. Unmittelbar daneben steht die um 705–715 errichtete al-Aqṣā-Moschee, das Ziel der „Nachtreise" – beides zentrale Erinnerungsorte des Islam, deren Bedeutung gerade zur Zeit des Maimonides unter der Herrschaft der Ayyubiden eine besondere Zunahme erfuhr.[60]

Muhammad", in *Zion – Ort der Begegnung* (wie Anm. 37), S. 227–270; Ammīqam Elad, *Medieval Jerusalem and Islamic worship. Holy places, ceremonies, pilgrimage* (Islamic history and civilization 8; Leiden etc.: Brill, 1995); Ammīqam Elad, „Pilgrims and pilgrimage to Jerusalem during the early Muslim period", in *Jerusalem. Its sanctity and centrality* (wie Anm. 34), S. 300–314; Angelika Neuwirth, „Jerusalem and the Genesis of Islamic Scripture", in *Jerusalem. Its sanctity and centrality* (wie Anm. 34), S. 315–325; Hartmut Bobzin, „Jerusalem aus muslimischer Perspektive während der Kreuzfahrerzeit", in *Jerusalem im Hoch- und Spätmittelalter* (wie Anm. 35), S. 203–218; Tilman Seidensticker, „Jerusalem aus der Sicht des Islams", in *Jerusalem im Widerstreit politischer und religiöser Interessen* (wie Anm. 38), S. 99–112.

59 Ora Limor, „The Place of the End of Days: Eschatological Geography of Jerusalem", in *The real and ideal Jerusalem in Jewish, Christian and Islamic art. Studies in honor of Bezalel Narkiss on the occasion of his seventieth birthday*, ed. Bianca Kühnel (Jewish art 23/24; Jerusalem: Center for Jewish Art, 1998), S. 13–22, hier S. 18–19; Elad, „Pilgrims and pilgrimage to Jerusalem" (wie Anm. 58).

60 Zu den Bauten und zur Archäologie Jerusalems siehe, mit weiterer Literatur: Klaus Bieberstein, *Jerusalem. Grundzüge der Baugeschichte vom Chalkolithikum bis zur Frühzeit der osmanischen Herrschaft* (3 Bände; Tübinger Atlas des Vorderen Orients. Beihefte B 100/1–3; Wiesbaden: Reichert, 1994); Andreas Kaplony, *The Haram of Jerusalem 324–*

3. Judentum

Für das Judentum schließlich – und damit kehren wir wieder zu Maimonides zurück – nimmt die Stadt Davids – der Ort, den der König den Jebusiten abnahm – eine singuläre Stellung ein. Der Berg Zion symbolisiert als gängiges Synonym für Jerusalem das davidische Königtum und den zentralen Kult, der gegen Ende der Zeit des Ersten Tempels (ca. 1004–586 v. Chr.) auf Jerusalem konzentriert wurde.[61] Auch in der Zeit des Zweiten Tempels (538 v. Chr.–70 n. Chr.) besaß die Stadt eine politisch wie kultisch herausragende Stellung, die sich nicht zuletzt in besonderen Reinheits- und Bebauungsvorschriften niederschlug.[62]

Doch neben dem Bild der Stadt als politischem und religiösem Zentrum des Judentums entwickelte die Aggadah bereits in der Zeit des Zweiten Tempels eine parallele Vorstellung, wonach neben dem irdischen ein himmlisches Jerusalem stand, das Zentrum der Welt, ein Ort ungeheurer Größe, der herabkommen werde, um den Platz der irdischen Stadt einzunehmen.[63] Im jüdischen Verständnis war spätestens seit dem Jubiläenbuch des zweiten vorchristlichen Jahrhunderts Jerusalem sogar der *umbilicus mundi*, der Nabel der Welt. Spätere rabbinische Texte deuteten dieses Bild nicht mehr geographisch, sondern kosmologisch und sahen in Jerusalem den Ort der unmittelbaren Verbindung mit Gott.[64] Dort, am Ölberg, werde der Messias wiederkehren und die Gottesherrschaft mit seinem Volk errichten.[65]

1099. Temple, Friday Mosque, Area of Spiritual Power (Freiburger Islamstudien 22; Stuttgart: Steiner, 2002).

61 Shemaryahu Talmon, „The Significance of Jerusalem in Biblical Thought", in *The real and ideal Jerusalem* (wie Anm. 59), S. 1–12, hier S. 6–7; Sara Japhet, „From the King's Sanctuary to the Chosen City", in *Jerusalem. Its sanctity and centrality* (wie Anm. 34), S. 349–370, hier S. 5–10; Yair Zakovitch, „The First Stages of Jerusalem's Sanctification under David: A Literary and Ideological Analysis", in *Jerusalem. Its sanctity and centrality* (wie Anm. 34), S. 16–35; William W. Hallo, „Jerusalem under Hezekiah: an Assyrological Perspective", in ibid., S. 36–52.

62 Shmuel Safrai, „Jerusalem in the Halacha of the Second Temple Period", in *The centrality of Jerusalem. Historical perspectives*, ed. Marcel Poorthuis (Kampen: Kok Pharos, 1996), S. 94–113; Stefan C. Reif, „Jerusalem in Jewish liturgy", in *Jerusalem. Its sanctity and centrality* (wie Anm. 34), S. 424–437; Lee I. Levine, „Second Temple Jerusalem: A Jewish City in the Greco-Roman Orbit", in ibid., S. 53–68, hier S. 54–56; Frédéric Manns, „A Response to Professor A. Shinan", in *Jerusalem. House of prayer* (wie Anm. 34), S. 72–80.

63 Limor, „The Place of the End of Days" (wie Anm. 59); Albert I. Baumgarten, „The Role of Jerusalem and the Temple in the ‚End of Days' Speculation in the Second Temple Period", in *Jerusalem. Its sanctity and centrality* (wie Anm. 34), S. 77–89, der allgemein auf den jüdischen Messianismus – auch ohne Fixierung auf Jerusalem – eingeht.

64 Söllner, „Jerusalem, die hochgebaute Stadt" (wie Anm. 44); Talmon, „The Significance of Jerusalem in Biblical Thought" (wie Anm. 61), S. 8–11; Philip S. Alexander, „Jerusalem as the Omphalos of the World: On the History of a Geographical Concept", in

Auch in der Diaspora nach der Zerstörung des Tempels äußerte und äußert sich jüdische Zionliebe und Zionsehnsucht sowohl in der Jerusalemallegorese des nachbiblischen Judentums als auch ganz konkret in Pilgerreisen oder der Immigration ins Heilige Land.[66] Die Vorstellung, sich durch die Anwesenheit an einem *locus sanctus* zu reinigen und selbst zu heiligen, ist älter als das Christentum und fand unter anderem in den Worten des Tobias (12:13) und des Isaias (2:2–5) seinen Niederschlag, wonach Jerusalem das Ziel der großen Pilgerfahrt der Völker sei. Die in der Bibel festgehaltene Vorschrift, wonach jeder erwachsene Jude dreimal im Jahr Jerusalem aufsuchen solle (Exodus 23:17; Deuteronomium 16:16), entfaltete schon zum Ende des Zweiten Tempels sowie endgültig mit der Diaspora des Jahres 70 nach Christus eine ganz eigene Wirksamkeit.[67] Manche Juden und Christen zogen nicht nur nach Palästina, sondern blieben auch dort und beschlossen ihre Tage im Lande des Herrn, andere gaben sich damit zufrieden, die Stätten gesehen zu haben, um dann in ihre Heimat zurückzukehren. Diese Tradition blieb auch im Früh- und Hochmittelalter ungebrochen, wie die zitierten Reisebeschreibungen und vielfältige Belege für die jüdische Emigration nach Palästina zur Zeit des Maimonides belegen.

Die Jerusalemallegorese der rabbinischen Literatur des Frühmittelalters wiederum lässt eine ähnlich zwiespältige Beurteilung der Stadt erkennen wie im Christentum.[68] Auch unter den jüdischen Gelehrten standen den positiven auch negative Deutungen der Stadt Davids gegenüber, in denen auf ihre Schwächen und Verfehlungen hingewiesen wird. Die Schicksalsschläge, die Jerusalem trafen – ihre Eroberung durch die persischen Sassaniden, durch die Muslime und später durch die Christen –, wurden von jüdischen Gelehrten unterschiedlich, auch apokalyptisch, gedeutet.[69] Diese Doppeldeutigkeit wird

---

Jerusalem. Its sanctity and centrality (wie Anm. 34), S. 104–119, der auf griechische Einflüsse hinweist. Die Stelle dürfte auf Äthiopischer Henoch 26:1 zurückgehen (ibid., S. 109).

65 Sanders, „Jerusalem and its Temple" (wie Anm. 40), S. 93–102.

66 Marianne Awerbuch, „Zionsliebe – Zionssehnsucht", in *Die Reise nach Jerusalem – Eine kulturhistorische Exkursion in die Stadt der Städte, 3000 Jahre Davidsstadt*, ed. Hendrik Budde und Andreas Nachama (Berlin 1995), S. 44–49; Haggai Ben-Shammai, „Jerusalem in early medieval Jewish Bible exegesis", in *Jerusalem. Its sanctity and centrality* (wie Anm. 34), S. 447–464.

67 Martin Goodman, „The Pilgrimage Economy of Jerusalem in the Second Temple Period", in *Jerusalem. Its sanctity and centrality* (wie Anm. 34), S. 69–76.

68 Avigdor Shinan, „The Many Names of Jerusalem", in *Jerusalem. Its sanctity and centrality* (wie Anm. 34), S. 120–131.

69 Günter Stemberger, „Jerusalem in the Early Seventh Century: Hopes and Aspirations of Christians and Jews", in *Jerusalem. Its sanctity and centrality* (wie Anm. 34), S. 260–273, der die Schriften des Strategius/Eustratius, Sophronius, Pseudo-Methodius auf christlicher Seite und den Sefer Zerubbabel, den Sefer Eliyahu und drei Piyyutim auf jüdischer Seite untersucht; die jüdischen Texte interpretierten die Ereignisse stark

auch an den vielen Bezeichnungen erkennbar, mit denen die rabbinische Literatur Jerusalem versah und die in bis zu siebzig Epitheta umfassenden Namenslisten gesammelt wurden.[70] Doch trotz aller Vorbehalte wurde die insgesamt herausragende Position der Stadt im jüdischen Denken nie ernsthaft in Frage gestellt. In liturgischen Kommemorationen und einer Vielzahl apokrypher Gesetze und Gewohnheiten stand die Stadt Davids im Mittelpunkt. Gerade die in der alltäglichen religiösen Praxis angesiedelten Bräuche, wie sie entweder in Jerusalem selbst oder fern von Israel zu besonderen Anlässen wie Hochzeiten und Trauerfeiern gepflegt wurden beziehungsweise werden, dienen dazu, Jerusalem im kollektiven Bewusstsein der Judenheit wach zu halten.[71]

Resümierend kann man also festhalten, dass das biblische, aber auch das nachbiblische Judentum wesentlich dazu beigetragen hat, die Stadt Jerusalem mit einer Vielzahl von – oftmals in ihrer Widersprüchlichkeit kaum auflösbaren – Sinngehalten aufzuladen.[72]

Vor diesem Hintergrund mag es erstaunen, dass Maimonides Israel verließ und auch nach der Eroberung Jerusalems 1187 in Ägypten blieb. Hierfür dürfte die herausragende Position verantwortlich gewesen sein, die er inzwischen unter den Weisen der großen Kairoer Gemeinde erlangt hatte. Dennoch gibt es genügend Aussagen des Maimonides, die seine besondere Beziehung zum Gelobten Land erkennen lassen, wie insbesondere Isadore Twersky herausgearbeitet hat.[73]

---

eschatologisch. Robert Chazan, „Jerusalem as Christian Symbol during the First Crusade: Jewish Awareness and Response", in *Jerusalem. Its sanctity and centrality* (wie Anm. 34), S. 382–391, der auch auf die Deutung der Pogrome im Rheinland durch eine auf Jerusalem deutende Bildersprache hinweist und dies als Transferprozess zwischen christlicher und jüdischer Jerusalemsehnsucht deutet; Burton L. Visotzky, „Jerusalem in Geonic Era Aggadah", in *Jerusalem. Its sanctity and centrality* (wie Anm. 34), S. 438–446, hier S. 442–444.

70 Shinan, „The Many Names of Jerusalem" (wie Anm. 68); Talmon, „The Significance of Jerusalem in Biblical Thought" (wie Anm. 61), S. 4–5 schließt ebenso von der Häufigkeit und der Verschiedenartigkeit der Bezeichnungen Jerusalems auf dessen Bedeutung im jüdischen Denken.

71 David Golinkin, „Jerusalem in Jewish Law and Custom: a Preliminary Typology", in *Jerusalem. Its sanctity and centrality* (wie Anm. 34), S. 408–423; Reif, „Jerusalem in Jewish liturgy" (wie Anm. 62); Andreas Gotzmann, „Zentrum in Abwesenheit – Jüdische Traditionen zu Jerusalem vor der Staatsgründung Israels", in *Jerusalem im Widerstreit politischer und religiöser Interessen* (wie Anm. 38), S. 59–72.

72 Mit weiterer Literatur: Francis E. Peters, *Jerusalem. The Holy City in the Eyes of Chroniclers, Visitors, Pilgrims and Prophets from the Days of Abraham to the Beginnings of Modern Times* (Princeton, N.J.: Princeton University Press, 1985); *City of the great king. Jerusalem from David to the present*, ed. Nitza Rosovsky (Cambridge, Mass. etc.: Harvard University Press, 1996); *Jerusalem. Its sanctity and centrality* (wie Anm. 34); *The centrality of Jerusalem* (wie Anm. 62); *The Holy Land, holy lands, and Christian history* (wie Anm. 33).

73 Twersky, „Maimonides and Eretz Yisrael" (wie Anm. 13).

IV. Maimonides und Jerusalem

Die Aussagen des Maimonides über Jerusalem lassen auf eine doppelte Bindung des Gelehrten an die Heilige Stadt schließen: zum einen auf eine abstrakte, theoretische Beziehung und zum anderen auf eine eher individuelle, spirituelle Anbindung. Die Überlegungen des Maimonides zur Rechtsgültigkeit der Halakhah berühren immer wieder das Gelobte Land – genauer: die Beziehung zwischen der politisch-institutionellen Herrschaft der Juden über Israel und dem in diesem Rahmen geschaffenen Recht. In dieser Facette des maimonidischen Denkens tritt uns Palästina – und zwar entweder als politisches Gebilde oder als geographischer Raum – als Grundlage des jüdischen Rechts entgegen. Auch in den Rechtskompilationen des Maimonides finden sich verschiedene Bezüge zum Heiligen Land, wobei nicht zwischen dem gegenwärtigen Zustand und einem zukünftigen, jüdisch beherrschten Israel unterschieden wird.[74] Twersky formuliert prägnant: „[...] anyone who plunges into the completely new sections of his Great Compilation [...] is returned to Eretz Yisrael in general and to Jerusalem in particular".[75]

Viel grundlegender als diese eher praktischen Überlegungen des Maimonides zur Rolle Palästinas für Kultus und Recht der Juden ist seine Haltung zur Heiligkeit Jerusalems. Zwar sah Maimonides nach Ausweis Gad Freudenthals im Gegensatz zu zeitgenössischen Denkern wie Juda ha-Levi oder Abraham Ibn Ezra Jerusalem nicht als den Ort der unmittelbaren Verbindung mit Gott.[76] Doch meinte auch er, dass das Göttliche dort auf ewig präsent und durch keine Macht der Welt zu vertreiben sei.[77] Neben diesen klaren, vielfach im Werk des Maimonides zu findenden Aussagen zur Heiligkeit und zur Zentralität Israels

---

74 Ibid., S. 264–265; vgl. die Stellen aus der *Mišneh Torah* bei Moses Maimonides: *A Maimonides reader*, ed. Isadore Twersky (New York 1972), S. 143, 176–177, 194–195. Zur Rolle, die Maimonides Jerusalem in messianischer Zeit zuerkennt, siehe Gad Freudenthal, „Jérusalem ville sainte? La perspective maïmonidienne", in *Revue de l'Histoire des Religions* 217 (2000), S. 689–705, hier S. 700–703 – herzlichen Dank an Gad Freudenthal für die Zusendung seines Beitrags.

75 Twersky, „Maimonides and Eretz Yisrael" (wie Anm. 13), S. 279.

76 Freudenthal, „Jérusalem ville sainte" (wie Anm. 74), S. 690–697. Zur Sicht der Glaubensgenossen vgl. Shalom Rosenberg, „The Link to the Land of Israel in Jewish Thought: A Clash of Perspectives", in *The Land of Israel: Jewish Perspectives*, ed. Lawrence A. Hoffmann (Notre Dame, Ind. 1986), S. 139–169.

77 Twersky, „Maimonides and Eretz Yisrael" (wie Anm. 13), S. 285–288. Vgl. die Stellen aus der *Mišneh Torah* bei Maimonides, *A Maimonides reader* (wie Anm. 74), S. 116–119, 148–149, 173, 216, 218–219 und insbesondere 142: „Because the sanctity of the Sanctuary of Jerusalem derives from the Divine Presence, which could not be banished". Gad Freudenthal weist mit Recht darauf hin, dass Jerusalem nach Ansicht des Maimonides nicht von Anbeginn der Zeiten heilig gewesen, sondern erst in der Epoche der Könige und durch deren Wirken auf ewig geheiligt worden sei: Freudenthal, „Jérusalem ville sainte" (wie Anm. 73), S. 698–700.

und Jerusalems für die Judenheit nehmen sich die Hinweise auf dessen persönliche, individuelle Erfahrungen und Motivationen eher bescheiden aus. Allerdings besitzen wir seine Selbstbezeichnung, er sei ein „nach Spanien gekommener Exulant Jerusalems";[78] und zu Beginn des *Iggeret Teman* hält er in einer seltenen, biographisch geprägten Passage fest, er sei seinerzeit aus dem Westen, also aus dem Maghreb, aufgebrochen, um „die Lieblichkeit des Herrn und seine Heiligen Stätten wahrzunehmen".[79] Ein weiteres Beispiel für den Wert, den Maimonides für seine eigene Person Palästina beimaß, bietet dessen Beschreibung der Reise, die er 1165/1166 nach Jerusalem und Hebron unternahm:

> Am neunten Tag des [hebräischen] Monats Cheschwan verließ ich Jerusalem in Richtung Hebron, um die Gräber meiner Vorväter [Abraham, Isaak und Jakob] in der Höhle von Machpela zu küssen. Ich legte das Gelübde ab, diese beiden Tage [als ich Jerusalem und Hebron besuchte] würden mir Feiertage sein, gewidmet dem Gebet und der Freude. So wie ich dort auf den Trümmern gebetet habe, so sei es mir und ganz Israel vergönnt, bald das Heilige Land zu schauen, aufgerichtet und aus seinem Verfall erhoben.

Mit diesen Überlegungen zum Zustand seines Volkes endet Maimonides seinen Bericht.[80] Und dennoch verließ der Gelehrte das Gelobte Land und zog nach Ägypten. Die Gründe hierfür sind bereits angesprochen worden, doch mutet es merkwürdig an, wenn Maimonides in der *Mišneh Torah* kategorisch erklärt: „Zu allen Zeiten soll man in Palästina leben, selbst wenn die Mehrzahl der Bevölkerung heidnisch ist, und nicht außerhalb Palästinas, selbst wenn die Mehrheit der dortigen Bevölkerung jüdisch ist; denn derjenige, der Palästina verläßt, betreibt gleichsam Idolatrie".[81] Hier wird eine Diskrepanz zwischen der Biographie des Gelehrten und seinen Vorschriften erkennbar, die nie ganz aufgehoben wurde.

Es ist daher vielleicht bezeichnend, dass Maimonides zwar nie nach Israel zurückkehrte, aber dennoch dort bestattet wurde. In Tiberias, am See Genezareth, wo auch andere jüdische Gelehrte wie Rabban Joḥanan ben Sakkai und der aus Navarra stammende Juda ha-Levi gebettet wurden,[82] fand er seine letzte Ruhe. Für diese posthume Rückkehr nach Israel lieferte Maimonides selbst eine Begründung und zugleich eine Entschuldigung: Im vierzehnten Buch der *Mišneh Torah* wies er darauf hin, dass derjenige die Versöhnung mit

---

78 Heschel, *Maimonides* (wie Anm. 3), S. 53.

79 Nach der englischsprachigen Übersetzung bei Twersky, *Maimonides and Eretz Yisrael* (wie Anm. 13), S. 288.

80 Heschel, *Maimonides* (wie Anm. 3), S. 68 nach *Kobez teshubot ha-Ramban ve-iggerotav*, ed. Abraham ben Aryeh Lichtenberg (Leipzig: H. L. Schnaus, 1859; Nachdruck Farnborough: Gregg, 1969), Band 2, S. V.

81 Übersetzt in *A Maimonides reader* (wie Anm. 74), S. 219.

82 Arbel, *Maimonides. A spiritual biography* (wie Anm. 3), S. 52.

Gott fände, der im Gelobten Land begraben werde. Es sei zwar besser, zu Lebzeiten dort zu weilen, als im Tode dort bestattet zu werden, doch hätten einige der Größten Israels ihre Toten dorthin überführt; man möge lediglich an Jakob oder Joseph denken.[83] Hier, im Gelobten Land, schloss sich also der Lebenskreis eines Mannes, der auf die vielfältigsten Arten mit der Stadt Davids und ihren Herrschern verbunden war.

Diese Verbindung endete jedoch keineswegs mit dem Tod des Maimonides, sondern lebte in positiver wie negativer Hinsicht fort. Als belastet dürfte man die Rezeptionsgeschichte des maimonidischen Werkes in Palästina bezeichnen, denn es sollte hier besonders scharfe Kritik erfahren. Das christliche Akkon des 13. Jahrhunderts brachte eines der bedeutendsten Zentren jüdischer Studien des Mittelalters hervor, dessen Verfügungen im gesamten Vorderen Orient autoritativen Charakter gewannen. Zum Ende des Jahrhunderts erlangte Rabbi Shelomo le Petit hier großen Einfluss. Dieser Gelehrte wandte sich scharf gegen die Werke des Maimonides und verkündete zur Mitte der 1280-er Jahre sogar ein Verbot aller seiner Schriften. Die Verfügung sollte die jüdischen Gemeinden des Vorderen Orients spalten und auch der Akkonenser Gemeinde schweren Schaden zufügen.[84]

Dieser Bekämpfung des Maimonides und seines Werkes steht die Verehrung gegenüber, die er im Heiligen Land und darüber hinaus nach seinem Tod unter den Juden genoss. Sie drückte sich auf vielfältige Weise aus, am eindrücklichsten aber in der Bedeutung, die seine Grablege am See Genezareth in der jüdischen Welt erlangte. Reisende des Spätmittelalters berichten, dass dieser Ort sich zu einer eigenen Station für jüdische Pilger entwickelte, zu einem geheiligten Platz, den man ausdrücklich ansteuerte, um den Ruheort des großen Gelehrten oder des „Heiligen" (*ṣaddiq*), wie ihn ein anonymer jüdischer Reisender des 14. Jahrhunderts bezeichnete, zu besuchen.[85] Das Grab des Maimonides wurde so zu einem weiteren sakralen Ort dieses ohnehin an geheiligten Räumen gesegneten Landes. Dieses aufschlussreiche, wenngleich weitgehend unbekannte Faktum mag sich als letzter Mosaikstein in das Bild eines Mannes einfügen, der nicht müde wurde, die Heiligkeit des Gelobten Landes zu betonen: Auch in der eigenen Person und im Tode trug Maimonides zur Sakralisierung Palästinas bei.

---

83 *A Maimonides reader* (wie Anm. 73), S. 218, vgl. auch Twersky, „Maimonides and Eretz Yisrael" (wie Anm. 13), S. 289. Zu den weiteren in Tiberias bestatteten Gelehrten vgl. Binyamīn Ben-Yōna Tudela, *Syrien und Palästina* (wie Anm. 5), S. 56. Es dürfte auch kein Zufall sein, dass gerade in Jerusalem auf die Nachricht von seinem Tode ein Sonderfasten verkündet wurde: Yellin und Abrahams, *Maimonides* (wie Anm. 3), S. 204.

84 Prawer, *The History of the Jews* (wie Anm. 4), S. 283–291; Schein, „Jewish settlement in Palestine" (wie Anm. 5), S. 34.

85 Prawer, *The History of the Jews* (wie Anm. 4), S. 182, 247; Meri, *The cult of saints* (wie Anm. 10), S. 65–66, 219. Zum Begriff des *ṣaddiq* vgl. ibid., S. 62–66 und den Eintrag „Zaddik" in *Encyclopaedia Judaica* (Jerusalem, 1971–1972), Band 16, S. 910–911.

Maimonides and Charity in the Light of the Geniza Documents

by

Mark R. Cohen

Princeton University

Maimonides is best known as a philosopher, a physician, and a legist. But he was also a public figure, a "man of action", in the title of one of Goitein's essays.[1] This paper seeks to blend the two images: Maimonides as a man of action in the Jewish community and Maimonides as an intellectual, particularly as codifier of Jewish law. It addresses the following question: how are Maimonides' activities in the realm of charity "on the ground", so-to-speak, reflected in his codification of the laws of charity in the *Mishneh Torah*? It is, therefore, a study of the interaction of normative law and social history. We are able to undertake this inquiry thanks to the documents from everyday life found in the Cairo Geniza, which include hundreds of letters of the poor and letters of recommendation on their behalf, as well as hundreds of alms lists and lists of donors to public charity.[2]

Maimonides' codification

As far as we know, Maimonides was the first to codify the dispersed laws of charity in the Bible, rabbinic, and geonic literature. He had no model, no prior codification of Jewish eleemosynary legislation before him. Precisely because there is no earlier corpus of laws on charity, Maimonides' creation stands as a

---

1 Shlomo D. Goitein, "Maimonides, 'Man of Action': A Revision of the Master's Biography in Light of the Geniza Documents", in *Hommage à Georges Vajda: Études d'histoire et de pensée juives*, ed. Gérard Nahon and Charles Touati (Collection de la Revue des Études Juives 1; Louvain: Peeters, 1980), pp. 155–167.

2 I have identified over 880 of these documents for a study I have just completed on poverty and charity: a monograph, *Poverty and Charity in the Jewish Community of Medieval Egypt* (Princeton: Princeton University Press, 2005), and a collection of sources in translation, *The Voice of the Poor in the Middle Ages: An Anthology of Documents from the Cairo Geniza* (Princeton: Princeton University Press, 2005).

ready candidate for investigating the relationship between normative law and contemporary reality.

The Biblical laws of charity are scattered in the Torah. They reflect an agricultural society. The poor have free access to what is left over after harvest. Because they often had to borrow in distress, the Torah legislates other acts of benevolence, including interest-free loans, cancellation of debts, and release from debt-servitude after seven years. Laws of charity are similarly dispersed in rabbinic literature. There is much discussion in the Mishnah and Tosefta *Pe'ah* and in the Palestinian Talmud on *Pe'ah,* for instance, but because these and other agricultural laws applied only in the Land of Israel, the Babylonian Talmud has no tractate on the subjects treated in those compilations.

Because Biblical legislation on charity comes from an agricultural setting, the laws of charity found their home in Maimonides' *Code* in the "Book of Seeds" ("Sefer Zera'im"). Since the Babylonian Talmud, which by Maimonides' time formed the constitution of Jewish life in the Islamic world, lacks a tractate on *Pe'ah,* the great codifier had to draw his material from different and disparate locations in that Talmud, where laws of charity were brought by association with something else. His sources included, most importantly, a section in the first chapter of *Bava Batra* (8a–11a), where a long discussion of charity is kicked off associatively by a question about the length of time necessary to establish residence in a town. Another source is in *Ketubbot* (67a–68a), where a *mishnah* about marrying off daughters and orphans mentions the charity fund and so gave rise in the Gemara to a discussion of charity in general. In these cases and all others in the Talmud, the material is hardly systematic or comprehensive. It is not surprising, therefore, as Twersky tells us, that Maimonides resorts to the Tosefta and the Palestinian Talmud and even to original interpretation in the "Book of Seeds" more so than elsewhere in the *Code.*[3]

I will argue that in ordering the laws of charity and in some of their details, Maimonides' codification bears the imprint of local practice as reflected in the Geniza documents. This represents an aspect of originality in the *Code* that has not been well recognized.[4] To illustrate the phenomenon, let me begin with a trifling example. In his laws of charity, "Hilkhot mattenot 'aniyyim" 7.14, Maimonides writes: "Whoever *travels on business (bi-seḥora) to another town* and is assessed for alms by the inhabitants of the town he went to, must contribute

3 Isadore Twersky, *Introduction to the Code of Maimonides* (*Mishneh Torah*) (Yale Judaica Series 22; New Haven: Yale University Press, 1980), p. 266.

4 Abraham Cronbach talks about aspects of originality represented by apparent deviations from rabbinic sources, some of which he suggests reflect current practice in Maimonides' time. Abraham Cronbach, "The Maimonidean Code of Benevolence", in *Hebrew Union College Annual* 20 (1947), pp. 471–540. My contribution is to show that many of these original features and deviations can be explained with the aid of evidence from everyday life from the Geniza.

to the poor of that town". The source for this *halakhah* is a precedent in Tractate *Megillah* (27a) of the Babylonian Talmud, as was recognized by the two sixteenth-century commentators, R. David ibn Abi Zimra (Radbaz), the Spanish exile who settled in Egypt and became chief Rabbi of Cairo at the beginning of the sixteenth century, and R. Joseph Caro (*Kesef Mishneh*) of Sefat, Palestine, the author of the *Shulḥan Arukh*. Their commentaries surround the Maimonidean text in the standard printed editions. But the Talmud states: "If the townsmen of one town *travel to another town* and are assessed for alms..." This sentence does not mention a business trip. It does not take much imagination to hear in the word *bi-seḥora* that was added by Maimonides an echo of the intensely commercial Jewish society of the Mediterranean which he inhabited, and whose contours are familiar to us from the documents of the Geniza. The constant preoccupation with business matters that permeates Maimonides' *responsa* appears here in the *Mishneh Torah* as well, in one short word amplifying a *halakhah* from the Talmud with reverberations from daily life in twelfth-century Egypt.

Pidyon shevuyim, "Ransom of Captives"

We learn from several Geniza documents that, no sooner did Maimonides arrive in Egypt in the mid-1160s than he found himself organizing charity drives to ransom Jewish captives. Goitein suggested that it was his central role in this humanitarian effort around 1169 that catapulted Maimonides shortly after his arrival in Egypt into the leadership of the Jewish community as *Raʾīs al-Yahūd*.[5] The evidence shows, too, that the problem of redemption of captives as a practical issue was much on his mind during the years he was compiling the *Mishneh Torah*.

Ransoming captives in Egypt appears abundantly in Geniza letters. These prisoners usually appeared in Alexandria, the main Egyptian port of call on the Mediterranean coast. They were either captives of pirates or captives of war. Pirates brought their human prizes to the Jewish community and demanded money for their release. Thirty-three and a third dinars was the price for one. Sometimes captors tortured their prisoners in order to force the community to pay for their release. Alexandria could not shoulder the burden on its own, and so commonly other communities were asked to pledge sums toward the expense. A list of contributions from ten towns or villages in the Rīf, the Egyptian country-side, during the time of the head of the Jews, Samuel the Nagid b. Ḥananya, who was in office from 1140 to 1159, totaled 225 3/8 dinars, a sizeable sum.

5 Goitein, "Maimonides, 'Man of Action'" (see above n. 1).

Maimonides' action on behalf of captives shortly after his arrival in the country took the form of circular letters, which he dispatched around Egypt with emissaries. These men were charged with collecting money pledged to meet the emergency that followed the Crusader invasion of Egypt in 1168 and the capture of many Jews, who were taken by the Franks back to Palestine.[6]

Several Geniza letters and other documents have been connected with this crisis. The most well known of them is a circular letter bearing the date of 1169, Goitein has convincingly argued. In it Maimonides addresses the communities of Egypt, urging them to contribute money to the cause at hand:

> Act upon it in the same way as we, all the *judges* and the *elders and the student(s)*, have acted, going around, night and day, urging people in the synagogues, the markets, and at the doors of dwellings, in order to collect something towards this great goal. *Having contributed as much as we ourselves are able, you, too, should do for them (the captives) as fits your generosity and your [renown] as seekers of merit [through] kindness and love.* Write to tell us the total amount you collect on their behalf, through God the ex(alted's) compassion and your own. Exert yourselves to collect it quickly and send it to us with *our above-mentioned dignitary* R. Aaron ha-Levi.[7]

---

6 Chapter Three in my monograph (see above n. 2).

7 JTS (Jewish Theological Seminary) Ms. 8254.7 (formerly: 2896), ed. Shlomo D. Goitein, *Ha-yishuv be-ereṣ yisrael be-reshit ha-islam uvi-tequfat ha-ṣalbanim* (Palestinian Jewry in Early Islamic and Crusader Times), ed. Joseph Hacker (Jerusalem: Yad Izhak Ben-Zvi, 1980), pp. 312–314 and translated by him into English in "Moses Maimonides, 'Man of Action'" (see above n. 1), pp. 156–157. Also *Iggerot ha-Rambam – maqor we-tirgum* [Epistles of Maimonides], ed. Isaac Shailat (2 volumes; Jerusalem: Mosad Harav Kook, 5747/1987–1988), vol. I, pp. 64–65. The translation from the Arabic above is my own. Hebrew phrases are italicized. The letter was originally published by S. H. Margulies, "Zwei autographische Urkunden von Moses und Abraham Maimuni", in *Monatsschrift für Geschichte und Wissenschaft des Judentums* 44 (1900), pp. 8–13. Goitein could not locate the letter in Cambridge, where he assumed it was still located since the time of Margulies. Using the facsimile in Margulies' article and in Norman Bentwich, *Solomon Schechter: A Biography* (Philadelphia: Jewish Publication Society of America, 1938), opp. p. 143, he read the date as Tammuz (1)480 (of the Era of Documents), that is, the summer of 1169, and connected the appeal with the Crusader sack of Bilbays the previous November. Margulies thought the date was (1)484 = 1173 and Bentwich wrote 1172. Shailat prefers to read (1)481, hence the summer of 1170, and connects the episode with a collection of money on behalf of captives which, according to another document, was sent to Maimonides from the city of al-Maḥalla in the Egyptian Delta (see below). His hypothesis about the date of the letter does not negate the significance of Goitein's interpretation of Maimonides' rise to prominence. I examined the letter at the Jewish Theological Seminary under bright light and also ultra-violet light and did not see any letter after the "tp", which stands for (1)480; hence I agree with Goitein's reading of the date. For a different opinion see Menahem Ben-Sasson, "Maimonides in Egypt: The First Stage", in *Maimonidean Studies*, ed. Arthur Hyman, vol. 2 (1991), pp. 4–5, following Mordechai A. Friedman, "New Sources from the

Around the same time, as described in a legal document dated the summer of 1170, Maimonides' emissary, Aaron ha-Levi, shows up fund raising for ransom of captives in the community of al-Maḥalla in the Nile Delta countryside – a sizeable community, where the Spanish-Jewish traveler, Benjamin of Tudela, encountered at just about this very time around 500 Jews. A list of the contributors from the pledge drive (called *pesiqa* in the document and in the Geniza generally) had been sent to Maimonides in the capital. One of the donors had been constrained to put his slave girl up for sale to pay part of his pledge. The court document testifies that he was sending Maimonides nine dinars from this sale through an agent empowered with his power of attorney. Nine dinars was a very respectable contribution from one person. On the back of the document Maimonides acknowledges receipt of the money and releases the agent from all further obligation.[8] We see, therefore, that Maimonides acted as the focal point of this humanitarian effort both by exhorting the communities of Egypt to contribute, and by collecting the funds and to be disbursed to the captors. In another letter Maimonides mentions a mission to Palestine by two veteran judges, who Goitein ingeniously surmises had been sent by Maimonides to negotiate with the Franks for release of the Egyptian Jews held prisoner there.[9]

Ten years later, in 1180, the year he completed the *Mishneh Torah*, Maimonides received a legal query, included in his *responsa*, which had its origins in an episode of ransoming a captive in Alexandria. A pirate had demanded from the Jews the exorbitant price of 100 dinars[10] for a single captive, three times the going and accepted rate. The man was suffering and his life stood in danger. The local elders conducted an emergency appeal in the city, but could only come up with sixty dinars. Standing surety, they signed a promissory note in the Muslim court for the balance so the captive could be released immediately. When time for payment arrived the pirate captor pressed the elders hard in the Muslim court. Meanwhile, they had appealed for contributions to other communities in Egypt, sending emissaries from place to place, "following what was

Geniza for the Crusader Period and for Maimonides and his Descendants" (Hebrew), in *Cathedra* 40 (1986), pp. 72–75, who, after studying a photograph of the document sent him by the Seminary librarian, reopened the case for the date proposed by Margulies–Bentwich and suggested, further, that Maimonides may already have been head of the Jews when he led the campaign to ransom the captives.

8 T-S (Taylor-Schechter Collection, Cambridge University Library) NS Box 309.12, ed. Goitein, *Ha-yishuv* (see above n. 7), pp. 316–318; cf. idem, "Moses Maimonides, 'Man of Action'" (see above n. 1), p. 160.

9 T-S 16.9, ed. Goitein, *Ha-yishuv* (see above n. 7), pp. 314–316; idem, "Moses Maimonides, 'Man of Action'" (see above n. 1), pp. 158–159.

10 *Peraḥim* in this medieval Hebrew translation of the lost Arabic original. The singular of the word, meaning "flower", translates "florin", a medieval gold coin patterned on the Florentine original.

always the custom". The anxious pirate captor would wait no longer, however. He demanded full payment immediately. But word had it that other communities were themselves hard pressed to come up with the ransom money. So, by communal agreement, the local elders decided to tap another resource: the estate (it amounted to 30 dinars) of a deceased Jew whose heirs (if he had any) had not yet shown up on the scene.[11]

I believe that Maimonides' personal involvement in ransoming captives – not just in 1169 at the beginning of his career in Egypt but many times afterwards – echoes in the pages of the *Mishneh Torah* in the laws of charity. Let me explain.

Ransom of captives is discussed in the Babylonian Talmud in the tractate *Bava Batra*. An anecdote relates that Hormiz, the mother of Shapur, King of Persia, sent a gift of gold coins to R. Joseph, asking that it be dedicated to a "great religious duty" (*miṣvah rabbah*). The rabbis decided that ransoming of captives qualified. The Talmud explains why, both textually (with Biblical quotations) and logically. It may be implicit from the discussion that the Talmud considers ransoming captives the most important form of charity of all, but it took Maimonides in his *Code* to make this explicit. We read in "Hilkhot mattenot ʿaniyyim" 8.10:

> The ransoming of captives has precedence over the feeding and clothing of the poor. Indeed there is *no religious duty more meritorious than the ransoming of captives*, for not only is the captive included among the hungry, the thirsty, and the naked, but his very life is in jeopardy. He who turns his eyes away from ransoming him transgresses the commandments "Thou shalt not harden thy heart, nor shut thy hand" (Deuteronomy 15:7), "Neither shalt thou stand idly by the blood of thy neighbor" (Leviticus 19:16), and "He shall not rule with rigor over him in thy sight" (Leviticus 25:53). Moreover, he nullifies the commandments "Thou shalt surely open thy hand unto him" (Deuteronomy 15:8), "That thy brother may live with thee" (Leviticus 25:36), "Thou shalt love thy neighbor as thyself" (Leviticus 19:18), "Deliver them that are drawn unto death" (Proverbs 24:11), and many other admonitions like these. To sum up, there is no religious duty greater than the ransoming of captives.[12]

Rarely in the *Code* does Maimonides marshal so many prooftexts from the Bible for a single law. Here he adduces seven biblical commandments, none of which constitutes a specific precept to redeem captives, and he alludes that

---

11 Moses ben Maimon, *Teshuvot ha-Rambam* (Responsa), ed. Joshua Blau (3 volumes; Jerusalem: Mekize Nirdamim, 1957–1961), vol. II, pp. 733–734 (no. 452); cf. Shlomo D. Goitein, *A Mediterranean Society: The Jewish Communities of the Arab World as Portrayed in the Documents of the Cairo Geniza* (5 volumes plus Index volume by Paula Sanders; Berkeley, Los Angeles: University of California Press, 1967–1993), vol. I, p. 329.

12 *Mishneh Torah*, "Hilkhot mattenot ʿaniyyim" 8.10.

there are many more. For Maimonides, this ethical act is more important than all other forms of almsgiving. It should not be supposed that Maimonides had the rabbinic precedent for this in mind. The story about the mother of Shapur King of Persia and the rabbis' response, which might have served the purpose, is used by him in the immediately preceding section as a precedent for a different *halakhah*: gifts from heathen rulers should be accepted, but redistributed to the heathen poor.

Following "Mattenot ʿaniyyim" 8:10 come eight more laws to the end of the chapter, seven of which include ransom of captives. But Chapter Eight has a topic sentence that reads: "Almsgiving is included in the category of vows". Maimonides embedded the dispersed rabbinic *halakhot* on ransoming captives in this chapter because in Egypt, as we learn from the Geniza documents and especially from those concerning Maimonides' coordination of the fund-raising for the captives of the Crusader invasion of Egypt in 1168, the principal vehicle for raising money for that cause was pledges – vows in the language of the Talmud.

I believe we are on safe ground, therefore, in concluding that Maimonides' emphasis on ransom of captives in the *Code*, his enhancement and reinforcement of the talmudic statement that ransom constitutes a "great religious duty", and his placement of the laws relating to ransom of captives in a chapter on vows, had much to do with his personal experience with the captive problem in Egypt. It illustrates how everyday life impacted on the formation of Maimonides' *Code* and provides an example of the interaction between normative law and social history.

Twenty-five years ago, in his *Introduction to the Code of Maimonides*, Isadore Twersky commented on exceptional cases of amplification in the *Mishneh Torah*. Among his examples, he noted that Maimonides' style of amplification in the laws of ransom of captives violates his principle of brevity.

> The statement about ransoming captives, with its repetition, stringing together halakic commands and prohibitions, and exhortation, has a deep pathos which gives the passage a rhythm of its own and almost produces a visual representation of the suffering and possible tragedy which prompt and unstinting giving of charity will prevent. *One is also tempted to conclude that only a person who had traveled the Mediterranean and experienced its hazards and anxieties could have written such moving prose.*[13]

Twersky was only "tempted to conclude". I think he was even closer to the truth than he was willing to concede. The Geniza confirms quite unequivocally, I think, that Maimonides had contemporary realia in mind when codifying the laws of ransom of captives in the *Mishneh Torah*.

---

13 Twersky, *Introduction to the Code of Maimonides* (see above n. 3), p. 340 (emphasis mine).

"Concealing" and "uncovering one's face"

One of the most interesting concepts of poverty revealed by the Geniza letters is the twin notion of *mastūr* and *kashf al-wajh. Mastūr* means, literally, "concealed". It is used in the Judaeo-Arabic context to represent those living above the poverty line, getting by, and maintaining their privacy through self-sufficiency. The word can be found in classical Islamic texts with the same meaning and also in modern Arabic dialects. When the *mastūr* or *mastūra* falls temporarily into poverty, usually because of what the French Annalistes call a *conjuncture,* he or she experiences shame, very much like the "shamefaced poor" in medieval European texts about poverty. In order to limit their shame, to avoid, in their words, "uncovering their face", *kashf al-wajh,* especially by resorting to the public dole, they write letters asking for private charity.

Scores of alms lists show us the names of the chronic poor, those who are indigent perpetually, or at least on a long-term basis, and cannot help it. On occasion, however, someone is registered on an alms list as *mastūr*. Why? In order to differentiate him or her from those who collect alms regularly. One recipient of alms, for instance, is called *Mu'ammala mara armala [ma]stūra mā akhadhat qaṭṭu shay*, "Mu'ammala, a *mastūra* widow, who has never, ever, taken anything".[14] The chronic poor, or "structural poor", to use the language of the Annalistes again, feel less shame than the "concealed" because, being sick, or lame, or blind, or foreigners, or orphans, or penniless widows, they are persistently needy and cannot help it. Not the widow Mu'ammala. She was normally self-sufficient and hence "concealed" from the shame of becoming a recipient of public charity. That is why she is listed as "Mu'ammala, a *mastūra* widow, who has never, ever, taken anything".

Maimonides captures the antinomy between being "concealed" and forced to "uncover one's face" in a brief but as far as I know overlooked passage in the "Book of Commandments", his prolegomenon to the *Mishneh Torah.* Because the book was written in Arabic it reproduces the technical terms exactly as they appear in Judaeo-Arabic letters of the Jewish "shamefaced poor". Positive commandment number 197 is the injunction to lend money to the poor. Maimonides writes:

> This is a greater and weightier obligation than charity; for the suppliant (*alladhī iltaja'a*) who has to "uncover his face" to beg from people (*wa-kashafa wajhahu li'l-su'āl min aydī al-nās*) does not suffer as acute stress in doing so as the one who is normally "concealed" (*al-mastūr*) and whose

14 T-S Arabic Box 30.67 verso, left-hand page, lines 5–7; cf. Goitein, *A Mediterranean Society* (see above n. 11), vol. II, pp. 456–457, Appendix B 6. Translated into English in Cohen, *The Voice of the Poor* (see above n. 2), no. 71.

need is for help that will save him from uncovering his condition (*ḥattā lā yankashifa ḥāluhu*) and from becoming a suppliant.[15]

The twin notion of "concealment" and "uncovering the face" is not to be found, as far as I know, in any Jewish source available to Maimonides. To be sure, the concept of shame associated with the temporary poverty of the normally well to do is already present in earlier Judaism. Rabbinic midrash speaks about the "person from a prominent family (*ben gedolim*) who fell from his wealth (*yarad mi-nekhasav*) and was too ashamed to take (alms)".[16] But the metaphor of "concealment" – *mastūr* – and "uncovering the face" is, I believe, a cross-cultural conception of poverty existing in the Islamic world and the Judaeo-Arabic world within it, as it did in the medieval Christian environment. I believe that Maimonides' commentary on positive commandment 197 reflects the real world he inhabited, one in which people regularly used these metaphors when speaking about poverty.

Concealing the poor from shame is also a major reason underlying Maimonides' novel "ladder of charity" at the end of the laws of charity in the *Mishneh Torah*. It ranks preferentially the various types of philanthropy beginning with the midrashically recommended giving of a gift or a loan to the poor or offering them remunerated work. This and the next several "rungs" on the ladder have as their main concern to shield the poor from feeling embarrassed about their plight.[17] Here, again, I claim that we can make a correlation

---

15 Moses b. Maimon, *Sefer ha-miṣvot*, edited and translated into Hebrew by Joseph Kafaḥ [= Y. Qafīḥ] (Jerusalem: Mosad Harav Kook, 1971), pp. 158–159; English translation, *The Commandments: Sefer Ha-Mitzvoth of Maimonides*, by Charles B. Chavel (London, New York: The Soncino Press, 1967), vol. I, p. 211. I have modified Chavel's translation to convey the metaphoric content of Maimonides' text, which is more closely preserved in Kafaḥ's Hebrew rendition.

16 *Vayiqra Rabbah* 34:1, ed. Mordekai Margoliot (5 volumes; New York: Bet ha-midrash le-rabanim ba-Amerikah), vol. 4, p. 773; also, with variations, in Elijah ha-Kohen b. Solomon Abraham, *Me'il ṣedaqah* (Smyrna, 1731 and later editions, e.g.: Druck und Verlag der hebäischen Buchdruckerei des F. Galński und S. L. Flecker, 1859, p. 6, no. 107).

17 See Naftali Tzvi Yehudah Bar-Ilan, *Niqdash bi-ṣedaqah* (Rehovot: N. Ts. Y. Bar Ilan, 1990), pp. 68–72. The third century (?) *midrash* Avot de-Rabbi Nathan (ed. Schechter, version A, chapter 41) states: "Three things were said of men: one gives charity, may blessing come upon him; superior to him is one who lends his funds; superior to all is one (who forms a partnership with the poor) on terms of one half the profits (for each) or on terms of sharing what remains"; translation by Judah Goldin, *The Fathers According to Rabbi Nathan* (Yale Judaica Series 10; New Haven: Yale University Press, 1955), p. 171. The novelty of Maimonides' formulation lay in the listing of the "gradations of benevolence" and in the last four of the eight categories themselves, for which no prior rabbinic source is known. The ladder image caught on in later rabbinic commentators. Abraham Cronbach, "The Gradations of Benevolence", in *Hebrew Union College Annual* 16 (1941), pp. 163–186.

between Maimonides' normative statements and real life as reflected in the rhetoric of the Geniza documents about the poor.

The *quppah* and the *tamḥui*

In the talmudic period, two main public institutions for relieving poverty existed side-by-side. The *quppah,* literally, "basket", served the local, resident poor (*'aniyyei ha-'ir*). Donors made cash gifts and the money was deployed by the community either directly to the poor for their expenses, or in the form of food or clothing purchased with the proceeds. *Quppah* disbursements could also include money for household furnishings and payment of government taxes. The distribution was made once a week, Friday, on the eve of the Sabbath.

The other entity, the *tamḥui,* literally "alms tray" (frequently rendered "soup-kitchen") was dedicated to "the poor of the whole world", *'aniyyei 'olam.* It consisted in direct, daily food distributions, mainly to wayfarers or other indigents from outside the city. Communal charity collectors gathered foodstuffs from donors and redistributed them on a daily basis. Foreigners could appear in town at any time and the community had to be prepared to feed them daily. Another procedure of the *tamḥui* may have entailed purchasing loaves of bread with monies donated for daily distribution to needy wayfarers.[18]

In the *Mishneh Torah* Maimonides discusses the *quppah* and the *tamḥui* in Chapter Nine of "Hilkhot mattenot 'aniyyim". In the third *halakhah,* he makes an astonishing statement that seems to fly in the face of the Talmud. "We have neither seen nor heard of a Jewish (Israelite) community that does not have a *quppah. As for the tamḥui, there are some localities where it is customary to have it, and some where it is not.* The custom widespread today is for the collectors of the *quppah* to go around every day, and to distribute every Friday". This statement caused consternation in the Radbaz. In his commentary he writes, "This is the custom in our time. But I wonder who gave them permission to do away with the *tamḥui,* for it is written in the Mishnah at the end of (Tractate) *Pe'ah* and in a *baraita* at the beginning of *Bava Batra* and quoted elsewhere in several places in the Talmud. It is possible to explain this as follows: Because there is a *baraita* that says 'The townspeople are permitted to make *quppah* (funds) *tamḥui* (funds) and *tamḥui* (funds) *quppah* (funds)' they got into the habit of contributing to the *quppah* for the *tamḥui* and to make everything *quppah*".[19]

---

18 Zeev Safrai, *Ha-qehila ha-yehudit be-ereṣ yisrael bi-tequfat ha-mishnah veha-talmud* (The Jewish Community in Palestine during the Period of the Mishnah and the Talmud) (Jerusalem: The Zalman Shazar Center for Jewish History, 1995), pp. 64–67.

19 Radbaz, *ad loc.* The *baraita* is quoted in *Bava Batra* 8b, and Rashi explains that permission to take from the *quppah* for the *tamḥui* is granted when the number of outsiders

In fact, the first three *halakhot* of Chapter Nine are all a little unusual. The sources for most of the other *halakhot* in that chapter that deal with *quppah* or *tamḥui* can be located in more or less the same wording in one of the Talmuds, in the Mishnah, or in the Tosefta. But not the first three. The language and formulation of these introductory *halakhot* are patently of Maimonides' own invention. I believe they can be elucidated with the aid of the documentary Geniza evidence. But first, what is that evidence?

We are at first glance confronted with a mystery. The term *quppah* is nearly absent from the Geniza, appearing not at all in Fusṭāṭ. It appears only in connection with Alexandria, representing a receptacle in which bread was collected for distribution to the poor (rather than small coins, which were scarce). Goitein suggests that in this as in other ways, Alexandria followed an old Palestinian custom because, along with Jerusalem, it was part of the Eastern provinces of the Roman Empire for centuries before the foundation of Islamic Fusṭāṭ and later (New) Cairo. *Quppah* crops up also in a letter from the provincial town of Minyat Zifta addressed to the judge Elijah b. Zechariah, but in that communication the reference is to an actual alms-box for weekly collections of money distributed to poor orphans, rather than to the institution of the alms dole. "Since we possess hundreds of records and letters referring to charity from [Fusṭāṭ]", Goitein writes, "this can only mean that the institution characterized by that word did not exist there"[20].

---

exceeds the number of local residents. Radbaz also noticed in "Hilkhot mattenot ʿaniyyim" 9.12 another discrepancy between Maimonides and the Talmud. He rules that thirty days residency in a town make one liable to contribute to the *quppah;* three months, to the *tamḥui*. This is the reverse of what the Talmud says in *Bava Batra* 8a, at the very beginning of the long section on charity. Radbaz notes that another Andalusian authority, R. Isaac al-Fasi (d. 1103), assumes the same text as Maimonides in his own epitome of the Talmud and that the Palestinian Talmud has it as well. He offers the opinion that the ruling sought to assure that there would be abundant food for the poor (the resident poor), "and it is for this reason that some places do not have the *tamḥui*". There is another nuance to be noted. In chapter 7:7, Maimonides adopts the Talmud's wording regarding the house-to-house beggar (*meḥazzer ʿal ha-petaḥim*), stipulating that "one is not obligated to give him a large gift, but only a small one" (from Babylonian Talmud, *Bava Batra* 9a). This passage in the Talmud was understood by most medieval commentators to refer to allocations from the *quppah* (see Rashi and other commentaries *ad loc.* in the standard printed Talmud with commentaries). Radbaz assumes a priori that Maimonides means just that, even though he left it out. Other commentators on Maimonides did not assume so and tried to interpret his omission in different ways. These debates are summarized by Joseph Kafaḥ in his own, modern edition and commentary on the *Mishneh Torah*, "Seder Zeraʿim" (Kiryat Ono: Makhon Mishnat ha-Rambam, 1990), pp. 242–243. Given what we shall say below, it is not unlikely that Maimonides omitted *quppah* on purpose.

20 Goitein, *A Mediterranean Society* (see above n. 11), vol. II, pp. 104–105. *Minyat Zifta*: T-S 8 J 17.6, lines 7–10, cf. Goitein, ibid., pp. 105–106. Apart from Alexandria and Minyat Zifta, the word *quppah* crops up elsewhere in the Mediterranean. For instance, a huge

The word *tamḥui* does not appear either. I have not encountered it once in the more than 880 documents that I collected and analyzed for my monograph. Nor does it appear in the historical documents currently in the database of the *Princeton Geniza Project*.[21] On the other hand, the old rabbinic term *mezonot*, literally, "maintenance" (the root of the word means "to feed"), occurs frequently. In rabbinic times, *mezonot* encompassed maintenance for wives, children, orphans, widows, wives with absentee husbands, laborers, and even work animals. In the Geniza it encompasses a seemingly new and wider range of distributions, from food for the poor to contributions towards the salaries of generally poorly paid communal officials, such as cantors, teachers of poor children, and kosher meat inspectors. Goitein found the application of the word *mezonot* to food for the poor "strange".[22]

How shall we account for the absence of the words *quppah* and *tamḥui* in the myriad of documents relating to charity in Fusṭāṭ and the ubiquitous appearance of the term *mezonot* for the weekly food dole? The apparent non-existence in the surrounding Muslim society of the equivalent of the famous soup kitchens (*ʿimārets*) of the later Ottoman period might have some relevance to the mysterious absence of the *tamḥui* in the Geniza world.[23] But other explanations must be also sought for the terminological enigma.

I believe a likely answer to this mystery can be found in the demographic realities of the Jewish poor in the Geniza world. The numbers of outsiders (*ʿaniyyei ʿolam* or *ʿaniyyei ʿir aḥeret* in the language of the Talmud) in medieval Fusṭāṭ were huge. This is abundantly clear from entries of newcomers in the alms lists. Large numbers of immigrants benefited from the community dole. There is an additional clue. Bread, the basic item of sustenance in the alms lists,

gift of 2000 dinars that was bequeathed to the poor through the *quppah shel ṣedaqah* by a man in Tunisia is reported in a letter from Tyre, Lebanon, that found its way into the Geniza. T-S 10 J 12.25, ed. Assaf, in *Yerushalayim*, ed. Michael Ish-Shalom, Meir Benayahu, Azriel Shohet (Jerusalem: Mosad Harav Kook, 1953), p. 109; cf. Goitein, ibid., p. 110.

21 www.princeton.edu/~geniza.

22 "[I]t seems strange that the collections for the semiweekly distributions of bread should have been called by this name" (Goitein, *A Mediterranean Society* [see above n. 11], vol. II, p. 544, n. 25). One example from among many of this broadening of the meaning of *mezonot*, a tiny fragment of a list of distributions of cash to the needy (or salary supplementation to the poorly paid; two cantors are listed, for example), using Coptic numerals, as was common: "The elder Menaḥem, collector (*jābī*) of the *mezonot*: In his possession (a balance of) 4 3/4 (dirhems)" (ENA [Elkan Nathan Adler Collection, Jewish Theological Seminary of America] NS 77.374). This fragment was unknown to Goitein, as it was only recently removed by me from a box of unpreserved, crumpled fragments at the Jewish Theological Seminary.

23 About the absence of the soup kitchen in the medieval Arab world see Norman Stillman, "Charity and Social Service in Medieval Islam", in *Societas* 5(2) (1975), pp. 105–115, esp. p. 111.

was distributed not once but twice a week, the traditional Sabbath eve and also Tuesday. This twice-weekly distribution exceeded the schedule prescribed by the Talmud for *quppah* distributions to local indigents and it also contradicted the talmudic standard of food distribution through the *tamḥui* for foreigners on a daily basis. What was going on here?

Burdened with an especially large influx of foreign Jewish poor, the collection and distribution of charity was better served by a unified system, rather than by separate funds for the local needy and poor arrivals from the outside. Since the Talmud made a distinction that the Jews of Fusṭāṭ no longer maintained, and neither rabbinic term was suitable to designate the unified system that existed, they simply did not use these words. Feeling a need for a term, however, they substituted the word, *mezonot*, which was neutral and had no particular connection in rabbinic sources with either locals or newcomers.[24]

This data from the Geniza documents now help elucidate the entire original presentation of *quppah* and *tamḥui* at the beginning of Chapter Nine of "Hilkhot mattenot ʿaniyyim" in the *Mishneh Torah*. Let us examine the introductory *halakhot* one by one. In the first *halakhah* Maimonides defines *quppah*.

> In every city inhabited by Jews (Israelites), it is their duty to appoint from themselves well known and trustworthy persons to act as alms collectors, to go around *collecting from the people every Friday*. They should demand from each person what is proper for him to give and what he has been assessed for, and should *distribute the money every Friday*, giving each poor man maintenance (*mezonot*) sufficient for seven days. This is what is called "alms fund" (*quppah*) (9:1).

Noticeably, Maimonides does *not* repeat here what the Talmud says, namely, that the *quppah* is reserved for local, resident poor. He reserves that for later on, in *halakhah* 6, when actually quoting the Talmud.

Next, he explains *tamḥui*. Here, too, he omits the talmudic principle that *tamḥui* is dedicated to "the poor of the world".

> They must similarly appoint collectors to *gather every day*, from each courtyard, bread and other eatables, fruits, or money from anyone who is willing to make a free-will offering at that time. They should *distribute these toward that same evening* among the poor, giving therefrom to each poor man his sustenance (*parnasato*) for the day. This is what is called "alms-tray" (*tamḥui*) (9:2).

---

24 Its use for "bread" for the poor might have lexical foundation in the passage from the Talmud (*Bava Batra* 9a): "Rav Huna said: We examine before giving food but not before giving clothing [...]. R Judah said: We examine before giving clothing but not before giving food", where *mezonot* is the word used for food.

Maimonides' formulation of the laws of *quppah* and *tamḥui* in the first two introductory *halakhot* of Chapter Nine in words of his own invention contains the first hint of the unification of the two institutions in practice in medieval Fusṭāṭ. Noteworthy, too, he uses the word *mezonot* to describe the *quppah*. This echoes the usage of *mezonot* in the Geniza lists to denote money for bread (the usage Goitein found "strange"). The association of the charity *quppah* with the term *mezonot* does not occur, as far as I have been able to determine, in the talmudic sources.

In the next *halakhah*, the one we began with, Maimonides confirms explicitly the consolidation of the talmudic *quppah* and *tamḥui* into a unified system of public charity.

> We have neither seen nor heard of a Jewish (Israelite) community that does not have a *quppah*. As for the *tamḥui*, *there are some localities where it is customary to have it, and some where it is not*. The custom widespread today is for the collectors of the *quppah* to *go around every day, and to distribute every Friday* (9:3).

In his endeavor to justify Maimonides' enigmatic statement about the relationship between *quppah* and *tamḥui* in this *halakhah*, Radbaz, as we have seen, found in the Talmud a halakhic dispensation – the permission to change the use of charity funds from one to the other – for a departure in practice from talmudic prescription that existed in Fusṭāṭ at least five centuries before he arrived in Egypt. It is not unlikely that Maimonides interpreted the *baraita* the same way.[25] Maimonides, a newcomer to Egypt, found there a community where the *tamḥui* and *quppah* were merged into one, unified institution, encompassing the functions that the two had fulfilled separately in talmudic times. He took cognizance of this consolidation in 9:1, when he omitted the essential talmudic principle that the *quppah* served the local poor. Nonetheless, since his goal was to codify all of Jewish law, he could not completely ignore the institution of *quppah*. At the same time, he included the actual term used in Egypt, *mezonot*, in his original formulation. Finally, with due attention to the realities of Egypt, he added (in 9:3): "The custom widespread today is for the collectors of the alms fund (*quppah*) to *go around every day*, and to *distribute every Friday*". This sentence in 9:3, combining wording from 9:1 about the *quppah* ("distribute the money every Friday") with wording from 9:2 regarding the *tamḥui* ("gather every day"), similarly reflects the merging of the *quppah* and *tamḥui* into a single system.

Three *halakhot* later, in 9:6, Maimonides brings the actual rabbinic laws that distinguish the *quppah* from the *tamḥui* and in the exact order and in the same

25 Maimonides codified the dispensation for interchanging charities in "Mattenot ʿaniyyim" 9:7.

language they appear in the Talmud:[26] "Contributions to the *tamḥui* are to be collected every day, those for the *quppah* each Friday. The *tamḥui* is for the poor of the whole world, while the *quppah* is to provide for the poor of the city alone". Why doesn't Maimonides say this at the beginning? I think that the introductory *halakhot* reflect, not the talmudic *halakhah,* but current practice in Fusṭāṭ, where the old distinction between alms for locals and alms for foreigners was no longer maintained.[27]

In short, Maimonides' subtle "transformation" of the *halakhah* of *quppah* and *tamḥui* at the beginning of Chapter Nine in three original introductory *halakhot* nearly exactly reflects what we find in the Geniza documents, except that, in Fusṭāṭ, as mentioned, distributions of bread were made on Tuesday as well as Friday. This, too, needs explanation. I suggest that this was a kind of compromise between the Talmud's once-a-week dole for the resident poor and the daily distribution to foreigners, who, in the extremely mobile Mediterranean society of the Geniza period, arrived in far greater numbers and far more frequently than in the talmudic period.

What we cannot know, however, is how early this consolidation of *quppah* and *tamḥui,* this departure from the talmudic system, took place. Did it begin early in the Islamic period, when Jews began to travel in the Near East and North Africa over much greater distances than during the talmudic period? Did the unification come about when the ratio of needy foreigners to needy local residents changed so drastically that the old system no longer made sense? Was the unified system already in place in Geonic Babylonia? Unfortunately there are very few Geonic sources on the subject of charity by which to judge. Was the unified system in place in Maimonides' Spain, so that what he found in Egypt was actually no surprise? Unfortunately, the Geniza unveils its sources only in the eleventh century. We cannot know how things were before that time.

Changing the use of charitable funds

With the unification of the *quppah* and the *tamḥui* into a single system of charitable disbursements, there still remained a question whether such funds could be used for any other purpose. This issue is discussed in the Talmud in that *halakhah* which Radbaz cited to explain Maimonides' enigmatic claim that some communities did not have the *tamḥui*.

---

26 In *Bava Batra* 8b.

27 The possibility of merging the two may already be alluded to in the Talmud, in the story of the charity collector who kept one purse for both the foreign poor and local indigents and stipulated with the community that the money could be used for both (*Bava Batra* 8b–9a).

The full statement begins: ראשים בני העיר לעשות קופה תמחוי ותמחוי קופה ולשנותה לכל מה שירצו – "The townspeople are permitted to make *quppah* (funds) *tamḥui* (funds) and *tamḥui* (funds) *quppah* (funds) and to change its use for whatever they wish"[28]. The words "for whatever they wish" led to different interpretations in the Middle Ages. Rabbenu Tam, the French Tosafist (d. 1171), permitted using charity funds even to pay the salary of the city watchmen.[29] Maimonides' Spanish predecessor, Rabbi Joseph ibn Megas (d. 1141), whose teachings he greatly admired, argued vociferously against using *quppah* or *tamḥui* receipts for anything other than the needs of the poor.[30]

The Geniza evidence shows that monies collected for the poor were often applied to other needs of the community, *ṣorkhei ṣibbur* in rabbinic language. This meant especially the payment of salaries of communal officials. Many Geniza accounts of charitable donations and expenditures include both disbursements for charity (such as purchase of bread for the communal dole) and salaries for communal servants (cantors, beadles, etc.).[31] Protesting against this practice, we find a poor man complaining that charity earmarked for him in the form of pledges for a whole week had been diverted to a cantor.[32]

If we read the *Mishneh Torah* ("Mattenot 'aniyyim" 9:7) very attentively, we discover that Maimonides responded to the broadened use of charity funds in Fusṭāṭ in a bold departure from the strict ruling of Joseph ibn Megas. He slightly altered the talmudic statement by the addition of two significant words at the end, to read, ולשנותה לכל מה שירצו מצורכי צבור – "[the townspeople are permitted to make *quppah* (funds) *tamḥui* (funds) and *tamḥui* (funds) *quppah* (funds)] and to change its use *for any need of the community* they wish." And he added for reinforcement: "even if they (the contributors) did not stipulate so at the time it was collected". Moreover, he went on in a somewhat novel way to say that "if there were in the city a great sage, whose judgment determines all collections and who distributes them to the poor as he sees fit, he is permitted to change their use for any need of the community he sees fit" (see *Megillah* 27b).

I believe that Maimonides' addition of the two words, a clear departure from the language of the Talmud and from the ruling of his admired forerunner in Spain, reflects the practice of his own time and place in Egypt and represents his effort to respond to this reality in his *Code*. Radbaz recognized Maimonides' departure from the Talmud. He added that this broadened use of charity funds was still the custom in his own time.[33] Of course, as he did in the matter of Maimonides' strange statement regarding the *tamḥui*, the sixteenth

28 *Bava Batra* 8b.

29 *Tosafot* to *Bava Batra* 8b.

30 Michael Hellinger, *Charity in Talmudic and Rabbinic Literature: A Legal, Literary and Historical Analysis* (Ph.D. dissertation, Bar-Ilan University, 1999), pp. 218–239.

31 One translated example in Cohen, *The Voice of the Poor* (see above n. 2), no. 72.

32 T-S 8 J 17.27, translated in ibid., no. 39.

33 See Radbaz, *ad loc.*

century Chief Rabbi of Cairo went on to find a logical rationalization for even this apparent deviation from the talmudic law. If the Talmud meant funds could be used only for *quppah* or *tamḥui*, it needn't have added the words "to change its use for whatever they wish". The language of the Talmud must therefore encompass uses other than direct charity. Maimonides simply makes this more explicit. It is not unlikely that Maimonides, like Radbaz after him, held to the same interpretation of the talmudic statement, and so felt quite comfortable bringing the *halakhah* in this case into conformity with Egyptian practice of his time.

Radbaz noticed anomalies in Maimonides' laws of charity and even recognized their connection with current practice in his own time five centuries later. His explanation of Maimonides' remarkable statement "As for the *tamḥui*, there are some localities where it is customary to have it, and some where it is not" comes tantalizingly close to the explanation I have offered on the basis of data from the Geniza. But Radbaz was a halakhist, not an historian. I am an historian not a halakhist. This case-study, I believe, shows that the interpretation of the *Code* in the light of contemporary historical realia is valid and useful. It must proceed very cautiously, to be sure. But when we have evidence from everyday life in the Geniza that makes what is obscure in Maimonides' work less obscure, I believe we are permitted to speculate. We are permitted to look for the interaction of normative law and social history, even to go beyond Twersky's rare and reluctant bow to this kind of interpretation. We must not lose sight of the purely intellectual aspect, the hermeneutics of codification, if you will. But we must also allow that Maimonides, a "man of action" in Goitein's words, was not immune to the world around him and made efforts, here and there, to adapt the language of the *halakhah* to current practice. I hope I have demonstrated with a few examples how this played itself out as he wrote the *Code*. Scholars have yet to pursue this type of work systematically. I believe it is a field offering the potential for fruitful results in understanding Maimonides the legist in the light of his contemporary environment. More work is left to be done.

Philologie

The Languages of Maimonides

by

Simon Hopkins

The Hebrew University, Jerusalem

I. Introduction

Let me begin with a personal anecdote. I was once employed by the University Library in Cambridge, the home of the celebrated Taylor-Schechter collection of geniza manuscripts. Among my duties was the task of showing visitors to the library around the collection. On one occasion a group of so-called ultra-orthodox Jews from a yeshiva in North London arrived. They had heard that several autographs of Maimonides were to be found in Cambridge and asked whether they could see some examples. I showed them one of several *responsa* in the collection, saying that here we have the very handwriting of Maimonides himself, including his signature at the bottom of the page. This was met with incredulity. How could it be that Maimonides didn't write the Hebrew letters we read in the printed books? I was asked to read the text aloud. On doing so, incredulity increased, and in the case of some members of the party even turned to indignation. Not only was the script unfamiliar, the text was in a language they did not know; as far as Maimonides was concerned, their visit to Cambridge had been a waste of time. To these people, who for years had been spending several hours a day studying the writings of Maimonides in Hebrew, the realization that the great halakhic authority of Rabbinic Judaism, the codifier of Jewish law and commentator on the Mishnah, had Arabic as his mother tongue and used this language in his writings was an unwelcome discovery.

There is nothing very unusual in this story; it is but an example of the huge gap which, by a series of historical accidents, may arise between the source of our material and the form in which we use it. It is a curious fact that scholars frequently pay very little attention to the linguistic circumstances of their subjects. They take it for granted that communication takes place, but do not always stop to ask what languages were spoken in a certain area at the period in question, in what language a given conversation may have occurred or in what script a particular text may have been written. How many biblical commentaries, for example, spend time discussing the identity of the language in which David addressed Goliath (I Samuel 17:43ff.) or the conversational medium used by Samson and Delilah (Judges 16:6ff.)?[1]

Accordingly, it may not be out of place to remind ourselves of the linguistic situation in which Maimonides lived, what languages he spoke, wrote and read, in what circumstances and in what scripts. We are in a rather favourable position in this regard, for a good deal is known about the life and times of Maimonides and most of his works are available in reliable editions. What is more, Maimonides has left behind a considerable number of autographs, so that we may often gain precise information about how exactly he used his languages.

II. "Old Castilian" and Greek?

But first we must ask about the linguistic situation of his early childhood. Maimonides was born in Córdoba in 1138, i.e. several centuries after the arrival of the Arabs and well before the Christian reconquest. Córdoba had long been an Arabic-speaking city and nobody will doubt that Maimonides's mother tongue was Spanish Arabic. But Córdoba was a socially complex place and we should not necessarily assume that the whole population was exclusively monoglot, speaking (and writing) only Arabic all of the time, at home as well as in the street. This applies particularly to the Christian and Jewish minorities, which perhaps resisted full Arabicization for longer than we imagine. Was there any Romance still spoken among them? If so, it is possible that Maimonides might have heard and even understood (some sort of) Spanish also. Although we have, admittedly, little or no solid evidence pointing in such a direction, it could be a trifle rash to assume that Romance during Maimonides's lifetime had disappeared entirely from the non-Muslim communities of Andalusia. In the light of the extraordinary tenacity of certain minority languages which have survived in the face of all odds,[2] the presence of a Romance-speaking element in twelfth-century Córdoba should not be dismissed out of hand. And it is not impossible to imagine that Maimonides could have been exposed to it in his early youth.[3] If, however, he did know some Andalusi Romance ("Old

1 Cf. Edward Ullendorff, "The knowledge of languages in the Old Testament", in *Bulletin of the John Rylands Library* 44 (1961–1962), pp. 455–465, reprinted in idem, *Is Biblical Hebrew a Language? Studies in Semitic Languages and Civilizations* (Wiesbaden: Harrassowitz, 1977), pp. 37–47.

2 The Neo-Aramaic of Christians and Jews in Kurdistan comes particularly to mind.

3 See in general David J. Wasserstein, "The language situation in al-Andalus", in *Studies on the Muwaššaḥ and the Kharja* [Proceedings of the Exeter International Colloquium], ed. Alan Jones and Richard Hitchcock (Oxford Oriental Institute Monographs 12; Reading: Ithaca Press, 1991), pp. 1–15. I gratefully acknowledge here some private correspondence on this disputed subject with Professors F. Corriente and D. J. Wasserstein.

Castilian") in his childhood, there is, as far as I know, no conclusive trace of it in his writings. The Romance plant-names listed in his herbal *Šarḥ asmā' al-'uqqār*[4] (and elsewhere)[5] as belonging to *'ajamiyyat al-Andalus*[6] and, less commonly, *laṭīnī*,[7] are inadmissible as evidence of his own vernacular, for Meyerhof has rightly pointed out that these cases of 'espagnol' = 'vieux castillan' were copied by Maimonides from the written sources of his Spanish predecessors in the field.[8]

This is a convenient point to dispose of another language about which it may occur to one at least to ask. The lives of great national heroes such as Maimonides tend rather quickly to become the stuff of legend.[9] For example, the biography of Rashi, who died almost exactly 100 years before Maimonides, has been embroidered to include polyglot talents of a high order; in addition to the languages of Jewish culture and his native French (all of which he certainly knew), Rashi is said to have known Latin, Greek, Arabic and Persian.[10] Of these, only Latin need be taken seriously. The evidence is scanty and scholarly opinion is divided; the balance of probability is that Rashi did not know Latin.[11] We could be tempted to ask a similar question with regard to Maimonides and Greek. The whole of Maimonides's philosophical and medical oeuvre is so

---

4 Max Meyerhof, *Šarḥ asmā' al-'uqqār* (Mémoires présentés à l'Institut d'Égypte ... XLI; Le Caire: Imprimerie de l'Institut Français d'archéologie orientale, 1940), with the 'Index des noms ibériques', pp. 230–232.

5 Zacharias Frankel, *Hodegetik zur Mischnah, Tosefta, Mechilta, Sifra und Sifri* (= דרכי המשנה) (Warsaw: M. L. Cailingold, ²1923), p. 342 (= Leipzig: Hunger, ¹1859, p. 322) [Hebrew] had already noted that Maimonides sometimes gives Spanish equivalents.

6 E.g. Meyerhof, *Šarḥ asmā' al-'uqqār* (see above n. 4), p. 25 no. 217: "*al-laḥlāḥu huwa l-fijlu l-barrīyu wa-smuhu l-'arabīyu l-hamaḏānu wa-bi-'ajamīyati l-andalusi labšanā*" – "*laḥlāḥ* is wild radish, whose Arabic name is *hamaḏān* (= *haymaḏān*) and in Andalusian vernacular *labšanā*" (= λαψάνη: *Wörterbuch der Klassischen Arabischen Sprache*, ed. Manfred Ullmann, vol. II, pt. 1 [Wiesbaden: Harrassowitz, 1983], p. 144b).

7 Ibid., p. 22 no. 189: *kamāḏariyūsun* [χαμαίδρυς] *huwa ballūṭu l-arḍi wa-bi-l-laṭīnīyi bertonica* ("*kamāḏariyūsū* is ground oak, and in Latin *bertonica*"), quoted in *Wörterbuch* (see note 6 above), p. 38a, s.v. *lāṭīnīy*, glossed as "altkastilisch".

8 Ibid., pp. lxiv, lxv. See too Manfred Ullmann, *Die Medizin im Islam* (Handbuch der Orientalistik, Abt. 1: Der Nahe und der Mittlere Osten, Ergänzungsband 6, Abschnitt 1; Leiden, Köln: Brill, 1970), p. 291.

9 See Isaiah Berger, "הרמב"ם באגדת העם", in *Massad* 2 (1936), pp. 216–238 and the series "Maimonides in Jewish folklore" by Yehuda Rassabi (sic), Jacob Atiel (sic) et al., in *Yeda-'Am* 2 (4–5) (Oct. 1954), pp. 191–204 [Hebrew]. The whole subject has been taken up in greater detail by Yitzhak Avishur, *In Praise of Maimonides: Folktales in Judaeo-Arabic and Hebrew from the Near East and North Africa* (Jerusalem: The Magnes Press, 1998) [Hebrew].

10 Maurice Liber, *Rashi*, trans. Adele Szold (Philadelphia: Jewish Publication Society of America, 1906; reprint New York: Hermon Press, 1970), p. 80.

11 Cf. e.g. Esra Shereshevsky, "Rashi's and Christian interpretations", in *Jewish Quarterly Review* 71 (1970–1971), pp. 76–86.

saturated with Hellenism, so full of quotations from Aristotle and Galen etc., that one wonders whether he may possibly have known some Greek. Well, the answer is surely negative. In the pre-Renaissance world language acquisition was almost exclusively utilitarian with immediate conversational or other practical aims in mind; even the learned did not as a rule engage in the serious study of languages foreign to their own cultures or beyond their own immediate environments.[12] For example, educated oriental Christians such as Ḥunayn b. Isḥāq learned Greek as part of their cultural heritage, and Ibn Ḥazm did not need to leave his native Córdoba in order to acquire whatever Latin he knew. The case of Maimonides and Greek, however, is entirely different. Greek played no part in the educational curriculum of Jews or Muslims; nor was it spoken in any of the places in which he lived. Unless some startling new facts come to light, we must assume that Maimonides's knowledge of Greek wisdom was acquired entirely through the intermediary of Arabic; there is no evidence, and indeed no real likelihood, that he himself read any Greek.[13] The occasional explanations of Greek words which he offers likewise reveal no knowledge of the language.[14]

III. Trilingual Culture: Arabic, Hebrew, Aramaic

We may now turn to the languages which Maimonides actually did know. Rabbinic Judaism is a trilingual culture: any male born into this culture, in addition to knowing the local language(s) of his community, will be well schooled in the written languages of traditional Jewish civilization, viz. Hebrew and Aramaic.

---

12 The very interesting list of names for God in various languages in Jacob Mann, *The Jews in Egypt and in Palestine under the Fatimid Caliphs*, vol. II (Oxford: Oxford University Press, 1922), p. 106 is an amateur curiosity only. The only Arab grammarian with any interest in non-Arabic languages seems to have been Abū Ḥayyān al-Ġarnāṭī. For the subject generally see Bernhard Bischoff, "The study of foreign languages in the Middle Ages", in *Speculum* 36 (1961), pp. 209–224, revised version in idem, *Mittelalterliche Studien: Ausgewählte Aufsätze zur Schriftkunde und Literaturgeschichte* (Stuttgart: Hiersemann, 1966–1981), vol. II, 1967, pp. 227–245.

13 Thus correctly Frankel, *Hodegetik* (see above n. 5), p. 342 (= ^{1}1859, p. 322); Meyerhof, *Šarḥ asmāʾ al-ʿuqqār* (see above n. 4), p. lxv. On the other hand, Tanḥūm Yerushalmi, who less than a century after Maimonides compiled a Hebrew–Arabic dictionary to *Mishneh Torah* (see below n. 65), certainly knew a few words of Greek, but this hardly amounted to actual reading ability; Wilhelm Bacher, *Aus dem Wörterbuche Tanchum Jeruschalmi's* (Strassburg: K. J. Trübner, 1903), pp. 92–93.

14 Wilhelm Bacher, "Beiträge zur semitischen Sprachvergleichung bei Moses Maimûni", in *Recueil des travaux rédigés en mémoire du Jubilé Scientifique de M. Daniel Chwolson [= Festschrift zu Ehren von Profess. Daniel Chwolson]* (Berlin: Calvary, 1899), pp. 144–147.

Arabic, Hebrew and Aramaic were the languages with which Maimonides was familiar, but his familiarity with them was of different kinds. Arabic he read, wrote and spoke; Hebrew he read and wrote;[15] Aramaic he only read.[16] We should remember that 'Arabic', 'Hebrew' and 'Aramaic' in this context are far from being uniform entities. The diglossic contrast within Arabic between the written language and the spoken dialects is well known and applies to the Middle Ages just as it does today – we shall return to Maimonides's use of Arabic later. A similar variety exists within Hebrew and Aramaic; both include several different layers and styles: Biblical, Mishnaic and Talmudic Hebrew are by no means the same and the differences between the Aramaic of the Bible, the Targumim, and the Babylonian and Palestinian Talmuds are even greater.

The closest modern parallel to the cultural and linguistic world in which Maimonides lived is provided by Yemenite Jewry, now no longer in their South Arabian homeland, but still (just) to be found in Israel. We find here a trilingual heritage and a linguistic virtuosity rather similar to that I have just mentioned for the Middle Ages. Unlike other Arabic-speaking Jewish communities, the Yemenites have continued the mediaeval Judaeo-Arabic culture and language of which Maimonides was such a luminous exponent. Among the Yemenites the classical compositions of Saadya Gaon and Maimonides are still studied in their original language.[17] It is no coincidence that so much of the Maimonidean legacy in Arabic is extant in Yemenite manuscripts, sometimes in Yemenite manuscripts only (cf. below p. 96, n. 50).

In such a culture, where traditional learning is valued for its own sake, linguistic attainments are both highly necessary and highly admired. When writing about the loss of his beloved younger brother David, drowned in the Indian Ocean, Maimonides does not omit to mention that in addition to other prized qualities, his brother was well versed in Talmud and expert in Hebrew: והבין בתלמוד במהרה והבין בדקדוק הלשון יתר – "and he understood the Jewish sources/Talmud with competence and well understood the niceties of the (Hebrew) language".[18] Maimonides is enthusiastically approving of the excel-

15 Like many learned Jews throughout the ages Maimonides was doubtless also capable of speaking Hebrew if necessary, but I know of no testimony to his ever having done so.

16 Reading in this context frequently implies reading aloud, or chanting; see e.g. Samuel Krauss, *Talmudische Archäologie*, vol. III (Leipzig: Fock, 1912), § 296; Israel Abrahams, *Jewish Life in the Middle Ages*, new edition enlarged and revised by Cecil Roth (London: Goldston, 1932), p. 379.

17 Though somewhat in decline in the twentieth century; Shelomo Dov Goitein, *The Yemenites: History, Communal Organization, Spiritual Life. Selected Studies* (Jerusalem: Ben-Zvi Institute for the Study of the Jewish Communities in the East, 1983), p. 261 [Hebrew].

18 *Letters and Essays of Moses Maimonides: A Critical Edition of the Hebrew and Arabic Letters* […] Based on all extant manuscripts, translated and annotated with introduction and

lence in Arabic and Hebrew attained by the translators Judah b. Tibbon and his son Samuel in Provence. Of Judah's language accomplishments he had personally heard from various scholars: והודיעונו ברב חכמותיו וצחות לשונו בלשון עברי ולשון הגרי אנשים ידועים – "and famous people have informed us of his many talents and his eloquence in the Hebrew and Arabic languages";[19] Samuel's linguistic abilities were to be applauded all the more because his Arabic was acquired in a country where Arabic was not spoken: ותמהתי היאך יהיה טבע בן שנולד בין העלגים כך וירדף אחר החכמות, ויהיה מהיר בלשון ערבי ... ועוד היאך יבין דקדוקי הלשון וענינים עמקים – "and I was astonished how the nature of a son born among non-Arabic-speakers could be like this, (how) he could pursue learning and be skilled in the Arabic language [...] and further how he could understand the niceties of the (Hebrew) language and profound matters".[20]

IV. Script

Beside the question of language, there is also the question of script. Traditional Jewish culture conducts its business in Hebrew script. Hebrew letters are the first the Jewish child learns, these are the letters he knows best, and out of sheer convenience these are the letters a traditional Jew will normally use in writing, be it Hebrew, Aramaic, Arabic, Yiddish, Persian, Ladino or whatever. Thus it was with Maimonides. He, of course, knew Arabic script perfectly well and there are even sporadic autograph examples of his Arabic handwriting,[21] but when writing for his Jewish readers and even when writing privately for himself it never occurred to him to use anything but Hebrew letters.[22]

---

cross-references by Isaac Shailat (Yiṣḥāq Shelat) (2 volumes; Maaleh Adumim, Israel: Maaliyot, 5747–5748 [1986–1988]), p. 230,4–5 [Hebrew]. Pace Wilhelm Bacher, "Die Bibelexegese Moses Maimûni's", in *Jahresbericht der Landes-Rabbinerschule zu Budapest für das Schuljahr 1895/6* (Budapest, 1896), p. 167 n. 4. דקדוק here need not imply formal grammatical study – grammar per se was of little interest to Maimonides; see below n. 84.

19 Shailat, *Letters* (see above n. 18), p. 530,7–8.

20 Ibid., p. 531,12–15. Further in praise of Samuel ibid., p. 558,10–15.

21 Simon Hopkins, "A new autograph fragment of Maimonides's *Epitomes* of Galen (*De locis affectis*)", in *Bulletin of the School of Oriental and African Studies* 57 (1994), p. 128 n. 17; Nehemya Allony, "אוטוגראף הרמב"ם מאוסף אדלר ומגניזת לנינגראד", in *Sinai* 92 (1982–1983), p. 191 n. 11.

22 Joshua Blau, *The Emergence and Linguistic Background of Judaeo-Arabic: A Study of the Origins of Middle Arabic* (Oxford: Oxford University Press, 1965; 2nd edition Jerusalem: Ben-Zvi Institute for the Study of the Jewish Communities in the East, 1981; 3rd edition 1999), p. 41 n. 6. What is said there about Maimonides's medical autographs doubtless applies also to the herbal *Šarḥ asmāʾ al-ʿuqqār*. Although this work – a multilingual glossary arranged according to the *abjad* sequence – is based on sources in Arabic script and

The fact that his Arabic works were written in Hebrew script (i.e. in Judaeo-Arabic) made them, of course, inaccessible to Muslim and Christian readers. But there were certain circles of inquiring Muslims and Christians who were very eager indeed to study the work of the great Sage of Fustat, especially the *Guide of the Perplexed*. One Muslim scholar of his acquaintance,[23] ʿAbd al-Laṭīf al-Baġdādi (d. 1231/1232), is said to have learned the Hebrew letters for this very purpose.[24] The transmission of the *Guide* is very interesting indeed from this cross-cultural point of view. The work was composed, as expected and as the autographs show, in Judaeo-Arabic for a Jewish public. Maimonides is said (by the aforementioned ʿAbd al-Laṭīf al-Baġdādi) to have issued an injunction forbidding the work to be transcribed into Arabic characters,[25] presumably lest Muslims read it and take offence at its contents.[26] The effect of this injunction – if it was ever made – did not last very long. Already during Maimonides's lifetime Samuel b. Tibbon, the Hebrew translator of the work in Provence, suspected that a faulty copy from which he had been working had been prepared, directly or indirectly, from a *Vorlage* in Arabic script.[27] Be that as it may,

---

survives in a unique manuscript likewise in Arabic script (in the autograph hand of Ibn al-Bayṭār, d. 1248 – see Meyerhof, *Šarḥ asmāʾ al-ʿuqqār* [see above n. 4], pp. lviiff.), there is no reason to suppose that Maimonides composed it in anything but Hebrew letters.

23 Maimonides was, of course, at all stages of his career in contact with Muslim scholars; see e.g. Simon Eppenstein, "Moses ben Maimon, ein Lebens- und Charakterbild", in *Moses ben Maimon. Sein Leben, seine Werke und sein Einfluss*, ed. Wilhelm Bacher, Marcus Brann, David Jacob Simonsen … (2 volumes; Leipzig: Fock, 1908–1914; reprint in one volume: Hildesheim, New York: Olms, 1971), vol. II, p. 11.

24 Israel Friedlaender, *Der Sprachgebrauch des Maimonides: Ein lexikalischer und grammatischer Beitrag zur Kenntnis des Mittelarabischen, 1. Lexikalischer Teil* (Frankfurt am Main: Kauffmann, 1902), p. xxi.

25 Salomon Munk, "Notice sur Joseph ben-Iehouda ou Abou'lhadjâdj Yousouf ben-Ya'hya al-Sabti al-Maghrebi, disciple de Maïmonide", in *Journal Asiatique* iii 14 (1842), p. 27 n. 1; Moritz Steinschneider, *Die arabische Literatur der Juden* (Frankfurt am Main: Kauffmann, 1902), p. xxxiii top; Salo W. Baron, *A Social and Religious History of the Jews* (18 volumes; New York: Columbia University Press, ²1952–1983), vol. VIII (1958), p. 314 n. 28.

26 David Kaufmann, *Gesammelte Schriften*, ed. Marcus Brann, vol. II (Frankfurt am Main: Kauffmann, 1910), p. 158 (an essay first published in 1898); Eppenstein, "Moses ben Maimon" (see above n. 23), p. 85.

27 Letter from Samuel b. Tibbon to Maimonides in קובץ תשובות הרמב"ם ואגרותיו, ed. Abraham ben Aryeh Lichtenberg (Leipzig: H. L. Schnaus, 1859; reprint Farnborough: Gregg, 1969), part II, p. 27a, col. 2: כי הראשונה כאשר הודעתי אל כבוד אדוננו נראה ממנה שנכתבה מספר כתוב ערבי או מספר שנכתב הוא מספר כתוב ערבי ולזה רבו טעיותיו כאשר יראה בה אדוננו – "for the first [copy], as I have informed our honourable master, seemed to have been written from a book written in Arabic [scil. script] or from a book which itself was written from a book in Arabic [script], and hence its mistakes are numerous, as our master will see"; cf. Moritz Steinschneider, *Die hebräischen Uebersetzungen des Mittelalters und die Juden als Dolmetscher* (2 volumes; Berlin: Bibliographisches Bureau, 1893; reprint Graz: Akademische Druck- und Verlagsanstalt, 1956), p. 416.

Maimonides's *Guide* was circulating in Arabic letters at an early period and, perhaps rather unexpectedly, soon found a readership outside the Jewish community for whom it was intended.[28]

The conversion of a book such as Maimonides's *Guide* to Arabic script is not without difficulty. A serious problem is caused by the large number of Hebrew quotations, especially Biblical quotations, which it contains. What is to be done with these? For the Muslim or Christian reader ignorant of Hebrew language and script the best solution would, of course, be to translate all such quotations into Arabic together with the rest of the text, just as e.g. Munk was to translate them into French or Pines into English. This, however, was very rarely done.[29] Instead, the Hebrew quotations were left in Hebrew, sometimes retaining the original Hebrew script, sometimes transliterated into Arabic letters. Copies of the former type in continually alternating Arabic-Hebrew language and script are extant in the geniza[30] and in 1974 a copy of the latter kind, containing the entire text of the *Guide* in Arabic script, Hebrew quotations and all, was published from an Istanbul manuscript written in the Yemen in 1477–1479.[31] Such productions represent an interesting cultural phenomenon. Who used them? For the Jews the Arabic script was unnecessary and unnatural; for Muslims and Christians the Hebrew quotations were illegible and incomprehensible. The natural *Sitz im Leben*, therefore, for these texts is as reading material for philosophical gatherings, literary *majālis*, at which the Muslim and Christian

28 Steinschneider, *Die arabische Literatur* (see above n. 25), p. 204 with literature on pp. 218–219 n. 12; Friedlaender, *Der Sprachgebrauch des Maimonides* (see above n. 24), p. xxi; Eppenstein, "Moses ben Maimon" (see above n. 23), p. 85 n. 1. As far as a Muslim readership is concerned, Georges Vajda, in *Encyclopaedia of Islam* (new edition; Leiden: Brill, London: Luzac), vol. III, (1971), col. 877a, is rather reserved.

29 Munk, "Notice sur Joseph" (see above n. 25), p. 27 n. 1 mentions a Paris manuscript (BN Ancien fonds 95) of this type in Arabic script = Gérard Troupeau, *Bibliothèque Nationale … Catalogue des manuscrits arabes*. Première partie: *Manuscrits chrétiens*, Tome I (Paris: Bibliothèque Nationale, 1972), no. 205.12.

30 Simon Hopkins, "Two new Maimonidean autographs in the John Rylands University Library", in *Bulletin of the John Rylands Library* 67 (1985), p. 713 n. 11 (T-S NS 306.252). Further leaves of the same manuscript are mentioned by Geoffrey Khan, *Karaite Bible Manuscripts from the Cairo Genizah* (Cambridge University Library Genizah Series 9; Cambridge: Cambridge University Press, 1990), p. 2 n. 17, to which add also T-S Ar. 18 (1).141.

31 Hüseyin Atay, *Delâlet'ü l-Hairîn. Filozof Musa ibn Meymun el-Kutrtubi 1135–1205* (Ankara Üniversitesi İlâhiyat Fakültesi Yayınları 93; Ankara: Ankara Universitesi Basimevi, 1974). The whole manuscript had earlier been described by Franz Rosenthal, "From Arabic books and manuscripts V: A one-volume library of Arabic philosophical and scientific texts in Istanbul", in *Journal of the American Oriental Society* 75 (1955), pp. 14–23.

participants for whom such copies were prepared had Jewish instructors to help them with the Hebrew portions.[32]

Certain other works of Maimonides have also been transmitted in Arabic as well as Hebrew script, notably his youthful treatise on logic and some of the medical compositions,[33] such as the treatise on poisons.[34] The *Šarḥ asmā' al ʿuqqār*, as we have seen above (pp. 90–91, n. 22), is extant only in Arabic script. These compositions, however, are in a completely different category from the aforementioned copies of the *Guide*. For example, the treatise on poisons was compiled at the behest of Maimonides's Muslim patron from material already extant in Arabic letters; it contains nothing whatever of specifically Jewish interest, it has no Hebrew quotations and although Maimonides doubtless wrote the work in Hebrew script, it was from the beginning intended to be read outside the Jewish community as well as within it.

V. Arabic vs. Hebrew in the works of Maimonides

Maimonides's views on the relative merits and functions of Arabic and Hebrew[35] are worth a short enquiry. He wrote in both languages and it is not uninteresting to ask after the reasons that governed his choice. He was, of course, aware that Arabic and Hebrew are closely related: ואמא אללגה̈ אלערביה̈ ואלעבראניה̈ פקד אתפק כל מן עלם אללגתין אנהמא לגה̈ ואחדה̈ בלא שך – "and as for the Arabic and Hebrew languages, all who know both of them are agreed that they are one language without a doubt".[36] On an ideal, theoretical level he was of the

32 Cf. Mark R. Cohen and Sasson Somekh, "Interreligious majālis in early Fatimid Egypt", in Hava Lazarus-Yafeh et al. (Eds.), *The Majlis: Interreligious Encounters in Medieval Islam* (Wiesbaden: Harrassowitz, 1999), pp. 128–136. One should probably think of learned Christians in this context rather than Muslims, cf. above n. 28; a Karaite readership seems unlikely.

33 Vajda (see above n. 28), col. 876b.

34 Steinschneider, *Die arabische Literatur* (see above n. 25), p. 214; Ullmann, *Medizin im Islam* (see above n. 8), pp. 338–339.

35 Maimonides did not write continuous original prose in Aramaic (אללגה̈ אלסריאניה̈; לשון ארמי – the term ארמאניה̈ as in other mediaeval writers is also used; Joseph Kafaḥ [= Qāfiḥ], *Rabbi Moshe Ben Maimon (Maimonides), Iggerot. Letters. Arabic Original with New Translation and Commentary* [Jerusalem: Mossad Harav Kook, 1972], p. 150, n. 12 [Hebrew]). The Aramaic in Maimonides's works consists merely of quotations from the sources, particularly, of course, Talmudic sources. For his use of the term לישנא דרבנן see below n. 70.

36 Bacher, "Bibelexegese Moses Maimûni's" (see above n. 18), pp. 163–164. The Arabic text is given in Qāfiḥ, *Iggerot* (see above n. 35), p. 150 (§ 25 of *Pirqe Moshe*) and two Hebrew translations in Suessman Muntner (Ed.), *Moshe Ben Maimon. (Medical) Aphorisms of Moses, in Twenty Five Treatises* (Jerusalem: Mosad Harav Kook, 1959), p. 362.

opinion that Hebrew, the language of Eden and of Holy Scripture, the medium in which God chose to reveal His will to mankind, was intrinsically superior to Arabic.[37] Indeed, he subscribed to the commonly held mediaeval Jewish view that "das Arabische ist verdorbenes Hebräisch";[38] in his famous letter to Samuel b. Tibbon he says (in a part preserved only in Hebrew translation): ... בלשון ערבי – שהיא ודאי לשון עברי שנשתבשה מעט – "[...] in Arabic, which is certainly Hebrew which has been corrupted a little".[39]

Belief in the abstract superiority of Hebrew is all very well as a philosophical tenet but lacks practicality. Now Maimonides was a very practical man; in his view effective communication of the message should always take precedence over the medium in which it is delivered. He never let extraneous considerations interfere with efficient communication. The rhymed Hebrew preface to *Iggeret Teman* ends with the words – ראיתי להשיב התשובה בלשון קדר וניבו למען ירוץ קורא בו – מכל האנשים – הטף והנשים – כי תשובת ענינו יחד – ראויה לעמוד עליה כל קהלותיכם כאחד – "I saw fit to make my reply in the Arabic tongue and idiom so that the reader – everybody, including women and children – may read it fluently, for it is proper that all your communities jointly understand the reply to the affair as a whole", whereupon the author immediately continues in Arabic. When Joseph b. Jābir of Baghdad wrote declaring that he spent much time studying Maimonides's Arabic *Commentary on the Mishnah* but, being an ignoramus, had difficulty with the Hebrew *Mishneh Torah*, Maimonides replied (in Arabic of course) reassuring his correspondent that he was far from being an ignoramus, that study is of itself a valuable activity, and that it matters not through which language understanding is achieved: אנך ליס בעם ארץ, בל תלמידֿנא וחביבנא אנת וכל מן יתעלק בטלב תלמוד ולו פהם פסוק אחד או הלכה אחת, לא פרק אן יפהם דֿלך אלמעני מן לשון הקודש או מלשון ארמי או מן ערבי, אלקצד פהם אלמעאני באי לגהֿ כאנת – "You are not an ignoramus, on the contrary, you are a pupil and friend of ours. Whoever concerns himself with the pursuit of learning, even if he only understands a single verse or a single *halakhah*, it makes no difference whether he understands the meaning via the Holy Tongue, Aramaic or Arabic – the point is to understand the meanings in whatever language it may be".[40] For this reason, Maimonides was not opposed

---

37 Maimonides's view of the sanctity of (Biblical) Hebrew as לשון הקדש "the Holy Tongue" is expressed in the *Guide of the Perplexed* III.8 *in fine*, on which see Bacher, "Bibelexegese Moses Maimûni's" (see above n. 18), p. 165 n. 2.

38 Steinschneider, *Die arabische Literatur* (see above n. 25), p. xxxiv and the quotation from Dunash b. Tamim, ibid., p. 72; see further Bacher, "Bibelexegese Moses Maimûni's" (see above n. 18), p. 164 n. 2; Eduard König, *Hebräisch und Semitisch: Prolegomena und Grundlinien einer Geschichte der semitischen Sprachen* ... (Berlin: Reuther und Reichard, 1901), p. 114.

39 Shailat, *Letters* (see above n. 18), p. 531,14.

40 Ibid., p. 404,11–15; cf. Steinschneider, *Die hebräischen Uebersetzungen* (see above n. 27), pp. 931–932.

to prayer in Arabic if this be helpful to understanding; and if prayer in Arabic is permissible, how much the more so the study of commentaries and codes in that language: קריית [שמע] גאיזה̈ בכל לשון נאהיך אלשרוח ואלתואליף.[41] And in the dispute concerning Hebrew vs. Arabic wedding etc. songs, Maimonides forcefully opposed those who permitted such jollity in Hebrew but forbade it in Arabic. Such a position, he says, reveals "sheer ignorance" (גֿהל מחץ̇), for the worth of any song should be judged by its content, not by its medium: ואעלם אן אלאשעאר אלמולפה באי לגה̈ כאנת אנמא תעתבר במעאניהא – "and know that songs composed in whatever language it may be should be considered according to their meanings only".[42]

In accordance with this principle of efficient communication, the great majority of Maimonides's works were composed by preference in the mother tongue and first literary language both of himself and his immediate readership, i.e. Arabic, to be more precise in Judaeo-Arabic – in what kind(s) of Arabic we shall see shortly.

While Maimonides was first and foremost an Arabic author, he did, of course, also write in Hebrew. Certain of his Arabic works, in accordance with literary convention, contain an introduction in Hebrew, e.g. the aforementioned letter to Samuel b. Tibbon about the translation of the *Guide of the Perplexed*[43] or

---

41 Shailat, *Letters* (see above n. 18), p. 404,15. Prayer in the Arabic vernacular was likewise approved in the *Letter of Consolation* attributed to Maimonides's father: Laurence M. Simmons, in *Jewish Quarterly Review* 2 (1890), p. 77 = Arabic text p. 9. Cf. Maimonides's *responsum* (R. Moses b. Maimon, *Responsa*, ed. Jehoshua Blau [4 volumes; Jerusalem: Mekitse Nirdamim, 1957–1988], vol. II, 1960), no. 254 = Shailat, *Letters*, p. 590,12 on *piyyuṭ*.

42 *Commentary on the Mishnah*, Avot 1:16 (Yosef Qāfih [Ed.], משנה עם פירוש רבינו משה בן מימון – סדר נזיקין (Jerusalem: Mosad Harav Kook, 1964), p. 419; cf. the discussion in Simon Federbush, הלשון העברית בישראל ובעמים (Jerusalem: Mosad Harav Kook, 1967) 107. Maimonides refers to this passage in his *responsum*, ed. Blau (see above n. 41), no. 224 = Shailat, *Letters* (see above n. 18), p. 426,15. We may note in passing that Maimonides generally cared little for poetry and song; nor was the *piyyuṭ* genre much to his liking, either linguistically or liturgically – see in general e.g. David Yellin and Israel Abrahams, *Maimonides* (London: Macmillan, 1903), pp. 141–142 with n. 83; Eppenstein, "Moses ben Maimon" (see above n. 23), pp. 10, 55 n. 5 (referring to the *responsum* Blau no. 254 mentioned in the preceding note), 70, 101 n. 3; Alexander Marx, *Studies in Jewish History and Booklore* (New York: Jewish Theological Seminary of America, 1944), p. 46 (an essay first published in 1935). This dislike did not, however, prevent him from composing occasional Hebrew verses of his own or from quoting those of others; Wilhelm Bacher, "Hebräische Verse von Maimuni", in *Monatsschrift für Geschichte und Wissenschaft des Judentums* 53 [N.F. 17] (1909), pp. 581–588; Eppenstein, ibid., p. 10 n. 4 = Shailat, *Letters*, p. 530,16. Maimonides also composed rhymed Hebrew prose, e.g. the prefaces to the *Commentary on the Mishnah* and *Iggeret Teman*.

43 On the bilingual structure of this document see the important discussion of Shailat, *Letters* (see above n. 18), pp. 513–515.

the rhymed prose which prefaces *Iggeret Teman*[44] and the *Commentary on the Mishnah*. The drafting of some of his *responsa* and letters in Hebrew was largely a case of practical good manners: such documents are written in reply to enquiries received in Hebrew or addressed to correspondents who either did not know Arabic,[45] or for whom communication in Hebrew was for one reason or another preferable.[46] The compendium *Hilkhot ha-Yerushalmi* was not written in Arabic for the simple reason that it consists almost entirely of abridged verbatim Hebrew and Aramaic extracts from the Palestinian Talmud.

We should not be misled – as some have been – into believing that the list of Maimonides's Hebrew works is longer than it actually is by the fact that certain of his compositions are extant in Hebrew only; there is no reasonable doubt that the treatise on the calendar, the so-called מאמר העבור,[47] and the אגרת השמד[48] were originally composed in Arabic and that the Hebrew texts which survive are but translations. It is quite possible that the Arabic originals of these compositions will yet be discovered. This is just what happened in the case of מאמר תחית המתים, of which the Arabic original was in Steinschneider's day considered lost,[49] but has meanwhile turned up in several Yemenite[50] copies and can now be read in at least three editions, those of J. Finkel,[51] the late Y. Qāfiḥ[52] and, most recently, I. Shailat.[53] On the other hand, the famous letter to the community of Montpellier on astrology, which according to the colophon of MS Leipzig 30 was translated from Arabic by Moses b. Tibbon, turns out to have been written in Hebrew by Maimonides himself.[54]

44 On this case see Mordechai Akiva Friedman, *Maimonides, the Yemenite Messiah and Apostasy* (Jerusalem: Ben-Zvi Institute, 2002), p. 153 n. 18 [Hebrew].

45 E.g. R. Pinḥas ha-Dayyan; Shailat, *Letters* (see above n. 18), p. 434.

46 Blau, *Responsa* (see above n. 41), vol. III, pp. 18–19; Shailat, *Letters* (see above n. 18), p. 219 n. 5 *in fine*.

47 Steinschneider, *Die hebräischen Uebersetzungen* (see above n. 27), § 377 ("wahrscheinlich [...] in arabischer Sprache") and hence registered in idem, *Die arabische Literatur* (see above n. 25), p. 213, against Yellin and Abrahams, *Maimonides* (see above n. 42), p. 21 "written in Hebrew".

48 Steinschneider, *Die hebräischen Uebersetzungen* (see above n. 27), § 554.3; idem, *Die arabische Literatur* (see above n. 25), p. 209; Qāfiḥ, *Iggerot* (see above n. 35), p. 105.

49 Steinschneider, *Die hebräischen Uebersetzungen* (see above n. 27), p. 431; idem, *Die arabische Literatur* (see above n. 25), p. 210.

50 Qāfiḥ, *Iggerot* (see above n. 35), p. 67 n. 15 notes that this work is preserved only in Yemenite copies.

51 Joshua Finkel, "Maimonides' Treatise on Resurrection", in *Proceedings of the American Academy for Jewish Research* 9 (1938–1939), pp. 57–105, א–מב.

52 Qāfiḥ, *Iggerot* (see above n. 35), pp. 63ff.; for the Yemenite source of the edition see there p. 67.

53 Shailat, *Letters* (see above n. 18), pp. 315ff.; for the Arabic sources see there pp. 317–318.

54 Alexander Marx, "The correspondence between the rabbis of southern France and Maimonides about astrology", in *Hebrew Union College Annual* 3 (1926), pp. 336–338; Shailat, *Letters* (see above n. 18), p. 476 n. 5.

There is one – only one – real exception to this state of affairs. In only one case did Maimonides *on principle* write in Hebrew and *on principle* object to Arabic. This exception is the great *Mishneh Torah*.[55] Maimonides was firmly of the opinion that Hebrew, and Hebrew only, was a suitable medium for his vast compendium of Jewish *fiqh*. It is worthwhile to ponder the reasons for this insistence. It was not merely a matter of national, religious sentiment and love of Hebraic beauty.[56] Nor was it a question of the technical subject matter dictating the use of the Holy Tongue of his forefathers for this huge halakhic encyclopaedia; were this the case, *Sefer ha-Miṣwot*, which served as a prelude, or pendant, to *Mishneh Torah* and deals with very much the same material, would have been written in Hebrew also. As it was, Maimonides wrote *Sefer ha-Miṣwot* in Arabic. When later he expressed regret for this, it was not because matter and medium were inherently unsuited, but because of the mundane practical consideration that the use of Arabic automatically restricted his readership to the Arabic-speaking world alone: וניחמתי הרבה על שחיברתיו בלשון ערבי מפני שהכל צריכין לקרותו – "and I much regret having composed it in the Arabic language, because everybody ought to read it".[57] Maimonides had no difficulty, either in principle or in practice, with using the Arabic language for the most intimate and sacred subjects of Judaism.

In the same way as the use of Hebrew script put Maimonides's Judaeo-Arabic works beyond the reach of Arabic-speaking Muslims and Christians, so the use of the Arabic language put them beyond the reach of his Jewish co-religionists outside the Arabic-speaking world, particularly in Europe. Maimonides was very happy to have his Arabic works translated into Hebrew; indeed, in the case of the *Guide*, though himself too busy to translate the book (and other books) personally,[58] he actively assisted in the process of translation[59] and tacitly gave his advance approval to the result,[60] which was completed on 30th November 1204, just a fortnight before he died.[61] The translation of Maimonides's *Guide* was quickly followed by translations of others of his works, not infrequently by several different translations. This translation activity, associated

---

55 Detailed discussion in Isadore Twersky, *Introduction to the Code of Maimonides (Mishneh Torah)* (New Haven, London: Yale University Press, 1980), chapter V, "Language and style", pp. 324–355.

56 As claimed by e.g. Federbush (see above n. 42), pp. 104, 108.

57 Blau, *Responsa* (see above n. 41), vol. II, p. 725 no. 447 = Shailat, *Letters* (see above n. 18), p. 223,9–10.

58 Shailat, *Letters* (see above n. 18), p. 558,1–7.

59 See especially the long letter to Samuel b. Tibbon, in Shailat, *Letters* (see above n. 18), pp. 511ff. no. 35. Maimonides's concrete suggestions for translations of his own work are discussed by David Zvi Baneth, "הרמב"ם כמתרגם דברי עצמו", in *Tarbiz* 23 (1952), pp. 170–191.

60 Cf. Shailat, *Letters* (see above n. 18), p. 514 top and Maimonides's letter itself, especially ibid., p. 531,5–11.

61 Steinschneider, *Die hebräischen Uebersetzungen* (see above n. 27), p. 420.

particularly with several generations of the Ibn Tibbon family in Provence, marks the opening of a new period in the history of the Hebrew language. Maimonides states that he would have liked to see Hebrew versions of at least two other of his Arabic compositions, *Sefer ha-Miṣwot* and the *Commentary on the Mishnah*, possibly even contemplating doing the job himself.[62] But the suggestion that *Mishneh Torah* be translated into Arabic provoked him into strong resistance. He would not tolerate the idea and in his reply to Ibn Jābir says: ואיני רוצה בשום פנים להוציאו ללשון ערבי, כי נעימותיו ייפסדו. ואני מבקש עתה להחזיר פרוש המשנה וספר המצוות ללשון הקודש, וכל שכן שאחזיר זה החיבור ללשון ערבי – אל תבקש זה כלל – "And I do not wish under any circumstances to translate it [scil. *Mishneh Torah*] into Arabic, for its beauties[63] will be lost. I am now looking[64] to convert the *Commentary on the Mishnah* and *Sefer ha-Miṣwot* to the Holy Tongue; all the more so, then, do not ask me at all to convert this composition to Arabic".[65]

Maimonides's insistence on Hebrew only as the medium of *Mishneh Torah* and his refusal to countenance an Arabic translation were the result neither of sentimental attachment to the ancestral language of his forebears nor of constraints imposed by the subject matter. The reason for the unique position of the Hebrew *Mishneh Torah* in his oeuvre must be sought elsewhere. That reason must surely be the status which Maimonides envisaged for his halakhic *magnum opus*. His colossal codification of Jewish law was not intended for

---

62 For *Sefer ha-Miṣwot*, in addition to the passage from the letter to Ibn Jābir immediately hereafter in n. 65, see Blau, *Responsa* (see above n. 41), vol. II, p. 725, no. 447 = Shailat, *Letters* (see above n. 18), p. 223,10: ואני מחכה עתה שאעתיק אותו ללשון הקדש בעזרת שדי – "and I am now waiting to translate it [scil. *Sefer ha-Miṣwot*], with God's help, into the Holy Tongue."

63 For the reading נעימותיו see Steinschneider, *Die hebräischen Uebersetzungen* (see above n. 27), pp. 931–932 n. 188.

64 Note that Bacher, "Zum sprachlichen Charakter" (see below n. 78), pp. 81–82, n. 2 reads ואיני מבקש, understanding "Nicht einmal seine arabischen Werke wolle er jetzt mehr ins Hebräische übertragen [...]".

65 Shailat, *Letters* (see above n. 18), p. 409,8–11 (the passage is missing by homoeoteleuton in the Arabic original of the letter). Parts of *Mishneh Torah*, however, were translated into Arabic; Steinschneider, *Die arabische Literatur* (see above n. 25), pp. 200, 281 § 53, 303 § 159. There are also Arabic commentaries to the work; Steinschneider, ibid., p. 200 (BL Cat. no. 498), p. 271 § 233 referred to by Hartwig Hirschfeld, in *Jewish Quarterly Review* 16 (1904), p. 412. Hebrew-Arabic lexicography based upon *Mishneh Torah* was rather well developed, notably by Tanḥum Yerushalmi's *al-Muršid al-Kāfi* (Steinschneider, ibid., § 174.2). The Yemenite dictionary of David b. Yeshaʿ (ibid., § 255) of which the section א–ב was published by Nathan Max Nathan, *Ein anonymes Wörterbuch zur Mišna und Jad haḥazaka* (Berlin: Itzkowski, 1905) can now be consulted in full in the facsimile edition מלון עברי–ערבי "אלגאמע" – המאסף, published by Shalom b. Saʿadya Gamliʾel (Jerusalem: Mekhon Shalom Le-Shiveṭey Yeshurun, 1988); for further information on the subject see the appendices ibid. by Yosef Tobi and Uri Melammed, pp. 175–187, 188–189 respectively, together with the references there [Hebrew].

Arabic-speaking Jewry alone, but planned as a monument to the Jewish nation as a whole, a code of law for all Israel everywhere,[66] so comprehensive as to make its predecessors redundant and any successors unnecessary. Maimonides's intentions are stated rather clearly at the end of the preface to the work: עד שתהא תורה שבעל פה כולה סדורה בפי הכל ... עד שיהיו כל הדינין גלויין לקטן ולגדול ... כללו שלדבר כדי שלא יהא אדם צריך לחיבור אחר בעולם בדין מדיני ישראל אלא יהא חיבור זה מקבץ לתורה שבעל פה כולה עם התקנות והמנהגות והגזרות שנעשו מימות משה רבינו ועד חיבורי התלמוד וכמו שפירשו לנו הגאונים בכל חיבוריהם שחיברו אחר התלמוד. לפיכך קראנו שם חיבור זה משנה תורה לפי שאדם קורא בתורה שבכתב תחלה ואחר כך קורא בזה ויודע ממנו תורה שבעל פה כולה ואינו צריך לקרות ספר אחר ביניהם – "so that the whole Oral Law shall be properly organized on the lips of all […] so that all laws shall be clear to young and old […] in sum, so that nobody shall need another book in the world concerning any law of Israel, but this book (חיבור) shall gather the whole Oral Law together with the ordinances, practices and decrees which have been made from the days of Moses until the composition of the Talmud[s], including what the Geonim interpreted in all the compositions of theirs which they composed after the Talmud. We have therefore called this book (חיבור) *Mishneh Torah*, because a person who first of all reads the Written Law and afterwards reads this [book] will know from it the whole Oral Law and will not need to read another book besides them".[67] As such, the fitting medium for *Mishneh Torah* was of course the national language of his people.[68] Only in Hebrew could the book attain the universal circulation Maimonides had conceived for it.

VI. Maimonides's Hebrew

(לשון הקודש, לשון עברי; אללגֿה אלעבראניה֗, אללגֿה אלמקדסה֗, לסאן כתב אלתנזיל, לגתנא, עבאני)

Mishneh Torah is distinguished as much by its marvellously fluent and limpid Hebrew prose as by its contents.[69] In the preface to the work the author is not very forthcoming about the kind of Hebrew in which he chose to write, saying only that he wrote "in clear language and concisely" (בלשון ברורה ודרך קצרה; cf. Zephaniah 3:9, Job 33:3). More information is given in the preface to *Sefer*

66 Its wide circulation is mentioned, with evident approval, in Maimonides's letter to Montpellier published in Shailat, *Letters* (see above n. 18), p. 478,17–18: שכבר פשט באי סיקיליאה כמו שפשט במזרח ובמערב ובתימן – "and it has already reached Sicily, just as it has reached the east, the west and the Yemen".

67 Much the same may be read, in Arabic, in the preface to *Sefer ha-Miṣwot*: *Sefer Hamitzvot. Book of Commandments. Arabic Original with New Translation and Commentary* by Joseph Kafih [= Y. Qāfiḥ] (Jerusalem: Mossad Harav Kook, 1971), pp. 2–3.

68 See in general e.g. Eppenstein, "Moses ben Maimon" (see above n. 23), pp. 68ff.

69 For the matters discussed here see also the chapter "Language and style", in Twersky, *Introduction* (see above n. 55), pp. 324–355.

ha-Miṣwot. Here Maimonides tells us that he avoided Biblical style on the one hand and Talmudic diction on the other, Biblical Hebrew being too limited for the purpose and the Talmudic idiom too full of Aramaic, much of which even the most learned can hardly cope with. Instead – with a very practical aim in mind – he chose to write in the language of the Mishnah so as to be readily intelligible to the rank and file. This is what he says: וכד̇לך ראית באן לא אולפה בלסאן כתב אלתנזיל, אד̇ תצ̇יק בנא אליום תלך אללגה̈ אלמקדסה̈ ען תכמיל מעאני אלפקה בהא, ולא איצ̇א אולפה בלגה̈ אלתלמוד, אד̇ ליס יפהמהא מן אהל מלתנא אליום אלא אחאד, ותשד̇ כלמאת כת̇ירה̈ ותצעב ולו עלי אלמברזין פי אלתלמוד, כל אולפה בלגה̈ אלמשנה כי יסהל ד̇לך עלי אכת̇ר אלנאס – "And so I saw fit not to compose it in the language of scripture, for that holy tongue is too restricted for us today for the full expression in it of matters of Halakhah; and [I saw fit] also not to compose it in Talmudic language, for today only a few individuals of our nation understand it, and many words are anomalous and difficult even for experts in Talmud[70] – but I would compose it in the language of the Mishnah[71] so that it will be easy[72] for the majority of people".[73]

The result was not only an intellectual achievement of gigantic proportions, but also a linguistic masterpiece of the highest order. Maimonides was

70 Cf. Maimonides's remarks on Talmudic language in the preface to *Mishneh Torah*: ועוד שהוא בלשון ארמי מעורב עם לשונות אחרות לפי שאותה הלשון היתה ברורה לכל אנשי שנער בעת שחובר התלמוד אבל בשאר מקומות וכן בשנער בימי הגאונים אין אדם מכיר אותה הלשון עד שמלמדין אותו – "furthermore (the Talmud) is in Aramaic mixed with other languages, for that language was intelligible to all the inhabitants of Babylonia at the period in which the Talmud was compiled but in other places and indeed even in Babylonia in the days of the Geonim there was nobody who knew that language without being taught". This language is called by Maimonides לישנא דרבנן (Shailat, *Letters* [see above n. 18], p. 558,5) and in it he composed several items of Talmud commentary; see Eppenstein, "Moses ben Maimon" (see above n. 23), pp. 12–13, Shailat, *Letters*, pp. 558, ad line 5, 653 ad line 1.

71 Cf. the letters to Ibn Jābir in Shailat, *Letters* (see above n. 18), p. 404,7: ואנה יתעד̇ר עליה פהם אלחיבור לכונה בלשון משנה – "and that the *Ḥibbur* [= *Mishneh Torah*] is difficult for him to understand because of its being written in the language of the Mishnah", and to R. Pinḥas ha-Dayyan, ibid., p. 440,6: שיהיה דרך המשנה ובלשון המשנה – "that it [scil. *Mishneh Torah*] should be according to the method of the Mishnah and in the language of the Mishnah". Maimonides's admiration for the Mishnaic language of Judah ha-Nasi is discussed by Bacher, "Bibelexegese Moses Maimûni's" (see above n. 18), pp. 165–167.

72 The simplicity of the Hebrew of *Mishneh Torah* is mentioned again in the letter to Ibn Jābir, in Shailat, *Letters* (see above n. 18), p. 404,20–21 = Qāfiḥ, *Iggerot* (see above n. 35), p. 136 § 26: וינבגי איצ̇א אן תתעלם הד̇א אלקדר מן לשון הקודש אלד̇י אלפנא בה אלחיבור פאנה סהל אלפהם קריב אלמראס – "and you ought also to learn the [necessary] amount of Hebrew, in which we have composed the *Ḥibbur*, for it is easy to understand and simple to manage". Ibn Jābir himself thought differently and would have preferred to have the work in Arabic.

73 Qāfiḥ, *Sefer Hamitzvot* (see above n. 67), p. 2.

perfectly aware that with *Mishneh Torah* he had produced a virtuoso performance the like of which had not been seen before;[74] and when he said of it (in a rather uncharacteristic expression of aesthetic judgement) that by translation to Arabic "its beauties will be lost" (נעימותיו ייפסדו, see above p. 98, n. 63), he was simply stating a fact.

But Maimonides's Neo-Mishnaic style – or, rather, the novelty of his casting Talmudic Aramaic material into Mishnaic Hebrew language[75] – did not meet with universal approval. Abraham b. David of Posquières, the leading figure in the ensuing Maimonidean controversy, objected in vitriolically polemic tones not only to the method of *Mishneh Torah* but also to its language.[76] Maimonides's *Code* nevertheless exerted a permanent and decisive influence on the language of everything that came after it.[77]

As far as the technical description of Maimonides's Hebrew usage in *Mishneh Torah* (and in his Hebrew letters) is concerned, research has not advanced much beyond two important studies written by W. Bacher some 100 years ago.[78] Although a great deal remains to be done in this field, circumstances are propitious. The manuscript tradition of *Mishneh Torah*, intricate though it is, is in rather a good state; several copies are known to have been made from the author's original (one of these includes the autograph affirmation of Maimonides himself) and there even exist autograph drafts in the hand of the author.[79]

---

74 See the verses with which he ended the work; Bacher, *Aus dem Wörterbuche* (see above n. 13), p. 23 n. 4; idem, "Hebräische Verse von Maimuni" (see above n. 42), pp. 582, 588.

75 Only rarely in *Mishneh Torah* did Maimonides retain the Talmudic Aramaic terminology; Bacher, "Der sprachliche Charakter" (see below n. 78), pp. 122–123.

76 Isadore Twersky, *Rabad of Posquières* (Philadelphia: Jewish Publication Society of America, ^{2}1980), pp. 170–171 (with further literature) and more briefly e.g. Bacher, "Zum sprachlichen Charakter " (see below n. 78), p. 281; Federbush (see above n. 42), p. 109; Eduard Yechezkel Kutscher, *A History of the Hebrew Language* (Jerusalem, Leiden: The Magnes Press et al., 1982), § 274.

77 For the *Shulḥan ʿArukh* see Jacob I. Dienstag, "ליחס מרן אל משנת הרמב"ם", in *Sinai* xxx 59 (1966), pp. 59–60.

78 Wilhelm Bacher, "Der sprachliche Charakter des Mischne-Tora" in idem, *Aus dem Wörterbuche* (see above n. 13), pp. 117–147, Hebrew part, pp. 36–38; idem, "Zum sprachlichen Charakter des Mischne Tora", in *Moses ben Maimon. Sein Leben, seine Werke und sein Einfluss* (see above n. 23), vol. II, pp. 280–305. Further items are mentioned by Dienstag (see above n. 77), pp. 60–61 n. 29; Angel Sáenz-Badillos, *A History of the Hebrew Language*, trans. John Elwolde (Cambridge: Cambridge University Press, 1993), pp. 208 n. 18, 263 n. 131.

79 Details *apud* Marx, *Studies in Jewish History and Booklore* (see above n. 42), pp. 52–53 n. 9 and the addition on p. 431; Baron, *History of the Jews* (see above n. 25), vol. VI, pp. 376ff. n. 114; Malachi Beit-Arié, "A Maimonides autograph in the Rylands Gaster *Genizah* collection", in *Bulletin of the John Rylands Library* 57 (1974), pp. 1–6. See also the review "הנוסח המנופה של היד החזקה" by Joshua Blau of Yosef Qāfiḥ's new edition of *Mishneh Torah*, in *Peʿamim* 25 (1985), pp. 146–147 and now the introduction to Y. Shailat, רמב"ם מדויק. כרך א: ספר המדע (Maʿale Adumim, Israel: Shailat, 2004), pp. א–כא.

The Mishnaic style used by Maimonides should be compared in detail with the recension(s) of the Mishnah upon which he based his *Commentary*, a work for which extensive autograph materials exist, in both draft and fair copies. The celebrated autograph fair copy of the *Commentary* contains the Mishnah vocalized in Maimonides's own hand.[80] This Mishnaic text in all probability represents the Spanish tradition of Isaac Alfasi and Ibn Migash, transmitted to the young Maimonides by his father. Maimonides's father, himself a scholar of no mean accomplishment,[81] had studied at the feet of Ibn Migash in Lucena and had composed Mishnaic scholia which were later used by his son in his great *Commentary*.[82]

The Neo-Mishnaic Hebrew of *Mishneh Torah* contains, of course, various elements which do not occur in the Mishnah itself; one finds there a certain number of Arabisms[83] and the occasional grammatical oddity.[84] It would be worthwhile to compare it in these respects with the Hebrew used in Maimonides's letters, which were not composed with the Mishnaic ideal in mind and are likely to reveal a greater degree of Arabic interference.[85] These letters, however, are themselves far from stylistically homogeneous; in particular one should distinguish between the flowery rhymed prose with which some begin and the humbler epistolary style of the messages themselves. A different

---

80 See on these matters Simon Hopkins, *Maimonides's Commentary on Tractate Shabbat: The draft commentary according to autograph fragments from the Cairo Geniza* (Jerusalem: Ben-Zvi Institute, 2001), p. xxx, nn. 61, 62 and the references there.

81 Steinschneider, *Die arabische Literatur* (see above n. 25), § 157; Eppenstein, "Moses ben Maimon" (see above n. 23), p. 4 n. 2.

82 For this intellectual lineage of Maimonides see Shailat, *Letters* (see above n. 18), p. 115 ad line 9. The Spanish Mishnaic tradition which he received from his father going back to Alfasi is mentioned in the *Commentary* in connection with the disputed pronunciation of מלא הין *Eduyot* 1:3: ואלקראה̈ אלאולי הי אלתי רוית ען אבא מארי זצ"ל ען רבו ען רבו זכרם לברכה – "and the first reading is that which has been transmitted from my late father, my master, from his teacher and his [teacher's] teacher – may their memory be blessed".

83 Bacher, "Der sprachliche Charakter" (see above n. 78), pp. 120ff. For the use of יש שם "there is" etc. mentioned there on p. 121 and the difficulties caused by it see Steinschneider, *Die hebräischen Uebersetzungen* (see above n. 27), p. 418; Friedlaender, *Der Sprachgebrauch des Maimonides* (see above n. 24), pp. xii–xiii n. 2.

84 Bacher, ibid., pp. 123–124. Maimonides, although acquainted with a certain amount of linguistic literature (e.g. Arab grammarians, Ibn Janāḥ, Ḥayyūj, Ibn Ezra – references in Bacher, "Bibelexegese Moses Maimûni's" [see above n. 18], pp. 170, 171–172 etc.), was not interested in grammatical study as such. Leaving aside the Hebrew – Aramaic – Arabic word comparisons treated by Bacher, "Beiträge zur semitischen Sprachvergleichung" (see above n. 14), pp. 124–144, the nearest he came to linguistic discussion is perhaps the treatment of synonyms at the beginning of the *Guide*.

85 Little has been done on the Hebrew of the letters since the notes of Alexander Marx on "The original language of Maimonides in the letter of astrology", in *Hebrew Union College Annual* 3 (1926), pp. 336–338.

register again is represented by the heavily Arabicized Tibbonic idiom used by Maimonides's translators. In the field of mediaeval Hebrew in general and that of Maimonides in particular a great deal remains to be done.

VII. Maimonides's Arabic

(לשון ערבי, לשון קדר, לשון הגרי; אללגה אלערביה)

Research on Maimonides's Arabic usage is somewhat more advanced than that on his Hebrew, but here too matters are still at a fairly preliminary stage.

The various layers and levels of Maimonides's Arabic make it an especially interesting object of study. Any writer in Arabic has to come to terms with the familiar conflict between the literary and the spoken language, and Maimonides is, of course, no exception. He writes neither in high classical nor in vulgar colloquial, but occupies a wide stylistic range ("Middle Arabic") between these two extremes, sometimes (as in the *Guide*) tending towards an elevated literary register, sometimes (as in certain of his *responsa*) approaching more the language of colloquial speech. In addition to this familiar diglossic tension, perfectly normal for anybody writing in Arabic, the Arabic of Maimonides is distinguished by marked regional factors. His mother tongue, as we have seen, was Spanish Arabic. He always regarded himself proudly as a Spaniard (אני קטן מקטני חכמי ספרד, אני משה בר׳ מימון הספרדי etc.),[86] retained his characteristically Spanish handwriting to the end of his life and continued to use expressions such as ענדנא פי אלאנדלס "among us Andalusians" for years after his arrival in Egypt,[87] where, after short periods in North Africa and Palestine, he spent most of his life. Maimonides's Arabic, accordingly, is dialectally heterogeneous, containing both Western (Spanish) and Eastern (Egyptian) elements.

It would be possible to write a full description of Maimonides's Arabic, based on the most reliable of materials, describing in detail how he oscillates stylistically between high (classical) and low (colloquial), and dialectally between east (Egypt) and west (Spain) and showing how he himself ironed out some of the linguistic differences and eliminated features to which he was particularly sensitive. Such a description should, of course, be based upon Maimonides's autographs, pride of place among which must be awarded to the sumptuous fair copy of the *Commentary on the Mishnah*. The text of this should be compared systematically with what survives of the autograph drafts of the *Commentary* –

86 Steinschneider, *Die hebräischen Uebersetzungen* (see above n. 27), p. 774; Shailat, *Letters* (see above n. 18), p. 115 ad line 9.

87 Joshua Blau, "A[t our place in al-Andalus, a]t our place in the Maghreb", in *Massorot* 7 (1993), pp. 43–50 [Hebrew]; idem, "Maimonides' 'at our place in al-Andalus' revisited", forthcoming in the proceedings of the conference *Maimónides y su época*, Córdoba 6–9 Sept. 2004.

the comparison is often extremely illuminating.[88] Autographs of other works are available too, e. g. certain *responsa* and parts of the *Guide*; where autographs are not extant, recourse may be had to the very reliable Yemenite transmission of the Maimonidean legacy. A description of Maimonides's Arabic usage should, however, make only sparing use of his technical writings, particularly the medical works. Although autographs of some of these are available too, the texts are largely digests of material already available elsewhere in Muslim Arabic sources and do not not necessarily represent genuine Maimonidean Arabic.

VIII. Conclusion

We see, then, that the works of Maimonides present a rather intricate picture of languages, styles and scripts. Research into these things still has a long way to go, but excellent materials are available in abundance[89] and the circumstances for significant progress are distinctly favourable.

To end this talk I should like to return to the anecdote with which I began. Unawareness of the fact that the mother tongue of Maimonides was Arabic, that Arabic is the language of the great majority of his works and that the Hebrew versions are but translations (not always very good translations) is not at all confined to Ashkenaz. Even Arabic-speaking Jewry – the Yemen of course very notably excepted – has largely lost sight of this simple reality. This may be illustrated by another anecdote.

In the Jewish world outside the Yemen transmission of the great Maimonidean heritage became more and more restricted to its Hebrew parts, i.e. (i) works originally written in Hebrew and (ii) the Hebrew translations of those originally composed in Arabic. The *Commentary on the Mishnah* is today usually read in the mediaeval Hebrew translations (ed. princeps Naples 1492) which have for centuries formed part of printed editions of the Babylonian Talmud. In this form it was read in the Arabic-speaking world too, where it became so well known in its Hebrew dress that its Arabic origin was quite forgotten. Thus, when Joseph Renassia (1879–1962)[90] of Constantine, Algeria, wanted to make e.g. the famous *Eight Chapters* (ת̇מאניה̈ פצול < שמונה פרקים) available to his flock in Arabic, he did not use Maimonides's original text (which he had surely never seen and which survived only in the Yemen), but translated Ibn Tibbon's Hebrew version back into his own North African vernacular, adding for good

88 Hopkins, *Maimonides's Commentary on Tractate Shabbat* (see above n. 80), p. xxx.

89 Already in 1893 Steinschneider, *Die hebräischen Uebersetzungen* (see above n. 27), p. 413 described the sources as an "Embarras de richesses".

90 *Encyclopaedia Judaica*, Yearbook 1990/91 (Jerusalem: Keter Publishing House, 1992), pp. 386–387.

measure an Algerian Judaeo-Arabic version of the commentary *Ḥesed Abraham* by Abraham b. Shabbetai Sheftel Horowitz (d. c. 1615).[91] For Renassia Maimonides's *Eight Chapters* was an original Hebrew text, no different in this respect from *Ḥesed Abraham* and quite on a par with *Mishneh Torah*, which he translated into Algerian Arabic as well. Nothing could illustrate more strikingly the changes which had occurred among the Jews of Arab lands after the sun had set on the mediaeval golden age of Judaeo-Arabic culture, which reached its peak during the period of Maimonides. The gap, linguistic and otherwise, between Maimonides's original text of the *Eight Chapters* and that of Renassia's twentieth-century recreation of it is enormous. Here is a specimen from the beginning of § 4:

Maimonides's original:

פי טב אמראץׄ אלנפס

א. אלאפעאל אלתי הי כׄיראת הי אלאפעאל אלמעתדלה̈ אלמתוסטה̈ בין טרפין המא גׄמיעא שרא אחדהמא אפראט ואלאכׄר תקציר

ב. ואלפצׄאיל הי היאה̈ נפסאניה̈ ומלכאת מתוסטה̈ בין היאתין רדיתין אחדהמא אזיד ואלאכׄר אנקץ וען הדׄה אלהיאה̈ תלזם תלך אלאפעאל

ג. מתׄאל דׄלך אלעפה̈ פאנהא כׄלק מתוסט בין אלשרה ובין עדם אלאחסאס באללדׄה̈ ...

ד. וכדׄלך אלסכׄא מתוסט בין אלתקתיר ואלתבדׄיר

ה. ואלשגׄאעה̈ מתוסטה̈ בין אלתהור ואלגׄבן

> Ibn Tibbon's Hebrew translation:

ברפואות חולי הנפש

א. המעשים הטובים הם המעשים השוים הממוצעים בין שתי קצוות ששתיהן רע האחת מהן תוספת והשנית חסרון

ב. והמעלות הן תכונות נפשיות וקניינים ממוצעים בין שתי תכונות רעות האחת מהן יתרה והאחרת חסרה מן התכונות האלה יתחייבו הפעולות ההן

ג. והמשל בו הזהירות שהיא מידה ממוצעת בין רוב התאוה ובין העדר הרגש ההנאה ...

ד. וכן הנדיבות ממוצעת בין הכילות והפיזור

ה. והגבורה ממוצעת בין המסירה לסכנות ובין רוך הלבב

---

91 יוסף בן דוד גְנאסייה: ספר תולדות יעקב יוסף. והוא פרקי אבות עם פירוש הרמב"ם ז"ל. ושמונה פרקים להרמב"ם והם הקדמה לפירושו. עם הקדמת רבי שמואל אבן תבון ופירוש חסד אברהם להרב ר' אברהם הורוויץ ז"ל = R. Yocef Renassia, *Commentaire du PEREK de Maïmonide, avec les 8 Chapitres (Traité Philosophique) avec la préface de R. Samuel Ben Thibbone, Traduits en Judés*(!)*-Arabe* (Djerba, Tunisie: Imprimerie Haddad, 1954). Cf. the curious mediaeval case mentioned by Steinschneider, *Die hebräischen Uebersetzungen* (see above n. 27), p. 431; idem, *Die arabische Literatur* (see above n. 25), p. 210; Baron, *History of the Jews* (see above n. 25), vol. VIII, p. 308 of Maimonides's מאמר תחית המתים translated from Arabic > Hebrew > Arabic > Hebrew.

> Y. Renassia's Arabic translation:

דווא מרץ̇ אלרוח

א. לפעאייל למלאח הומאן לפעאייל למסתוויין לווסטיין בין אלזוג̇ ג̇יהאת אלי תנינהם דוניין וחדה מנהם אלזיאדה ואלתאנייא אלנקצאן

ב. וצ̇רג̇את אטבוע *les bons caractères* הומאן רתבאת רוחאנייאת (נפס מליחה) ומכאסב וסטיין בין זוג̇ רתבאת דונייאת וחדה מנהם זאידה ולאוכ̇רה נאקצה מן האד אלרתבאת יתלזמו לפעאייל האדוך̇

ג. ולמתל פי האד לאמר אשטארה אלי הייא טביעה מואסטה בין כתרת אלשהווה ובין נקץ̇ חססת למנפעה ...

ד. והאכדאך̇ אלסכ̇אייא *la générosité* מווסטה בין אלתמשחיח ואלתפרית

ה. ולגבורה בין אלי ירמי רוחו פי סכנה ובין רטב לקלב *poltron*

Such episodes are a natural part of Jewish cultural history and should be accepted for what they are, viz. innocent accidents caused by altered circumstances, just as in the Christian Middle Ages the oeuvre of Moses Egyptius was read in Latin, and in the yeshivot of Eastern Europe the *Commentary on the Mishnah* has always been studied in Hebrew translation. These cases should be distinguished sharply, in my view, from examples of the same syndrome in academic circles, for here the cause is probably not unconscious ignorance of the linguistic facts, but rather a deliberate unwillingness to face them. There is surely a great difference between not knowing a certain fact and not caring about it. M. Friedländer's translation of Maimonides's *Guide*, which is still used in the English-speaking world even after the publication of the vastly superior version of L. Strauss & S. Pines, announces on its title page that it has been "translated from the original Arabic text". Inspection of the contents, however, will show that much of the book has been translated from Ibn Tibbon's Hebrew rather than from Maimonides's Arabic. And in our own day, university courses are delivered and studies of Maimonides are published by professional academics for whom the originals are a sealed book and whose knowledge of the material is derived entirely from translations.

There is something not altogether healthy about such a situation.[92] The originals of Maimonides's writings, whether in Arabic or in Hebrew, are the carefully crafted works of a master "der Gedankentiefe und Formenschönheit in meisterhafter Weise miteinander in Einklang zu bringen versteht".[93] As such they deserve our closest attention. The more closely we stick to them the more honour will accrue to their author, and the better will be the state of our subject.

---

92 Cf. the remarks of Daniel J. Lasker, "The interpretation of Maimonides – past and present", in *Alei Sefer* 19 (2001), pp. 209–213 [Hebrew].

93 Israel Friedlaender, "Der Stil des Maimonides", in *Moses ben Maimon. Sein Leben, seine Werke und sein Einfluss* (see above n. 23), vol. I, p. 429.

Averroes' mittlerer Kommentar (*talḫīṣ*) zur *Rhetorik* des Aristoteles: Die hebräische Übersetzung

von

Ahmed Chahlane

Université Mohamed V, Rabat

In Ibn an-Nadīms *Fihrist* werden die Werke des Aristoteles in die Kategorien Logik (*manṭiqīyāt*), Physik (*ṭabīʿīyāt*), Metaphysik (*ilāhīyāt*) und Ethik (*ḫuluqīyāt*) eingeteilt. Ibn an-Nadīm schreibt:

> Seine Bücher zur Logik sind acht: *Qāṭīgūriyās*, das heißt: die Kategorien (*al-maqūlāt*); *Barʾirminiyās*, das bedeutet: der Ausdruck (*al-ʿibāra*); *Anālūṭiqā*, das bedeutet: die Analyse der Analogie (*taḥlīl al-qiyās*); *Abūdiqṭīqā*, das ist die zweite *Anālūṭiqā* und es bedeutet: die Demonstration (*al-burhān*); *Ṭūbīqā*, das heißt: die Dialektik (*al-ǧadal*); *Sūfisṭīqā*, das bedeutet: diejenigen, die andere von ihrer Fehlerhaftigkeit zu überzeugen suchen (*al-muġāliṭīn*); *Rīṭūrīqā*, das heißt: die Redekunst (*al-ḫaṭāba*); *Abūṭīqā* oder *Būṭīqā*, das bedeutet: die Dichtung (*aš-šiʿr*).[1]

Im weiteren Fortgang seiner Biographie des Aristoteles führt Ibn an-Nadīm die arabischen Übersetzungen und Übersetzer der Werke der aristotelischen Logik auf. Zur Übersetzung der *Rhetorik* schreibt er: „Hiervon gibt es eine alte Übersetzung; angeblich soll Isḥāq es ins Arabische übertragen haben; außerdem gibt es die Übersetzung von Ibrāhīm Ibn ʿAbdallāh".[2]

Auf diese Stelle nimmt ʿAbd ar-Raḥmān Badawī in seiner Edition des arabischen Textes unter dem Titel *Die alte arabische Übersetzung der „Rhetorik"*[3] Bezug. Er weist darauf hin, dass Ibn an-Nadīm den Verfasser der „alten Übersetzung" nicht benannt habe und dass er mit Isḥāq „Isḥāq Ibn Ḥunayn" meine. Badawī bezweifelt die Existenz einer Übersetzung dieses Textes durch Isḥāq. Er deutet die Bezeichnung „alt" als Hinweis darauf, dass diese Übersetzung auf die Zeit vor Ḥunayn (gest. 194/869) zurückgehen müsse. Badawī verneint darüber hinaus die Möglichkeit, dass der von ihm edierte Text mit der von Ibn an-

1 Ibn an-Nadīm, *Kitāb al-Fihrist* (Beirut: Dār al-Maʿrifa li-ṭ-Ṭibāʿa wa-n-Našr, 1978), S. 347.

2 Ibid., S. 349.

3 Arisṭūṭālis, *Al-Ḫaṭāba: At-tarǧama al-ʿarabīya al-qadīma* (Kairo: Maktabat a-Nahḍa al-Miṣrīya, 1959).

Nadīm erwähnten Übersetzung des Ibrāhīm Ibn ʿAbdallāh identisch sein könnte. Daraus folgert er, dass es sich bei seiner Edition um jenen Text handelt, den Ibn an-Nadīm mit den Worten „hiervon gibt es eine alte Übersetzung" (*yuṣābu bi-naqlin qadīm*) bezeichnet.[4] Badawī geht auch auf die mögliche Existenz einer weiteren Übersetzung ein, ohne jedoch Einzelheiten zu nennen. In seiner Einleitung zur Edition von Averroes' mittlerem Kommentar (*talḫīṣ*) zur *Rhetorik* kehrt er zu dieser Thematik zurück. Er sagt über die von Averroes benutzte Übersetzung: „Wir wissen nicht genau, ob der von ihm [Averroes] benutzte Text mit der von uns edierten alten Übersetzung identisch ist. Mehr noch: Wir vermuten, ja wir halten es sogar für gewiss, dass er eine andere arabische Übersetzung benutzt haben muss, und zwar entweder die des Isḥāq Ibn Ḥunayn – wenn er es tatsächlich übersetzt hat (woran wir zweifeln) – oder die des christlichen Schriftstellers Ibrāhīm Ibn ʿAbdallāh".[5]

Ibn Rušd interessierte sich für die *Rhetorik* im Rahmen seiner Beschäftigung mit dem aristotelischen Korpus insgesamt. Er hat in der Regel drei verschiedene Arten von Kommentaren zu den aristotelischen Werken verfasst: 1. Paraphrasen beziehungsweise Kurzkommentare (arabisch *muḫtaṣar* beziehungsweise *ǧawāmiʿ*), 2. mittlere Kommentare (*talḫīṣ*), 3. längere Kommentare (*šarḥ* beziehungsweise *tafsīr*). Im Fall der *Rhetorik* hat er sich jedoch auf die zwei zuerst erwähnten Arten von Kommentaren beschränkt. Die Paraphrase der *Rhetorik* ist Teil eines größeren Werkes, das sämtliche Schriften des Aristoteles zur Logik mit der *Eisagoge* des Porphyrios umfasst. Üblicherweise trägt diese Schriftensammlung den Titel *Organon*.

Das arabische Original der *Organon*-Übersetzung ist verloren. Glücklicherweise sind aber zwei Handschriften des Textes in hebräischer Schrift erhalten, eine davon in Paris, die andere in München. Auf diese beiden Handschriften stützte sich Butterworth bei seiner Edition der Kurzkommentare (*muḫtaṣarāt*) zur *Topik, Rhetorik* und *Poetik*.[6]

Der Kurzkommentar des Averroes zum aristotelischen *Organon* unter dem arabischen Titel *Aḍ-Ḍarūrīy fī l-manṭiq* wurde zweimal ins Hebräische übersetzt. Als erster übertrug ihn Yaʿqūb Ibn Maḫīr, bekannt als „Profatus Judeus", im Jahr 1289, dann folgte eine Übersetzung durch Samuel Ibn Yehuda Ibn Mešallem al-Marsīlī (aus Marseille) 1329. Ibn Maḫīrs Übersetzung wurde 1559 in Riva di Trento gedruckt.[7]

---

4 Siehe die Einleitung zu *al-Ḫaṭāba* (wie Anm. 3), S. (ز).

5 Abū l-Walīd Muḥammad Ibn Rušd, *Talḫīṣ al-ḫaṭāba* (Kuwait: Wikālat al-Maṭbūʿāt, Beirut: Dār al-Qalam, 1979]), S. (ط). Auf Badawīs Edition des mittleren Kommentars Averroes' zur *Rhetorik* folgte eine weitere durch Muḥammad Salīm Sālim: Abū l-Walīd Muḥammad Ibn Rušd, *Talḫīṣ al-ḫaṭāba* (Kairo: al-Maǧlis al-Aʿlā li-š-Šuʾūn al-Islāmīya, 1967).

6 Charles E. Butterworth, *Averroës' Three short commentaries on Aristotle's „Topics" „Rhetoric", and „Poetics"* (Albany, N.Y.: State University of New York Press, 1977).

7 כל מלאכת הגיון לארסטו מקצורי אבן רשד ... ריווא דרינטו, שנת ש"ׁ כלפ"ק.

Der mittlere Kommentar des Averroes zur *Rhetorik* (*Talḫīṣ al-ḫaṭāba*) wurde von Todros Todrosi 1337 in Trinquetaille ins Hebräische übersetzt. Diese Übersetzung diente Abrahamo de Balmes als Vorlage für dessen Übersetzung des Textes ins Lateinische.[8] Die hebräische Übersetzung wurde von J. Goldenthal ediert.[9] Zu Beginn seiner Einleitung erinnert der Herausgeber an die Bedeutung der Juden Andalusiens für die Wissenschaften allgemein und insbesondere auf dem Gebiet der Übersetzungen. Im weiteren Verlauf spricht er über die jüdische Philosophie, Maimonides und Aristoteles, sowie die islamische Mystik.[10] Goldenthal widmet der Biographie des Averroes einen eigenen Abschnitt: Averroes habe das Amt des Kadi bekleidet, habe während seiner Verbannung im jüdischen Viertel gewohnt (?!), sei nach Fez ausgewandert (ist Marrakesch gemeint?), dort gefangengesetzt und wieder freigesprochen worden, bevor er in Marrakesch erneut ins Richter-Amt eingesetzt worden sei, wo er 603 d. H. starb. Offensichtlich gibt Goldenthal hier zahlreiche Nachrichten wieder, die der Phantasie des Leo Africanus entstammen.

Goldenthal geht des Weiteren auf die Bücher und Kommentare des Averroes sowie auf seine Bedeutung in der Philosophie ein, behandelt die hebräischen Übersetzungen der Schriften des Averroes und stellt – nach der Lektüre des griechischen Textes der *Rhetorik* sowie einiger lateinischer Kommentare – fest, dass Averroes Aristoteles besser verstanden habe als alle seine Nachfolger. In seiner Einleitung listet Goldenthal außerdem Fehler der Übersetzung auf und korrigiert sie. Er macht Bemerkungen zur Sprache der hebräischen Übersetzer und erwähnt, dass die Sprache der jüdischen Philosophie ein Kind dieser Übersetzungsbewegung und darum das mittelalterliche Hebräisch ein Abbild der arabischen Sprache sei. Viele Übersetzer hätten deshalb den Fehler begangen, für identische Ausdrücke in den beiden Sprachen dieselbe Bedeutung zu unterstellen. Darüber hinaus habe der relativ eingeschränkte Wortschatz des Hebräischen zu zahlreichen Entlehnungen aus dem Arabischen geführt. Im Hinblick auf die Übersetzung des *Rhetorik*-Kommentars sei der zuvor erwähnte arabische Einfluss das eigentlich bestimmende Element der Übersetzung gewesen, bis hin zu den typischen Verständnis- und Formulierungsfehlern. Bei dieser Gelegenheit betont er die Notwendigkeit einer kritischen Überprüfung dieser Texte.

Auch der Übersetzer Todros Todrosi hatte seiner Übersetzung eine Einleitung vorausgeschickt, in der er vier verschiedene Beweggründe für seine Arbeit nennt:

---

8 Diese Übersetzung wurde 1553 und 1574 mit den anderen Schriften des Averroes in Venedig publiziert.

9 Todros Todrosi Arelatensi, *Averrois Commentarius in Aristotelis de Arte Rhetorica libros tres*, ed. Jacob Goldenthal [Hebräisch] (Leipzig: H. Franke, 1842).

10 Siehe meinen Aufsatz: „kitāb *Mīzān al-ʿamal* li-Abī Ḥāmid al-Ġazālī, at-tarǧama al-ʿibrīya: *Al-Mīzān* bayn al-mafāhīm al-islāmīya wa-t-taqālīd al-yahūdīya", in *Ghazālī. La raison et Le miracle. Table ronde UNESCO, 9.–10. déc. 1985* (Paris: Maisonneuve et Larose, 1987), S. 93–117.

1. die Liebe zur Wahrheit. Denn auch wenn die poetischen und rhetorischen Prämissen wahr zu sein schienen, so sei die Wahrheit doch eine andere; sie seien der Wahrheit nur ähnlich. Die Kenntnis der Logik verhindere Fehler.
2. den Wunsch, den der Philosophie zugeneigten Juden zum Glück der Erkenntnis der Wahrheit zu verhelfen, welches das höchste Glück auf der Welt sei. Seine Glaubensgenossen hätten bei der Lektüre von Büchern der Ethik, Physik und Metaphysik die Bedeutung der Dialektik, Analogie und Demonstration erkannt und verlangten nun nach der Übertragung der Wissenschaft der Logik, wegen deren rhetorischer Bedeutung, die den Menschen in den Stand setze, andere zu überzeugen. Dies sei ja der eigentliche Zweck der Rhetorik, so wie der Zweck der Demonstration die Erkenntnis sei, der Zweck der Dialektik das Denken, der Zweck der Sophistik das Erkennen von Fehlern und der Zweck der Poesie die Imitation. Aus all diesen Gründen verlangten die Juden nach der Übersetzung der Logik.
3. Aufgrund ihrer Unkenntnis des Arabischen verlangten die Vorsteher der Juden nach dem averroistischen Text in einer verständlichen hebräischen Sprache. Sie baten Todros, diese Aufgabe zu übernehmen. Er habe es jedoch zunächst abgelehnt, sowohl wegen der Schwierigkeit der Themen als auch, weil er sich wegen mangelhafter Kenntnis des Arabischen nicht im Stande gesehen habe, eine solch schwierige Aufgabe zu bewältigen. Als er aber auf das Buch *Kitāb al-ʿayn*[11] gestoßen sei, das Rabbi Schlomo Ibn Tibbon aus dem Osten mitgebracht habe, habe er davon viel profitiert. Ihm seien bei der Übersetzung keine nennenswerten Schwierigkeiten begegnet, bis auf den dritten Traktat (*maqāla*), in dem Averroes spezielle Themen der arabischen Sprache sowie die unterschiedlichen Gattungen der Poesie und Prosa bei den Arabern und besonders bei den Andalusiern behandele. Er habe sich deshalb erlaubt, zahlreiche Stellen in Prosa und Poesie auszulassen. Er sei dabei dem Beispiel des Averroes gefolgt, der an vielen Stellen der *Rhetorik* und der *Poetik* dasselbe getan habe, besonders an denjenigen Stellen, die Aristoteles der Behandlung von Themen der griechischen Sprache und Poesie oder Fragen der Redekunst widmet. Averroes begründe dies damit, dass es sich um ein anderes System der Sprache und Redekunst handele, das dem arabischen Stil und Geschmack fremd sei.
4. Die arabischen Wissenschaften, insbesondere die Bücher der Logik wie die *Rhetorik* und *Poetik*, hätten den jüdischen Vorstehern die Augen geöffnet. Todros sei deshalb dem Wunsch seiner Glaubensgenossen nachgekommen, indem er beide Texte übersetzt und seinen Glaubensgenossen zugänglich gemacht habe.

---

11 Badawī vermutet in der Einleitung zu *Talhīṣ al-ḫaṭāba* (wie Anm. 3), S. يب, dass das *Kitāb al-ʿayn* eine Schrift des Ibn Tibbon sei. Todros meint aber in Wirklichkeit das *Kitāb al-ʿayn* des al-Ḫalīl Ibn Aḥmad.

Über den Text der Handschrift

Vom mittleren Kommentar des Averroes zur *Rhetorik* (*Talḫīṣ al-ḫaṭāba*) sind nur zwei Handschriften erhalten, eine davon befindet sich in Leiden, die andere in Florenz. ʿA. Badawī legte beide seiner Edition zugrunde. Von der hebräischen Übersetzung existieren einige Handschriften in verschiedenen Bibliotheken wie zum Beispiel Leipzig 41A sowie Paris 932A und 933A.[12]

Ich werde mich bei der folgenden Darstellung auf den Umgang des Übersetzers mit Zitaten und Eigennamen beschränken.

A. Zitate

Die *Rhetorik* des Aristoteles enthält zahlreiche Zitate aus Poesie und Prosa sowie Sprichwörter und Ausdrücke aus dem gewöhnlichen Sprachgebrauch. Averroes tauscht die meisten griechischen Zitate gegen arabische Beispiele aus Poesie und Prosa, belässt in seinem Text jedoch einige griechische Sprichwörter. Dennoch fällt auf, dass er alles auslässt, was ihm Geschmack und Kultur der Araber nicht zu entsprechen scheint.

I. Koran

Folgende Stellen des Kommentars von Averroes, die Belege aus dem Koran enthalten, werden vom hebräischen Übersetzer übergangen:

قال تعالى حاكيا عن هود: وأنا لكم ناصح أمين (Koran 7:68) S. 267/189[13] ؛ أما الضد فمثل قوله تعالى: كانا يأكلان الطعام (Koran 5:75) S. 267/189 ؛ مثال قوله تعالى: وتظنون بالله الظنون (Koran 33:10) S. 287/204 ؛ قوله تعالى: الحاقة ما الحاقة وما أدراك ما الحاقة (Koran 69:1–3) S. 288/204 ؛ قوله تعالى: وبشروه بغلام عليم فأقبلت امرأته في صرة فصكت وجهها وقالت عجوز عقيم (Koran 51:28–29) S. 288/204.

12 Moritz Steinschneider, *Die hebraeischen Übersetzungen des Mittelalters, und die Juden als Dolmetscher* (Berlin: Bibliographisches Bureau, 1893; Nachdruck Graz: Akademische Druck- und Verlagsanstalt, 1956), S. 62–65.

13 Die Zahl links vor dem Schrägstrich ist die Seitenzahl im Kommentar des Averroes nach Badawīs Edition, die Zahl rechts nach dem Schrägstrich ist die Seitenzahl in der hebräischen Übersetzung (in der Edition von Goldenthal)

Eine weitere Stelle wird vom Übersetzer folgendermaßen gekürzt:

אמרו ית' לא תהו בראה לשבת יצרה וזה שבראה ויצרה הם כלם על שמוש אחד. ורוב הדבור (S. 204) .	فمثال المفصل بالصيغ المتفقة قوله تعالى: فاصبر صبرا جميلا إنهم يرونه بعيدا ونراه قريبا (المعارج ٥- ٧) وذلك أن «جميلا» و«بعيدا» و«قريبا» هي كلها صيغة واحدة وشكل واحد. وهذا كثير في الكتاب العزيز. وأكثر الكلام (S. 288).

II. Prophetische Sprüche (ḥadīṯ)

Der Übersetzer modifiziert folgende Stelle mit einem Spruch des Propheten Muhammads dahingehend, dass dessen Urheber anonym wird:

כי בעל תורה ע"ה כבר אמר שהכביד האבות מוסיף בחיים (S. 92) .	فإن صاحب الشرع عليه السلام قال: صلة الرحم تزيد العمر (S. 122).

Eine andere Stelle mit einem weiteren Spruch des Propheten wird hingegen völlig ausgelassen:

كما روي عن النبي (ص) أنه قال في آخر خطبة: بعثت أنا والساعة كهاتين [...] (S. 250/179).

III. Arabische Poesie

Averroes führt in seinem Kommentar eine Reihe von Beispielen aus der arabischen Dichtung auf, die weggelassene griechische Beispiele ersetzen und die enthaltenen Thesen belegen sollen. Der hebräische Übersetzer modifiziert einige solcher Stellen stark, er lässt jedoch die meisten davon völlig unbeachtet.[14]

---

14 Die Belege aus der arabischen Dichtung, die samt Einleitungsworten in der hebräischen Übersetzung völlig fehlen, sind:

- نفس عصام سودت عصاما (S. 78/60).
- كما قال الشاعر:
  عليكم بداري فاهدموها فإنها تراث كريم لا يخاف العواقبا (S. 101/78).
- ولذلك قيل:
  إن الريح إذا ما استعصفت قصفت عيدان نجد ولم يعبأن بالرتم (S. 120 des arabischen Kommentars).
- مثل قول ابن المعتز:
  يا دار أين ظباؤك اللعس؟ قد كان في إنسها أنس
  فإن العرب جرت عادتهم أن يشبهوا النساء بالظباء فلربما أتوا به على جهة الإبدال، مثل ما تقدم من قول ابن المعتز، وربما أتوا بذلك مع حرف التشبيه (S. 255/182).
- مثل قول امرئ القيس يصف حمار الوحش:

So übersetzt er aus den zwei folgenden Versen nur den ersten sinngemäß ohne Beibehaltung der poetischen Form, den zweiten lässt er aus:

كما قال الشاعر:
لسنـا وإن كرمت أوائلنا   يوما على الأحساب نتكل
نبني كما كانت أوائلـنـا   تبني، ونفعل مثلما فعـلوا[15]

= כמו שיאמר המשל:
אין לנו ואם כובדו ראשוני אבותינו הפראשים [הראשונים]
להשען על היחסים (S. 78/60).

يهيل ويزري تربه ويثيره   إثارة نباث الهواجر مخمس
فإن نباث الهواجر إنما تعرفه العرب ومن هو مثلهم ممن يسكن الصحاري (S. 255/182).

- مثل قوله [الحطيئة] في داليته المشهورة:
  وهند أتى من دونها النأي والبـعد (S. 263/187).
- مثل ما عرض في قول امرئ القيس:
  وفيها صـــمـاء ابنة الجبـــل (S. 265/188).
- أو كما قال:
  من كف جارية كأن بنانها من فضة قد طـوقت عنابـــها (S. 268/190).
- مثل قول النابغة:
  سقط النصيف ولم ترد إسقاطه   فتناولته واتقـــتنا باليد
  ومثل قول أبي تمام:
  أعيدي النوح معولة أعيـــدي   وزيدي من عويلك ثم زيدي
  وقومي حاسرا في حاســرات   خوامش للنحور وللـــخدود
  ومثل [...] قول القائل:
  إذا ما هبطن الأرض قد مات عودها بكين بها حتى يعيش هشيم (S. 293/207).
- ومثل قول أبي الطيب:
  مغاني الشعب طيبا مغاني   بمنزلة الربيع من الزمـــان (S. 294/207).
- وهذا مثال قول المعري:
  توهم كل سابغة غديـــرا   فرنق يشرب الحلق الدخـــالا
  ومثل قول أبي الطيب
  إذا ما ضربت به هامـــة   براها وغناك في الكـــاهل (S. 295f./208).
- ومن هذا الموضع عيب على أبي العباس التطيلي الأندلسي قوله:
  أما والهوى وهو إحدى الملل لقد مـــال قدك حـــتى اعـــتدل (S. 299/210).
- مثل قولهم:
  ذكرتنـــي الطعن وكنت ناسيا (S. 301/211).
- مثل استقباح عبد الملك بن مروان لاستفتاح جرير:
  أتصـــحو أم فؤادك غير صاح
  ومثل ما استقبح استفتاح أبي الطيب:
  أوه بديل من قولتي واها
  وقوله:
  كفى بك داء أن ترى الموت شافيا (S. 312/218).
- قول أبي تمام:
  فلو صورت نفسك لم تزدها   على ما فيك من كرم الطباع
  [...] وقريب من هذا قول أبي نواس:
  وليس لله بمستنـــكر   أن يجمع العالم في واحد (S. 321/224).

15 Die beiden Verse werden Maʿn Ibn Abī Aus al-Maznī zugeschrieben. Vgl. Abū ʿUbaydallāh al-Marzabānī, *Muʿǧam aš-šuʿarāʾ* (Kairo: ʿĪsā al-Bābī al-Ḥalabī, 1960), S. 400.

Vom Original abweichend stellt sich die Übersetzung des folgenden Halbverses dar:

ولذلك قيل:
يواسيك أو يسليك أو يتفجع = יכלכלך או ישאלך או ידאג לצרתך (S. 140/104).

Des Weiteren hat der hebräische Übersetzer eine längere Stelle, in der Averroes zur Erklärung komplexer Metaphern (*al-murakkaba*) einen Vers des vorislamischen Dichters Imruʾ al-Qays und den Kommentar al-Fārābīs dazu zitiert, drastisch gekürzt, indem er daraus nur deren Anfang und wenige Sätze übernommen hat.[16]

IV. Arabische Sprichwörter

Ähnlich verhält es sich mit arabischen Sprichwörtern, die Averroes in seinem Kommentar als Belege vorführt und die vom Übersetzer ungenau übertragen oder sogar völlig übergangen werden, wie folgende Vergleiche zeigen:

מעוט ההוצאה מזל מעשיר (S. 29)	ولذلك قيل: قلة العيال أحد اليسارين (S. 35).
	مثل ما يقال: إن الخيار يولد في الخيار (S. 79). إن الحية تلد الحية (S. 79).
משרש נחש יצא צפע (S. 61)	ولذلك يقال في المثل: إن الشر اليسير يستثير الكثير، وإن الشر قد تبدوه صغاره (S. 104).
שהרע המועט יעזור הרב (S. 80)	ولذا قيل: البادي أظلم (S. 105/81).

Weitere arabische Sprichwörter werden überhaupt nicht übersetzt.[17]

16 Nur die in Klammern stehenden Sätze erscheinen in der Übersetzung:
وأنشد أبو نصر في مثال المركبة البعيدة التركيب الخفية الاتصال، بيتا لامرئ القيس، والبيت:
بدلت من وال وكندة عد وان وفيها صماء ابنة الجبل
قال، فإن هذا التغيير فيه تركيب كثير. وذلك أنه جعل «ابنة الجبل» بدلا من قوله «الحصاة»، وجعل قوله «صماء» بدلا من «عدم صوت الحصاة»، فإن عدم الصوت وعدم السمع يتقاربان فإنه قسيمه، إذ كان عدم السمع إما أن يكون عن عدم الصوت، وإما لفساد في الحاسة. وجعل عدم صوت الحصاة بدلا من ابتلال الأرض، فإن الأرض إذا ابتلت وطرحت فيها الحصاة لم تصوت (وجعل ابتلال الأرض بدلا من انصباب الدماء على الأرض) فإن ابتلال الأرض لاحق من لواحق انصباب الدماء عليها (وجعل انصباب الدماء عليها بدلا من القتال الشديد، لأن انصباب الدماء يكون عن القتال الشديد. وجعل القتال الشديد بدلا من الأمر العظيم) فكأنه أراد «وفيها أمر عظيم» فأبدل مكان ذلك «وفيها صماء ابنة الجبل» واستعمل في ذلك هذا الإبدال الكثير (وهذا- كما قلنا- إنما يليق بالشعر) (S. 256/182f.).

17 Diese sind:

- ولو من الميت أكفانه (S. 121).
- إنما الخزي مما تراه العين (S. 124).
- بلغ الماء الزبى (S. 213/153).

V. Nichtarabische Sprichwörter, die Averroes durch arabische Pendants ersetzt

Aristoteles zitiert in der *Rhetorik* zahlreiche Verse altgriechischer Dichter sowie geläufige Sprichwörter. Averroes ersetzt sie durch arabische Beispiele, die in den Kontext passen. Aristoteles führt darüber hinaus weitere Beispiele an, die er konstruiert oder seinen eigenen Beobachtungen entnommen hat. Einige von diesen lässt Averroes stehen, andere tauscht er gegen eigene Sätze aus. Daher wimmelt es im Buch der Rhetorik sowohl im aristotelischen Text als auch im averroistischen Kommentar von Aussprüchen, Sprichwörtern und Redewendungen, die den verschiedensten Situationen und Umständen menschlichen Lebens entspringen. Ich kann im Rahmen dieser Arbeit nicht umfassend demonstrieren, wie der hebräische Übersetzer mit all diesen Sätzen umgeht. Deshalb beschränke ich mich im Folgenden auf einige Beispiele, die in drei Gruppen eingeteilt seien: 1. Griechische Aussprüche, 2. arabische oder islamische Aussprüche und 3. allgemeine Aussprüche und Beispiele.

1. Griechische Aussprüche

Der Übersetzer versucht, diese Aussprüche sinngemäß und allgemein zu übersetzen, er überspringt jedoch stillschweigend viele Abschnitte, die er offensichtlich nicht verstanden hat. Darüber hinaus unterlaufen ihm viele Fehler bei der Lesung des arabischen Textes. Ich beschränke mich auf folgendes Beispiel. Averroes bezieht sich auf *Rhetorik* 1393b, 10–18,[18] wo Maultiere einmal als Pferdetöchter (*banāt al-ḫayl*) und einmal als Eselstöchter (*banāt al-ḥamīr*) angesprochen werden.

مثل ما حكى أرسطو عن بعض القدماء أنه قال في حكاية حكاها عن البغال أنها كانت مسرورة بانضمامها إلى بنات الخيل على أنها قد كانت أيضا بنات الحمير. قال فإن قوله في البغال: «بنات الخيل» تشريف لها. وقوله: «بنات الحمير» تخسيس لها (S. 268).

Der hebräische Übersetzer liest fälschlich *nabāt* (Pflanze) für *banāt* (Töchter) und überträgt die Stelle wie folgt:

שהיה שמח באכלו צמח הסוס על שהיא גם כן כבר היה צמח החמור. אמר הנה אמרו בפרד «צמח הסוס» הגדלה לו, ואמרו בצמח החמור הבחתה לו (S. 190).

- ولى حارها من تولى قارها (S. 218/157).
- القتل أنفى للقتل (S. 288/205).
- طويل النجاد (S. 290/205).
- يقال زهيري الأفعال وحاتمي الكرم (S. 295/208).
- وقد ساوى الماء الزبى وبلغ الحزام الطبيين (S. 301/211 und 309/216).

18 Aristoteles, *Ars Rhetorica*, ed. William David Ross (Oxford: Clarendon Press, 1959).

2. Arabische oder islamische Aussprüche

Der Übersetzer übergeht einen Großteil der Stellen, die solche Aussprüche beinhalten.[19] An den Stellen, die er ins Hebräische übersetzt, unternimmt er gravierende Änderungen, wie folgende Beispiele zeigen:

مثل أن يقول القائل في شيء دفعه لغيره: إنما دفعته لك عارية، ويقول الآخر: إنما دفعته لك هبة.

= וכמו שיאמר אומר בדבר נתנו אדם לזולתו: אמנם נתת אותו אליו להכלים ולהבאישו، כי גחלים אתה הותה על ראשו! ויאמר אחר שמתנתו היא מתנת אוהב[20] (S. 233/167).

Im folgenden Beispiel, das die arabischen Verkleinerungsformen für die Worte Gold (*ḏahab*/*ḏuhayb*), Gewand (*ṯawb*/*ṯuwayb*) und Mensch (*insān*/*unaysān*) demonstrieren soll, entfernt sich der hebräische Übersetzer deutlich von seiner Vorlage. Das erste und das letzte Beispiel ersetzt er durch hebräische Personennamen. Für das mittlere Beispiel erfindet er nach dem morphologischen Muster des Arabischen das hebräische Wort בגיד (*buggayd*):

وينبغي أن تستعمل من التعظيم في الخطابة ومن التصغير بقصد، مثل من يقول في ذهب «ذهيب» وفي ثوب «ثويب» وفي إنســــــان «أنيسان».

=כמו שאמר מאברהם «אברהים» [אבריהם], ומאמנון: «אמינן» ומבגד «בגיד» (S.269/190).

Eine Geschichte über den abbasidischen Kalifen al-Manṣūr in der Kaaba wird dahingehend geändert, dass sie von einem „berühmten König im Tempel“ handelt:

---

19 Einige Beispiele seien im Folgenden genannt:

- وكذلك يشبه أن يكون الأمر عندنا في قطع اليد في النصاب وبخاصة في المطعومات (S. 113/86).
- ولذلك زيد في عقاب الفرية عندنا التفسيق ورد الشهادة (S. 117/88).
- ولذلك ليس في العذاب شيء يوثق به [ولمكان هذا درأ الشرع عندنا الحدود التي تتعلق بالإقرارات التي تحت الإكراه] (S. 127/95. In Klammern [ ] stehendes fehlt in der Übersetzung).
- وهذا الضرب من النغم ضروري في أوزان أشعار من سلف من الأمم ما عدا العرب، فإن من سلف من الأمم كانوا يزنون أبياتهم بالنغم والوقفات، والعرب إنما تزنها بالوقفات فقط (S. 251/180).
- مثال أن يستعمل الحجازي لغة حمير (S. 257/183).
- وذلك كما أن التأسي في الخير يوجب مدح بعض بعضا - كذلك التأسي في الشر يزيل ذم بعض بعضا [ومن هذا الموضوع أمر أردشير بن بابك الملك حيث قال في كتابه: إن الطاغين على الملوك بالدين ينبغي أن يؤتوا من الدنيا ويوسع عليهم حتى يكون هو الذي يقتلهم ويريح الملوك منهم] (S. 228/164).
- لأنه محتاج إلى الاستعانة بجميع الأشياء المقنعة في موضوع المنازعة لتحصل الغلبة [وأمثال هذه الخطب هي الخطب التي كانت بين علي ومعاوية وأمثال ذلك في الأشعار التي كانت بن جرير والفرزدق] (S. 252).

20 Der hebräische Übersetzer hat hier offensichtlich das Adjektiv *al-ʿāriya* (etwas, das, ohne eine Gegenleistung zu erwarten, verschenkt wird) nicht verstanden. Er ersetzt es durch das bedeutungsferne hebräische להכלים ולהבאישו (um ihn zu demütigen). Dabei bezieht er sich auf Proverbien 25:22.

مثال ذلك [تفاضل الألفاظ] ما يحكى أن المنصور لما دخل الكعبة رأى رجلا قد سبقه بالدخول، وكان قد أمر أن لا يدخل إليها أحد قبله من العامة، فقال له «أما سمعت النداء؟» فقال «بلى». فقال «أو ما تعرفني؟» فقال «بلى». فقال له «فكيف تجاسرت؟» فقال له الرجل «وكيف لا أتجاسر عليك؟ وهل أنت في أول أمرك إلا نطفة مذرة (فاسدة)، وفي آخر أمرك إلا جيفة قذرة، وأنت فيما بين ذلك تحمل عذرة؟» فخلى عنه، إذ صغرت بهذا القول نفسه عنده، أعني نفس المنصور (S. 261).

= מה שסופר ממלך מפורסם שהוא למה שהכניס עקבו במפתן ההיכל (...) (S. 185).

3. Allgemeine Aussprüche und Belege

Der hebräische Übersetzer übersetzt die meisten Belege dieser Art, macht jedoch dabei Fehler, die darauf hindeuten, dass er den arabischen Text falsch gelesen oder dessen Bedeutung nicht verstanden hat. Folgende Beispiele mögen dies zeigen:

a) مثال ذلك أن العدل في سياسة التغلب أنه لا شيء على الرئيس إذا لطم المرؤوس، وفي سياسة الحرية: العدل في ذلك أن يلطم الرئيس مثل اللطمة التي لطمها (S. 68).

In der Übersetzung wird الرئيس zu שוטר, المرؤوس zu תחת שוטר (S. 157).

b) لو وضع واضع أن الرياسة خير، وأنه أن يكون الإنسان مرؤوسا خير، فإنه إن أبطلها بالكلية قال: كون الإنسان مرؤوسا يحتاج إلى غيره. والحاجة شر، فالرياسة شر. وإن أبطلها بالخير قال: ليس كل رئاسة نافعة، وذلك أن التغلب رياسة، فليست خيرا (S. 243).

= הנה כמו אלו הנח מניח שהראשות טוב ושהיות האדם בעל ראשות טוב כי הוא אם בטול בכללות אמר היות האדם בעל ראשות יצטרך אל זולתו וההצטרכותו רע הנה הראשות רע ואם בטלו חלק אמר אין כל ראשות (S. 174).

c) مثل قول القائل في الخطب المشاورية: هذا قولي فاسمعوا والحكم إليكم فاحكموا (S. 332).

= כה מאמרי וכך מכווני פקחו עיניכם וראו ואזניכם הטו והמשפט אליכם משפט אמת שפטו (S. 231).

B. Eigennamen

Der hebräische Übersetzer überträgt die meisten griechischen Eigennamen, die im Kommentar des Averroes enthalten sind. Die meisten arabischen und islamischen Namen übergeht er hingegen, samt den Zitaten, in denen sie vorkommen. Es handelt sich beim Großteil davon um Dichtungsverse, Sprichwörter oder geläufige Redewendungen, die er nicht verstanden oder in ihnen gar keinen Nutzen für seine Übersetzung gesehen haben dürfte. Es seien im Folgenden einige Beispiele genannt:

I. Griechische Eigennamen werden in ihrer arabisierten Form übernommen: *Arisṭū* (Aristoteles) wird an zahlreichen Stellen erwähnt; *Homirus* (S. 54/42, 65/51, 93/71, 97/75, 147/109, 321/224); *Afrūṭāġus* (S. 167/232); *Zenon* (S. 208/150); *Suqrāṭ* (S. 223/320, 227/325, 227/326); *Hiraql* (S. 189/138).

II. Arabische und islamische Eigennamen werden, wie bereits erwähnt, in den meisten Fällen nicht übertragen. So lässt der Übersetzer beispielsweise folgende Namen aus: *Imru' al-Qays* (S. 255/182); *Abū Tammām* (S. 293/207); *Ǧarīr* (S. 252/180, 312/212); *al-Farazdaq* (S. 252/180); *al-Mutanabbī* (S. 294/207, 296/213); *Ibn al-Muʿtazz* (S. 254–255/182); *al-Maʿarrī* (S. 295/208); *an-Nābiġa aḏ-Ḏubyānī* (S. 293/207); *Abū Nuwās* (S. 321/224); *ʿAlī Ibn Abī Ṭālib* (S. 252/180); *ʿAbd al-Malik Ibn Marwān* (S. 312/212); *Muʿāwiya Ibn Abī Sufyān* (S. 252/180); anstelle von *ʿUmar Ibn al-Ḫaṭṭāb* kommt *Suqrāṭ* vor (S. 317/221). Der in grammatikalischen Beispielsätzen verwendete Name *Zayd* wird übernommen. Nur einmal wird er durch ראובן ersetzt (S. 273/193). Der Name ʿAmr wird ebenfalls durch שמעון ersetzt (S. 273/179). Der Name *Hūd*, nach dem im Koran eine Sure benannt ist, wird ausgelassen (S. 17/15).

Schlussbemerkungen

Die dargestellten formellen Bemerkungen zur hebräischen Übersetzung von Averroes' mittlerem Kommentar (*talḫīṣ*) zu Aristoteles' Buch der *Rhetorik* können eine sorgfältige Untersuchung der in diesem Werk angewandten Übersetzungsmethode nicht ersetzen. Eine solche Untersuchung müsste sich in erster Linie kritisch mit Fragen des literarischen Stils und der rhetorischen Begrifflichkeit beschäftigen. Das Problem, dass sich beide Sprachen im Hinblick auf den Reichtum ihres Wortschatzes und ihre Semantik voneinander unterscheiden, sollte auch dabei besondere Aufmerksamkeit erhalten. Dieses Problem nämlich bereitete den jüdischen Übersetzern im Mittelalter bei der Übertragung islamischer wissenschaftlicher Werke ins Hebräische oder später ins Lateinische große Schwierigkeiten. Ich konnte während meiner Erforschung der hebräischen Übersetzungen von Schriften des Averroes beobachten, dass die jüdischen Übersetzer damals kein Interesse an der Übersetzung des Korans ins Hebräische hatten. Die erste hebräische Koranübersetzung aus dem Arabischen stammt erst aus dem 17. Jahrhundert. Sie ist in einer geistigen Atmosphäre entstanden, in der wissenschaftlich-dogmatische Diskussionen zwischen Anhängern verschiedener Religionen nicht mehr in einem hebräischen, vom Judentum geprägten Rahmen, sondern in einer vom lateinischen Denken geprägten Umgebung stattfanden.

Die Übersetzung von koranischen Zitaten in Schriften von Averroes wie *Tahāfut at-tahāfut*, *Faṣl al-maqāl*, *al-Kašf ʿan manāhiǧ al-adilla* und *Kitāb aš-šiʿr* war keineswegs ein systematisches Unternehmen, das in den verschiedenen Schriften eine einheitliche Übersetzungsmethode aufweisen würde. Keiner der Übersetzer bemühte sich darum, koranische Bedeutungen genau zu übersetzen – nicht einmal diejenigen Sinngehalte, die mit dem Judentum zusammenhängen. Die Übersetzer bemühten sich vielmehr ausschließlich darum, Ausdrücke zu finden, die den zu übersetzenden Worten ähnlich waren. Komplizierte Ausdrücke blieben unübersetzt; meist wurden Leerstellen frei gelassen – vielleicht weil die Übersetzer hofften, später noch einmal auf sie zurückkommen zu können.

Die bereits genannten Bücher enthalten 198 koranische Zitate (die Zahl steigt auf 215, wenn die Wiederholungen berücksichtigt werden). *Tahāfut at-tahāfut* enthält 34 Belege aus dem Koran, von denen der anonyme Übersetzer 33 Belege ins Hebräische übersetzte und nur einen ausließ. Kalonymus ben Todros, der das Werk erneut ins Hebräische übersetzte, tauschte 15 koranische Zitate gegen Texte aus der Torah und der jüdischen Überlieferung und ließ 14 Zitate aus dem Koran ersatzlos aus.

Die Abhandlung *Faṣl al-maqāl* enthält 16 koranische Zitate. Sie wurden alle ins Hebräische übertragen. Die Übersetzung ist von zahlreichen Missverständnissen und falschen Lesarten gekennzeichnet. *Al-Kašf ʿan manāhiǧ al-adilla* hat 120 Zitate aus dem Koran (132 zusammen mit den Wiederholungen), 119 davon wurden übersetzt, ein Zitat geändert und neun ausgelassen. Der Kommentar zur *Poetik* umfasst 13 koranische Zitate, nur eins davon wurde übersetzt, während der Rest übergangen wurde. Im Kommentar zur *Rhetorik* stehen sechs Belege aus dem Koran, der Übersetzer versucht, einen davon zu übersetzen, und lässt fünf völlig aus.

Die beiden mittleren Kommentare (*talḫīṣ*) zur *Poetik* und zur *Rhetorik* enthalten ebenfalls eine Reihe von Zitaten aus der arabischen Dichtung. Der Kommentar zur *Poetik* umfasst 86 Verse und sieben Halbverse. Der hebräische Übersetzer übersetzte nur zwei dieser Verse, ersetzte zwei weitere durch ähnliche Belege aus der jüdischen Tradition und ließ den Rest völlig unbeachtet. Im mittleren Kommentar zur *Rhetorik* kommen 17 Verse und acht Halbverse vor, die vom Übersetzer, wie bereits dargestellt, behandelt wurden. Die umfangreichen Auslassungen, die weitgehend zur Verdunkelung des hebräischen Textes und Verständnisschwierigkeiten bei seinem Leser führten, erklären sich aus den sprachlichen und inhaltlichen Schwierigkeiten, die diese dichterischen Zitate bergen, sowie aus der Inkompetenz des hebräischen Übersetzers in der arabischen Sprache und Kultur.

Die hebräische Übersetzung von Averroes' Kommentar zur aristotelischen *Rhetorik* stellt ein historisches Dokument aus einer wichtigen Epoche der Geistesgeschichte dar, in der die arabische Kultur großen Einfluss auf das hebräische Denken hatte. Dieses wiederum wurde zu einer Brücke, über die die wichtigsten Texte des arabisch-islamischen Denkens an das lateinische Denken vermittelt wurden. Mein Interesse galt in der vorliegenden Studie daher zunächst den Absichten des Übersetzers bei seiner Übersetzung.

Mein historisches Interesse gilt aber auch der Zeit, in der Goldenthal die hebräische Übersetzung herausgegeben hat. Denn diese Arbeit, die eine hebräische Übersetzung eines arabischen Textes einem breiteren Leserkreis zugänglich machte, hat eine gewisse Bedeutung für die jüngere Geschichte bis in unsere heutige Zeit.

Was mich jedoch in erster Linie interessiert, ist die Übersetzungsmethode und die Art und Weise, in der die jüdischen Übersetzer die Texte des Averroes und andere Texte verstanden – wobei bemerkt werden soll, dass einige von ihnen zum Zweck des Broterwerbs, andere aber aus wissenschaftlichem Interesse für sich selbst und ihre Gleichgesinnten übersetzten und dass dieser Unterschied nicht ohne Einfluss auf die Übersetzungen blieb. Der im Rahmen dieser Studie dargestellte Übersetzungsprozess verursachte vielfältige Begriffsverwirrung. Dies hatte insofern Auswirkungen auf die Geschichte der arabischen Kultur, als die Lateiner dem arabischen Denken Unverständnis der griechischen Kultur vorwarfen. Die lateinischen Kritiker beachteten dabei jedoch nicht, dass die meisten arabischen Werke ihnen nicht im arabischen Original, sondern in hebräischen Übersetzungen vorlagen und dass die begriffliche Verwirrung, die sie dem arabischen Denken anlasten wollten, viel eher in den Übersetzungen als in den Originalquellen ihren Ursprung hatte. Ihr Urteil steht im Widerspruch zu einem anderen Urteil, wonach Aristoteles zwar die Natur erklärt habe, er jedoch von Averroes erst erklärt worden sei. Ein verwirrtes Denken hätte die Logik, Physik und Metaphysik des Aristoteles nicht erklären und darüber nicht so urteilen können, wie es Averroes tat und wie es Goldenthal bestätigt.

In der vorliegenden Untersuchung habe ich Unregelmäßigkeiten in den übersetzten Texten aufgedeckt, um Vorurteile abzubauen. Die vorgeführten Beispiele zeigen den Umgang des hebräischen Übersetzers mit arabischen Texten aus Koran, Ḥadīṯ und Poesie sowie mit Eigennamen, Sprichwörtern und Redewendungen. Ein solcher Umgang, der stillschweigend erfolgt, verursacht unmittelbar Verwirrung im Verständnis der betroffenen Texte, beeinträchtigt im Allgemeinen den historischen Verlauf der Kultur, der die Texte entstammen, und führt schließlich dazu, dass dieser Kultur bei der kritischen historischen Betrachtung Unrecht widerfährt. Der Übersetzer meinte es bei seinem Unternehmen wahrscheinlich gut, war aber entweder nicht in der Lage, den Text richtig zu verstehen, oder beabsichtigte bewusst, Begriffe aus einer anderen Kultur und Religion der eigenen Kultur und Religion anzupassen. Er konnte jedoch nicht ahnen, welche negativen Konsequenzen für die Geistesgeschichte überhaupt und den Verlauf der menschlichen Kultur daraus entstehen würden. Denn die Kultur ist ein gemeinsames Erbe aller Menschen, dessen unbeschadeter Erhalt in der Verantwortung aller Generationen liegt.

Philologen haben in diesem komplexen Problemfeld gerade heute eine besondere Verantwortung. Sie besteht darin, mangelhaft überlieferte Texte zu revidieren, um im zweiten Schritt falsche Begriffe und daraus resultierende Fehler der Geschichtsschreibung zu korrigieren. So verhelfen wir der Kultur, ja sogar der Menschlichkeit zu ihrem Recht.

Unter Mitwirkung von Dr. Claudia Ott von Dr. Georges Tamer aus dem Arabischen ins Deutsche übertragen.

Der jüdische Kontext / Jüdisches Denken

God and the Good Life: Maimonides' Virtue Ethics and the Idea of Perfection

by

Lenn E. Goodman
Vanderbuilt University, Nashville, Tennessee

Maimonides opens his analysis of biblical anthropomorphisms with a discussion of *image and likeness*.[1] His aim is to show that there are spiritual rather than merely physical senses to the language the Torah applies to God. He follows Saʿadya's inductive method,[2] scanning the text for usages that clearly exclude the surface meaning (*ẓāhir*) and single out a specific figurative sense, not only as possible but as actually in use in the Hebrew of the canon. Then, parsing the senses he discovers, he applies the classic demand of natural theology, that one must say of the divine only what is worthy of it, that is to say, only the highest sense.

To'ar, he explains, is clearly a physical term. Thus Genesis (39:6) describes Joseph as "fair of form", and Isaiah (44:13) describes a craftsman marking out the form of an idol with line and compass.[3] *To'ar* is never applied to God. But *ṣelem*, Maimonides writes,

1 Maimonides, *Guide of the Perplexed* I.1, edited with French translation by Salomon Munk, *Le guide des égarés: Traité de théologie et de philosophie* (3 volumes; Paris: Franck, 1856–1866; reprint Osnabrück: Zeller, 1964). Citations below are to this edition, by volume and page in the Arabic, after giving the part, chapters and where relevant the section number: here, ed. Munk, vol. 1, pp. 12a–13a. Munk's pagination is recorded in the running heads of the English translation by Shlomo Pines (Chicago: University of Chicago Press, 1963). Translations in the present essay are my own.

2 For Saʿadya's inductive method of exegesis, see Saʿadya, *The Book of Theodicy: Translation and commentary on the book of Job*. Translated from the Arabic with a philosophic commentary by Lenn E. Goodman (Yale Judaica Series 25; New Haven: Yale University Press, 1988), pp. 131–132; and Lenn E. Goodman, "Saadiah Gaon's Interpretive Technique in Translating the Book of Job", in *Translation of Scripture: Proceedings of a Conference at the Annenberg Research Institute May 15–16, 1989* (Jewish Quarterly Review. Supplement; Philadelphia: Annenberg Research Institute, 1990), pp. 47–76.

3 Ed. Munk (see above n. 1), p. 12a. So in the traditional renderings, and in Saʿadya's translation.

> denotes the natural form, the factor that substantiates a thing, i.e., makes it what it is. This is the reality of that thing as such a being. In man's case, this is the source of human awareness. It is in virtue of this intellectual awareness that it is said of man "In the image of God created He him" (Genesis 1:27).[4]

As a prooftext, the Rambam offers a line from the Psalms (73:20) that speaks of God's despising the form of the wicked. "For contempt applies to the soul, which is the specific form, not to the shape and lineaments of the body." Similarly *demut*, likeness, can clearly have a non-physical sense. When the psalmist says "I am like a pelican in the desert" (102:7), "he does not mean that he has feathers and wings like a pelican, but that he is as desolate" as a pelican in the desert.

Maimonides' aim here is not to refute the notion of God's physicality. As he explains:

> All that needs to be said against corporealism and in support of God's true unity – which cannot be true unless corporealism is rejected – you will find proved as this discussion unfolds. Here in this chapter I wanted only to alert you to this clarification of the meaning of *image and likeness*.[5]

Maimonides' scriptural disproof of corporealism comes in the *Mishneh Torah*:

> It is clearly explicit in the Torah and the Prophets that the Holy One, blessed be He, is not a body or anything physical, as it is written: "For the Lord is God in the heavens above and on earth below"(Deuteronomy 4:39). But a body cannot be in two places at once. And it is also said, "You saw no shape (*temunah*) [when the Lord your God spoke to you out of the fire]" (Deuteronomy 4:15). And again, "To whom will you liken or compare Me?" (Isaiah 40:25). For if He were a body He would be comparable to other bodies.[6]

As for the conceptual proof, that will depend, as Maimonides foreshadows, on the idea of God's absolute unity – itself a corollary of God's necessary existence. That is recognized once we grasp the ontic hierarchy that is just hinted in this first assay of biblical language.

It would be premature just at the outset of the *Guide* for Maimonides to telegraph his rejection of the very idea of divine attributes. That outcome will emerge from his inductive survey, as he assays the Torah's language about God and skims off each layer of more intellectual and spiritual sense, leaving behind all that is less perfect. But it is not too soon even here for him to suggest the equation of reality with perfection, ontic potency and causal puissance. Pointing to a reality beyond the physical as the source of all contingent existence, Maimonides

---

4 *Guide* I.1 (ed. Munk [see above n. 1], p. 12b).

5 *Guide* I.1 (ed. Munk, p. 12a).

6 *Mishneh Torah* I.1, "Hilkhot Yesodei ha-Torah" 1.8.

lays the groundwork for the recognition of God as the goal of all strivings.[7] But he is also proposing that the gradient of reality or perfection is intellectual rather than physical. For the derived reality of all contingent things *is* rationality objectified, refracted into specificity in their natural forms, and rendered subjective once again in the rational intelligence that makes us human. As he writes in laying out the conceptual groundworks of the Law in his great legal code:

> The soul of every mortal creature is its Godgiven form; and the higher consciousness of man, found in his soul, is the form of a mentally unimpaired human being. It is of this form that it is said in the Torah: "Let us make man in our own image, after our likeness" (Genesis 1:26). This means that man's form can grasp and know nonphysical ideas.[8]

When Moses asked God's name, and God told him *I am that I am*, "Thus shalt thou say to the Israelites: *I am* hath sent me to you" (Exodus 3:13–15), Moses, by Maimonides' account, was using courtly diction, avoiding baldly saying that the question that concerned him was not about God's name but about His reality.[9] The answer he was given to address the doubts that the Israelites would rightly voice, was no proper name (readily dismissed as common knowledge had it been familiar, and as gibberish had it been unknown) but the heart of the biblical idea of God – not a name in the usual sense at all but an argument, which the elders would understand, even if they could not have framed it for themselves.[10]

The reasoning, spelled out in the affirmation of God's absoluteness and encapsulated in the Tetragrammaton, was that the Being that stands at the peak of the ontic hierarchy[11] cannot fail to exist. The necessity of God's existence entails His absolute simplicity and uniqueness; thus, the utter inappositeness of any of the notions that we humans use to class and categorize the contingent realities we encounter in our daily lives. Of course a being that is utterly simplex will not be extended. But "true unity" has more radical implications. It means that God is indivisible even conceptually. So the very idea of divine attributes is absurd and, as the Rambam will argue, a greater affront to God's unity than idolatry.[12]

Maimonides might have chosen any of a number of biblical anthropomorphisms for his opening shot. He might have addressed God's presumed

---

7 See *Mishneh Torah* I.2, "Hilkhot De'ot" 3.2–3: "A person should direct all his actions toward the knowledge of God", citing Proverbs 3:6, and *Mishnah Avot* 2:17.

8 *Mishneh Torah* I.1, "Hilkhot Yesodei ha-Torah" 4.8.

9 *Guide* I.63 (ed. Munk [see above n. 1], p. 81a).

10 *Guide* I.61–63 (ed. Munk, pp. 77b–82b). For those who follow an argument even if they cannot frame one for themselves, see al-Fārābī, *K. Mabādi' Ārā' Ahl al-Madīna 'l-Fāḍila* (The Book of the Principles Underlying the Beliefs of the People of the Virtuous State), § 17.2, ed. and trans. Richard Walzer as *Alfarabi on the Perfect State* (Oxford: Oxford University Press, 1985), Arabic p. 278, lines 11–12, English p. 279.

11 See *Guide* I.11, 15, 16, 20.

12 *Guide* I.51–53.

enjoyment of the sweet savor of sacrifices (Genesis 8:21, Exodus 29:18, etc.), or God's fatherhood (as in Malachi 1:6, 2:10), or God's regret over his creation (Genesis 6:6), or the kindling of His wrath – more literally, the fire in His nose (Exodus 32:10–12). But Maimonides chose *image and likeness* because it singles out the affinity between man and God. And that, as Narboni explains, is the Rambam's intended goal. For, as Narboni explains, paraphrasing the well known liturgical and Midrashic trope, what was first in design was last in execution.[13] This particular likening of man to God, the reference to the affinity to God of the human mind or spirit, will not be dissolved by analysis as a mere accommodation. It will be taken seriously as a pointer orienting us in the ontic hierarchy, the Jacob's ladder by which humanity and divinity are conjoined.

If we want to see how the negative theology of the *Guide* comports with Maimonides' acceptance of any discourse about God, even in the Torah, or bracketed in quotations from scripture in our prayers, or how it is possible for Maimonides to conceive the ultimate goal of human life and of all rational human endeavor as a pursuit of the knowledge of God and of imitation of His ways,[14] we need to start from the ontic and epistemic hierarchy that Maimonides adopts from his neoplatonic predecessors. He projects that hierarchy concisely when he speaks in neoplatonic mode about the ontology of angels:

> If you told one of those men who purport to be the Sages of Israel that the Deity sends an angel that enters the womb of a woman and there forms the foetus, that would impress him and he would accept it as an expression of God's greatness and power and an instance of His wisdom – although still convinced that an angel is a body of flaming fire one-third the size of the entire world – supposing that all this was perfectly possible for God. But if you told him that God placed a formative power in the semen, by which limbs and organs are shaped and demarcated, and that this is the angel, or if you told him that the forms of all things are the work of the Active Intellect and that this is the angel constantly mentioned by the Sages as the magistrate of the world, he would recoil at such a view. For he does not understand the real meaning of greatness and power.[15]

Angels, in Maimonides' view, are forms and forces.[16] The evanescent angels of the Rabbis, who "sing their song before Him and go their way" are natural forces. These include impulses and urges like the "angel appointed over lust" which the

---

13 Moses Narboni, on Maimonides' *Guide*, edited and translated by Maurice-Ruben Hayoun, *Moshe Narboni* (Texts and Studies in Medieval and Early Modern Judaism 1; Tübingen: J. C. B. Mohr [Paul Siebeck], 1986), Hebrew text p. 132, French translation p. 42.

14 See *Mishneh Torah* I.2, "Hilkhot De'ot", first commandment, and 1.6.

15 *Guide* II 6 (ed. Munk [see above n. 1], vol. 2, p. 18b).

16 For Maimonides' Platonic and Aristotelian naturalization of angels, see my "Maimonidean Naturalism", in Lenn E. Goodman (Ed.), *Neoplatonism and Jewish Thought* (Albany: SUNY Press, 1992), pp. 139–172, and in Robert Cohen and Hillel Levine (Eds.), *Maimonides and the Sciences* (Boston: Kluwer, 2000), pp. 57–85.

Sages introduce to explain Judah's resort to a prostitute.[17] The enduring angels are Platonic Forms, afforded by the Active Intellect, the source of those forms by which things are substantiated, given definite natures as what they are, as Maimonides explains. The sense to be derived from the Rabbinic dictum that angels are the third part of the world is a reference not to their size but to the tripartite ontology in which angels mediate between God and nature.[18]

The Active Intellect is the philosophers' name for the wholesale source of that mediation, the active and activating distributor of all forms, including the unique essence that makes man what he is, the human intellect. Maimonides focuses on the human form not just because it is ours but because it holds the key to understanding our role in the universe. For, while it is not true that all things were made for man and man that he might worship God,[19] we humans do play an unequaled part in the cosmic drama, and the reason lies in the human mind.[20]

The human form is unique in three ways (beyond its uniqueness as the form of just one species): 1) It is subjective as well as objective. That is, it is conscious and self-conscious. 2) It is individual as well as universal. For subjectivity brings with it intentionality, and that, as Avicenna argued,[21] imparts an individuality not dependant on our embodiment. For both of these reasons 3) man's intellectual awareness, human rationality, the mind, gives us an affinity with God quite beyond that of all other beings. All beings derive unity and reality from God. All are God's creatures and all display God's grace and wisdom in the intricacy of their design and peculiarities of their natures. But only mankind, being consciously aware of God, is capable of realizing the affinity with Him. Our individuality, the quirks of our personalities, our strengths and weaknesses of impulse and imagination, all arise from our embodiment, which Maimonides' finds that we

17 *Guide* II.6 (ed. Munk [see above n. 1], p. 17b), citing Genesis 38:15–16 and *Genesis Rabbah* §§ 50, 78, 85.

18 See *Guide* II.10 (ed. Munk [see above n. 1], vol. 2, p. 22a–b): "The Sages' dictum that the angel is the third part of the world in *Genesis Rabbah* [§ 10] […] is now clear as can be […]. There are three kinds of created beings: 1) disembodied intellects, i.e., angels; 2) the bodies of the spheres; 3) prime matter, the constantly changing bodies beneath the sphere of the moon." Angels impart the forms by which matter is differentiated into specific substances with definite natures. The spheres are the material vehicles through which the intellectual influences of the disembodied Forms/angels/intellects are transmitted.

19 *Guide* III.12 (ed. Munk [see above n. 1], p. 18a–b); cf. *Guide* I.2 (ed. Munk, pp. 13a–14b).

20 *Mishneh Torah* I.1, "Hilkhot Yesodei ha-Torah" 4.9: "This spiritual form is not compounded of the elements, so as to dissolve into them. Nor is it of the vital spirit and so dependent on it as that spirit depends on the body. It comes from God in Heaven. Thus, when the body breaks down into its elements, and physical life ends, unable to continue without the body, on which all its functions depend, this form is not obliterated. For its acts do not depend on animal vitality. It still knows and recognizes the disembodied Ideas and the Creator of all, and it endures eternally. As Solomon so wisely said: 'The dust returns to the earth, whence it came. But the spirit returns to God, who gave it' (Ecclesiastes 12:7)."

21 See Lenn E. Goodman, *Avicenna* (London and New York: Routledge, 1992), chapter 3.

must conceptualize in terms of God's will.[22] But our intelligence is our affinity with God's wisdom. The possibility of realizing that affinity is what makes life worthwhile and outweighs all the sufferings and hardships to which our embodiment makes us vulnerable.[23]

Moses asked to see God's face. But this request was denied. Man cannot see God's face and live.[24] What Moses was vouchsafed was the vision of God's "back" – that is, as Maimonides glosses, what follows in God's wake, the effects of God's work in nature.[25] This, after all, is what Moses needed to fulfill his mission of governance: Not to behold God's ipseity, which would transcend all finite apprehension, but rather to see nature *as* God's work. By grasping the mercy and justice of God's rule in nature, he would be enabled to see mercy and justice as the two great themes of human governance as well.[26] The notions are human, of course. But that is hardly inappropriate, if they are to have human application. It is because mankind, male and female, is made in God's image that the human image can serve as the mirror of God – above all, for ethical purposes.

Once we know that God is perfection and have seen that the biblical anthropomorphisms deconstruct themselves to yield only the perfections they signify, while purging themselves of every suggestion of finitude that the language of human perfections would normally connote,[27] we are prepared to understand what it would mean to pursue the goal of becoming as like to God as humanly possible, as Plato puts it (*Theaetetus* 176),[28] or of knowing God, pursuing fulfillment of the biblical command: "You shall be holy, for I the Lord thy God am holy" (Leviticus 19:2).[29]

Holiness, in biblical parlance, means transcendence. If defined merely negatively, that idea becomes vacuous and ethically useless. But if we know the

---

22 See Lenn E. Goodman, "Matter and Form as Attributes of God in Maimonides' Philosophy", in Ruth Link-Salinger (Ed.), *A Straight Path: Studies in Medieval Philosophy and Culture. Essays in honor of Arthur Hyman* (Washington: The Catholic University of America Press, 1987), pp. 86–97.

23 *Guide* III.17–18, 22–23.

24 *Mishneh Torah* I.1, "Hilkhot Yesodei ha-Torah" 1.10 glossing Exodus 33:18 and 33:23.

25 *Guide* I.38 (ed. Munk [see above n. 1], p. 45a–b).

26 *Mishneh Torah* I.2, "Hilkhot De'ot" 1.6: "As He is called gracious, so be thou gracious; as He is called merciful, so be thou merciful." The source texts: *Sifre* to Deuteronomy 10:12; Babylonian Talmud, *Sota* 14a, glossing Deuteronomy 13:5; Babylonian Talmud, *Shabbat* 133b; *Leviticus Rabbah* 24.

27 *Guide* I.26 (ed. Munk [see above n. 1], pp. 29a–b); *Guide* III.19 (ed. Munk, p. 39a–b).

28 Cf. Plato, *Laws* 716, *Republic* 500B–501C, 589D; cf. *Phaedrus* 273; *Timaeus* 90B.

29 As Maimonides explains (*Guide* I.54 [ed. Munk (see above n. 1), pp. 65a–b]), the Sages explicate the commandment, in terms of familiar and appropriate human virtues: "They glossed: as He is gracious, so do you be gracious; as he is compassionate, so do you be compassionate." Cf. *Guide* III.54 (ed. Munk [see above n. 1], pp. 134b–135a); *Eight Chapters*, chapters 5, 7, edited and translated by Joseph I. Gorfinkle (New York: Columbia University Press, 1912; repr. New York: AMS Press, 1966), pp. 69–74, 79–84; Lenn E. Goodman, *God of Abraham* (New York: Oxford University Press, 1996), p. 88.

direction in which transcendence lies, we are positioned to pursue the imitation of God. We then see that our quest is for human perfections, and we have a basis for recognizing such perfections. We are no longer without a compass. We know what God is through our knowledge of perfection, and what perfection is in us, through our knowledge of God and human nature. Here arises the possibility of that chimneying between our ethical knowledge and our religious experience (communal as well as personal) which has been so prominent a theme in my own philosophical work.[30]

The two questions asked about Maimonides, perhaps more frequently than any other, once the questioner has gained a basic familiarity with the lay of the land, is how we can know God if God cannot be described, and how we can imitate God, if, as the Rambam seems to say, there is no relationship between God and any other being. Maimonides himself suggests the beginnings of an answer to the first question, when he projects the path of an asymptotic approach to God via the very project of negative theology itself.[31] For the further we rise above the categories of limitation and particularity the closer we come to God and the further removed we are from matter, here construed, Platonically, as otherness, the polar opposite of God's unity and perfection. But Maimonides does not address the second question, since the terms in which it is asked are foreign to his thinking. They rest, in fact, on a misconstrual of his language.

Maimonides considers four kinds of predicates that might be applied to God: definitions, properties, accidents, and relations. God, he argues, has no definition. For definitions, as Aristotle taught us to construct them, depend on analysis. They assign a genus and species, naming the kind a thing belongs to and then differentiating it from others of its kind. But God, being unique, is a member of no class; and, being simplex, is beyond analysis. There is no opening for thought to make inroads into any composition on which God depends, precisely because God is not contingent, as all composites are. Ultimately, Maimonides argues, all definitions refer to causes. But "He has no prior causes of His existence, by which He might be defined. That is why it is acknowledged by every thinker who has studied the question that God is undefinable."[32]

What is definable is finite, contingent, composite, even temporal. Were Maimonides to pursue Aristotle's equation of existence with definiteness, he might even have followed the Platonists in placing God beyond being. But that would be too misleading a locution. He simply says that existence is said of God in a sense quite different from the familiar one[33] and holds out the inviting prospect of an asymptotic climb, higher and higher, towards infinity. For it is not

30 See ibid., pp. 83–89.

31 *Guide* I.59 (ed. Munk [see above n. 1], pp. 72a–73b); *Guide* I.73 (ed. Munk, p. 115a); *Eight Chapters* (see above n. 29), chapter 5.

32 *Guide* I.52 (ed. Munk [see above n. 1], p. 59a).

33 *Guide* I.52 (ed. Munk [see above n. 1], pp. 60b, last line – 61a, first line).

the case, as Maimonides reads the dynamic of existence, that only emptiness rather than plenitude stands at the summit of the ontological ladder, the Source and Goal of all.

Just as God has no definition, so does He have no properties. This too is universally agreed among all who have reflected on the matter. For properties are elements in a definition: "if God had a part of an essence, His essence would be composite."[34] Bear in mind what Maimonides said at the very opening of his discussion of biblical anthropomorphisms: that an essence is what makes a thing what it is. So essences are imparted, and their components are constituents in the composition of a (contingent) being, a thing that is what it is because they are combined within it, and that would be destroyed – denatured – were they lacking or disarranged. The force of the objection is not only logical but theological: At stake is not just God's simplicity but His absoluteness. There will be no suffering God here.

Thirdly, Maimonides argues, we must judge all accidental predicates inapplicable to God. Accidents are the characteristics that do not make a thing what it is, traits without which it would still belong to its kind. That again would demand compositeness, but now, of a baser kind: "if God had an attribute of this sort, He would be the substrate of accidents."[35] That yields a variable and a constant: trait and substrate. So, does God vary? And is this putative substrate anything other than matter, making God not only temporal but corporeal? How rapidly we descend to the grossest materialism:

> How odd that those who assign attributes to God still reject describing Him in creaturely terms or in any way that would qualify His absoluteness. But what does it mean for them to affirm that His reality is not to be qualified, unless it means that He has no qualities?[36]

What else can it mean to affirm God's infinite transcendence but to deny the pertinence of any notion that would limit Him?

Skepticism would see no way forward here. But Maimonides has left one door open to the path he expects us to follow. He sees a bright ray of light marking his path, laid out by the principle he elicits from the poetics of the prophets: Only predicates of perfection will be assigned to God, shorn of all their familiar connotations of finitude and deficiency. Hence the wisdom of the Rabbinic rule that even scriptural epithets are permissible only by prophetic license (which sees the need for some suggestion of the direction in which God lies), and of the further demand that even these be applied seriously, as in prayer, only by Rabbinic sanction (again prophetic in standing).[37] For without the context and catena of

34 Ibid.

35 *Guide* I.52 (ed. Munk [see above n. 1], p. 59b).

36 Ibid.

37 *Guide* I.59 (ed. Munk [see above n. 1], p. 73b), citing Babylonian Talmud, *Berakhot* 33b.

prophetic discourse, these anthropomorphisms would not deconstruct one another. The language would fail to shear away the privative connotations of its ordinary usage and would not point the way toward God.

Now for the matter of relations. This is where I find a misconstrual of Maimonides' language, in an effort at literalism that results in serious anachronism. Today we use the word 'relation' in a sense so broad and abstract that we readily say that two things are completely unrelated, and that is the relationship between them. We often treat identity as a relation and include reflexivity among its properties. Implication and equivalence are relations, although their terms are not things but propositions. If the correspondence account is true, knowledge relates in a certain way to its object. And, of course, there are all sorts of relations in logic and mathematics – greater than, lesser than, square root of – each with interesting properties of its own, not to mention the relations dealt with by geographers, genealogists, and geomancers.

Maimonides uses the term "relation" in a far more restricted sense when he writes: "The matter we must investigate and reflect on is whether there is any real relation (*nisba*), in terms of which God might be characterized, between Him and any of the substances He created."[38] At a glance, unless he is flatly contradicting himself, he clearly posits at least one relation right here: that of creator and object of creation, a classic asymmetrical relation readily compared with that of parent and child or artist and handiwork, two of the familiar tropes prophetically applied to God and the world, or humanity. Indeed, as soon as he has made his point about relations, Maimonides accepts descriptions of God as a creator, since predication of authorship need not pin down or delimit the author. That is the heart of Maimonides' concern.

Obviously, as he argues, there is no spatial or temporal connection between God and his creatures. For these would entail physicality. A fortiori is there no physical connection. But the general category of relation is not ruled out but held in reserve, since relations need not entail multiplicity or change in the relata: Zayd may be the father of one man, brother of another, master of a third; his partner may die without any change in him. That is the advantage with relations: They are not definitions, properties or accidents. Yet even many relations that do not overtly presume temporality or physicality remain inapplicable to God. Maimonides singles out two cases that are heavy with the scent of the Arabic *nisba,* namely, correlation and comparison. For etymologically, *nisba* means kinship or linkage, and more technically, proportion.

Plainly there can be no correlativity between God and any contingent object, since that assumption would violate the strong asymmetry of the creator relation: With correlatives, the non-existence of one member entails that of the other. So God would not exist unless the world did. That was very much the reasoning of the neoplatonists, who held that the world must be eternal if God is by His very

38 *Guide* I.52 (ed. Munk [see above n. 1], p. 60b).

essence its creator. That made God as dependent on His creation as it was on him.[39] Some mystics find that idea titillating. But it contravenes God's absoluteness, and Maimonides will none of it.[40]

The idea of comparison does have a certain specious appeal, Maimonides writes. For people readily enough think that God is like us, only more so – greater, more powerful, more universal.[41] But, as the incident of Rabbi Ḥanina's reproof to his disciple's essays in creative liturgy underscores, the difference between God and creation is not just a matter of degree.[42] It is a real difference. In a modern, abstract sense that *is* a relation – but not one that allows any delimiting characterization. We need to speak strictly when we speak of God, as the Rambam sees things, and strictly speaking,

> comparisons can be made only between two members of the same infima species. Even if the two fall under the same genus there is no comparing them. That is why we do not say that this red is redder than that green, or less so, or equally so – even though both belong to the same genus, namely color.[43]

We do compare different colors in intensity or saturation. But if asked how red something is, we need to compare it with other reds, not greens. Higher up the tree of Porphyry the point grows sharper:

> If two things fall under different genera, there is no comparison of any sort between them [...] between, say, a hundred cubits and the hotness of peppers. For the one belongs to the category of quality, and the other to that of quantity. Again, there's no comparison between knowledge and

39 In *Mishneh Torah* I.1, "Hilkhot Yesodei ha-Torah" 1.2–3, Maimonides argues that if God did not exist, nothing else would exist, but if nothing else existed, God would still exist. That does describe a relation, *in our terms*, the utter dependence of all things upon God. The implication Maimonides draws is God's uniqueness (ibid., 1.4), as proclaimed by Jeremiah (10:10): "The Lord God is truth." What this means, as Maimonides understands it, is that God alone has true reality: none other has truth like His: "As the Torah says, 'There is none but He'(Deuteronomy 4:35)."

40 At *Categories* 4, 2a 1, Aristotle offers 'double and half' and 'greater than' as opening illustrations of the idea of relation. These do involve co-relativity and proportion. For there is no double unless there is a half; and 'greater than' invites the question: 'By how much?' In *Metaphysics* V,15, Aristotle adds causal relations to his list, speaking of the relation of what heats to what is heated, "and in general, the active to the passive." But causal relations of this kind involve interaction, reciprocal effects and affectedness. God, for Maimonides, is never passive. If God gives actuality without Himself being diminished or entering into the process of becoming, then a causal idea is not inapplicable to God. That is what Aristotle proposes in the idea of the Unmoved Mover and what Maimonides values in the Plotinian idea of emanation.

41 *Guide* I.56 (ed. Munk [see above n. 1], p. 68a).

42 *Guide* I.59 (ed. Munk, p. 73b).

43 *Guide* I.52 (ed. Munk, p. 61).

> sweetness, or clemency and bitterness, although these do fall under the general category of qualities. So how could there be a comparison between Him and any of His creatures, given the enormity of the difference between them in the character of their existence – than which there is none greater.[44]

Poets do, of course, compare knowledge with sweetness – and cruelty, at least, with bitterness. But that means fictively placing the objects on the same scale. For God and His creatures there is no such scale. Even at the most general level, that of existence, a broader class (in the scheme Maimonides uses) than any of Aristotle's ten categories, the gulf between God and creatures is absolute, since God's existence is necessary and the rest, contingent. It's never a difference of degree. There is no scale of comparison.

Hence the inappositeness here of the idea of proportion, lingering from the Greek idea of *logos*. Creation is not the case of an iron bar heated by a furnace, where the heat of the bar is proportioned to the heat of the flames. The reasoning is spelled out by Thomas Aquinas, for in Thomas, as in Maimonides, God is known by His works: "When the existence of a cause is demonstrated from an effect, this effect takes the place of the definition of the cause in proving the cause's existence."[45] That is why, Thomas argues, following in the Rambam's footsteps, "the names given to God are derived from His effects."[46] Yet "God's effects are not proportioned to Him, since He is infinite and His effects are finite."[47] Thus Moses' confinement to the vision of God's "wake", and the reason, voiced in the Torah's characteristically concrete language: "Man cannot see God's face and live." In more abstract terms: Human finitude precludes any direct intuition of the divine aseity.

Yet we do have a window on the Infinite, and although there is no scale of comparison there is that Jacob's ladder which rises from finitude toward the Infinite. Granted we know God only through His effects. But one of those effects is our own intelligence, and that does link us with God. The divine Infinite is not merely the undefined. It is the infinitely real. In keeping with the Torah's central teaching about God, what is most real (and thus divine) is purely and absolutely good.[48] And, in keeping with Plato's central teaching, what is most perfect is most real. We know what God is to the extent that we know what perfection is. In our world that is not a mystery. So God's infinitude itself is not a mystery in the sense

44 *Guide* I.52 (ed. Munk [see above n. 1], p. 61a).

45 *Summa Theologica,* qu. 2 a. 2 reply obj. 2.

46 Ibid.

47 *Summa Theologica,* qu. 2 a. 2, obj. 3.

48 Some readers make much of the fact that we humans, by Maimonides' account (*Guide* I.2), characteristically use the ideas of good and evil in a subjective, animal like way, to name our likes and dislikes. But that is not the only way these notions are applied. There is also the sense they must be given when, for example, God, in Genesis judges light and life to be good – or when we humans are told, as we are by the Torah, what is good and what is bad for us, the life and death, the blessing and the curse.

that we have no inkling of its direction or the demands it makes on us, but only in the sense that its fullness is beyond our grasp.

We know – we have been told, as Micah (6:8) puts it – not only what is right but what God expects of us and, beyond that, invites us to achieve. We pursue God's infinite perfection by pursuing perfection in ourselves. That is why no knowledge is more needful to us than the study of man – not a cynical, reductive study, but the study of human potential and perfectibility, strengths and weaknesses. We mark the Torah as a divinely inspired law because it pursues not just our civil security and material well being but also the perfection of our character and enlightenment of our understanding that will allow us to pursue our affinity with God.

The biblical law, on Maimonides' account, embodies a virtue ethics aiming at the refinement of our character and advancement of the intellectual standing that is the true measure of our ontic worth and propinquity to God. It does, to be sure, lay down civil and penal laws, aiming at containing force and controling fraud. But these, as Ibn Tufayl had argued, are the most minimal requirements of a law. They are necessary, as are those regulations that will actually enhance our material well being, by promoting trade and fostering other modes of cooperation. For, as Maimonides argues, no human being can reliably expect to contemplate higher things while living in fear or penury, or suffering the pangs of hunger or ill health.[49]

But the Torah distinguishes itself as divine law (and other systems derived from it show their parentage by their concerns) when it aims to cap material welfare with moral betterment, and that in turn with spiritual awakening, the intellectual apprehension that realizes our human potential.[50] For Aristotle was right, Maimonides believes, in holding that no activity can claim rationality if it does not pursue an aim ultimately worthwhile in itself. To Maimonides this means: "A man ought to subordinate all the powers of his psyche to reason [...]. He ought always to hold out before himself a single goal: to come as close to God as humanly possible."[51]

What this means may want a little spelling out. It does not demand a life of solid mystic meditation. For we know God through nature, and through human nature specifically. Study of nature, then, becomes not just a mode of worship but a way of approaching God. Further, subordination of all our powers to reason means commitment to the refinement of our moral character and perfection of our social natures. For moral development is a prerequisite of intellectual perfection, and the moral virtues are distinguished by a habitual, spontaneous, even pleasurable responsiveness to the counsels and judgments of reason.[52] Man, moreover,

---

49 *Guide* III.27–28.

50 *Guide* II.40 (ed. Munk [see above n. 1], pp. 86a–b).

51 *Eight Chapters* (see above n. 29), chapter 5.

52 *Eight Chapters* (see above n. 29), chapter 6.

as Aristotle argued, is a social creature. The moral virtues arise and flourish, meet their characteristic challenges and grow to their full height only in a social context. Nor do we secure even our most basic needs, let alone find the sphere for cultivating our talents, the theater for exercise of our concerns, or the vehicle for achievement of our potential, in isolation from our fellow human beings. Saʿadya saw this when he argued that the eremite or anchorite who seeks spiritual perfection in isolation from society typically defeats his own purpose by thwarting his own nature, more likely becoming bitter and misanthropic rather than spiritually fulfilled.[53] Maimonides adopts Saʿadya's reasoning here, arguing that an asceticism that leans away from the normal mean and even pursues some measure of isolation from humanity may be therapeutic for those who seek to cleanse themselves of sensate impulses or purge the influence of corrupt neighbors (for our social natures do lead us to internalize the norms and values practiced around us) but is nonetheless a deviation from the mean, ultimately, in need of correction.[54]

Maimonides' counsel that we must direct all our activities toward a single goal is thus to be read in an inclusive rather than exclusive sense. There are, after all, only certain ends that integrate all our actions. The good life that finds a proper place for all human goods is the most credible contender. Its singleness results from the adequate subordination and coordination of the many aims and values that may seem to compete for our energies and attentions. Knowing what is a means and what is worthy of being made an end is what makes this integration possible.[55] Thus Maimonides argues, pleasant company, a comely spouse, attractive clothing, decorous surroundings, healthful and tasty food, good music, and wholesome amusements, contribute to the good life.[56] They are not ultimate ends. But neither are they "temptations" or "distractions." Just as pains are real evils, but not ultimate evils,[57] so these external things and human relationships are real goods, but not ultimate goods. They have value intrinsically, and they contribute to our well being, but (as Saʿadya showed[58]) they become evils when treated as the be-all and end-all of our existence. They need to be situated in the larger framework of a life, and the pursuit of our likeness to God is the organizing and orienting principle that allows us to do just that.

---

53 Saʿadya, *Kitāb al-Mukhtār fī l-amānāt wa-l-iʿtiqādāt* (The Book of Critically Chosen Beliefs and Convictions, commonly known as *Sefer Emunot ve-Deʿot*), X; see the discussion in Goodman, *God of Abraham* (see above n. 29), pp. 143–144.

54 *Eight Chapters* (see above n. 29), chapters 3–4; *Mishneh Torah* I.2, "Hilkhot Deʿot" 3.1, citing Numbers 6:11 and Ecclesiastes 7:16.

55 See Goodman, *God of Abraham* (see above n. 29), pp. 165–166.

56 *Eight Chapters* (see above n. 29), chapter 5.

57 *Guide* III.16.

58 See Goodman, *God of Abraham* (see above n. 29), pp. 142–152.

The Biological Limitations of Man's Intellectual Perfection According to Maimonides

by

Gad Freudenthal

Châtenay-Malabry

Please allow me to put scholarly practice and customs aside for one moment and begin with a personal word. For me, this conference is not one among many. For two reasons. The first is its location at the Friedrich-Alexander Universität Erlangen-Nürnberg. The name "Nürnberg" has been a synonym for "hatred" – it is indissolubly associated with the 1935 racial laws named after it. Also Hitler's diatribes delivered not far away from here still ring in my ears. I say this with my mind turned not only to the past, but above all to the future. In being devoted to Maimonides, the emblematic Jew, this conference has the considerable merit to deliver, at Nürnberg, a forceful message redeeming the town's Nazi past. No less important, this conference is unique because, as far as I can see, it is the only one, among many organized this year on the occasion of the 800th anniversary of Maimonides' death, in which participate Arab and Jewish scholars. This is a significant symbol: by its very existence, this conference tells us that we all share a common cultural heritage in that we are committed to the ideal of rational thought. The organizers are to be commended for having initiated and realized this scholarly gathering, whose value is not scholarly alone.

***

Like most contemporary *falāsifa*, Maimonides was a declared elitist. In the very beginning of the *Guide* he says that he will teach a *demonstrated truth* to a single virtuous man (*fāḍil*), even if this means displeasing ten thousand ignoramuses (*jāhil*) who cannot follow such a high-level teaching.[1] Almost two centuries

1 Maimonides, *The Guide of the Perplexed*, "Instruction with respect to this treatise". Text in Joseph Kafaḥ (Ed. and Trans.), *Rabbenu Moshe ben Maimon, Moreh ha-nevukhim. Dalālat al-ḥā'irīn* (Jerusalem: Mosad Harav Kook, 1972), vol. 1, p. 17; translation quoted from Moses Maimonides, *The Guide of the Perplexed*. Translated with an Introduction and Notes by Shlomo Pines (Chicago and London: University of Chicago Press, 1963), p. 16. In what follows, all translations from the *Guide* are Pines' (occasionally with modifications).

before Maimonides, the great scientist Ibn al-Haitham (965–c. 1041), in his autobiography composed in 1027, similarly wrote that he did not wish to address himself to "the totality of men", but only to the "most virtuous (*al-fāḍil*)" among them. Ibn al-Haitham adds the following remark:

> With respect to this I say what Galen has said in his book on *Megapulsus*: "In this book I do not address the totality of men, but the man who outweighs thousands of men, nay tens of thousands of men."[2]

Ibn al-Haitham and Maimonides both follow in the footsteps of Heraclitus, whose fragment 22B49 states: "One man is as ten thousand for me, if he is best."[3] This fragment is preserved notably in one of the sixteen treatises making up Galen's *Megapulsus*,[4] which Ibn al-Haitham, and presumably Maimonides too, knew in its Arabic translation.[5] Maimonides was thus in good company: His elitism, so shocking to our modern ears informed by the Enlightenment and by the French Revolution, was a politically correct posture of his own day.

This elitism was purely intellectual. The view that men are born unequal with respect to their intellectual capacities appeared to most *falāsifa* (notably to the Aristotelians among them) as an indisputable *fact*. Maimonides clearly expressed this view, e.g. in the following passage:

---

2 Quoted after Ibn Abī Uṣaibiʿa, *ʿUyūn al-ʾanbāʾ fī ṭabaqāt al-ʾaṭibbāʾ* (Beirut: Dār Maktābat al-Ḥayāt, n.d. [1980]), p. 558. Ibn al-Haitham's autobiography is translated in Eilhard Wiedemann, "Ibn al-Haitam, ein arabischer Gelehrter", in *Festschrift J. Rosenthal zur Vollendung seines siebzigsten Lebensjahres gewidmet* (Leipzig: Thieme, 1906), pt. 1, pp. 147–178 (= idem, *Gesammelte Schriften zur arabisch-islamischen Wissenschaftsgeschichte.* 1. Band: *Schriften 1876–1912*, ed. Dorothea Girke [Frankfurt am Main: Institut für Geschichte der Arabisch-Islamischen Wissenschaften an der Johann Wolfgang Goethe-Universität, 1984]), on p. 168.

3 Translation quoted after Geoffrey S. Kirk, John Earle R. Raven and Malcolm Schofield, *The Presocratic Philosophers* (Cambridge: Cambridge University Press, 2nd edition 1983), p. 211n. See also Gad Freudenthal, "Four Implicit Quotations of Philosophical Sources in Maimonides' *Guide of the Perplexed*", in *Zutot: Perspectives on Jewish Culture* 2 (Dordrecht, Boston, London: Kluwer Academic Publishers, 2003), pp. 114–125.

4 The statement is in *De dignoscendis pulsibus*, ed. Carl Gottlob Kühn (*Claudii Galeni Opera omnia* [20 volumes; Leipzig: Knobloch, 1821–1833]), vol. VIII, pp. 766–961, on p. 773. There are two parallel texts which confirm the authenticity of the quotation, but which were not available in Arabic and thus do not concern us here.

5 Under the titles *Kitāb fī nabḍ al-ʿurūq* or *Kitāb an-nabḍ al-kabīr*. See Fuat Sezgin, *Geschichte des arabischen Schrifttums.* Band III: *Medizin — Pharmazie — Zoologie — Tierheilkunde* (Leiden: Brill, 1970), pp. 91–94; Manfred Ullmann, *Die Medizin im Islam* (Handbuch der Orientalistik, Abt. 1: Der Nahe und der Mittlere Osten, Ergänzungsband 6, Abschnitt 1; Leiden, Köln: Brill, 1970), pp. 43–44; Elinor Lieber, "Galen in Hebrew: The Transmission of Galen's Works in the Mediaeval Islamic World", in Vivian Nutton (Ed.), *Galen: Problems and Prospects* (London: Wellcome Institute for the History of Medicine, 1981), pp. 167–186, on p. 173.

> The difference in the capacity existing between the individuals of the [human] species with regard to sensory apprehensions and all other bodily faculties is manifest and clear to all men. [...] The same holds of human intellectual apprehensions. There are great differences in capacity between the individuals of the [human] species. This is also manifest and very clear to the men of knowledge. It may thus happen that whereas one individual discovers a certain notion by himself through his speculation, another individual is not able ever to understand that notion [...].[6]

Why is this so? For Maimonides and his contemporaries the answer was clear: the fact that men are unequal with respect to their intellectual potentials is a matter of biology. Maimonides often states that individuals are born with an innate biological constitution, which conditions their intellectual capacity. A prophet, he says for instance, is, biologically speaking, someone "whose brain in its *original constitution* (*fī aṣl jiblatihi*) is extremely well proportioned because of the purity of its matter and of the particular temperament (*mizāj*) of each of its parts".[7] Similarly, Maimonides says that the portion of emanation (*fayḍ*) that an individual receives depends first and foremost on "the disposition of his matter".[8] To signal an individual having a superior intelligence Maimonides says that he has "a most perfect natural disposition (*kāmil al-fiṭra jiddan*)".[9] Conversely, when Maimonides considers the case of an individual whose rational faculty is defective, he remarks that this can be due either to the imperfect "original natural disposition" (*min aṣl al-jibla*), or to the insufficiency of training.[10] Maimonides mitigates this biological determinism, but only very slightly, by holding that the original natural disposition can be somewhat modified through an appropriate regimen: one can improve his temperament, but only within very narrow limits; someone born with a defective constitution will never be able to achieve intellectual perfection, whatever his efforts.[11] There thus are between men irreducible differences, which all go back to "the difference of the[ir] mixture[s] [or: temperament(s): *ikhtilāf al-mizāj*]".[12] The bodily perfection is famously the second among the four human perfections identified by Maimonides (in the sequel of Ibn Bājja).[13]

---

6 Maimonides, *Guide* I.31; trans. Pines (see above n. 1), p. 65.

7 *Guide* II.36; trans. Pines, p. 371.

8 *Guide* III.18; trans. Pines, p. 475.

9 *Guide* II.17; trans. Pines, p. 295.

10 *Guide* II.37; trans. Pines, p. 374.

11 *Guide* II.36; trans. Pines, pp. 369–370.

12 *Guide* II.40; trans. Pines, p. 382.

13 *Guide* III.54. See Alexander Altmann, "Maimonides's 'Four Perfections'", in idem, *Essays in Jewish Intellectual History* (Hanover: University Press of New England, and London: Brandeis University Press, 1981), pp. 65–76.

The question now naturally arises: What determines one's constitution or temperament? Why are some individuals fortunate to have a much better constitution than most others? Why at a given moment at a given place an individual like Moses is born, whereas most newborns are not capable of becoming even philosophers? Here Maimonides is extremely brief, indeed evasive. All he has to say is that a perfect constitution is a "*divine gift*": "If it so happens (*idhā ittafaqa*) that the matter of a man is excellent, and suitable, neither dominating him nor corrupting his constitution", Maimonides writes, then "that matter is a divine gift" (*mawhiba ilāhīya*).[14] A case in point seems to be King Solomon, of whose wisdom Maimonides writes that it was a "divine power" (*quwwa ilāhīya*).[15] In the *Book of Knowledge* Maimonides expresses much the same idea when he affirms that the human intellect "comes from God and has its origin in the heavens".[16]

In the following remarks I wish to point out in what respect Maimonides' position was singular. The idea that intellectual capacities depend on the bodily constitution, it will be seen, was scientifically grounded in a number of entrenched theories that were shared by contemporary *falāsifa*. But whereas someone like al-Fārābī combined these theories into a climatological explanation of the distribution of intellectual excellence among men, Maimonides rejected this naturalistic and determinist account.[17]

* * *

The first pillar of the theories linking one's intellectual potential with his bodily constitution comes from Aristotle.[18] Through a cluster of very elaborate theories the Stagirite establishes that the *scala naturae* of species, and of individuals within a species, depends on their vital heat. According to Aristotle, an individual's innate vital heat, and hence his intellectual and psychological potential, depends first and foremost on the vital heat of the male parent. Aristotle's embryology posits that the male semen is food that had been concocted by the vital heat and thereby *informed*. The embryo is formed when the male's *form*

14 *Guide* III.8; trans. Pines, p. 433.

15 Isaac Shailat [= Yiṣḥāq Shilat], *Haqdamot ha-Rambam la-Mishnah* (Jerusalem: Maaliyyot, 1992), p. 352.

16 "Hilkhot yesodey ha-Torah" 4.9.

17 A fuller treatment of the questions discussed here can be found in Gad Freudenthal, "Maïmonide: La détermination, partielle, biologique et climatologique (mais non pas astrale) de la félicité humaine", in Tony Lévy and Roshdi Rashed (Eds.), *Maïmonide: savant, philosophe* (Louvain: Peeters, 2004), pp. 494–544, and idem, "Biological Foundations of Intellectual Elitism: Maimonides vs. al-Fārābī", in Arthur Hyman (Ed.), *Maimonidean Studies*, vol. 5 (New York: Yeshiva University Press, 2005) (in press).

18 For what follows see Gad Freudenthal, *Aristotle's Theory of Material Substance* (Oxford: Clarendon Press, 1995), and the references there.

carried by the semen acts on and informs the material supplied by the female, viz. the menstrual blood (itself also concocted food). The semen concocts this blood by its formative vital heat, thereby informing it into an embryo having the male parent's form. In the ideal case, this form is transmitted without loss, and the offspring will resemble the father, in particular in being a male. But if the male's vital heat fails to master the female material completely, then the form is transmitted inadequately or not at all, and "monstrosities" result. Here the impact of the environment is crucial. A cold bath, for instance, may be enough to refrigerate the semen with the unfortunate result being, e.g., a female. Thus, differences of the vital heat of the semen produce differences of the resulting souls and their capacities.

The upshot is clear enough: an individual's vital heat, and with it all his psychological capacities, including intelligence, essentially depend on the innate vital heat he or she has received through the father's semen. So far the theory of vital heat.

Another Greek theory relevant to our concerns is the medical theory of the body's four humours, which defined health of both body and soul as a state in which an individual's *temperament*, or *complexion*, is balanced.[19] If one of the humours predominates, then the body is ill, and often the soul, too, is so as a result. For instance, a predominant black bile produces melancholy. More generally, the noetic capacities of an individual whose organism is not in a state of equilibrium will be impaired. This is one of the many propositions of the generally accepted Doctrine of the Mean.[20]

Galen systematized the medical doctrine, including its part relating the temperament to psychical qualities. I cannot do here more than merely mention two of his treatises bearing on our topic, both of which were very widely diffused in Arabic. One is entitled "That the Powers of the Soul Follow Upon the Temperament [or: Complexion] of the Body" (*Fī anna quwā an-nafs tābiʿa li-mizāǧ al-badan*): its title very well captures the entire doctrine expounded therein, and Maimonides quotes it with approval.[21] Another treatise by Galen, entitled *Peri Ethon* (*Kitāb al-akhlāq*), elaborates the idea that a man is born with a given

19 See e.g. Georg Wöhrle, *Studien zur Theorie der antiken Gesundheitslehre* (Hermes Einzelschriften 36; Stuttgart: Franz Steiner Verlag, 1990); Rudolph E. Siegel, *Galen on Psychology, Psychopathology, and Function and Diseases of the Nervous System* (Galen's System of Physiology and Medicine 3; Basel, New York: S. Karger, 1973), especially pp. 173ff.

20 See Theodore J. Tracy, *Physiological Theory and the Doctrine of the Mean in Plato and Aristotle* (The Hague and Paris: Mouton, 1969).

21 Hans Hinrich Biesterfeldt (Ed. and Trans.), *Galens Traktat 'Dass die Kräfte der Seele den Mischungen des Körpers folgen' in arabischer Übersetzung* (Abhandlungen für die Kunde des Morgenlandes 40,4; Mainz: Deutsche Morgenländische Gesellschaft, 1973). See also idem, "Galīnūs *Quwā an-nafs*, zitiert, adaptiert, korrigiert", in *Der Islam* 63 (1986), pp. 119–136.

temperament, which can be modified, albeit only slightly, and which thus remains largely constant throughout one's life.[22]

The biological theory of vital heat and the medical theory of temperament have in common the doctrine that an individual's psychical qualities depend on his biological make-up, namely on the strength of his vital heat and on the equilibrium of his temperament. They also share the doctrine that an impact received from the environment may modify the initial inner state of a living body, thereby altering its cognitive capacities. This proposition provided the theoretical grounds for the widely accepted climatological theory, which offered determinist causal accounts of the dependence of intellectual (and other qualities) of human groups on the environment.

The locus classicus of the climatological theory is the Hippocratic *Airs Waters, and Places*,[23] whose main theses already reverberate in Aristotle's *Politics* (VII,7, 1327b23–33). This Hippocratic treatise was translated into Arabic,[24] in more than one version, and Galen's commentary on it was also available in Arabic.[25] An important discussion is also found in the *Problemata*, a work that goes back to the Aristotelian school, and which was also available in Arabic. All these works have in common that they posit causal relationships between climatological factors and anthropological traits, and in particular affirm a

---

22 Paul Kraus (Ed.), "Kitāb al-akhlāq l-ǧālīnūs", in *Bulletin of the Faculty of Arts of the University of Egypt* 5(1) (1937), Arabic section, pp. 1–51. English translation: John N. Mattock, "A Translation of the Arabic Epitome of Galen's *Peri Éthon*", in Samuel M. Stern, Albert Hourani and Vivian Brown (Eds.), *Islamic Philosophy and the Classical Tradition: Essays Presented by His Friends and Pupils to Richard Walzer on His Seventieth Birthday* (Oxford: Cassirer, 1972), pp. 235–260. See also Richard Walzer, "New Light on Galen's Moral Philosophy", in idem, *Greek into Arabic* (Oxford: Cassirer, 1962), pp. 142–163.

23 For an excellent introduction see Jacques Jouanna, *Hippocrates*, trans. M. B. DeBevoise (Baltimore and London: Johns Hopkins University Press, 1999), especially pp. 210–232.

24 See *On Endemic Diseases (Airs, Waters and Places)*, edited and translated with Introduction, Notes and Glossary by John N. Mattock and Malcolm C. Lyons (Cambridge: Heffer, 1969), pp. xxxv–xxxviii.

25 Gotthard Strohmaier, "La question de l'influence du climat dans la pensée arabe et le nouveau commentaire de Galien sur le traité hippocratique des *Airs, eaux et lieux*", in Ahmad Hasnawi, Abdelali Elamarni-Jamal and Maroun Aouad (Eds.), *Perspectives arabes et médiévales sur la tradition scientifique et philosophique grecque* (Actes du colloque de la SIHSPAI [Société internationale d'histoire des sciences et de la philosophie arabes et islamiques], Paris, 31 mars–3 avril 1993) (Louvain, Paris: Peeters, 1997), pp. 209–216. One looks forward to the edition of the text promised by Professor Strohmaier. An epitome was published in Hebrew translation: *Galen's Commentary on the Hippocratic Treatise "Airs, Waters, Places": In the Hebrew Translation of Solomon ha-Me'ati*. Edited with introduction, English translation and notes by Abraham Wasserstein (Proceedings of the Israel Academy of Sciences and Humanities 6[3]; Jerusalem: Israel Academy of Sciences and Humanities, 1982).

causal dependence of intellectual qualities on the climate. To give only one example: according to the *Problemata*, the inhabitants of hot regions have a cold constitution, which induces them to study, but most intelligent of all are the inhabitants of the temperate climates.[26]

It is easy to see that this theory accounts causally for the intellectual capacities of individuals and human groups. Drawing on it and on the other theories mentioned, al-Fārābī in the tenth century indeed offers us a deterministic account of the different intellectual capacities of what he calls *umam* and of individuals, differences, he explicitly says, that condition their possibility to attain "the most noble thing", viz. intellectual perfection. Fārābī developed his views on the question mainly in his work variously known under the titles *al-Siyāsa al-madanīya*, i.e. the "Political Regime", or *Kitāb mabādi' al-maujūdāt*, i.e. the "Principles of Existing Things".[27] I will use it as a back-drop against which to assess Maimonides' views.

Like Maimonides, Fārābī takes for granted the assumption that the inborn physical constitution of an individual conditions his intellectual capacities: a person born with a well-balanced temperament will be able to excel in intellectual achievement, while one born with an imbalanced temperament will not be able to, whatever his efforts. Like Maimonides he holds that some people, "owing to their nature (*bi-l-ṭabī'a*)" are not capable to avail themselves even of the first intelligibles. Intellectual excellence and, therefore, felicity (*sa'āda*), can be attained only by those whose constitution (*fiṭratuhum al-insānīya*) is perfect (*salīma*).[28] The problem of accounting for intellectual diversity among men is thus a problem in biology.

All biological differences among men, Fārābī argues, ultimately go back to differences between the zones of the sky situated at their respective zeniths. Fārābī, who opposed astrology, emphasizes that although the celestial bodies are all of the fifth substance and hence have no qualities, they are yet capable

26 F. S. Filius (Ed. and Trans.), *The Problemata physica attributed to Aristotle* (Leiden: Brill, 1999), pp. 640–643.

27 Fauzi M. Najjar (Ed.), *Al-Fārābī's "The Political Regime" (Al-Siyāsa al-Madanīya, Also Known as The Treatise On the Principles of Beings)* (Arabic) (Beirut: Imprimerie Catholique, 1964). This work has been translated into Hebrew by Samuel Ibn Tibbon under the title *Hatḥalot ha-nimṣa'im*. Samuel Ibn Tibbon's Hebrew translation was edited on the basis of two manuscripts by Zvi Filipowsky in the almanach *Sefer ha-asif* for the year 5609 (Leipzig: K. F. Köhler, 1849), pp. 1–64. The treatise has also been translated into German and modern Hebrew: *Die Staatsleitung von Alfārābī.* Deutsche Bearbeitung ... aus dem Nachlasse des Dr. F. Dieterici herausgegeben ... von Dr. Paul Brönnle (Leiden: Brill, 1904); Shukri B. Abed (Trans.), Abū Nasr Muhammad Alfārābī, *The Political Regime* (*also known as The Treatise on the Principles of Beings*) (Hebrew) (Tel Aviv: University Publishing Projects, 1992). (This translation indicates the page numbers of the Arabic edition.)

28 *Al-Siyāsa* (see above n. 27): ed. Najjar, 74,16–75,3; Hebrew: Filipowsky, pp. 36–37.

of producing contrary qualities in the sublunar world.[29] Fārābī reasons as follows. The celestial realm is to some extent heterogeneous, e.g. in the distribution of the stars in the eighth sphere, in the inclinations and motions of the planets, etc. This heterogeneity up there produces a heterogeneity of the parts of the earth below: for example, one region is hot and arid, another cold and humid. As a result, the exhalations produced at different places are different too. Differences between the exhalations, in their turn, bring about differences in the air and the water at these places. These differences of the water and the air naturally produce differences in the fauna and the flora. Consequently, people who dwell at different places are nourished by different kinds of food. The differences in nourishment in turn have crucial effects on man: they produce differences of the semen and the menstrual blood, which according to the prevailing (Aristotelian) embryology result from the nutrition through concoction and which provide the embryo with its form and matter, respectively.[30] The differences of the semen and the menses going into individuals are, Fārābī concludes, the formal and material causes of the differences in intellectual excellence.

Fārābī has thus shown that the diversity of individuals and of *umam*, both on the physical and on the psychical and cognitive levels, goes back to the heterogeneity of the heavenly realm. Through a necessary causal chain, the structure of a given supralunar region has been shown to determine the temperaments of animal and human bodies and thus determine the capacity of individuals to receive influences reaching them from the active intellect. The bottom line is that *the place of residence determines whether an individual or a community can reach intellectual perfection.* To be sure, an excellent inborn potentiality is a necessary, but not a sufficient condition for attaining felicity: Fārābī emphasizes that each individual also has to make use of his freedom of choice and conduct his life appropriately in order to attain this intellectual excellence effectively.[31] Yet, although the innate potential can be modified, e.g. by exercise, intake of substances, etc., still the basic intellectual capacity is pre-determined and can be modified only within a narrow latitude.

* * *

Against the backdrop of Fārābī's deterministic theory, consider now the views of Maimonides. Let me first recall that Maimonides held Fārābī in great esteem

29 *Al-Siyāsa* (see above n. 27): ed. Najjar, 55,13–56,12; Hebrew: Filipowsky, p. 21.

30 See e.g. Freudenthal, *Aristotle's Theory of Material Substance* (see above n. 18), pp. 22–26 and the references there. Like his contemporaries, Fārābī subscribes to this theory; see e.g. Richard Walzer (Ed. and Trans.), *Al-Farabi on the Perfect State. Abū Nasr al-Fārābī's Mabādi' ārā' ahl al-madīna al-faḍila* (Oxford: Oxford University Press, 1985), pp. 188–193.

31 *Al-Siyāsa* (see above n. 27): ed. Najjar, 72,9–14; Hebrew: Filipowsky, pp. 34–35.

and explicitly recommended his treatise *Mabādi' al-maujūdāt*.[32] Maimonides also shared most of Fārābī's theoretical premises: he was familiar with, and endorsed Hippocrates' *Airs, Waters, Places*,[33] and he in different contexts drew on the climatological theory.[34] He also shared the Galenic idea "that the faculties of the soul follow upon the [physiological] temperament",[35] a title he explicitly quotes in the *Guide*. We should thus expect Maimonides to endorse also the consequences which Fārābī had derived from the conjunction of these elements and to subscribe to his naturalistic theory of the distribution of intellectual excellence.

Maimonides, as we have seen, indeed concurs with Fārābī that an individual is born with given, innate, physical *cum* intellectual capacities. By contrast, he opposes the idea that intellectual excellence is related to geographic location. Contrary to Juda ha-Levi, for example, Maimonides famously did not think that the people of Israel was given prophecy because it dwelt at a specific place, nor that prophecy ceased because it lived far away from the Holy Land. Maimonides rather held that prophecy in Israel ceased after the destruction of the Temple owing to the Israelites' melancholy in exile, which unfavourably influences the psychical faculties required for prophecy.[36] This is an altogether psychological explanation, which denies at its basis the very idea of a climatological account.

Maimonides rejected this account: he did so because it was an integral part of Fārābī's necessitarian philosophy of nature, which sought to show how the entire world emanates with necessity from the First Cause, with the consequence that it was eternal.[37] Maimonides wanted to disprove this view and

32 Cf. Maimonides' letter to Samuel Ibn Tibbon, in *Letters and Essays of Moses Maimonides: A Critical Edition of the Hebrew and Arabic Letters*. Translated and annotated with introduction and cross-references by Isaac Shailat (Hebrew) (2 volumes; Ma'aleh Adumim, Israel: Maaliyot Press of Yeshivat Birkat Moshe, 5747–5748 [1987–1988]), vol. 2, p. 553. Indeed, some passages of the *Guide* can readily be identified as carrying its mark; see Freudenthal, "Four Implicit Quotations of Philosophical Sources in Maimonides' *Guide of the Perplexed*" (see above n. 3).

33 Cf. Joseph Schacht and Max Meyerhof, "Maimonides Against Galen, on Philosophy and Cosmogony", in *Bulletin of the Faculty of Arts of the University of Egypt* 5(1) (1937), pp. 53–88, on p. 59, as well as Maimonides, *Commentary on Hippocrates' "Aphorisms"*, 23,15; Hebrew translation in Maimonides, *Ketavim Refu'iyim*, ed. Suessman Muntner (4 volumes; Jerusalem: Mosad Harav Kook, 1961ff.), vol. 2, p. 281.

34 For details see my paper "Maïmonide: La détermination" (see above n. 17).

35 See *Guide* III.12 (ed. and trans. Kafaḥ [see above n. 1], vol. 3, p. 484 [Arabic text]) and Pines' translation, p. 445: "[…] it having already been said that the moral qualities of the soul are consequent upon the temperament of the body". Maimonides' Arabic wording reads: *anna akhlāq an-nafs tābi'a li-mizāğ al-badan*; the Arabic title of Galen's treatise (see above p. 141): *fī anna quwā an-nafs tābi'a li-mizāğ al-badan*.

36 *Guide* II.36.

37 The view one takes on the issue we now touch upon directly depends on one's global interpretation of Maimonides as an exoteric or esoteric thinker. My account here assumes the view of Maimonides forcefully argued in Herbert A. Davidson, *Moses Mai-*

drew on arguments from particularization to show that the world cannot have resulted from natural necessity. Maimonides' rejection of Fārābī's account of the distribution of intellectual excellence on earth is thus part and parcel of his denial of the necessitarian philosophy of nature.

Maimonides offered an original alternative to the necessitarian philosophy of nature, namely a non-determinist natural philosophy. I here follow the remarkable suggestion by the late Amos Funkenstein, who identified in Maimonides' philosophy of nature a "principle of indeterminacy": the essential element in Maimonides' natural philosophy, Funkenstein argued, is the construal that there is "an objective indeterminacy *within nature itself*".[38] This means that natural necessity does not determine nature down to the last detail, but rather leaves open a range of possibilities that depend upon chance. This view of nature has momentous theological consequences. "The principle of indeterminacy", Funkenstein wrote, "allowed [Maimonides] [...] to introduce most miracles – or more generally, instances of special providence – without violating laws of nature".[39]

Elsewhere I seek to corroborate and complement Funkenstein's insight by pointing out another indeterminist element in Maimonides' natural philosophy.[40] It is implied, I argue, by Maimonides' original four-globe cosmology presented in the *Guide* II.9–10. To summarize very briefly: Maimonides posits four globes, each of which exerts its influence on a single element: the globe carrying the sun exerts its influence on the element fire, the globe carrying the moon exerts its influence on the element water, and the globe carrying all the fixed star exerts its influence on the element earth. The remaining element, air, is moved by a globe which groups together the spheres of five planets (which Maimonides supposes to be all situated above the sun). With respect to the motion produced by this globe Maimonides writes: "it is because of the multiplicity of the motions of these planets – their differences, their retrogressions, their direct progressions, and their stations – that the shapes of the air, its

monides: The Man and His Works (New York: Oxford University Press, 2005). A similar position is held by Eliezer Schweid in his *Ha-filosofim ha-gedolim shelanu: Ha-filosofia ha-yehudit bi-yemey ha-beynayim* (Tel Aviv: Yedioth Aharonoth/Sifrey Hemed, 1999).

38 Amos Funkenstein, "Maimonides: Political Theory and Realistic Messianism", in *Miscellanea Mediaevalia* 11 (1977), pp. 81–103; reprinted in idem, *Perceptions of Jewish History* (Berkeley: University of California Press, 1993), pp. 131–155, on pp. 89, 140, respectively.

39 Ibid., pp. 90, 141, respectively. See Alfred Ivry, "Neoplatonic Currents in Maimonides' Thought", in Joel L. Kraemer (Ed.), *Perspectives on Maimonides: Philosophical and Historical Studies* (Oxford: Oxford University Press, 1991), pp. 115–140, especially pp. 119, 121, 127 for the suggestion that this aspect of Maimonides' philosophy of nature goes back to Plotinian sources.

40 Gad Freudenthal, "Maimonides' Four Globes (*Guide* 2:9–10): Sources and Purposes" (Hebrew), forthcoming in a volume to be edited by Aviezer Ravitzky (Jerusalem: Merkaz Zalman Shazar, 2005).

differences, and its rapid contractions and expansions are multiple."[41] I take this to imply that in Maimonides' view the (apparent) irregular motions of the planets produce the irregular motions of the air. This is a strong anti-determinist move: the very variables that Fārābī took to participate in producing the *determinate* natural order on earth are taken by Maimonides to globally produce mere haphazard movements of the element air. Now according to medieval biology, the air inhaled by man is of great importance for his physical constitution and, especially, for his mental capabilities at each moment.[42] Consequently, the motions of the air have momentous consequences for man's intellectual capacities. It follows that the astral indeterminism, in bringing about irregular motions of the air, produces an indeterminacy of the psychical and intellectual functioning of man. The stochastic environment in which man dwells rules out a deterministic theory of mental functioning *à la* Fārābī. In a word: through his four-globe cosmology, *Maimonides replaces Fārābī's astral determinism with an astral indeterminism.*

This indeterminist philosophy of nature, I submit, is the context in which we have to place Maimonides' answer to the question what determines the different inborn dispositions of individuals. We have noted that Maimonides writes that an excellent constitution "is a divine gift" (*mawhiba ilāhīya*). Now the notion of "divine gift" goes back at least to Plato and Aristotle.[43] In the *Meno*, Socrates states that virtue is acquired neither by nature nor by teaching, but "whoever has it gets it by divine dispensation".[44] Aristotle, in the *Nicomachean Ethics*,[45] asks whether happiness is acquired through our own doing or "comes by some divine dispensation (θεῖα μοῖρα)" and is "a gift of the gods (θεῖον δώρημα) to mankind", expressions translated into Arabic as *ḥaẓẓ min Allāh* and *mawhiba min Allāh*.[46] Aristotle opts for the view that happiness "comes through some process of learning or training", but inasmuch as he considers utmost happiness to be the activity of the intellect which is "the divinest of the things in us" and that happiness is "most divine", he at least points into the direction of

---

41 *Guide* II.10; trans. Pines, p. 270. This topos was common in medieval natural philosophy; see my "Maïmonide: La détermination" (see above n. 17).

42 See, e.g., Maimonides, *Hanhagat ha-Beri'ut*, § 4,1: ed. Muntner, *Ketavim Refu'iyyim* (see above n. 33), vol. 1, pp. 65–66 and the sources indicated in my "Maïmonide: La détermination" (see above n. 17). See also Gerrit Bos, "Maimonides on the Preservation of Health", in *Journal of the Royal Asian Society*, series 3, 4(2) (1994), pp. 213–235, especially p. 225.

43 The following references I owe to the erudition and helpfulness of my colleague Ahmed Hasnaoui, to whom I am much indebted.

44 *Meno* 99e (trans. William Keith Chambers Guthrie [Harmondsworth: Penguin, 1956]).

45 For what follows see *Nicomachean Ethics* I,9, 1099b10ff.; X,7, 1177a13ff. I used the translation in Christoph Rowe and Sarah Broadie, *Aristotle, Nicomachean Ethics* (Oxford: Oxford University Press, 2002), with the commentary on pp. 282, 441.

46 The Arabic is in Aristotle, *al-Akhlāq*, ed. ʿAbd ar-Raḥmān Badawī (Al-Kuwait: Wakālat al-Maṭbūʿāt, 1979), p. 73.

the idea that intelligence itself and its activity are both a divine gift. Averroes, in his Middle Commentary on the *Nicomachean Ethics*, repeats the same account.[47] It thus seems that Maimonides borrowed the notion of "divine gift" from Aristotle, presumably indirectly, although he attributes to it a very different meaning: Aristotle had in mind the origin of human happiness and intelligence *as such*, whereas for Maimonides the "divine gift" is an excellent bodily constitution, and hence superior intelligence, bestowed upon specific *individuals*. We thus have a terminological continuity but an ideational discontinuity and we should ask how Maimonides construed the notion of "divine gift" within the framework of his own philosophy.

Taking our clue from Funkenstein's explication of Maimonides' natural philosophy, the "divine gift" of a perfect bodily constitution in an individual appears as yet another exemplification of the deity's intervention in nature: it follows from God's sovereign will, the same will that operated also creation, the "particularization" of certain celestial phenomena, and miracles. The "divine gift" is a fact of nature following not from natural necessity, but rather from divine "particularization".

[Students of Maimonides who see in the *Guide* an esoteric text whose author hid (among other things) his belief in the eternity of the world will of course reject this interpretation. They may interpret the notion of "divine gift" as alluding to the fact that an embryo results from the necessary natural action of the body's "formative forces" (a notion taken over from Galen), which Maimonides identifies with the angels, who act by God's order. "All this – including [...] even the creation of limbs of animals as they are – has been brought about through the intermediation of angels. For all forces are angels", Maimonides writes.[48] This holds specifically of the "formative force shaping the limbs and giving them their configuration" that the deity has placed in the sperm via the active intellect.[49] Seeing that the constitutions or temperaments of living beings thus all ultimately go back to God (and are thus "divine"), interpreters holding that Maimonides denied divine intervention in the order of nature may construe the expression "divine gift" as merely signaling that a particularly good bodily constitution is a "gift" in the sense that it is both rare and invaluable.]

Maimonides, let me note in conclusion, seems to have thought of himself as someone who benefited from the "divine gift". In his letter to R. Jonathan ha-Kohen of Lunel he writes in 1199 that even before he was formed in the womb, the Torah had already chosen him and sanctified him to her study and

---

47 Laurence V. Berman (Ed.), *Averroes' Middle Commentary on Aristotle's* Nicomachean Ethics, *in the Hebrew Version of Samuel ben Judah* (Hebrew) (Jerusalem: The Israel Academy of Sciences and Humanities, 1999), p. 80, ll. 472–473; p. 337, ll. 393–399.

48 *Guide* II.6; trans. Pines, p. 263.

49 *Guide* II.6; trans. Pines, pp. 263–264.

teaching.[50] Maimonides ably plays on similes and language drawn from Jeremiah 1:5 to suggest that like the prophet he was given talents and obligations independent of his free choice.[51]

The theological consequences of Maimonides' stance are far-reaching. The apprehension of intelligibles is the highest good humans can attain, and it may even afford the immortality of one's soul. The statement that a good constitution is a divine gift thus means that it is by divine will that humans are unequal both in this world and in the world to come.

50 Maimonides, *Letters and Essays*: ed. Shailat (see above n. 32), vol. 2, p. 502.

51 I leave it to others to decide whether Maimonides also believed that he had in fact attained prophecy. See Abraham Joshua Heschel, "Did Maimonides Believe that he Had Attained Prophecy?" (Hebrew), in *Louis Ginzberg Jubilee Volume* (New York: The American Academy for Jewish Research, 1945), Hebrew Section, pp. 159–188.

Skeptical Motifs Linking Together Maimonides' *Guide* and his *Mishneh Torah*

by

Aryeh Botwinick
Temple University, Philadelphia

I shall be addressing a central question that has consistently tantalized and vexed students of Maimonides over the past eight centuries: namely, how can the major theorist of the literal unapproachability of God in his *Guide of the Perplexed* become so labyrinthine and explicit in his codification of Jewish law in his *Code* (*Mishneh Torah*)? This problem is on the same order of magnitude as that classified by German scholars as "The Problem of the two Adam Smiths" – the Adam Smith of *The Wealth of Nations* and the Adam Smith of *The Theory of the Moral Sentiments* – and the long-standing problem confronted by readers and scholars of Plato, of how to reconcile the Plato of *The Laws* with the Plato of *The Republic*. From a number of different but interrelated perspectives, I shall attempt to theorize the unity of content and logical and presuppositional structure that links together Maimonides' *Code* with his *Guide*.

What needs to frame our discussion as we begin our analysis of the relationship of the *Guide* to the *Code* is an awareness of how paradoxical an entity the Maimonidean negative theological God is. The utter conceptual removal of the monotheistic God, which renders Him totally unlike anything human, requires some kind of grammatical subject concerning whom the continual divestiture of predicates can take place. The closest categorical analogue to monotheism in the Western stock of ideas – the one whose logical behavioral properties bears the closest resemblance to it – is skepticism. In order to emerge as properly consistent, skeptical doctrine must encompass a reflexive maneuver whereby skeptical critical canons are turned against the tenets of skepticism themselves – forcing them into a movement of recoil and thereby inhibiting their adequate formulation. Skepticism is a doctrine of radical critique that both presupposes and denies a stable subject (in a grammatical sense): tenets of skepticism. By the same token, monotheism is also a doctrine of radical critique that simultaneously presupposes and denies a stable grammatical subject, namely, God. Although Maimonides says that none of the traditional theological terms apply literally to God – God does not see, hear, or even exist in the way that traditional religious understanding projects – Maimonides nonetheless wants all of his negative criticisms to apply to God: The subject of all of his negative, paring-down work is the traditional (mono-) theistic God. In order for Maimonides' critical apparatus to have a viable target, he needs precisely to maintain in some form, to some extent, whatever it is that his apparatus shoots down. In bold outline, comparable paradoxes of self-referentialism seem to render incoherent both the notions of skepticism and of God. The holistic thrust of both doctrines (even though their overt contents ostensibly contradict each other) puts us theoretically out of commission. We are not able to proceed further in accordance with the protocols of the traditional Aristotelian logic which enshrine the law of non-contradiction and the law of the excluded middle.

If what I am saying makes sense to any degree, then we have an immediate basis for transition between the *Guide* and the *Code*. Jewish theology in its attempt to vindicate God's existence issues forth in a string of irresolvabilities – and its province then gets taken over by Jewish law. A god that we cannot theoretically engage devolves upon a set of legalistically-delimited behavioral patterns and practices that become the experientially-registered functional equivalents of the conceptually non-negotiable God. Of course, the theoretical sequence that I am painting is exactly the opposite of the biographical sequence – where the *Mishneh Torah* (1180) precedes the *Moreh Nevukhim* (1190) by ten years. Nonetheless, the theoretical line of development that I am sketching might still offer us a valuable hermeneutic gloss for plotting the biographical sequence.

At the beginning of the *Code* – in Chapter Four, *halakha* Thirteen, of his "Laws Concerning the Basic Principles of the Torah" – Maimonides self-consciously situates the *Code* as a stepping-stone – a facilitator – for entry into the more broadly metaphysical and speculative domains delineated in the *Guide*:

> And I say that it is not proper to dally in Pardes [the highest reaches of metaphysical and cosmological speculation] till one has first filled oneself with bread and meat; by which I mean knowledge of what is permitted and what forbidden, and similar distinctions in other classes of precepts. Although these last subjects were called by the sages "a small thing" – when they say "A great thing, Maaseh Merkabah [metaphysics]; a small thing, the discussions of Abaye and Rava" – still they should have the precedence. For the knowledge of these things gives primarily composure to the mind. Moreover, they are the precious boon bestowed by God to promote social well-being on earth, and enable men to obtain bliss in *'olam habah* [the life hereafter]. Moreover, the knowledge of them is within the reach of all, young and old, men and women; those gifted with great intellectual capacity as well as those whose intelligence is limited.[1]

1 Moses Maimonides, *Mishneh Torah. Volume 1: The Book of Knowledge.* Edited and translated by Moses Hyamson (Jerusalem: Feldheim, 1974), pp. 39b–40a (with some minor emendations on my part).

We can imagine Maimonides in drawing up his *Code* as being as much riveted by philosophical concerns as he is by more intermediate Halakhic issues. The first volume in the *Code,* after all, is the "Sefer Hamada", which addresses dense metaphysical and theological issues such as the nature of God and human free-will of the sort addressed in the *Guide* – and, moreover, adopts positions on them that are in many ways strictly continuous with those defended in the *Guide.* It is within this metaphysical framework that the more narrow Halakhic investigations and formulations proceed. In writing the *Code,* Maimonides is testing limits (the limits of the legally rationally resolvable and statable given the initial limits imposed by the monotheistic conception of God) – as much as he is exploring what lies between the legal limits that he discerns. In the *Guide* ten years later, Maimonides is still probing limits – is still mesmerized by the prospect of going beyond the limits that he had implicitly delineated ten years earlier. The upshot of his huge thought experiment carried out in the *Guide* is that the earlier limits cannot be pierced or transgressed – but in the *Guide* the validation of those limits comes more systematically from the other side, from a deliberately studied and fashioned attempt in a work of philosophical exploration to move beyond them.

In part of the story that I have to tell, I will try to highlight how the very skeptical factors that make God conceptually impenetrable by us also confer elements of irredeemable opacity upon the legalistic texts that become the surrogates for Divine connection. The words that we employ are as defiantly transcendent in their reach as the concept of God Himself. The underdetermination of human words by human things microcosmically recapitulates the everlasting aloofness of God from the universe from which and for which we invoke Him. In the end, the pathos of the fully-worked out and systematized legal system approximates to the pathos that is attached to the fully-elaborated theological system. When we translate both into the cases and dramas of practical affairs and everyday life, it is almost as if we start from scratch in achieving the orientation and directedness that motivated the construction of these vast intellectual edifices of law and theology in the first place.

It is important to note that in Aggadah (in its homiletic portions) and in Halakhah (its more strictly legal portions) the Talmud implicitly embraces the full-scale consequences of a negative theological reading of God. The location of the believer vis-à-vis such a God is beautifully captured by the Talmudic dictum that "Everything is in the hands of Heaven except the fear of God."[2] Everything falls under the jurisdiction of the monotheistic God except the holding of Him in awe as the Creator of heaven and earth. Whatever occurs in the world comes under the tutelage of the monotheistic God – except the affirmation of His role as God. In order for the interrelated system of beliefs and practices that go to constitute Judaism to work, there is one background

---

2 Babylonian Talmud, *Berakhot* 33b; *Megillah* 25a; *Niddah* 16b.

premise that must be put in place – namely, an acknowledgment of God as Creator and Ruler of the universe. Given the irredeemably metaphoric nature of all of our descriptions of God, it is only our acquiescence in the centrality and significance of the symbol of God that sets the system in motion. Any imputation of action or initiative to Him is just another metaphor whose "cash value" is being deferred. The only "hard currency" for which the invocation of God can finally be exchanged is human consent in the establishment of the God symbol. Maimonides thus has a very striking Rabbinic pedigree as well as an Islamic and Greek one for the tenets of negative theology.

There is a Talmudic precursor for Maimonides' negative theological understanding of God which harbors the implication that *miṣvot* conjoin local rationality with global arbitrariness. In the Babylonian Talmudic tractate of *Horayot* 3b, we find the following *mishnah*:

> If the court ruled that an entire principle was to be uprooted; if they said, for example, that [the law concerning the] menstruant is not found in the Torah or the [law concerning the] sabbath is not found in the Torah or [the law concerning] idolatry is not found in the Torah, they are exempt. If, however, they ruled that a part [of a commandment] was to be annulled and a part retained, they are liable.[3]

Maimonides in summarizing the ruling of this *mishnah* in his "Laws Concerning Offerings for Transgressions Committed Through Error", straightforwardly follows the line of interpretation pursued in the Talmudic discussion of the *mishnah*. The "uprooting of an entire principle" has to do with forgetting a Biblical verse whose import is so clear and unequivocal that even the Sadducees who were gross literalists converge with the Pharisees in acknowledging its force. The court is liable only in a case where they forget an interpretation that the Sadducees dispute.[4] What is at stake in the *mishnah* is the scope of the law pertaining to the *par helem davar shel ṣibbur* – the bull sacrifice that a court has to bring when it inadvertently misleads its litigants concerning the content of Jewish law.[5] So the Mishnah in *Horayot* as interpreted in the Talmud and as codified by Maimonides[6] emphasizes that the court is only culpable and needs to bring the bull sacrifice when it strayed with regard to a law that the Rabbis deduce from a Biblical verse whose meaning is ambiguous and therefore susceptible to a variety of different interpretations. But where the meaning appears so transparent that even the Sadducees concur in it, then the court's action seems more like a matter of willful forgetting and is therefore in the

3 *Hebrew-English edition of the Babylonian Talmud: Tractates Abodah Zarah, Horayoth, Eduyyoth, Aboth*, trans. Israel W. Slotki (London: The Soncino Press, 1988).

4 Babylonian Talmud, *Horayot* 4a.

5 Leviticus 4:13–21.

6 Maimonides, *Code*, The Book of Offerings, "Laws Concerning Offerings for Transgressions Committed through Error", Chapter 14, Paragraphs 1 and 2.

words of Rashi (which Maimonides approximates to on his own) *karov l'mazid*[7] – close to an intentional transgression. In such a case, members of the court are debarred from bringing the sacrifice prescribed in the Book of Leviticus, but the individual Jews who transgressed Jewish law in accordance with the erroneous ruling handed down by the court need to bring sacrifices in order to achieve atonement.

The depth analytical distinction in this Halakhic formulation seems to be between a framework rule that is constitutive of a set of practices and a substantive rule that comes within the purview of a particular framework or set of practices.[8] Since it is not self-evident where frameworks end and substantive rules begin (this whole categorial dichotomy is ambiguous and open-ended), the Talmud followed by Maimonides seeks to register the difference between the two categories in terms of the literalness and explicitness of the Torah's language with regard to particular areas of Jewish law. Where the Torah's language is "unmistakable", the sentence in question is regarded as constitutive of (establishing a framework for) a particular area of Jewish law. For example, the verse in Exodus 16:29 when read without vowels and vocalization can be translated as "A person should not carry out from his place on the seventh day." Carrying as exemplifying prohibited labor is therefore constitutive of the halakhic category of the Sabbath. The various categories and subcategories of labor that are prohibited on the Sabbath that are often derived by the rabbis through traditional patterns of inference from the Biblical text would be consigned to the category of substantive rules. Similarly with regard to idol-worship the verse in Exodus 34:14 says "thou shalt prostrate thyself to no other god." The normal connotation of "prostrating" is spreading out one's arms and legs – in other words, a gesture suggesting total subordination to a strange god. This verse can be taken as enunciating a framework rule in relation to idolatry. By contrast, the prohibition of merely kneeling before an idol without prostrating oneself would be consigned to the category of substantive rule pertaining to the laws of idolatry.

There is something deeply anomalous about the category of *karov l'mazid* ("close to an intentional act") which according to both Rashi and Maimonides accounts for why an erring court is not culpable (by human hands, even though it is vulnerable from a Divine perspective) if it strays with regard to a framework rule. Not being conversant with a textually-based framework rule cannot easily be subsumed under the category of "inadvertence" nor is it intentional in the full-fledged sense. The upshot of the court's "ignorance" is that they are left off the hook – and the "buck" of culpability is passed to the individual transgressors who acted in accordance with the court's ruling.

7 Rashi, *Horayot* 4a.

8 John Rawls, "Two Concepts of Rules", in idem, *Collected Papers*, ed. Samuel Freeman (Cambridge, Mass.: Harvard University Press, 1999), pp. 20–46.

The category of *karov l'mazid* seems to be one of numerous legal fictional categories in Halakhah. What it accomplishes is the sleight of hand of making in a legally actionable sense the outcome better for the defendants because what they did was worse than what the average defendants in such a case usually transgress. The average defendants mistakenly overlook a particular substantive law – and the defendants in this case mistakenly overlook a whole halakhic framework under which many substantive laws are included. The Halakhah by subsuming their action under the rubric of a transgression *karov l'mazid* somehow stipulates that by making it worse for themselves they have actually made it better – because now they are exempt from any humanly-imposed atonement, even an animal sacrifice, for a transgression committed in error. What I am trying to unravel in this case is the strange alchemy by which the more stringent (transgression) is transmuted into the less stringent (penalty).

From the perspective of an analytical jurisprudence, "transgression" and "penalty" are correlative terms. If there is no penalty, then in some sense waiting to be defined there is also no transgression. Can we specify what this sense might be with regard to *miṣvot*? What is the relationship between culpability understood from this augmented perspective and justification (the justification or validation of *miṣvot* as Maimonides practices it in the *Guide* and in the *Code*)?

We might say that the structure of justification duplicates or parallels the structure of culpability. Just as a court is only culpable if they show cognizance of the framework rules establishing the Halakhic categories and institutions pertaining to the menstruant woman, the Sabbath, idolatry and so on but are only ignorant concerning particular substantive rules falling under these rubrics (but if they are not aware of the framework rules themselves establishing these Halakhic institutions they are exempt), so too appropriately conceived justifications or rationales for *miṣvot* are internal to prior validation of the frameworks within which those *miṣvot* fall – but do not extend to external justification of the frameworks themselves. Once one accedes to the validity and sanctity of the Sabbath and the prohibition against worshipping idols, then *ta'amei hamiṣvot* (rationales for commandments) can spell out the benefits and utilities that accrue from performing particular *miṣvot* or avoiding particular prohibitions that exemplify the larger principles and categories. But the province of *ta'amei hamiṣvot* ceases if their task is defined as justifying from some external synoptic perspective (from a "view from nowhere") why the abstract category of *miṣvah* needs to be complied with or particular framework rules such as those establishing the Sabbath or idolatry need to be affirmed. Just as the culpability of a court is restricted to cases where it acknowledges the framework rules but shows ignorance of particular substantive rules falling under them, so too justification of *miṣvot* can only proceed relative to the embrace of the theological-Halakhic framework or horizon wherein the particular *miṣvah* in question falls.

In the cases of culpability and justification, a relevant factor for limiting the scope of both seems to be epistemological. Given the negative theological understanding of the nature of the monotheistic God, all the terms that we invoke to refer to Him are consistently metaphoric. The metaphors can have "cash value" in our lives and bind us and render us culpable for transgressions committed under their rubric only if we consent to regard the metaphors as harboring such cash value. On their face, they are only figures of speech. So when a court displays ignorance of one of the substantive laws of the Sabbath such as throwing from one jurisdiction to another but affirms the institution of the Sabbath as exemplified in the laws of carrying from one jurisdiction to another, their affirmation of the institution establishes a basis for culpability. The court has at least implicitly shown acquiescence in the basic category and some of its legal ramifications and can therefore be duly held to account (in the form of having to bring a sacrifice) for neglecting some additional requirement of the law derived by the Rabbis out of the larger category and its supportive texts. But if the court is oblivious of the Halakhic framework or category itself, then there is no basis for reconstructing consent and therefore assigning responsibility and culpability. If the court overlooks a whole category of Judaism, as exemplified by its forgetful jettisoning of an explicit verse in the Torah, we lack a significant trace of their having transformed metaphor into obligation and therefore cannot assign them culpability.

Analogously – with regard to justification – external justification (justification of categories from an external, detached perspective that proposes to illustrate why they should be binding upon us) opens the floodgates to an infinite regress. Unless we voluntarily assume upon ourselves the yoke of religious obligation by entering the Jewish theological system of representations and rules, the search for external justification would only duplicate itself endlessly without providing satisfactory closure, as the metaphors for Divinity piled up without end. Internal justification – justifying a religious framework/category such as the Sabbath in terms of the utilities and satisfactions to be reaped from performing the commandments associated with it; or justifying a particular law within the framework by elaborating upon its relationship to the framework as a whole – seals off a regress by invoking mechanisms of consent implied by one's not questioning the larger framework. My discussion is not meant to suggest that internal justification is skeptically invulnerable. Grounding religious authority in consent might itself be a supreme manifestation of skepticism. But internal justification at least manages to ward off one version of an infinite regress – even though it might be vulnerable on other grounds.

Even beyond the Mishnah and the Talmud, there is a verse in the Psalms that prefigures the idea that both God and His commandments stand in a relationship of unbridgeable distance to the community of Jewish believers. Psalm 119:138 says: *ṣivita ṣedek edotekha, v'emunah me'od* – "You commanded the justice of Your testimonies, and great faithfulness." The justice of Your testimonies is a function of Your command: You decreed that Your testimonies are just. Justice is not something intrinsic to them by virtue of their content.

The same is true for *emunah* – faith. We are believers because You commanded us to be such. We do not follow Your commandments because we are believers. We believe because we follow Your commandment to have faith.

Faith evokes the specter of an infinite regress. Why do we have faith? Because we have faith in the idea of having faith. Why do we have faith in the idea of having faith? Because we have faith in the idea of having faith in the idea of having faith, and so on *ad infinitum*. The infinite regress can only be broken by acknowledging or stipulating that God commands that we have faith. "Commandment", just like faith, also evokes the specter of an infinite regress. In order to answer the question as to why I (for every individual member of a faith community) am obligated to obey a particular commandment, we would need to invoke a commandment to obey a particular commandment – and to legitimate and validate the second commandment to obey the first commandment, we would need to invoke a third commandment to obey the second commandment, and so on *ad infinitum* – so that, in the end, we would be bereft of any basis in commandment to obey any commandment. The upshot of this analysis of the verse in Psalms is that "faith" and "commandment" are both circular categories, parasitically feeding-off each other's circular character. What sets both circles in motion is acquiescence in the idea of God who commands us both to have faith and to conform to His commandments.

In the light of this discussion of Maimonides' Biblical and Rabbinic predecessors, it is not surprising that in "Hilkhot Sanhedrin" (Laws Pertaining to Legal Tribunals) he implicitly embraces the notion of Law as grounded and nurtured in skepticism – rather than certainty. In this section of the *Mishneh Torah,* Chapter 9, Paragraph 1, Maimonides codifies the following law: "If in trying a capital case all the members of the Sanhedrin forthwith vote for conviction, the accused is acquitted. Only when some cast about for arguments in his favor and are outvoted by those who are for conviction is the accused put to death."[9] The commentators on Maimonides' text uniformly trace the source of his codification of the law to the following Talmudic dictum of R. Judah's in the name of Rab: "None is to be given a seat on the Sanhedrin unless he is able to prove the cleanness of a reptile from Biblical texts."[10] The *Midrash Shmuel* – a classic commentary on *Pirkei Avoth* (the Ethics of the Fathers) – cites a teaching of Maimonides which amplifies on the connection between R. Judah in the name of Rab's statement and Maimonides' codification of the law in capital cases:

---

9 *The Code of Maimonides: Book 14: The Book of Judges*, trans. Abraham M. Hershman (New Haven: Yale University Press, 1949), p. 28. See the discussion of this law in Samuel K. Mirsky, *Siyumei H'Mesekhtot B'Mishnah U'V'Talmud Bavli: Sefer Hadranim* [Tractate Endings of the Mishnah and the Babylonian Talmud] (Jerusalem: Sura, 1961), pp. 204–208.

10 *The Babylonian Talmud: Sanhedrin*, translated by Jacob Shachter and Harry Freedman (London: The Soncino Press, 1987), p. 17a.

> The explanation that I heard in the name of Maimonides seems eminently correct. And it is exactly what I myself have written to underscore that when there isn't a group that resists on the basis of questions and counter-arguments in one of its inquiries it is impossible that the matter should come out right. And it is possible that they [the judges] will all fall into error. This is analogous to the reason that is given[11] as to why our holy teacher [R. Judah the prince, the editor of the Mishnah] cites the dissenting opinion alongside the majority view, even though the law is not like the dissenter in relation to the majority.[12]

Maimonides' gloss as to how the processes of judicial decision and legal determination work provides us with a skeptical framework for grasping the content of law. Legal and judicial formulations can be construed from an entirely negative perspective. It is not as if we know with certainty at any level of legal or judicial formulation what the law is or should be. As the Talmud states in *Menahot* with regard to a particular view of the Tanna Rabbi Simeon: "Can we fathom R. Simeon's mind?"[13] From the original discussion of a legal issue in the Babylonian academies as reflected in the pages of the Talmud to its codification by a legist such as Maimonides what gets crystallized as the optimal legal and judicial opinion are the statements that manage to withstand criticism the best. What proves least vulnerable to logical, legal, exegetical, and historical counterattacks attains the threshold of legal utterance and consensus in the Talmud and gets confirmed or revised in successive codes.[14]

The Halakhah codified in the *Mishneh Torah* is thus not an outgrowth of certainty but represents the distillation of the skeptical cross-fire exchanged between disputing Rabbis. Almost after the manner of the ancient Sophists who considered the goal of argument to be to make the weaker argument the stronger, Maimonides in his meta-legal gloss on the nature of law suggests that what gets promulgated as law in each individual case is merely what "gets knocked down the least" in the agonistic confrontations between scholars. "Law" just like "God" can be theorized entirely within an ambit that takes into account the central roles played by human limitation and ignorance.

I am suggesting that the model for making sense of the Halakha (the laws enshrined in Maimonides' *Code*) is God – the negative theological way in which Maimonides conceives of God. But his way of understanding God seems to eventuate (as we have seen) in inescapable paradox. How does one wend one's

---

11 Babylonian Talmud, *Eduyot*, Chapter One, *mishnah* Five.

12 Cited in Mirsky, *Sefer Hadranim* (see above n. 9), pp. 206–207.

13 Babylonian Talmud, *Menahot* 4a.

14 These relativized judgments are largely pragmatically motivated – and do not presuppose or require knowledge of any absolutes such as the true, the good, the just, or the will of God. For a discussion of the most consistent version of pragmatism as a generalized agnosticism see my *Postmodernism and Democratic Theory* (Philadelphia: Temple University Press, 1993), Chapter Two.

way around the paradoxes I have described? A suggestive approach that is covertly prefigured in both the *Guide* and the *Code* is spelled out in the writings of Emmanuel Levinas and Gilles Deleuze.

Levinas in the priority that he assigns to ethics over all other branches of philosophizing invokes skeptical argument as internal support for his thesis. Levinas says that "It is as if the correlation of the Saying and the Said were a diachrony of the unassemblable."[15] As I read him, Levinas's argument seems to go something like this: The best internal (by "internal" I mean internal to philosophical argument and exploration itself) support for the ideas of God and the Other come from the breakdown of what Levinas calls synchrony – and the triumph of diachrony. What the history of philosophy shows to be the most consistent and dramatic expression of the urge toward synchrony – encompassing all of the moves that it is dialectically inviting and metaphysically compelling to make in one concentrated philosophical vision – are formulations of skepticism. However, it is precisely here that the urge toward synchrony trails off into incoherence, as the skeptic in order to remain consistent needs to skeptically interrogate the tenets of skepticism, which aborts his attempt at synchronous formulation of skepticism as a vision of the whole. Only some move in the direction of diachrony – of in a barely intelligible sense separating-out the saying from the said – can salvage skepticism.

The breakdown of synchrony as manifested most glaringly in the case of skepticism creates metaphysical space for the notions of the Other and of God. Since formulations of skepticism give rise to dilemmas of consistency which are best resolved by imagining logical grids that enable us to dissociate the "saying" of skepticism from the "said" of skepticism – logical grids that offer us an alternative to the binary constraints of the traditional Aristotelian logic, so that contradiction is normalized – then indirect support is received for a generalized agnosticism which engenders receptivity to such logics. A generalized agnosticism leaves the door open to an endlessly unfolding future which might be the most cogent way to construe Levinas's notion of infinity – and its attendant openness to the ideas of the Other and of God.

Michel Foucault's summarizing of Deleuze's philosophy in *Difference and Repetition* and *The Logic of Sense* gives us an illuminating analogue to Levinas's notion of dissociating the saying from the said of skepticism. In order to formulate a coherent theory of difference – of plurality in all of its manifold cultural, personal, and metaphysical senses – one confronts the paradox that the categorical notion of "difference" already introduces a homogenizing element – an expression of the impulse toward Sameness – into the very delineation of difference. How would it be possible to formulate an understanding of difference

15 Emmanuel Levinas, *Proper Names*, trans. Michael B. Smith (Stanford: Stanford University Press, 1996), p. 59.

that was reflexively uncontaminated? This is the way Foucault (paraphrasing Deleuze) formulates the dilemma – and resolves it:

> What if it conceived of difference differentially, instead of searching out the common elements underlying difference? Then difference would disappear as a general feature that leads to the generality of the concept, and it would become – a different thought, the thought of difference – a pure event. As for repetition, it would cease to function as the dreary succession of the identical, and would become displaced difference.[16]

Apropos of our previous discussion, Foucault states very pointedly that the problem of conceiving "difference differentially"

> cannot be approached through the logic of the excluded third, because it is a dispersed multiplicity; [...] The freeing of difference requires thought without contradiction, without dialectics, without negation; thought that accepts divergence; affirmative thought whose instrument is disjunction; thought of the multiple – of the nomadic and dispersed multiplicity that is not limited or confined by the constraints of similarity; thought that does not conform to a pedagogical model (the fakery of prepared answers), but that attacks insoluble problems – that is, a thought that addresses a multiplicity of exceptional points, which are displaced as we distinguish their conditions and which insist and subsist in the play of repetitions.[17]

What methodological principle is at work in Deleuze's and Foucault's resolutions of the problem of conceiving of difference differentially? Foucault states it very sharply and succinctly: "What is the answer to the question? The problem. How is the problem resolved? By displacing the question."[18] In their discerning of this methodological principle, Deleuze and Foucault are prefigured by a great rabbinic sage of the late nineteenth/early twentieth century – Rav Simcha Zissel of Kelm – who said that "Every question that is especially strong and does not have a solution, then the question is (becomes) the solution."[19] Deleuze's and Foucault's resolution of the problem of delineating difference differentially which involves "the suppression of categories, the affirmation of the univocity of being, and the repetitive revolution of being around difference"[20] consists in a reinsertion of the constitutive features of the problem in the infrastructure of its solution – a revised set of logical protocols that normalizes contradiction.

---

16 Michel Foucault, *Language, Counter-Memory, Practice*, ed. Donald F. Bouchard (Ithaca, N.Y.: Cornell University Press, 1977), p. 182.

17 Ibid., p. 185.

18 Ibid.

19 Cited as epigraph in Aryeh Botwinick, *Skepticism, Belief, and the Modern: Maimonides to Nietzsche* (Ithaca, N.Y.: Cornell University Press, 1997).

20 Foucault, *Language* (see above n. 16), p. 187.

The solution as it were stabilizes and institutionalizes the problem – thereby transforming it from problem to solution.

Karl Popper in his essay, "What is Dialectic?" (included in his volume, *Conjectures and Refutations*), offers us (in a way that Popper would want to disown) a very economical perspective from which to acknowledge the same point that Levinas and Deleuze make. Popper argues that once contradiction is admitted into any one of our premises, no argumentative move can be precluded (we can go on blithely proliferating contradictions without having to incur any visible costs), since by admitting contradictory premises into our argument we have effectively deprived ourselves of all logical or argumentative mechanisms to flag contradiction as inadmissible. In Popper's idiom: "If two contradictory statements are admitted, any statement whatever must be admitted; for from a couple of contradictory statements any statement whatever can be validly inferred."[21] The admission of contradiction leads inexorably, if perversely, to the normalizing of contradiction, as the internal censoring mechanisms of the traditional Aristotelian logic have been subverted by the incorporation of the first contradiction into our argument. In the case of the negative theological conceptualization of God, its very contradictory character neutralizes the acids of criticism that can be mobilized against it – and insinuates the possibility of formulating alternative logical frameworks that are governed by protocols other than those of the traditional logic.

Maimonides' theorizing in his very early work, *Millot HaHigayon* ("Treatise on Logic") – written (according to some scholars) when he was sixteen – coheres very well with the reading of his pathbreaking later works I am adducing here, that emphasizes the centrality of contradiction and the consequent breakdown or irrelevance of the traditional Aristotelian logic for grasping the nature of man's relationship to reality. In trying to carve out a role for the traditional syllogism in argument, Maimonides says the following:

> A little reflection will make it evident that from any two distinct propositions nothing else will ever result, as when we say, "Every man is an animal," and "Every fire is hot," and "Every snow is cold." Even if the number of the distinct propositions is indefinitely increased, nothing will result from their combination.[22]

According to Maimonides, the only way that the brute distinctness of propositions can be overcome is through combining them in such a way that a minor premise is followed by a major premise which generates a legitimate inference or consequent, which is then formally stated in the conclusion of the argument.

21 Karl R. Popper, *Conjectures and Refutations* (London: Routledge and Kegan Paul, 1965), p. 317.

22 Israel Efros, *Millot HaHigayon: Maimonides' Treatise on Logic* (New York: American Academy for Jewish Research, 1938), p. 40.

This structuring of argument is called a syllogism – and it constitutes the primary means through which thought is able to synthesize its multiple awareness of and modes of response to the world. A traditional example of this type of argument which Maimonides cites is "'Every man is an animal,' and 'Every animal is sentient,' it necessarily results from this combination that 'Every man is sentient,' which is the conclusion."

This understanding of the role of syllogism in overcoming the utter disparateness of our sentences, which seems so straightforward and even simplistic, gets called into question twenty pages later in Maimonides' treatise when he discusses the meaning of λόγος. Maimonides points to the compressed ambiguity of the term – and delineates three separate strata of meaning within it:

> The term logos technically used by the thinkers of ancient peoples is a homonym having three meanings. The first is the faculty, peculiar to man, whereby he conceives ideas, learns the arts, and differentiates between the ugly and the beautiful, it is called the rational faculty. The second is the idea itself which man has conceived; it is called inner speech. The third is the interpretation in language of that which has been impressed on the soul; it is called external speech.[23]

What emerges from Maimonides' analysis of λόγος is that, according to him, external speech is already a phenomenon evincing underdetermination. It is underdetermined by the "idea itself" – what Maimonides calls "inner speech". The manner in which inner speech receives outward expression is a matter of "interpretation". Apparently, there are no fixed sets of protocol that determine in advance how inner speech is to be externally articulated.

The syllogism which is supposed to rescue us from the indefinite proliferation of heterogeneous, distinct propositions by mapping legitimate patterns of inference between them breaks down as a result of Maimonides' theorizing of the relationship between inner and outer speech. The building blocks of propositions, after all, are the tokens of external speech whose underdetermined relationship to the traces of inner speech means that they can also be articulated in ways that contradict the actual constellation of external speech that was chosen. However, the placement of contradiction in the heart of every logico-linguistic construction called the syllogism means that the process of coherent derivation of patterns of inference between propositions breaks down – and we are restored to a process of endless proliferation of distinct propositions. We are in the uncemented universe of Levinas and Deleuze and Popper – where infinite "sayings" can be parsed out of infinite "saids" and contradiction cannot be contained (or even registered as contradiction).

As a not untypical example of contradiction in the *Code* – and how the pattern of resolution exhibits the same kind of logical features as those that

23 Ibid., p. 61.

enable us to make sense of negative theological argument generally – I would like to turn to Chapter Three, Paragraph One of the "Laws Concerning Creditor and Debtor", where Maimonides states the following:

> One must not take a pledge, either at the time the loan is made or afterwards, from a widow, whether she be poor or rich; nor must one take a pledge from her by order of the court. For it is written, Thou shalt not take the widow's raiment to pledge (Deuteronomy 24:17). And if one takes a pledge from a widow, he is compelled to return it against his will.[24]

The Rabad in the standard published texts of Maimonides' *Code* raises an immediate, very strenuous objection to Maimonides' formulation of the law. Taking a pledge "at the time of the loan" does not come within the purview of the verse that Maimonides cites from Deuteronomy. The Hebrew phrase which is translated into English as "Thou shalt not take" is *lo taḥbol*. *Laḥbol* means "to seize" – and it is etymologically linked to the word *ḥabalah* which means "wound" or "injury". The Rabad's objection is that seizing a pledge from a widow after the terms of the loan have been agreed upon and sealed as a further assurance that the loan is going to be repaid comes within the parameters of *lo taḥbol*. The involuntary expropriation of collateral makes it a kind of *ḥabalah*. However, if at the time that the terms of the loan are being negotiated the widow voluntarily agrees to provide collateral to the lender as an additional inducement or reward for his providing her with a loan, that appears to have nothing to do with – and even to run completely contrary to – the moral depravity being outlawed by the verse *lo taḥbol*. From the Rabad's perspective, what Maimonides cites as a prooftext actually undermines his formulation of the Halakha.

In order to situate Maimonides' text in the *Code*, one must turn to the Talmudic source from which in one way or another it derives. The following are the relevant *mishnah* and the short Talmudic discussion of it in the Babylonian Talmudic tractate of *Baba Meṣiah* 115a:

> *Mishnah:* A man may not take pledge from a widow, whether she be rich or poor, for it is written, Thou shalt not take a widow's raiment to pledge.
>
> *Gemara:* Our rabbis taught: Whether a widow be rich or poor, no pledge may be taken from her: This is R. Judah's opinion. R. Simeon said: A wealthy widow is subject to distraint, but not a poor one, for you are bound to return (the pledge) to her, and you bring her into disrepute among her neighbors. Now shall we say that R. Judah does not interpret the reason for the Writ, whilst R. Simeon does? (i.e., R. Judah applies the law to all, whilst R. Simeon seeks the reason for any Scriptural law,

24 Jacob J. Rabinowitz (trans.), *The Code of Maimonides: Book Thirteen: The Book of Civil Laws* (New Haven: Yale University Press, 1949), p. 85.

> and having found it, exempts those to whom it is inapplicable.) But we know their opinion to be the reverse. For we learnt: "Neither shall he multiply wives to himself that his heart turn not away (Deuteronomy 17:17); R. Judah said: He may multiply (wives), providing that they do not turn his heart away. R. Simeon said: He may not take to wife even a single one who is likely to turn His heart away; what then is taught by the verse, Neither shall he multiply wives to himself? Even such as Abigail! (This shows that R. Judah interpreted the scriptural reason, whilst R. Simeon did not.) – In truth, R. Judah does not interpret the reason of Scripture; but here it is different, because Scripture itself states the reason: Neither shall he multiply wives to himself, and his heart shall not turn away. Thus, why "shall he not multiply wives to himself"? So "that his heart turn not away." And R. Simeon argues thus: Let us consider. As a general rule, we interpret the Scriptural reason (on his view, i.e., when it is not stated): then Scripture should have written, "Neither shall he multiply, etc.", whilst "and his heart shall not turn away" is superfluous, for I would know myself that the reason why he must not multiply is that his heart may turn away. Why then is "shall not turn away" explicitly stated? To teach that he must not marry even a single one who may turn his heart.[25]

The Mishnaic and Talmudic texts that I have cited make no reference to the time the loan is made, which is explicitly mentioned in Maimonides' *Code*. After citing the Mishnaic and Talmudic passages that clearly serve as the precursor-texts for Maimonides' formulation, we seem to be as much in the dark as we were before.

Perhaps a clue for deciphering Maimonides' formulation in the *Code* can be found in his commentary on this *mishnah* which appeared in 1168, twelve years before the *Code*. In his *Commentary on the Mishnah*, Maimonides says that "It is prohibited to distrain on a widow in order that she should not come under suspicion when she goes after the holder of the pledge to retrieve her pledge. Or their relationship might lead to *kilkul* (sin; disgrace; corruption). Therefore, the Mishnah draws no distinction in this matter between a rich widow and a poor one."[26]

The language of Maimonides in his *Commentary on the Mishnah* seems crucial for understanding his formulation of the Halakhah in his *Code*. The two factors that Maimonides cites in prohibiting the taking of collateral from a widow appear to be independent of her class status as being rich or poor. The first of two interrelated factors is that she should not be viewed suspiciously in the eyes of the community if she has to go after the creditor to retrieve her collateral after she has repaid her loan. The second consideration has to do

---

25 Babylonian Talmud, *Baba Meṣiah* 115a (*Hebrew-English edition of the Babylonian Talmud: Baba Mezia*, translated by Salis Daiches and Harry Freedman [London: The Soncino Press, 1986]).

26 My translation.

with how a relationship of dependency that begins with a loan and extends to the giving of collateral to secure her loan can tempt the "superior" male and the "subordinate" female into corrupting further contacts – where (more likely) the strong exploits the weak, or (less likely, but still possible) the weak party to the relationship tempts and exploits the strong, or some inextricable mixture between the two constellations of temptation occurs. These further contacts are even mandated by the Torah itself – in terms of its requiring the restoration of a daytime collateral garment by day and a nighttime collateral garment at night.

Given these considerations that in this case seem central to Maimonides' scheme of Halakhic calculation, it looms as plausible that when he came to compose the *Code* he saw no reason to consider the distinction between "at the time of the loan" and "after" as being particularly significant. The widow might be so needy and vulnerable at the time of the loan that in order to secure it she deludes herself into believing that giving collateral to her male creditor will not be fraught with potential damage to her reputation – and poses no danger of landing her in moral and physical entanglements from which it will be hard to distance and extricate herself. Her "real interest" that Maimonides discerns – as opposed to her self-declared and perhaps even self-diagnosed interest – is to be relieved of the need to provide collateral (through the imposition of a blanket prohibition upon her creditor) altogether. So in the *Code* Maimonides takes a policy leap beyond the official language of the Mishnah in *Baba Meṣiah* and his explication of it in his *Commentary on the Mishnah* and prohibits taking a pledge from a widow at all times, whether "at the time of the loan" or afterwards. The question still remains how the texts of the Mishnah and Gemara from *Baba Meṣiah* 115a can be rendered amenable to (or compatible with) this sort of daring and innovative policy extension? And also how the text of the Torah can be reconciled with it?

The mini-*sugya* that I have recorded above from *Baba Meṣiah* 115a is a classic instantiation out of the numerous *sugyot* that one could cite from the Babylonian Talmud of the principle of the underdetermination of meaning by text. The *braita* with which the Talmudic discussion of the *mishnah* begins immediately shows us that our anonymous *mishnah* codifies the view of R. Judah in contrast to R. Simeon. Since the law is generally in accord with a *stam* (anonymously stated) *mishnah*, we can assume that despite the unusual extension that he provides Maimonides sees himself as codifying the view of R. Judah. R. Judah holds that one may not take a pledge from a widow whether she be rich or poor. Maimonides inserts this clause into his formulation of the law in the "Laws of Creditor and Debtor" – and adds another clause concerning how the prohibition against taking a pledge extends to the time of the loan itself – as well as afterwards. Can this clause be linked to R. Judah?

What Maimonides imbibes from the Talmudic *sugya* itself is how the methodological principle of the underdetermination of meaning by text is the chief animating force behind it. The Gemara citing an additional *braita* assumes that R. Judah's limiting the scope of the Biblical prohibition against a king taking many wives to those cases where they "turn his heart away" is symptomatic of his subscribing to the principle that one does interpret the reason of the Writ (of Scripture) – which appears to contradict his view in the case of taking a pledge from a rich widow. The Talmud responds by saying that our original reading of R. Judah is correct; that he does not attempt to openly project the rationale of a Scriptural law as a basis for fixing its scope and limits. The Talmud proceeds to distinguish the case of a king taking many wives where the Torah itself outlines the reason for the prohibition from the case of taking a pledge from a widow where the Torah remains silent about the specific injunction it addresses to judges and creditors, so as to reinstate our understanding of R. Judah's allegiance to the principle that one "does not interpret the reason of the Writ." The fact that the text of the *braita* concerning a king taking many wives is susceptible to contradictory readings (that R. Judah does/does not interpret the reason of the Writ) is indicative of the principle of the underdetermination of meaning by text.

The two inferences that one can legitimately draw from the Talmudic *sugya* are (a) that R. Judah whose view is codified into law can be postulated as adhering to the principle that one does not interpret the reason of the Writ and (b) that the methodological principle of "underdetermination" is a key operative factor in Talmudic interpretation. Conjoining these two factors together, how can one account for the legal formulation one finds in Maimonides' *Code*?[27]

Following the lead of Rav Shmuel Ashkenazi in his work, *Mekom Shmuel*,[28] we might say the following: Maimonides himself, exemplifying a principle of

---

27 Rabbi Boruch Halevi Epstein in his commentary on the Torah called *Torah Temimah* reconciles Maimonides' formulation in his *Code* which prohibits taking collateral from a widow even at the time that the loan is being negotiated with the verse in the Torah which seems to countenance the taking of collateral from her at that juncture by saying that Maimonides is simply responding to the duplication of the prohibition. In Deuteronomy 24:10, the Torah had already informed us that when we lend our "fellow man a loan of anything, you shall not go into his house to fetch his pledge." How then shall we account for the repetition of this prohibition concerning the taking of pledges with regard to a widow in Deuteronomy 24:17? According to the *Torah Temimah*, Maimonides interprets the force of the repetition as insinuating an extension of the scope of the prohibition with regard to a widow: Taking a pledge at the time of the loan is prohibited alongside the taking of collateral afterwards. What the *Torah Temimah* leaves crucially unexplained, however, is how this extension is to be reconciled with the overt language of the verse in the Torah, which suggests that only forcible expropriation of a pledge is prohibited but not one voluntarily acquiesced in by the widow at the time of the loan. It is this central interpretive question that I address in the text. See Boruch Halevi Epstein, *Chumash Torah Temimah. Volume Five: Sefer Devarim* (Tel Aviv: Am Olam, 1972), p. 374, n. 151.

28 Shmuel Ashkenazi, *Sefer Mekom Shmuel* (Monroe, N.Y.: Hasefer, 1989), Sh`elah Lamed Bet [Question 32].

"underdetermination", confines R. Judah's principle that one "does not interpret the reason of the writ" only to cases that result in limiting the scope of a Biblical prohibition – such as taking a pledge from a rich widow, but not from a poor one. But one can impute to Maimonides the understanding that where supplying a reason for a Biblical verse enables one to make better sense of the full literal scope of the Biblical formulation, R. Judah embraces it. The Torah's language with regard to "*lo taḥbol beged almanah*" ("Do not take in pledge the garment of a widow") is all-inclusive and unconditional. The literal language of the Torah does not restrict its application to a poor widow rather than to a rich one; or to "not at the time of the loan", rather than to "the time of the loan". It is true that as many commentators on Maimonides' *Code* starting with the Rabad point out, the term *laḥbol* – "seizing a pledge" – suggests "not at the time of the loan", because if the widow voluntarily agrees to provide collateral at the time of the loan, then almost by definition it is not being seized. The way Rav Ashkenazy explicates R. Judah's position (in Maimonides' reconstruction of him), the lack of exceptions in the Torah's formulation is suggestive of the factors emphasized by Maimonides in his *Commentary on the Mishnah*: The aspect of *ḥshad* – "Suspicion" – when the male lender and female borrower come together for purposes of retrieving her collateral after she repays her loan – and also creating a climate favorable to sexual transgression by proliferating the occasions (if it is a daytime garment, it needs to be restored to the borrower by day; if it is a nighttime garment it needs to be returned to her at night) when the lender and borrower might come together. These sorts of factors are all-encompassing in character. They would be operative whether the borrower were rich or poor – and independently of the circumstances whether the pledge was tendered at the time that the loan originally took place – or afterward.

According to Rav Ashkenazy, there is a kind of tacit principle of *palginan dibura* (splicing in novel and unexpected ways the order of significations of a sentence or phrase) that Maimonides effectuates with regard to the words *lo taḥbol*. The all-inclusiveness of the prohibition of *lo taḥbol* is logically detached – dissociated – from the literal connotations of the verbal command *lo taḥbol* – with the upshot being that even at the time the loan was being worked-out, a lender would not be allowed to take a pledge from a widowed borrower who voluntarily agreed to give it to him. This logical move of dissociation of the literal import of the phrase *lo taḥbol* from the comprehensiveness of the prohibition it registers constitutes further evidence of the need to supplement the role of two-place logical schemata in meta-halakhic discourse with an awareness of the central role performed by multivalued logical schemata in normalizing the contradictions that are often endemic to halakhic argument.

The meaning of the prohibition stated in the Torah – *v'lo taḥbol beged almanah* – is underdetermined by the text of this prohibition. The Rabad and many other rabbinic commentators interpret the text literally – so that a widowed borrower agreeing at the time of the loan to give her creditor collateral does not fall within the purview of the prohibition. Maimonides interprets this phrase metaphorically – as an expression of the Torah's revulsion against subjecting a widow to any potentially compromising and humiliating sets of circumstances, and therefore as implicitly ruling-out the giving of collateral even at the time of the loan. Maimonides implicitly applies the methodological principle of underdetermination of meaning by text in construing a verse of the Torah. From a Popperian perspective, the very flouting of the original logical limits in interpreting the injunction of *lo taḥbol* has ended up legitimating the moves that have resulted from that flouting. If we have no place to go, we simply have to devise logical protocols to capture where we are.

In Rav Ashkenazy's commentary on the paragraph of Maimonides' *Code* that we are discussing, there is also the intimation that Maimonides is following through on his well-attested predilection for the Jerusalem Talmud over the Babylonian Talmud in determining the Halakhah in a particular case. It is well documented that in cases of dispute between the two Talmudim with regard to particular Halakhic matters, Maimonides often decides in favor of the Jerusalem Talmud. The preferential treatment that Maimonides often accords the Jerusalem Talmud over the Babylonian one might prima facie be regarded as a function of the mode of presentation in the Jerusalem Talmud being held superior to the one followed in the Babylonian Talmud. In the Jerusalem Talmud, what is most characteristic of the order of presentation are bald statements of Halakhic views, rather than systematic attempts (which is definitive of the Babylonian Talmud) to explore their background assumptions and presuppositions and immediate and mediate implications. Maimonides in relation to the *sugya* in *Baba Meṣiah* 115a takes the unadorned Halakhic implications as found in the Mishnah as binding, and considers it entirely methodologically and theologically legitimate to counterpose his understanding of the presuppositions and implications of the statements found in the Mishnah to that developed in the Gemara.

Many modern analysts have said that Maimonides' preference for the Jerusalem over the Babylonian Talmud as a source for Halakhah is a function of the greater clarity and certainty that is endemic to the Jerusalem Talmud's largely un-dialectical and more ostensibly straightforward presentation of Halakhic views. I would argue in the light of the evidence supplied by the case of "taking a pledge from a widow" that the case is exactly the opposite. Maimonides prefers the Yerushalmi's presentation of sources over the Bavli's orderings of them precisely because by their very open-endedness and indeterminacy they are less likely to engender false consciousness than their Bavli counterparts. The Bavli through its very exhaustiveness and elaborateness often gives the impression that it has pinned-down presuppositions and implications, whereas in fact it hasn't. The Bavli gives us readings – but hardly ever a final reading of a Biblical or Tannaitic or earlier Amoraic text. In any event, given Maimonides' tacit allegiance to the principle of underdetermination, we would have to say that in the case of taking a pledge from a widow, the Talmudic dissection of the relevant *mishnah* constitutes the unfolding of one set of possibilities that enjoys no logical or any other kind of priority to that worked out by later commentators and interpreters.

An unsuspected section of Maimonides' *Code* can also be linked to negative theology and the skeptical motifs encapsulated within it. In Chapter Seven, Paragraph Two of the "Laws Pertaining to Moral Dispositions and to Ethical Conduct", Maimonides says the following:

> Whoever tells tales about another person violates a prohibition, as it is said "Thou shalt not go up and down as a tale bearer among thy people" (Leviticus 19:16). And although no stripes are inflicted, it is a grave offense, and leads to the death of many souls in Israel. Hence, this precept is followed immediately by the sentence "neither shalt thou stand idly by the blood of thy neighbor" (Leviticus 19:16) ... Who is a tale-bearer? One who carries reports and goes about from one person to another and says "So-and-so said this"; "Such and such a statement have I heard about so-and-so." Even if what he says or repeats may be true, the tale-bearer ruins the world. There is still a graver offense that comes within this prohibition, namely, the evil tongue [*lashon harah*]. This means talking disparagingly of anyone, even though what one says is true.[29]

The vehement reaction provoked by *lashon harah* – and the centrality that Maimonides assigns to the laws guarding against it – are evidenced even more forcefully in his commentary on *Avoth*, Chapter One, *mishnah* Sixteen, where he cites the language of the Tosefta to the Babylonian Talmudic Tractate of *Arkhin*: "There are three offenses for which one is punished in this world and forfeits his portion in the World to Come [*'olam habah*]. These are idolatry, incest, and murder; but the evil tongue is equal to all three put together."

One could argue that Maimonides' (inspired by his Rabbinic precursors') thrusting of the laws of *lashon harah* to center stage of Rabbinic attention is at least partially a function of his (and their) adherence to negative theology. From a negative theological perspective, *v'halakhta b'drakhav* and *u'ledavka bo* (walking in God's ways and cleaving unto Him) cannot be construed literally, since God's utter transcendence rules out any direct, literal commerce with Him. Therefore, these Scriptural requirements are displaced unto a general commandment to imitate His attributes – to try and approximate to those actions that the canonical texts of the tradition and their Rabbinic commentaries and elaborations attribute to Him. In this context, noticing how speech is the prime instrumentality of Divine creativity – "With ten utterances the world was created" – becomes a major "meeting-ground" between us and God. For us, too, creativity is supremely manifested through speech. How does the negative theological God who cannot be grasped by us in any sense – on any level –

29 Moses Maimonides, *Mishneh Torah: The Book of Knowledge* (see above n. 1), p. 56a.

create through speech? The normative Rabbinic as well as mystical understanding is that He has to withdraw into Himself – engage in a stupendous act of *ṣimṣum* (contraction) – to enable what is other than Himself – the world, which represents extraordinary *hitpashtut* (expansion) – to come into being. With Creation-through-Speech-and-Withdrawal together serving as the model of Divine action, the principle of *v'halakhta b'drakhav* would suggest that in order for our speech to be maximally efficacious, we, too, need to engage in stupendous and sustained acts of *ṣimṣum* by observing all of the self-restraining disciplines enshrined in the laws of *lashon harah*. It is the pulling-back that is part and parcel of the creating. Hence, the centrality accorded to the laws of *lashon harah* in Rabbinic and Maimonidean discourse.

One can make sense of the laws of *lashon harah*, which seem to be exceedingly idealistic and other-regarding in character, from an egoistic perspective that is the moral psychological correlative to the skepticism which is integral to my genealogical account as to why these laws occupy such prominence in the metaphysical-theological landscape of Judaism. From the Talmudic discussion of *lashon harah* in *Arkhin* 15a–17a, to Maimonides' codification of them, and, most especially, to the Chofetz Chaim's elaborate systematization of them utilizing nearly all of the materials of his Rabbinic predecessors, it becomes evident how intricate patterns of character development are insinuated by relationships between the multiple verses in Scriptures that impinge upon the theme of *lashon harah* and the Rabbinic commentaries and expansions upon them. When you consider what the common denominator is in these verses and the Rabbinic exegeses thereon, you end up with a vision of how flexibility and humility – flexibility nurtured in a psychological seedbed of deep humility – are central to the proper conduct of a human life. The humility and flexibility help to engender and foster charitableness and forgiveness toward the other, and, equally importantly, toward the self. By recognizing that we need to be charitable and forgiving to ourselves in order to extricate ourselves from whatever ruts we might have landed ourselves into, we are able to empathize with the need to be charitable and forgiving toward others to enable them to grapple with situations that are not that different from those we confront. Being good and kind toward others enables us to complete the job of being good and kind toward ourselves. By displaying these attitudes toward others, we legitimate and reinforce our mobilizing them in relation to ourselves. The famous verse in Leviticus (19:18) says, *v'ahavta l'reiaḥa komokha* – "Love your fellow human being as yourself." The relationship between self-love and love of the other is so dense and mutually inter-penetrating that both injunctions – the need to cultivate a healthy self-affirmation and love for the other – can only be jointly formulated as one unit of ethical and theological discourse. The laws of *lashon harah* are one integral component of that encompassing unit.

A not-fully-appreciated source in Maimonides that underscores the underlying unity of the projects of justification of *miṣvot* in the *Guide* and the *Code* as stemming from and reflective of his negative theological theorizing of God is his commentary on the first *mishnah* of the first chapter of *Pe'ah*, which is incorporated into the Jewish daily liturgy. The Mishnah reads as follows:

> These are the precepts that have no prescribed measure: the corner of a field [which must be left for the poor], the first-fruit offering, the pilgrimage, acts of kindness (*gemillut ḥasadim*), and Torah study. And these are the precepts whose fruits a person enjoys in this world but whose principal remains intact for him in the World to Come (*'olam habah*): the honor due to father and mother, acts of kindness (*gemillut ḥasadim*), bringing peace between man and his fellow, and the study of Torah is equivalent to them all.

In his *Commentary on the Mishnah*, Maimonides says the following:

> If a person fulfills the *miṣvot* that are addressed to him in a solitary capacity that pertain to his relation to the Creator, he receives a reward which *Hashem* will mete out to him in the World to Come (*'olam habah*) as we will explain in the chapter Chelek [the last chapter of the tractate *Sanhedrin*]. And if he fulfills the *miṣvot* that are dependent upon improvement of relations between people with each other he receives for this reward in the World to Come for fulfilling the commandment. And he receives benefit in this world for pursuing good conduct with other people, since if he follows this path and the other also follows it, the other will receive a comparable benefit. And all of the *miṣvot* pertaining to relations between one human being and the next are included under the rubric of acts of kindness (*gemillut ḥasadim*).[30]

This passage as a whole has the effect of deflating the categorical scheme of rewards and punishments as it pertains to the performance of *miṣvot*. The six hundred and thirteen *miṣvot* teased out and elaborated upon by the Rabbis out of the text of the Torah fall into two broad categories: *bein adam l'makom* (between man and God) and *bein adam l'ḥaveiro* (between man and man). Maimonides says in this passage that the *miṣvot* that come within the sphere of between man and God are rewarded *l'olam habah* (in the World to Come) – a sheer disembodied realm that is neither empirically accessible to us nor fully rationally graspable by us, since it is so dissimilar to the conditions governing our earth-bound existence. Reward for this category of *miṣvah* is therefore beyond human calculation. We mouth the words pertaining to it without being able to fully fathom their cash value.

With regard to the second half of the mutually exhaustive dichotomous categorization of *miṣvot* – *miṣvot sh'bein adam l'ḥaveiro* (*miṣvot* affecting relations between one human being and the next) – Maimonides explicates the scheme

30 *Mishnah Im Perush HaRambam* [Mishnah with Maimonides' Commentary]. *Volume One: Zeraim and Mo'ed*. Translated into Hebrew by Yosef Kafiah (Jerusalem: Mossad Harav Kook, 1963), p. 55; my translation into English.

of rewards and punishments in a mutually self-interested, instrumentalized way, where reward is conceived as a deliberately designed consequence of the mode of relating itself. "If he follows this path and the other also follows it, the other will receive a comparable benefit." Maimonides seems to be alluding in proto-social-contract fashion to the most minimalist set of principles under which the cooperation of the other in the institution and maintenance of an ordered and mutually-beneficial system of social relations can be purchased. Reward in the very capacious domain of *bein adam l'ḥaveiro* is a function of the deliberate design of the social system and does not represent any kind of supernatural gift or bestowal. Since social contractarian modes of argumentation had already been put in circulation in Western thought in the Glaucon and Adeimantus section of Plato's *Republic,* Maimonides would have a historical focal point with which to connect in articulating this system of ideas.

Ta'amei hamiṣvot (rationales for commandments) and *schar v'onesh* (reward and punishment) appear to be at least to some extent mutually implicative notions. If we can have an authentic grasp of rewards and punishments, that would suggest that we can rationally plot and reconstruct the factors that are/should be conducive in the first instance to our performance of *miṣvot*. But if as Maimonides insinuates in his commentary on the first *mishnah* of *Pe'ah* that rewards and punishments on a Divine level remain an enduringly inscrutable domain – and that on a human level they are more a function of what we do in designing a mutually egoistically-supportive social system, rather than literally referring to something that we directly receive – then a skeptical gloss has been cast upon how we need to interpret *ta'amei hamiṣvot*.

Maimonides' causal dissection of *miṣvot* in the *Guide* – seeking to answer the question of what would prompt a lawgiver to promulgate the particular commandments and prohibitions that he does – coheres very well with this understanding of a conceptual linkage between rewards and punishments and rationales for commandments. The attenuating of the first leads to the enervation of the second. But with Maimonides' *Commentary on the Mishnah* in *Pe'ah* as a guide, we can also read his discussion of *ta'amei hamiṣvot* in the *Code* in a comparable light. In the *Code,* Maimonides is not telling us what the compelling antecedent factors are that should persuade us to perform *miṣvot*. He is rather pointing to the worlds of sensibility and value that our compliance with *miṣvot* will generate as a basis for doing them. The justificatory discourse in the *Code* is future rather than past oriented. The structure of Maimonides' justificatory argument in the *Code* is implicitly tautological. We do because we do – but if there are enough of us conforming to *miṣvot,* then we mutually contribute toward fashioning multiple worlds of Halakhic observance, where different but related constellations of social, cultural, and theological values are manifested.

In Maimonides' reckoning in his commentary to the first *mishnah* of *Pe'ah,* all *miṣvot sh'bein adam l'ḥaveiro* are included under the rubric of *gemillut ḥasadim,* and reward in each of these cases is a function of the play of mutually self-interested calculation that is evocative of social contract theorizing. All *miṣvot* that are not included in this category come under the rubric of *miṣvot sh'bein adam l'makom* and are subject to all of the acts of discounting and deliteralization characteristic of negative theology generally. We are not able to fathom what our performance of these *miṣvot* signifies for God – nor are we able to figure out how He is able to channel rewards and punishments to us, nor, indeed, what "reward" and "punishment" signify to the mind of God altogether. In this context, it seems plausible to maintain that *miṣvot* are performed in a vacuum or suspension of rationality – where it is collective doing in common directions that conjures up patterns of meaning, rather than universally received and acknowledged meanings that inform the doing.

Hermann Cohen, Leo Strauss, Alexander Altmann: Maimonides in Germany

by

Alfred L. Ivry
New York University

The three persons whose work this essay commemorates encompass a century and more of German-Jewish scholarship. Hermann Cohen lived from 1842–1918; Leo Strauss from 1899–1973, and Alexander Altmann from 1906–1987. I should like to show how each one's view of Maimonides reflects in part their reaction to the crises of their time. In what follows, I do not presume to offer a psychological or historical analysis of these men, but rather wish to illustrate how their work on Maimonides offers a prism through which the philosophical perspectives of each one can be appreciated.

I.

By the beginning of the twentieth century, there had been a considerable amount of critical Maimonidean scholarship, in Germany, France, and elsewhere in Europe. On the occasion of the 700th anniversary of Maimonides' death (a hundred years ago), plans were made in Breslau to present a comprehensive evaluation and critique of his oeuvre.[1] Though much was anticipated, the only publication actually to see light in this project was a two-volume collection of essays, one of which was by Hermann Cohen.

Cohen at that time was one of Germany's leading philosophers, identified with the Marburg school of Neo-Kantian thought. His Jewish identification had been more of a private affair throughout his career, as necessitated by the prejudices of the age. However, towards the end of his university career and increasingly in his retirement, Cohen became publicly identified as one passionately concerned to teach and interpret Jewish tradition in a manner congruent with modern, rational thought and humanitarian ideals. For Cohen this meant

1 Hermann Cohen, *Ethics of Maimonides*, trans. Almut Sh. Bruckstein (Madison, Wisc.: University of Wisconsin Press, 2004), p. XXV.

viewing the Jewish tradition within an ethic guided by Kantian and Platonic teachings.

Cohen's essay, "Charakteristik der Ethik Maimunis", published in 1908, is a tour de force of Cohenian exegesis, presenting for the first time a full portrait of his understanding of Maimonides.[2] Here we find adumbrated many of Cohen's central views of Judaism, as developed fully in his *Religion der Vernunft aus den Quellen des Judentums*, a work published posthumously some eleven years later.[3] It is clear that Maimonides' philosophy, as Cohen reads it, expresses many of what Cohen believes to be the essential teachings of the Jewish faith. This includes the fundamental idea of God which Cohen believes Maimonides shares with him, as well as an allegedly similar religious epistemology; a similar view of what constitutes human perfection; a shared view of the priority of ethical action to theoretical contemplation; and a similar attitude to history and the messianic age.

Accordingly, the *Religion der Vernunft* appears often as a Cohenian elaboration of Maimonides' idea of God; the book being a select conflation of writings found in the *Guide of the Perplexed*, the Code of Jewish law known as *Mishneh Torah* and the treatise "Fathers" (*Avot*) of Maimonides' *Commentary on the Mishnah*.[4] The physical and the Platonic connection is evinced at the very beginning of Cohen's 1908 Maimonides essay, the entire first chapter being devoted to an exposition of Plato's idea of the good as *anupotheton*,[5] that which is without or beyond hypothesis. It is a reality (in some ideal sense) unconditioned and absolute, beyond being of any other sort, the fundamental postulate of knowledge and ethical consciousness. This construal of ethics, founded on the concept of the transcendence of the good, leads on a "straight road" ("ein gerader Weg") to Kant, Cohen says in *Religion of Reason*.[6] And, we may add, from Kant to Cohen.

---

2 Hermann Cohen, "Charakteristik der Ethik Maimunis", in *Moses ben Maimon: Sein Leben, seine Werke und sein Einfluß*, ed. Wilhelm Bacher et al. (Leipzig: Fock, 1908; reprinted in *Hermann Cohens Jüdische Schriften*, ed. Bruno Strauss [Berlin: C.A. Schwetschke & Sohn, 1924]), vol. III, pp. 221–289; translated (after a fashion) into Hebrew by Ṣvi Weissalewski, *Hermann Cohen, Iyyunim beyehadut ubeva'ayot haddor* (Jerusalem: Mōsad Byālīk, 1977), pp. 17–59. Now translated into English, with commentary, by Bruckstein (see above n. 1).

3 This work received a new edition in 1928, following the manuscript and galley proofs left by the author. A reprint was published in Wiesbaden in 1995. This second edition served as the basis for the English translation of Simon Kaplan, *Religion of Reason: Out of the Sources of Judaism* (New York: Frederick Ungar, 1972; second edition: Atlanta: The American Academy of Religion, 1995).

4 See Leo Strauss' "Introductory Essay" to the English translation of Simon Kaplan (see above n. 3): in the second edition, pp. xxiii–xxxviii.

5 *Republic* VI, 511b, and see Cohen, "Charakteristik der Ethik Maimunis" (see above n. 2), p. 225 and generally, pp. 221–231.

6 Cf. Hermann Cohen, *Religion of Reason* (see above n. 3), p. 291; idem, *Religion der Vernunft* (see above n. 3), p. 339.

Aristotle's place along the road is acknowledged, though Cohen is critical of Aristotle's allegedly self-indulgent virtue of contemplation. Maimonides, of course, was much impressed with Aristotle's ethics, following his doctrine of the mean for most virtues. However, in Maimonides' introduction to his Mishnaic commentary on *Avot,* as well as in "Hilkhot De'ot", the "Treatise on Beliefs" in the first Book ("Sefer HaMaddah") of his *Mishneh Torah.* Maimonides repudiates the mean as regards humility and forbearance from anger;[7] and in the latter work he distinguishes the *ḥasid* from the *ḥakham,* the pious from the wise person, as one who in religious principle practices supererogatory actions.[8]

It is the *ḥasid,* of course, whom Cohen views, correctly, as Maimonides' ideal ethical type. He is the person who goes beyond the letter of the law, the person who does for another more than is required, without ulterior purposes, as an act of *ḥesed. Ḥesed,* loving-kindness, together with *ṣedakah* and *mishpat,* righteousness and judgment, are singled out by Maimonides in III.53 of the *Guide* as the preeminent expressions or attributes of Divine action; and the following, final chapter of the *Guide* bids us to emulate these traits. Indeed, the person who has achieved perfection (that is, intellectual perfection) will as a matter of course live with these virtues in mind and presumably seek opportunities to enact them, Maimonides concludes.

For Cohen, the God of Maimonides must be a God whose primary concern, besides justice, is with supererogatory acts of loving-kindness and righteousness; all are expressions of the goodness that is the defining attribute of His being.

The ultimate wisdom, Cohen believes Maimonides is saying, is not only of God as the unique one, an object of metaphysical knowledge, to whatever degree possible; but also and more so, knowledge of an ethical deity whose attributes are to be imitated as best one can. For Cohen, *ḥesed, mišpat* and *ṣedakah* are more than divine attributes, they are expressions of God's very essence, of the goodness that for Cohen is the defining characteristic of Divinity.

Cohen identifies his God, as well as Maimonides', with the personal God of the Hebrew Bible, a volitional deity who is passionately concerned with suffering mankind, on a one-to-one basis. It is this *Mitmenschlichkeit,* this with-it-ness with a person, which differentiates religion's perspective on ethics from that of philosophy, for Cohen. In language which prefigures Buber, Cohen

7 Cf. *Avot commentary* 4:4, "Hilkhot De'ot" 2.3, and see *The Eight Chapters of Maimonides on Ethics.* Edited, annotated and translated with introduction by Joseph I. Gorfinkle (New York: Columbia University Press, 1912; reprinted in New York: AMS Press, 1966), p. 60, n. 2. Cf. too Maimonides' *Mishneh Torah: The Book of Knowledge.* Edited according to the Bodleian (Oxford) Codex with introduction, biblical and talmudic references, notes and English translataion by Moses Hyamson (Jerusalem: Boys Town Publishers, 1962), p. 48b.

8 "Hilkhot De'ot" 1.5, and Gorfinkle (see above n. 7), p. 60, n. 2; Hyamson (see above n. 7), p. 49a.

states that the ethical self has no I without thou: "[Für dieses] gibt es kein Ich ohne Du. *Rea* heißt der andere; er ist wie Du; er ist das Du zum Ich." "*Re'a* means the other; he is as thou, he is the thou in I."[9]

The *re'a* one is commanded to love as oneself is not just the Jewish neighbor, the messianic goal not a Jewish happening only. It is a universal brotherhood towards which the messianic ideal is pointed, and the Jewish mission is to work eternally towards this end.

Cohen's Maimonides may be seen in part as a response to what Cohen considered the atheism and consequent materialism of modern society, and as expressing a belief in the possibility, even necessity, of good manifesting itself in human affairs. Cohen was to die before that belief was put to its most severe test, but our other two figures were not to be spared the destruction of that German-Jewish cultural symbiosis of which Cohen was the prime example and exponent.

II.

Leo Strauss had disowned the premises of that symbiosis or *Bildung* in which Cohen and most others of his generation believed, even before the rise of fascism made a mockery of it.[10] Initially accepting the Zionist repudiation of Jewish life outside of the land of Israel, Strauss soon came to consider political Zionism as itself the product of the Enlightenment, and as such essentially secular and atheistic. He viewed all attempts to modify traditional Judaism in light of modernity as concessions and distortions of the primary beliefs of the faith. These beliefs could not be rationalized in terms of modern philosophies or Enlightenment values. The premises of the faith were immune, he believed, to rational and scientific challenges.

At the same time, Strauss believed deeply in the role of reason and rationalism. He found in Maimonides a person who he believed maintained both an appreciation of and critical attitude towards science, and a deeply held religious conviction. Strauss therefore adopted Maimonides as a model for his generation, a figure with which to challenge the secular premises of the Enlightenment, the

---

9 Cohen, "Charakteristik der Ethik Maimunis" (see above n. 2), p. 275. See Bruckstein's translation and references (see above n. 1), pp. 152, 153.

10 The biography of Strauss' life in Germany and analysis of his early writings has only recently been explored in scholarly detail. Cf. Michael Zank, *Leo Strauss: The Early Writings (1921–1932)* (Albany: State University of New York Press, 2002), pp. 3–49. See too David Biale, "Leo Strauss: The Philosopher as Weimar Jew", in Alan Udoff (Ed.), *Leo Strauss' Thought: Toward a Critical Engagement* (Boulder, London: Lynne Rienner Publishers, 1991), pp. 31–40.

impending anarchy of society and the corruption of an authentic Judaism.[11] Strauss also discerned in Maimonides and in his Islamic predecessors, particularly al-Fārābī, a predilection for esoteric writing, a mannerism occasioned by the political climate and biases of the society in which they lived. This literary style, which Maimonides boldly announces in the Introduction to his *Guide of the Perplexed*,[12] in effect gives all of medieval philosophy, or nearly all of it, a political dimension that should not be ignored. At the same time it also makes it much more difficult to discern the author's real position on any given issue.

Strauss' *Persecution and the Art of Writing*, published in 1952,[13] forcefully brings out this aspect of Maimonides' style, and with it puts into question Maimonides' position on many key issues, such as his belief in creation, revelation, miracles, etc. Such is Strauss' dedication to Maimonides, however, that he does not explicitly tell the reader what he then believed Maimonides' true beliefs were. Strauss imitates his master, or keeps faith with him, in writing in an esoteric manner himself; becoming famous, or infamous, some would say, in this respect.

The public face Strauss puts on his interpretation of Maimonides is evident in two compositions that Strauss wrote in a span of some thirty years: *Philosophie und Gesetz* published in 1935,[14] and "How to Begin to Study *The Guide of the Perplexed*", the introductory essay he wrote to Shlomo Pines' translation of Maimonides' *Guide*, published in 1963. In the earlier work, Strauss critiques the Enlightenment and political Zionism along the lines mentioned, and opposes the illusory freedom an atheistic modernity offers with an appreciation for a revealed law such as traditional Judaism affirms.[15]

For Strauss, it is the revelation granted the biblical prophets, and particularly Moses, that provides man with "those truths that transcend rational knowledge and that he needs for his life [...]. Above all, Revelation teaches the existence, unity, and incorporeality of God just as it teaches the createdness of the world."[16] Strauss appears to claim that Maimonides believed in the latter doctrine as much as in the former, and that it is the very inexplicable nature of

---

11 For a more comprehensive treatment of Strauss' relation to Maimonides, cf. Kenneth Hart Green, *Jew and Philosopher: The Return to Maimonides in the Jewish Thought of Leo Strauss* (Albany: State University of New York Press, 1993). See too Alfred L. Ivry, "Leo Strauss on Maimonides", and Rémi Brague, "Leo Strauss and Maimonides", in *Leo Strauss' Thought* (see above n. 10), pp. 75–91 and 93–114, respectively.

12 Cf. the translation of Shlomo Pines, *Moses Maimonides: The Guide of the Perplexed* (Chicago, London: University of Chicago Press, 1963), pp. 6–7.

13 Published in Glencoe, Ill., by The Free Press.

14 Translated by Fred Baumann as *Philosophy and Law* (Philadelphia: The Jewish Publication Society, 1987). See the critique and suggested revisions offered by Eve Adler, "Leo Strauss' *Philosophie und Gesetz*", in *Leo Strauss' Thought* (see above n. 10), pp. 183–226.

15 Cf. *Philosophy and Law* (see above n. 14), p. 16.

16 Ibid., p. 47.

creation from nothing, as Maimonides presents it, that insulates it from attack, and that establishes the validity of miracles and revelation in general.

Moses' prophecy is unique in that through it the law is given, and society afforded the controls and rationale for a civilized life. Strauss believes Maimonides fully appreciated this, and came to understand politics as "the seal of metaphysics", Jewish law being seen as encompassing both metaphysical and practical concerns.[17]

Strauss considers the centrality of law and concern for the public weal in Maimonides as a theme taken philosophically from Plato, by way of al-Fārābī. As does Cohen, so Strauss claims Plato as the main philosophical influence upon Maimonides. Now, however, it is Plato's political philosophy, not his ethics, that is seen as the key to understanding Maimonides.

Strauss reiterates a number of these views in his much later introduction to the English translation of the *Guide*. Written for those about to embark on a study of the text, Strauss cautions them about its esoteric nature, saying it is "sealed with many seals."[18] It is a Jewish book, he affirms, not a philosophic book, and one must wait thirty-six pages before Strauss qualifies that claim.[19] Nor is he willing to open any of the seals to which he alludes, the reader must find out Maimonides' true views by himself.

Strauss does elaborate upon Maimonides' hermeneutical methodology, understanding his radical allegorizing of the Biblical text as a bold attempt to rid Judaism of a corporealized image of the deity. Strauss identifies this as the struggle against idolatry, personified for Maimonides by Sabianism, and Strauss appears to believe that Maimonides succeeded in ridding Judaism of this belief.[20]

Strauss does not tell the reader, however, just what it is in idolatry, or for that matter in the notion of divine corporeality, that so disturbed Maimonides. Strauss offers no explanation of the logical problem such an image offers to the divine unity, as Maimonides conceives it. One therefore has the impression that Strauss is using Sabianism as a front for another faith, a religion that his Jewish readers considered, or ought to consider, idolatrous.

In this manner, Strauss places Maimonides' struggle against an anthropomorphic view of God in a political context of both historical and contemporary significance. The *Guide* is depicted, even if in passing, as resonating with Maimonides' concerns for his people. Accordingly, Strauss states with a minimum of references that Maimonides "did not forget the disastrous effect of the exile"

---

17 Cf. ibid., p. 50.

18 Strauss, "How to Begin to Study *The Guide of the Perplexed*", in Pines, *The Guide of the Perplexed* (see above n. 12), p. xiii.

19 Cf. ibid., p. l.

20 Cf. ibid., p. xlii.

in the *Guide*, and that "it goes without saying that Maimonides also never forgot the Messianic future."[21]

Strauss' most striking attempt to sway the reader's sympathy for his reading of Maimonides is found in his description of the shared assertions of the existence, unity and incorporeality of God, in the arguments of both the *kalam* and the philosophers which Maimonides presents in the *Guide*.[22] Finding both sides have inadequate arguments yet agree upon what is sought, Maimonides opts (at least exoterically) for a Creator God whose will is dominant, over an Aristotelian eternally unmoved mover that is characterized as intellect.

Strauss remarks upon the different entailments of these opposing positions of the *mutakallimūn* and the philosophers, despite their shared assertions. Surprisingly, he compares this situation to the common fate of post-war prosperity that would have befallen either a triumphant Nazi Germany or a defeated one, however different the character of the country would have been. In other words, Strauss likens the difference between believing in a creator God or in Aristotle's god to the difference between a democratic and a fascist state.

This bizarre comparison can only have issued from Strauss' personal experience. It is a reminder of the impact the Shoah had upon him, and how it affected and reinforced his reading of Maimonides. Creation is necessary for Strauss, whether true or false, for with it mankind has a God who through revelation provides the moral and political anchor society requires.

III.

Alexander Altmann was personally affected by the rise of Nazism in Germany no less than Strauss. Indeed, Altmann had to flee for his life from the Gestapo.[23] He was pursued because of his very public leadership of the Berlin Jewish community, both as a rabbi and as the founder of a *Lehrhaus* similar to that established in happier days by Franz Rosenzweig in Frankfurt. Altmann named his institute the "Rambam-Lehrhaus", and offered courses in Maimonides there, among a wide range of Jewish studies.

---

21 Ibid., p. xlii, citing *Guide* I.71 and XI.11 for references to exile, and I.61 and XI.27 for the messianic future.

22 Cf. ibid., p. lii.

23 Cf. Paul Mendes-Flohr, "Theologian before the Abyss", in Alexander Altmann, *The Meaning of Jewish Existence: Theological Essays 1930–1939*, ed. Alfred L. Ivry (Hanover, N.H., London: Brandeis University Press, 1991), pp. xiii–xlvii.

This was to be expected of Altmann, who published a German translation of selections of *The Guide of the Perplexed* in 1935, and followed it the next year with a major study of "Maimonides' Attitude toward Jewish Mysticism".[24]

Besides writing these historically oriented publications, Altmann wrote a number of articles in the thirties addressing contemporary theological and social concerns.[25] His response to Nazism was a reaffirmation of the classical faith of Judaism, coupled with a very modern, critical appreciation of the demands of objective scholarship. This scholarly aspect of Altmann's personality dominated his published work, once he left Germany. He became a leading authority on the historical investigation of Jewish Philosophy and mysticism, particularly in the medieval period, as well as on the work of Moses Mendelssohn and his contemporaries.[26]

Altmann was drawn to Maimonides throughout his life, becoming an expert medievalist and Maimonidean scholar. His methodology was that of a comparativist and historian of philosophy. He located Maimonides within a broad spectrum of thinkers: Greek, Muslim, Jewish and Christian. Thus, his celebrated 1972 article on "Maimonides' Four Perfections"[27] identifies the „letter of Farewell" by the Muslim philosopher Ibn Bājja as Maimonides' source. Altmann finds an essentially complete congruence between the two men on this theme, which identifies intellectual cognition, namely, the contemplation of Divine truths, as the ultimate perfection of man.[28] Ethical behavior and moral virtues constitute the third perfection, and are seen as subservient to the final perfection and subsumed within it. Aristotle's contemplative ideal is that to which both medieval philosophers subscribe, and Altmann has no problem with that.

In his 1974 article on "Free Will and Predestination in Saadia, Bahya and Maimonides"[29] Altmann distinguishes between Maimonides' remarks on the topic in his theological compositions, and in the *Guide*. In the former,

---

24 Published originally as "Das Verhältnis Maimunis zur jüdischen Mystik", in *Monatsschrift für Geschichte und Wissenschaft des Judentums* LXXX, Neue Folge XLIV (1936), pp. 305–330. The English translation first appeared in *Studies in Jewish thought: An Anthology of German and Jewish Scholarship*, ed. Alfred Jospe (Detroit: Leo Baeck Institute, 1981).

25 Many of these articles, translated into English by Edith and Leonard Ehrlich, are found in Altmann, *The Meaning of Jewish Existence* (see above n. 23).

26 Cf. Manfred Altman, "Bibliography of the Published Writings of Alexander Altmann", in *Perspectives on Jewish Thought and Mysticism*, ed. Alfred L. Ivry, Elliot R. Wolfson and Allan Arkush (Amsterdam: Harwood Academic Publishers, 1998), pp. 1–19.

27 First published in *Israel Oriental Studies* II (1972), pp. 15–24, republished in A. Altmann, *Essays in Jewish Intellectual History* (Hanover, N.H.: University Press of New England, 1981), pp. 65–76.

28 Cf. Altmann, *Essays* (see above n. 27), p. 71.

29 First published in *Religion in a Religious Age*, ed. Shlomo D. Goitein (Cambridge, Mass.: Association for Jewish Studies, 1974), pp. 25–51. Reprinted in Altmann, *Essays* (see above n. 27), pp. 35–64.

particularly in Maimonides' *Eight Chapters* introduction to the Mishnaic tractate *Avot*, Altmann argues that Maimonides holds to a doctrine of free will, while acknowledging a limited sense of Divine predestination; whereas in the *Guide*, Maimonides inclines (esoterically) to a doctrine of strict causality, or determinism.[30] As a philosopher, Maimonides is thought by Altmann to restrict God's will to the initial act of creation, an action in which future "miracles" are also somehow programmed. Altmann calls this an "almost deistic stance",[31] and feels no compunction to qualify his remark.

To take a third example, in his 1978 article on "Maimonides and Thomas Aquinas: Natural or Divine Prophecy",[32] Altmann contrasts the naturalistic presentation of prophecy in Maimonides with the supernatural understanding of it found in the Scholastic philosopher. Even while acknowledging the political function of the prophet in Maimonides' philosophy, Altmann sees it as a frequent theme in all Islamic philosophy, naturalized within a metaphysics of emanationism. "Maimonides subscribes to the Avicennian type of ontology", Altmann declares without apology.[33]

Altmann is consistent, then, in placing Maimonides within a context of medieval Aristotelianism, a philosophy that accepts Neoplatonic elements, but that emphasizes natural science in both its physics and metaphysics. There are limits to man's knowledge, but they are not such to warrant the theological exegesis of a Hermann Cohen or the radical politicization of a Leo Strauss. Thus, in his last major article, published in 1987, "Maimonides on the Intellect and the Scope of Metaphysics",[34] Altmann rose to defend the integrity of Maimonides' metaphysics and his vision of the happiness to be found in the activity of intellection.

IV.

Of our three philosophers' relations with Maimonides, then, Altmann may be said to be the most scholarly and historically rooted; Cohen the most religiously driven, and Strauss the most politically stricken. Each one has his disciples today, testimony to their enduring contributions.

---

30 Cf. ibid., pp. 49–58.

31 Ibid., p. 52.

32 First published in *AJS Review* III (1978), pp. 1–19. Reprinted in Altmann, *Essays* (see above n. 27), pp. 77–96.

33 Altmann, *Essays* (see above n. 27), p. 81.

34 Alexander Altmann, *Von der mittelalterlichen zur modernen Aufklärung* (Texts and Studies in Medieval and Early Modern Judaism 2; Tübingen: J. C. B. Mohr [Paul Siebeck], 1987), pp. 60–129.

Der arabische Kontext / Arabische Kultur

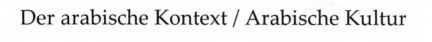

Maimonides and the Development of Jewish Thought in an Islamic Structure

by

Oliver Leaman
University of Kentucky, Lexington

There is a characteristic form of writing that is very common in Islamic theology and philosophy, and takes the nature of the summary or commentary. Many thinkers do not address other thinkers directly, but rather through discussing some other thinker entirely. Whole controversies have taken place in this indirect way, and it is all too easy to characterize this sort of technique as unoriginal and derivative. After all, if a writer concentrates on the thought of another author, even a very distinguished one such as God, and spends a great deal of time outlining that thought, surely he is doing something a lot less original and exciting than someone who undertakes a creative and new exploration of those same issues.

In Islamic philosophy, for example, we have a situation where the commentary is the major form of expression. This has often led to criticism of this sort of philosophy as rather unexciting and unoriginal, since after all a commentary can only go so far, and the ideas expressed by the commentator do have to try to stick as close as they can to the ideas of the text they are explicating. Along with the commentary there is another important form of writing, the summary. The summary brings out in relatively short form the essence of a book or a whole metaphysical and/or theological view, for instance, and again it looks like a rather unexciting form of intellectual work. The summary depends for its interest, after all, on what it summarizes, and however skilled the summarizer, he could never do more than represent briefly what the original author presents at length. Like the commentator, the summarizer looks like very much an underlabourer, someone who works in a secondary occupation and is firmly in the background.

One of the most famous occasions in which someone was called onto summarize is when the Amīr al-mu'minīn, Abū Ya'qūb, told his physician and court philosopher Ibn Ṭufayl that it would be an excellent idea if someone were to *yulakhkhiṣuha* (summarize) the works of Aristotle, and as a result of that Ibn Rushd set out his efforts at *talkhīṣ* or summary. Presumably the original aim of Abū Ya'qūb was for Ibn Ṭufayl to undertake the task, but he was really not a good person for the job. For one thing he was engaged in work with rather more mystical leanings than would cohere nicely with Aristotle. It was also a job for a younger man, and one that Ibn Rushd jumped at, enthusiastic as he was about the thought of Aristotle and recognizing that here was an opportunity for him to study at length the works of his hero. Ibn Rushd wrote commentaries of varying lengths – long, medium and short – so he participated in two characteristic activities of Islamic culture, writing commentaries and producing summaries.

A summary is not only a shortened version of what it summarizes. This is an important point, and one thus far insufficiently understand. When Abū Yaʿqūb suggested that someone summarize Aristotle he was not just asking for a shortened version of Aristotle. He was asking for Aristotle to be represented in such a way that his thought would be available to a much wider public. A summary does not only do that, but it also represents that thought in a particular way. That seems obvious, surely, a summary represents its object in a briefer way, so it has to take a decision on how to represent it.

Let us look at how this works visually. A map both represents and summarizes a landscape. In *Alice in Wonderland* Alice contemplates the nature of the perfect map, which she suggests would be the same size as what it represents, and in a sense that is true. If one could actually place a representation of a spatial area on the area so that the names corresponded precisely with the places, that would be a perfectly accurate map. And also a totally useless one. Or we could take a picture of something and wonder whether it would be a better picture if it was the same size as the object it is representing. Would a picture of Erlangen that was the same size as Erlangen be a better picture than a picture of Erlangen that was smaller than the town itself? Perhaps more reasonably we could ask whether a picture of a mouse that is the same size as a mouse is preferable to a picture of a mouse that is smaller, or bigger, than a mouse. In this case there is no answer, size really does not matter. The quality of the picture is unaffected by its actual size. We would have to ask what the picture is for, what it is trying to do, and size would be important then, but only as part of the whole form of representation.

When we compare pictures from different periods of Persian art, we often prefer the work of Bihzad to that of the earlier Timurid painters, perhaps because Bihzad's work is more realistic and employs ideas of perspective familiar to us today. The Timurid paintings are flat, highly stylized and concentrate more on rich and fanciful color rather than accurate spatial representation. But perhaps the earlier Persian paintings were trying to do something different from the later ones. Perhaps they were trying to summarize a scene or series of events, perhaps they are giving a view of the world that holds everything together at once, a view that in effect presents a facsimile of the divine point of view. But is not a summary merely a shorter version of something else? In art not necessarily, a summary is a specific form of representation that has its own logic and metaphysics. Its structure is based on a set of ideas and presuppositions which might be very different from those employed by someone else trying to describe the same situation. Saying that a summary is just a shortened version of something is equivalent to saying that a picture of a house is just a shortened version of the house. It is more than that, though, it is how the artist sees the house, which details he thinks worthy of notice, from what side he paints it, and so on.

When we think about Maimonides and his controversial views we tend to concentrate on the *Guide* and the specific topics he discusses there on the creation of the world, prophecy and so on. This was not the only aspect of his work that his contemporaries and later generations found difficult to accept. There was also the way he had summarized *halakhah*, Jewish law, in his *Mishneh Torah* and Jewish belief in his "13 Principles" In doing this Maimonides was copying specifically Islamic models. The different schools of *fiqh* had long ago summarized and determined the legal answers to a variety of issues, albeit in a particular way according to the views of each specific school. Similarly, creeds were written that determined what one had to believe if one was a Muslim, and they differed from school to school.

Let us look at some of Maimonides' work in the summary line. He produced three major halakhic works, the *Sefer Hamiṣvot* (Book of Commandments), his *Commentary on the Mishneh* and the *Mishneh Torah*. The *Sefer* has as its aim the delineation of the 613 commandments in the Torah. According to the Talmud 248 are positive and 365 negative. Yet the Torah seems to include far more laws than this and the Talmud does not really tell us what the commandments are or how they are arrived at. The *Sefer* fills this gap. Maimonides first of all establishes the criteria on the basis of which a rule may be considered to be a *miṣvah* or otherwise. He produces fourteen rules in operation here, using the Talmud as his source. So by working through the whole of the Talmudic literature he arrives at the principles that the Talmud itself uses, but does not make explicit, or so he claims. Then he produces the 613 *miṣvot,* dividing them up in the appropriate way as between negative and positive injunctions.

This work, written in Arabic, was the product of Maimonides' twenties. When he was thirty-two he started working on the *Mishneh Torah,* a project that took him ten years to complete. The *Mishneh Torah* codifies the Talmud and is written in a highly clear form of Hebrew. What is interesting about this work's structure is that Maimonides reverses the normal way of setting out to discuss the Talmud. The normal method is to see the Talmud's structure as something to be replicated. Yet Maimonides adopts the form of the earlier rabbinic text, the Mishnah, and uses that to divide up the Talmud. So the way in which the Mishnah is divided up into *sedarim,* tractates, chapters, and sections (*mishnayot*) is followed. The *Mishneh Torah* is divided up into fourteen volumes, each volume into categories of related laws, each section into chapters, and each chapter into *halakhot* or specific laws. When one compares this to the organization, or rather disorganization of the Talmud, the result is clear. One achieves a perspicuous grasp of the whole of the Talmud in a way that brings out its inherent coherence and the general thrust of its argumentation.

The *Mishneh Torah* proved to be both popular and controversial. It was popular because it brought out for the first time for a lot of readers what *halakhah* was all about. But this led to problems. For example, it might be thought that if one had the *Mishneh Torah,* one needs not bother with the halakhic text itself, rather in the way that American undergraduates sometimes stick to Cliff's Notes rather than studying the text itself. Another issue his opponents raised was that Maimonides' rather breathless pace throughout his text makes it impossible to state why he came to the decisions that he did. He does not go into the sources of his decisions on what the laws are, and this means that readers might not understand the principle that was in action here, and so might go awry when they have to use their own interpretive power in difficult cases that come before them. This objection at least was easily resoluble, since later works were written that filled in the gaps, as it were, and pointed to the parts of the Talmud where Maimonides had derived his decisions. Readers then had the opportunity to understand where in the original to look and what sorts of principles for action were then operative.

This objection in any case is entirely besides the point. Naturally, a summary will not contain all the information present in the original; it is after all a summary of the original, not the original itself. But it would be a mistake to see a summary as only a summary. After all, the *Mishneh Torah* is not the only summary of the law in Jewish history. There is also the *Halakhot* by Yitzhak al-Fasi (the Rif), which came before the *Mishneh Torah,* and the *Shulḥan Arukh* by Yosef Karo that came after. These are also summaries, but far less complete than Maimonides' work. The latter includes all of Jewish law, both written and oral, including laws that cannot be performed in the absence of the Temple and laws that will become practicable once the Messiah comes. That means that the *Mishneh Torah* represents a guide to Jewish law at all times and all places, and so presents a view of the entire scope of Jewish law.

If there is a theme to Maimonides' writings, that theme is summarization. In his *Commentary on the Mishnah* he sorts out and organizes the text so that the final halakhic decision becomes evident. In his introduction, and in the text itself, the emphasis is definitely on explaining what basic principles are in play in the Mishnah and how those principles may be used to bring out the meaning of the text as a whole. This feature is perhaps nowhere more obvious than in his introduction to the tenth chapter of the Tractate *Sanhedrin.* Here Maimonides produces the Thirteen Principles of Jewish Belief, principles that he argues underlies the whole of Judaism. His introductions really set out what he takes to be the basis of what follows. These prolegomena are very helpful in understanding what follows, and often plays a significant role in what follows. For example, in the "Seder Taharot", twelve tractates of complex legislation on the laws of purity, Maimonides cuts through the mass of verbiage and elaboration to what he takes to be the core of the matter, and he uses that notion of a core as an organizing principle around which the explanation of the text is organized.

This principle of organization is of course very familiar from *fiqh*, Islamic jurisprudence. Here the distinction between *uṣūl* or basic principles and *furū'* or branches of the law is commonplace, as is the writings of creeds, lists of basic beliefs that characterize being a Muslim. It is the contention here that Maimonides set out to copy this model, to show that *halakhah* was no different in these respects from Islamic law and that Judaism as a system of belief was at least no less perspicuous than Islam. One of the reasons he himself gives for writing his extensive works of commentary is the need to provide the Jewish community in the Islamic world with a series of texts that would help them cope with the difficult conditions in which they found themselves. In just the same way that the Jewish poets tried to resist the ubiquity of Arabic as a cultural language, so Maimonides tried to resist the argument by Muslims that Judaism had been superceded by Islam. One of the criticisms that people made then, as now, of Jewish law and religion is that they are excessively complicated, difficult to understand and hard to apply. No doubt this argument, along with physical coercion, was very effective in leading to the conversion of many Jews in the Islamic world. Maimonides sought to show that Judaism could be presented in just as clear a manner as Islam, and Jews could gain just as perspicuous a grasp of their faith as could Muslims. The route to this goal was the summary, the *talkhīṣ*, an account of the subject matter of Judaism that presented it with just the same clarity and coherence as commentaries on the Qur'an presented the Book.

Opposition to Maimonides often centered on particular positions that he was supposed to hold, such as a denial of the resurrection of the dead or a general elitism that led him to advocate a lax attitude to Halakhah. This latter is clearly based on a mistake, and the former is something that could be deduced from some of his arguments, but not from anything he wrote directly. There is no way that Maimonides would question resurrection in a legal work, since what is important about the doctrine is not its literal formulation but its appropriate interpretation. That interpretation is certainly not given a philosophical explication in the *Mishneh Torah*, since that would hardly be appropriate as part of a legal discussion. One of the methodological principles that Maimonides adopted from al-Fārābī was the idea that one should always carefully distinguish between the different sorts of discipline within which one operates, so that a theological discussion is carried out differently from a philosophical discussion, and a philosophical discussion bears little relation to a legal discussion. So the defenders of Maimonides in the so-called Maimonidean controversy were right to point to the unfairness of the general critique of his legal work, since this is exoteric and would not really raise the sorts of doubts about doctrine that his critics suggest.

That is the standard response, but it is not correct. In fact the *Mishneh Torah* and the other legal work of Maimonides is much more radical than the *Guide* and his more specifically philosophical output. Here his critics are really perceptive. They say that Maimonides has obviated the sort of discussion about law that one finds in the Talmud by presenting the community with answers. It must have looked very much as though the *Mishneh Torah* was a methodological advance that would put a lot of professionals out of a job. Who needs rabbis and scholars to pore over the Talmud to seek the answers to difficult problems if one could just look them up in Maimonides? What need is there for *teshuvot* (*responsa*) to topical issues if the *responsa* are already available in the *Mishneh Torah*? Would this not put out of work a large body of people who were used to being in work, and highly respected members of the community? It is hardly surprising that many august members of the rabbinic community did not leap with joy at the arrival of the *Mishneh Torah.* As we know, they need not have worried. On the whole attempts to simplify law merely make it more complicated. The new system of legislation has to be reconciled with the old, thus creating yet another level of complexity which requires a set of specialists for its resolution. This is why bureaucracies tend to expand whatever is done to shrink them.

These practical points aside, the *Mishneh Torah* is a genuinely radical work, not so much for the particular conclusions that it comes to but because it comes to particular conclusions on legal issues and represents those conclusions as *the* solutions to the problems. The Mishnah and the Talmud do not tend to do this, nor do the *responsa* of the Geonim. They tend to outline a variety of views and then indicate their preference for a particular opinion, yet someone else is not obliged to accept that opinion as settling the issue. The Talmud itself is often difficult to interpret, and the accompanying commentaries that run along the sides of the text serve as a sort of supercommentary that needs to be consulted also. It is very much part of the tradition of talmudic discussion for a particular passage to be discussed in tandem with the commentaries by Rashi etc. and also with the *Mishneh Torah,* and for a final adjudication of the issue to be based on an argument that takes all these sources of information into account and then provides a plausible technique for resolving all these different points.

Issues are determined in a variety of ways, but the overriding principle seems often to be a majority of informed opinion, of those qualified to judge. Many of the conclusions that are reached are provisional, even majority decisions may be later overturned if it is decided that they are unsatisfactory. Minority decisions are recorded and their authors are not in any way derided. In fact, no distinctions are made between the rabbis as far as status is concerned. Although some rabbis are quoted more often than others, and some even have supernatural events connected to them, these are not taken as indicating different levels of legal skill. Rabbi Akiva is regarded very highly in Jewish culture yet in the Talmud his colleagues are always making fun of him. He is bitterly criticized in the Yerushalmi Talmud for supporting Bar Kochba's claim to be the messiah. In the Bavli he is attacked with particular venom on occasion, being told that he is not competent enough to herd cattle. Akiva replies that he is not even up to herding sheep (Babylonian Talmud, *Yevamot* 16a), his previous occupation. Moses is said to have visited Akiva's college and listened to his lecture about the law of Moses from Mount Sinai, and not to have understood a thing. When he heard that the law was acknowledged as originating with Moses he was relieved, but the story can be taken to criticize Akiva's far-fetched elaboration of law out of very skimpy original material. Even Moses has no idea what he is talking about, and yet Moses knows the law if anyone does.

Akiva is said to have derived many laws from the crowns that are flourishes on the top of the Hebrew letters in a *sefer Torah*. It is not clear if this is meant literally, presumably not, but the implication is that he was capable of making a lot out of a little. This could be regarded as a positive or a negative skill. Clearly some of his colleagues thought he went too far, and that his method produced significant results out of very weak premises, and so was basically unsatisfactory. Rabbi Ishmael suggests that Akiva took a superfluous *vav* ("and") in a biblical passage to show that the daughter of a priest who had been found guilty of adultery should be burnt alive as a means of execution. So the penalty of death by fire arises through a reading of a superfluous *vav*, the astounded Ishmael says (Babylonian Talmud, *Sanhedrin* 51b). Yet this is the same Akiva who is said to have been the only rabbi who entered Paradise and returned to earth while still alive, and was unharmed by the experience, and the same Akiva who died a death which was clearly *kiddush ha-shem*.

This is not the place to discuss why the Talmud is so critical of Akiva. Perhaps it was to preserve a more democratic atmosphere where no particular rabbi dominated the rest. Perhaps the negative comments made about him are not be taken as definitive but just as the stray remarks of people who resented Akiva's status in the community. What we do need to discuss is how different the style of the Talmud is from what is supposed to describe its conclusions, the *Mishneh Torah*. As soon as it is formulated in this way one should become suspicious, since the Talmud does not really come to any conclusions in the sense of answers to questions that remain the answers to those questions for ever and ever. What Maimonides does is use his great skill as a codifier to assess the various discussions, work out what the majority or plausible conclusion is to legal issues, and then present us with those conclusions. The Talmudists themselves would probably have treated him in the way in which they treated Rabbi Akiva. Who is one legal authority like Maimonides to say what the final resolution of these problems is? Perhaps he would also have been told that he was not even good enough to herd cows!

As we know, some of the rabbinic authorities did criticize the *Mishneh Torah* for this very reason, arguing that just as the solution to all these legal issues is not in heaven (Babylonian Talmud, *Bava Meṣiah* 4.59a–b) so it is also unlikely to be in Maimonides. Maimonides is seen as taking on a status vis-à-vis his colleagues and successors that is entirely unsatisfactory. One may dismiss this objection as *ressentiment*, but it is based on something of a tradition, as we have seen, in the Talmud of respect for other opinions and those who provided them. Maimonides seems to bypass this entirely by ignoring much of the discussion, and cutting to the chase, as it were. What is often called the sea of the Talmud is thoroughly charted and organized, and only one course across it is shown to be acceptable. Yet this lies in total contradiction to the free and open nature of the text itself. Although many commentators on the Talmud have gone so far as to see it as prefiguring movements such as deconstruction, this is going much too far. The Talmud does not adopt a laisser-faire attitude to the law, nor does it regard the issue of the law as subjective and mutable. Quite the reverse, it is because the issue of law is so important the rabbis spend so much time and effort arriving at the correct adjudication.

It is important to understand that Maimonides should not have been accused of being another Akiva, trying to dominate the legal scene with his opinions and interpretations. Maimonides was not just giving his take on the law, he was doing more than that. He was giving his view of what the law, and Judaism, is all about. He set out to describe the essence of the law, and the essence of religion, in a way that gives the reader a grasp of how it operates as a whole. That is why it is wrong to criticize him for not giving his sources or entering into the Talmudic fray, his purpose was not to add to the discussion but to summarize it. What we should concentrate on is not the content of the *Mishneh Torah* and Maimonides' other halakhic works, but their design.

If we think in terms of design we could think of the Talmud and associated legal texts as representing a map of Jewish law and belief, while the *Mishneh Torah* is a diagram. If you travel on the London Underground you will see on the walls and in the carriages the famous Harry Beck representation of the system, or at least later developments of Beck's original design. This is often called the London Underground map, but it is not a map. It is a diagram. It is not a map because the representation of the distances between the stations is uniformly inaccurate. The earlier representations of the Underground system were maps, since then the system was still relatively unfamiliar and people had to be encouraged to link the stations to streets and the different parts of London. But once this hurdle was overcome the main point was to provide passengers with an overall view or summary of the system, and for this a diagram is useful. Harry Beck was initially an electrician, and he based the diagram on a circuit diagram, where of course distance is of no significance, but the links between the different things on the circuit is. This is precisely what makes the diagram so often pointed to as a masterpiece of design; it does precisely what one wants it to do. It helps passengers get around the system, because it gives them a view of the whole system. Another aspect of it that must have occurred to Beck who lived in Finchley, on what were the outskirts of the network, is that the diagram helps passengers or potential passengers see the system as an integrated whole which they themselves can visit and use. At the same time as the diagram was becoming popular London Transport produced posters to encourage people to visit the more rural and relatively less known parts of London, now easily accessible through the Underground.

What is the relevance of this to Maimonides? The thesis should be pretty clear, that what he was setting out to do in much of his halakhic work (and we should not really use that term, as though some of his work were kosher and some was treyf!) was present a diagram or summary of the law. He was not contributing to the law, he was contributing to the understanding of the law by the Jewish community. He was making the law more user-friendly and available. In writing in this way Maimonides was following a pattern of writing that had become very popular in the Islamic world. The authors of the main texts of the four *sunnī* legal schools, for example, present their understanding of legal issues without going through all the reasoning and competing opinions, rather like the *Mishneh Torah*. But this is not just limited to legal works. There is a fascination with summarizing in Islamic culture. So many books are based on other books, and present those other books in a summary manner. Often the criticism is made that this direction of effort is not creative and represents a decline in Islamic culture from the time of the great original thinkers. The whole Ottoman period is often dismissed as a period of stagnation in intellectual life, since the primary form of literature during this time was the commentary and consisted of examining and re-examining other people's writings. We should really be careful about making points like this, since exciting arguments can and do appear in the form of a commentary. The commentary and the summary are literary devices that can contain a good deal of both original and brilliant material. Even a glossary (*hashiyah*), again a familiar literary device in the Islamic theological world, is interesting in the concepts it decides are worth discussing and those that are omitted, and the sorts of accounts it gives of those concepts. One of the stylistic features of Islamic theology is the careful analysis of the key terms and arguments that it uses, often not so much to assess their validity but to take them apart and carefully reassemble them. The placing of terms and positions in different categories is an activity that takes up a lot of time and effort in many books, and still does today. Anyone who has attended a lecture in Qom or al-Azhar will have quite likely heard the lecturer spend a good deal of the lecture dividing up the topic into its constituent parts, and then taking those parts in turn to pieces, before putting the whole issue back again, but not before the audience is invited to see it in a rather different sort of way, in a way that allows the audience to get hold of the topic perhaps for the first time.

Why was there such a concentration on these literary devices? One reason is the overwhelming significance of the Book, the Qur'an, and since that represented a miraculous quality of writing, it is not something that could be equaled. Another reason is that many of the books that were produced were part of a teaching process that involved lectures, and what one does in such a context is often to produce material that is expository rather than original. Yet quite a lot of the writing that took place within this tradition is actually original, without eschewing a relationship with some other text on which it appears to be derivative. In fact, though, the text on which the book is based is often irrelevant to the "commentary" itself, it provides the excuse for writing the "commentary", and within the context of being a commentary it allows the author to say what he wants to say. Commentators on commentaries often comment that they are evidence of a lack of creativity or new work in the area. Why produce a commentary or gloss (*hashiyah*) if it is possible to write an original work of one's own? This is a silly question, since the commentary form was during much of this period the way in which thinkers would produce original works of their own, albeit within the style of the time, which is the commentary. Saying that commentaries cannot be original is like saying that photography cannot be an art form.

> A main source of our failure to understand is that we do not perspicuously overview ["übersehen"] the use of our words. — Our grammar is lacking in this sort of perspicuity ["Übersichtlichkeit"]. A perspicuous representation ["übersichtliche Darstellung"] produces just that understanding which consists in "seeing connections". Hence the importance of finding and inventing intermediate cases. The concept of a perspicuous presentation is of fundamental significance for us. It earmarks the form of account we give, the way we look at things. (Is this a Weltanschauung?)[1]

Maimonides sees the *Mishneh Torah* is bringing out the connections that already exist in the Talmud, albeit for the first time in a perspicuous manner. The *Mishneh Torah* is then genuinely a *Weltanschauung*, it presents all at once an account of how the law hangs together and what it rests on. As we know, although the *Mishneh Torah* is now widely respected and accepted, this was not the case originally, and the opposition to it was based on a variety of motives. One was to preserve the independence of legal thinkers to interpret the Talmud and not necessarily accept Maimonides' approach. But a more significant motive was the sense that the *Mishneh Torah* is a basically subversive work not because of its content but because of its form. Its form is to present a rational model of the law, and as Maimonides says in his introduction, the point of this

---

1 Ludwig Wittgenstein, *Philosophical Investigations*, trans. G. E. M. Anscombe (Oxford: Blackwell, 1958), p. 122.

is to succor the worldwide Jewish community who no longer perhaps know how to approach the Talmud and Mishnah or who are poorly guided by their rabbis. That rational model is based on particular principles, principles that Maimonides says underpin Judaism, and here we see the subversive turn that his argument takes. Once we start to base law and practice on principles, we can start to wonder whether that statement of principles is in fact the right one. Suppose someone were to argue that different principles are the bases of the system of Judaism, or even that no principles were? These arguments were to be put, and they came to have significant implications. If religious practice is only meaningful if it is based on particular rational principles, as Maimonides argues, then arguing for different principles produces an alternative understanding of Judaism. We know what legs this debate came to have, and continues to have, in the Jewish community.

There is a word I absolutely detest when I hear or read it in discussions like this, and that word is "influence". It is thrown about far too easily and without any clear idea of what it actually shows. What I have argued here, though, is that Maimonides did employ a novel structure for his work that does display something of his cultural context in an Islamic environment. In just the same way that Jewish thinkers would have no compunctions about learning from Muslim astronomers and physicians, so they also learnt a great deal from the rich and conceptually powerful system of Islamic theology and law. Maimonides' *Mishneh Torah* is an excellent example of the fruits of such learning.[2]

2 *Bibliography:* Dan H. Frank (Ed.), *Maimonides* (special issue). *American Catholic Philosophical Quarterly* 76 (2002); David Hartman, *Maimonides: Torah and Philosophic Quest* (Philadelphia: Jewish Publication Society, 1976); Menachem Kellner, *Maimonides on Human Perfection* (Atlanta: Scholars Press, 1990); Joel Kraemer (Ed.), *Perspectives on Maimonides: Philosophical and Historical Studies* (Oxford: Oxford University Press, 1991). Oliver Leaman, *Moses Maimonides* (London: Routledge, 1990); Yeshayahu Leibowitz, *The Faith of Maimonides* (New York: Adama Books, 1987); ʿAbd al-Wahid al-Marrakushi, *Kitāb al-Muʿjib fi talkhīṣ akhbar al-maghrib*, ed. Reinhart Dozy (Leiden: Brill, 1885); Shlomo Pines and Yirmiyahu Yovel (Eds.), *Maimonides and Philosophy* (Dordrecht: Nijhoff, 1986); Kenneth Seeskin, *Searching for a Distant God: The Legacy of Maimonides* (New York: Oxford University Press, 2000); Isadore Twersky, "Some Non-Halakhic Aspects of the *Mishneh Torah*", in *Jewish Medieval and Renaissance Studies*, ed. Alexander Altmann (Cambridge: Harvard University Press, 1967), pp. 95–118; idem, *Introduction to the Code of Maimonides (Mishneh Torah)* (New Haven: Yale University Press, 1980); idem (Ed.), *Studies in Maimonides* (Cambridge, Mass.: Harvard University Press, 1991); Ludwig Wittgenstein, *Philosophical Investigations*, trans. G. E. M. Anscombe (Oxford: Blackwell, 1958).

Das Fārābī-Bild des Maimonides

Ideentransfer als hermeneutischer Weg zu Maimonides' Philosophie

von

Hans Daiber

Johann Wolfgang Goethe-Universität, Frankfurt am Main

Die philosophischen Traditionen des Fārābī in ihrer Auswirkung auf Maimonides' enzyklopädisches Werk *Moreh Nevukhim*, „Führer der Unschlüssigen", sind schon verschiedentlich Gegenstand der Forschung gewesen. Hierbei ist Maimonides' ausdrücklicher Rückgriff auf Fārābīs *Abhandlung über den Intellekt* und auf drei verlorene Schriften des Fārābī, seinen Kommentar zu Aristoteles' *Physik* und *Nikomachischer Ethik* und seine Abhandlung über *Die veränderlichen seienden Dinge*, diskutiert worden.[1] In der Zwischenzeit sind weitere Texte des Fārābī identifiziert worden, deren Titel Maimonides nicht nennt.[2]

Für Details eines zentral stehenden Themenkomplexes, nämlich Maimonides' Diskussion der Prophetie, ist auf Fārābīs Buch über den Musterstaat verwiesen worden oder auf Ibn Sīnās diesbezügliche und letztlich von Fārābī inspirierte Erörterungen.[3] Maimonides nennt keine der politischen Schriften des

1 Vgl. Shlomo Pines in der Einleitung zu seiner Übersetzung von Moses Maimonides, *The Guide of the Perplexed.* With an Introductory Essay by Leo Strauss (2 Bände; Chicago, London: Chicago University Press, 1963), S. lxxviii ff.

2 Vgl. Sarah Stroumsa, „Al-Fārābī and Maimonides on the Christian Philosophical Tradition: a Re-evaluation", in *Der Islam* 68 (1991), S. 263–287 (zu *Moreh* I.71); Gad Freudenthal, „Four Implicit Quotations of Philosophical Sources in Maimonides' *Guide of the Perplexed*", in *Zutot: Perspectives on Jewish Culture* 2 (Dordrecht etc.: Kluwer Academic Publishers, 2003), S. 114–125, hier S. 123–125 (al-Fārābī, *as-Siyāsa al-madanīya*, benutzt in Maimonides, *Moreh* I.31); Rémi Brague, „Mise à jour", in Shlomo Pines, *La liberté de philosopher. De Maïmonide à Spinoza* (Paris: Desclée de Brouwer, 1997), S. 227–233, hier S. 228–229: zu Fārābī, *Kitāb al-ǧadal* als Quelle von *Moreh* II.15, mit Verweis auf Georges Vajda, „À propos d'une citation non identifiée d'Al-Fārābī dans le «Guide des Égares»", in *Journal asiatique* 253 (1965), S. 43–50; dazu ergänzend Sarah Stroumsa, „Al-Fārābī and Maimonides on Medicine as a Science", in *Arabic Sciences and Philosophy* 3 (1993), S. 235–249, hier S. 247–249.

3 Vgl. Pines, *Guide* (wie Anm. 1), S. lvii ff., besonders S. lxxviii ff.; zu Ibn Sīnā S. xciii ff. und Idit Dobbs-Weinstein, „Maimonides' Reticence Toward Ibn Sīnā", in *Avicenna and His Heritage. Acts of the International Colloquium, Leuven – Louvain-La-Neuve, September 8 – September 11, 1999*, ed. Jules Janssens and Daniel De Smet (Ancient and Medieval Philosophy. Series 1. XXVIII; Leuven: Leuven University Press, 2002), S. 281–296.

Fārābī, ebenso keine von Fārābīs zahlreichen logischen Schriften, obgleich er Letztere in einem Brief an den hebräischen Übersetzer seines *Moreh Nevukhim* für unübertroffen hält.[4] Wir sind also gut beraten, nochmals das jetzt zugängliche Œuvre des Fārābī mit Maimonides zu vergleichen, an einem ausgewählten Detail zu prüfen, was Maimonides ausgewählt hat, was er weggelassen hat und warum.

In früheren Vergleichen zwischen Fārābī und Maimonides, die teilweise auch Maimonides' *Mišneh Torah*[5], seine *Maqāla fī Ṣināʿat al-manṭiq*[6] und seine *Šemonah peraqim*[7] einbezogen haben, ist man je nach Einschätzung der farabianischen Gedanken zu unterschiedlichen Ergebnissen gekommen. Grundlegend ist hierbei Leo Strauss' Interpretation geworden, der in drei in den Jahren 1934, 1935 und 1936 erschienenen Veröffentlichungen die Prophetologie beider Denker verglichen hat.[8] Shlomo Pines hat 1965 in seiner Einleitung zur englischen Übersetzung von Maimonides' *Moreh Nevukhim* weitere Details zugefügt.[9] Maimonides stütze sich auf Fārābīs Lehre von der Vollendung des Menschen, seiner Glückseligkeit durch größtmögliche Annäherung an den göttlichen Aktiven Intellekt; von Fārābī habe er seinen abstrakten und bewusst Widersprüchlichkeiten in Kauf nehmenden Stil übernommen, um die Ungebildeten abzu-

4 Mitgeteilt bei Pines, *Guide* (wie Anm. 1), S. lx oben.

5 So Joel L. Kraemer, „Alfarabi's Opinions of the Virtuous City and Maimonides' Foundations of the Law", in *Studia Orientalia memoriae D.H. Baneth dedicata* (Jerusalem: Magnes Press, 1979), S. 107–153.

6 Vgl. Harry A. Wolfson, *Studies in the History of Philosophy and Religion*, Band I (Cambridge, Mass.: Harvard University Press, 1973), S. 551–560 („Note on Maimonides' Classification of the Sciences"); Joel L. Kraemer, „Maimonides on the Philosophic Sciences in his Treatise on the Art of Logic", in idem (Ed.), *Perspectives on Maimonides. Philosophical and Historical Studies* (Oxford: Oxford University Press, 1991), S. 77–104.

7 Vgl. Herbert Davidson, „Maimonides' *Shemonah Peraqim* and Alfarabi's *Fuṣūl al-Madanī*", in *Essays in Medieval Jewish and Islamic Philosophy*. Selected, and with an Introduction by Arthur Hyman (New York: Ktav, 1977), S. 116–133; Jeffrey Macy, „The Theological-Political Teaching of *Shemonah Peraqim*: a reappraisal of the text and of its Arabic sources", in *Proceedings of the Eighth World Congress of Jewish Studies (Jerusalem, August 16–21, 1981)*, Division C (Jerusalem: The World Union of Jewish Studies, 1982), S. 31–40.

8 Leo Strauss, „Die philosophische Begründung des Gesetzes. Maimunis Lehre von der Prophetie und ihre Quellen", in idem, *Philosophie und Gesetz. Beiträge zum Verständnis Maimunis und seiner Vorläufer* (Berlin: Schocken, 1935), S. 87–122 (auch erschienen in *Monde Oriental* 28 [Uppsala 1934], S. 99–139). Ferner: Strauss, „Quelques remarques sur la science politique de Maïmonide et de Fārābī", in *Revue des études juives* 100 (Paris 1936), S. 1–37. – Strauss' Arbeiten verdrängten die ungefähr gleichzeitig, im Jahr 1935 erschienene vergleichende Studie von Erwin J. Rosenthal, „Maimonides' Conception of State and Society", in *Moses Maimonides, 1135–1204. Anglo-Jewish papers in connection with the 8th centenary of his birth*, ed. Isidore Epstein (London: The Soncino Press, 1935), S. 191–206.

9 Pines, *Guide* (wie Anm. 1), S. lxxviii ff.

schrecken.[10] Doch in den politischen Theorien gebe es Unterschiede zwischen beiden. So sei Moses der einzige Gesetzgeber, der eine authentische Offenbarung, nämlich das göttliche Gesetz des Judentums, empfangen habe, wogegen die anderen Propheten Plagiaristen seien.[11] Moses bedürfe im Unterschied zu den anderen Propheten nicht der vermittelnden Funktion der Einbildungskraft, die prophetische Eingebungen in Form von Bildern weitervermittle.

Hier wollen wir jetzt anknüpfen und dazu Maimonides selbst zu Worte kommen lassen. Er schreibt: „Aber Moses vernahm die Stimme, ohne sich der Einbildungskraft zu bedienen, vom Deckel der Bundeslade zwischen den beiden Cherubim".[12] Moses wird daher in religiösem oder politischem Zusammenhang als „Herr der Propheten" (*sayyid an-nabiyīn*) bezeichnet[13] oder in einem philosophischen Zusammenhang[14] „Herr der Wissenden" (*sayyid al-ʿālimīn*), wobei es einen Gradunterschied zu den anderen Propheten gibt;[15] diese verdienen nur dann den Namen eines Propheten, wenn die göttliche Vernunftemanation (*al-fayḍ al-ʿaqlī*) auf das Denkvermögen (*al-quwwa n-nāṭiqa*) und die Einbildungskraft (*al-quwwa l-mutaḫayyila*) in vollkommener Weise wirkt; Maimonides zufolge[16] müsse derjenige, der eine Einwirkung der Vernunftemanation nur auf das Denkvermögen, nicht oder in mangelhafter Weise aber auf die Einbildungskraft erfährt, lediglich zu der Kategorie „der Gelehrten und Theoretiker" (*al-ʿulamāʾ ahl an-naẓar*)[17] gerechnet werden; und wer eine Einwirkung der göttlichen Vernunftemanation lediglich auf die Einbildungskraft erfahre, aber von Natur oder wegen mangelnder Übung über zu wenig Denkvermögen verfüge, gehöre zu den „Staatslenkern, den Gesetzgebern, Wahrsagern und Zauberern sowie denjenigen, die wahre Träume haben" (*al-mudabbirūn li-l-mudun wa-wāḍiʿū n-nawāmīs wa-l-kuhhān wa-z-zāǧirūn wa-arbāb al-aḥlām aṣ-ṣādiqa*).[18]

10 Ibid., S. lxxix.

11 *Moreh* II.39–40; vgl. Pines, *Guide* (wie Anm. 1), S. xc–xci.

12 *Moreh* II.45, Ende; arabischer Text: ed. Hüseyin Atay (Ankara Üniverseitesi Ilâhiyat Fakültesi Yayınları 93; Ankara: Üniverseitesi, 1974), S. 447,9; englische Übersetzung: Pines, *Guide* (wie Anm. 1), S. 403; vgl. Exodus 25:22. – Hier und in den nachfolgenden Verweisen auf Pines' englische Übersetzung wurde jeweils auch die wertvolle deutsche Übersetzung von Adolf Weiss, *Mose Ben Maimon, Führer der Unschlüssigen* (2 Bände; Leipzig: Meiner, 1923; Nachdruck Hamburg: Meiner, 1995) herangezogen.

13 Zum Beispiel *Moreh* II.19; arabisch: ed. Atay (wie Anm. 12), S. 336,19.

14 Zum Beispiel *Moreh* II.28; arabisch: ed. Atay (wie Anm. 12), S. 363,9.

15 Diese Stufung beschreibt Maimonides auch in der später als *Moreh* verfassten arabischen und nur hebräisch erhaltenen „Abhandlung über die Einheit": siehe *Maamar ha-Jichud*, ed. Moritz Steinschneider (Berlin: Friedländer, 1847), Kapitel 2 (Inhaltsübersicht S. XII).

16 *Moreh* II.37; englisch: Pines, *Guide* (wie Anm. 1), S. 373ff.

17 Arabisch: ed. Atay (wie Anm. 12), S. 410,8.

18 Arabisch: ed. Atay (wie Anm. 12), S. 410,13–14.

Diese Differenzierung, die im Grunde genommen Fārābīs Gedanken von der Unterschiedlichkeit der Menschen weiterführt,[19] ist von modernen Interpreten in unterschiedlicher Weise missverstanden worden. Abweichend von L. Strauss[20] sieht Shlomo Pines[21] hier einen Widerspruch: Warum entbehre der Prophet Moses der Einbildungskraft und erfahre die direkte Einwirkung der göttlichen Vernunftemanation, nicht aber der Regent, der im Gegenteil durch die Einbildungskraft qualifiziert sei? Erwin I. J. Rosenthal geht in seinen 1957 gehaltenen Franz-Delitzsch-Vorlesungen[22] nicht hierauf ein; ebenso Alvin J. Reines in einem 1970 erschienenen Aufsatz über „Maimonides' Concept of Mosaic Prophecy";[23] Lawrence V. Berman konnte in seinem 1974 erschienenen Aufsatz über „Maimonides, the Disciple of Alfārābī"[24] hierauf keine Antwort geben und begnügte sich mit dem Hinweis, dass für Maimonides Moses sowohl „Herr der Propheten" war als auch Herr der demonstrativen Philosophie, der in Fārābīs System der Stellung des Philosoph-Regenten entspreche und somit eine Verbindung zwischen vollkommener spekulativer Vernunft und vollkommener praktischer Aktivität forme.[25]

Die widersprüchliche Auffassung vom Propheten Moses und von den anderen Propheten erscheint bis heute ungeklärt. Auch die umfangreiche, 2001 erschienene Monographie von Howard Kreisel *Prophecy. The history of an idea in medieval Jewish philosophy*[26] vermag keine Antwort zu geben. Jeffrey Macy hatte in seinem 1986 veröffentlichten Vergleich zwischen Fārābīs und Maimonides' Prophetentum[27] die Erklärung vorgeschlagen, dass Maimonides hier einer Ambiguität bereits bei Fārābī gefolgt sei; dieser habe in seinen Schriften in uneinheitlicher Weise über Offenbarung als Quelle rationaler Erkenntnis für

---

19 Vgl. zu dessen Echo bei Maimonides Freudenthal, „Four Implicit Quotations" (wie Anm. 2), S. 124.

20 Vgl. dessen *Philosophie und Gesetz* (wie Anm. 8), S. 95–96.

21 *Guide* (wie Anm. 1), S. xci.

22 Veröffentlicht unter dem Titel *Griechisches Erbe in der jüdischen Religionsphilosophie des Mittelalters* (Stuttgart: Kohlhammer, 1960), Kapitel 4 („Sendungsprophetie und Natürliche Prophetie").

23 In *Hebrew Union College Annual* 40–41 (1969–1970), S. 325–361.

24 In *Israel Oriental Studies* 4 (Tel Aviv 1974), S. 154–178, hier S. 166, zu Anm. 42.

25 Vgl. auch Berman, „The Political Interpretation of the Maxim: The Purpose of Philosophy is the Imitation of God", in *Studia Islamica* 15 (1961), S. 53–61, besonders S. 59–60; idem, „Maimonides on Political Leadership", in *Kinship and Consent. The Jewish Political Tradition and Its Contemporary Uses*, ed. Daniel J. Elazar (Ramat Gan, Philadelphia [etc.]: Turtledove, 1981), S. 113–125.

26 Kreisel, *Prophecy* (Amsterdam Studies in Jewish Thought 8; Dordrecht etc.: Kluwer, 2001), S. 210ff.

27 Jeffrey Macy, „Prophecy in al-Farabi and Maimonides: The Imaginative and Rational Faculties", in *Maimonides and Philosophy. Papers Presented at the Sixth Jerusalem Philosophical Encounter, May 1985*, ed. Shlomo Pines and Yirmiyahu Yovel (Archives Internationales d'Histoire des Idées 114; Dordrecht etc.: Nijhoff, 1986), S. 185–201.

den Philosophen gesprochen, der nicht immer als Prophet dargestellt werde und der die Phantasie, die Einbildungskraft lediglich benutze, um mit den Bildern der Religion die nichtphilosophische Masse zu überreden.

Diese Erklärung setzt ein Fārābībild voraus, das nicht dem Textbefund und der ihm angemessenen Interpretation entspricht. Es ist schon ein fundamentaler Irrtum anzunehmen, dass bei Fārābī die Verwendung des Begriffes „Offenbarung" „nicht mehr sei als eine Anpassung an volkstümlichen Glauben" – „nothing more than an accomodation to popular beliefs".[28]

Im Gegenteil, für Fārābī ist die Offenbarung, die Eingebung des göttlichen aktiven Intellekts, Quelle aller Erkenntnis.[29] Wenn ihm zufolge die nachahmende Einbildung auf die gegenwärtigen und zukünftigen Partikularien (*al-ǧuz'iyāt*), auf die „getrennten Intelligibilia" (*al-maʿqūlāt al-mufāriqa*) und auf „alle erhabenen Dinge" gerichtet sei, kurzum auf dasjenige, was vom göttlichen Intellekt inspiriert sei, spreche man von Prophetie (*nubūwa*). Diese trete dann auf den Plan, wenn die philosophische Erkenntnis dessen, was gut ist, nicht ausreiche und der Ergänzung bedürfe durch die Eingebung (*waḥy*) des göttlichen aktiven Intellekts.

Es ist daher kein Wunder, dass für Fārābī der Regent des Musterstaates nicht nur Philosoph, sondern auch Prophet sein muss. Da den Regenten die göttlichen Eingebungen des aktiven Intellekts in der Form von Nachahmungen der Wahrnehmungen und Intelligibilia erreichen, kann er sie auch in dieser Form an die Menschen, seine Untertanen, weitergeben. Er hat die Aufgabe, in philosophischen Beweisführungen den philosophisch Gebildeten zu überzeugen und die Masse, die nur ein „bildhaftes Wissen" habe, durch „Warnungen" und „Vorschriften" zu überreden. Als Philosoph kann er sich in seiner Instruktion des Bürgers verschiedener Hilfsmittel der Logik und Beweisführung bedienen, als Prophet bedient er sich der Metaphern der rhetorisch-poetischen Sprache.

Hierbei entpuppen sich die prophetischen Warnungen nicht als unvollkommenes, der Philosophie unterlegenes Wissen, das auf die Anhänger der Religion und deren Unzulänglichkeit im Verstehen philosophischer Wahrheit zugeschnitten ist; im Gegenteil: Da sie vom göttlichen aktiven Intellekt gespeist sind, ergänzen sie das philosophische Wissen. Dies geschieht in einer Weise, die der Ergänzung der theoretischen Erkenntnis durch die praktische Orientierung, die moralische Einsicht und praktische Klugheit dient. Die Religion und ihre Partikularien werden so zu einer „Nachahmung", zu einem ergänzenden Bild der Philosophie, der Universalien, ohne mit dieser identisch zu sein. Sie

---

28 Macy, „Prophecy" (wie Anm. 27), S. 192.

29 Vgl. zu den nachfolgenden Ausführungen Hans Daiber, *The Ruler as Philosopher. A new interpretation of al-Fārābī's view* (Mededelingen der Konklijke Nederlandse Akademie van Wetenschappen, Afd. Letterkunde, Nieuwe Reeks, d. 49, no. 4; Amsterdam etc.: North Holland Publishers, 1986).

ist ein „Instrument" der Philosophie und verhilft dieser, zur Wirklichkeit zu werden. Denn Philosophie ist primär praktische Ethik.

Nun muss – wie schon gesagt – ein guter Philosophenherrscher auch ein Prophet sein – dies sowohl im Hinblick auf die Anhänger der Religion, die Masse, als auch angesichts der Grenzen philosophischen Wissens. Philosophie und die rhetorisch-poetischen Mittel der Sprache erscheinen als unvollkommene Hilfen beziehungsweise Werkzeuge der Religion.

Philosophisches Wissen muss durch den göttlichen *intellectus agens*, nämlich durch prophetische Eingebungen vermittelt und ergänzt werden. Hierbei kann das Wissen, das der Regent so erhält, in Form von nachahmenden Bildern an den Untertan vermittelt werden. Diese Nachahmungen ersetzen das Original, das nur in der Form von Abbildern wahrgenommen und weitervermittelt werden kann. Diese Abbilder erscheinen orientiert an der Wirklichkeit – ebenso wie das philosophische Denken in seiner Interdependenz von Theorie und Praxis.

Diese Analogie zwischen Religion und Philosophie – Fārābī spricht von Religion als Nachahmung der Philosophie – erlaubt den philosophischen Beweis für religiöse Wahrheiten sowie die Verwirklichung philosophischer Erkenntnis in der Religion. Daher ist der Regent im Musterstaat nicht nur ein Philosoph, sondern auch ein Prophet, der mit Hilfe von Gottes Eingebung – durch „Angleichung" an Gott, das heißt, indem er Gottes Vorschriften nacheifert und diese weitervermittelt – den Staat regiert.

Gleichzeitig hat Fārābī das Wissen des Regent-Philosophen und Regent-Propheten als Nachahmungen klassifiziert, deren Original die Idee des Musterstaates ist. Hier erscheint die Wirklichkeit des Menschen als politisches Wesen (ζῷον πολιτικόν) mit ethischen Verpflichtungen in der Gemeinschaft des Staates betont. Philosophie ist nicht mehr ein Privileg der Spezialisten, der Elite, sondern kann durch den Regent-Philosophen an den Bürger vermittelt werden – nämlich in der Gestalt der Religion, der von ihr vorgeschriebenen Regeln und Gesetze. Als eine Nachahmung der Philosophie erscheint Religion als eine Verwirklichung der wahren Philosophie, die sich an der Praxis orientiert weiß, als Ethik.

In seiner Diskussion hatte Fārābī in der Nachfolge von Aristoteles' *Nikomachischer Ethik* die drei Seelenkräfte Sinneswahrnehmung, Verstand und Streben eingeführt, die das ethische Handeln des Menschen sowie seine Erkenntnis des Richtigen steuern. Fārābī integrierte hier den aristotelischen Begriff der φρόνησις, der praktischen „Einsicht": Die Intelligibilien sind nicht nur ein Gegenstand wissenschaftlicher Erkenntnis, sondern vermitteln auch sittliche Einsicht, Erkenntnis des erstrebenswerten Guten und des zu meidenden Schlechten. Wissenschaftliche Erkenntnis und sittliche Einsicht hängen zusammen; der Mensch kann nicht allgemein tugendhaft sein, sondern nur, indem er das Gute praktiziert. Theorie und Praxis gehören zusammen, wobei einerseits die Vernunft, die philosophische Erkenntnis das tugendhafte Handeln bestimmt und andererseits die vernunftorientierte Einsicht in das erstrebenswerte Gute und das zu meidende Schlechte auf das Handeln des Menschen gerichtet ist; es orientiert sich an der Wirklichkeit und ist nicht rein theoretisch.

In dieser an der Praxis orientierten Philosophie der Ethik kann Fārābī sich auf eine aristotelische Lehre stützen, die in der Fārābīforschung bislang übersehen worden ist, nämlich auf die Interdependenz von Denken und Wahrnehmung: Ihm zufolge ist das allgemein Gute, die Idee des Guten nicht denkbar ohne sinnliche Wahrnehmung. Daher haben Aristoteles und in seiner Nachfolge Fārābī die Einbildungskraft (φαντασία) eingeführt; diese schickt als Vermittler zur Denkseele die „Sinneswahrnehmungen" (Aristoteles: αἰσθήματα) beziehungsweise die „Vorstellungsbilder" (Aristoteles: φαντάσματα) des wahrgenommenen Objektes.[30]

Diese „Vorstellungsbilder" nennt Fārābī „Nachahmungen" (*muḥākāt*) – eine terminologische Neuschöpfung des Fārābī. Alles sinnlich Wahrnehmbare, aber auch alle Intelligibilia (*al-ma'qūlāt*) werden von der Einbildungskraft nachgeahmt. Denn nicht das Wahrgenommene oder das Gedachte selbst gelangt in die Denkseele des Menschen, sondern lediglich eine Imitation, ein Bild. Die Seele denkt nur in Bildern.

Die hier zugrunde liegende Interdependenz von Denken und Wahrnehmung ist für Fārābī eine weitere Rechtfertigung für die aristotelische Kombination von wissenschaftlicher Erkenntnis (ἐπιστήμη) und sittlicher Einsicht (φρόνησις), von theoretischer und praktischer Vernunft. Dieses Miteinander von wissenschaftlicher Erkenntnis und sittlicher Einsicht kommt in Fārābīs Musterstaat (*al-madīna al-fāḍila*) und in seiner „Musterreligion" (*al-milla al-fāḍila*) zum Ausdruck. Denn die Partikularien (*al-ǧuz'iyāt*) der Religion entsprechen den Universalien (*kulliyāt*) der Philosophie, die die Partikularien beweist.[31] Insofern erscheint die Musterreligion als Nachahmung der Philosophie; sie ist ihr „ähnlich" (*šabīha*).[32]

Diese Ähnlichkeit beruht, wie wir gesehen haben, auf gemeinsamer Struktur. Gleichzeitig aber entpuppt sich die Religion keineswegs als wertloses Abbild der Philosophie. Denn sie allein kann die Bürger des Musterstaates überzeugen, das zu glauben und zum Erreichen der höchsten Glückseligkeit das zu tun, was sich von der Philosophie her beweisen, aber nicht von ihr herleiten lässt.

Dies bedeutet keineswegs, dass Philosophie eine Dienerin der Religion ist. Denn die Wirklichkeitsbezogenheit der Philosophie ist Fārābī zufolge nicht nur erkenntnistheoretisch beweisbar, nämlich mit der aristotelischen Lehre von der Interdependenz von Denken und Wahrnehmung; die Musterreligion ist auch ein praktisches, durch die Philosophie als gültig erwiesenes Beispiel

30 Vgl. auch Deborah L. Black, *Logic and Aristotle's Rhetoric and Poetics in Medieval Arabic Philosophy* (Islamic Philosophy and Theology 7; Leiden etc.: Brill, 1990), S. 189ff.

31 Vgl. Fārābī, *al-Milla al-fāḍila*, ed. Musin Mahdī (Beirut: Dār al-Mašriq, 1968), S. 47,12–17.

32 Vgl. ibid., S. 46,22; Daiber, *Ruler* (wie Anm. 29), S. 11.

für den Zusammenhang von wissenschaftlicher Erkenntnis und sittlicher Einsicht, insofern eine Nachahmung der Philosophie. Mit ihren Vorschriften und Regeln sorgt sie für die Praxisbezogenheit der Ethik und hat das Ziel, die sittliche Einsicht der Philosophie zu verwirklichen.

Hier zeigt sich, dass der Zusammenhang von Theorie und Praxis in Philosophie und Religion auch Religion und Philosophie strukturell miteinander verbindet. Philosophie und Religion sind ebenso aufeinander angewiesen wie Denken und Wahrnehmung, Theorie und Praxis, wissenschaftliche Erkenntnis und sittliche Einsicht, religiöser Glaube („Meinungen") und Handeln nach den Vorschriften der Gesetze. Der Nachweis dieser Zusammenhänge ist die originelle Leistung des Fārābī.

Bei Maimonides ist von diesen Gedanken des Fārābī recht wenig übrig geblieben. Die erkenntnistheoretischen Überlegungen des Fārābī vermisst man, und an die Stelle der farabianischen Religion als Komplex von Vorschriften und „vorzüglichen Gesetzen" (*šarā'i' fāḍila*)[33] sowie als Abbild der Philosophie ist bei Maimonides[34] das wegen seiner „gewissen Nützlichkeit"[35] universell gültige und göttliche jüdische Gesetz getreten. Dieses ersetzt seit Moses die anderen Gesetze, kann aber später durch einen Propheten oder durch die Versammlung der Weisen (*ḥakhāmīm*) allenfalls vorübergehend suspendiert oder ergänzt werden.[36] Es führe den einzelnen durch Spekulation (*an-naẓar*) und rationale Forschung (*al-baḥṯ*) zu menschlicher Vollkommenheit, nämlich zu einer Vollkommenheit in der Vernunft und Erkenntnis.[37] Diese setze die „erste Vollkommenheit" nämlich in materieller Hinsicht voraus, die nur in der Gemeinschaft im Zusammenspiel mit der Gemeinschaft[38] erreicht werden könne.[39]

Maimonides integriert einzelne Traditionen der farabianischen Philosophie, hat aber die farabianische Offenbarung, Quelle der theoretischen Erkenntnis und sittlichen Einsicht durch Vermittlung der Einbildungskraft, ersetzt durch

---

33 Fārābī, *al-Milla al-fāḍila*, ed. Mahdi (wie Anm. 31), S. 47,2ff.

34 Vgl. zu Maimonides Jeffrey Macy, „The Rule of Law and the Rule of Wisdom in Plato, al-Fārābī, and Maimonides", in *Studies in Islamic and Judaic Traditions. Papers presented at the Institute for Islamic-Judaic Studies*, ed. William M. Brinner and Stephen D. Ricks (Atlanta: Scholars Press, 1986), S. 205–232.

35 *Moreh* III.26; arabisch: ed. Atay (wie Anm. 12), S. 576,15ff.; englisch: Pines, *Guide* (wie Anm. 1), S. 508.

36 Vgl. Macy, „Rule" (wie Anm. 34), S. 218.

37 *Moreh* III.27; arabisch: ed. Atay (wie Anm. 12), S. 580; englisch: Pines, *Guide* (wie Anm. 1), S. 511; zitiert bei Macy, „Rule" (wie Anm. 34), S. 216. – Vgl. Menachem Kellner, *Maimonides on Human Perfection* (Brown Judaic Studies 202; Atlanta: Scholars Press, 1990).

38 Vgl. auch *Moreh* II.40; arabisch: ed. Atay (wie Anm. 12), S. 419ff.; englisch: Pines, *Guide* (wie Anm. 1), S. 381ff. und Aristoteles, *Politik* I,2.

39 *Moreh* III.27; arabisch: ed. Atay (wie Anm. 12), S. 579,18ff.; englisch: Pines, *Guide* (wie Anm. 1), S. 511.

die Vernunftemanation direkt an Moses, den Propheten par excellence, der nicht der vermittelnden Einbildungskraft bedarf. Denn die Einbildungskraft vermittelt sozusagen nicht die nackte Wahrheit, sondern nur Bilder, die in Maimonides' Augen wegen der Unterschiedlichkeit einer wörtlichen oder figürlichen Deutung zu Widersprüchlichkeiten führen[40] und daher ebenso wenig als gleichrangig mit der direkten Vermittlung der Wahrheit an den Propheten Moses gelten können wie das Hören von Gottes Wort durch Vermittlung eines Engels.[41] Hier ist Aristoteles' Wechselbezug zwischen Denken und Wahrnehmung und Aristoteles' Konzept von der Einbildungskraft aufgegeben zugunsten einer Epistemologie,[42] in der die Einbildungskraft wegen ihrer bildhaften und deswegen verfälschenden Darstellung nicht den Rang einer direkten Wahrheitsvermittlung einnimmt und somit nicht mit dem direkten Sprechkontakt zwischen Gott und Moses vergleichbar ist.

Im Gegensatz hierzu hatte Fārābī in seiner Schrift *al-Alfāẓ al-mustaʿmala fī l-manṭiq*[43] zu einem bestimmten Grade die bildhafte Darstellung schwieriger Dinge, das Ersetzen schwieriger Dinge durch leichter Vorstellbares und Vergleichbares für möglich gehalten. Hierin sah Maimonides jedoch eine der Ursachen für Widersprüche, die man in Büchern finden kann. Maimonides diskutiert dies offensichtlich unter dem Eindruck der genannten Fārābīschrift; deren These von der Gleichheit von Ding und Abbild und die damit begründete pädagogische Theorie vom Bild als Hilfsmittel zur Erleichterung des Lernens wird kritisiert, weil sie zu Widersprüchen führe.

Als Folge dieser Kritik an der Wertigkeit des Vorstellungsbildes können wir jetzt verstehen, warum Moses in den Augen des Maimonides nicht der Einbildungskraft bedarf und damit den anderen Propheten überlegen ist, aber auch den „Staatslenkern und Gesetzgebern", die Maimonides zufolge zu denen gehören, „die eine Einwirkung der göttlichen Vernunftemanation lediglich auf die Einbildungskraft erfahren, aber von Natur oder wegen mangelnder Übung über zu wenig Denkvermögen verfügen".[44] Deutlich ist der Unterschied zu Fārābī, für den der Regent des Musterstaates ein Philosoph und Prophet ist, der durch Vermittlung der Einbildungskraft, der nachahmenden Einbildung, die

---

40 Vgl. *Moreh* I, Vorwort; arabisch: ed. Atay (wie Anm. 12), S. 22,13ff.; englisch: Pines, *Guide* (wie Anm. 1), S. 17ff.

41 Vgl. *Moreh* II.45, Ende; arabisch: ed. Atay (wie Anm. 12), S. 445ff.; englisch: Pines, *Guide* (wie Anm. 1), S. 402–403.

42 Vgl. zu ihr auch Joel L. Kraemer, „Maimonides on Aristotle and Scientific Method", in *Studies in Philosophy and the History of Philosophy* 19 (Washington: The Catholic University of America Press, 1989), S. 53–88, besonders S. 62ff. und 80; Shlomo Pines, „The Limitations of Human Knowledge According to Al-Farabi, Ibn Bajja, and Maimonides", in *Studies in Medieval Jewish History and Literature*, ed. Isadore Twersky (Cambridge, Mass., London: Harvard University Press, 1979), S. 82–109, hier S. 89ff.

43 Ed. Mahdi (wie Anm. 31), S. 88–91; vgl. Daiber, *Ruler* (wie Anm. 29), S. 8–9.

44 Siehe oben zu Anm. 18.

Emanationen des göttlichen aktiven Intellekts empfängt. Ein Charakteristikum von Fārābīs Lehre von der Prophetie, nämlich die Nachahmung der Einbildungskraft, spielt bei dem Propheten par excellence, Moses, keine Rolle mehr und nimmt bei den im Rang nachfolgenden Empfängern der Emanationen des göttlichen aktiven Intellekts lediglich eine vermittelnde Rolle ein.

Auffälligerweise hat diese negative Einschätzung der Einbildungskraft eine Parallele bei dem älteren, gleichfalls in Cordoba geborenen Zeitgenossen Abraham Ibn Daud (1110–1180). In einer 1990 von Resianne Fontaine veröffentlichten Quellenanalyse[45] von Ibn Dauds in Toledo um 1160, also 30 Jahre vor Maimonides' *Moreh* geschriebenem Werk *ha-Emunah ha-ramah*[46] ist auf diese Abweichung von Fārābī hingewiesen worden, ohne allerdings die Parallele bei Maimonides zu notieren. Nun gibt es, worauf Fontaine[47] hinweist, in Ibn Dauds Diskussion der Prophetie eine ganze Anzahl von Parallelen zu Ibn Sīnā; sie zählt dazu auch Ibn Dauds von Fārābī abweichende Einschätzung der Einbildungskraft. Hier sollten wir allerdings darauf hinweisen, dass Ibn Dauds Einschränkung der Rolle der Einbildungskraft kein Erbe Ibn Sīnās ist; denn Ibn Sīnā folgt im Großen und Ganzen Fārābī.[48]

Angesichts weiterer Parallelen zwischen Ibn Dauds und Maimonides' allerdings wesentlich detaillierterer und teilweise erheblich abweichender Diskussionen der Prophetie,[49] aber auch anderer Themen[50] könnte Maimonides in diesem Punkt von Ibn Daud inspiriert gewesen sein.[51] Hierfür spricht manches, wobei wir uns bewusst bleiben sollten, dass Maimonides auf dieselben Quellen wie Ibn Daud zurückgegriffen und offensichtlich weitere Texte zur Verfügung hatte. Die Abhängigkeit Maimonides' von Ibn Daud ist daher nicht eindeutig klärbar; überdies betont Ibn Daud mehr die Tugendhaftigkeit des Propheten Moses, nicht aber seine intellektuelle Überlegenheit über die anderen Propheten. Diese hatte Maimonides mit der Nähe zu Gott begründet, weswegen Moses nicht der Vermittlung der Einbildungskraft bedürfe.

---

45 Resianne Fontaine, *In Defence of Judaism: Abraham Ibn Daud. Sources and Structures of Ha-Emunah ha-Ramah* (Studia Semitica Neerlandica 26; Assen, Maastricht: van Gorcum, 1990), S. 143–144.

46 Fünfte Grundlehre, Abschnitte I und II; vgl. die deutsche Übersetzung von Simson Weil (*Das Buch Emunah Ramah oder: Der erhabene Glaube* [Frankfurt am Main: Typographische Anstalt, 1852]), S. 88ff.

47 *In Defence of Judaism* (wie Anm. 45), S. 144–145.

48 Vgl. Black, *Logic* (wie Anm. 30), S. 201ff.; und zu Ibn Sīnā auch John Peter Portelli, *The Concept of Imagination in Aristotle and Avicenna* (Diss. Montreal, McGill University, 1979), S. 32ff., besonders S. 57ff.

49 Vgl. Fontaine, *In Defence of Judaism* (wie Anm. 45), S. 149ff.

50 Vgl. ibid., Register s.n. Maimonides.

51 Auf einen solchen Einfluss hat bereits A. Weiss (einer Anregung von Jacob Guttmann folgend) in der Einleitung zu seiner oben (Anm. 12) genannten deutschen Übersetzung des *Moreh* hingewiesen, allerdings mit der Einschränkung, dass beide aus einer gemeinsamen Quellen geschöpft haben könnten (S. CLXXVI– CLXXVII).

Bei dieser Pointierung handelt es sich um eine Neuerung des Maimonides, die wie gesagt seiner Kritik an Fārābīs Theorie vom Bild als pädagogischem Hilfsmittel entspringt; ferner seiner Kritik an Fārābīs Übertragung der Abbildtheorie im Rahmen der Lehre von der Einbildungskraft auf seine Doktrin von der Prophetie.

Abweichend von Fārābī betont Maimonides hier die direkte Kommunikation zwischen Gott und dem Propheten, nämlich Moses; die Einbildungskraft als vermittelnde und damit mehr oder weniger verfälschende Instanz ist den übrigen Propheten zu eigen, aber auch in variierender Weise den „Gelehrten und Theoretikern", den „Staatslenkern, den Gesetzgebern, Wahrsagern und Zauberern sowie denjenigen, die wahre Träume haben".[52]

Die von uns herausgearbeitete Neubewertung der Einbildungskraft bei Maimonides und die Konsequenz für Maimonides' Fārābībild lässt Zweifel aufkommen an der von Pines Fārābī zugeschriebenen inneren Widersprüchlichkeit in ihrer Auswirkung auf Maimonides. Sie lässt auch Zweifel aufkommen an Pines' offensichtlich von Leo Strauss[53] initiierten These, dass beide sich eines schwer verständlichen Stils bedienten, um nicht qualifizierte Leser nicht zu Fehldeutungen zu verleiten, die für den Autor und die Gesellschaft verhängnisvoll werden könnten.[54] Eine solche These lässt sich nicht aus Fārābīs Werken begründen; sie verdankt offensichtlich ihre Entstehung Maimonides' Diskussion der Ursachen der Widersprüchlichkeiten im Vorwort zum *Moreh Nevukhim*;[55] eine davon ist Maimonides zufolge der Trugschluss, eine schwierige Sache durch ein für die Vorstellungskraft des Lesers oder Zuhörers leichter verständliches, aber verfälschendes Bild erklären zu wollen. Diese kritische Einschätzung des Bildes und der Einbildungskraft hat Maimonides zu erheblichen Abweichungen von Fārābī veranlasst. Es ist daher falsch, Maimonides als uneingeschränkten Schüler des Fārābī einzustufen. Ideentransfer erscheint hier als modifizierte Adaption, die es im vorliegenden Fall verbietet, Fārābī durch die Brille des Maimonides zu sehen. Die analysierende Beschreibung der Unterschiedlichkeit und ihrer Ursachen verhilft gleichzeitig zu einem besseren Verständnis der beiden Denker Maimonides und Fārābī.

52 Siehe oben zu Anm. 18.

53 Vgl. zu diesem hier Georges Tamer, *Islamische Philosophie und die Krise der Moderne. Das Verhältnis von Leo Strauss zu Alfarabi, Avicenna und Averroes* (Islamic Philosophy, Theology and Science 43; Leiden etc.: Brill, 2001), besonders S. 244ff.

54 Vgl. Pines, *Guide* (wie Anm. 1), S. lxxix und lxxxvi.

55 Vgl. zu dieser Marvin Fox, *Interpreting Maimonides: Studies in Methodology, Metaphysics, and Moral Philosophy* (Chicago, London: University of Chicago Press, 1990), S. 67–90 („Maimonides' Method of Contradictions").

Maimonides' Knowledge of Avicenna

Some Tentative Conclusions About a Debated Question

by

Mauro Zonta

Università degli Studi di Roma "La Sapienza"

The question of the relationship of Maimonides to Avicenna's thought has been debated in the last decades by a number of scholars of Medieval Jewish philosophy (but apparently it has not raised so much interest among scholars of Medieval Islamic philosophy).[1] However, up to now it seems that none of them has been able to give a solution to what appears to be the core of this question: how and by which way did Maimonides know Avicenna's thought? Did Maimonides read Avicenna's philosophical and scientific works, or had he only an indirect knowledge of their contents? A definitive answer to these questions is very difficult. An analysis of Maimonides' extant works shows that he was very reticent about Avicenna: although a number of passages of these works have been related to the contents and even to precise passages of Avicenna's works, Maimonides' direct, literal quotations of Avicenna are really very few; they concern mostly Avicenna's medical themes and works, and even in this case, rather surprisingly, they do not concern Avicenna's main and mostly quoted and employed writings (to begin with the *Canon*).

Very recently, a short essay by Idit Dobbs-Weinstein[2] about the question of the relationship between Maimonides and Avicenna has appeared, where, probably for the first time, a tentative general approach to the question of

1 See the short list of articles and books partially or totally devoted to the question found in the recent bibliographical essays on Avicenna by Jules L. Janssens, *An Annotated Bibliography on Ibn Sīnā (1970–1989)* (Leuven: Leuven University Press, 1991), p. 259, and *An Annotated Bibliography on Ibn Sīnā. First Supplement (1990–1994)* (Textes et études du Moyen Âge 12; Louvain-la-Neuve: F.I.D.E.M., 1999), pp. 162–164. Cf. also Hans Daiber, *Bibliography of Islamic Philosophy* (2 volumes; Handbuch der Orientalistik, Abt. 1, vol. 43; Leiden, Boston: Brill, 1999), vol. II, Index; Thérèse-Anne Druart, "Brief Bibliographical Guide in Medieval Islamic Philosophy and Theology (1998–2002)", s.v. "Avicenna" (http://philosophy.cua.edu/faculty/tad/biblio.cfm).

2 Idit Dobbs-Weinstein, "Maimonides' Reticence Towards Ibn Sīnā", in Jules L. Janssens and Daniel De Smet (Eds.), *Avicenna and His Heritage. Acts of the International Colloquium, Leuven – Louvain-La-Neuve, September 8 – September 11, 1999* (Ancient and Medieval Philosophy 1/XXVIII; Leuven: Leuven University Press, 2002), pp. 281–296.

Maimonides' direct knowledge of Avicenna is found. As Dobbs-Weinstein rightly observes at the very beginning of her paper, "any attempt to discuss Ibn Sīnā's substantive influence upon Maimonides' thought [...] may risk the incredulity of the scholarly community [...] in the absence of *explicit* references to Ibn Sīnā". However, one of the conclusions of her valuable paper, affirming that "we can be reasonably certain that he [i.e. Maimonides] would have read all those Arabic works of Ibn Sīnā available in al-Andalus, Fez and Cairo after 1138", appears to be rather far-fetched, or at least not supported by irrefutable proofs (as a matter of fact, this particular question appears not to be discussed by Dobbs-Weinstein in detail). Among the other scholarly works concerning the general question of the relationship of Maimonides' thought to Avicenna, one should consider in particular Shlomo Pines' section on Avicenna in the introduction to his English translation of the *Guide of the Perplexed*,[3] and his short passage on Maimonides' knowledge of Avicenna in his item on Avicenna in the *Encyclopaedia Judaica*;[4] but, although Pines arrives at the conclusion that "Avicenna had considerable influence upon Maimonides",[5] he himself admits that "a number of Maimonidean teachings that medieval and modern commentators on the *Guide of the Perplexed* attribute to Avicenna, are, in fact, already found in al-Fārābī",[6] and that Avicenna's general influence on Maimonides might have been mediated through the reading of some of al-Ġazālī's works. More recently, aspects of the question of Maimonides' knowledge of Avicenna have been discussed in some pages of the newest (and very original) book on Maimonides' life and works, by Herbert A. Davidson,[7] and Davidson has already devoted at least parts of two other essays to the question of Avicennian influences on Maimonides.[8] However, he too seems not to have solved the question of the real extent of Maimonides' direct knowledge of Avicenna's works.

In this paper I do not claim to give a definitive answer to this question. I will only try (i) to give a concise *status quaestionis*, especially through a survey of

3 Shlomo Pines, "Translator's Introduction. The Philosophic Sources of The Guide of the Perplexed", in idem (trans.), Moses Maimonides, *The Guide of the Perplexed* (2 volumes; Chicago, London: Chicago University Press, 1963), vol. I, pp. lvii–cxxxiv, on pp. xciii–ciii.

4 Shlomo Pines, "Avicenna", in *Encyclopaedia Judaica* (Jerusalem: Keter Publishing House, 1971), vol. III, cols. 955–960, on col. 958.

5 See Pines, "Translator's Introduction" (see above n. 3), p. cii.

6 See Pines, "Avicenna" (see above n. 4), col. 958.

7 Herbert A. Davidson, *Moses Maimonides. The Man and His Works* (Oxford, New York: Oxford University Press, 2005), in particular on pp. 86, 94–95, 102–104, 113, 115, 466–467, 496, 500, 528, 536.

8 Herbert A. Davidson, *Alfarabi, Avicenna, and Averroes, on Intellect. Their Cosmologies, Theories of the Active Intellect, and Theories of Human Intellect* (Oxford, New York: Oxford University Press, 1992), pp. 197–207; idem, "Maimonides, Aristotle, and Avicenna", in Régis Morelon and Ahmad Hasnawi (Eds.), *De Zénon d'Elée à Poincaré. Recueil d'études en hommage à Roshdi Rashed* (Louvain, Paris: Peeters, 2004), pp. 719–734.

recent scholarly papers where precise suggestions of Maimonides' reading of Avicenna's passages are found, and (ii) to arrive at some tentative conclusions about Maimonides' direct knowledge (if any) of Avicenna's writings, in order to suggest what might have been the real extent of Avicenna's much-claimed "influence" on him.

***

In recent research about Maimonides' knowledge of Avicenna's works and thought, scholarly attention is devoted both to a number of "implicit" references to Avicenna (be they precise traces of reading of Avicennian passages, or more vague ones), and to the very few "explicit" references to him and his writings. Let us begin our survey from the former.

The most claimed relationship between Maimonides' and Avicenna's thoughts concerns the doctrines of the distinction between essence and existence, and between necessary and contingent (or possible) beings – and, generally speaking, the various aspects of Avicennian metaphysics. These doctrines are evidently found in Maimonides' *Guide*: here, they are the object of some detailed, although not extensive discussions in the first paragraphs of chapter 57 of part I of the *Guide*.[9] As recently shown by Yair Shiffman,[10] the Avicennian origin of such doctrines was already acknowledged by the 13th-century Spanish Jewish philosopher Shem Tov Ibn Falaquera in his *Guide to the Guide* (*Moreh ha-Moreh*), one of the first complete and systematical Hebrew commentaries on Maimonides' masterpiece, where he refers to passages of the metaphysical section of Avicenna's major encyclopaedic work, *The Cure* (*aš-Šifā'*). In modern times, Pines first gave evidence of the fact that these doctrines were closer to Avicenna's relevant ones, than to doctrines found e.g. in al-Fārābī;[11] he has also affirmed that Maimonides "holds, with Avicenna, that God's essential attributes are to be understood negatively, and uses the Avicennian proof for the existence of God, known as the proof from necessity and contingency".[12] In the last decades, this point has become the most examined and affirmed evidence of Maimonides' dependence on Avicenna's philosophical thought. In a 1992 paper, Alfred L. Ivry has tentatively connected Avicenna's doctrine about possible and necessary existences to Plotinus' Neoplatonism, and has claimed that

9 See Maimonides, *Guide*, trans. Pines (see above n. 3), vol. I, p. 132. Maimonides affirms here: "It is known that existence is an accident attaching to what exists. For this reason it is something that is superadded to the quiddity of what exists [...]. His [i.e. God's] existence is necessary. Accordingly, His existence is identical with His essence and His true reality, and His essence is His existence" etc.

10 Yair Shiffman, "'Od 'al ha-Rambam we-Ibn Sina (Again on Avicenna and Maimonides)", in *Tarbiz* 64 (1995), pp. 523–534, in particular on pp. 524–526.

11 See Pines, "Translator's Introduction" (see above n. 3), pp. xciv–xcviii.

12 See Pines, "Avicenna" (see above n. 4), col. 958.

this might be the reason for which Maimonides has accepted and defended it.[13] The same point is one of the most discussed evidences given by Dobbs-Weinstein for explaining Avicenna's "influence" on Maimonides' thought, although in any case she has not examined the question if Maimonides really read the relevant passages by Avicenna.[14] As a matter of fact, in the relevant passage of the *Guide* Maimonides does not refer explicitly to Avicenna's name, and no scholar has yet been able to prove that Maimonides' treatment of the subjects of essence/existence and necessary/possible, as found there, literally depends upon some passage of Avicenna's works.

Davidson has recently re-examined the whole question of the dependence of some aspects of Maimonides' metaphysical doctrine in the *Guide* upon Avicenna's. In a 1992 book about the doctrine of the intellect in Al-Fārābī, Avicenna and Averroes, he affirms that metaphysical "theses and details in Maimonides for which Avicenna is the source include the explicit formulation of the principle that from the one only one can necessarily proceed, the emanation of the matter of the sublunar region from the active intellect, and the designation of the active intellect as the *giver of forms*".[15] Later on, in a 2004 article, he has studied some of Maimonides' twenty-five philosophical propositions on Aristotelian physics and metaphysics at the beginning of part II of the *Guide*, and has shown that three of them at least (propositions 19, 20 and 21)[16] are surely not taken from Aristotle, and their contents are very similar to some peculiar aspects of Avicennian metaphysical doctrine; in other cases too (the notion of a natural form not subject to generation and corruption; the doctrine that unity is an accident attached to the essence of what exists; the

13 See Alfred L. Ivry, "Maimonides and Neoplatonism: Challenge and Response", in Lenn E. Goodman (Ed.), *Neoplatonism and Jewish Thought* (Studies in Neoplatonism 7; New York: State University of New York Press, 1992), pp. 137–156, in particular on pp. 146–154.

14 See Dobbs-Weinstein, "Maimonides' Reticence" (see above n. 2), pp. 286–293.

15 See Davidson, *Alfarabi, Avicenna, and Averroes* (see above n. 8), pp. 199 and 206. Surprisingly, these doctrines, as Davidson himself has pointed out in "Maimonides, Aristotle, and Avicenna" (see above n. 8), pp. 730–731, are ascribed to Aristotle in the *Guide*, part II, chapters 4, 21 and 22: see Maimonides, *Guide*, trans. Pines (see above n. 3), vol. II, pp. 256–258, 315–320.

16 See Maimonides, *Guide*, trans. Pines (see above n. 3), vol. II, p. 238: "Everything that has a cause for its existence is only possible with regard to existence in respect to its own essence [...]. Everything that is necessarily existent in respect to its own essence has no cause for its existence [...]. Everything that is composed of two notions has necessarily that composition as the cause of its existence as it really is [...]". In his recent Hebrew translation of the *Guide*, Michael Schwarz has pointed out the possible Avicennian origin also of proposition 22 (see ibid.: "Every body is necessarily composed of two things and is necessarily accompanied by accidents [...]"). See Maimonides, *Guide*, Hebrew translation ... by Michael Schwarz (2 volumes; Tel Aviv: Tel Aviv University Press, 2002), vol. I, pp. 253–254, nn. 30–33.

hypothesis that the celestial spheres are "approximately fifty"),[17] when in the *Guide* Maimonides explicitly refers to "Aristotle" and/or to his *Metaphysics*, in reality he is referring to doctrines found not in Aristotle, but in Avicenna.[18] As observed by Shiffman, Falaquera had already identified Avicenna as a source of some of these doctrines in his commentary on the *Guide*.[19] Other aspects of Maimonides' metaphysics as "influenced" by Avicenna are occasionally noted by scholars: e.g., in 1991 Warren Zev Harvey has pointed out the "Avicennizing" character of Maimonides' idea of the "Creator", including the crucial point that the "First Mover" is not God himself, but something "created" by Him (chapter 69 of part I, and chapter 4 of part II).[20]

The question of the direct source of these doctrines is not easy to solve. Of course, Maimonides might have found them by perusing Avicenna's *The Cure* and his other well-known (and shorter) philosophical encyclopaedia, *The Salvation (an-Naǧāt)*, where a number of traces of them have been identified by medieval (Falaquera) and modern historians of Jewish philosophy; but apparently no one of the above-mentioned scholars has been able to give proof of this fact. As a matter of fact, some of the most recent studies on the "Avicennian" origin of the above affirmations found in the *Guide* have admitted that Maimonides could find almost all of Avicenna's metaphysical doctrines in another, well-known medieval Islamic philosophical source: the *Intentions of the Philosophers* (*Maqāṣid al-falāsifa*) by al-Ġazālī, where Avicenna's doctrines are reported and discussed in detail.[21] Moreover, Davidson has pointed out that, when in chapter 22 of part II of the *Guide* Maimonides, after having explained Avicenna's doctrine of emanation, rejects it, he employs the same arguments of al-Ġazālī.[22] This is valid also for what Pines assumes to be a sure quasi-explicit quotation of Avicenna found in the *Guide* (part I, chapter 74), where Maimonides ascribes to "some of the later philosophers" the claim (criticized by him) that the doctrine of the eternity of the world is not incompatible with belief in

17 For these doctrines, see Maimonides, *Guide*, trans. Pines (see above n. 3), vol. I, pp. 168–169 (part I, chapter 69) and p. 132 (part I, chapter 57); vol. II, p. 257 (part II, chapter 4).

18 See Davidson, "Maimonides, Aristotle, and Avicenna" (see above n. 8), pp. 728–732; see also idem, *Moses Maimonides* (see above n. 7), pp. 102–104.

19 See Shiffman, "Again on Avicenna and Maimonides" (see above n. 10), pp. 533–534.

20 See Warren Z. Harvey, "Why Maimonides Was Not a *Mutakallim*", in Joel L. Kraemer (Ed.), *Perspectives on Maimonides. Philosophical and Historical Studies* (Oxford: Oxford University Press, 1991), pp. 105–114, on pp. 113–114 and n. 28.

21 This is noticed by Davidson, "Maimonides, Aristotle, and Avicenna" (see above n. 8), p. 732 ("Virtually every of a metaphysical character attributed by Maimonides to Aristotle but actually deriving from Avicenna was available to him through Ghazali's *Maqāṣid*"; in n. 49, Davidson notes the "striking similarities", *even in phraseology*, between Maimonides and al-Ġazālī about some of these points); see also idem, *Moses Maimonides* (see above n. 7), p. 104, n. 146; Dobbs-Weinstein, "Maimonides' Reticence" (see above n. 2), p. 282.

22 See Davidson, *Alfarabi, Avicenna, and Averroes* (see above n. 8), pp. 199–200.

the afterlife of the individual soul:[23] very probably, the source of this passage is found in al-Ġazālī's *Incoherence of the Philosophers* (*Tahāfut al-falāsifa*), where this question is discussed and Avicenna's opinion about it is mentioned.[24] Therefore, one should conclude that Maimonides' *direct* dependence on Avicenna about the above-mentioned crucial questions has not yet been demonstrated, and has even been (although cautiously) cast into doubt.

Of course, there are other points where similarities between Avicenna's and Maimonides' philosophical doctrines have been found; in some minor cases, scholars have explained them by referring to precise passages of Avicenna's works.

One of the recently debated points concerns Maimonides' doctrine of the human intellect, especially as far as its conjunction with the Agent Intellect is concerned, which is found in several passages of the *Guide*, and is discussed in particular in chapter 51 of part III.[25] Davidson claims that, on this point, Maimonides completely followed Avicenna in "the thesis that man obtains actual intellectual thought by entering into conjunction with the active intellect and receiving the active intellect's emanation".[26] Here, Davidson has found a very similar example in both authors: the analogy of "the skilled scribe when he is not writing",[27] which Maimonides and Avicenna employ for describing the state of potentiality of human intellect close to actuality; this example is found also in a passage of Maimonides' *Treatise on Logic*,[28] but one has to remark that the Maimonidean authorship of this work has been recently challenged.[29] However,

23 See Pines, "Translator's Introduction" (see above n. 3), p. ciii; see also Maimonides, *Guide*, trans. Pines (see above n. 3), pp. 220–221: "One of the creationists maintains that the creation of the world in time is established by what the philosophers say regarding the permanent existence of the souls. He says: if the world is eternal, the number of the men who died in the limitless past is infinite. There would therefore be an infinite number of souls existing simultaneously. Now this is [...] false [...]. Now *some of the later philosophers* have resolved this doubt by saying that the soul endowed with continued existence were not bodies so that they would have place and position; and that in regard to their existence, infinity in number would be impossible for them" (Italics by the author).

24 See Herbert A. Davidson, *Proofs for Eternity, Creation and the Existence of God in Medieval Islamic and Jewish Philosophy* (Oxford, New York: Oxford University Press, 1987), p. 123 and n. 69 (referring to *Incoherence of the Philosophers*, question 1, § 22); see also ibid., pp. 368–369 (referring to *Incoherence of the Philosophers*, question 4, §§ 8 and 19), and Maimonides, *Guide*, trans. Schwarz (see above n. 16), vol. I, p. 232, n. 43.

25 See Maimonides, *Guide*, trans. Pines (see above n. 3), vol. II, pp. 618–628, in particular on p. 621.

26 See Davidson, *Alfarabi, Avicenna, and Averroes* (see above n. 8), pp. 200–203, 206 (where the quotation is found).

27 See Maimonides, *Guide*, trans. Pines (see above n. 3), vol. II, p. 625.

28 See Maïmonide, *Traité de logique*. Traduit de l'arabe, avec une introduction et des notes par Rémi Brague (Paris: Desclée de Brouwer, 1996), p. 80.

29 See Davidson, *Moses Maimonides* (see above n. 7), pp. 313–322.

as affirmed by Dobbs-Weinstein, Avicenna's influence upon Maimonides' noetics is "bracketed [...] by differences"[30] as far as the nature of the human soul, the status of the acquired intellect and the question of the conjunction are concerned. What can we conclude from this? There is no doubt that Maimonides knew Avicenna's quoted example, but this is neither a proof of the fact that he found it directly in Avicenna's work, nor that he perused all of Avicenna's many treatments on noetics and employed them as his major source. One should remember that Avicenna's doctrine of the human intellect was well-known among several 12th-century Islamic authors.

Probably, the same conclusion can apply also to the doctrine of prophecy as found in the *Guide* (part II, chapters 32–48, in particular chapters 36–38),[31] which has been connected to Avicenna's own doctrine by modern scholars. About this doctrine, Pines first declared that "there are several points in which Avicenna's influence on Maimonides may be discerned with some degree of precision".[32] According to Pines, "Maimonides agrees with Avicenna that man must live in a community, and that prophets are needed to establish the law of the community" (a general point which was already noticed by Falaquera in his commentary).[33] "Maimonides further agrees with Avicenna that the appearance of prophets is due to teleological provisions of nature. Avicennian influences also seem to be at work in Maimonides' contention that prophets can reach knowledge of reality without having previously grasped the theoretical premises for such knowledge, and in his view that meditation is superior to worship".[34] However, as rightly observed by Pines himself, although Avicenna briefly deals with prophecy in several of his extant works, most of the similarities between these passages and the detailed treatment of prophecy found in the *Guide* are really very limited, are often vague, and might have been drawn from non-Avicennian sources.[35] As a matter of fact, Davidson has found in Maimonides a theoretical knowledge about prophecy that "recalls Avicenna's intellectual prophecy, but Maimonides' version has peculiarities of his own".[36] Up to now, it seems that scholars have identified a close relationship of Maimonides' doctrine on prophecy to Avicenna in one particular point only: it is the idea, found in chapter 38 of part II of the *Guide*, that the prophet has a specific aptitude of

30 About this point, see Dobbs-Weinstein, "Maimonides' Reticence" (see above n. 2), pp. 293–296 (quotation from p. 293).

31 See Maimonides, *Guide*, trans. Pines (see above n. 3), vol. II, pp. 369–378.

32 See Pines, "Translator's Introduction" (see above n. 3), pp. xcviii–xcix, and in general pp. xcviii–cii.

33 See Shiffman, "Again on Avicenna and Maimonides" (see above n. 10), pp. 529–531.

34 See Pines, "Avicenna" (see above n. 4), col. 958.

35 See Pines, "Translator's Introduction" (see above n. 3), pp. ci–cii.

36 See Davidson, *Alfarabi, Avicenna, and Averroes* (see above n. 8), pp. 203–206 (quotation is found on p. 205).

"insight" (Arabic *ḥads*), which gives him the capacity of receiving the emanation of the Active Intellect (that is, the genuine truth) without any effort.[37]

Another Maimonidean treatment of a philosophical doctrine which has been related to Avicenna is the question of the immortality of the human soul, as discussed in particular in Maimonides' *Commentary on the Mishnah*, treatise *Sanhedrin*, chapter 10, introduction (the so-called *Introduction to Pereq Ḥeleq*). A connection between Maimonides' and Avicenna's solutions of this question was first suggested by Harry Blumberg in a paper first published in 1965, and then reprinted several times.[38] However, the first detailed study about the possible employment of an Avicennian source in this case has been made by Dov Schwartz. In a recent article, Schwartz has compared the identification of immortality as pleasure as found in the above-mentioned Maimonidean passage and in Avicenna's *The Salvation*: "like Avicenna, Maimonides too draws a sharp line between the physical pleasure of man's internal and external senses [...] and the pleasure in intellectual attainment and knowledge enjoyed by the supernal beings [...]. Like Avicenna, Maimonides holds that it is within man's power to achieve pleasure of this second kind and apprehend spiritual knowledge".[39] Schwartz has even found in both authors the same examples: "the analogy of the blind man who cannot envisage visual beauty [...]; the fact that people are willing to suffer in order to gain respect or praise from their peers; [...] the pleasure derived by the separate intellects from their intellectual activity".[40] Schwartz concludes that Maimonides did surely read the relevant passages of Avicenna's *The Salvation*, either in their original text or in an Arabic paraphrase; however, he modified one component at least of Avicenna's doctrine according to his own views. On the contrary, Amira Eran has then pointed out that

37 See Maimonides, *Guide*, trans. Pines (see above n. 3), vol. II, p. 376 (where this term is translated as "conjecturing"). The closeness to Avicenna's doctrine on "insight" has been pointed out in Pines, "Translator's Introduction" (see above n. 3), p. ci, n. 73, and in Davidson, *Alfarabi, Avicenna, and Averroes* (see above n. 8), p. 205; see also Maimonides, *Guide*, trans. Schwarz (see above n. 16), vol. II, p. 331, n. 9, quoting, among others, the recent study by Binyamin Abrahamov, "Maimonides and Ibn Sina's Theory of *Ḥads*: A Re-Examination of the *Guide of the Perplexed* II, ch. 38", in Paul Fenton (Ed.), *Proceedings of the Seventh International Conference of the Society for Judaeo-Arabic Studies, Strasbourg 1995* (forthcoming).

38 See Harry Blumberg, *The Problem of Immortality in Avicenna, Maimonides, and St. Thomas Aquinas*, in *Harry A. Wolfson Jubilee Volume* (2 volumes; Jerusalem: American Academy for Jewish Research, 1965), vol. I, pp. 165–185; reprinted in Jacob I. Dienstag (Ed.), *Studies in Maimonides and St. Thomas Aquinas* (New York: Ktav Publishing House, 1975), pp. 29–49, and in Harry Blumberg, *Essays in Medieval Jewish and Islamic Philosophy*, ed. Arthur Hyman (New York: Ktav Publishing House, 1977), pp. 95–115.

39 See Dov Schwartz, "Avicenna and Maimonides on Immortality: A Comparative Study", in Richard Nettler (Ed.), *Medieval and Modern Perspectives on Muslim-Jewish Relations* (Luxembourg: Harwood Publishers, 1996), pp. 185–197 (quotation on pp. 187–188).

40 See ibid., p. 188.

some of al-Ġazālī's affirmations about the immortality of the human soul are apparently closer to Maimonides' doctrine about this question than Avicenna's.[41] More recently, Davidson has re-examined the whole point and has come to a more complicated solution. He concludes that Maimonides' "parallels with Avicenna and Ghazālī are too distinctive to be accidental, but the analogies are so appealing that they could have circulated independently of the books in which they originated".[42] Therefore, in this case too the existence of similar examples and doctrines in Maimonides and Avicenna does not prove that the former read them directly in the writings of the latter.

This suggested explanation, according to which in this case Maimonides did probably not read Avicenna but a source close to Avicenna, should be valid in some other cases, which have been already pointed out by scholars. For example, in 1979 Miriam Galston suggested that, in chapter 14 of the *Treatise on Logic,* Maimonides (provided that he is the real author of this book) adopted the distinction between theoretical and practical philosophy, as well as the tripartition of the latter, from Avicenna's *On the Division of the Intellectual Sciences* (*Fī aqsām al-ʿulūm al-ʿaqlīya*);[43] but Joel Kraemer rightly identified al-Fārābī as the main source of this doctrine.[44] Other supposed Maimonidean references to Avicenna are vague and uncertain. Very recently, Gad Freudenthal has found a passage of the commentary on the *Guide* by the 14th-century Provençal Jewish philosopher Moses Narboni (1300–ca. 1360), who affirmed that Avicenna was the source of the doctrine of the four celestial spheres and of their relationship to the four elements, found in chapter 10 of part II of the *Guide;*[45] however, as pointed out by Freudenthal, there seems to be no trace of this precise doctrine in Avicenna's philosophic-scientific encyclopaedias (to begin with *The Salvation*) or in other works.[46]

Serious doubts about the extent of Maimonides' knowledge of Avicenna's writings are raised even from the examination of the very few direct, explicit quotations of Avicenna found in Maimonides' works other than the *Guide.* As a matter of fact, in his *Treatise on the Resurrection,* Maimonides explicitly affirms

41 See Amira Eran, "Al-Ghazali and Maimonides on the World to Come and Spiritual Pleasures", in *Jewish Studies Quarterly* 8 (2001), pp. 137–166.

42 See Davidson, *Moses Maimonides* (see above n. 7), pp. 94–95 (quotation from p. 95).

43 See Miriam Galston, "Realism and Idealism in Avicenna's Political Philosophy", in *Review of Politics* 41 (1979), pp. 561–577, on pp. 570–572.

44 See Joel L. Kraemer, "Maimonides on the Philosophic Sciences in His Treatise on the Art of Logic", in idem (Ed.), *Perspectives on Maimonides* (see above n. 20), pp. 77–104. See also Maïmonide, *Traité de logique,* trans. Brague (see above n. 28), pp. 96 and 99–102, in particular n. 217 (where it results that here practical philosophy is divided not into three, but into *four* parts, as in al-Fārābī's *Book on Religion*).

45 See Maimonides, *Guide,* trans. Pines (see above n. 3), vol. II, pp. 270–271.

46 See Gad Freudenthal, "Maimonides' Four Globes (Guide II: 9–10): Sources and Purposes" (forthcoming in a volume to be edited by A. Ravitzky; Jerusalem: Merkaz Zalman Shazar, 2005).

that Samuel ben ʿEli, his rival in the book, was mentioning "things taken from Avicenna's *al-Maʿād*", without giving any precise information about the contents of these "things". Davidson, who has studied this passage, has concluded that it appears impossible even to ascertain which of the two or three Avicennian works having a similar title it refers to.[47] Possibly, just like in the case of the mention of (Abū l-Barakāt al-Baġdādī's) *Kitāb al-muʿtabar* in the same passage, Maimonides had only an indirect knowledge of the existence of an Avicennian writing having that title, and of some of its contents. Therefore, the only explicit and direct quotations of Avicenna in Maimonides are found in the latter's medical works: they are medical recipes ascribed to him. Some of these recipes, taken from chapter 4 of Avicenna's short treatise *On Cardiac Drugs*,[48] are quoted in Maimonides' *On the Causes of Symptoms*; some other recipes attributed to Avicenna are found in an untitled treatise on sexual performance, whose ascription to Maimonides, according to Davidson, is even doubtful.[49] Evidently, these short references do not prove that Maimonides had an extensive knowledge of Avicenna's medical writings as he had, e.g., of Galen's. In particular remarkable is the apparent total absence of any clear reference to Avicenna's best known medical encyclopaedia, the *Canon*.[50]

From the data given above one might be lead to conclude that, in a number of fields (not only in medicine), Avicenna was not regarded as a useful *direct* source by Maimonides. This conclusion appears to be confirmed by Maimonides' one single explicit remark on Avicenna's thought and work, as found in his well-known and often quoted letter to his "authorized" Hebrew translator, Samuel Ibn Tibbon, written in 1199 and preserved in two Hebrew versions.[51] Here, Maimonides affirms that, although the books of Avicenna are precise and subtle, they are not like those of al-Fārābī (or, according to another, apparently more critical version, "Avicenna's books can raise objections and

47 See Davidson, *Moses Maimonides* (see above n. 7), p. 528, n. 194.

48 See Avicenna, *Liber Canonis, De medicinis cordialibus, et Cantica*. Latin translation by Gerard of Cremona, ed. Andrea Alpago (Venetiis: Apud Juntas, 1555; reprint Cambridge, Mass.: Omnisys, n.d. [1990?]), fol. 566r–566v.

49 See Davidson, *Moses Maimonides* (see above n. 7), pp. 466–467.

50 See ibid., p. 86, pointing out Maimonides' "noteworthy failure to mention Avicenna's substantial, authoritative medical encyclopedia". Salomon Munk pointed out the apparent similarity between a short statement of Maimonides' *Guide* (part I, chapter 26, according to Pines' translation: "[a living being] requires eating and drinking in order to replace what has been dissolved") and a passage of the *Canon*, but obviously this is not a proof of the fact that Maimonides read and employed the latter as a medical source. See Maimonides, *Guide*, trans. Schwarz (see above n. 16), vol. I, p. 63, n. 8.

51 A classical edition of these two versions (whose contents have some important variants) is found in Alexander Marx, "Texts by and about Maimonides", in *The Jewish Quarterly Review* n.s. 25 (1934–1935), pp. 371–428, on pp. 378–380. A re-edition is now available in Yishaq Shailat (Ed.), *Iggerot ha-Rambam* (2 volumes; Jerusalem: Hotsa'at Ma'aliyyot, 1987–1988), vol. II, pp. 552–554.

are not like al-Fārābī's"); however, they are usable and deserve attention and reflection. Dobbs-Weinstein has recently re-examined the relevant passage in her study on Maimonides and Avicenna. Her claim is that, from an analysis of Maimonides' affirmations found in this letter, he regarded the writings of Avicenna, like those of Plato, to be "superior both in form and in content" not for the teaching of philosophy, but "for instruction in 'divine science', where philosophical clarity is not only impossible but may […] be misleading".[52] As a matter of fact, it seems to me that Dobbs-Weinstein's ingenious interpretation of the two versions of Maimonides' judgement of Avicenna is based upon a diffused but doubtful interpretation of Maimonides as an "esoteric writer", but does not change substantially the facts. As observed by Davidson, here "Maimonides rates Avicenna's writings as inferior to Alfarabi's, although he grants that they have 'value' and are worthy of study".[53] A literal, factual interpretation of Maimonides' affirmations shows that he was rather reserved with regard to Avicenna's books, which he did not regard to be so authoritative as those of Aristotle ("roots and foundations of all works on the sciences"), Al-Fārābī (whose books on logic are "faultlessly excellent"), Ibn Bajja (whose writings are "all […] of high standard").[54] So, did he really think that they deserved to be systematically read and perused? Apparently, he did not.

* * *

What is the relationship between Maimonides and Avicenna resulting from the above mentioned data? It seems to me that there is no reason to deny that Maimonides was in some way "influenced" by Avicenna, in the sense that he had an *indirect* knowledge at least of the main contents of Avicenna's philosophical thought. This influence – which was well-known to some of the most learned medieval Hebrew commentators of Maimonides – concerned especially such crucial points as the nature of God, the emanation concept, and the relationship between human intellect and the Active Intellect; it also involved some particular aspects of prophecy and the question of the immortality of the human soul. However, the fact that Maimonides had a general idea of some important Avicennian philosophical doctrines does not imply that he directly read and perused Avicenna's most important philosophical works, such as *The Cure* or *The Salvation*. More probably, he might have read some isolated passages of Avicenna's minor works, having a direct knowledge of some of his

52 See Dobbs-Weinstein, "Maimonides' Reticence" (see above n. 2), pp. 283–286 (quotation from p. 286).

53 See Davidson, *Moses Maimonides* (see above n. 7), p. 113.

54 These translations of Maimonides' judgements of Aristotle's, al-Fārābī's and Ibn Bajja's books are taken from Dobbs-Weinstein, "Maimonides' Reticence" (see above n. 2), p. 284.

medical writings. Surely, Maimonides knew some examples which are found also in Avicenna, but these examples are common to a number of Islamic philosophical authors after Avicenna, in particular to al-Ġazālī.

One can even suppose that al-Ġazālī was the real, direct source of many, if not all of Maimonides' "Avicennian" doctrines. This supposition might be supported by some considerations. Al-Ġazālī surely played an important role in the shaping of Maimonides' philosophical and theological thought, as it has been pointed out by some scholars from the nineteenth century onwards, more recently by Charles Manekin;[55] and, as said, Davidson and others admitted the possibility that Maimonides found in al-Ġazālī a number of "Avicennian" ideas. Moreover, it results that al-Ġazālī's *Intentions of the Philosophers* were among the major sources through which another 12th-century Jewish philosopher, Abraham Ibn Daud, completed his knowledge of Avicenna's thought.[56] As it has been recently pointed out by Steven Harvey, among European Jewish philosophers after Maimonides, especially in the 14th century, al-Ġazālī's *Intentions* seem to have been employed for substituting the direct reading of Avicenna's philosophical encyclopaedias.[57] Maimonides might have adopted the same solution: he could not, and in fact did not ignore Avicenna's philosophical thought – which, as shown by recent research,[58] directly or indirectly influenced a number of authors of 12th-century Islamic philosophy in the Near East, where Maimonides lived and worked – but al-Ġazālī might have been a more useful and easier way for knowing, understanding and employing it.

---

55 See Charles Manekin, "Al-Ghazali and Maimonides Revisited", paper read at the 36th Annual Conference of the American Association for Jewish Studies (Chicago, 19th–21st December, 2004).

56 See the recent study of Ibn Daud's main philosophical work, *The Exalted Faith,* in Amira Eran, *Me-emunah tammah le-emunah ramah. Haguto ha-qdam-Maimonit shel ha-Rabad (From Simple Faith to Sublime Faith. Ibn Daud's Pre-Maimonidean Thought)* (Hakibbutz Hameuhad, Israel, 1998), in particular pp. 27 and 76.

57 See Steven Harvey, "Why did Fourteenth-Century Jews Turn to Alghazali's Account of Natural Science?", in *The Jewish Quarterly Review* n.s. 91 (2001), pp. 359–376.

58 See the recent survey by Dimitri Gutas, "The Heritage of Avicenna: The Golden Age of Arabic Philosophy, 1000 – ca. 1350", in Janssens and De Smet (Eds.), *Avicenna and His Heritage* (see above n. 2), pp. 81–97.

Averroes and Maimonides in Defense of Philosophizing

by

Ralph Lerner

The University of Chicago

In honor of Joel L. Kraemer

We need a latter-day Plutarch to oblige us with a "parallel lives" of Córdoba's most notable native sons. The thoughts and acts of those almost exact contemporaries, Averroes and Maimonides, invite sustained scrutiny. Their points of convergence and divergence solicit reflection and repay analysis. Yet, after eight centuries we still have only the rudiments, not the comprehensive and searching account we crave.[1] That project awaits a master yet to come.

The theme of the present paper is necessarily modest. I will consider some of the activities of Averroes and Maimonides as exegetes, jurists, and statesmen in one specific respect. I want to witness their determined efforts to make room in their world for philosophers and philosophizing. Although the evidence I can adduce is hardly new, the shift in perspective may suggest a shared interest between these two thinkers that deserves forceful restatement.

True, the *ra᾽īs al-Yahūd* in Fusṭāṭ never issued a formal ruling comparable to that of the jurist in Córdoba. Nevertheless, the themes and concerns raised in Averroes' *Decisive Treatise* are familiar to readers of Maimonides as well. This is hardly surprising given the parallels in these two thinkers' situations. Each lives and acts within a communal world defined by its sacred text. In coming to terms with that ineluctable presence, each is obliged to confront anew the problem of how best to read that text. Each understands the search for meaning to be ultimately a quest to establish a writer's or speaker's intention. Needless to say, the stakes are raised very high when the text and its author or speaker are invested with divinity. The exalted character of Holy Writ should preclude unqualified individuals from indulging their interpretive fancy. Yet they feel free to do so, and

1 Shlomo Pines, "Translator's Introduction", in Moses Maimonides, *The Guide of the Perplexed* (Chicago, London: University of Chicago Press, 1963), pp. cviii–cix, cxvi–cxx; Warren Zev Harvey, "Averroes and Maimonides on the Obligation of Philosophic Contemplation (*i'tibār*)", in *Tarbiz: A Quarterly for Jewish Studies* 58(1) (Oct.–Dec. 1988), pp. 75, 80 (Hebrew); Leo Strauss, *Philosophie und Gesetz* (Berlin: Schocken, 1935), chapter 2(a)(b).

the consequent instability and uncertainty afflicting their communities prompt these two philosophers to intervene. They offer their publics a corrective lesson in the form of a philosophically informed commentary on a sacred text. It is noteworthy that while engaging in interpretation, each also effectually legislates on behalf of his special cause.

I.

The locus classicus for this campaign on behalf of philosophy is Averroes' *Decisive Treatise* (*kitāb faṣl al-maqāl*).[2] From the outset Averroes speaks as a jurist delivering a formal legal opinion. He leaves no doubt that his theorizing in this work has as its point of departure the revelation that literally constitutes his community. Indeed, his inquiry as a whole bears silent witness to the Muslims' omnipresent sacred texts and traditions by being ever mindful of their presumed bounds. Hence any dissatisfaction we readers may have with Averroes' way of making his case and pressing his argument has to allow for the special circumstances attending this production. However we characterize this work – as a *fatwā*, or as a public address to a favorably disposed ruler, or as yet another of Averroes' efforts to put the dialectical theologians in their place – this much is clear: the *Decisive Treatise* is not a private communication of one philosopher to another. To begin as he does by asking – What is the legal status of human wisdom? – is tantamount to acknowledging that the study of philosophy and perhaps even of logic is a matter of general misgiving or suspicion. It is as it were to put philosophy on trial. A significant body of public opinion holds that the defendant in the dock has much to answer for. Averroes accordingly mutes any features of philosophizing that might make it seem more alien in Muslim eyes than it already does. Further, he enlarges upon any scriptural language that might appear to comport with (or even welcome) the philosophers' aims.

Averroes hastens to engage in creative exegesis. Invoking the Koranic injunction, "Consider, you who are able to see" (59:2), he ignores this verse's commonly understood meaning (look back upon the scriptural texts and draw the appropriate lessons from their examples).[3] Rather, he would have us read the verse as enjoining the use of our intellect to gain a greater understanding of the art embedded in all existing things. The surer our grasp of that art, the more certainly are we

2 Parenthetical citations are to the page and line numbers of Marcus J. Müller's 1859 edition of the Arabic text (Averroes, *Philosophie und Theologie* [München: Franz]), which have been carried over in the following: Ibn Rushd (Averroes), *Kitāb faṣl al-maqāl*, ed. George F. Hourani (Leiden: Brill, 1959); and Averroes, *On the Harmony of Religion and Philosophy*, trans. George F. Hourani (London: Luzac, 1961).

3 Harvey, "Averroes and Maimonides" (see above n. 1), p. 78.

pointed toward the Artisan whose works they are. And given that this activity of theorizing about existing things constitutes philosophizing itself, the verse must be read as calling us, like Abraham, to engage in that very activity. More radically stated, the Law *commands* that we come to know all existing things *demonstratively*.

Here is a heavy obligation. It already presupposes that I, for one, am able to distinguish the various kinds of syllogistic reasoning and that I can assess their relative validity and certainty. This is as much as to say that there is a prior legal obligation to master the art of logic. Even if this were baldly asserted it would not necessarily shock or alarm. After all, Muslim jurists have long engaged in analogical reasoning when deriving rules and settling cases. But Averroes insists on pressing his point. The mastery of logic that he is speaking of cannot be passed off as an Islamic science, let alone as something an individual might work out on his own. On the contrary, intellectual syllogistic reasoning has to be recognized as a multigenerational bequest, a product of the cumulative collaborative efforts of a long line of thinkers. While it is indeed an indispensable tool for one who is trying to know God, it is admittedly a bequest from a pre-Islamic world, a world of nonbelievers. Averroes brings his readers to a paradoxical conclusion: Only by stepping outside the Islamic milieu and by reflecting upon the works of the Ancients, can one then be positioned to fulfill the Law's command.

This is a prospect fraught with dangers – and not only those arising from the cries of outraged literalists. Believers generally are wary of alien imports. Their misgivings and suspicions extend far beyond the Ancients' works on logical reasoning. More incomprehensible and reprehensible for them is Averroes' bold conclusion that the aim and intention of the Ancients, as expressed in their books, "is the very intention to which the Law urges us" (p. 5,13–14). To be sure, Averroes quickly stipulates a proviso lest he be misunderstood. In no way is he issuing a *laissez-passer* for anyone and everyone to engage in these studies. The Law's injunction to "consider" is directed to those "who are able to see", to those who combine the requisite innate intelligence with the integrity and moral virtue that would be expected of a witness testifying in a court of law. To forbid this kind of qualified individual from reflecting upon those works of the Ancients amounts to slamming shut the gate that leads to the truest knowledge of God. Doing so makes as little sense as denying the thirsty a fresh, sweet, life-giving drink just because some people have choked on water (pp. 5,14–18; 6,6–9).

Averroes boldly declares that the Law's intention is to teach "true science and true practice" (p. 19,10). His insistence that sound interpretation is the deposit or trust that mankind is charged with holding (p. 23,16–17), comes close to asserting that the end of man as man is true interpretation, or philosophy. Yet Averroes proceeds with caution in trying to mark off a place where those rare few, the select, can fulfill their "obligation" (pp. 1,14; 2,9.11; 26,14), or their "duty" (20,14.16), to engage in a thorough investigation of the root of the Law. A wisdom that would teach sobriety to others must itself first exhibit sobriety. Rather than act in the spirit of some sophist or village atheist eager to disabuse the great multitude of their cherished images and beliefs, the select must exercise social responsibility. They must forbear from broadcasting the refined conclusions of philosophic interpretations and stifle any expressions of contempt for generally held beliefs. For when the wise come to understand the *necessity* of these opinions and images they develop the proper respect for the Law's wisdom. At the same time they will appreciate how swiftly and how far Averroes' argument has slipped its initial moorings in the safe harbor of Law-based theorizing.

At first, let us recall, Wisdom is hauled before the bar of the Law to justify itself. But this very legitimation of intellectual syllogistic reasoning leads to an exaltation of philosophic inquiry as a way of life. Averroes even asserts in his own name that the apparent sense of the Law has to yield whenever it is at odds with the conclusions of demonstrative reasoning (pp. 7,21–8,1). His argument's point of departure has been inverted. Now it is the sacred text that has to be interpreted to conform to the findings of philosophic investigation. Some of Averroes' readers may find this line of argument paradoxical, even an inducement to puzzle out its unsettling implication. The recommended activity of unearthing the Law's inner meaning through true interpretation may be but an optional way of acquiring knowledge of the whole of existence. Those few readers are left to draw their own quiet conclusions about how best to conduct their philosophical pursuits.[4]

Averroes stresses the universality of the Koran's message. As the tradition has it, the Prophet was sent to "the Red and the Black". Now since the Law aims to address all people, it has to take account of their different natures. Each must be spoken to according to that person's abilities and acquired capacities. Each will be brought to assent to the Law's message if it is couched for him or her in fitting language and at the appropriate level. A rhetorical presentation will be intelligible and persuasive to most; a dialectical argument to some; and a demonstration to but a few. It follows that it is precisely because the Law intends to teach *everyone* that it cannot be presumed to speak in only one voice. Rather, it has to contain all kinds of methods of bringing about assent and all kinds of methods of forming a concept (p. 19,17–18). The Law accomplishes its great end by using language that bears both an apparent sense and an inner sense. The former conveys images of its truths. Addressed to mankind at large, these representations must be taken at face value by anyone belonging to the subdemonstrative classes. The inner sense, on the other hand, conveys the Law's true meanings, but these reveal themselves

4 It is striking that Averroes extends this scholarly freedom of interpretation to encompass one of the principal roots of the Law. A man of the demonstrative class may engage freely in private interpretation of the promised life in the hereafter (however understood), provided only that he not lead others to deny its *existence* (pp. 16,19–17,1; 17,7–9). In the Introduction to his translation of this text, Hourani sees clearly the chasm that this line of argument opens for philosophizing in Islam, but draws back from the precipice (Hourani, *On the Harmony* [see above n. 2], pp. 25–26).

only to members of the demonstrative class. Herein lies the beautiful artfulness of the Law.

Yet for all the privileges Averroes accords the demonstrative class, he takes pains to limit his claims on their behalf. The promotion of demonstrative science is only a secondary intention of the Law. Its primary intention is to take care (*'ināya* – p. 19,21) of the greater number, the subphilosophic multitude.[5] Toward them the Lawgiver acts as a physician of the soul, preserving and restoring health by instilling pious assent (pp. 22,8–13; 23,5–8). At the same time the Lawgiver has not neglected to alert (*tanbīh* – pp. 8,12; 19,21) the select few – "those adept in demonstration", "those adept in the truth" (p. 25,16–17). He has signaled them that there is more to the scriptural text than meets the untrained eye. This invitation to dig and discover the true interpretation embedded in the Law's images and words is conveyed with exquisite reserve and discrimination to a class that is itself expected to display reserve and discrimination.

This great Farabian motif appears more than once in Averroes' other writings. His paraphrase of Plato's *Republic* details the devices to which the teaching philosopher has to resort in order to effect even a modest degree of popular enlightenment.[6] Likewise, the theme of the reticent philosopher is raised briefly at the end of the *Incoherence of the Incoherence* where Averroes sketches the public face that philosophy must present to a world that neither trusts nor understands it.[7] Here in the *Decisive Treatise*, however, Averroes lays bare an exegetical tactic that would create a preserve for the learned while keeping all others from trespassing where they do not belong and can do themselves no good. What purport to be alternative interpretations of a Koranic verse are in truth little short of legislative enactments by this philosopher-jurist-exegete.[8] Averroes cites an ambiguous verse no fewer than four times in an effort to account for seemingly contradictory statements in scripture. But in the process of doing so he succeeds in highlighting his own ambiguous and contradictory presentation. As it stands, this verse (3:7) invites an interpreter or editor to supply some punctuation:

---

5 On the tension between the highest intention of the divine Law and what Averroes calls its primary intention, see Muhsin Mahdi, "Remarks on Averroes' *Decisive Treatise*", in *Islamic Theology and Philosophy: Studies in Honor of George F. Hourani*, ed. Michael E. Marmura (Albany: SUNY Press, 1984), pp. 200–201.

6 *Averroes on Plato's "Republic"*, trans. Ralph Lerner (Ithaca: Cornell University Press, 1974), pp. 25,14–33; 29,17–26; 60,25–61,1 (references are keyed to Erwin I. J. Rosenthal's 1956 edition of the Hebrew text); and see the analysis on pp. xxv–xxvii.

7 *Tahāfot at-Tahāfot*, ed. Maurice Bouyges (Beirut: Imprimerie Catholique, 1930), 582,5–583,6. An English version is in *Averroes' Tahāfut al-Tahāfut (The Incoherence of the Incoherence),* trans. Simon Van den Bergh (London: Luzac, 1954), vol. 1, pp. 360–361.

8 "[...] although Averroes appears in the *Decisive Treatise* to perform the more limited function of a judge or jurist who merely draws inferences from the divine law, in fact, he interprets the divine law in a manner that takes into account the new conditions and the intention of the divine lawgiver, which is more appropriate as a function of a legislator or a successor of the divine lawgiver" (Mahdi, "Remarks" [see above n. 5], p. 308 n. 16).

> He it is who has sent down to you the Book, containing certain verses clear and definite – they are the essence of the Book – and others ambiguous. Now those in whose hearts is mischief go after the ambiguous passages, seeking discord and seeking to interpret them. But no one knows their interpretation except God and those who are well grounded in science they say, "We believe in it, it is all from the Lord; but only men of intelligence give heed."[9]

Twice Averroes inserts a full stop so that the sentence reads: "But no one knows their interpretation except God and those well grounded in science" (pp. 8,13–14; 10,6–9). In this version the text is assuring members of the demonstrative class that it suffices for the great mass of believers to learn to keep away from scriptural obscurities. They have no cause to preoccupy themselves with what is none of their business; this is the domain of men of intelligence. Most people are best left undisturbed at the level of figures of speech and symbols. Secure in their faulty understandings, let them continue to enjoy untroubled sleep, however inferior their assent is to that of the learned. Yet Averroes does not leave it at this bold act of circumscribing popular exegesis. He also offers a cautious alternative interpretation, one that acknowledges publicly that finite human intelligence necessarily must falter in the presence of the infinite. Thus in his two other citations of this verse, he punctuates as follows: "But no one knows their interpretation except God" (pp. 16,12–13; 21,16–19). By putting the period after the word "God", the learned assure the subdemonstrative classes that we are *all* in the dark and that only God knows how scripture's abstruse or ambiguous language ought to be interpreted.

We are obliged to wonder at Averroes' equivocation. Can both of these readings be equally serviceable? Yes, if we think of the *Decisive Treatise* as addressing two audiences and as having a distinct message for each. If its author's intent is to help abate public agitation over religious doctrine, then enlisting his cautious gloss on verse 3:7 serves him well. The last thing the multitude of believers need is the welter of confusion generated by contending allegorical interpretations, whether promoted by rogue philosophizers or by intemperate dialectical theologians.[10] On the other hand, if the author's intent is to shore up with scriptural authority the exposed and vulnerable position of those who would philosophize in his religious community, then his bold gloss on verse 3:7 also serves him well. Given the diverse ends in view, both readings are necessary. For all his concern that philosophers find a secure space in the House of Islam where they can follow *their* pursuit, Averroes is no less concerned that popular beliefs not be undercut by those who have nothing better to supply in their place (pp. 21,20–23,4). I

9 Averroes, *On the Harmony* [see above n. 2], p. 97 n. 87.

10 Averroes, *Kitāb al-kashf 'an manāhij al-adilla*, pp. 124,10–125,13; 126,5–127,3, excerpted in idem, *Kitāb faṣl al-maqāl* (see above n. 2), pp. 48–51 (Arabic); and idem, *On the Harmony* (see above n. 2), pp. 79–81.

conclude that Averroes' philosophical politics might well be characterized as bold in thought and moderate in practice. As such, it exhibits traits of the highest kind of statesmanship.

II.

Like Averroes, Maimonides laments and disdains the uninformed, irresponsible talk among his co-religionists as partisans rummage about in Holy Writ searching for proof-texts. A disregard for context might be prompted by ignorance or haughtiness, but in either case will likely lead to absurdities and gross misunderstandings.[11] Again and again Maimonides insists that one take due note of the setting in which a statement appears with a view to better perceiving its intended meaning.[12] Never is this disciplined reading more indispensable than when confronting the Law of God and attempting to discern the divine Legislator's intention. Failing that, readers might be perplexed and misled by the external resemblances of two allegedly divine Laws. The one commands and prohibits, promises and threatens, just as does the other. Impressed by these similarities, such readers might succumb to the argument that the more recent Law completes, perfects, and supplants the earlier one. They would be unable to extricate themselves from their confusion of mind unless and until they come to grasp that "our Law" has an inner meaning. Someone who understood that inner meaning "would recognize that the entire wisdom of the true divine Law is in its inner [or: esoteric] meaning."[13] Access to

---

11 See, for example, his strictures against "such rubbish and such perverse imaginings" as make one both laugh and weep. Maimonides, *Guide* I.59 (ed. Munk, pp. 74a–b; trans. Pines, p. 141). Citations are to this work's part and chapter numbers; the page number in the Munk edition of the Judeo-Arabic text (Salomon Munk, *Le guide des égarés: Traité de théologie et de philosophie* [2 vols.; Paris: Franck, 1856–1866; reprinted Osnabrück: Zeller, 1964]) and the corresponding page number in the Pines translation (see above n. 1) follow in parentheses.

12 Maimonides, *Guide* I.25, 39 (ed. Munk, pp. 29a, 46a; trans. Pines, pp. 55, 89). See also his *Epistle to Yemen* (*Moses Maimonides' Epistle to Yemen: The Arabic Original and the Three Hebrew Versions.* Edited from manuscripts with introduction and notes by Abraham S. Halkin and an English translation by Boaz Cohen [New York: American Academy for Jewish Research, 1952], pp. 46–48); *Treatise on Resurrection* (*Maimonides' Treatise on Resurrection: The original Arabic and Samuel ibn Tibbon's Hebrew translation and glossary.* Edited with critical apparatus, notes and introduction by Joshua Finkel [New York: American Academy for Jewish Research, 1939], pp. 19–20). The Judeo-Arabic texts of the latter two works are in Isaac Shailat (Ed.), *Letters and Essays of Moses Maimonides* (Maaleh Adummim, Israel: Maaliyot Press of Yeshivat Birkat Moshe, 5748/1988), vol. 1, pp. 95, 328. English translations are in Ralph Lerner, *Maimonides' Empire of Light: Popular Enlightenment in an Age of Belief* (Chicago: University of Chicago Press, 2000), pp. 114, 165.

13 Maimonides, *Epistle to Yemen* (ed. Halkin [see above n. 12], p. 16). Arabic: Shailat, *Letters* (see above n. 12), p. 87; English: Lerner, *Empire* (see above n. 12), p. 105.

the divine intent thus is predicated on an understanding of the *ways* of divine speech.

Maimonides draws his readers' attention to the challenge of addressing members of a heterogeneous audience with divergent possibilities. Precisely because scripture's reports of God's speech are directed to both the many and the elite, each according to their distinct capacities, a univocal reading of its words must necessarily miss the point. Hence Maimonides has to insist on the twofold perfection to which the Law calls and directs its adherents. One is the inculcation of those ethical virtues requisite for leading a fitting human life in this world. The other is the inculcation of the rational virtues through which an individual might apprehend the intelligibles as much as is humanly possible.[14] To be sure, these two aims differ in nobility and urgency. Maimonides makes this abundantly clear in his classic account in the *Guide of the Perplexed*, part III, chapter 27. If his readers keep that distinction constantly in mind, they will be spared the blunders and confusions that beset the common people and even some purported members of the elite. The uninstructed, however, remain ignorant of the Law's distinct aims and its consequent need to display different faces in public and in private. As a result most people fail both to discern scripture's use of parabolic language and to evaluate it properly. That failure in turn redoubles their perplexity – both about the Law's language and about the message it means to convey (I. Introduction [ed. Munk, p. 2b–3b; trans. Pines, pp. 5–6]).

To start to emerge from this impasse, one must go back to the beginning. First, one must develop the healthy habit of being attentive to the context in which a statement appears. If people are baffled or misled by prophetic pronouncements, it is for want of understanding the kind of speech characteristic of each. Every prophet makes his own distinctive use of parable, metaphor, hyperbole, and figurative speech; and these in turn need to be recognized and then correctly understood. Here, then, is the context – a lengthy examination of Isaiah's manner of speaking, taken as a case in point – into which Maimonides inserts a silent quotation. They are, strange to say, the words of Koran 59:2, those very words Averroes cites in the opening pages of the *Decisive Treatise*: "Consider, you who are able to see."[15]

When we look more narrowly at what Maimonides says we ought to "consider", we find him once again crafting different recommendations for different audiences. And since we would expect the object of our preoccupation to manifest itself in our adopting a certain way of life, we are prepared to see Maimonides

14 Maimonides, *Epistle to Yemen* (ed. Halkin [see above n. 12], pp. 14–18). Arabic: Shailat, *Letters* (see above n. 12), pp. 86–87; English: Lerner, *Empire* (see above n. 12), p. 105.

15 Maimonides, *Guide* II.29 (ed. Munk [see above n. 11], p. 61b; trans. Pines [see above n. 1], p. 340). For a discussion of Maimonides' surprising use of this silent quotation in the *Guide*, see Harvey, "Averroes and Maimonides" (see above n. 1), pp. iv (English summary), 80–81.

recommending different ways of life as well. Needless to say, his understanding of human nature rules out the possibility that one size can fit all.[16] Accordingly, his recommendations range from those attainable by most people to those that for all practical purposes are attainable by none, or by only the highest imaginable exemplar of humanity.

The alternatives are encapsulated – for believers, at least – in Maimonides' very brief discussion of the positive commandment that we love God. We fulfill that, he says, by "considering" divine commandments, exhortations, and works. Each of these objects of contemplation leads to a recognition of the Creator. With that recognition we can move on to achieve some comprehension of Him, and that in turn leads to our coming to love Him. But as the objects of consideration might be thought of as being of unequal rank, so too are the degrees of perfection that their devotees might achieve. It is significant, I suspect, that the consideration of "works" in Maimonides' triad does not appear in our text of the rabbinic source he cites in the *Book of Commandments*.[17] Similarly, when addressing correspondents who wonder whether there is any utility in studying astronomy, Maimonides cites an otherwise unknown dictum of Rabbi Meir to the effect that one ought to "contemplate His works, for thus you recognize Him who spoke and the world came into being." He also directs his correspondents' attention to the beginning of "our great compilation" where they will find an explication of these roots.[18] And indeed the *Mishneh Torah* does not disappoint expectations.

The sheer scale of that vast work permits Maimonides an amplitude that he does not ordinarily grant himself.[19] In "Laws Concerning Character Traits" he discusses the ways in which one might govern one's life and addresses in turn the wise man, the disciples of the wise, and man simply. To the latter he has a message as apparently simple as it is daunting: Cleave to Him! But what can this mean? Is it even conceivable as a positive commandment? By recurring to the talmudic sages'

---

16 It suffices to point to *Guide* II.36 (ed. Munk [see above n. 11], p. 79b; trans. Pines [see above n. 1], p. 372).

17 Positive Commandment no. 3, in *Sefer Hamiṣvot, Book of Commandments*. Arabic original with new Hebrew translation and commentary by Rabbi Joseph Kafaḥ [= Y. Qāfiḥ] (Jerusalem: Mosad Harav Kook, 1971), p. 59. See Harvey, "Averroes and Maimonides" (see above n. 1), p. 79.

18 Query no. 32, in "Responsa to the disciples of Rabbi Ephraim of Tyre", in Shailat, *Letters* (see above n. 12), vol. 1, pp. 208, 216–217. – In the plain, succinct language of *Guide* III.28 (ed. Munk, p. 61a; trans. Pines, pp. 512–513): "We have already explained in *Mishneh Torah* that this love becomes valid only through the apprehension of the whole of being as it is and through the consideration of His wisdom as it is manifested in it. We have also mentioned there the fact that the Sages, may their memory be blessed, call attention to this notion."

19 "If it were possible for us to put all of the jurisprudence of the Law in one chapter we would not put it in two chapters" (*Treatise on Resurrection* [ed. Finkel (see above n. 12)], pp. 24–26; Arabic: Shailat, *Letters* [see above n. 12], p. 332; English: Lerner, *Empire* [see above n. 12], p. 169).

glosses on this biblical command, Maimonides is able to specify an object for everyone to "consider". Learn from the actions and words of the wise men and their disciples by associating with them and bonding with them in every aspect of ordinary life. Thus understood, this injunction is within the reach of many.[20] But what of those thoughtful individuals to whom Maimonides (along with Averroes) addresses the call, "Consider, you who are able to see"? Maimonides' own injunction to them is more challenging by far than that prescribed for ordinary folk. "Man needs to direct every single one of his deeds solely toward attaining knowledge of the Name, blessed be He" (*Mishneh Torah*, "Hilkhot De'ot" 3.2/49b; trans. Weiss, p. 34). Here, in a centrally situated discussion of how to conduct one's life according to the mean, Maimonides points to an all-absorbing life devoted to *theoria.* This interpretation reaffirms the peak of human achievement held forth in his *Eight Chapters.* There he prescribes subordinating all the powers of one's soul to thought, focusing on a single goal: "the perception of God (may He be glorified and magnified), I mean, knowledge of Him, in so far as that lies within man's power."[21] By living in a manner that perfects and strengthens one's body, a man positions his upright soul to come to know the Lord ("Hilkhot De'ot" 3.3/50a; trans. Weiss, p. 35). Or as somewhat otherwise expressed in the *Guide*: It is with a view to that intellectual apprehension of the deity, of the angels, and of His other works that you should arrange and direct all your actions, impulses, and thoughts. This is what is required of man. It is your abiding business to take as your very own end that which is the end of man qua man.[22]

The confluence of these discrete but related themes occurs in Maimonides' invocation in the *Guide* of Deuteronomy 6:5, where the faithful are enjoined, in stunningly summary fashion, "to love the Lord". Maimonides explains: This tersest of commandments encapsulates all the correct opinions promoted by the Law through which an individual might attain his ultimate perfection. Oddly enough, as regards these matters of the highest possible human importance, the divine Legislator apparently is content to give only the barest indication. It takes a Maimonides (or someone instructed by a Maimonides) to develop in detail the implied correct opinions – and at that "only after one knows many opinions" (III.28 [ed. Munk, pp. 60b–61a; trans. Pines, p. 512]). Alternatively stated, only a reader trained in attending to the ways in which the Law needs to be read will

20 Maimonides, *Mishneh Torah: The Book of Knowledge*, ed. and trans. Moses Hyamson (reprint edition, Jerusalem: Boys Town Jerusalem Publishers, 1965), "Hilkhot De'ot" 6.2/54b. References are to the part name, chapter and section numbers, and page number of the Hebrew text printed in this edition. Wherever applicable, reference is made to the reliable English translation of the text in: *Ethical Writings of Maimonides*. Edited Raymond L. Weiss by with Charles E. Butterworth (reprint edition, New York: Dover Books, 1983), p. 47.

21 *Eight Chapters*, chapter 5, title and beginning. An English translation is in Weiss, *Ethical Writings* (see above n. 20), p. 75.

22 Maimonides, *Guide* I.39, III.8 (ed. Munk [see above n. 11], pp. 46a, 12a–b; trans. Pines [see above n. 1], pp. 89, 432–433).

grasp the opinions taught by the Law and come at last to apprehend God's being as He is in truth. The knowledge conveyed by these opinions leads to that very love to which the Law both summons and commands. Speaking directly to his addressee, Maimonides says, "You know to what extent the Torah lays stress upon love" (III.52 [ed. Munk, p. 130b; trans. Pines, p. 630]).

One can hardly fault Maimonides for failing to hold high the love which the Torah so exalts. But students of what he calls the legalistic study of the Law might well be surprised by his prescription for achieving that love. His emphatic message in the "Book of Knowledge" comes down to this: Live, above all else, a life of *theoria*. This highly assertive and conspicuous injunction is one of those notable moments in his writings when Maimonides abstracts from considerations of family and community, even from the performance of deeds as such, when recommending a way of life for others to follow. He urges, rather, a single-minded preoccupation with acquiring the kind of knowledge by which one might come to know God. The would-be lover's focused devotion to understanding the sciences will point him to an understanding of the Maker. He must guide himself with an awareness of the following divine calculus: "According to the knowledge will be the love – if little, little; if much, much." It is at this point, at the very end of the "Book of Knowledge", that Maimonides explicitly refers the aspirant back to the opening of his book ("Hilkhot Teshuvah" 10.10–11/93a).

Those four initial chapters contain Maimonides' thumbnail sketch of divine science and natural science – that is, metaphysics and physics. In gaining that knowledge, the lovesick seeker gains an avenue to fulfill his yearning. Yet gratification is not instantaneous; if anything, the intensity of his desire will increase. The more the aspirant for perfection studies God's wondrous great works and reflects upon the infinite wisdom implicit in all that handiwork, the greater will be his yearning and the nearer will he draw to the object of his desire ("Hilkhot Yesodei ha-Torah" 2.2/35b, 4.12/39b; English: Lerner, *Empire* [see above n. 12], pp. 144, 152). The impression, overall, is that this immersion in the study of physics and metaphysics is a prescription for a solitary's way of life, or at least for a man who is not encumbered by any hostages to fortune. Yet even in his more moderate formulation of a work-and-study program for an artisan who *is* encumbered and who has to earn a living to support his dependents, even there Maimonides makes it possible for the studier to aim high. He creates space for the esoteric studies called "*Pardes*" and subsumes all that under the rubric "*talmud*". It is fair to say that Maimonides' *Mishneh Torah* not only reconceptualizes the tradition's curriculum of study but also proposes itself as the indispensable replacement for a significant part of that legacy.[23]

It is startling to see with what address and boldness Maimonides employs his acknowledged mastery as a jurist and exegete to legitimize philosophical studies

23 "Talmud Torah" 1.11–12/58a. See the translation and analysis in Lerner, *Empire* (see above n. 12), pp. 38–41.

by those Jews who are capable of such. The *Mishneh Torah* carves out a space for pursuing those concerns within the broad framework of the Law's commanded and prohibited actions. The *Guide of the Perplexed,* in turn, fills that space so memorably and impressively as to eclipse any precedent, rival, or successor effort. But for all his solicitude for the rare individual – that one man in ten thousand whom alone, he says, he in truth cares to satisfy (I. Introduction [ed. Munk, p. 9b; trans. Pines, p. 16]) – Maimonides also has a message for a broader population of his misguided co-religionists. It is a message urging them to arm themselves with reason and not fall victim to the delusions and distractions fostered by unreason. Thus he confronts their unthinking fatalistic belief in the powers of judicial astrology by commanding his brethren, "out of my knowledge", to move with determination into dangerous but stirring territory.

> Hew down the tree and cut off its branches, and so on [Daniel 4:11]. Plant in its stead the tree of the knowledge of good and evil, and eat of its goodness and its fruit, and put forth your hands and take also from the tree of life. The Holy One (blessed be He) will absolve us and will absolve you for plucking off its fruit and for eating our fill of its goodness until we live forever.[24]

Maimonides cites no authority for this remarkable rhetorical flight – other than his own knowledge. In urging his fellows to seek to realize their highest potentiality, he transforms the Bible's primal act of disobedience into a case of doing one's duty to oneself. The philosopher's love of God demands no less.

III.

In stressing as I have the parallels between Averroes and Maimonides, I have perforce neglected to do justice to their divergent approaches. That kind of investigation would require a different point of departure from that adopted here. It would have to note the absence from Averroes' surviving writings of any responses to queries that might have been posed to him by agitated or perplexed Muslim communities. It would have to dwell upon these jurists' differing reactions to popular delusions. Averroes accepts without audible misgiving that the bulk of his co-religionists are condemned to mistaking the shadows projected on their cave's wall for objects as they truly are. For Maimonides, on the other hand, this condition is at least a matter of expressed regret as he tries to combat an unthinking corporealist view of God wherever it appears. Finally, that other kind of investigation would have to come to terms with this striking fact: Averroes

24 *Letter on Astrology*, end. The Hebrew text is in Shailat, *Letters* (see above n. 12), vol. 2, p. 490. An English translation is in Lerner, *Empire* (see above n. 12), p. 187.

boldly reads his scripture as imposing, upon some at least, an obligation to philosophize. But Maimonides' muted defense of *theoria* as a way of life stops short of that. It is enough for him that he makes it possible for a patient and careful reader to make that choice on his own.

Yet for all these and other differences that might be explored, there remains their shared commitment. Each thinker, working within the context of his religious community, labors to legitimize philosophizing while simultaneously using the teachings of philosophy to challenge certain prevalent and even cherished popular beliefs most hostile to thoughtful questioning. This effort – at once tedious, risky, and indispensable – might be thought of as an instance of *imitatio Dei*, as an expression of those great men's aspiration to cleave to God by coming to love, to know, Him.[25] But their labors might no less be thought of as another striking instance of a phenomenon to which Leo Strauss drew attention more than fifty years ago. In a volume of essays he rather playfully characterized as contributions toward a future sociology of philosophy, he raised anew "the possibility that all philosophers form a class by themselves". More radically and without demurrer, he reported the message of Fārābī's *Plato* that philosophers "defended the interests of philosophy and of nothing else. In doing this, they believed indeed that they were defending the highest interests of mankind."[26] A year later Strauss, speaking in his own name, expanded on this notion. He declined to contest the Marxist or crypto-Marxist impulse to search for a thinker's particular class bias as a necessary step in identifying what may lie behind a particular political doctrine. But, he wrote, "It suffices to demand that the class to which the thinker in question belongs be correctly identified." Strauss insisted in no uncertain terms that "there is a class interest of philosophers qua philosophers." Almost paradoxically he limned that *class* interest as the selfish interest of the *solitary*, the *mutawaḥḥid*. "Philosophers as philosophers do not go with their families. The selfish or class interest of the philosophers consists in being left alone, in being allowed to live the life of the blessed on earth by devoting themselves to investigation of the most important subjects."[27]

It is not far-fetched to view Averroes' and Maimonides' efforts in this light. Nor is it far-fetched to understand their activity as being legislative in the highest sense. We do well to begin by taking up Montesquieu's hint in the *Spirit of Laws*. In his little chapter titled "Of Legislators" (book 29, chapter 19), he concludes as a matter of fact that legislators always indulge and express their "passions and prejudices" through their very acts of legislating. Remarkably, all the examples of

---

25 See Lerner, *Empire* (see above n. 12), p. 76.

26 Leo Strauss, *Persecution and the Art of Writing* (Glencoe, Ill.: The Free Press, 1952), pp. 7–8, 17–18.

27 Leo Strauss, *Natural Right and History* (Chicago: University of Chicago Press, 1953), p. 143. For Strauss's earlier and fuller formulation, see "Persecution and the Art of Writing", in *Social Research* 8(4) (Nov. 1941), p. 503 n. 21.

legislators whom Montesquieu adduces in support of that assertion are philosophers. Can Averroes and Maimonides justly be included in that cohort? How would one weigh their self-serving, as against their philanthropic, intentions? In what sense can their activities be properly characterized as legislative? Since the furthest thing from their minds would have been to proclaim themselves discoverers of new worlds to conquer, any intimations of profound change, let alone originality, had to remain heavily veiled. Yet these two were individuals with radically independent minds. Looking at their world from a distance but with piercing eyes, they saw thoughtfulness and genuine greatness everywhere besieged. If it was not theirs to make a fresh start, neither was it beyond their ambition to bend their community's regnant religion to further their own project of cultivation and education. Their aspirations were indeed high; they took into consideration generations yet unborn. These two preeminent sons of Córdoba did not need a Nietzsche to rouse them to assume their highest potentialities as philosophers. They had before their eyes the teaching of "the second master", Fārābī. The virtuous regime established by the prophet-philosopher-ruler who founded a religious community could not remain frozen in time. Circumstances must and do alter. The very hopes fostered by the religion's yearning for perfection create their own destabilizing and self-consuming changes. The question necessarily arises: what would the original supreme ruler-founder have done in response to these newly arising conditions? Fārābī taught that rare, qualified successors – the embodiments of living wisdom – would see and seize the opportunity to further the original Legislator's intentions.[28] One may, if so inclined, view this intervention by the philosopher as the fulfillment of a duty. But it is no belittling of either an Averroes or a Maimonides to solemnly concede that for each it was as much a duty to oneself as to others.

---

28 See Friedrich Nietzsche, *Beyond Good and Evil*, Aphorisms 61, 211, 212; and Muhsin S. Mahdi, *Alfarabi and the Foundation of Islamic Political Philosophy* (Chicago: University of Chicago Press, 2001), pp. 136–139, 166–168.

Zur Interpretation von Heiligen Schriften bei Averroes und Maimonides

von

Georges Tamer

Universität Erlangen-Nürnberg

Das Verhältnis von Religion und Philosophie stellt für das Denken im Mittelalter eine Herausforderung dar, die erstmals in der arabisch-islamischen Welt zum philosophischen Problem wurde.[1] Selbst die Beschäftigung mit rein theoretischen Bereichen der antiken Philosophie, die mit der Religion keine unmittelbare Beziehung aufzuweisen scheinen, geschieht dort auf eine Weise, die von religiösen Bezügen nicht unberührt bleibt. Auch die Logik fand Zugang zu den religiösen Wissenschaften. Es musste zur ersten Auseinandersetzung zwischen dem antiken Erbe des Rationalismus und dem Glauben des Monotheismus kommen, als die Philosophie in den islamisch geprägten Kulturkreis eingeführt wurde, in dem der religiöse Anspruch erhoben wird, dass Gottes Buch, das dem Propheten wörtlich übermittelt wurde, die ganze Wahrheit enthält und menschliches Tun und Handeln regelt. Mit einem solchen Gedanken kann sich selbstverständlich nur die Religion zufrieden geben. Ein rationaler Mensch stellt jedoch Fragen; er möchte sogar manchmal Wahrheiten hinterfragen, obwohl sie aus religiöser Sicht als absolut gelten müssen. Von einem Konflikt zwischen Glauben und Wissen zu sprechen, bleibt der Rationalität vorbehalten, die durch die Konfrontation mit dem Anspruch der Religion auf exklusiven Wahrheitsbesitz dazu veranlasst wird.

Die Frage nach der Interpretation von heiligen Schriften scheint ein konkreter Grenzpunkt zu sein, an dem besonders deutlich gezeigt werden kann, inwiefern sich Religion und Philosophie voneinander unterscheiden und wie sie miteinander in Einklang gebracht werden könnten. Denn ebenso wie der philosophische Beweis immer mit Worten geführt wird, kommen auch Gottesoffenbarungen in den monotheistischen Religionen mit Worten zum Ausdruck.

---

1 Vgl. zum Thema überhaupt: Leo Strauss, *Philosophie und Gesetz. Beiträge zum Verständnis Maimunis und seiner Vorläufer* (Berlin: Schocken, 1935); Etienne Gilson, *Reason and Revelation in the Middle Ages* (New York: Charles Scribner's Sons 1938); Arthur J. Arberry, *Revelation and Reason in Islam* (London: Allen and Unwin, 1957); Alain de Libera, *Denken im Mittelalter* (München: Fink, 2003).

So erhält Moses Gebote, auf Tafeln geschrieben,[2] und der mündliche Vortrag, den Muhammad vernimmt, stammt ursprünglich von einer „wohlbewahrten Tafel".[3] Zwischen beiden Schriftzeugnissen tritt die Verkündigung von dem Fleisch gewordenen *Wort* auf.[4] Ob wirklich am Anfang das Wort oder, wie Goethe seinem *Faust* voranstellte, „die Tat"[5] war, mag nunmehr offen bleiben. Dennoch könnte man über Goethes Gedanken reflektierend kurz sagen, dass, wenn die Tat tatsächlich am Anfang war, es doch eine Wort-Tat war. Denn vernünftiges Sein äußert sich erst durch das Wort. Dieses ist das Medium, in dem sich die Offenbarung nicht nur äußert, sondern auch in dem ihr die Vernunft begegnet.

Besonders an der philosophischen Deutung von theologischen Inhalten, die in den heiligen Schriften enthalten sind, zeigt sich der rationale Umgang mit der Religion. In der letzten Phase der klassischen Epoche der arabischen Philosophie im Mittelalter geben Averroes (1126–1198) und Maimonides (zwischen 1135 und 1138–1204) zwei beachtenswerte Beispiele dafür, die nicht zuletzt wegen des gemeinsamen Kontexts ihrer Entstehung in Andalusien über weite Strecken miteinander übereinstimmen. Trotz ihrer weitgehenden Konvergenz sind die von dem muslimischen und dem jüdischen Denker entwickelten Umgangsweisen mit den heiligen Schriften unterschieden. Der Unterschied geht zweifelsohne zum Teil auf den unterschiedlichen religiösen Rahmen zurück, in dem sich beide jeweils bewegten. Daraus leiten sie spezifische Konzeptionen für die philosophische Behandlung von Offenbarungsschriften ab, die im Folgenden diskutiert werden sollen. Zunächst sollen aber die philosophischen Voraussetzungen dafür, die über zwei Jahrhunderte zuvor angelegt wurden, kurz dargestellt werden.

Für den ersten Systematiker der islamischen Philosophie, Abū Naṣr al-Fārābī (870–950),[6] stellt sich die Interpretation von heiligen Schriften noch nicht als theoretisches Problem dar. Sein harmonisierendes Anliegen gilt zuerst den Ansichten von Platon und Aristoteles, um im zweiten Schritt die vereinheit-

2 Exodus 20:1–17.

3 Der Koran 85:22.

4 Johannesevangelium 1:1, 14.

5 Goethe, *Faust*. Erster Teil. Kommentiert und herausgegeben von Erich Trunz (München: Beck, 1986), V. 1237.

6 Zu seinem Leben und Werk vgl. *Al-Fārābī on the Perfect State: Abū Naṣr al-Fārābī's Mabādi' 'ārā' 'ahl al-madīna al-fāḍila*. A revised Text with introduction, translation, and commentary by Richard Walzer (Oxford: Oxford University Press, 1985); Ian Richard Netton, *Al-Farabi and his School* (London, New York: Routledge, 1992); Deborah L. Black, „Al-Fārābī", in Seyyed Hossein Nasr und Oliver Leaman (Eds.), *History of Islamic Philosophy* (London, New York: Routledge, 1996), S. 178–197; jetzt auch Ulrich Rudolph, *Islamische Philosophie: Von den Anfängen bis zur Gegenwart* (München: Beck, 2004), S. 29–36.

lichte Philosophie mit der Religion zusammenzubringen.[7] Die vollkommene Leitung, am Begriff des *ra'īs al-awwal* paradigmatisch präsentiert, kommt seiner Ansicht nach durch die Vereinigung der perfekten intellektuell-theoretischen und der imaginativ-abbildenden Fähigkeit zustande. Während Erstere den Erwerb von wissenschaftlicher Erkenntnis ermöglicht und wiederum dadurch gestärkt wird, bewirkt Letztere unter anderem die pädagogische Vermittlung von schwer verständlichen theoretischen Inhalten an Nichtphilosophen durch Gleichnisse, besonders im Falle der Religion.[8] Auf diese Weise bringt al-Fārābī eine theoretisch-musterhaft entwickelte Kompetenzenteilung zwischen Religion und Philosophie zustande, die die ganze Epoche hindurch fortwirkte. Ihre wesentlichen Züge werden von Averroes auf die Interpretation des koranischen Textes übertragen.

Averroes ist der einzige arabisch-muslimische Philosoph, der diesem Thema eine eigene Schrift, *Faṣl al-maqāl wa-taqrīr mā bayn aš-šarī'a wa-l-ḥikma min al-ittiṣāl* sowie Teile seiner anderen Schrift *al-Kašf 'an manāhiǧ al-adilla fī 'aqā'id al-milla* widmet.[9] Die erstgenannte Abhandlung soll vor 1179–1180 entstanden sein.[10] Sie scheint hauptsächlich eine Antwort auf die Schrift *Kitāb fayṣal at-tafriqa*[11] (geschrieben zwischen 1096 und 1106) zu sein, in der wie auch in anderen Schriften[12] Abū Ḥāmid al-Ġazālī (1058–1111) die Frage nach der religionsgesetzlichen Zulässigkeit der allegorischen Interpretation des Koran erörtert und diese allgemein für unzulässig erklärt. Da eine Darstellung von al-Ġazālīs Ansichten und deren Einfluss auf Averroes den aktuellen Rahmen sprengen würde, muss ich mich auf den allgemeinen Hinweis beschränken, dass alle theologisch-philo-

---

7 Al-Fārābī, *Kitāb al-ǧam' bayna ra'yay l-ḥakīmayn*, ed. Alber Naṣrī Nādir (Beirut: al-Maṭba'a al-Kāṯūlīkīya, 1960). Deutsche Übersetzung von Friedrich Dieterici, *Alfārābī's philosophische Abhandlungen* (Leiden: Brill, 1892), S. 1–53.

8 *Al-Fārābī on the Perfect State* (wie Anm. 6), S. 244.

9 Beide Schriften sind zuerst von Marcus Joseph Müller 1859 in München ediert worden. Darauf folgten in Ost und West weitere Editionen. Hier wird folgende Edition benutzt: Ibn Rushd (Averroes), *Kitāb faṣl al-maqāl with its Appendix (Ḍamīma) and an Extract from kitāb al-Kashf 'an manāhiǧ al-adilla.* Arabic text edited by George F. Hourani (Leiden: Brill, 1959). Die Angaben zu Seiten- und Zeilenzahlen folgen den Angaben von Müllers Edition, die Hourani am Rande aufführt.

10 Averroes, *On the Harmony of Religion and Philosophy. A translation with introduction and notes, of Ibn Rushd's Kitāb faṣl al-maqāl, with its appendix (Ḍamīma) and an extract from Kitāb al-kashf 'an manāhij al-adilla,* by George F. Hourani (London: Luzac, 1961), S. 1.

11 Al-Ġazālī, *Kitāb fayṣal at-tafriqa bayn al-Islām wa-z-zandaqa*, ed. S. Dunyā (Kairo, 1381/1961). Deutsche Übersetzung: *Über Rechtgläubigkeit und religiöse Toleranz. Eine Übersetzung der Schrift Das Kriterium der Unterscheidung zwischen Islam und Gottlosigkeit*, eingeleitet und übersetzt mit Erläuterungen von Frank Griffel (Zürich: Spur-Verlag, 1998).

12 Es sei beispielsweise genannt: *Al-Muṣṭafā min 'ilm al-uṣūl* (Kairo, 1904); *al-Qisṭās al-mustaqīm* (Kairo, 1925). Englische Übersetzung: *The Just Balance.* A Translation with introduction and notes by David Pearson Brewster (Lahore: Ashraf, 1978).

sophischen Schriften des Letzteren[13] als Erwiderung auf des Ersteren Kritik an den griechischen und islamischen Philosophen verstanden werden müssen. Die darin enthaltenen Argumente werden in ständiger Rücksicht auf Abū Ḥāmid entwickelt, so dass man doch wohl sagen kann, dass in Averroes ein al-Ġazālī steckt, genauso wie beispielsweise ein Hegel in Marx oder Kierkegaard.

Besonders wichtig für unseren Zusammenhang ist in *Faṣl al-maqāl* die Behandlung der Frage nach der Schriftauslegung (*ta'wīl*). Averroes wird bei diesem Unternehmen von der Absicht geleitet, zwei offensichtlich verschiedene Denksysteme durch die Bestimmung der unterschiedlichen Bereiche ihrer theoretischen Handlung miteinander zu harmonisieren. Er bringt seine Absicht zu Beginn der Abhandlung in bestechender Klarheit zum Ausdruck. Zweck des Buches ist es, „aus der Perspektive des Religionsgesetzes zu überprüfen, ob das Studium der Philosophie und der logischen Wissenschaften durch das Religionsgesetz erlaubt, verboten oder befohlen wird und ob dieses Studium ein freiwilliger Auftrag oder sogar eine notwendige Pflicht ist."[14] Averroes möchte also hier ein Rechtsurteil sprechen.[15] Er bestimmt daraufhin die Tätigkeit der Philosophie als die, „die seienden Dinge zu studieren und zu bedenken, inwiefern sie auf den ‚Hersteller' (*ṣāniʿ*) hinweisen".[16] Eine solche Philosophie, die neben der Logik die Physik und Metaphysik umfasst und durch die Untersuchung der seienden Dinge auf deren Urheber aufmerksam macht, ist nach averroistischer Auffassung teleologisch identisch mit der Religion.[17] Sie stellt sich wie diese als ein Weg zur Erkenntnis Gottes dar. Warum sollte sie also – so der Tenor der Argumentation – der Koran verbieten?

Gerade das Gegenteil will Averroes zeigen. Auf koranische Äußerungen gestützt erklärt er, dass die Philosophie, die den Betrachter auf Gott hinführt, aus der Sicht des Religionsgesetzes nicht nur erlaubt, sondern Pflicht ist.[18] Mit Blick auf die den Arabern vermittelten Wissenschaften der heidnischen Griechen bekräftigt Averroes weiter, dass es ebenso Pflicht ist, sich die Erkenntnisse

---

13 Zu den bereits erwähnten Schriften sei noch Averroes' großes Werk genannt: *Tahāfut at-tahāfut*, ed. Maurice Bouyges (Beirut: Imprimerie catholique, 1930; Nachdruck Frankfurt am Main: Institute for the History of Arabic-Islamic Science, 1999). Englische Übersetzung: *Tahafut al-Tahafut* (*The Incoherence of the Incoherence*). Translated from the Arabic with introduction and notes by Simon van den Bergh (London: Luzac, 1954). Es ist eine Antwort auf al-Ġazālīs philosophiekritische Abhandlung *Tahāfut al-falāsifa*, ed. Maurice Bouyges (Beirut: Imprimerie catholique, 1927). Nachdruck mit einer Einleitung von Māǧid Faḫrī (Beirut: Dār al-mašriq, 1990). Englische Übersetzung: *The Incoherence of the Philosophers/Tahāfut al-falāsifa. A parallel English-Arabic text*. Translated, introduced, and annotated by Michael E. Marmura (Provo, Ut.: Brigham Young University Press, 1997).

14 *Faṣl al-maqāl* (wie Anm. 9), S. 1,7–9. Alle Zitate sind von mir ins Deutsche übersetzt.

15 Vgl. den Beitrag von Ralph Lerner in diesem Band, S. 224.

16 *Faṣl al-maqāl* (wie Anm. 9), S. 1,10–11.

17 Ibid., S. 5,13–14; 18,20–22.

18 Ibid., S. 2,2,9–12.

Früherer und Andersgläubiger anzueignen, ohne dass daran Anstoß genommen werden solle.[19] Diese offene Haltung der Wissenschaft gegenüber erhebt sie über ethnische und religiöse Grenzen und sieht keinen Widerspruch zwischen ihr und der Religion. Einer solchen Position liegt die Überzeugung von der Einheit der Wahrheit zugrunde, welche gleichermaßen von der Religion und der Wissenschaft angestrebt wird. Averroes bringt diese Auffassung in *Faṣl al-maqāl* deutlich zum Ausdruck. Aufgrund ihrer Bedeutung nicht nur für unser Thema, sondern auch darüber hinaus für das averroistische Verständnis der Beziehung von Religion und Philosophie soll die viel zitierte, oft missverstandene Stelle im Folgenden ausführlich zitiert werden:

> Da diese Schrift (*šarīʿa*) [der Koran] wahr ist und zu dem Studium der theoretischen Wissenschaften (*naẓar*) auffordert, welches zur Erkenntnis der Wahrheit führt, so wissen wir, die Gemeinschaft der Muslime, definitiv, dass das Studium der theoretischen Wissenschaften mittels der Demonstration nicht zu einem Widerspruch zu dem in der Schrift (*šarʿ*) Enthaltenen führt; denn das Wahre (*al-ḥaqq*) kann dem Wahren nicht widersprechen, sondern es stimmt mit ihm überein und legt Zeugnis von ihm ab.
>
> Wenn bei einer solchen Situation das Studium der theoretischen Wissenschaften mittels der Demonstration zu irgendeiner Art von Erkenntnis von irgendeinem Seienden führt, so kann bloß folgende Alternative eintreten: Entweder schweigt die Schrift (*aš-šarʿ*) [der Koran] darüber, oder sie gibt davon Kunde. Schweigt sie darüber, so ist hier kein Widerspruch; und es verhält sich damit ebenso wie mit den religiösen Bestimmungen (*aḥkām*), die in der Schrift nicht erwähnt werden und die der Jurist (*faqīh*) mittels des religionsgesetzlichen Syllogismus (*bi-l-qiyās aš-šarʿīy*) entwickelt hat. Wenn aber die Schrift [der Koran] davon spricht, so wird der äußere Wortlaut mit dem, wozu die Demonstration führt, übereinstimmen oder ihm widersprechen. Stimmt er mit ihm überein, so ist weiter nichts zu sagen. Ist er aber im Widerspruch mit ihm, so ist es erforderlich, ihn zu interpretieren.[20]

Der Name Averroes wird bekanntlich meistens mit der Lehre der doppelten Wahrheit assoziiert.[21] Grob gesagt bedeutet diese Lehre, dass es zwei entgegengesetzte Wahrheitssysteme gibt, die sich gegenseitig ausschließen. Averroes scheint jedoch die Ansicht zu vertreten, dass es nur eine Wahrheit gibt, deren Vermittlungszugänge die Religion und die Philosophie bilden. Die eine Wahrheit kann in unterschiedlichen Graden gemäß menschlichem Vermögen erreicht werden. Die Philosophen verfügen über den höchsten Grad der Erkenntnis.

19 Ibid., 3,20–4,7.

20 Ibid., 7,7–15.

21 Für einen knappen, aber durchaus lesenswerten Überblick über die Entstehung des „Mythos der doppelten Wahrheit" siehe de Libera, *Denken im Mittelalter* (wie Anm. 1), S. 94–99.

Dennoch unterscheidet sich das letzte Wahrheitsziel, das sie anstreben, nicht vom Wahrheitsgehalt der Offenbarungsschrift. Auf der Grundlage der Einheit der Wahrheit kann Averroes für die Interpretation der heiligen Schrift folgendes Prinzip entwickeln: Den Philosophen ist es erstens erlaubt, sich über alles zu äußern, worüber die Schrift schweigt, und zweitens den Text des Korans im Sinne der Vernunft zu interpretieren, wenn er Äußerungen enthält, die im Widerspruch mit den Postulaten der Vernunft stehen. Die Schrift beinhaltet dieselbe Wahrheit, die die Philosophen suchen. An einer anderen Stelle bezeichnet Averroes die Philosophie und die *šarīʿa* als „Milchschwestern", die dieselbe Nahrung aus derselben Quelle schöpfen. „Sie sind in der Natur (*bi-ṭ-ṭabʿ*) befreundet und lieben einander im Wesen (*bi-l-ğawhar*) und Instinkt (*wa-l-ġarīza*)."[22]

Averroes flicht beide gewonnenen Fäden, nämlich den von der religiösen Pflicht zu studieren und den von der Übereinstimmung zwischen Philosophie und Religion, zusammen mit dem Faden der Notwendigkeit, den Koran zu interpretieren. Diese Notwendigkeit wird aus der Natur des koranischen Textes abgeleitet, der ein Äußeres (*ẓāhir*) und ein Inneres (*bāṭin*) aufweist. Während das Äußere in jenen Allegorien besteht, die zum Ausdruck von Bedeutungen verwendet werden und jedem zugänglich sind, besteht das Innere aus jenen Bedeutungen, welche sich nur den Leuten der Demonstration, das sind die Philosophen, enthüllen.[23] Die Doppelbödigkeit des Korantextes korrespondiert in seiner Konzeption mit der Klassifizierung der Menschen nach ihrem Erkenntnisvermögen in drei Gruppen: 1. die große Masse, die sich nur das sinnlich Wahrnehmbare vorstellen kann und der nur rhetorische Argumente (*al-aqāwīl al-ḫaṭābīya*) zugänglich sind; 2. die Dialektiker, die über ein höheres Abstraktionsvermögen verfügen, aber bei der dialektischen Argumentation (*al-aqāwīl al-ğadalīya*) stehen bleiben; 3. die Philosophen, die das Wesen der Dinge erfassen und aufgrund demonstrativer Beweise (*al-aqāwīl al-burhānīya*) Urteile bilden.[24] Während das Textäußere allen Menschen zugänglich ist, erschließt sich dessen Inneres nur den Philosophen.

Der Offenbarungstext will alle Menschen ansprechen,[25] weil er vor allem auf die Fürsorge der Mehrheit (*al ʿināya bi-l-akṯar*) abzielt, ohne die Ermahnung der Elite (*tanbīh al-ḫawāṣṣ*) zu vernachlässigen.[26] In erbarmender Rücksicht (*talaṭṭafa*) auf diejenigen, die keinen intellektuellen Zugang zur Demonstration haben, brachte Gott die Dinge, die nur durch die Demonstration erkannt werden können, durch Gleichnisse und Metaphern zum Ausdruck und rief sie dazu auf,

22 *Faṣl al-maqāl* (wie Anm. 9), S. 26,4–7. Vgl. Alfred Ivry, „Towards a Unified View of Averroes' Philosophy", in *The Philosophical Forum* IV,1 (1972), S. 87–113, besonders 108–111.

23 Ibid., S. 15,14–16.

24 Ibid., S. 6,17–21. Vgl. Aristoteles, *Analytica Prior* II,23; idem, *Topica* I,1; al-Fārābī, *Iḥṣāʾ al-ʿulūm*, ed. ʿUṯmān Amīn (Kairo: Dār al-Fikr al-ʿArabīy, 1948), S. 63–69.

25 Ibid., S. 7,3.4; S. 9,10–12 mit Bezug auf *Ṣaḥīḥ al-Buḫārī* III,49.

26 Ibid., S. 19,20–21.

daran zu glauben.[27] Die Mehrdeutigkeit von Versen führt zur Entstehung von verschiedenen Lesarten und zwingt dazu, solche Verse zu interpretieren. Niemand ist dafür qualifizierter als die Leute der Demonstration, das sind die Philosophen, die zum Wesen der Dinge hineindringen und zur natürlichen Intelligenz auch religiöse Integrität und moralische Tugendhaftigkeit besitzen.[28] Sie werden sogar vom Koran selbst damit beauftragt, wie es Averroes im Koranvers 3:7 begründet sieht.[29] Für Averroes kommt es hier auf den Punkt im dritten Satz an. Wird der Punkt nach „Gott" gesetzt, lautet der Satz: „Aber niemand weiß es zu deuten außer Gott."[30] Die Menschen werden dann von der Deutung solcher Stellen ausgeschlossen. Im Falle der Philosophen jedoch setzt er den Punkt (*al-waqf*) an eine spätere Stelle. So lautet dann der Satz: „Aber niemand weiß es zu deuten außer Gott und denjenigen, die ein gründliches Wissen haben." Die Philosophen werden damit von der Offenbarung selbst ermächtigt, mehrdeutige Koranstellen zu interpretieren.[31]

Averroes wäre überhaupt nicht in der Lage, durch veränderte Punktierung die Bedeutung einer Koranstelle seinen Zwecken entsprechend zu variieren,

---

27 Ibid., S. 15,9–13.

28 Ibid., S. 5,15.21. Al-Fārābī setzt für das Studium der Philosophie eine tugendhafte Lebensführung voraus (*Alfārābīs philosophische Abhandlungen* [wie Anm. 7], S. 88). Er unterscheidet den wahren Philosophen dadurch vom eitlen, dass Ersterer zur Aufnahme der theoretischen Wissenschaften mit den in der *Politeia* erwähnten intellektuellen und ethischen Eigenschaften ausgestattet und darüber hinaus fromm und gemäß den religiösen Gesetzen und Überzeugungen erzogen wird: *Kitāb taḥṣīl as-sa'āda*, ed. Ǧa'far Āl Yāsīn (Beirut: Dār al-Andalus, 1401/1981), S. 94–95. Die Eigenschaften, über die in der Auffassung des Averroes der Philosoph verfügen soll, um zweideutige Koranstellen interpretieren zu dürfen, unterscheiden sich merklich von den Eigenschaften, die Platon für seinen Philosophenkönig und al-Fārābī für den *ra'īs al-awwal*, das Oberhaupt der tugendhaften Stadt, fordern. Vgl. Hourani in Averroes, *On the Harmony* (wie Anm. 10), S. 89–90, Anm. 48; Georges Tamer, „Monotheismus und Politik bei Alfarabi", in Aziz Al-Azmeh und János M. Bak (Eds.), *Monotheistic Kingship: The Medieval Variants* (Budapest, New York: Central European University Press, 2005), S. 191–214.

29 Ibid., S. 8,12–14. Der Vers lautet in Rudi Parets Übersetzung: „Er [Gott] ist es, der die Schrift [den Koran] auf dich herabgesandt hat. Darin gibt es (eindeutig) bestimmte Verse (…) – sie sind die Urschrift (…) – und andere, mehrdeutige (…). Diejenigen nun, die in ihrem Herzen (vom rechten Weg) abschweifen, folgen dem, was darin mehrdeutig ist, wobei sie darauf aus sind, (die Leute) unsicher zu machen und es (nach ihrer Weise) zu deuten. Aber niemand weiß es (wirklich) zu deuten außer Gott. Und diejenigen, die ein gründliches Wissen haben, sagen: ‚Wir glauben daran. Alles (was in der Schrift steht) stammt von unserem Herrn (…).' Aber nur diejenigen, die Verstand haben, lassen sich mahnen." Siehe den Beitrag von Ralph Lerner, S. 228.

30 Ibid., S. 16,13–14.

31 In der oben dargelegten Interpretation des Koranverses wird die Begründung der Lehre von der doppelten Wahrheit gesehen. Vgl. hierzu Friedrich Niewöhner, „Zum Ursprung der Lehre von der doppelten Wahrheit: Eine Koran-Interpretation des Averroes", in idem, Loris Sturlese (Eds.), *Averroismus im Mittelalter und in der Renaissance* (Zürich: Spur-Verlag, 1994), S. 23–41.

wenn die Überlieferung des Korantextes dies nicht ermöglichen würde. Dieser war ursprünglich in der Konsonantenschrift ohne Vokale, Verseinteilungen und Surenüberschriften geschrieben. Sie wurden erst später hineingefügt.[32] Nach islamischem Verständnis also ist die Punktierung im Koran Menschenwerk; sie verdient es im Gegensatz zum Konsonantentext deshalb nicht, als Bestandteil der Offenbarung betrachtet zu werden.[33] Der andalusische Philosoph stützt sich stillschweigend auf dieses Faktum aus der Entwicklungsgeschichte des Korantextes und präsentiert zwei Lesarten desselben Verses, die seine Position, dass nur Wissende die mehrdeutigen Koranstellen auslegen, während andere davon ausgeschlossen bleiben müssen, bestätigen sollen. Er behandelt den Offenbarungstext nicht willkürlich und unternimmt nichts, was mit der traditionellen Auffassung des Korans im Islam nicht vertretbar wäre. Ganz im Gegenteil: Er bewegt sich in zulässiger Weise innerhalb eines Handlungsrahmens, in dem die historisch begründete Lage des heiligen Textes freien Raum lässt. Dies zeigt auf der einen Seite, dass er als gläubiger Muslim mit seiner Interpretation den überlieferten Status der heiligen Schrift nicht verletzt. Auf der anderen Seite erweist er sich als guter Aristoteliker, der Geschichtsrealitäten ernst nimmt und Konsequenzen daraus für die Entwicklung seines Denkgebäudes zieht. Für ihn steht das Muslimsein nicht im Widerspruch mit dem Aristotelismus.[34]

Wie bestimmt Averroes die Interpretation (*ta'wīl*)? Sie besteht darin, „den Sinn des Ausdrucks vom wirklichen in den metaphorischen Sinn herauszuführen, ohne dass dadurch der arabische Sprachgebrauch beeinträchtigt würde."[35] Wenn die Bedeutung eines mehrdeutigen Ausdrucks den Anforderungen der Vernunft nicht entspricht, muss der Ausdruck als Metapher gedeutet werden. In *al-Kašf* teilt Averroes den Text des Koran in zwei Kategorien ein: 1. die Kategorie der Texte, in denen der zum Ausdruck gebrachte Sinn der wirklich gemeinte Sinn ist. Hier erübrigt sich die Interpretation. 2. Die Kategorie der Texte, in denen sich das Äußere (*al-ma'nā al-muṣarraḥ bihi*) vom Inneren (*al-ma'nā al-mawǧūd*) des Korans (*fī-š-šar'*) unterscheidet und es symbolisiert (*'alā ǧihat at-tamṯīl*). Diese Kategorie besteht aus vier Unterteilen, die sich vonein-

32 Theodor Nöldeke, Friedrich Schwally et al., *Geschichte des Qorans* (Leipzig: Dieterich, ²1909–1938; Nachdruck Hildesheim etc.: Olms, 2000), Band III, S. 257ff.; François Déroche, *The Abbasid Tradition. Qur'ans of the 8th to the 10th centuries AD* (London: The Nour Foundation, 1992).

33 Vgl. Michael Cook, *Der Koran. Eine kurze Einführung* (Stuttgart: Reclam, 2002), S. 80ff.

34 Beide Lesarten werden in Korankommentaren erwähnt. Die Lesart „*wa-mā yala'mu ta'wīlahu illā-llāhu wa-r-rāsiḫūna fī-l-'ilm*" (Aber niemand weiß es zu deuten außer Gott und denjenigen, die ein gründliches Wissen haben) wird sogar Muhammads Vetter Ibn 'Abbās, der traditionell als Begründer der Korankommentierung gilt, zugeschrieben. Einer Überlieferung zufolge soll Muhammad Gott gebeten haben, Ibn 'Abbās gründliches Wissen in der Religion und die Kunst der Interpretation zu schenken. Vgl. dazu die Kommentare von aṭ-Ṭabarī, az-Zamaḫšarī, ar-Rāzī und al-Qurṭubī zur Stelle 3:7.

35 *Faṣl al-maqāl* (wie Anm. 9), S. 7,15–17.

ander nach dem Grad der Schwierigkeit unterscheiden, in dem die Symbolisierungen und ihre Bedeutungen erfasst werden.[36]

Die Philosophen allein mit der Aufgabe der Koranauslegung zu betrauen bedeutet im Zusammenhang der islamischen Ideengeschichte, eine vor allem von *al-aš'arīya* vertretene Lehre einzuschränken. Dieser Lehre zufolge wird der Konsens (*iǧmā'*) der Muslime zur absoluten Autorität in dogmatischen Fragen erklärt.[37] Averroes lehnt den Konsens nicht ab. Als Jurist muss er ihn akzeptieren. Er unterzieht ihn jedoch dem historischen Beweis, dass es von Anfang an in der islamischen Gemeinschaft keine Übereinstimmung über spekulative Glaubensfragen gab. Indem er der Elite geeigneter, mit theoretischen Mitteln ausgestatteter Philosophen das Exklusivrecht der Interpretation zuschreibt, unterscheidet er sich auch von al-Ġazālī, der die Interpretationsberechtigung nicht vom intellektuell-theoretischen Vermögen, sondern von mystischen Erfahrungen abhängig macht.[38]

Verfügt dennoch der Koran-Interpret über die Möglichkeit, seine Tätigkeit ohne jegliche Einschränkung auszuüben? Die Frage, die anfangs rein dogmatisch zu sein schien und bei deren Behandlung die historische Entwicklung des koranischen Textes berücksichtigt werden musste, erhält im weiteren Verlauf der Argumentation hermeneutische Züge. Averroes stellt für die philosophische Auslegung des Korans fünf Bedingungen auf, welche im Folgenden kurz dargestellt und auf ihre Tragweite hin geprüft werden:

1. Die erste Bedingung ist sprachlicher Natur. Die Interpretation müsse dem arabischen Sprachgebrauch nicht zuwider, sondern solle den Regeln der Interpretationskunst im Arabischen gerecht werden.[39] Bei genauerer Betrachtung wird es jedoch deutlich, dass die Interpretationsfreiheit durch diese Einschränkung gar nicht ernsthaft gefährdet wird, weil es kaum möglich ist, dass eine solche Interpretation dem arabischen Sprachgebrauch widerspricht. Selbst wenn dies vorkäme, sollte jede Aussage des Korans, die nach den Sprachregeln nicht interpretiert werden kann, als rhetorisch bezeichnet werden. Averroes selbst verweist auf diese Möglichkeit, wenn er durch die Interpretation des Koranverses 16:125 „Rufe zu dem Weg deines Herrn durch die Weisheit und durch die schöne Ermahnung und streite mit ihnen durch das, was das schönste ist", die Rhetorik zusammen mit der

---

36 *Al-Kašf 'an manāhiǧ al-adilla,* Teile in Houranis Edition von *Faṣl al-maqāl* (wie Anm. 9, Müllers Seiten- und Zeilenzählung), S. 125,10–126,17.

37 Vgl. Iysa A. Bello, *The Medieval Islamic Controversy between Philosophy and Orthodoxy. Ijmā' and Ta'wīl in the Conflict between al-Ghazālī and Ibn Rushd* (Islamic Philosophy and Theology 3; Leiden: Brill, 1989), besonders S. 17–28, 44–51.

38 Al-Ġazālī, *Iḥyā' 'ulūm ad-dīn*, ed. 'Abd ar-Raḥīm Ibn al-Ḥusayn al-'Irāqī (5 Bände; Kairo: Dār al-Ḥadīṯ, 1938–1939), Band I, S. 180.

39 *Faṣl* (wie Anm. 9), S. 7,16–17.

demonstrativen Argumentation und der Dialektik als Überzeugungsmethoden zulässt.[40]

2. Eine weitere Bedingung besteht darin, die Interpretation einer Koranstelle durch eine andere Stelle, die mit ihrem Wortlaut (*ẓāhir*) diese Interpretation bezeugt, zu bestätigen.[41] Angesichts der Tatsache, dass kaum eine der relevanten Lehrmeinungen nicht von mehreren Schriftstellen bezeugt oder sinngemäß bestätigt werden kann, stellt sich diese Bedingung in Wahrheit als gar keine dar.
3. Die dritte Einschränkung verbietet die Interpretation von Stellen, die nach dem Konsens (*iǧmāʿ*) der Muslime wörtlich zu verstehen sind. Wie bereits dargelegt wurde, leugnet Averroes die Existenz eines solchen Konsenses unter den muslimischen Gelehrten im Hinblick auf spekulativ-theologische Fragen.[42]
4. Der vierte Vorbehalt betrifft die Interpretation von Lehren, welche durch alle drei Arten der Argumentation, der demonstrativen, dialektischen und rhetorischen, bestätigt werden kann.[43] Es ist dabei auffällig, dass es sich hier gar nicht um eine Einschränkung der Interpretation handelt. Da eine Stelle überhaupt nur und erst dann interpretiert werden soll, wenn sie dem Ergebnis der Demonstration widerspricht, erübrigt sich die Interpretation, wenn der Sinn der Stelle durch die Demonstration bereits als bestätigt gilt.
5. Die Interpretation wird nach Averroes schließlich nicht zugelassen, wenn sie zur Verleugnung der Existenz der Dinge führt, welche zu den Prinzipien der Religion gehören. Darunter fallen Gottes Sein, die Prophetien und die Sanktionen. Lediglich die Qualität dieser Dinge, das heißt ihre durch die Offenbarung vermittelte Beschaffenheit, darf vom Interpreten behandelt werden.[44] Da die von Averroes zum Beginn seiner Abhandlung propagierte Philosophie nicht das Ziel hat, Gottes Existenz zu verneinen, sondern sie eher mittels theoretischer Forschung zu beweisen, wird sie von dieser Bedingung gar nicht betroffen.

Aus den bereits aufgeführten, zum Teil nur scheinbaren Bedingungen wird deutlich, dass Averroes den Philosophen einerseits die Freiheit gibt, den Wortlaut des Korans gemäß ihren vernunftorientierten Überzeugungen zu interpretieren, dass sie dabei allerdings bestimmte Grenzen nicht überschreiten und keine Ideen verbreiten dürfen, die gegen die Existenz Gottes, der Prophetien und der ewigen Sanktionen verstoßen.[45] Der philosophischen Freiheit der Interpretation werden damit Grenzen gesetzt, deren Überschreitung an der Autorität

40 Ibid., S. 15,5–7.
41 Ibid., S. 8,6.
42 Ibid., S. 8,15–22.
43 Ibid., S. 15,17–18.
44 Ibid., S. 17,8–9.
45 Ibid., S. 14,20–21.

der Religionsschrift scheitert. Das, was die Schrift erlaubt, bleibt an ihre Vorgabe gebunden. Die Textoberfläche ist ein gemeinsames Feld für Philosophen und Nichtphilosophen, deshalb können Konflikte um Bedeutungen nicht ausgeschlossen werden. Im Gegenteil: Sie scheinen quasi vorprogrammiert zu sein. Das bedeutet für den Philosophen, in voller Verantwortung Vorsichtsmaßnahmen zu ergreifen, um von vorneherein Interpretationskonflikte abzuwenden. Denn für ihn steht viel auf dem Spiel. Am interpretatorischen Umgang des Philosophen mit religiösen Schriften wird die philosophische Tätigkeit schlechthin demonstriert. Aus diesem Grunde muss Averroes die philosophische Interpretation der heiligen Schrift aus dieser heraus rechtfertigen, wenn er die Philosophie aus der Religion heraus begründen und die Vereinbarkeit beider beweisen will.

Averroes gibt in diesem Zusammenhang eine vorbeugende Maßnahme bekannt, indem er erklärt, dass die Philosophen durch den Koran zu dessen Interpretation ermächtigt sind, während diese den übrigen Menschen, die nur mittels rhetorischer und dialektischer Argumente die Wahrheit erkennen können, verboten bleiben soll. Interpretationen dürfen nicht jedem Menschen offengelegt werden, sondern nur denjenigen, die sie verstehen können. Sonst seien sie schädlich.[46] Der Arzt Averroes vergleicht denjenigen, der seine Interpretation vorbehaltlos veröffentlicht, mit einem Menschen, der ein für viele Menschen nützliches Medikament jemandem gibt, dem es wegen schlechter Mischung der Temperamente nicht zugute kommt, woraufhin an der Nützlichkeit der Medizin überhaupt gezweifelt wird.[47] Den Verstoß gegen dieses Gebot hält er für Unglauben oder wenigstens Häresie.[48] Er begründet sein Urteil damit, dass allegorische Interpretationen der Schrift aus zwei Gründen vor der Allgemeinheit geheim gehalten bleiben müssen. Sie gefährden zum einen den Glauben einfacher Menschen, die infolgedessen der Gefahr allgemeinen Zweifels ausgesetzt werden. Zum anderen könnten vieldeutige Interpretationen weitere Spaltungen in der Religionsgemeinschaft hervorrufen – für Averroes ein weiterer, nicht unwichtiger Grund, al-Ġazālī zu kritisieren.[49]

---

46 Ibid., S. 22,1–7.

47 *Al-Kašf ʿan manāhiǧ al-adilla*, ed. Muḥammad ʿĀbid al-Ǧābirī (Beirut: Markaz Dirāsāt al-Waḥda al-ʿArabīya, 1998), S. 149.

48 *Faṣl al-maqāl* (wie Anm. 9), S. 16,3–4; 17,11–14.

49 Ibid., S. 17,15–18,10. Platon, *VII. Brief* 341d–344d, lehnt die Verbreitung aller philosophischen Ansichten in der Öffentlichkeit ab. Die in der Spätantike bekannte Tendenz der Philosophen, bestimmte Ansichten vor Nichtphilosophen zu verheimlichen, erreichte auch die islamischen Philosophen. Al-Fārābī nennt drei Gründe für die dunkle Ausdrucksweise des Aristoteles: die Prüfung, ob der Schüler die erforderliche Anlage besitzt, um unterrichtet zu werden, die Beibehaltung der Philosophie für Geeignete und schließlich die intellektuelle Übung des Schülers durch die Mühen der Forschung (*Mā yanbaġī an yuqaddam qabla taʿallum falsafat Arisṭū*, in *Mabādiʾ al-falsafa al-qadīma* [Kairo: al-Maktaba as-Salafīya, 1328/1910], S. 1–17, hier S. 14. Deutsche Übersetzung von F. Dieterici in *Alfārābī's philosophische Abhandlungen* [wie Anm. 7], S. 82–91, hier S. 89).

Averroes selbst wollte den Koran nicht auslegen; seine Vorliebe galt der Kommentierung von aristotelischen Schriften. Er legte jedoch die Prinzipien philosophischer Interpretation von mehrdeutigen Koranstellen fest und wollte an der Schriftauslegung (*ta'wīl*),[50] von Philosophen durchgeführt und durch die Schrift selbst legitimiert, die Aufhebung des scheinbaren Widerspruchs zwischen Philosophie und Religion demonstrieren. Maimonides, ein Landsmann von ihm, knapp zehn Jahre nach ihm geboren und sechs Jahre nach ihm gestorben, begab sich durch das Tor, das Averroes öffnete, ins Reich der philosophischen Bibelauslegung. Auch er wollte die aristotelische Philosophie in seinen religiösen Rahmen integrieren. Sein Unternehmen war allerdings nicht weniger spannungsreich als das seines älteren Zeitgenossen, dessen Schriften er gekannt haben dürfte.[51] Im Hinblick auf den gemeinsamen Entstehungskontext und kulturellen Hintergrund beider Denker im Spanien des 12. Jahrhunderts darf es nicht verwundern, dass viele der Probleme, die sie behandelten, trotz unterschiedlicher Religionszugehörigkeit und damit zusammenhängender Lebensführung identisch sind.[52] Das gilt besonders für die Zweckidentität von Religion und Philosophie sowie die Frage der Interpretation von heiligen Schriften durch Philosophen.

Maimonides kommentierte die *Mischna*, die erste Sammlung von jüdischen Religionsgesetzen, und erfasste in seinem großen Kodex *Mišneh Torah* alle Religionsgesetze des Judentums. Sein Werk mit ausgeprägtem philosophischem Charakter ist *Dalālat al-ḥā'irīn*, das er auf arabisch spätestens 1191 verfasste.[53] Es ist seinem Schüler Joseph bin Jehuda gewidmet, den er für würdig hielt, in die „Geheimnisse der Bücher der Prophetie" eingeweiht zu werden. Seine besondere Qualifikation bestand in seiner philosophischen Bildung.[54] Das Buch

---

Weiterführende Hinweise finden sich in Hourani, *On the Harmony* (wie Anm. 10), S. 106–107, Anm. 142.

50 Eine ausführliche Beschreibung seiner Theorie ist bei Bello, *The Medieval Islamic Controversy* (wie Anm. 37), S. 66–82.

51 Shlomo Pines, „Translator's Introduction: The Philosophic Sources of The Guide of the Perplexed", in Moses Maimonides, *The Guide of the Perplexed*. Translated by Shlomo Pines (Chicago: Chicago University Press, 1963), S. lvii–cxxxiv, hier S. cviii; Alfred Ivry, „The Utilization of Allegory in Islamic Philosophy", in Jon Whitman (Ed.), *Interpretation and Allegory: Antiquity to the Modern Period* (Brill's Studies in Intellectual History 101; Leiden: Brill, 2000), S. 153–180, hier S. 178.

52 Siehe hierzu: Joel Kraemer, „Maimonides and the Spanish Aristotelian School", in Mark D. Meyerson und Edward D. English (Eds.), *Christians, Muslims, and Jews in Medieval and Early Modern Spain. Interaction and Cultural Change* (Notre Dame, Ind.: University of Notre Dame Press, 2000), S. 40–68.

53 Verwendet wird die von Ḥusayn Atay besorgte arabische Edition: *Dalālat al-ḥā'irīn, ta'līf al-ḥakīm al-faylasūf Mūsā bin Maymūn al-Qurṭubī al-Andalusī* (Ankara Üniverseitesi Ilāhiyat Fakültesi Yayınları 93; Ankara: Üniverseitesi, 1974; Nachdruck: Kairo: Maktabat at-Taqāfah ad-Dīnīya, o.J.).

54 Ibid., S. 3,12.

richte sich – so der Autor – an Leser, die sowohl der Welt der Torah als auch der der Philosophie angehören und angesichts biblischer Stellen, deren wörtliche Bedeutung philosophischen Ansichten widerspricht, ratlos (*ḥā'irīn*) werden.[55]

Für Maimonides ist die Bibel kein einheitliches Buch wie der Koran für Averroes. Dennoch finden sich bei beiden dieselben theoretischen Hauptelemente der Schriftauslegung. Maimonides ist wie Averroes bemüht, einheitliche Kriterien für die Bibelauslegung zu entwerfen. So stellt er der Metaphysik (*al-ʿilm al-ilāhīy*, der göttlichen Wissenschaft), deren vornehmlicher Gegenstand Gott ist, die Physik aus der Überzeugung voran, Gott könne durch die Erkenntnis der Natur erkannt werden.[56] Er macht neben der moralischen und religiösen Vollkommenheit das Studium der Philosophie und jener Wissenschaften zur Bedingung für die Möglichkeit, die heilige Schrift richtig zu verstehen. Dass die Bibel nicht von allen Menschen gleichermaßen verstanden werden kann, liegt daran, dass sie zwei Sprachen spricht: eine für Philosophen und eine für Nichtphilosophen.[57]

Die methodischen Prinzipien, die Maimonides der Bibelinterpretation zugrunde legt, können folgendermaßen zusammengefasst werden:

1. Das erste Prinzip betrifft die Natur des Textes. Entsprechend der Absicht seines Werkes, die Ratlosigkeit der philosophisch Gebildeten, die in der Bibel Verwirrendes finden, zu beseitigen, erklärt Maimonides gleich am Anfang von *Dalālat al-ḥā'irīn*, dass die Torah Wörter enthält, die in drei Gruppen eingeteilt werden: 1. die mehrdeutigen Wörter (*asmā' muštaraka*), denen die Ignoranten jeweils eine ihrer Bedeutungen zuschreiben. 2. Die Metaphern (*mustaʿāra*), die von den Ignoranten in ihrem unmittelbaren Sinn genommen werden. 3. Die zweifelhaften Wörter (*mušakkika*), die einmal für „univocal" und einmal für „equivocal" gehalten werden.[58] Vor allem die wörtlich verstandenen Ausdrücke widersprechen sich oft und sind außerdem unvereinbar mit der philosophischen Auffassung derselben Sachverhalte, die sie ausdrücken.
2. Maimonides bietet für die Lösung des Problems die allegorische Interpretation.[59] Somit wird die Vernunft eingeschaltet, die darüber bestimmt, ob der Text einfach oder allegorisch behandelt werden soll. In Rücksicht auf das unterschiedliche Auffassungsvermögen ihrer Adressaten bringt die Bibel die metaphysischen Inhalte metaphorisch zum Ausdruck. Ebenso sind biblische Geschichten Allegorien, die nicht wörtlich verstanden, sondern

55 Ibid., S. 5,15–6,15; 11,13–15.

56 Ibid., S. 9,20–10,3. Vgl. Rémi Brague, „Maimonides. Bibel als Philosophie", in *Philosophen des Mittelalters. Eine Einführung*, ed. Theo Kobusch (Darmstadt: Primus-Verlag, 2000), S. 96–110.

57 Ibid., S. 10,10–12.

58 Ibid., S. 5,6–11.

59 Ibid., S. 6,10–12.

nach ihrem inneren Sinn befragt werden sollen.[60] Maimonides steht damit in der Tradition der Bibelinterpretation, die mit Philo von Alexandria begonnen hat und im arabischen Sprachraum durch Saadya Gaon fortgesetzt wurde.

3. Ein weiteres Prinzip ist die Widersprüchlichkeit der Interpretation, die der biblischen Widersprüchlichkeit entspricht. Maimonides führt in der Einleitung zu *Dalālat al-ḥā'irīn* sieben Arten des Widerspruchs auf.[61] In seinem Werk kommen nach seiner eigenen Äußerung die fünfte und die siebte Art vor. Ersterer wird von den Philosophen für pädagogische Zwecke verwendet, Letzterer ist nötig, wenn die Rede von geheimnisvollen Inhalten ist, die besser verborgen bleiben und deshalb nur teilweise geoffenbart werden können.[62] Wenn Maimonides sein Buch die eben genannten zwei Arten des Widerspruchs enthalten lässt, bedeutet dies, dass er seinem Werk zweifelsohne einen philosophisch-theologischen Charakter verleiht. Es kann sich somit an junge philosophisch Gebildete richten, ohne dass damit Geheimnisse des Glaubens Nichteingeweihten offengelegt werden müssen. Maimonides versucht damit, gleichermaßen der Forderung der Philosophie nach intellektueller Anstrengung und der Forderung seiner Religion nach Geheimhaltung bestimmter Lehren gerecht zu sein.[63]

Ein wichtiges Anliegen der Bibelauslegung des Maimonides ist, eine philosophische Lösung für das Problem der Körperlichkeit Gottes anzubieten, die aus dem Standpunkt der Philosophie heraus strikt abgelehnt wird.[64] Der Grund dafür, dass Gott überhaupt Körpereigenschaften zugeschrieben werden, liegt darin, dass die Torah „in der Sprache der Menschen spricht"[65] und mit allgemein verständlichen Bildern göttliche Eigenschaften vorstellt. Damit der Glaube an die Existenz, Allwissenheit und Allmacht Gottes in dem Bewusstsein des einfachen Menschen verwurzelt wird, beschreibt sie Gott als einen Menschen, der mit seinen Augen sehen, mit seinen Ohren hören und mit seinen Händen schlagen kann. Denn die Vorstellung eines Gottes, der mit vortrefflichen omnipotenten Körpereigenschaften versehen wird, dient zur moralischen Leitung der Menschen.[66] Maimonides hingegen hält die Auffassung von der Körper-

60 Ibid., S. 14ff.

61 Ibid., S. 18,13–20,3.

62 Ibid., S. 21,18–20.

63 Maimonides stellt seinem Werk Verse voran, in denen er diejenigen, die sich auf dem Feld der Torah nicht zurecht finden, dazu einlädt, seinen geraden Pfad, nämlich den Pfad der Erkenntnis einzuschlagen. Er bezeichnet ihn als einen heiligen Pfad, den weder ein Unreiner noch ein Leichtsinniger gehen darf. *Dalālat al-ḥā'irīn* (wie Anm. 53), S. 2. Vgl. Jesaja 35:8. Zu Maimonides und der Poesie siehe Kraemer, „Maimonides and the Spanish Aristotelian School" (wie Anm. 52), S. 40ff.

64 *Dalālat al-ḥā'irīn* (wie Anm. 53), Teil I, Kapitel 68–69.

65 Ibid., S. 58,7.

66 Ibid., Teil I, Kapitel 51.

lichkeit Gottes für schlimmer als den Götzendienst und möchte konsequent den Gottesbegriff von allen körperlichen Attributen reinigen. Er kann sich das in diesem Kontext erlauben, weil er sich an gebildete Leser richtet, die zur theoretischen Erkenntnis fähig sind und ein moralisches Leben führen.

Solchen Lesern will Maimonides vermitteln, dass der philosophische Gottesbegriff mit dem Gott der Torah übereinstimmt. Darum unternimmt er über viele Kapitel des *Führers der Unschlüssigen* die Umdeutung anthropomorpher Eigenschaften Gottes im Sinne aristotelischer und neoplatonischer Begrifflichkeit. Er muss jedoch einräumen, dass ein solches Unternehmen nicht allen zugute kommt. Deshalb adoptiert er von Onqelos einen Kompromiss, wonach die ursprüngliche Bedeutung der körperlichen Eigenschaften beibehalten wird, jedoch nicht auf Gott selbst, sondern auf geschaffene Seiende bezogen wird, die in Beziehung zu Gott stehen wie „das geschaffene Licht" oder die „geschaffene Stimme".[67] Die Einschaltung solcher Entitäten ermöglicht Maimonides, die Beschreibung Gottes auf Wirkungsattribute, das heißt auf Verben, die Gottes Handlungen beschreiben, und negative Eigenschaften der apophatischen Theologie zu beschränken.

Für Maimonides ist die allegorische Schriftauslegung (*taʾwīl*) notwendig, wenn der Wortlaut der Schrift (*ẓāhir*) mit der Demonstration (*burhān*) im Widerspruch steht, das heißt irrational ist. Die Tore der *taʾwīl* seien nicht geschlossen.[68] Diese Ansicht beruht im Grunde genommen auf der Auffassung, dass die Torah zwar ewig ist, dass aber die Veränderung historischer Umstände Modifikationen mit sich bringt, welche die Anwendung des Gesetzes betreffen und erneute Interpretation erfordern. So haben zum Beispiel die Opfergesetze nur noch formale Gültigkeit, weil sie an den Vollzug des Gottesdienstes im Tempel gebunden sind. Auch Maimonides trägt in seiner Behandlung der heiligen Schrift geschichtlichen Entwicklungen Rechnung. Religiöse Bestimmungen gelten nach seiner Auffassung nicht als unveränderbarer Bestandteil der Offenbarung, sondern als Handlungen, die die Offenbarung unter bestimmten Umständen vorgeschrieben hat. Sie sind deshalb zum Teil historisch bedingt und können bei veränderter Geschichtslage geändert, ja sogar aufgehoben werden. Ebenso wie Averroes betrachtet auch Maimonides seine Religion als eine Komposition von ewigen und historischen Elementen.

Maimonides zeigt sich in *Dalālat al-ḥāʾirīn* als gläubiger Rationalist.[69] Seine Interpretation der Bibel in diesem Werk ist – mit einem Ausdruck von Josef Stern – „a compound" aus Philosophie und Exegese und von jeder der beiden

---

67 Jakob S. Levinger und Hanna Kasher, „Maimonides (1135–1204)", in Friedrich Niewöhner (Ed.), *Klassiker der Religionsphilosophie* (München: Beck, 1995), S. 172–173.

68 *Dalālat al-ḥāʾirīn* (wie Anm. 53), S. 350,4–5.

69 Vgl. beispielsweise die rationalen Erklärungen der Gesetzesgebote in ibid., Teil III, Kapitel 36–49.

unterschieden.[70] Darin werden philosophische Erkenntnis und biblische Inhalte gleichermaßen aufgehoben, wobei sich beide Seiten offensichtlich gegenseitig beeinflussen. So ist seine Auffassung von der Bibel, wie bereits erläutert, philosophisch geprägt. Die Bibel bestimmt wiederum sein philosophisches Interesse, das sich ausschließlich religiösen Themen widmet. Der Modus, in dem hier Philosophie und Exegese betrieben werden, unterscheidet sich grundsätzlich von der traditionellen Art beider Richtungen. Er ist von einer Spannung zwischen philosophischer und imaginativer Sprache gekennzeichnet, die sich durch das ganze Unternehmen zieht und schließlich zur Bevorzugung der negativen Ausdrucksweise von Gott und seinen Eigenschaften führt. Dennoch zeigt sich, dass Maimonides' allegorische Interpretationen oft kreativ sind. Seine philosophische Orientierung verleiht ihm eine gewisse Souveränität dem biblischen Text gegenüber, die allerdings Wurzeln in der Tradition des rabbinischen *Midrasch* besitzt und nicht selten vom *Targum* des Onqelos Gebrauch macht. Der biblischen Allegorie folgend beansprucht er für seine Bibelinterpretation, die goldenen Äpfel, das heißt die innere Bedeutung des Textes, in den silbernen durchsichtigen Schalen, das ist das Äußere des Textes, zu zeigen. Das schöne Bild von den Äpfeln in durchsichtigen Schalen vermittelt eine Auffassung von der biblischen Allegorie, der auch Maimonides in seinem Werk folgt und die dem Autor ermöglicht, Sinngehalte sowohl zu offenbaren als auch zu verbergen.[71]

An dem Punkt gelangen wir zur Frage nach der Esoterik in Maimonides' Interpretation der Bibel. Es war in erster Linie Leo Strauss, der im vergangenen Jahrhundert auf diesen Aspekt des maimonidischen Denkens aufmerksam wurde.[72] Strauss beschränkte sich nicht darauf, die von ihm beobachtete Esoterik des mittelalterlichen Denkers zum Gegenstand wissenschaftlicher Forschung zu machen, sondern orientierte sich darüber hinaus in seinen eigenen Interpretationen früherer Schriften daran. Wie bereits erwähnt gibt Maimonides selbst zu erkennen, dass sein Buch methodische Widersprüche enthält, die sowohl mit dem esoterisch-exoterischen Charakter der Bibel wie auch mit seiner theo-

70 Josef Stern, „Philosophy or Exegesis: Some Critical Comments", in Norman Golb (Ed.), *Judaeo-Arabic Studies. Proceedings of the Founding Conference of the Society for Judaeo-Arabic Studies* (Amsterdam: Harwood Academic Publishers, 1997), S. 213–228, hier S. 215.

71 *Dalālat al-ḥā'irīn* (wie Anm. 53), S. 13,6–18; Proverbien 25:11.

72 Leo Strauss, „The Literary Character of the Guide of the Perplexed", in idem, *Persecution and the Art of Writing* (Glencoe, Ill.: The Free Press, 1952), S. 38–94. Dagegen Oliver Leaman, *Moses Maimonides* (revised edition; Richmond: Curzon, 1997), besonders S. 2–15; Joseph A. Bujis, „The Philosophical Character of Maimonides' *Guide* – A Critique of Strauss' Interpretation", in *Judaism* 27 (1978), S. 448–457. Vgl. weiter zum Thema Leonard S. Kravitz, *The Hidden Doctrine of Maimonides' Guide for the Perplexed. Philosophical and Religious God-Language in Tension* (Lewiston, N.Y.: Edwin Mellen Press, 1988).

logisch-philosophischen Herangehensweise an die Schrift zusammenhängen. Würde man die Position Maimonides' genauer betrachten, stellt sich folgende Charakterisierung seiner Esoterik dar. Die Mehrdeutigkeit biblischer Texte ist im Anspruch der Bibel begründet, die Menschen gemäß ihres unterschiedlichen Auffassungsvermögens verständlich anzusprechen. Sie ist auch der Grund dafür, dass der Vernunft Macht über den Vorgang des Verstehens der Bibel zugesprochen wird. Das vernünftige Interpretieren des biblischen Textes wird somit aus dessen esoterischem Charakter legitimiert. Aus der Sicht des Maimonides ist dieser Charakter ein absichtlicher, um den einfältigen Lesern unnötige Schwierigkeiten zu ersparen. Leser, die Nichtphilosophen sind, können auch die philosophische Auslegung der Bibel nicht akzeptieren, ohne dass ihr Glaube erschüttert würde. Für Maimonides ist die Vernunft das Alpha und Omega der biblischen Esoterik sowie einer esoterischen Interpretation derselben. Sowohl deren Ausgangspunkt als auch deren Ergebnis sind von der Vernunft bestimmt. Dementsprechend *muss* jede vernünftige Interpretation der Bibel aus diesem Grunde esoterisch sein. Die Vernunftwahrheit ist wiederum das Kriterium der Bibelinterpretation. Dieser Bestimmung liegt die Überzeugung zugrunde, dass es zwischen der Torah und der Vernunft im Wesentlichen keinen Widerspruch gibt. Daraus ergibt sich, dass Esoterik in einem solchen Kontext zu einem ganz natürlichen Modus der Kommunikation wird.[73]

Averroes und Maimonides treffen sich im gemeinsamen Bemühen, die Übereinstimmung zwischen der eigenen Religion und der Philosophie zu zeigen und diese somit in die eigene Religionsgemeinschaft zu integrieren. Einen konkreten Ausgangspunkt für dieses Anliegen bildet für Maimonides die Überzeugung, die Propheten seien auch Philosophen – eine Eigenschaft, die übrigens Averroes in seinen Schriften für Muhammad nicht beansprucht. Dennoch vertreten beide die Ansicht, dass die einheitliche Wahrheit in der Philosophie universellen Ausdruck findet und in der Religion mittels partikularer Vorstellungen den Menschen vermittelt wird. Auch das Mittel zur Begründung der Philosophie auf dem Boden der jeweiligen Religion ist unterschiedlich. Während Averroes das Studium der Philosophie unmittelbar an Stellen begründet sieht, die zum Betrachten und Bedenken von Gegenständen aus der Erfahrungswelt durch Begriffe wie *iʿtibār*, *tafakkur* und *naẓar* im Koran anregen, argumentiert Maimonides für die Philosophie mit der Liebe zu Gott. Gerade sie führt in seiner Konzeption dazu, dass sich Menschen der theoretischen Betrachtung des Seins verstärkt widmen.[74]

Beide Philosophen erkennen unzweideutig den Zusammenhang zwischen ihrem Philosophieren und der Offenbarung an. Damit zeigen sie auch ein enges und vielleicht deshalb spannungsreiches Verhältnis zwischen Philosophie und Religion im Mittelalter. Zugleich kann beobachtet werden, dass die

---

73 Vgl. Kraemer, „Maimonides and the Spanish Aristotelian School" (wie Anm. 52), S. 47.
74 Vgl. den Beitrag von Ralph Lerner (S. 232–233).

Philosophie in beiden Konzeptionen nicht bedingungslos der Religion untergeordnet wird. Schwer verständliche, dogmenhaltige Schriftstellen müssen mit Mitteln der Demonstration interpretiert werden. Die Aussagen der Schrift müssen mit den Postulaten der Vernunft kompatibel sein. Damit scheint die Vernunft gegenüber der Offenbarung sogar die Oberhand zu behalten. Letztere stellt jedoch das Gleichgewicht her, indem sie beansprucht, das vernünftige Eingreifen in ihre Werke selbst zu legitimieren. Dieser Anspruch kommt bei Averroes explizit vor; Maimonides setzt ihn seinem *Dalālat al-ḥā'irīn* offensichtlich voraus. Das Handeln der Vernunft wird dadurch gerechtfertigt, dass diese gar nicht von Gott wegführt, sondern durch Erkenntnis der Schöpfung zur Verherrlichung des Schöpfers beiträgt und die von Gott geschaffene Vernunft durch ihre interpretative Tätigkeit nichts Weiteres tut, als den rationalen Sinn der Offenbarungsschrift, der sich zunächst lediglich dem Auge des Wissenden erschließt, ans Licht zu bringen und ihn damit intellektuell fähigen Mitgliedern der Religionsgemeinschaft sichtbar zu machen.[75]

Erkennt Averroes der Philosophie ihre Priorität an, so kann er dies nur auf der Basis ihrer natürlichen Verpflichtung zur Erkenntnis Gottes unternehmen. Er betrachtet die vernunftorientierte Interpretation von heiligen Schriften als Korrektiv für traditionelle Glaubensansichten. Ihm gelingt es, dem koranischen Text die klare Aufforderung abzugewinnen, dass Geeignete philosophieren und darüber hinaus dunkle Stellen im Koran auslegen müssen, weil er an der Einheit der wahren Inhalte von Religion und Philosophie festhält. Die Bestimmung der Wahrheit ist eine Tätigkeit der Vernunft, die sich ihrer von der Offenbarung abgesteckten Grenzen bewusst ist und dementsprechend handelt.[76] Auch Maimonides ist der Ansicht, dass sich die Lehren der Philosophie und der heiligen Schrift überlappen und dass Glaubensinhalte stufenweise verstanden werden können. Er geht allerdings nicht so weit wie Averroes, um der heiligen Schrift das Gebot zur philosophischen Interpretation zu entnehmen, sondern begnügt sich damit, dass der aufmerksame Leser selbst die Ermutigung dazu aus der heiligen Schrift herausliest. Der Grund dafür dürfte in seiner Auffassung liegen, dass sich der Glaube auf Dinge bezieht, die sich der Vernunfterkenntnis entziehen. Die Wahrheit, die die Philosophie erreicht, unterscheidet sich in ihrem Wesen nicht von der Wahrheit der Torah. Unterschiedlich ist jedoch die Art, in der die Wahrheit in beiden Bereichen artikuliert wird. Während die Schrift die Wahrheit auf Gottes den Propheten mitgeteilte Offen-

75 Siehe hierzu Oliver Leaman, *An Introduction to Medieval Islamic Philosophy* (Cambridge: Cambridge University Press, 1985; Nachdruck 1992), S. 169ff., 177–178.

76 Averroes scheint wohl die Ansicht zu vertreten, dass die menschliche Vernunft von der Natur her unfähig ist, alles zu begreifen, und dass sie deshalb auf die Offenbarung angewiesen bleibt, die übervernünftige Wahrheiten vermittelt: *Tahāfut at-tahāfut* (wie Anm. 13), S. 255–256. Hourani, „Introduction", in Averroes, *On the Harmony* (wie Anm. 10), S. 26–27, unterschätzt die Bedeutung der Stelle.

barung bezieht, ist für die Philosophie das wahr, was die Vernunft mittels der Demonstration erfasst.

Sind Philosophie und Religion im Wesentlichen miteinander vereinbar, so ist der Unterschied zwischen ihnen in der Situation *ad hominem* begründet. In Rücksicht auf die unterschiedliche Rezeptionsfähigkeit der Menschen vermittelt die Schrift die Wahrheit durch Bilder, Metaphern und mehrschichtige Ausdrücke, will sie doch alle Menschen, Gebildete wie Ungebildete, erreichen. Die Philosophie erhebt einen solchen Anspruch nicht. Sie ist die Wissenschaft der geistigen Elite, die geeignet ist, die Wahrheit zu begreifen. Die Differenz zwischen Religion und Philosophie ist also von den Rezipienten abhängig. Sie ist deshalb nicht wesenhaft, sondern quasi zufällig. Sie besteht nicht in der Substanz der Wahrheit, sondern in ihrer Vermittlung. Eine solche Bestimmung des Unterschieds zwischen Religion und Philosophie erschließt den Philosophen einen weiteren Horizont. Für Averroes und Maimonides ist das Kriterium für richtiges Verstehen der mehrdeutigen Schriftäußerungen deren Vereinbarkeit mit den Prinzipien der Vernunft. Die Philosophen verfügen über die richtigen Bedeutungen. Ihr Glaube beruht nicht auf imaginativ vermittelten Vorstellungen, sondern ist von rationaler Gewissheit untermauert.[77] Ihr Wissen ist aber nicht uneingeschränkt. Themen wie zum Beispiel die, welche die Natur Gottes betreffen, übersteigen ihr Auffassungsvermögen. Sie sind hierbei auf die Schrift angewiesen, wie es bei Averroes heißt. Maimonides räumt den Propheten explizit einen höheren Rang an Erkenntnis ein als den Philosophen.[78] Letztere übertreffen jedoch alle anderen Menschen beim Verständnis des schriftlich fixierten Offenbarungskorpus. Ihre Interpretation ist eine wichtige Aufgabe für eine Philosophie, die sich selbst als *imitatio dei* versteht. Die Grenzen zwischen Religion und Philosophie sind aus der Sicht beider Philosophen durchlässig.

77 *Faṣl al-maqāl* (wie Anm. 9), S. 10,11–14.

78 *Dalālat al-ḥā'irīn* (wie Anm. 53), Teil II, Kapitel 36.

The Politico-Religious Context of Maimonides

by

Sarah Stroumsa

The Hebrew University, Jerusalem

Since Leo Strauss, one has become used to interpreting the thought of Maimonides, and in particular his prophetology, in terms of political theory. More than others, Strauss dwelt on the fact that, like some other contemporaneous philosophers in the Islamic world, Maimonides viewed the prophet as the ideal statesman. Elaborating on Plato's model of the philosopher-king, Maimonides and other medieval Arab philosophers substituted the philosopher by a prophet. As noted by Strauss, and more recently by Shlomo Pines, the medieval opponents of these philosophers criticized them for being interested primarily in the economy of this world's affairs rather than in the economy of salvation.[1] The recurrence of such criticism in medieval Arabic texts led Pines to suggest that indeed, for Maimonides and for some other medieval philosophers, like al-Fārābī and Ibn Bājja, the belief in the afterlife held mainly an educational purpose, and that in fact they believed that the ultimate good must be sought in the establishment of a healthy society.[2]

The assumption underlying modern scholarly approaches (both that of Strauss and Pines and that of their critics) is that Maimonides' political thought was embedded in the philosophical legacy of which he was the recipient, and thus was shaped mainly by reinterpretations of the Hellenistic philosophical tradition current in the Islamic world.

Maimonides' life, however, evolved within the political reality of his time, under Muslim (and not under Hellenistic) rule. In what follows I will attempt to analyze the components of this politico-religious reality, and the impact it

---

1 Leo Strauss, *Persecution and the Art of Writing* (Glencoe, Ill.: The Free Press, 1952), pp. 9–14; Shlomo Pines, "The Limitations of Human Knowledge according to Al-Fārābī, ibn Bājja, and Maimonides", in *Studies in Medieval Jewish History and Literature*, ed. Isadore Twersky (Cambridge, Mass.: Harvard University Press, 1979), pp. 82–109.

2 Pines' view has been strongly criticized in Herbert Davidson, "Maimonides on Metaphysical Knowledge", in *Maimonidean Studies* 3 (1992/93), pp. 49–103, especially p. 89. See also Sarah Stroumsa, "'True Felicity:' Paradise in the Thought of Avicenna and Maimonides", in *Medieval Encounters* 4 (1998), pp. 51–77.

had on Maimonides' thought in general and on some aspects of his political thought in particular.

* * *

The Islamic polity which Maimonides encountered during his lifetime was far from being made of one cloth. Four major political entities dominated his life:

1. From his birth in 1138 in Córdoba and until 1148, Maimonides lived under the rule of the Berber dynasty of the *Murābiṭūn* (known to the Latins as the Almoravids) in al-Andalus.
2. In 1148 Córdoba was captured by another Berber dynasty, that of the *Muwaḥḥidūn* (or Almohads). The whereabouts of the Maimūn family in the following few years are unclear; it may have stayed in Seville at some stage.[3] At any rate, in 1160 the family moved to Fez, the North African capital of the Almohads, where it remained for five years.
3. In 1165 Maimonides and his family left Fez, and after a short period in Palestine, they moved to Egypt and settled in Cairo, which was then still ruled by the Fāṭimids.
4. Egypt was conquered by the Ayyūbids in 1171, and it is under their rule that Maimonides lived until his death in 1204.

Each of these political entities is closely associated with a specific school of religious law (*madhhab*), and with a particular school of thought:

1. The Almoravids are identified with Mālikī law, and typically (or stereotypically) described as opposed to rational speculation in all its forms. An extreme manifestation of this attitude was the public burning of the books of Abū Ḥāmid al-Ġazālī (d. 1111) during the reign of ʿAlī b. Yūsuf b. Tāshufīn (d. 1106).[4]
2. Like the Almoravids, the Ayyūbids were Sunnī Muslims; they, however, followed Shāfiʿite law, and adopted Ashʿarite *kalām* or speculative theology.[5]

---

3 See Maimonides' reference to the ships loading oil at Seville and leaving on the Guadalquivir to Alexandria; R. Moses b. Maimon, *Responsa*, ed. Jehoshua Blau (3 volumes; Jerusalem: Mekitse Nirdamim, 1957–1961), vol. II, 1960, p. 576. See also his autobiographical note in the *Guide of the Perplexed*, Part II, Chapter 9 (translated by Shlomo Pines [Chicago, London: University of Chicago Press, 1963], on p. 269), according to which he has met the son of Ibn al-Aflaḥ of Seville.

4 See Pedro Chalmeta, "The Almoravids in Spain", s.v. "Al-Murābiṭūn", in *Encyclopedia of Islam*, New Edition, vol. VII (Leiden: Brill, 1993), pp. 589–591, especially p. 591, col. 1.

5 Cf. Joseph Drory, "The Early Decades of Ayyūbid Rule", in *Perspectives on Maimonides: Philosophical and Historical Studies*, ed. Joel L. Kraemer (Oxford: Oxford University Press, 1991), pp. 295–302, especially p. 296.

3. The Fāṭimids, as Ismā'īlī Shi'ites, belonged to "the fifth *madhhab*" in law, and their theology reflected a wholesale adoption of Neoplatonic philosophy.[6]
4. And last, the Almohads were Sunnī Muslims who developed their own brand of legal system, although this system cannot exactly be called a school.[7] Their jurisprudence reveals some affinity with the Zāhirī school, (although it cannnot be identified as Zāhirī). They also developed their own particular theological-philosophical stance. Regarding theology, they are associated mostly with al-Ġazālī (i.e. with Ash'arite *kalām*), but some of the Arab historiographers also associate them with the Mu'tazila school of *kalām*, while others connect them (probably with much exaggeration) with Aristotelian philosophy.[8]

Maimonides's attitude to *kalām* in general and to al-Ġazālī in particular has been studied extensively.[9] Scholarly attention has also been given to Maimonides' attitude to the Ismā'ilīya,[10] and to the impact of Sunnī law on his thought.[11] The impact of the Almohad regime on Maimonides' thought has remained almost unnoticed, and it is on this impact that I wish to focus here.

---

6 See, for example, Farhad Daftary, *The Ismā'īlīs: Their history and doctrines* (Cambridge: Cambridge University Press, 1990), especially pp. 144–255; Heinz Halm, *The Fatimids and their Traditions of Learning* (London: Tauris and The Institute of Ismaili Studies, 1997), especially pp. 30–40.

7 Cf. Maribel Fierro, "The Legal Policies of the Almohad Caliphs and Ibn Rushd's *Bidāyat al-Mujtahid*", in *Journal of Islamic Studies* 10 (1999), pp. 226–248.

8 Cf. Madeleine Fletcher, "Ibn Tūmart's Teachers: The Relationship with al-Ghazālī", in *al-Qanṭara* 18 (1997), pp. 305–330.

9 Cf. Franz Rosenthal, "Maimonides and a Discussion on Muslim Speculative Theology", in *Jewish Tradition in the Diaspora: Studies in Memory of Professor Walter J. Fischel*, ed. Mishael Maswari Caspi (Berkeley etc.: Judah L. Magnes Memorial Museum, 1981), pp. 109–112; Michael Schwartz, "Who Were Maimonides' Mutakallimūn? Some Remarks on 'Guide of the Perplexed', part 1, chapter 73", in *Maimonidean Studies* 2 (1992), pp. 159–209; 3 (1995), pp. 143–172; Hava Lazarus-Yafeh, "Was Maimonides influenced by al-Ghazālī", in *Tehillah le-Moshe: Biblical and Judaic Studies Presented to Moshe Greenberg*, ed. Mordekai Cogan et al. (Winona Lake, Ind.: Eisenbrauns, 1997), pp. 163–193 (in Hebrew); Amira Eran, "Al-Ghazālī and Maimonides on the World to Come and Spiritual Pleasures", in *Jewish Quarterly Review* 8 (2001), pp. 137–166; Steven Harvey, "Al-Ghazālī and Maimonides and their Books of Knowledge", in *Studies in Memory of Professor I. Twersky by His Students* (Cambridge, Mass.: Cambridge University Press [forthcoming]), n. 11 (I am grateful to Steven Harvey for allowing me to consult his manuscript before publication).

10 Cf. Alfred I. Ivry, "Neoplatonic Currents in Maimonides' Thought", in *Perspectives on Maimonides* (see above n. 4), pp. 115–140.

11 See, for example, Gideon Libson, "Parallels between Maimonides and Islamic Law", in *The Thought of Moses Maimonides: Philosophical and Legal Studies*, ed. Ira Robinson et al. (Lewiston, N.Y.: Edwin Mellen Press, 1990), pp. 209–248; Joel Kraemer, "The

The Almohad movement was not yet another wave of renovation, in a cycle of such waves emerging from the desert to restore old mores and values in the corrupt cities.[12] Ibn Tūmart presented himself as the Mahdī: his leadership retained aspects of millenarian messianism, and his movement was revolutionary in all domains.[13]

The Almohads, who aimed at overthrowing the Mālikīs, sought to reform their legal system.[14] Instead of the Mālikī reliance on precedents, the Almohads returned to the sources (*uṣūl*) of jurisdiction (*Qur'ān* and *sunna*). They strove to do away with the accumulated casuistics (*furū'*) and, claiming that Truth is one and not multiple, they rejected the legitimacy of legal controversy (*ikhtilāf*), and admitted no pluralism of schools. Ibn Tūmart and his followers summarized their legal opinions in small manuals of law (which together form "The Book of Ibn Tūmart"[15]). Much of the Almohad legal system remains unclear to us, mainly because of the process of extensive "de-almohadization" which presumably took place after the fall of the dynasty. Their peculiar interpretation of the law is nevertheless well documented, as in the case of their abolition of the status of *ahl al-dhimma*, and the ensuing persecution of religious minorities.[16]

The revolutionary zeal which informed Almohad law is also manifest in Almohad theology. There too the Almohads called to a return to the sources, indoctrinating the multitudes and introducing a compulsory Credo about the Unity of God (*tawḥīd*) against what they presented as the anthropomorphism (*tajsīm*) of the Almoravids. This Credo circulated in small manuals of catechism (*murshida* and *'aqīda*), and served for the indoctrination of the various strata of

Influence of Islamic Law on Maimonides: The Case of the Five Qualifications", in *Te'udah* 10 (1996), pp. 225–244 (in Hebrew).

12 Cf. Ernest Gellner, *Muslim Society* (Cambridge: Cambridge University Press, 1981).

13 See Maribel Fierro, "Le Mahdī Ibn Tūmart et al-Andalus: l'élaboration de la légitimité almohade", in *Mahdisme et millénarisme en Islam*, ed. Mercedes García-Arenal (Revue des Mondes Musulmans et de la Méditerranée 91/94; Aix-en-Provence: Édisud, 2000), pp. 107–124.

14 Cf. Maribel Fierro, "Proto-Mālikīs, Mālikīs and Reformed Mālikīs in al-Andalus", in *The Islamic School of Law: Evolution, Devolution, and Progress* (Cambridge, Mass.: Harvard University Press, 2004).

15 See *Le Livre de Mohammed Ibn Toumert, Mahdi des Almohades*, ed. Jean-Dominique Luciani, with an Introduction by Ignaz Goldziher (Alger: Imprimerie Orientale Pierre Fontana, 1903).

16 On the Almohad persecutions, see David Corcos, "The Attitude of the Almohads Towards the Jews", in his *Studies in the History of the Jews of Morocco* (Jerusalem: Rubin Mass, 1976), pp. 136–160 (in Hebrew); Jean-Pierre Molénat, "Sur le rôle des almohades dans la fin du christianisme local au Maghreb et en al-Andalus", in *Al-Qanṭara* 18 (1997), pp. 389–413; Maribel Fierro, "Spiritual Alienation and Political Activism: the *Gurabā'* in al-Andalus during the Sixth/Twelfth Century", in *Arabica* 47 (2000), pp. 230–260, especially p. 231.

Almohad society.[17] A close-knit elite (the *ṭalaba*) served as the cadre for Almohad administration.[18] This elite was educated on the higher lever of theology, based on an adaptation of al-Ġazālī (i.e. *Ash'arite kalām*). Unlike the Almoravids, the Almohad regime was tolerant of philosophy (although it was probably not itself committed to philosophy, contrary to the way it is depicted in some of the Arabic sources as well as in some modern scholarship).[19]

Maimonides spent almost twenty years of his life as a young adult under the Almohads, and he retained contacts with Jews living under this regime after he had moved to Egypt. According to Muslim sources, Maimonides' family underwent forced conversion, like the rest of the Jewish community, and thus the young Maimonides read Qur'ān and studied *fiqh*.[20] Under such circumstances, it is inconceivable that he would not have been influenced by the Almohads, and even less conceivable that he would have remained unaware of the intricacies of their revolution. The existence of such influence must therefore be our working hypothesis, although Maimonides never mentions the Almohads by name, and when he alludes to their regime it is only in the context of their persecution of the Jews. In the remaining part of this paper I will try to demonstrate that this working hypothesis allows us to see that indeed many of Maimonides' innovations (large scale as well as peculiarities in detail) reflect Almohad influence.

* * *

Maimonides presents his major halakhic work, the *Mishneh Torah*, as a pioneering composition ("in which none in our nation had preceded me") and his claim for innovation is accepted by modern scholarship.[21] Maimonides' explicitly declared aim in this book was to replace the written "oral law", that is to say, the Mishnah and the Talmud (while reaffirming their authority), and to make redundant later legal literature, a body of texts which accumulated over the ages. Maimonides' explicit declaration refers to the Talmudic and post-Talmudic literature. But in fact, as the name "*Mishneh Torah*" reveals, and as

17 See Henri Massé, "La profession de foi (*aqīda*) et les guides spirituels (*morchida*) du Mahdi Ibn Toumart", in *Mémorial Henri Basset*, vol. 2 (Paris: Librairie Orientaliste Paul Geuthner, 1928), pp. 105–121.

18 See Eric Fricaud, "Les *ṭalaba* dans la société almohade (Le temps d'Averroes)", in *Al-Qanṭara* 18 (1997), pp. 331–388.

19 On this question, see Sarah Stroumsa, "Almohad Philosophers? Ibn Rushd, Maimonides, and Almohad Ideology" in *Les Almohades: Doctrine, activité intellectuelle et pratiques religieuses,* ed. Maribel Fierro (Madrid: Casa de Velázquez [forthcoming]).

20 See, for example, Ibn Abī Uṣaybi'a, *'Uyūn al-Anbā' fī ṭabaqāt al-aṭibbā'*, ed. Nizār Riḍā (Beirut: Dār Maktabat al-ḥayāt, n.d.), p. 582.

21 See Isadore Twersky, *Introduction to the Code of Maimonides (Mishneh Torah)* (New Haven, London: Yale University Press, 1980), p. 3; idem, "The Mishneh Torah of Maimonides", in *Proceedings of the Israel Academy of Sciences and Humanities* 5 (1976), pp. 265–295.

the introduction to the book says clearly, Maimonides saw the role of this book as making the whole body of written "oral law" redundant, "so that a person may first read the written Torah, then read this book and know by it the whole oral Torah, requiring no book between them." In the Introduction to his *Book of Laws*, Maimonides spells out his methodology in the *Mishneh Torah*:

> [...] I saw fit to prepare also a composition that includes all the laws and precepts of the Torah [...] and to proceed as I am wont to do, namely, avoiding mentioning disagreements (*ikhtilāfāt*) and positions that were rejected, and listing only the finite ruling [...]. And I also opt for omitting the justifications and arguments in support of each ruling, and the names of transmitters.[22]

Maimonides also declares his intention to go back to the sources of legislation (*uṣūl*) and to avoid casuistics (*furū'*) as much as possible, and he gives precedence to rulings that rely on earlier sources (*de'orayta*) over those presented as relying on later interpretation (*de-rabbanan*). When speaking of the *Mishneh Torah* he says:

> We also mentioned in it all the religious and legal principles (*uṣūl*), intending all those who are called "Disciples of the sages", or "Sages", or "Geonim", or however you wish to call them, to establish their derivative legal ruling (*furū'*) on legal principles (*uṣūl fiqhiyya*).[23]

The Arabic terminology highlights the affinity of this legal methodology with that of the Almohads, an affinity which is unexpected particularly in the domain of Jewish religious law. It appears that in his decision to compose a comprehensive manual of law, as well as in the methodological principles which guided him in this composition (namely, going back to the *uṣūl*, presenting a final ruling, and dispensing with the traditional scaffolding that accompanied it) Maimonides was following closely the Almohad example.

The similarity, however, is not restricted to terminology and methodology, but is attested also in the domain of religious indoctrination. Maimonides chose to begin his legal Codex with a manual of theological, philosophical and even scientific catechism, *The Book of Knowledge*. A parallel structure can be found in al-Ġazālī's *Ihyā' 'ulūm ad-dīn*, but although the *Ihyā'* contains matters of religious law, it is not a codex of law. Ibn Tūmart, the Mahdī of the Almohads who was influenced by al-Ġazālī, also opens his "*Book*" with a *Book of Knowledge*, and as the "*Book of Ibn Tūmart*" includes manuals for everyday law, it can be said to offer a closer parallel to the *Mishneh Torah*. It thus seems plausible that al-Ġazālī's influence reached Maimonides through the Almohad channel.

22 Maimonides, *Book of Commandments*, ed. Josef Kafaḥ [= Y. Qāfiḥ] (Jerusalem: Mosad Harav Kook, 1971), pp. 1–2.

23 *Maimonides' Treatise on Resurrection (Maqāla fī teḥiyyat ha-metim)*, ed. Joshua Finkel (New York: American Academy for Jewish Research, 1939), p. 4.

The most obvious case of influence of Almohad indoctrination can be seen in Maimonides' unwavering rejection of anthropomorphism, which he presents as incumbent on all levels of society. According to him,

> The negation of the doctrine of the corporeality of God and the denial of His having a likeness to created things and of His being subject to affections are matters that ought to be made clear and explained to everyone according to his capacity, and ought to be inculcated in virtue of traditional authority upon children, women, stupid ones, and those of defective natural disposition, just as they adopt the notion that God is one.[24]

Maimonides, just like the Almohads, identified true monotheism with a non-corporeal perception of God, and he included this understanding among the thirteen principles *(qawāʿid)* of faith,[25] the belief in which are preconditions for belonging to the Jewish people. Maimonides was not, of course, the first Jewish thinker to reject anthropomorphism, but none of his predecessors had defined this article of faith as the *conditio sine qua non* for salvation. Maimonides' doctrinal approach was revolutionary, and it is most probable that in this approach he followed the Almohads.[26]

By shaping a compact and decisive legal Codex, and by including indoctrination in this Codex, Maimonides was playing the role assigned to the ruler according to the Platonic philosophical tradition: the role of the law-giver who builds a virtuous city, the one who guides his flock towards true opinions. The idea that the philosopher must play this role was, as mentioned above, part of the Hellenic legacy. The parameters of what exactly this role meant, however, and some of the details of its implementations, reflect, I suggest, a strong Almohad influence.

If this suggestion is accepted, and if it is recognized that the image Maimonides had of true politico-religious leadership was indeed influenced by the Almohads, then it is likely that, in addition to the fact that his overall perception of the role of the ruler is modeled according to the Almohad thought, various details will also be found that reflect this influence.

Maimonides' depiction of Messianic era is a case in point. Contrary to Maimonides usual methodology of revealing only chapter-heads, in what concerns the Days of the Messiah Maimonides goes out of his way to make public his demythologizing reading of the scriptures. Maimonides has been criticized for

---

24 *The Guide of the Perplexed*, II, p. 35 (p. 81 in Pines' translation).

25 *Mishnah with Maimonides' Commentary*, Tractate *Sanhedrin*, Introduction to *Pereq Ḥeleq*, ed. Josef Kafaḥ [= Y. Qāfiḥ] (Jerusalem: Mosad Harav Kook, 1964), p. 211.

26 As suggested already by Isaak Heinemann, "Maimuni und die arabischen Einheitslehrer", in *Monatschrift für Geschichte und Wissenschaft des Judentums* 79 (1935), pp. 102–148; and Shlomo Pines, "A Lecture on the Guide of the Perplexed", in *Iyyun* 47 (1998), pp. 115–128 (in Hebrew), on p. 116.

his interpretation of the World to Come, and was accused of denying the resurrection of the dead. In this context, Maimonides complained that the storm against him rose despite his outspoken declaration of his belief in the resurrection.[27]

In what concerns the Messianic era, however, Maimonides says explicitly that the text of the scriptures must not be taken literally, but should rather be read as a parable, and he even hints at what it is a parable of. In the Introduction to the *Guide of the Perplexed* Maimonides presents such a procedure as equivalent to divulging the secret of the Torah. And yet, regarding the Days of the Messiah, Maimonides consistently adopts this procedure, and he does so clearly and outspokenly, in the last chapters of *Mishneh Torah*, as well as in the *Guide of the Perplexed*.[28]

One could of course argue, in a Straussian way, that here too Maimonides adopts an esoteric technique of "uncovering a cubit, covering two". A more plausible explanation, however, seems to be offered by reading Maimonides in his historical context. Maimonides believed that the true head of state has to teach "true beliefs". He clearly was an elitist,[29] but he also believed that some fundamentals (*uṣūl*) ought to be taught to people belonging to all levels of society. As mentioned above, Maimonides adopted Almohad fundamentalism in imposing the rejection of anthropomorphism as an article of faith. Apparently, he viewed the demythologizing interpretation of scriptures regarding the messiah as belonging to the same category.

Maimonides' approach to this question may be reflected in yet another aspect of his description of the messiah. As noted by Joel Kraemer, Maimonides'

---

27 See, for example, *Treatise on Resurrection* (see above n. 23), pp. 10–15. On the Controversy, see also Sarah Stroumsa, "Twelfth-Century Concepts of Soul and Body: The Maimonidean Controversy in Baghdad", in *Self, Soul and Body in Religious Experience*, ed. Albert I. Baumgarten et al. (Studies in the History of Religions 78; Leiden: Brill, 1998), pp. 313–334; eadem, *The Beginnings of the Maimonidean Controversy in the East: Yosef Ibn Shim'on's Silencing Epistle Concerning the Resurrection of the Dead* (Jerusalem: Ben Zvi Institute, 1999; in Hebrew, with English Introduction).

28 *Mishneh Torah*, "Hilkhot melakhim" 12.1 (p. 208). Cf. Joel Kraemer, "On Maimonides' Messianic posture", in *Studies in Medieval Jewish History and Literature*, vol. II, ed. Isadore Twersky (Cambridge, Mass., London: Harvard University Press, 1984), pp. 109–142; Aviezer Ravitzki, "'As much as is humanely possible' – The Messianic Era in Maimonides' Teaching", in *Messianism and Eschatology*, ed. Zvi Baraz (Jerusalem: Merkaz Zalmān Shāzār, 1983), pp. 191–220 (in Hebrew), especially pp. 194 and 204, and n. 33. Ravitzki stresses Maimonides' claim that "all these things, no one knows how they will be until they come to be", which Ravitzki sees as "Maimonides' agnostic stance". In fact, there is very little agnosticism in Maimonides' saying. He is very clear in saying that the things described in the verse will *not* happen as they are described, and that the verse must therefore be taken out of its literal sense.

29 Twersky, *Introduction to the Code of Maimonides* (see above n. 21), pp. 469–471: "Overt acknowledgement of elitism".

depiction of the messiah is characterized by an overwhelming insistence on the messiah's military role.[30] One suspects that the frequent military campaigns of the Almohads, in which they were accompanied by a magnificent copy of the Qur'ān and advancing under the banner of the Mahdī, offered Maimonides a messianic model that went well with his reading of the *Laws of Kings*, both in Deuteronomy and in the Talmud.

* * *

The material presented above imposes on us a slight modification of our somewhat bookish image of Maimonides as a political philosopher. As "the disciple of al-Fārābī", Maimonides "took the Alfarabian theory of the relationship between philosophy, religion, jurisprudence and theology and applied it in a thoroughgoing manner to a particular religion, Judaism."[31] Both the Platonic and the Jewish models, however, remained for him abstract constructions. The Almohads, on the other hand, presented a living model: a political regime which, despite the fact that it persecuted Maimonides' own people, presented some traits with which Maimonides could identify.

The status of Maimonides within his own community was strikingly different from that of the Muslim philosophers of his generation within their society. While the latter had no communal authority unless it was bestowed upon them by a Muslim ruler, Maimonides was (besides his role as a physician at the Ayyūbid court) the undisputed leader of the Jewish community. As the spiritual leader of a minority group, Maimonides could feel, perhaps more than a Muslim philosopher marginalized in the court could, that he was able to shape the minds of his flock. Moreover, as I have argued elsewhere, the position of the leader of a minority group allowed him, paradoxically, more freedom to adopt Almohad ideology than that left to his Muslim counterparts.[32] For Maimonides, the Almohad revolution could serve as a source of inspiration, precisely because (unlike an Ibn Rushd, for example) his applications of Almohad ideas were not monitored and could not be manipulated by Almohad rulers. He watched Almohad practices just as he read Arabic political philosophy, and both of these sources served him as building blocks for constructing his own ideology. Integrating both models into his reading of the Jewish texts, he could thus construct a model image of Kingship and sovereignty, which he could uphold as the true image of the Jewish polity.

30 Kraemer, "On Maimonides' Messianic Posture" (see above n. 28), pp. 130–131 ("a warrior-Messiah, an armed prophet").

31 Cf. Lawrence V. Berman, "Maimonides the Disciple of al-Farabi", in *Israel Oriental Studies* 4 (1974), pp. 154–178.

32 See Sarah Stroumsa, "The Literary Corpus of Maimonides and Averroes", in *Maimonidean Studies* 5 (forthcoming).

Maimonides' Critique of the Mutakallimūn in *The Guide of the Perplexed*

by

Hassan Hanafi

Cairo University

I. Introduction

The identity between revelation, reason and nature is an Islamic model built especially by Muʿtazilite Theology and Philosophy and carried on in medieval Christian and Jewish cultures contact with Islamic culture, whether directly through Arabic texts (like the case of Maimonides), or indirectly through Latin translations (Beranger de Tours, Anselm de Bestate in the eleventh century, Abelard in the twelfth century) before generating the reaction of Thomas Aquinas in the thirteenth century, but again carried on by Latin Averroists till the European Renaissance in modern times. This model is also carried on, although in a different manner, by the other two Islamic sciences, methodology of Jurisprudence (*uṣūl al-fiqh*) through the deductive-inductive method, and mysticism through pantheism and metaphysics of unity, the last phase in the mystical road.

The Jewish model before this cultural interaction, first in Spain, second in Sicily and southern Italy, third in the Byzantine Empire, was that theology, philosophy, law and even mysticism are essentially religious sciences based on revelation and depending on scriptural arguments. The absolute will of God has no rational justification. The literal meaning of the text is absolutely true. Doctrines such as election, covenant, and promised land were not questionable. Anthropomorphic interpretation of texts regarding God was generally accepted. The law was practised as Divine Imperatives and dictum of the tradition, via Shabbat, dietary practices and festivals. Mysticism was purely spiritual exercises and visions intertwined with magic and superstition. The argument of authority, not the argument of reason, was the only valid argument.

The Christian model was similar to the Jewish one. The credo is a mystery which goes beyond reason. Belief is an act of will, not an act of reason. Canonic law is promulgated by the authority of the Church. Even the canonization of the tradition, the performance of sacraments and the adhesion to religious community are made by the Church. The God of the philosophers is not the God of the fathers, Abraham, Isaac and Jacob. The heart has its own reasons, which reason ignores. Scriptures were accepted without external or internal criticism. The scriptural argument, not that of reason, was also the only valid argument. Pauline theology and its major doctrines Incarnation, Trinity, redemption, salvation, fall, original sin are unchallenged even by new interpretations considered as heresies.

The relation between the three traditions are clear in the *Guide of the Perplexed*. According to Maimonides, the *creatio ex nihilo* interests the three religions, Judaism, Christianity and Islam, in order to support their beliefs in miracles and in other doctrines. However, every religion was also interested to defend its own specific doctrine, such as Trinity in Christianity and "the Word" in Islam. Maimonides does not want to criticize the beliefs of every religion, but he only wants to show that their propositions are not based on the investigations of the real properties of things.[1]

Reference to Christianity is very minimal and depends on whether it is due to the transmission of Greek philosophy through the Syrian scholars to the Muslims, or to the foundation of the Christian dogma.[2] Both Christians and Jews lived within Islamic culture as a general intellectual framework. The reference to the overall umbrella and the common cultural heritage, namely Islamic culture, was natural. Both Christianity and Judaism in Andalusia refer to Islamic culture more than they refer to each other.

In spite of Maimonides' historical and cultural initiative to transform traditional sciences to rational sciences, he was still limited by his parochialism, describing the nations in which the Jews lived as barbarous, and other nations as Gaonim including the Qaraites, the closest sect to Islamic tradition.[3]

Maimonides did not change the Arabic names as examples such as Zayd and ʿAmr, as did the translators of Averroes' commentaries on Aristotle, by changing the Arabic names and examples to Hebrew names and examples.[4] Alexandria, Al-Fusṭāṭ, Cairo, Córdoba, Seville, Saladin are geo-historical terms

---

1 Maimonides, *Guide of the Perplexed*. Translated and with an Introduction and Notes by Shlomo Pines (Chicago, London: The University of Chicago Press, 1963) (it will be referred to as *Guide*), pp. 177–178.

2 "[…] inasmuch as the Christian community came to include those communities, the Christian preaching being what it is known to be, and inasmuch as the opinions of the philosophers were widely accepted in those communities in which the philosophy had first risen, and inasmuch as kings rose who protected religion – the learned of those periods from among the Greeks and the Syrians saw that those preachings are greatly and clearly opposed to the philosophic opinions. Thus there arose among them this science of kalām. They started to establish premises that would be useful to them with regard to their belief and to refute those opinions that ruined the foundations of their Law" (*Guide*, p. 177).

3 "[…] which you will find in the writings of some *Gaonim* and in those of the Qaraites" (*Guide*, p. 176).

4 *Guide*, p. 184.

determining the cultural Islamic atmosphere in which Maimonides lived. The high reference for Arabic Writings and sources made Arabic important in both communities, Jewish and Christian. It is a language of culture, even if it is written in Hebrew sacred characters as in *Dalālat al-ḥā'irīn*.

A commentary is an old *genre littéraire* practiced in classical traditions. In Islamic philosophy, it does not mean textual explanation, term by term, phrase by phrase. It also does not mean tautological paraphrasing and repetition of the same meanings in other words, but a more complex cultural phenomenon implying openness to other cultures and the translation of their major works, the assimilation of other cultures to reintegrate them in the local culture in order not to fall into cultural dualism between the exogenous and the endogenous, and to create a unified human culture, total and integral, a result of cultural interaction and mutual exchange, according to the dialectics between language, meaning and things. A commentary is a reading. A reading is an interpretation and a transposition.[5] As Maimonides read the Mutakallimūn, I am reading Maimonides back through the same Mutakallimūn, having in mind the old Andalusian model and the contemporary Palestinian counter-model, with the socio-cultural cohabitation and the geo-doctrinal exhabitation.

II. A Model from Andalusia

It is only in Spain, that a new model from Andalusia came out. This model was essentially built in Toledo, Granada and Córdoba. The three Abrahamic traditions, Judaism, Christianity and Islam, lived together in an atmosphere of Islamic Tolerance. It is in Andalusia that comparative history of religions began.

The expression "Andalusian scholars" is always repeated by Maimonides to indicate a cultural region with a possible model in physics, medicine, mathematics, linguistics, theology or philosophy which can be adopted by the Jewish community, since the model does not contradict the principles of Jewish faith. The openness of Jewish faith to cultural interaction strengthens it and makes it departing from the practical creed to reach the universal principles of reason.[6]

Maimonides' courage appears in the transformation of Jewish tradition to cultural sciences, against the prohibition of transforming the oral tradition to a written science. According to Maimonides, these sciences, once begun by the

5 This theme will be referred to in the conclusion only as a possible revival of the Andalusian model.

6 "Some of the men of Andalusia interpret the verse as meaning that his breath was suspended so that no breath at all could be perceived in him" (*Guide*, p. 92). "As for the Andalusians among the people of our nation, all of them cling to the affirmations of the philosophers and incline to their opinions, in so far as these do not ruin the foundation of the Law" (*Guide*, p. 177).

forefathers, were neglected because of the domination of the Jewish people by "barbarous" nations. The political situations of the Jews prevented them from dealing with speculative matters. Second, these sciences were only the privilege of the elite, not of the masses, a well known distinction in Islamic sciences between the *khāṣṣa* and the *ʿāmma*. Written tradition was prohibited by the Rabbis, since oral tradition was sufficient.[7] Maimonides wrote the *Guide* to enlighten his pupil and to form the enlightened religious man, before Spinoza and modern Jewish enlightenment. The perplexed is the one who is still wondering between tradition and reason, between *naql* and *ʿaql*. Here Maimonides, in his desire to show contradictions in the Gemara, is a precursor of Abelard and his application of reason in Patristic tradition according to its identity (*Sic*) and difference (*Nunc*) with reason, which later lead to rational textual criticism in Spinoza.[8]

Maimonides' choice for Islamic theology was pertinent since philosophy existed already via the Greeks and was carried on by Christian dogma. However, Maimonides adopts in philosophy the same method he adopted in theology, the expositions of major philosophical propositions called methods (eight in philosophy and twelve in theology).[9]

Already in Jewish law Jewish tradition had a discipline similar to Islamic Jurisprudence. However, Maimonides' classification of all the Commandments in the Torah into 613, dividing them into fourteen classes and then into positive and negative Commands, is an echo of Islamic *uṣūl al-fiqh* classifications of the Divine Imperatives to Prescriptions and Proscriptions (*amr-nahy*).[10] Jewish mysticism as explained in the *Zohar* was similar also to Islamic mysticism as formulated by Ibn Arabi in Andalusia. The only discipline Jewish tradition left out was that of theology, namely the work of reason and nature in revelation.

Maimonides leaves aside jurisprudence and mysticism, well dominant in Jewish tradition. He concentrates only on rational theology and philosophy, to be incorporated in Jewish tradition. For the first time since Philo, the figurative meaning comes ahead again. Philo began under the influence of Hellenism and Maimonides followed, under the direct influence of Islamic Muʿtazilite rational theology, or the indirect influence of Islamic philosophy. His initiative was to reconstruct Jewish tradition according to reason, transforming traditional sciences (*ʿulūm naqlīya*) to rational sciences (*ʿulūm ʿaqlīya*). This appears very

---

7 Part III begins with Maimonides' apology for publishing, contrary to the teaching of the Mishnah, an interpretation of the Account of the Beginning and the Account of the Chariot: *Guide*, pp. 415–416; also, Part I, p. 176: "This was the cause that necessitated the disappearance of these great roots of knowledge from the nation."

8 *Guide*, p. 19.

9 "I shall not write at length, but only draw your attention to the methods that they aim at, as I did for you regarding the opinions of the Mutakallimūn" (*Guide*, p. 285).

10 Maimonides ends the *Guide* by dividing the Precepts into fourteen classes: *Guide*, pp. 535–613.

clearly in the commentary on the Torah before ending Part 1 with the Islamic rational model of the Mutakallimūn and the continuation of exposing figurative style and allegorical acts in prophetic writings. Maimonides' distinction between partial simile and total simile is a step towards a total allegorical interpretation of the scriptures.[11]

Reference to Islamic philosophy is very little, since philosophy existed already by the Greeks, in Christian tradition and since Islamic philosophers, according to Maimonides, followed the same track.[12] However, Maimonides uses philosophy against theology in support of his own criticism of theology. He refers to Al-Fārābī's distinctions between several meanings of intellect, the dialectical and imaginative used by theologians and the demonstrative used by philosophers.[13] Maimonides also adopts al-Fārābī's commentary on Aristotle, that the Active Intellect, an incorporeal being, acts in one time and does not act at another time. He refers to him also as a rational philosopher criticizing the weak arguments, like the seventh proving the creation of the world from the immortality of the soul, in his book *The Changeable Being,* also alluded to by Averroes.[14]

Maimonides depends on al-Fārābī as commentator of Aristotle. The eternity of the world is undoubted, according to al-Fārābī, and has been expressed by

---

11 Figurative expressions applied to angels (*Guide,* pp. 108–110); on the allegories of the prophets (pp. 391–393); allegorical acts of prophets receive Divine messages (pp. 394–396); on figurative style of the prophetic writings (pp. 407–409). "Know that the prophetic parables are of two kinds. In some of these parables each word has a meaning, while in others the parable as a whole indicates the whole of the intended meaning. In such a parable very many words are to be found, not every one of which adds something to the intended meaning. They serve rather to embellish the parable and to render it more coherent or to conceal further the intended meaning; hence the speech proceeds in such a way as to accord with everything required by the parable's external meaning" (*Guide,* p. 12).

12 "Thus they found the kalām of John Philoponus, of Ibn ʿAdī, and of others with regard to these notions, held on to it, and were victorious in their own opinion in a great task that they sought to accomplish" (*Guide,* p. 178).

13 "[…] just as Abū Naṣr has noted when speaking of the notion to which the Mutakallimūn apply the term 'intellect'" (*Guide,* p. 207); "A proof of this is provided by the Active Intellect as it is conceived by Aristotle and his followers. For the Active Intellect, on the one hand, is separate from the matter; and, on the other, it acts at a certain time and does not act another time, as Abū Naṣr has explained in his treatise *'On the Intellect'*. For there he has set down a statement that runs literally as follows. He says: it is clear that the Active Intellect does not always act; rather it acts at a certain time and does not act at another time. This is literally what he says, and it is clearly true. But even if this is so, it cannot be said that the Active Intellect undergoes change or that it was acting potentially and became actual, because it did at a certain time what it did not do before" (*Guide,* p. 299).

14 "Abū Naṣr al-Fārābī has demolished the premise in question and has laid bare what belongs to fantasy in all its various details. You will find a clear limpid exposition of his argument if you study without partisanship in his well-known book, *'The Changing Beings'*" (*Guide,* p. 222).

Aristotle, in spite of Galen's doubts.[15] He also depends on al-Fārābī in his commentary on the *Physics* of Aristotle, adding a distinction between stars and spheres. The stars are opaque while the spheres are transparent, because of the difference between them in substance and forms. According to al-Fārābī, it is a small difference, but Maimonides sees it as a big one.[16]

Maimonides refers also to Abū Bakr Ibn al-Ṣā'igh (Ibn Bājja) in his doctrine of the immortality of the soul, the seventh argument proving the creation of the world.[17] But his major dependence on the Muslim philosopher is on astronomy and physics. A whole band of Andalusian scientists were around him studying the same scientific problems such as the position of Venus and Mercury, *vis-à-vis* the sun.[18] Maimonides depends on Abū Bakr in his rejection of the epicycles, quoting and summarizing his criticism.[19] He depends on him also as a reader of Aristotle's theory of the eccentricity of the sun, while expressing some doubts about it, and as a commentator of the *Physics*.[20]

---

15 "However, you know Abū Naṣr [al-Fārābī's] interpretation of this example, what he made clear with regard to it, as well as the fact that he considered disgraceful the notion that Aristotle could have doubted of the eternity of the world. He had an extreme contempt for Galen because of the latter's saying that this was an obscure question with regard to which no demonstration is known. As Abū Naṣr holds, it is clear and manifest, being proved by demonstration, that the heavens are eternal whereas that which is within them is subject to generation and passing-away" (*Guide*, p. 292).

16 "In fact Abū Naṣr al-Fārābī in his glosses on the 'Akroasis', has made a statement of which the literal text is as follows. He said: There is a difference between a sphere and the stars for a sphere is transparent whereas the stars are not transparent. The cause for this lies in the fact that there is a difference between the two matters and the two forms. But this difference is very small. This is literally the text of his statement. I, however, do not say 'small', but say that they are very different" (*Guide*, p. 309).

17 "However, what remains of Zayd is neither the cause nor the effect of what remains of Umar. Consequently all are one in number, as Abū Bakr Ibn al-Ṣā'igh and others who were drawn into speaking of these obscure matters have made clear" (*Guide*, p. 221).

18 "Then came latter-day groups of people in Andalusia who became very proficient in mathematics and explained, conforming to Ptolemy's premises, that Venus and Mercury were above the sun. In fact, Ibn Aflaḥ of Sevilla, whose son I have met, has written a celebrated book about this. Thereupon the excellent philosopher Abū Bakr Ibn al-Ṣā'igh, under the guidance of one of whose pupils I have read texts, reflected on this notion and showed various ways of argumentation – transcribed by us from him – by means of which the opinion that Venus and Mercury are above the sun may be shown to be improbable" (*Guide*, pp. 268–269).

19 "For this reason Abū Bakr Ibn al-Ṣā'igh states in his extant discourse on astronomy that the existence of epicycles is impossible. He points out the necessary inference already mentioned. In addition to this impossibility necessarily following from the assumption of the existence of epicycles, he sets forth there other impossibilities that also follow from that assumption. I shall explain them to you now" (*Guide*, p. 323).

20 "You know already that in speaking of natural science, Abū Bakr Ibn al-Ṣā'igh expresses a doubt whether Aristotle knew about the eccentricity of the sun and passed over it in silence – treating of what necessarily follows from the sun's inclination,

Islamic philosophy divided wisdom into three parts: logic, physics and metaphysics. The *Guide of the Perplexed* contains also three parts: the first on theology, the second on philosophy and the third on ethics. Only the second part is referring directly to philosophy.[21] Neither the first part nor the second refer directly to theology or to ethics. Theology comes in relation to Islamic Kalām, and ethics are deduced directly from the scriptures. Since both theology and philosophy deal with the same topic, namely God and the world, the first part of the *Guide* is indeed on metaphysics, while the second is on physics. In the first part, the Attributes of God are exposed and in the second part the *creatio ex nihilo* is defended against the eternity of the world, plus the theory of prophecy. The third part on ethics is indeed the theory of Acts, since it deals with the creation of Good and Evil and the Precepts of the Law.

A question remains: What about logic? It is true that in the triadic division of wisdom into logic, physics and metaphysics, logic is only an instrument to all sciences, discovering laws of thought to protect reason from errors in thinking. However, logic is incorporated in classical wisdom as prolegomena to physics and metaphysics. Maimonides' initiative did not go so far. It was enough for him to expose rational theology and to create rational philosophy from within the tradition, through metaphoric interpretations of the texts in the tradition of Philo, without substituting logic for tradition. This radical rationalism, switching from argument of authority to argument of reason, has to wait till the coming of Spinoza. However, Maimonides refers to logic in his introductory letter to his pupil. He promises to take him to a course in logic in order to know the esoteric ideas in the prophetic books, and in order to become a perfect man.[22] Logic, according to Maimonides, is the method of interpretation, the allegorical method which is indeed the logic of revelation, at least partly. Logic leads to esotericism and unveils the hidden meaning of the text. Maimonides wanted to give only applied studies of rational method of interpretation, not a theoretical exposition of the science of logic. That would be too much for the Jewish community to accept. Logic can also be exposed within natural philosophy, not alone, indirectly, in order to be accepted in a community still believing in the argument of authority (the law), not the argument of reason (logic).[23]

---

inasmuch as the effect of eccentricity is not distinguishable from that of inclination – or whether he was not aware of eccentricity" (*Guide*, p. 326). "Abū Bakr Ibn al-Ṣāʾigh has mentioned this in the commentary of the 'Akroasis'" (*Guide*, p. 515).

21 The twenty-six propositions employed by the philosophers to prove the existence of God: *Guide*, pp. 235–241.

22 "When thereupon you read under my guidance texts dealing with the art of logic, my hopes fastened upon you, and I saw that you are one worthy to have secrets of the prophetic books revealed to you so that you would consider in them that which perfect men ought to consider" (*Guide*, p. 3).

23 "It is not the purpose of this Treatise to make its totality understandable to the vulgar or to beginners of speculation, nor to teach those who have not engaged in any study

The Islamic model of the triadic division of wisdom to logic, physics and metaphysics was in the background of Maimonides thought, serving as a motivation to introduce the use of reason in understanding the tradition.[24]

III. Identity Between Reason and Revelation

For the first time in the history of Judaism, a rational Jewish theology and philosophy begins, with clear reference to its Islamic sources, especially to Muʿtazilism. It is not by chance that Maimonides devotes the last six chapters of the first part of the *Guide* (LXXI–LXXVI) to Kalām, transliterating the Arabic word, not translating it to keep the original Islamic source. Maimonides mentions the Mutakallimūn more than the Kalām.[25] Kalām is a method of thought to understand by reason the foundations of belief, to find rational arguments for their validity, and to argue against opposite doctrines. Kalām is also theories resulting from its method, such as the theory of substance and accidents.[26] Kalām is also stereotyped arguments to substantiate certain propositions, such as the three arguments proving the unity of God, or other arguments which are not in the Kalām such as arguments for the incorporeality of God. Kalām is finally a coherent system, built upon propositions and arguments, doctrines and methods, exempt of internal contradictions.[27]

The word Mutakallimūn according to Maimonides refers to a general trend more than to an abstract science like Kalām. Mutakallimūn represent a dynamic cultural movement in Islamic societies, carrying intellectual pluralism and the art

---

other than the science of the Law – I mean the legalistic study of the Law. For the purpose of this Treatise and of all those like it is the science of Law in its true sense" (*Guide*, p. 5).

24 "Accordingly it is certainly necessary for whoever wishes to achieve human perfection to train himself at first in the art of logic, then in the mathematical sciences according to the proper order, then in the natural sciences, and after that in the divine science" (*Guide*, p. 75). "Know, my son, that as long as you are engaged in studying the mathematical sciences and the art of logic, you are one of those who walk around the house searching for its gate" (*Guide*, p. 619).

25 The word Mutakallimūn in these six chapters on Kalām is mentioned 77 times in plural and only six times Mutakallim in singular, while the word Kalām is mentioned only five times.

26 "There does not exist at all, contrary to what you think, any form constituting a substance so that a variety of substances is thereby brought about. On the contrary everything that you consider as a form is an accident – as we have made clear from their assertion in the eighth premise" (*Guide*, p. 208).

27 "If, however, every single particle of that body were required for its constitution, there would be many deities and not one deity. But they [the Mutakallimūn, Ed.] have already made clear that he is one" (*Guide*, p. 227).

of dialogue between propositions and counter-propositions. They had the lead in inventing this "admirable science" a long time before Descartes, to prove the veracity of doctrines by rational arguments. They were followed by Jewish and Christian thinkers alike. However, masters stayed masters and disciples stayed disciples. The works of the imitators are insignificant compared to the works of the creators.[28]

In spite of the differences in conclusions between the Mutakallimūn, they all follow the same method.[29] This is why Maimonides does not mention the proper names of theologians. He is only satisfied with Kalām as a discipline, with the Mutakallimūn as a dynamic rationalist trend in every religious community, and with these two major trends in every theology, namely rationalists (Muʿtazila) versus "Fideists" (Ashʿarīya), liberals versus conservatives.

Indeed, Maimonides refers to these two major sects in Islamic theology.[30] But, he quickly falls into the famous but erroneous judgement that Islamic theology is based on propositions taken from the works of the Greeks to refute philosophy! If Maimonides made such a judgement on philosophy, that would be understandable. Islamic theology, *ʿilm uṣūl ad-dīn*, is authentically Islamic. The exogenous, namely Greek philosophy was translated, assimilated and reintegrated in the endogenous.

Maimonides describes the development of Islamic theology in three steps. First, there was the Kalām, undivided into sects. Second, the Muʿtazila appeared as a separatist movement in the Kalām. Third, the Ashʿarīya appeared as a revisionist movement from within the Muʿtazila. According to Maimonides, only the Muʿtazila had their influence on Jewish scholars, since they were at the origin of Islamic theology and the most rationalist. Ashʿarīya had their peculiar views and were not followed.[31]

---

28 "[…] it should be noted that the subject matter of this argument was taken over by them from the Mutakallimūn of Islam and that this bit is very scanty indeed if compared to what Islam has compiled on this subject" (*Guide*, p. 176).

29 "This is the way of every Mutakallim from among the Moslems in anything concerning this subject. […] While the ways in which they adduce the arguments in favor of the inference as to, and propound the premises with regard to, the establishment of the temporal creation of the world or to the refutation of its pre-eternity, differ from one another the universal thesis of all of them consists in the first place in the affirmation of the temporal creation of the world. And by means of its temporal creation, it is established as true that the deity exists" (*Guide*, pp. 179–180).

30 Maimonides in these six chapters on Kalām mentions the Muʿtazila six times and the Ashʿarīya five times. "Know also that all the statements that the men of Islam – both the Muʿtazila and the Ashʿariyya – have made concerning these notions are all of them opinions founded upon premises that are taken over from the books of the Greeks and the Syrians who wished to disagree with the opinions of the philosophers and to reject their statements" (*Guide*, p. 177).

31 "Also it has so happened that Islam first began to take this road owing to a certain sect, namely, the Muʿtazila, from whom our coreligionists took over certain things

Maimonides' dialectical thought considers reason represented by the Mutakallimūn, namely, the radicals as a source of the doctrine of *creatio ex nihilo* in the same title and the same virtue as the other source well known in tradition, namely prophecy. Once Maimonides makes room for reason represented by the Mutakallimūn, he argues against them in a second battle, namely, which proof is more rational, the opinion of the Mutakallimūn or the real properties of things proposed by him? The main contradiction is between reason and tradition, in which Maimonides sides himself with the Mutakallimūn and gives the choice to his community to do so. The difference in view between Maimonides and the Mutakallimūn regarding the type of proof to be used to demonstrate the *creatio ex nihilo* is a secondary consideration.[32]

Maimonides' art was to expose Islamic theology in order to make a cultural shock in his tradition for his community, showing them how to use reason in understanding revelation in spite of divergence of view between theologians inside every community and between theologians of different religious communities. It would then be difficult to know if Maimonides is with the Mutakallimūn or against them. He is with them *de jure*, since they use reason to understand revelation, but against them *de facto*, since they do not use reason properly, the same criticism addressed to them by Averroes.

The Mutakallimūn had their limits. They used propositions without proving the premises on which these propositions were founded. They proved only propositions which they thought true and disproved others which they thought untrue. Once the truth is known in advance, demonstrations follow. Dialectical arguments have their limits.[33] That is why Maimonides prefers returning to the properties of things, to nature, in order to have a criterion of validity beyond opinions. After studying the methods of the Mutakallimūn, he

---

walking upon the road the Muʿtazila had taken. After a certain time another sect arose in Islam, namely, the Ashʿariyya, among whom other opinions arose. You will not find any of these latter opinions among our coreligionists. This was not because they preferred the first opinion to the second, but because it so happened that they had taken over and adopted the first opinion and considered it a matter proven by demonstration" (*Guide*, pp. 176–177).

32 "The proofs of the Mutakallimūn, on the other hand, are derived from premises that run counter to the nature of existence that is perceived so that they resort to the affirmation that nothing has a nature in any respect. [...] for I reach the goal that every Mutakallim desires without abolishing the nature of existence [...]. For whereas the proof, with the aid of which some Mutakallimūn prove by inference the creation of the world in time and which is their most powerful proof, is not consolidated for them until they abolish the nature of all existence and disagree with everything that the philosophers have made clear" (*Guide*, p. 182).

33 "[The] predecessors toiled to establish the truth of what they desired to refute because of the harm that would come if this were not done – even if it were after a hundred propositions – to an opinion whose recognition as correct was desired by them. These ancient Mutakallimūn did away with the disease starting with its root" (*Guide*, p. 179).

concludes that, for them, the real existence of things proves nothing since they are different opposite forms, every one is equally true.[34] They follow the imagination, thinking that they follow the intellect.

Since the method proposed by Maimonides is that one returning to the real properties of things, physics look over metaphysics and all the twelve propositions selected from the Mutakallimūn are related to physics. Maimonides, then, shifts from the dialectical theology of the Mutakallimūn to physical theology, similar to that in philosophy. Dialectical theology is a waste of time and life of several generations.[35]

However, Jewish scholars of Andalusia adopted rather the views of philosophers than the methods of the Mutakallimūn, since philosophers' views are more adequate to Jewish doctrines than the Mutakallimūn's.[36] The purpose of the Mutakallimūn was to defeat philosophers' views. However, philosophers according to Maimonides are the Greek philosophers. It is possible that he may have in mind the common idea that Islamic philosophers are the followers of the Greeks. Maimonides would analyze in the second part of his treatise the same problems he studied already in the first part according to the Mutakallimūn.[37]

Maimonides' project for the foundation of a new Jewish theology following the Islamic model after its reconstruction from the level of dialectics to the level of demonstration is very similar to Averroes' project in *Manāhij al-adilla*.[38] The historical question of a possible influence on Maimonides, that Maimonides was far advanced in age when he knew Averroes, is purely factual. What

---

34 "When I studied the books of these Mutakallimūn, as far as I had the opportunity […] I found that the method of all the Mutakallimūn was one and the same in kind, though the subdivisions differed from one another. For the foundation of everything is that no consideration is due to how that which exists is, for it is merely a custom; and from the point of view of the intellect, it could well be different. Furthermore, in many places they follow the imagination and call it intellect" (ibid.).

35 "Likewise you should not desire that I should let you hear in this Treatise the argumentation of the Mutakallimūn that is intended to establish the correctness of their premises. For their lives passed away in this argumentation, and the lives of those who will come after them will likewise pass away in this, and their books have grown numerous" (*Guide*, p. 183).

36 "You will not find them in any way taking the path of the Mutakallimūn" (*Guide*, p. 177).

37 "Now as we have finished setting forth the end at which their discourse arrives, we shall start upon a presentation of the philosophic premises and of their demonstration proving the existence and the oneness of the deity and the impossibility of its being a body; whereby we shall grant them for their benefit that the world is eternal, though we do not believe in it" (*Guide*, p. 231).

38 "Now when I considered this method of thought, my soul felt a very strong aversion to it, and had every right to do so. For every argument deemed to be a demonstration of the temporal creation of the world is accompanied by doubts and is not a cogent demonstration except among those who do not know the difference between demonstration, dialectics and sophistic argument" (*Guide*, p. 180).

matters is the similarity of the two projects of Maimonides and Averroes, given the common cultural milieu in which they were living and the common opponent they were fighting, namely traditionalism.

IV. Identity Between Revelation and Nature

Maimonides' initiative was also to show the identity between revelation and science, between scriptures and nature, between Jewish tradition and modern physics, following the Muʿtazilite physical theology and Averroes' defense of the determinism of the laws of nature, continued on till Spinoza. That is why the Muʿtazila were preferred, because they were closer to physics than the Ashʿarīya. A whole subsect, namely the naturalist *Aṣḥāb aṭ-ṭabāʾiʿ* (Muʿammar, Thumāma, an-Naẓẓāam, Hishām) have greatly used physical concepts defending the autonomy of nature. They have introduced the atom theory in order to lay the foundation for the physical theology Maimonides is looking for.[39] Maimonides also refers to mathematical sciences as a part of the whole science, as a discipline, comparing the mathematical demonstration as a rational accurate argument with pseudo-rational arguments of the theologians, in connection with the third proposition in physical theology of the Mutakallimūn.[40]

Maimonides begins by exposing a certain kind of parallelism between the universe and man, which is a well known theme in Islamic philosophy, especially al-Fārābī in his parallelism between man and society. The study of the body is similar to the study of the thing. However, since the body refers to the soul, the thing also refers to God. This parallelism then was possible thanks to an unmentioned third part, God. Thinking in man and the world would lead to wisdom and providence, namely to the attributes of God. What Maimonides calls the real properties of things is indeed the "ascendant way" by opposition to the "descendant way" in thinking, the relation between the world and God. It is the same duality between induction and deduction, between the ontological argument and the cosmological or the physico-teleological arguments.[41]

Maimonides mentions twelve propositions held by the Mutakallimūn, all of them belonging to the theory of substance and accidents in order to begin his ascending way by the real properties of things. The chosen way may express the Jewish soul in its affirmation of the material world distinct from Greek idealism and the Mutakallimūn's hypothetical propositions.

39 "However, some of them belonging to the Muʿtazila assert that some accidents last for a certain time, whereas others do not last during two units of time" (*Guide*, p. 201).

40 "Know, moreover, that the Banū Shākir have composed the famous 'Book of Ingenious Devices', which includes one hundred odd ingenious devices, all of them demonstrated and carried into effect" (*Guide*, p. 198).

41 *Guide*, pp. 184–193.

In spite of the differences between the Mutakallimūn in methods, they share the same twelve propositions in order to establish the four principles as follows.[42]

1. Everything is composed from atoms. Some Mutakallimūn proposed that if two atoms were joined, they become a body and each atom would also become a body. All bodies are composed of similar atoms.[43] Indeed, atom theory was used in Islamic theology in order to prove the contingency of nature and consequently the existence of Necessary Being. It also helps in explaining the creation and the end of the world by composition and decomposition of the atoms.
2. The original Mutakallimūn affirmed the existence of vacuum. They were compelled to do so for the composition and the movement of the atom.[44] However, in Islamic theology, it is a debatable question, since for other trends vacuum does not exist, since God is everywhere. This poses the question of physical theology and its dependence on different feelings of the Divinity, which change according to individuals, groups, societies, cultures and periods of history. A moment would come to consider any feeling of the Divinity as an alienation in the feeling of nature. Every theology is a reversed anthropology.
3. Time is also composed of atoms as the Mutakallimūn saw Aristotle combining time with space, which is a complete misunderstanding by the Mutakallimūn of the nature of time.[45]

   However, these three propositions can be refuted. A line with an odd number cannot be bisected.[46] Geometry based on the invisibility of space

---

42 "The common premises laid down by the Mutakallimūn, in spite of the diversity of their opinions and the multiplicity of their methods, that are necessary with a view to establishing what they wish to establish with regard to the four problems in question, are twelve in number" (*Guide*, p. 194).

43 "If two particles are aggregated together, then according to the statement of some of them [i. e. some of the Mutakallimūn, Ed.], every particle has in that case become a body. And, as they say, it is impossible that a body should exist in any respect except it be composed of these particles, which are alike in such a way that they are adjacent to one another" (*Guide*, p. 195).

44 "The men concerned with the roots [the Mutakallimūn] believe likewise that vacuum exists [...]. Accordingly they must of necessity resort to the affirmation of vacuum so that it should be possible for these particles to aggregate and to separate and so that it should be possible for a moving thing to move in this vacuum in which there is no body and none of these substances" (*Guide*, pp. 195–196).

45 "For they [the Mutakallimūn, Ed.] undoubtedly had seen Aristotle's demonstrations, by means of which he has demonstrated that distance, time, and locomotion are all three of them equal as far as existence is concerned. [...] In fact they have no knowledge at all of the true reality of time" (*Guide*, p. 196).

46 "For in the case in which the number of its atoms is odd, the division of the line into two equal parts is impossible according to their assumption" (*Guide*, p. 198).

would be impossible. A lot of technical devices based on the negation of vacuum, such as waterworks, would also be impossible.

4. The accidents of things have real existence. This is true if the Mutakallimūn have left it as a clear and simple proposition, without deducing from it other propositions such as a substance, which does not have life, as accident must have death.[47] In Islamic theology, especially the Ashʿarite, the accidents were added to the substance, as the Attributes of God are added to His Essence, in order to affirm the additional relationship, not the equational, as the Muʿtazila do, between Essence and Attributes of God. This proves once more that physics is indeed reversed metaphysics.
5. Every atom is provided by accidents which cannot exist by themselves. Such a proposition helps in conceiving Necessary Being from behind the scene, sustaining the whole world of substances. However, objections arise regarding the soul, the intellect and knowledge. Are they also accidents or substances? That was the reason why theologians conceived "separated substances".
6. The accidents do not exist during two time-atoms. When God desires to deprive a thing of its existence, he discontinues the creation of its accidents, according to some Mutakallimūn. One thing cannot be the cause of the other, such as the indigo as cause of the blackness of a cloth.[48] In man, will and power are also accidents without duration. In Islamic theology, one atom cannot exist in two times since duration is an attribute of God. No accident can be the cause of the other, since God is the only cause. Both theories aimed at opposing the physical theory of "natural force". God is the efficient cause of everything.[49]
7. The absence of a property is a property such as life and death, with the exception of some Muʿtazila.[50] Theologians wanted to conceive God as the

---

47 "If this premise did not mean more than this, it would be a correct, clear, evident premise, and give rise to no doubt and no difficulty" (*Guide*, p. 198).

48 "They [the Mutakallimūn, Ed.] say that every atom of the atoms that God creates is provided with accidents from which it cannot be exempt" (*Guide*, p. 199).

49 "According to some of them, when God wishes to cause the nonexistence of a substance, He does not create an accident in it, in consequence whereof the substance becomes nonexistent" (*Guide*, p. 201). "There is unanimity among them with regard to their belief that a white garment that has been put into a vat full of indigo and has become dyed, has not been blackened by the indigo [...]. To sum up: it should not be said in any respect that this is the cause of that" (*Guide*, p. 202). "As all of them think, the created will and the created power and – in the opinion of some of them – also the created act, are accidents that do not last, God constantly creating in that way motion after motion in the pen in question as long as the pen is in motion" (*Guide*, p. 203).

50 "The position is also completely analogous with regard to life and death. For both of these are, according to them, accidents, and they clearly assert that a unit of life disappears and another is created as long as a particular living being is alive" (*Guide*, p. 204). "However one Muʿtazilite says that certain privations of habitus are not

creator of life and death alike, not only life and leaving death as a natural absence of life.

8. Everything has substance and accidents in the physical world, including heavenly bodies and even the Divine Throne. God alone is a substance without accidents.
9. No accident can be a substance to another accident. There is no indirect relation between accidents and substance.[51] The multiplicity of accidents returns to the unity of substance.
10. Everything conceived by imagination is admitted by the intellect as possible, as if imagination and intellect were the same.[52] However philosophers followed by Maimonides make a distinction between them. A dialogue between a Mutakallim and a philosopher ends by the victory of the philosopher and the defeat of the Mutakallim. The Mutakallimūn know the distinction, but they do not admit it. Theologians indeed defended imagination in order to facilitate the understanding of prophecy. Philosophers, even more, considered imagination as a higher faculty which can perceive and express through images, more than the intellect can do. Maimonides' defense of the intellect distinct from imagination makes him more a Muʿtazilite rationalist, since reason can interpret the images transforming them to meanings.
11. The existence of infinity in things is impossible without any distinction between the infinity of the body and its divisibility ad infinitum, between the coexistence of an infinite number of things and the infinite number of beings successively existing. Infinity is the privilege of God.[53]

---

existent things. He does not, however, say this consistently with regard to every privation" (ibid.).

51 "In their opinion all accidents, in the first place and in the same way, have substance as a substratum" (*Guide*, p. 205).

52 "They further assert that it is impossible and cannot be admitted by the intellect that an accident should exist without there being any accident in it; or, as some of them say, it is also impossible and cannot be admitted by the intellect that an accident should exist without being in a substratum" (*Guide*, p. 207). "[...] just as Abū Naṣr has noted when speaking of the notion to which the Mutakallimūn apply the term 'intellect'" (ibid.). "The explanation of this is in accordance with what I shall set forth to you while I reveal to you the secrets of these matters in the form of a dispute taking place between a Mutakallim and a philosopher. The Mutakallim said to the philosopher [...]. Thereupon the Mutakallim controverted this entire reply" (*Guide*, pp. 207–208). "Then when, according to the Mutakallim, everything he wishes with regard to his premises is established as true, the resultant conclusion is that the substance of iron and the cream are the same substances, substances similar to one another in every respect" (*Guide*, p. 208). "The greater or smaller number of the atoms does not in this point constitute a significant addition to the final result, as an accident subsists in every atom – as we have made clear on the basis of their assertion in the fifth premise" (*Guide*, p. 209). "Do not think that the Mutakallimūn are not aware of anything concerning this point" (*Guide*, p. 211).

53 "This is their saying that the existence of that which is infinite in any mode whatever is impossible" (*Guide*, p. 212). "As for the Mutakallimūn, there is no difference, in their

12. The senses are always not to be trusted. Sense errors are due to the misperception of existing objects and the absence of others. Intellect has to correct sense errors.[54]

By these twelve propositions, held in Islamic theology, Maimonides wanted to prove for his Jewish community that:

1. There is no danger at all in adopting physics as a foundation of their traditions, that theology is not a closed dogmatic science but a physical theology. Maimonides by this motivation would have paved the way for the continuity to switch from the closed book, namely, the Torah to the open book, namely Nature.
2. Reason and senses are the way by which nature can be understood and perceived. Once a proposition is put as an axiom or as an experience, other series of propositions can be deduced from it. A coherent system can consequently be built, forming a whole world view based on reason and nature, by opposition to another world view based on tradition and transmission. Since both world views claim revelation, it is up to the community to choose.
3. These twelve propositions are mostly from Ash'arīya theology, that means a halfway rational and natural theology, not a radical Mu'tazilite theology, depending only on reason and nature. Maimonides apparently wanted to initiate the Jewish community to Rationalism and Naturalism, but gradually, by the simple acceptance of the use of reason and the perception of nature. Once the principle is admitted, radical reason can take over "fideist" reason and independent nature can prevail over the dependent nature. Even if Ash'arīya was a revisionist movement in Islamic theology, it is here proposed for the Jewish community as the bad work of reason in revelation in order to defend the right one.

---

opinion, between saying that a certain infinite magnitude exists and saying that bodies and time are liable to be divided to infinity. There likewise is no difference, in their opinion, between asserting the simultaneous existence of things infinite in number, arranged, [at the same time] in orderly fashion [...]. Some of them wish, in a way that I shall explain to you in the present Treatise, to establish the correctness of the last of these divisions – I mean to say, they wish to make clear its impossibility" (*Guide*, pp. 212–213).

54 "For the Mutakallimūn have been suspicious with regard to the apprehension of the senses on two accounts" (*Guide*, p. 213). "Do not think that agreement of the Mutakallimūn in affirming this premise is gratious. That would be similar to the belief of the majority of the later Mutakallimūn that the wish of their predecessors to establish the existence of the indivisible particle did not correspond to a need" (*Guide*, pp. 213–214). "For whenever we apprehend with our senses things controverting their assumptions, they are able to say: no attention should be paid to the senses as the matter – which, as they think, has been proven by the testimony of the intellect – is demonstrated" (*Guide*, p. 214). "Consequently the answer to all this is, when answer is possible, that the particular thing one is concerned with has been missed by the senses" (ibid.).

4. Sometimes theology imposes itself on physics, such as the negation of causality, of natural force, and even of the free will in order to conceive God as the sole efficient and prime cause. And sometimes physics imposes itself on theology, such as the theory of substance and accidents in physics transformed to the theory of essence and attributes in theology. Maimonides' undeclared purpose may have been the exposition of such mutual dependence between these two sciences in order that the future generation, that of Spinoza, would choose the complete independence of both.

V. The Identity Between Reason, Revelation and Nature

The identity between Reason, Revelation and Nature is a combination of the two previous identities: Reason and Revelation, and Nature and Revelation, since both have Revelation as a middle term. Here the Islamic model culminates as the unity between the rational, the revealed and the real, between philosophy, religion and science. Once this model is built, any belief can easily be understood. Maimonides gives in his theology, following the Mutakallimūn, three beliefs: the creation of the world, the unity of God, and the incorporeality of God.

A. The Creation of the World

The creation of the world is proved *ad absurdum*, by proving the impossibility of the eternity of the world by the following seven arguments.[55]

1. By proving the creation of one thing, the *creatio ex nihilo* of the entire universe is proved, given the hidden analogy between the part and the whole.[56]
2. The proof of the creation of one thing is equally valuable for proving the *creatio ex nihilo* of the whole universe, given also the hidden analogy between the question about the origin of one thing and the question about the origin of the whole universe.[57]
3. Since there is no reason why atoms should be combined or separated, this proves that they are created from nothing, that the reason of their existence is not themselves.[58]

---

55 "In this chapter I shall include for your benefit a narration of the proofs of the Mutakallimūn showing that the world is created in time" (*Guide*, p. 215).

56 "Some of them think that any single happening occurring in time may be adduced as proof that the world has been created in time" (ibid.).

57 "Accordingly this constitutes, as they say, a demonstration of the world's having come into existence after pure and absolute nothingness" (*Guide*, p. 216).

58 "Thus this is, as they say, as proof of the world's being created in time. It is already clear to you that the author of this method used the first of their premises and all that

4. Since the whole universe is composed of substance and accidents, and since the accidents are not eternal, the substratum of the accidents cannot be eternal either.[59]
5. Since everything is determined in its place, size and composition, that proves that its existence has been determined not by itself. According to Maimonides this is the best argument.[60]
6. Since existence triumphed over non-existence, this triumph is called *creatio ex nihilo*. This argument as well as the previous one are based on the principle of determination.[61]
7. If the world were eternal, the number of the dead would be infinite and consequently an infinite number of souls would coexist. Since it has been proved that the co-existence of an infinite number of things is impossible, then the world is finite. This argument is based on the philosophical doctrine of the immortality of the soul.[62]

Maimonides does not refute these seven arguments. He only shows their weaknesses, asking for a better use of reason and nature. He just gives an example of the capacity of natural reason to prove the creation of the world, the second major belief after the existence of God.

---

necessarily follows from it" (*Guide*, pp. 216–217). "Those Mutakallimūn, as I have made known to you, do not imagine nonbeing other than the privations of all the habitus as privations" (*Guide*, p. 438).

59 *Guide*, p. 217.

60 "This is the method of particularization. And it is a method to which they [the Mutakallimūn, Ed.] accord very great preference. [...] They ramify this method into very many subdivisions of a general or a particular nature" (*Guide*, p. 218).

61 "One of the later ones thought that he had come upon a most excellent method superior to all the methods known before. This method is concerned with the preponderance given to existence over nonexistence. [...] For our adversary who believes in the eternity of the world, when he says that the world is possible in respect of existence, uses the term 'possible', as we shall make clear, in another sense than that in which it is used by the Mutakallim" (*Guide*, p. 219).

62 "[...] if the adversary would concede to him who tried to arouse the doubt that the imaginings that that individual entertains about his [to wit, the adversary's] speech concerning the continued existence of the souls were well-founded. [...] Know that whoever wishes to establish as true the coming-into-being of the world in time or to prove false its eternity by means of these methods of the Kalām must necessarily use one of these two premises or both of them [...] being the tenth [...] or the eleventh" (*Guide*, p. 221). "[...] the foregoing are the principal methods of the Mutakallimūn in establishing the coming-into-being of the world in time" (*Guide*, p. 222). "I have already set forth for your benefit the methods of the Mutakallimūn in establishing the newness of the world, and I have drawn your attention to the points with regard to which they may be attacked" (*Guide*, p. 293).

B. The Unity of God

The unity of God can be proved by the following five arguments, according to the Mutakallimūn:[63]

1. The argument of mutual neutralization, that means the impossibility of having two gods since one will make the atom warm and the other would make it cold, and since the atom having one quality, then God is the one who gave the quality to the atom.[64] Such an argument exists indeed in Ash'arīya theology, but Maimonides applied it specifically to the atom.
2. In case of two gods, they will share some attributes and one will have some attributes absent in the other, in order to conceive the difference between both. The perfect one is God, namely the one having the prime cause as attribute.
3. Since the will of God is independent of things willed, and since the will of God wills many things, the will is One while things willed are many.[65]
4. The existence of an action is a positive evidence of the existence of one agent, but does not prove necessarily the existence of more than one.[66]
5. The impossibility of two deities creating the world, otherwise both will be imperfect. Since the world is created, the creator should be one and perfect.

For Maimonides all these proofs can be accepted or rejected, since they are not based on the analysis of the property of things. They show the importance of the use of reason, but in the right way. The same argument is held by Averroes against the Ash'arīya.

---

63 "I shall explain to you likewise in this chapter the proofs of the belief in unity according to the opinion of the Mutakallimūn" (*Guide*, p. 223).

64 "Namely, the method referring to reciprocal hindering is the one preferred by the multitude [of Mutakallimūn]. [...] This kind of argumentation meant to lead to a proof is founded on the doctrine of the atoms, which is the first of their premises, and on the premise concerning the creation of accidents" (*Guide*, p. 223). "As [the Mutakallimūn] became aware of the weakness of this method, in spite of their having some incentive to choose it, they adopted another method" (*Guide*, p. 224).

65 "For some of them, namely, the ancients among them, believe that God wills by a will that is not something superadded to the essence of the creator, but is a will that does not subsist in a substratum" (*Guide*, p. 224).

66 "One of the later ones thought that he had found a demonstrative method for the belief in unity, namely, the method starting from need" (*Guide*, p. 225). "For just as we do not say that God, may He be cherished and magnified, is incapable because He is not able – according to their opinion – to bring a body into existence otherwise than through creating atoms and aggregating them by means of accidents that He creates in them. [...] One of [the Mutakallimūn] was so wearied by those tricks that he affirmed that the belief in unity was accepted in virtue of the Law. The Mutakallimūn considered this statement as very disgraceful and despised him who made it. [...] For these groups of people did not leave being with any permanent nature so that arguments could be adduced from it with a view to correct proof, nor did they leave the intellect with a sound" (*Guide*, p. 226).

C. The Incorporeality of God

The arguments proving the incorporeality of God are weak, not in the same strength as those proving the unity of God.[67]

The argument based on the corporeality requiring composition of substance and forms is not from the Mutakallimūn, and so a naive argument *ad absurdum*. However, the incorporeality of God can be proved by the following three arguments:

1. If God were corporeal, His Essence would exist in each atom or in one. In the last case, the existence of other atoms would be superfluous. In the former case, we will have many deities according to the number of atoms, which is against the unity of God already proved.
2. God cannot be compared to any of his creatures. Since creatures are corporeal, God will be incorporeal. This simple argument is based on the negation of the participation of two opposites in the same qualities.[68]
3. If God were corporeal, He would be finite. Since God is infinite, He is incorporeal. This argument is a conditional one since it depends on the demonstration of another. Incorporeality is a simple deduction of Infinity.

In these arguments, Maimonides appears less critical in order to give the simple reason his right to think and his credit in thought.

VI. Conclusion

The Islamic model is not only related to theology, physics, metaphysics, astronomy, and mathematics but it is also related to ethics and politics. Maimonides deals with ethics only in the third part of the *Guide*. However, the Islamic model appears through direct references to Islamic philosophy and theology. He refers to the theory of the attainment of human perfection through the intellect, unifying itself with the Intellect Agent as an example of human perfection. Raising one's soul from virtue to virtue will bring Divine protection.[69]

---

67 "The methods and the argumentations of the Mutakallimūn purporting to refute the doctrine of corporeality are very feeble, even feebler than their proofs in favor of the belief in unity […]. Now whoever refutes the doctrine of corporeality because a body is necessarily composed of matter and form and thus is compound – while, on the other hand, it is clear that there can be no composition in the essence of the deity – is, in my opinion, no Mutakallim. […] In this chapter our purpose is only to mention the proofs, according to their premises and argumentations, of the Mutakallimūn concerning the refutation of corporeality" (*Guide*, p. 227).

68 "Would that I knew how this feeble opinion can be controverted by means of these wondrous methods of theirs, which I have already let you know" (*Guide*, p. 229).

69 "Abū Naṣr [al-Fārābī] says in the Introduction to his Commentary on Aristotle's 'Nicomachean [Ethics]': Those who have the capacity of making their soul pass from

Mankind can be unified through Universalism, not ethnocentrism, sectarianism, parochialism and chauvinism. Universalism has long been defended by the prophets since Noah, Abraham and Moses, reaffirmed by Christ in the name of the new covenant and realized in Islam in the Andalusian model of Spain. It is a permanent virtue in a Palestinian model in which Jews, Christians and Muslims can live again under its protection.

Maimonides in his ethics makes a second reference to Islamic theology regarding free will. According to Ash'arīya, God creates in the hand holding a pen, four accidents, none of them the cause of the other. The four are only coexisting: the Wwll, the power, the motion of the body and the motion of the pen. According to the Mu'tazila and a sub-sect of Ash'arīya rejected by their majority, man acts by a power created in him.[70] The Ash'arīya theory of causality giving the absolute priority to the prime cause falls into absurdities.[71]

The freedom of man agreed upon in the Andalusian model by the three Abrahamic religions can continue in the Palestinian model, the freedom of all. The convergence of the three traditions in the Andalusian model can be a real alternative coming from history, to the actual divergence and exclusiveness.

The Andalusian model is not a utopia, since it existed in the past. The challenge is how to be authentically Jewish, Christian and Muslim, asserting respective traditions away from cultural alienation carrying ideas of ethnic nations surrounded by geographical boundaries, making war to each other. In the Andalusian model, the freedom of man is linked to the universalism of his intellect, which corresponds to the life in the desert under the starry sky looking for water and grass, settling in tents, wandering everywhere. That was the life of the Semite nomads, Arabs and Hebrews, intermarrying clans and allying tribes. The Andalusian model is an expression of the Semite nomadic life in which the Nation-State is completely alien.

---

one moral quality to another are those of whom Plato has said that God's providence watches over them to a higher degree" (*Guide*, p. 476).

70 "The doctrine of the majority and in particular that of the multitude of the Ash'ariyya is that when the pen is put into motion, God creates four accidents, one of which is a cause of any other" (*Guide*, p. 202). "On the other hand, the Mu'tazila maintain that man acts in virtue of the power created in him; and one of the Ash'ariyya says that this created power has a certain influence on, and connection with, the act. But they regard this as abhorrent" (*Guide*, p. 203).

71 "This is the opinion of the Islamic sect, the Ash'ariyya. Great incongruities are bound up with this opinion" (*Guide*, p. 466). "In consequence of this opinion, they [the Ash'ariyya, Ed.] are obliged to think that every motion and rest of animals has been decreed and that man has in no way the ability to do or not to do a thing" (*Guide*, p. 467). "The Mu'tazila also hold this opinion though, according to them, the ability of man to act of his own accord is not absolute" (*Guide*, p. 468).

„Das Siegel der Propheten"

Maimonides und das Verständnis von Mohammeds Prophetentum

von

Hartmut Bobzin

Universität Erlangen-Nürnberg

In der Anekdotensammlung *Nihāyat al-arab fī funūn al-adab* von an-Nuwayrī[1] findet sich folgende Anekdote, die am Hof des Kalifen al-Maʾmūn (reg. 813–833) spielt:

> Eine Frau, die sich als Prophetin ausgab, wurde vor den Kalifen geführt. Er fragte sie: „Wer bist du?" Sie sagte: „Ich bin die Prophetin Fatima." – „Glaubst du an die Botschaft Mohammeds?" – „Ja", erwiderte sie, „alles, was er verkündet hat, ist wahr!" – „Aber weißt du denn nicht, daß Mohammed gesagt hat: ‚Nach mir wird es keinen Propheten mehr geben?' [*lā nabīya baʿdī*]" – „Das weiß ich wohl; aber hat er auch gesagt: ‚Nach mir wird es keine Prophetin geben?' [*lā nabīyata baʿdī*]"

Diese Anekdote ist ein amüsanter Beleg für die bekannte islamische Auffassung von Mohammed als dem *letzten* Propheten, – eine Auffassung, die bekanntlich auf Sure 33, Vers 40 zurückgeht, wo Mohammed als „Gesandter Gottes und Siegel der Propheten" (*rasūl allāh wa-ḫātam an-nabīyīn*) bezeichnet wird. Auch die von Nuwayrī überlieferte Anekdote stützt die heute vorherrschende Ansicht, *ḫātam* („Siegel") sei im Sinne der „Letztgültigkeit" zu verstehen, daß es also keinen Propheten nach Mohammed mehr geben werde (beziehungsweise geben dürfe). Aber das bloße Faktum, daß es im Islam immer wieder prophetische Bewegungen gegeben hat, zeigt, daß das Wort *ḫātam* auch anders verstanden werden konnte und verstanden wurde, nämlich als „Besiegelung" im Sinn der „Bestätigung", also eine Anknüpfung an frühere Propheten und die Bestätigung von deren Sendung durch Mohammeds Prophetentum. Ein Blick in den umfangreichen, vor allem auf Ḥadīṯen beruhenden Korankommentar *ad-Durr al-manṯūr fī t-tafsīr al-maʾṯūr*[2] des bekannten ägyptischen Enzyklopädisten

---

1 Lebensdaten: 667–732/1279–1332; cf. H. Kilpatrick, in *Encyclopedia of Arabic Literature* (London, New York: Routledge, 1998), S. 590–591; vgl. *Geschichte der arabischen Litteratur*, ed. Carl Brockelmann, Band II (Leipzig: Amelang, ²1909), S. 175, sowie Supplementband II (Leiden: Brill, 1938), S. 173–174.

2 Siehe *Geschichte der arabischen Litteratur* (wie Anm. 1), Band II², S. 182, Nr. 2.

Ǧalāl ad-Dīn as-Suyūṭī[3] zeigt verschiedene Auslegungen des „Siegelwortes" (wie ich Sure 33:40 im Folgenden nennen will). So zum Beispiel diejenige, die auf ʿĀʾiša, die Lieblingsfrau Mohammeds, zurückgeführt wird: „Sagt ‚Siegel der Propheten', nicht: ‚Nach ihm wird es keinen Propheten mehr geben!'"[4]. Ein anderer Ḥadīṯ lautet wie folgt:

> Ein Mann sagte in Anwesenheit von Muġīra [b. Šuʿba, einem Prophetengenossen aus dem Stamm der Ṯaqīf]: „Gott segne Mohammed, das Siegel der Propheten; es gibt keinen Propheten nach ihm!" Muġīra entgegnete: „Begnüge dich zu sagen: Siegel der Propheten! Man überlieferte uns nämlich, daß Jesus (Heil sei über ihm!) einst (wieder)kommen wird, und wenn er (nun früher) schon aufgetreten ist, ist er also vor Mohammed und nach ihm!"[5]

Wer das ganze Spektrum der Auslegungsmöglichkeiten des „Siegelwortes" kennen lernen möchte, sei auf Johanan Friedman's 1989 erschienene Studie *Prophecy Continuous. Aspects of Aḥmadī Religious Thought and its Medieval Background* verwiesen; dort wird der ganze Problemkreis auf breiter Materialbasis erörtert, und zwar im Hinblick auf die moderne „prophetische" Bewegung der Aḥmadīya.

Die Wendung „Siegel der Propheten" hat vor einiger Zeit auch der Religionshistoriker und Iranist Carsten Colpe behandelt.[6] Er hat sie in der „bald nach 208 verfaßten" Schrift *Adversus Iudaeos* des nordafrikanischen Theologen Tertullian (gest. nach 220) ausgemacht;[7] dort wird sie auf Jesus angewandt, und zwar polemisch gegen die Juden gerichtet. Dies geschieht in der Auslegung der wichtigen Stelle Daniel 9:24,[8] die im frühen Christentum weithin messianisch ausgelegt wurde.

Ich möchte hier die Frage nach der Plausibilität von Colpes Ableitung nicht ausführlich diskutieren, sondern nur hinzufügen, daß sich ganz ähnliche Gedanken auch bei dem syrischen Theologen Afrahat[9] in einem nahezu gleichen

3 Lebensdaten: 849–911/1445–1505; vgl. R. Irwin, in *Encyclopedia of Arabic Literature* (wie Anm. 1), S. 746.

4 *qūlū ḫātam an-nabīyīna wa-lā taqūlū lā nabīya baʿdahū.*

5 *Qāla raǧulun ʿinda l-Muġīra … ṣallā llāhu ʿalā Muḥammadin, ḫātami l-anbiyāʾi lā nabīya baʿdahū. Fa-qāla l-Muġīra: ḥasbuka iḏā qulta ḫātamu l-anbiyāʾ. Fa-ʾinnā kunnā nuḥaddaṯu anna ʿĪsā (ʿalayhi s-salām!) ḫāriǧun fa-in huwa ḫaraǧa fa-qad kāna qablahū wa-baʿdahū.*

6 „Das Siegel der Propheten", in *Orientalia Suecana* XXXIII–XXXV (= FS Rundgren) (1984–1986), S. 71–83.

7 Ibid., S. 77–78.

8 „Siebzig [Jahr-]Wochen sind über dein Volk und über deine heilige Stadt bestimmt, bis der Frevel vollendet und das Maß der Sünde voll ist, bis die Schuld gesühnt und ewige Gerechtigkeit gebracht, bis Gesicht und Prophet bestätigt [ולחתם חזון ונביא] und ein Hochheiliges gesalbt wird."

9 Gestorben kurz nach 345; vgl. Peter Bruns, Art. „Afrahat", in *Religion in Geschichte und Gegenwart*, 4. Auflage (8 Bände; Tübingen: J.C.B. Mohr [Paul Siebeck], 1998–2005), Band I, 1998, Sp. 138–139.

Zusammenhang finden, und zwar in dessen „Taḥwəyāṭā" (Homilien) gegen die Juden und über die Verfolgungen.[10] Diese Feststellung erscheint mir insofern wichtig, als schon vor längerer Zeit der schwedische Islamforscher Tor Andrae (1885–1947) auf die Bedeutung der Gedankenwelt Afrahats und überhaupt der syrischen Mönchsfrömmigkeit für die frühe Verkündigung Mohammeds aufmerksam gemacht hat. So sind für Afrahat Mose wie Jesus die zwei größten Propheten schlechthin, – und genau diese prophetische Konzeption findet sich auch im Koran, wo Mose als Leitfigur der „Kinder Israel" (*Banū Isrāʾīl*) fungiert und Jesus als die der Christen, der *Naṣārā*. Auch findet sich bei Afrahat in ganz charakteristischer Weise eine typologische Auslegung des Alten Testaments, das heißt in der Geschichte der früheren Propheten ist die Geschichte Jesu *präfiguriert*[11] – und nicht lediglich ganz allgemein vorhergesagt. In ganz ähnlicher Weise legt der Koran die Prophetengeschichten der jüdisch-christlichen Überlieferung im Blick auf Mohammed aus.

Im folgenden soll der bisher von der Forschung kaum beachtete zweite Bestandteil des „Siegelwortes" im Mittelpunkt stehen, nämlich der Begriff des „Propheten" (arabisch *nabīy*). Auffällig ist, daß *nabīy* in Sure 33:40 in unmittelbarer Nachbarschaft zu dem anderen Begriff steht, der ebenfalls auf Mohammed angewendet wird, nämlich „Gesandter" (arabisch *rasūl*). Der ganze Vers lautet:

> Mohammed ist nicht Vater irgendeines von euren Männern, sondern Gesandter Gottes und Siegel der Propheten.[12]

Auf die Bedeutung des ersten Teiles dieses Verses und den größeren Zusammenhang, in dem dieser Vers steht, werde ich später zurückkommen. Zunächst möchte ich etwas genauer auf das Wortpaar „Gesandter" (*rasūl*) und „Prophet" (*nabīy*) eingehen. Beide Bezeichnungen werden heute auf Mohammed angewendet, oft ohne erkennbaren Bedeutungsunterschied. So gibt zum Beispiel A. Th. Khoury in seiner Koranübersetzung das Wort *rasūl* an einer Stelle mit „Prophet" wieder.[13] Daß beide Wörter jedoch nicht in jedem Fall austauschbar sind, zeigen bestimmte Alltagswendungen.[14] So heißt das Geburtstagsfest Mohammeds *mawlid an-nabīy* „Geburt des Propheten", und die Aufforderung zum Segensspruch über Mohammed[15] lautet: *ṣallū ʿalā n-nabīy* „Betet für den

10 Vgl. *Aphrahat's, des persischen Weisen, Homilien.* Aus dem Syrischen übersetzt und erläutert von Georg Bert (Texte und Untersuchungen zur Geschichte der altchristlichen Literatur 3/3–4; Leipzig: Hinrichs, 1888). Neueste Übersetzung von Peter Bruns, *Aphrahat, Unterweisungen* (2 Bände; Fontes Christiani 5,1/2; Freiburg im Breisgau: Herder, 1991).

11 Vgl. zu dieser Art der Auslegung Adalbert Merx, *Die Prophetie des Joel und ihre Ausleger* (Halle an der Saale: Verlag der Buchhandlung des Waisenhauses, 1879), S. 135.

12 *Mā kāna Muḥammadun abā aḥadin min riǧālikum wa-lākin rasūla llāhi wa-ḫātama n-nabīyīn.*

13 So in Sure 38:14. Vgl. *Der Koran,* Übersetzung von Adel Theodor Khoury (Gütersloh: Gütersloher Verlagshaus, 1987), S. 346.

14 Vgl. auch Moshe Piamenta, *Islam in Everyday Arabic Speech* (Leiden: Brill, 1979).

15 Vgl. Sure 33:56.

Propheten!" Anders hingegen ist es im Glaubensbekenntnis, der *šahāda*, denn dort wird Mohammed als „Gesandter", *rasūl*, bezeichnet: „Ich bezeuge, daß es keinen Gott gibt außer Gott, und daß Mohammed der Gesandte Gottes ist" (*ašhadu an lā ilāha illā llāh wa-anna Muḥammadan rasūlu llāh*). Auch in der frühen biographischen Literatur zu Mohammed, der *Sīra*, ist überwiegend vom „Gesandten" Gottes (*rasūl allāh*) die Rede. Nur am Rande sei angemerkt, daß diese Wendung zwar im Koran sehr häufig vorkommt, nicht aber ihr Gegenstück „Prophet Gottes", *nabīy allāh*; sie begegnet erst, soweit ich sehe, im Ḥadīṯ[16] und bei Ṭabarī (gest. 923).

Es ist nun ein guter philologischer Grundsatz, zunächst einmal davon auszugehen, daß zwei verschiedene Wörter auch jeweils etwas Unterschiedliches bezeichnen, daß also im „Siegelwort" nicht ohne Grund die Formulierung „Siegel der *Propheten*" gewählt ist. Näheren Aufschluß kann hier eigentlich nur die Analyse des gesamten Korantextes liefern. Bezüglich des Gebrauchs der beiden Bezeichnungen *nabīy* und *rasūl* sind dabei die folgenden drei Punkte auffällig:

a. Das Wort *rasūl* kommt mit insgesamt 332 Belegen[17] mehr als viermal so häufig vor wie das Wort *nabīy* mit 75 Belegen.[18]
b. Geht man von Theodor Nöldekes Chronologie der Suren aus,[19] so zeigt sich, daß *nabīy* ganz überwiegend in medinensischen Suren begegnet und in der frühen Verkündigung Mohammeds praktisch keine Rolle spielt.
c. Auf Mohammed selbst angewandt, begegnet das Wort *nabīy* erst in medinensischen Suren (beziehungsweise Einschüben).

Damit steht der Sprachgebrauch des Korans, wenn man ihn ernst nimmt, in eindeutigem Widerspruch zu der häufig geäußerten Ansicht, es gäbe zunächst den „Propheten" von Mekka, später hingegen den „Staatsmann" von Medina. Diese Periodisierung, die sich nahezu unhinterfragt bei einer ganzen Reihe neuerer Biographen findet – von Karl Ahrens[20] über Hans Heinrich Schaeder[21]

---

16 Vgl. Arent J. Wensinck et al., *Concordance et Indices de la Tradition Musulmane* (Leiden: Brill, 1967), Band 6, s.v. *nabīy*, S. 332ff.

17 Im Einzelnen: Singular *rasūl* 236 Vorkommen, Plural *rusul* 96 Vorkommen.

18 Im Einzelnen: Singular *nabīy* 54 Vorkommen, Plural *nabīyūna* 16 Vorkommen, Plural *anbiyā`* 5 Vorkommen.

19 Theodor Nöldeke, *Geschichte des Qorāns*. Zweite Auflage bearbeitet von Friedrich Schwally. Erster Teil: *Über den Ursprung des Qorāns* (Leipzig: Dieterich, ²1909; Nachdruck Hildesheim etc.: Olms, 2005).

20 Karl Ahrens, *Muhammed als Religionsstifter* (Abhandlungen für die Kunde des Morgenlandes XIX,4; Leipzig: Deutsche Morgenländische Gesellschaft, 1935; Nachdruck Nendeln, Liechtenstein: Kraus, 1966). Ahrens periodisiert Mohammeds Leben in die Stationen „Der Prophet", „Der Lehrer" und „Der Gesetzgeber".

21 Hans Heinrich Schaeder, „Muhammed", in *Arabische Welt* 5 (Heidelberg 1944), S. 1–72; wiederabgedruckt in idem, *Der Mensch in Orient und Okzident. Grundzüge einer eurasiatischen Geschichte* (München: Piper, 1960), S. 307–396.

bis hin zu William Montgomery Watt[22] –, geht oft mit der Annahme eines grundlegenden „Bruchs" in Mohammeds Wirken einher.

Eine solche Auffassung von Mohammeds Wirksamkeit ist – kurz gesagt – eng verknüpft mit dem Prophetenverständnis der modernen westlichen, vor allem protestantischen, Theologie. Danach ist der Prophet eine göttlich inspirierte oder jedenfalls bevollmächtigte Person, deren Aufgabe in der Verkündigung einer bestimmten – auf die Zukunft gerichteten – Botschaft besteht, die durchaus politisch-sozialen Charakter haben kann, wie es etwa bei den „klassischen" Schriftpropheten Amos, Jesaja oder Hosea der Fall ist. Aber die Propheten sind nicht selber „Politiker". Der Alttestamentler Walter Zimmerli hat gerade diesen Punkt als – wie er sich ausdrückt – entscheidenden „Fehler" Mohammeds herausgestellt:

> Der Fehler Mohammeds besteht darin: In dem Augenblick, wo die Macht ihm angeboten wird, ist er nicht mehr Prophet.[23]

Man wird ohne weiteres einsehen, daß es methodisch fragwürdig ist, mit dem Vorverständnis alttestamentlicher Prophetie zu arbeiten, wenn man Mohammeds Prophetentum verstehen will. Aber ebenso fragwürdig ist es auch, das Prophetenverständnis der muslimischen Mohammed-Biographen, das heißt des Ibn Isḥāq und seiner Nachfolger, unhinterfragt zum Ausgangspunkt für das Verständnis des koranischen „Gesandten und Propheten" Mohammed zu machen, so wie das in der Islamwissenschaft noch häufig geschieht. Eben dies hat schon vor längerer Zeit Rudolf Sellheim in seiner Arbeit „Prophet, Chalif und Geschichte. Die Muhammed-Biographie des Ibn Isḥāq"[24] implizit kritisiert.

In der *Sīra,* so wie Ibn Isḥāq sie als Gattung geschaffen hat, findet sich nämlich bereits eine ganz bestimmte Vorstellung davon, wie ein Prophet beschaffen sein muß und wie – nach dieser Vorstellung – das Leben Mohammeds verlaufen ist. Von daher ist die *Sīra* für die Analyse der koranischen Vorstellungen von Prophetie nur mit allergrößter Zurückhaltung zu gebrauchen. Das einzig legitime Verfahren ist die sorgfältige Untersuchung des koranischen

---

22 William Montgomery Watt, *Muhammad. Prophet and Statesman* (London etc.: Oxford University Press, 1961). Watt faßt hierin die Ergebnisse seiner beiden vorhergehenden umfassenden Studien *Muḥammad at Mecca* (Oxford: Clarendon Press, 1953) und *Muḥammad at Medina* (Oxford: Clarendon Press, 1956) für ein breiteres Publikum zusammen.

23 „Der Prophet im Alten Testament und im Islam", in Walther Zimmerli, *Studien zur Alttestamentlichen Theologie und Prophetie. Gesammelte Aufsätze,* Band II (Theologische Bücherei 51; München: Kaiser, 1974), S. 310. Ursprünglich erschienen unter dem Titel „Le prophète dans l'Ancien Testament et dans l'Islam", in *Collection „Le Christianisme et l'Islam"* (Lausanne: Édition de la Mission de Bâle, 1945), S. 5–32, hier S. 32: „La faute de Mahomet consiste en ceci: au moment où la puissance lui fut offerte, il n'est pas resté un prophète."

24 In *Oriens* 18–19 (1965/66), S. 33–91.

Wortgebrauchs selber und der darauf aufbauende Versuch, die dem Koran eigene theologische Konzeption von Mohammeds Prophetentum aufzuzeigen. Ob es auf diesem Wege allerdings auch gelingen kann, Mohammeds *Selbstverständnis als Prophet* zu eruieren, möchte ich offen lassen. Um es in äußerster Kürze zu formulieren: Selbst wenn der Koran als „historische Quelle" unbestreitbaren Rang besitzt,[25] so ist er jedoch in erster Linie ein kerygmatischer Text, das heißt er stellt die Übermittlung einer religiösen Botschaft dar, er ist „Verkündigung".

Als was erscheint nun Mohammed im Koran? In den frühesten Suren[26] findet man bekanntlich rein beschreibende Bezeichnungen für Mohammed. Die älteste und klarste ist „Warner" (*naḏīr* 51:50–51 beziehungsweise *munḏir* 79:45), sodann „Mahner" (*muḏakkir* 88:21); erst danach tritt die Bezeichnung „Bote" beziehungsweise „Freudenbote" hinzu (*bašīr* beziehungsweise *mubaššir*) – interessanterweise jedoch nie unabhängig, sondern immer zusammengeordnet mit „Warner". Und schließlich das Wort „Gesandter" (*rasūl*): Zweimal wird es mit dem Beiwort *mubīn* (44:13 und 43:29) verwendet, und das heißt „unzweideutig, vollkommen klar verständlich, offenkundig". Noch häufiger tritt dieses Beiwort übrigens zum „Warner".

Vor dem Hintergrund der „Klarheit" von Mohammeds Aufgabe, wie sie in diesen Bezeichnungen zum Ausdruck kommt, gewinnen auch die Abgrenzungen eine neue Deutlichkeit. Mohammed ist weder ein „Dichter" (*šāʿir* 69:41; 52:30) noch von einem Dämonen (*ǧinn*) „besessen", das heißt *maǧnūn* (68:2, 51; 52:29), wie das für Dichter galt,[27] noch ist er ein „Zauberer" (*sāḥir*), noch ein altarabischer „Orakelpriester" (*kāhin*). Wenn man diese abgrenzenden Äußerungen zusammenfassend charakterisieren will, dann gilt für sie zweierlei:

a. Sie umreißen das Spektrum altarabischer Ekstatiker, für die bestimmte Bezeichnungen feststanden und die mit bestimmten kultischen oder sozialen Institutionen verbunden waren. Genau das aber gilt für Bezeichnungen wie „Warner" und vor allem auch „Gesandter" nicht. Denn sie bezeichnen in sprachlich eindeutiger Form bestimmte Aufgaben und Funktionen, die Mohammed für sich selber reklamiert oder aber früheren Gestalten beilegt.
b. Die „Rede" (*qawl*) dieser „Ekstatiker" war in jedem Fall „kunstvoll". Die Qasiden der Dichter waren metrisch gebunden und voller Bilder und Ver-

---

25 Vgl. dazu Rudi Paret, „Der Koran als Geschichtsquelle", in *Der Islam* 37 (1961), S. 24–42 (Neudruck in idem [Ed.], *Der Koran* [Wege der Forschung CCCXXVI; Darmstadt: Wissenschaftliche Buchgesellschaft, 1975], S. 137–158); William M. Watt, *Muḥammad's Mecca. History in the Qurʾān* (Edinburgh: Edinburgh University Press, 1988), hier vor allem das erste Kapitel „The Qurʾān as Historical Source" (S. 1–4).

26 Im Folgenden wird die Chronologie Nöldekes vorausgesetzt – aber nur deshalb, weil es, trotz insgesamt enormen Erkenntnisfortschrittes, noch keinen überzeugenderen Gesamtentwurf gibt.

27 Vgl. Sure 37:36: „Sollen wir etwa einem besessenen Dichter (*šāʿir maǧnūn*) zuliebe unsere Götter aufgeben?"

gleiche; auch die Reimprosa (*saǧ*) der „Orakelpriester“ (*kāhin*) war, soweit sich das am spärlichen Material zeigen läßt, keineswegs kunstlos. Demgegenüber bezeichnet Mohammed seine Rede als „klar“ (*mubīn*).

Die Eigenart von Mohammeds Tätigkeit in Mekka läßt sich noch schärfer herausarbeiten, wenn man systematisch die Imperative beziehungsweise die Verbote sammelt, mit denen sich nach koranischem Zeugnis Gott an Mohammed wendet. Nach inhaltlichen Kriterien lassen sich dabei zwei Gruppen unterscheiden.

Die erste umfaßt Befehle, die mit Mohammeds öffentlichen Aufgaben verbunden sind, und zwar in Begriffen, die mit den zitierten Funktionsbezeichnungen wie „Warner“ oder „Mahner“ korrespondieren: „Steh auf und warne“ (*qum fa-anḏir* 74:2); „verkünde ihnen schmerzliche Strafe“ (*fa-bašširhum bi-ʿaḏābin alīm* 84:24), oder ganz kurz und absolut: „Mahne!“ (*ḏakkir* 87:9; 88:21; 51:55; 52:79). Das heißt, hier wird Mohammeds Aufgabe als „Bußprediger“ für seine „Stadt“ (*qarya*) beziehungsweise sein „Volk“ (*umma*) beschrieben.

Die zweite Gruppe bezieht sich auf Mohammed als Person und sein Verhältnis zu Gott. In diesen „Befehlen“ werden von Mohammed bestimmte Tugenden gefordert, zum Beispiel *ṣabr* „Geduld, Standhaftigkeit“ oder *tawakkul* „Gottvertrauen“, oder daß Mohammed Gott das Handeln überlassen soll (*ḏarnī* …). Gefordert sind aber auch bestimmte Frömmigkeitsübungen, wie sie vor allem in den Verben *sabbaḥa* „preisen, loben“, *ḏakara* „erwähnen“[28] und später auch *saǧada* „niederfallen“ zum Ausdruck kommen: „Preise deinen Herrn, wenn du aufstehst“ (52:48: *sabbiḥ bi-ḥamdi rabbika ḥīna taqūm*); „Gedenke morgens und abends des Namens deines Herrn; und wirf dich in Anbetung vor ihm nieder, wenn der Tag um ist, und preise ihn die lange Nacht!“ (76:25–26: *wa-ḏkur-i sma rabbika bukratan wa-ʾaṣīlan wa-min-a l-layli fa-sǧud lahū wa-sabbiḥhu laylan ṭawīlan*). Gerade bei diesen Anweisungen zeigen sich ganz klar Züge eines asketischen, um nicht zu sagen mönchischen Frömmigkeitsideals. Dazu sind die nächsten Parallelen im Mönchtum der syrischen Christenheit zu finden.

Wenn man also aufgrund dieser an den frühen mekkanischen Suren gemachten Beobachtungen Mohammed charakterisieren will, so könnte man ihn einen asketischen Bußprediger nennen. Er warnt vor einem herannahenden Gericht, an dem es für den Menschen keinen Fürsprecher gibt vor dem gerechten Richtergott, dem Schöpfer des Himmels und der Erde, der töten und wieder zum Leben auferwecken kann. Mit dieser Botschaft stößt Mohammed bei den Mekkanern auf Unglauben und Widerstand. Um seine Sendung zu legitimieren und ihr das nötige Gewicht zu geben, greift er auf das Beispiel früherer Gottgesandter (*rusul*) zurück. Das geschieht in Form von Geschichten, die seit den Forschungen von Josef Horovitz als „Straflegenden“ bezeichnet werden. In diesen Geschichten findet sich mit später zunehmender Systematisierung der

28 Verbunden mit dem Namen Gottes; vgl. 73:8; 76:25.

Gedanke, daß jedem „Volk“ sein Gesandter (*rasūl*) von Gott geschickt wird, um es zu warnen. In den sieben gleichsam „klassischen“ Fällen, die der Koran erwähnt, bezichtigt „das Volk“ (oder dessen Repräsentanten) den Gesandten der Lüge, und die Strafe folgt auf den Fuß. Das Volk geht zugrunde und der Gesandte überlebt, zum Teil, wie im Falle Noahs, mit einer kleinen Schar gläubiger Anhänger des Gesandten.

Im Zusammenhang dieser Geschichten taucht nun erstmals auch explizit der Begriff des „Propheten“ (*nabīy*) auf, – am eindrücklichsten in einer Art „Katalog“ in Sure 19.

Betrachtet man nun die Gestalten genauer, denen im Koran die Titel „Prophet“ (*nabīy*) beziehungsweise „Gesandter“ (*rasūl/mursal*) zuerkannt werden, dann ergibt sich folgender Befund:

Explizit als *rasūl* beziehungsweise *mursal* werden bezeichnet: Noah, Lot, Ismael, Mose, Aaron, Elia, Jona, Hūd, Ṣāliḥ, Šuʿayb, Jesus und Mohammed.

Explizit als *nabīy* werden bezeichnet: Idris, Noah, Abraham, Ismael, Isaak, Jakob, Mose, Aaron, David, Salomo, Jona, Hiob, Johannes der Täufer, Jesus und Mohammed. Aus verschiedenen Listen geht hervor, daß die Bezeichnung *nabīy* auch für Adam, Lot, Joseph, Samuel, Elia, Elisa und Zacharias gilt.

Alle *nabīy*-Gestalten entstammen also der jüdisch-christlichen Überlieferung; Arent Jan Wensinck hat alle diese Propheten übrigens sehr anschaulich als „Bibelheilige“ bezeichnet.

Für die „Gesandten“ gilt dieser Bezug zur jüdisch-christlichen Überlieferung jedoch nicht in dieser generellen Weise, wie man an den drei „arabischen“ Gestalten Hūd, Ṣāliḥ und Šuʿayb sehen kann; ihre Zahl ist im übrigen wesentlich geringer. Die eben gegebene Zusammenstellung zeigt aber auch, daß der immer wieder zu hörende Satz: „Nicht jeder *nabīy* ist ein *rasūl*, aber jeder *rasūl* ist ein *nabīy*“ in dieser Form nicht zutreffend ist.

Versucht man nun, die Charakteristika dieser beiden Gruppen ausschließlich auf koranischer Grundlage herauszuarbeiten, dann ist zunächst eine Reihe von Gemeinsamkeiten zu beobachten, die für „Propheten“ wie für „Gesandte“ gelten, wie zum Beispiel die „Schrift“ (*kitāb*), „Wunderzeichen“ (*āyāt*) oder „Inspiration“ (beziehungsweise Offenbarung, *waḥy*). Allein aufgrund dieser Merkmale ist keine scharfe Abgrenzung zwischen den Begriffen *nabīy* und *rasūl* möglich. Hingegen ist für den *rasūl* die Sendung zu einem bestimmten Volk (*umma*) konstitutives Merkmal. Das kann nun für die namentlich genannten Propheten schon deshalb nicht gelten, weil bei ihnen das genealogische Moment entscheidend ist, das heißt sie stammen alle aus einer ganz bestimmten „Nachkommenschaft“ (*ḏurrīya*):

> Wir schenkten ihm [das heißt Abraham] Isaak und Jakob und machten in seiner Nachkommenschaft die Prophetie (*nubūwa*) und die Schrift (*kitāb*) (29:27).
>
> Wir sendeten Noah und Abraham und machten in ihrer Nachkommenschaft die Prophetie (*nubūwa*) und die Schrift (*kitāb*) (57:26).

Für die im Koran namentlich genannten Propheten läßt sich nun ein weiteres wichtiges Merkmal festhalten, nämlich die „Erwählung".[29] Für die spätere Verehrung Mohammeds im Islam spielt genau dieser Gesichtspunkt keine geringe Rolle: Mohammed ist der „Erwählte", und zu seinen Ehrennamen zählen *al-muṣṭafā* oder *al-muḫtār*. Drei weitere Gruppen gelten als „erwählt", nämlich: das Geschlecht Abrahams, die Kinder Israel und das Geschlecht ʿImrāns. Man könnte diese Gruppen auch mit anderen Etiketten versehen, man könnte sprechen von den jüdischen Patriarchen beziehungsweise dem vormosaischen Judentum, dem mosaischen Judentum und dem nachjesuanischen Juden- beziehungsweise Judenchristentum. Das heißt: Ein wesentliches Merkmal der im Koran genannten Propheten und ihrer Nachkommenschaft ist ihre „Erwählung".

Es gibt aber noch ein weiteres Charakteristikum der koranischen Propheten. Gott nimmt nämlich von ihnen eine „Verpflichtung" (*mīṯāq*) beziehungsweise einen „Bund" oder „Vertrag" (*ʿahd*) entgegen. Ein solcher „Bund" ist nun aber nicht nur auf „Propheten" beschränkt, sondern bezieht sich in vollem Umfang auf die gerade genannten „Erwählten". Im Koran gibt es also das Konzept eines „Bundes" ebenso wie das einer „Erwählung": Damit ist die Kennzeichnung der Muslime in ihrer Gesamtheit als auserwähltes Gottesvolk und Träger der Verheißung gemeint.

Das koranische Konzept der Propheten, wie es sich uns bis jetzt dargestellt hat, ist, und das ist das wichtigste Ergebnis, verknüpft mit der „Erwählungsgeschichte" des Gottesvolkes: des Alten Bundes wie des Neuen Bundes. Zu einem ganz ähnlichen Ergebnis kann man im Übrigen auch gelangen, wenn man die Begriffe der „Nachfolge" und die des „Erbes" genauer untersucht. Das haben in anderen Zusammenhängen bereits Karl Prenner,[30] Heribert Busse[31] und Wolfdietrich Fischer[32] getan.

Der Titel „Gesandter" (*rasūl*) hingegen hat, trotz gewisser Anklänge an den Apostelbegriff des Neuen Testaments und der Alten Kirche, diese Vorgeschichte nicht; denn er kann ohne weiteres auch für Gestalten der arabischen Geschichte Verwendung finden, für Hūd, Ṣāliḥ, Šuʿayb – und eben auch Mohammed, für den ja zunächst ganz überwiegend die Bezeichnung *rasūl* Verwendung findet.

Wie also kommt es zur Übernahme des Prophetenbegriffs durch Mohammed beziehungsweise auf Mohammed? Es sei hier noch einmal in Erinnerung geru-

---

29 Die dafür verwendeten Verben sind *iṣṭafā*, *iǧtabā* und *iḫtāra*.

30 Karl Prenner, *Muhammad und Musa. Strukturanalytische und theologiegeschichtliche Untersuchungen zu den mekkanischen Musa-Perikopen im Qurʾān* (Altenberge: Verlag für Christlich-Islamisches Schrifttum, 1986).

31 Heribert Busse, *Die theologischen Beziehungen des Islams zu Judentum und Christentum. Grundlagen des Dialogs im Koran und die gegenwärtige Situation* (Darmstadt: Wissenschaftliche Buchgesellschaft, 1988 = ²1991).

32 Wolfdietrich Fischer, „Das geschichtliche Selbstverständnis Muhammads und seiner Gemeinde. Zur Interpretation von Vers 55 der 24. Sure des Koran", in *Oriens* 36 (2001), S. 145–159.

fen, daß die Verwendung des Titels „Prophet" (*nabīy*) für Mohammed selbst nach koranischem Befund erst in Medina stattfindet.[33] Die medinensischen Suren sind nun, wenn man ihren Inhalt auf die wichtigsten thematischen Schwerpunkte reduziert, durchzogen von der Auseinandersetzung mit dem Gedankengut, um nicht zu sagen: den Einwänden der dort in Medina ansässigen Juden. Natürlich ging es in Medina, rein politisch gesehen, um die Macht. Diese Auseinandersetzung spiegelt sich auch im Koran wider, jedoch nicht als historischer Bericht, sondern – sozusagen „verfremdet" – in theologischer Form, die diese Geschichte zugleich in heilsgeschichtlicher Perspektive deutet. Und danach steht Erwählungsanspruch gegen Erwählungsanspruch, oder, um es noch pointierter zu formulieren: Welche Gemeinde ist das wahre erwählte Gottesvolk, die Juden von Medina oder die muslimischen Neuankömmlinge aus Mekka? Um seinen eigenen Anspruch und den seiner Gemeinde, der Muslime, zu begründen, greift Mohammed, so möchte ich es sehen, zum Titel des „Propheten", und das hat, so merkwürdig es zunächst klingen mag, *genealogische* Gründe! Da nämlich alle Propheten Bestandteil der biblischen Heilsgeschichte und mithin „erwählt" sind, reiht sich Mohammed nun selber als (bisher letztes) Glied in diese Geschichte ein.

Und genau dafür findet man in Sure 33, der das „Siegelwort" entstammt, wichtige Hinweise. Rein äußerlich ist dabei zu beachten, daß knapp ein Viertel aller Belege für *nabīy* (nämlich 17 von 75) auf diese Sure entfallen; man könnte sie regelrecht als „Prophetenermahnung" verstehen: Sechsmal markiert die Anrede „Prophet!" (*yā ayyuhā n-nabīy*) neue und jeweils wichtige Abschnitte dieser Sure. Auffällig ist im übrigen, daß in dieser Sure eine ganze Reihe von „Vorrechten" des Propheten, auch und gerade im Verhältnis zu Frauen, begründet werden, aber auch andere, vor allem für die spätere Prophetenverehrung außerordentlich wichtige Aussagen sich hier finden: (1) Mohammed ist „das schöne Vorbild" (*al-uswa al-ḥasana*), dessen Leben es nachzueifern gilt (33:21); (2) Mohammed wird als „leuchtende Lampe" (*as-sirāǧ al-munīr*) bezeichnet: Ausgangspunkt für die später in Volksglaube und Mystik verbreitete, mit Mohammed verknüpfte Lichtsymbolik (33:46); (3) über Mohammed sprechen, so 33:56, „Gott und seine Engel den Segen" (*inna llāha wa-malāʾikatahū yuṣallūna ʿalā n-nabīy*): Ausgangspunkt für den obligatorischen Segenswunsch über den Propheten bei seiner Erwähnung.

Aber die in unserem Zusammenhang wichtigsten Verse sind das „Siegelwort" (33:40) sowie Vers 7, der zunächst zitiert werden soll:

> Und als wir von den Propheten ihre Verpflichtung entgegennahmen, – und zwar von dir, von Noah, von Abraham, von Mose und Jesus, dem Sohn der Maria, – da nahmen wir von ihnen eine feste Verpflichtung entgegen.

---

33 Zu den beiden Versen 7:157 und 158 siehe unten.

Mit diesem Satz, bei dem das „von dir" (*minka*), das heißt „von Dir, Mohammed!", geradezu emphatisch am Anfang, also vor Noah und den anderen Propheten steht, reiht sich Mohammed in die Genealogie der „erwählten" Propheten ein; die Verpflichtung gilt zugleich für sein Volk, seine *umma*. Und in *diesem* Sinne wird Mohammed in einem medinensischen Zusatz in Sure 7 zweimal (Vers 157–158) als *ar-rasūl an-nabīy al-ummī* bezeichnet, das heißt als „der Gesandte, der Prophet, der seiner [arabischen] *umma* zugehört",[34] nicht jedoch den „Schriftbesitzern" (*ahl al-kitāb*); insofern ist Mohammed also ein den „Heiden" (*ummīyīn*) entstammender Prophet.[35]

Und von diesem Propheten heißt es nun in Sure 7:157 im Hinblick auf die Juden und Christen, daß sie „bei sich von ihm geschrieben finden, in Thora und Evangelium".[36] Auf welche konkreten Schriftstellen hier Bezug genommen wird, soll später erörtert werden. Jedenfalls dürfte erst vor dieser Positionsbestimmung in vollem Umfang klar werden, worum es in Medina in der Auseinandersetzung mit den Juden vor allem ging, nämlich um die uralte Abgrenzung zwischen „wahrer" und „falscher" Prophetie oder, wie es Johan Bouman ausgedrückt hat,[37] um die „Weigerung der Juden, Muhammad als Prophet in der Tradition des Judentums anzuerkennen". Dafür waren nach Bouman, der hier zum Teil an Wensincks Forschungen zu den Juden in Medina[38] anknüpft, vor allem zwei Gründe maßgebend: „Nach jüdischer Tradition strebt ein Prophet nicht nach politischer Herrschaft. Daß Mohammed dies tut, erbringt den Beweis, daß er kein Prophet ist. Und ein Prophet [...] folgt nicht seinen fleischlichen Gelüsten, wie Muhammad dies tut."[39]

Ich beginne mit dem letzten Punkt, der untrennbar mit Mohammeds Polygamie verbunden ist, und hier insbesondere Mohammeds Heirat mit der schönen Zaynab bint Ǧaḥš. Nach Auskunft der muslimischen Historiker war sie zunächst mit Mohammeds Adoptivsohn Zayd b. Ḥāriṯa verheiratet. Während Zayd einmal abwesend war, so berichtet Ibn Saʿd (gest. 845) in seinem großen biographischen Werk,[40] habe Mohammed diesen in seinem Haus besuchen

---

34 Vgl. Carlo Alfonso Nallino, *Chrestomathia Qorani Arabica* (Lipsiae: Gerhard, 1893; korrigierter Nachdruck Roma: Istituto per L'Oriente, 1963), S. 20, s.v. *ummī*: „ad *umma* pertinens, λαϊκός. Itaque *al-ummīyūn* sunt Arabes gentilicii, nullos sacros libros habentes, oppos. *ahl al-kitāb*."

35 Zur Bedeutung von *ummī* vgl. die Diskussion bei Rudi Paret, *Der Koran. Kommentar und Konkordanz* (Stuttgart: Kohlhammer, 1971), S. 21–22.

36 *ar-rasūl an-nabīy al-ummī allaḏī yaǧidūnahū maktūban ʿindahum fī t-taurāh wa-l-inǧīl.*

37 Johan Bouman, *Der Koran und die Juden. Die Geschichte einer Tragödie* (Darmstadt: Wissenschaftliche Buchgesellschaft, 1990), S. 69.

38 Arent Jan Wensinck, *Mohammed en de Joden te Medina* (Leiden, 1908); englische Ausgabe: *Muhammad and the Jews of Medina*, translated and edited by Wolfgang H. Behn (Berlin: W. Behn et al., ²1982).

39 Bouman, *Der Koran und die Juden* (wie Anm. 37), S. 70.

40 *Kitāb aṭ-Ṭabaqāt al-kabīr*, ed. Eduard Sachau et al. (9 Teile; Leiden: Brill, 1904–1940; Ausgabe Beirut: Dār Beirūt, 1985, Band VIII, S. 101ff.); vgl. auch aṭ-Ṭabarī, *Annales*, ed. Michael Jan De Goeje et al. (Leiden: Brill, 1879–1901), Band I, S. 1460–1461.

wollen, dort aber nur Zaynab angetroffen. Daraus habe sich so etwas wie „Liebe auf den ersten Blick" entwickelt:[41] Man könnte sich nun denken, das Ganze nähme einen ähnlichen Fortgang wie die im Alten Testament erzählte Geschichte zwischen David und Bathseba, jedoch ist dem nicht so. Denn Zayd – als Mohammeds Adoptivsohn – ist nach altarabischem Recht (soweit rekonstruierbar) einem leiblichen Sohn gleichgestellt. Mohammeds Heirat mit Zayds Frau wäre damit „tabu".

In Sure 33:4 heißt es jedoch:[42] „Und er [Gott] hat eure Adoptivsöhne nicht zu euren wirklichen Söhnen gemacht." Dies könnte man als eine Art Einleitung verstehen zu der in den Versen 37–40 ausführlich behandelten Frage, ob es einem Gläubigen (*mu'min*) erlaubt ist, die Frau seines Adoptivsohnes zu heiraten. Und dieser Text mündet schließlich in das „Siegelwort" ein:

> Und als du zu demjenigen, dem Gott Gnade erwiesen hatte, und dem auch Du Gnade erwiesen hattest, sagtest: „Behalte deine Gattin für dich und fürchte Gott!", – insgeheim aber dachtest, was Gott offenbar macht, und die Menschen fürchtetest – (während du eher Gott fürchten solltest)! Als dann Zayd seine Angelegenheit mit ihr beendet hatte, gaben wir sie dir zur Frau, damit für die Gläubigen kein Anstoß (*ḥarağ*) darin bestünde, Frauen ihrer Adoptivsöhne zu heiraten, wenn diese ihre Angelegenheiten mit ihnen beendet haben. Gottes Befehl ist auszuführen. Der Prophet braucht keinen Anstoß (*ḥarağ*) daran zu nehmen, was Gott ihm als Brauch Gottes mit denen verordnete, die vor ihm dahingingen – Gottes Befehl ist Maß und Ziel! –, und die die Botschaften Gottes übermittelten und ihn und niemand sonst – als Gott allein – fürchteten. Genug an Gott als Richter! Und Mohammed ist nicht der Vater eines eurer Männer, sondern Bote Gottes und Siegel der Propheten. Und Gott weiß alle Dinge.

In dieser Passage ist durch das zweimal vorkommende Wort *ḥarağ* „Anstoß, Anstößigkeit" auf das Problematische der Situation eindeutig verwiesen. Die von Bouman gewählte Charakterisierung („fleischliche Genüsse") sollte man hier allerdings nicht verwenden; sicher ohne es zu wollen, ist Bouman das Opfer einer christlichen Auslegungstradition dieser Stelle geworden, die sich bis auf Johannes von Damaskus (gest. um 750) zurückverfolgen läßt.[43] Anderseits läßt freilich die Tatsache, daß zum Beispiel Ibn Isḥāqs Bearbeiter Ibn Hišām (gest. 830) diese Episode, die von Ibn Sa'd ausführlich geschildert wird,

41 So Fatima Mernissi, *Der politische Harem. Mohammed und die Frauen* (Frankfurt: Dagyeli, 1989), S. 137–138.

42 Hier und im folgenden folge ich der Übersetzung von Rudi Paret, *Der Koran*, Zweite, verbesserte Auflage (Stuttgart: Kohlhammer, 1982), nur in der Textauffassung, nicht jedoch im Wortlaut.

43 Vgl. Daniel J. Sahas, *John of Damascus on Islam. ‚The Heresy of the Ishmailites'* (Leiden: Brill, 1972), S. 91; Adel Theodor Khoury, *Les théologiens byzantins et l'islam. II. Polémique Byzantine contre l'Islam* (Münster, Lyon: Nauwelaerts, 1966), S. 91ff.

nicht bietet, die Schlußfolgerung zu, daß dieser Passus bereits in irgendeiner Weise als anstößig galt. Eine apologetische Tendenz des Korantextes ist sicherlich anzunehmen, doch dürfte diese ursprünglich nicht gegen Mohammeds eigene Anhängerschaft gerichtet gewesen sein. Dagegen spricht nämlich vor allem das als Abschluß fungierende „Siegelwort“. Das heißt, wenn Mohammed in dem zitierten Abschnitt bestreitet, daß sein Vorgehen etwas „Ehebrecherisches“ an sich hat, und daran eine theologisch so gewichtige „prophetologische“ Aussage anschließt, kann sich der Text nur an eine Adresse richten, die ihm gerade wegen dieses seines Verhaltens die Anerkennung seines prophetischen Anspruchs verweigert. Also bleiben nur die Juden von Medina als plausible „Adresse“.

Da es nun, außer dem Koran, keine direkten zeitgenössischen Quellen über die in Medina lebenden Juden gibt,[44] ist ein Umweg vonnöten. In der Mischna findet sich am Ende des Traktats *Sanhedrin*, der über Gerichtsangelegenheiten handelt, ein kurzer Abschnitt über den „falschen Propheten“ (*nabīʾ šäqär;* נביא שקר); unter den Merkmalen, an denen falsche Propheten zu erkennen sind, wird auch der Ehebruch genannt:[45] Im babylonischen Talmud findet sich dazu allerdings kein weiterer Kommentar. Dabei ist ganz allgemein zu berücksichtigen, daß das talmudische Material zu Fragen der Prophetie ziemlich spärlich ist, denn nach einer weit verbreiteten Ansicht, die zum Beispiel im Traktat *Baba Batra* (12a) dokumentiert ist, gibt es seit der Zerstörung des Tempels durch die Römer keine Prophetie mehr: „Nachfolger“ der Propheten sind die Weisen (*ḥākhamīm*, חכמים), das heißt die Rabbiner.[46] Für das rabbinische Judentum war die alte Prophetie primär der Gegenstand systematisierender Spekulation, die zum Beispiel folgende Fragen behandelten: War Prophetie auf Israel beschränkt? Was war der Charakter von Prophetie? Wie mußte ein Prophet beschaffen sein? Auf diese und ähnliche Fragen gibt das talmudische Material weit verstreute, oft anekdotenhafte Antworten. So heißt es zum Beispiel im Traktat *Šabbat* (92a), ein Prophet könne nur ein „weiser, tapferer, reicher und schön gewachsener Mann“ sein.[47] Die Nähe zum späteren islamischen Prophetenideal liegt hier auf der Hand. Aber darauf möchte ich nicht weiter eingehen.

Vielmehr möchte ich, zum Verständnis dieser Stelle, einen Umweg machen über Moses Maimonides (1135–1204). In zwei seiner arabisch geschriebenen

44 Vgl. noch immer Julius Wellhausen, „Medina vor dem Islam“, in idem, *Skizzen und Vorarbeiten*, Viertes Heft (Berlin: Reimer, 1889 = Nachdruck Berlin, New York: de Gruyter, 1985), S. 3–64. Siehe außerdem Michael Lecker, *Muslims, Jews & Pagans. Studies on Early Islamic Medina* (Islamic History and Civilization 13; Leiden: Brill, 1995).

45 Nur nebenbei sei erwähnt, daß er mit Erdrosseln zu ahnden ist.

46 Man fühlt sich dabei an den bekannten Ḥadīṯ von den „Gelehrten“ als den Erben des Propheten erinnert!

47 אין השכינה שורה אלא על חכם גבור ועשיר בעל קומה; siehe dazu Ernst Bass, *Die Merkmale der israelitischen Prophetie nach der traditionellen Auffassung des Talmud* (Berlin: Lamm, 1917) (Diss. Prag), S. 22.

Werke, dem großen Mischna-Kommentar und dem *Führer der Unschlüssigen* (*Dalālat al-ḥā'irīn*), entwickelt Maimonides eine ausführliche, philosophisch untermauerte Lehre von der „Prophetie";[48] dabei interpretiert und kommentiert er natürlich auch talmudisches Material,[49] so daß mit einer gewissen Vorsicht bestimmte Rückschlüsse möglich erscheinen. Im übrigen steht im Hintergrund von Maimonides' Überlegungen immer auch die Gestalt Mohammeds, und zwar in der Art, wie er von Alfarabi und Avicenna gezeichnet ist.[50] In unserem Zusammenhang ist zunächst eine Stelle aus Buch II (Kapitel 36) von Interesse, wo die ethisch-intellektuellen Voraussetzungen für einen Propheten dargelegt werden:[51]

> Ein [...] Mensch wird, durch Einwirkung von Erziehung und Wissenschaft, aus dem Vermögen zur Wirklichkeit gelangt, dann ein Prophet, wenn die menschliche Vernunft in ihm im vollkommensten und vollendetsten Zustande vorhanden, seine Charaktereigenschaften rein und gleichmäßig sind, wenn sein Verlangen ganz auf die Erkenntnis der Geheimnisse dieses Seienden und seiner Ursachen geht, seine Gedanken immer auf erhabene Dinge hinzielen und sein Augenmerk auf die Erkenntnis Gottes, auf die Betrachtung seiner Werke und dessen, was man von ihm glauben muß, gerichtet sind, und er zu denjenigen gehört, dessen Denken und Verlangen nach den tierischen Dingen bereits überwunden ist, nämlich das Verlangen nach Ergötzung an Speise, Trank oder Beischlaf [...].

Maimonides' Kommentator Isaak Abravanel (1437–1509) führt dazu Folgendes aus:

> There is no doubt that Maimonides, in this (proposition), by stipulating that he (the prophet) stand aloof both from all bodily pleasures and from the quest for domination and glory, refers to the nature of the prophet of the muslims, who was steeped in wickedness [...].[52]

Maimonides wird gegen Ende des 40. Kapitels jedoch noch konkreter; denn um den „wahren" Propheten vom „falschen" zu unterscheiden, ist das wichtigste Unterscheidungszeichen das Folgende, nämlich

---

48 Vgl. dazu Leo Strauss, „Maimunis Lehre von der Prophetie und ihre Quellen", in *Le Monde Orientale* XXVIII (1934), S. 99–139.

49 Vgl. dazu Bass, *Merkmale* (wie Anm. 47), S. 13.

50 Das sind die beiden wichtigsten Quellen für die Prophetologie des Maimonides; cf. Strauss, „Maimunis Lehre von der Prophetie" (wie Anm. 48), S. 112.

51 Moses Ben Maimon, *Führer der Unschlüssigen*. Übersetzung und Kommentar von Adolf Weiß (Philosophische Bibliothek 184a–c; Hamburg: Meiner, 1923–1924; Nachdruck 1972), Band II, S. 243.

52 Alvin Jay Reines, *Maimonides and Abrabanel on Prophecy* (Cincinnati: Hebrew Union College Press, 1970), S. 142.

> ob dieser die leiblichen Genüsse fahren läßt und sie verachtet, denn dies ist die erste Stufe für die Männer der Wissenschaft und umso mehr für die Propheten, – und insbesondere die Sinnlichkeit, die uns, wie Aristoteles sagt, zur Schande gereicht, und umso mehr den verächtlichsten von allen, den Beischlaf. Und deshalb hat Gott durch diesen mit besonderer Deutlichkeit jeden gekennzeichnet, der sich der Prophetengabe rühmt, damit die Wahrheit den Wahrheitsliebenden offenkundig werde, damit sie nicht selbst in Irrtum geraten und nicht andere irreführen.[53]

Daß Maimonides in seiner Ethik – man könnte sie geradezu „leibfeindlich“ nennen – hier mehr der aristotelischen als der genuin jüdischen Tradition verpflichtet ist, ist in diesem Zusammenhang nur am Rande von Belang. Entscheidend ist allein, daß er seiner Argumentation einen wichtigen alttestamentlichen Beispieltext anfügt, nämlich den Fall der beiden so genannten „Lügenpropheten“ Ahab Ben Kolaja und Zedekia Ben Maaseja, die, wie es bei Jeremia in einer Gottesrede (29:23) heißt,

> mit den Frauen ihrer Nächsten Ehebruch getrieben und in meinem Namen Worte geredet haben, die ich ihnen nicht aufgetragen habe.

Ich verkenne nicht die Problematik, die darin liegt, aus späteren literarischen Zeugnissen auf frühere Zustände schließen zu wollen. Aber dieses Zitat, das Maimonides im Zusammenhang des Themenkomplexes „Wahre versus Falsche Prophetie“ anführt, kann mit einiger Sicherheit als bereits altbekannt angesehen werden. Man könnte also vermuten, daß Mohammed mit der ausführlich zitierten Stelle aus Sure 33 jüdischen Vorwürfen, er sei wegen Ehebruchs als „falscher“ Prophet zu betrachten, entgegengetreten sei. Damit könnte der Zusammenhang, in dem das „Siegelwort“ steht, die prophetologische Relevanz gewinnen, die Colpe in dem oben genannten Aufsatz in ihm nicht sehen kann.[54]

So bliebe noch der von Wensinck wie von Bouman genannte zweite Aspekt zu behandeln, daß ein Prophet nach jüdischem Verständnis nicht nach politischer Herrschaft strebe. Diese Anschauung aber gründet sich nicht auf genuin jüdische Quellen, sondern zum größten Teil auf Äußerungen, die von den frühen arabischen Historikern als Äußerungen von Juden gekennzeichnet sind. Viel einleuchtender scheint mir die gerade aus jüdischen Quellen reichlich belegbare Auffassung, „Prophetie“ sei ein im Wesentlichen auf Israel beschränktes Phänomen. Diese Ansicht wird von Ibn Isḥāq auch – durchaus sachgerecht – den Juden in den Mund gelegt, die ʿAbdallāh Ibn Sallām, den damals prominentesten jüdischen Konvertiten, nach seiner Annahme des Islam zur Rede

53 Moses Ben Maimon, *Führer der Unschlüssigen* (wie Anm. 51), S. 266 (Kapitel 40, Ende).

54 Colpe, „Das Siegel der Propheten“ (wie Anm. 6), S. 71.

stellen:[55] „Prophetie gibt es unter den Arabern nicht, sondern dein Herr ist ein König", – das heißt jemand, der mit der spezifisch prophetischen Tradition der Juden gar nichts zu tun hat. In umgekehrter Akzentuierung findet sich bei aṭ-Ṭabarī (gest. 923) eine noch interessantere Stelle. Als Abū Sufyān, der Führer der mekkanischen Gegner Mohammeds, kurz vor seiner Annahme des Islam zu Mohammeds Oheim ʿAbbās sagt: „Die Macht (*mulk*) deines Neffen ist aber gewaltig geworden", antwortet dieser: „Wehe dir! Es ist das Prophetentum (*nubūwa*)."[56] Das heißt, dem heidnischen Mekkaner wird hier verdeutlicht, daß es sich hier um eine besondere Art der Macht handelt, der er sich jetzt beugen muß, einer Macht, die zugleich „Prophetie" ist.

Es steht hier nicht zur Diskussion, wie Mohammed seinen Anspruch als *nabīy* gegenüber den medinensischen Juden politisch durchgesetzt, sondern wie er diesen Anspruch theologisch begründet hat. Darauf gibt der Koran eine klare Antwort. Sie liegt in der Gestalt des „Gesandten und Propheten" Mose. Es kann wohl kaum auf Zufall beruhen, daß Mose die Prophetengestalt ist, von der im Koran am häufigsten die Rede ist. Es ist der bereits früher genannten Untersuchung von Prenner zu verdanken, daß die Mosegeschichten im Koran heute als Metaphern für die heilsgeschichtliche Konzeption der Sendung von Mohammed viel klarer verstehbar geworden sind. Liest man die Mosegeschichten unter diesem Gesichtspunkt, dann leuchtet es unmittelbar ein, daß es nach koranischer Konzeption keinen „Bruch" in der Entwicklung Mohammeds gibt: Mose als der Bußprediger vor dem Pharao, dann als der Herausführer seines Volkes aus Ägypten, dann als der Gesetzesverkünder in der Wüste. Eines ergibt sich zwingend aus dem anderen. Wenn es einen vergleichbaren „Wendepunkt" im Leben beider gibt, der aber eben keineswegs als „Bruch" interpretiert werden darf, so ist es der Exodus, der Auszug aus Ägypten hier, die Hiǧra, die Auswanderung nach Medina dort.

Ist die paradigmatische Bedeutung von Mose für Mohammed auf theologischer Ebene erst einmal erkannt, dann lassen sich leicht weitere Analogien finden. Dafür nur ein in meinen Augen besonders bedeutsames Beispiel. Zu Beginn von Sure 5, in der eine Reihe von Speisevorschriften eingeführt wird, häuft sich in auffälliger Weise der Gebrauch von *al-yawma* „heute"; der theologisch bedeutsamste Satz lautet: „Heute habe ich (an) euch eure Religion vollendet und meine Gnade an euch zu Ende gebracht und Gefallen gefunden am Islam als Religion für euch." Auf welchen Tag wird hier Bezug genommen? Nöldeke-Schwally gehen von irgendeinem Tag im letzten Lebensjahr Moham-

---

55 *Mā takūnu n-nubūwa fī l-ʿArab wa-lākinna ṣāḥibaka malik*, in *Das Leben Muhammed's nach Muhammed Ibn Ishâk bearbeitet von Abd el-Malik Ibn Hischâm*, ed. Ferdinand Wüstenfeld (Göttingen: Dieterich, 1858; Nachdruck Frankfurt am Main: Minerva, 1961), S. 400; vgl. Alfred Guillaume, *The Life of Muhammad. A translation of Ibn Isḥāq's Sīrat Rasūl Allāh* (Oxford: Oxford University Press, 1955 = Karachi, [6]1980), S. 270.

56 aṭ-Ṭabarī, *Annales* I (wie Anm. 40), S. 1633.

meds aus,[57] Erwin Gräf[58] – mit mehr Recht – von einem Datum kurz nach der Hiǧra, „als Mohammed noch um die Gunst der Juden geworben hat, als er sich noch zu zeigen bemühte, wie sehr er mit ihren Gesetzen vertraut war und mit ihnen übereinstimmte".

Meiner Ansicht nach ist jedoch die Frage als solche falsch gestellt. Um hier mehr Klarheit zu gewinnen, greife ich eine Anregung von Hartwig Hirschfeld auf.[59] Er spricht vom „deuteronomistischen" Charakter dieser Passage.[60] Was ist damit gemeint? Im 5. Buch Mose, dem Deuteronomium, beginnt Mose seine große Gesetzesrede, an deren Beginn die Zehn Gebote stehen, so: „Höre Israel, die Satzungen und Rechte, die ich euch heute verkündige ..." (Deuteronomium 5:1); und dieses „heute" zieht sich durch die ganze Rede, die der Erneuerung des Bundes am Horeb dient. In gleicher Weise scheint mir der Anfang von Sure 5 Teil einer solchen „Bundesrede" zu sein, auf die auch der bereits zitierte Vers aus Sure 33:7 verweist:

> Und als wir von den Propheten ihre Verpflichtung entgegennahmen, – und zwar von dir, von Noah, von Abraham, von Mose und Jesus, dem Sohn der Maria, – da nahmen wir von ihnen eine feste Verpflichtung entgegen.

Ein solcher Bundesschluß ist nun aber, pointiert formuliert, nicht Teil der Geschichte, sondern der Heilsgeschichte, er ist sozusagen ein „kerygmatisches" Datum und als solches historisch nicht festzumachen.

Hirschfelds Hinweis kann aber heute in noch ganz anderer Weise fruchtbar gemacht werden. Unter dem „Deuteronomisten" ist ein Bearbeiter der historischen Bücher des Alten Testaments zu verstehen, in dessen Konzeption den Propheten als den Predigern des Einen Gottes eine besondere Rolle zufällt. Hier findet sich erstmals der Gedanke vom „gewaltsamen Geschick" der Propheten, der auch im Koran wiederkehrt. Im Buch Deuteronomium (5. Mose) selber aber findet sich eine äußerst wichtige Passage über Wahrsager aller Art und wahre und falsche Propheten (Kapitel 18,9ff.). Und in diesem Kapitel

57 Nöldeke, *Geschichte des Qorāns* (wie Anm. 19), S. 228.

58 Erwin Gräf, *Jagdbeute und Schlachttier im islamischen Recht. Eine Untersuchung zur Entwicklung der islamischen Jurisprudenz* (Bonn: Orientalisches Seminar, 1959), S. 52.

59 Hartwig Hirschfeld, *New Researches into the Composition and Exegesis of the Qoran* (Asiatic Society Monographs 3; London: Royal Asiatic Society, 1902), S. 133.

60 „Such speeches of a deuteronomic character form the framework of Sûra V., the bulk of which was preached on the occasion of the last pilgrimage in the presence of a huge congregation. – We can take it for granted that Muhammad was acquainted with the Jewish interpretation of the character of the Deuteronomy as a repetitional injunction of the Law (*Mishnêh Tôrâh*). Why not follow this example? As an exterior deuteronomic feature in the first portion of our *sûra* I regard the three instances of *alyauma* ('today,' vv. 4.5.7 [i.e.: 3 bis. 5]), which in the same application is particular frequent in the Biblical book of Deuteronomy."

verkündet Mose den „Kindern Israel“: „Einen Propheten wie mich wird dir der Herr, Dein Gott, aus der Mitte deiner Brüder erstehen lassen; auf den sollt ihr hören“ (Deuteronomium 18:15).

Ich hatte vorhin den wichtigen Satz aus Sure 7:157–158 über den „arabischen“ beziehungsweise „heidnischen Propheten“ zitiert, in dem gesagt wird, daß die „Buchbesitzer“ „von ihm bei sich geschrieben finden in der Thora und im Evangelium“. Es ist keineswegs abwegig, darin einen Hinweis auf die eben zitierte Stelle aus Deuteronomium 18:15 zu sehen, so wie es die muslimische Apologetik übrigens schon immer tat.[61]

Um zusammenzufassen: Mohammeds Prophetentum, so wie der Koran es darstellt, ist auf charakteristische Weise mit der Gestalt des Mose in eine typologische Beziehung gebracht. Das uns hier begegnende Bild des Mose ist deutlich den Anschauungen des Judentums und Judenchristentums verpflichtet. Und an dieser Mosegestalt konnte für Mohammed die Idee der Theokratie reifen: „Fürchtet Gott und folgt seinem Gesandten!“ Und wie Jesus nach judenchristlicher Anschauung als Prophet die Prophetie des Mose „bestätigte“ und „vollendete“, so vollendete aus koranischer Sicht auch Mohammed das Werk des Mose.

61 Vgl. Hava Lazarus-Yafeh, *Intertwined Worlds. Medieval Islam and Bible Criticism*, (Princeton: Princeton University Press, 1992), S. 104.

Kulturtransfer: Die Sendung des Propheten und die Antwort des Rabbi*

von

Friedrich Niewöhner

Herzog August Bibliothek Wolfenbüttel

Vorwort

Abraham Geiger veröffentlichte 1833 in Bonn eine inzwischen berühmt gewordene Schrift mit dem Titel *Was hat Muhammed aus dem Judenthume aufgenommen?* Zahlreiche Untersuchungen mit ähnlichen Fragestellungen sind seitdem erschienen, ich erwähne nur Hartwig Hirschfelds *Jüdische Elemente im Qoran* (1878), Joseph Horovitz' *Koranische Untersuchungen* (1926), Abraham I. Katsh's *Judaism in Islam* und Heinrich Speyers bis heute maßgebliche Untersuchung über *Die biblischen Erzählungen im Qoran.*[1] Eine grundlegende Abhandlung mit umgekehrter Fragerichtung fehlt bis heute jedoch: „Was haben die Juden dem Koran entnommen?" Diese Frage scheint auf den ersten Blick etwas eigenartig, ist doch die historische Abfolge der Religionen diese: Judentum – Christentum – Islam. Sieht man jedoch genau hin, dann fällt Folgendes auf: Die erste Formulierung jüdischer „Dogmen"-*Ikkarīm* („Grundlehren") – geschah in den sechziger Jahren des 12. Jahrhunderts durch Mose ben Maimon (Maimonides, 1135–1204) in dessen *Kommentar zur Mischna,* das heißt exakt 533 Jahre *nach* dem Tod Muhammads und 33 Jahre vor dem Tod des letzten großen islamischen Philosophen, Ibn Rušd (Averroes), den Maimonides sehr bewunderte. Maimonides schrieb diesen Kommentar auf Arabisch (mit hebräischen Buchstaben) in Kairo, also in einer muslimischen Umwelt,

---

* [Krankheitsbedingt konnte der Autor seinen Beitrag nicht weiter bearbeiten. G. T.]

1 Abraham Geiger, *Was hat Mohammed aus dem Judenthume aufgenommen?* [Bonn 1833] Mit einem Vorwort herausgegeben von Friedrich Niewöhner (Jüdische Geistesgeschichte 5; Berlin: Parerga, 2005); Hartwig Hirschfeld, *Jüdische Elemente im Qoran* (Berlin: Selbstverlag, 1878); Joseph Horovitz, *Koranische Untersuchungen* (Berlin: de Gruyter, 1926); Abraham I. Katsh, *Judaism in Islam: Biblical and Talmudic Backgrounds* (New York: New York University Press, 1954; 2. Auflage unter dem Titel *Judaism and the Koran* [New York: Barnes, 1962]); Heinrich Speyer, *Die biblischen Erzählungen im Qoran* (Gräfenhainichen: Schulze, 1931; Hildesheim: Olms, ²1961).

die er sehr aufmerksam verfolgte. Auch wenn er den Koran nicht zitiert, so kann doch nachgewiesen werden, dass er ihn gut gekannt hat. Darüber hinaus war Maimonides auch ein intimer Kenner der verschiedenen Strömungen der islamischen Theologie (der Muʿtazila und der Ašʿarīya), wie die letzten sechs Kapitel seines philosophischen Hauptwerkes, dem *Führer der Unschlüssigen*, eindrucksvoll zeigen. Man muss weiterhin davon ausgehen, dass viele Formulierungen des Maimonides „*stillschweigende* Zurückweisungen der von den muhammedanischen Theologen ausgehenden Angriffe" gegen die jüdischen Glaubensinhalte sind, auch wenn „eine *offene* Bezugnahme auf dieselben [...] sich bei den älteren jüdischen Dogmatikern nicht" findet – so Ignaz Goldziher 1900 in einem Aufsatz über „Die Sabbath-Institution im Islam".[2]

Um die jüdische Philosophie des Mittelalters – mit Ausnahme von Joseph Albo, er schrieb sein *Sefer ha-Ikkarīm* („Buch der Grundlehren") 1425 auf Hebräisch in einem spanisch-christlichen Umfeld – zu verstehen, muss man also, das ist meine generelle Forderung,

1. die Schriften der jüdischen Philosophen im *arabischen* Original lesen; nur so können die sprachlichen und terminologischen Anspielungen auf islamische Positionen verstanden werden. Die maimonidischen *loquentes* bei Thomas von Aquin sind keine Schwätzer oder Vielredner, wie die hebräische Version des *Führers* durch Ibn Tibbon (*medabberīm*) nahe legt, sondern es sind die islamischen Theologen, die *mutakallimūn*, die Maimonides studiert hat und zitiert.
2. Wer die jüdischen Philosophen des Mittelalters studiert, sollte außerdem etwas vertraut sein mit den islamischen Denkrichtungen – wie es Maimonides selbst ja auch war. Vor allem aber sollte ein solcher Forscher den Koran kennen. Diese Forderung ist, so weit ich sehe, bis jetzt noch nicht erhoben worden, und der Grund dafür scheint mir folgender: Die jüdischen Philosophen zitieren den Koran nicht, und es fällt einem Leser darum gar nicht auf, wenn in einem philosophischen Text „stillschweigend" eine Beziehung zum Koran hergestellt wird. Der „Philosoph" – *al-faylasūf* – wird oft genannt (Aristoteles), und man muss ihn kennen. Muhammad wird nie genannt, höchstens als „der Verrückte" (*maǧnūn*) verhöhnt – dennoch ist er allgegenwärtig, denn er und seine Anhänger, nicht Aristoteles oder Platon, waren diejenigen, die für die Juden im islamischen Kulturraum die eigentliche Gefahr darstellten – gerade weil Muhammad viel dem Judentum entnommen hatte, er von sich behauptete, die Nachfolge des Moses angetreten zu haben, er sich selbst als „Siegel der Propheten"[3] verstand (Sure 33:40). Das Entstehen von jüdischen Grundlehren

2 In *Gedenkbuch zur Erinnerung an David Kaufmann*, ed. Marcus Brann et al. (Breslau: S. Schottlaender, 1900), S. 86–101.

3 Vgl. dazu den gleichnamigen Beitrag von Hartmut Bobzin, oben S. 289–306.

(Glaubensartikeln) kann nicht nur inner-jüdisch erklärt werden, erst die Einbeziehung des Islam in seiner Gegnerschaft zum Judentum macht auch schwer zu erklärende Formulierungen dieser Grundlehren deutlich. Im Mittelalter steht Moses immer im Schatten Muhammeds.

Moses

„Dies ist eine Schrift, die wir (als Offenbarung) zu dir hinabgesandt haben, damit du die Menschen mit der Erlaubnis ihres Herrn aus der Finsternis heraus ins Licht bringst." So spricht Gott in Sure 14, Vers 1 zu *Muhammad*. Vier Verse später heißt es: „Und wir haben den *Moses* mit unseren Zeichen gesandt (mit dem Auftrag): Bring dein Volk aus der Finsternis heraus ans Licht."

Der göttliche Auftrag an Muhammad scheint identisch zu sein mit dem an Moses. Nicht nur Muhammad ist Gottes Prophet (*nabīy*) und Gesandter (*rasūl*), auch von Moses heißt es in Sure 19, Vers 54: „Er war ein Auserlesener und ein Gesandter (*rasūl*) und ein Prophet (*nabīy*)": *wa-kāna rasūlan nabīyan*. Diese doppelte Funktion haben im Koran nur Muhammad und Moses. Die Sonderstellung des Moses unter allen anderen Propheten wird in der Torah zweimal betont:

1. Numeri 12:6–8: „Hört meine Worte: Ist jemand unter euch ein Prophet des Herrn, dem will ich mich kundmachen in Gesichten oder will mit ihm reden in Träumen. Aber so steht es nicht mit meinem Knecht Mose [...]. Von Mund zu Mund rede ich mit ihm, nicht durch dunkle Worte oder Gleichnisse [...]."
2. Deuteronomium 34:10: „Und es stand hinfort kein Prophet in Israel auf wie Moses, den der Herr erkannt hatte von Angesicht zu Angesicht."

Diese Verse demonstrieren die Sonderstellung Moses unter den Propheten. Da ist aber ein kleines Problem, das die Rabbiner schon früh erkannt hatten: In der *Sifra* zu Deuteronomium 34:10 heißt es: „Es stand aber kein Prophet mehr auf in Israel wie Moses – in Israel nicht, aber wohl unter den anderen Nationen (und dies ist Bileam)". Um die Sonderstellung des Prophetentums Moses ein für alle Mal zu garantieren, bedarf es also eines weiteren Zusatzes, der ein „außerhalb Israels" (unter den anderen Nationen) ausschließt. Dieser Zusatz findet sich in

3. Exodus 33:16–17: „Denn woran soll erkannt werden, dass ich [Moses] und dein Volk vor deinen Augen Gnade gefunden haben, wenn nicht daran, dass du mit uns gehest, so dass ich und dein Volk erhoben werden vor allen Völkern, die auf dem Erdboden sind? Der Herr sprach zu Moses: Auch das, was du jetzt gesagt hast, will ich tun."

Dieses Versprechen Gottes an Moses macht sicher: Da ganz Israel über alle Völker erhaben ist, kann gar kein Prophet außerhalb Israel auftreten, der größer ist als der einzigartige Moses in Israel.

Über Jesus braucht nicht geredet zu werden, denn er war Jude, erhob sich in Israel und hatte keinen Erfolg. Doch dann passierten zwei Katastrophen:

a) Der Tempel wurde im Jahre 70 zerstört, und die Juden wurden zerstreut in alle Welt. „In Israel" war nun kein Kriterium mehr, da es dieses schlichtweg nicht mehr gab.
b) „Unter den anderen Nationen", außerhalb Israels, stand ein Prophet auf, der ab dem Jahr 622 einen ganz ungeheueren Erfolg hatte: Muhammad. Dieser verglich sich mit Moses und behauptete, *größer* als dieser zu sein. Und Muhammad gründete ein Reich, das viel herrlicher und mächtiger war als das des Moses. Konnten die Juden nach Muhammad noch an der Einzigartigkeit der Person des Moses festhalten? Man konnte an dieser Tatsache „Islam" nicht einfach vorbeischauen. Nicht, dass nun die Singularität des Moses geschmälert wurde, doch man sah sie in einem neuen Licht – und sie bedurfte einer Stütze.

Maimonides

Die Sonderstellung des Moses unter den Propheten wird von Maimonides in seinem *Kommentar zur Mischna* im Rahmen der von ihm formulierten *13 Grundlehren* (*Ikkarīm*, arabisch: *uṣūl*) ausdrücklich hervorgehoben. In der 7. Grundlehre schreibt Maimonides, die Prophetie des Moses, des „Vaters aller Propheten", unterscheide sich in vier Punkten von der Prophetie aller übrigen Propheten:

1. Mit Moses hat Gott nicht durch ein Medium sondern „von Mund zu Mund" gesprochen (Numeri 12:8).
2. Zu Moses kam die Prophetie nicht im Schlaf, sondern in einem wachen Zustand.
3. Während alle anderen Propheten während der prophetischen Inspiration zitterten und sich fürchteten, hatte Moses keine Furcht.
4. Über alle anderen Propheten kam die Prophetie nach Gottes Willen. Moses aber prophezeite „zu jeder Zeit, da er wollte".

In dieser Reihung fällt auf: Von *Wundern* des Moses ist in diesem Abschnitt *nicht* die Rede. 25 Jahre später schreibt Maimonides die *Mišneh Torah,* worin er noch einmal fragt: „Wie unterscheidet sich Moses von den anderen Propheten?" Wieder werden diese vier Punkte aufgezählt. Wieder werden irgendwelche *Wunder* mit *keinem* Wort erwähnt. Um Wunder nicht erwähnen zu *müssen,* vermeidet Maimonides im Mischna-Kommentar wie in der *Mišneh*

Torah auch den Hinweis auf den Torah-Vers, den der Leser in einer Abhandlung über die Sonderstellung des Moses eigentlich erwarten musste: Deuteronomium 34:10 „Und es stand hinfort kein Prophet in Israel auf wie Moses". Und er stand nicht auf, Perfekt, *we-lo qām*. Denn die nächsten zwei Verse des Deuteronomiums thematisieren „all die Zeichen und Wunder, mit denen der Herr Moses gesandt hatte, dass er sie täte". Maimonides zitiert Deuteronomium 34:10 darum nicht, weil er die Wunder Moses' nicht erwähnen *wollte*.

Diese vier Punkte der speziellen Prophetengabe des Moses sind zu einem *locus classicus* geworden, auch Josef Albo wird sie 1425 in seinem *Sefer Ikkarīm* („Buch der Grundlehren") mit ausdrücklicher Berufung auf Maimonides aufzählen. Albo spricht im Anschluss an diese Aufzählung zwar dann auch von Wundern, da aber bei Albo die Besonderheit des Prophetentums des Moses – im Gegensatz zu Maimonides – *keine* Grundlehre des Judentums ist, spielt diese Wundererwähnung als Anhang zu den vier Charakteristika eigentlich keine wesentliche Rolle. Albo sagt an anderer Stelle auch ausdrücklich, dass „alle Zeichen und Wunder" des Moses „*vor* der Gesetzgebung" geschehen seien und nur zeigten, dass Moses Zeichen und Wunder vollbringen konnte. „Dennoch lieferten sie keinen wesentlichen Beweis für seine Prophetengabe."

Die Wunder des Moses sind *vor* seiner Gesetzgebung am Sinai geschehen. Für seine Legitimation als Gesetzgeber spielen sie keine Rolle, für die Beschreibung seiner Sonderstellung unter den Propheten werden sie bei Maimonides überhaupt nicht, bei Albo nur als Anhang um der Vollständigkeit willen erwähnt.

Vergangenheit und Zukunft

Maimonides schreibt im *Führer der Unschlüssigen*, im 2. Buch, Kapitel 35: „Ich habe bereits für jedermann die vier Unterschiede klar gemacht, durch welche sich die Prophetie Moses' von der der übrigen Propheten unterscheidet, und habe es im *Mischnakommentar* und in der *Mišneh Torah* begründet und klar gemacht. Es ist also nicht notwendig, es zu wiederholen." Und dann spricht Maimonides – von den *Wundern* Moses, denn sie seien „nicht von der Gattung der Wunder, welche die übrigen Propheten vollbrachten". Und nun endlich zitiert Maimonides Deuteronomium 34:10–12, um die Verse mit seinen Worten zu paraphrasieren: „und keiner *wird* auftreten, der das erkennen *wird*, was Moses erkannt hat, und keiner *wird* das tun, was er getan hat." Die Aussage der Torah steht im Perfekt (stand auf), Maimonides paraphrasiert sie im Futur („wird aufstehen"), *yaqūm*. Dieser Tempus-Wechsel scheint Maimonides wichtig, denn er wiederholt ihn kurz darauf.

Halten wir fest: Moses zeichnet sich jetzt von allen Propheten dadurch aus, dass er Wunder getan hat, die so einmalig sind, dass sie nie wieder von einem Propheten übertroffen werden können. Warum spricht Maimonides jetzt von Wundern und warum formuliert er im Futur? Einen Hinweis auf die mögliche Beantwortung dieser Fragen gibt Maimonides in seiner Interpretation von „in Israel" („Und es stand hinfort kein Prophet in Israel auf wie Moses"): Die Wunder des Moses unterscheiden sich von denen der anderen jüdischen Propheten wie von denen „seiner *Nachfolger unter den übrigen Völkern*". Welche Propheten anderer religiöser Nationen, nichtjüdischer Völker, kann Maimonides hier meinen? In der *Mišneh Torah* unterscheidet Maimonides zwischen Propheten „aus Israel" (*mi-yisrael*) und Propheten „aus den Völkern" (*min ha-ummōt*), wobei *ha-ummōt* für „Nicht-Juden" steht. Wer ist der Prophet, der von Maimonides als „Nachfolger" des Moses bei den *ummōt* bezeichnet wird? Es kann nur der Prophet gemeint sein, von dem der in Fusṭāṭ (Kairo) lebende Autor ständig hörte und der sein Prophetentum in geradezu exzeptioneller Weise mit der Sendung des Moses verglichen und sich als dessen Nachfolger verstanden hatte: Muhammad.

Die Höhen

Mūsā (Moses) ist die biblische Gestalt, die im Koran am häufigsten erwähnt wird. Er wird 136-mal genannt (Abraham nur 69-mal), in 35 Suren wird sein Leben detailliert geschildert. Im Mittelpunkt der koranischen Moses-Erzählungen stehen die „Zeichen" und Wunder, die Moses vollbracht hat. Die Gesetzgebung am Sinai wird dagegen nur beiläufig abgehandelt. Muhammad war nicht interessiert an den Inhalten der sinaitischen Offenbarung, sondern allein an der Person Moses als wundertätiger Führer seines Volkes – das heißt an dem Moses vor den Ereignissen am Sinai. In dem „Staatsmann" Moses fand Muhammad sein Vorbild. Wie eng er seine eigene Sendung mit der des Moses verknüpft sah, geht besonders aus Sure 7 („Die Höhen") hervor, in der er lange die Moses-Geschichte erzählt. Die Moses-Erzählung in Sure 7, Vers 154–158 endet folgendermaßen:

> Und als sich Moses' Zorn gelegt hatte, nahm er die Tafeln [wieder auf]. In ihrem Text ist Rechtleitung und Barmherzigkeit enthalten für diejenigen, die vor ihrem Herrn Angst haben. [...] „Du bist unser Freund. Vergib uns nun und erbarme dich unser! Du kannst am besten vergeben. Und bestimme uns hier im Diesseits Gutes, und [ebenso] im Jenseits! Wir haben [in gläubiger Hingabe] an dich das Judentum angenommen." Gott sagte: „Mit meiner Strafe treffe ich, wen ich will. Aber meine Barmherzigkeit kennt keine Grenzen. Und ich werde sie denen zukommen lassen, die gottesfürchtig sind und die Almosensteuer geben

> und die an unsere Zeichen glauben, – [denen,] die dem Gesandten, dem heidnischen Propheten, folgen, den sie bei sich in der Torah und im Evangelium verzeichnet finden und der ihnen gebietet was recht ist, verbietet, was verwerflich ist, die guten Dinge für erlaubt und die schlechten für verboten erklärt und ihre drückende Verpflichtung und die Fesseln, die auf ihnen lagen, abnimmt. Denen nun, die an ihn glauben, ihm Hilfe und Beistand leisten und dem Licht folgen, das mit ihm herabgesandt worden ist, wird es wohl ergehen.
>
> Sag: Ihr Menschen! Ich bin der Gesandte Gottes an euch alle, [desselben Gottes,] der die Herrschaft über Himmel und Erde hat. Es gibt keinen Gott außer ihm. Er macht lebendig und lässt sterben. Darum glaubt an Gott und seinen Gesandten, den heidnischen Propheten, der [seinerseits] an Gott und seine Worte glaubt, und folgt ihm! Vielleicht werdet ihr euch [dann] rechtleiten lassen."

Dieser Text ist erklärungsbedürftig, auf drei Aspekte möchte ich hinweisen:

1) Muhammad sagt, der Text der Tafeln, die Moses empfangen habe, enthalte „Rechtleitung und Barmherzigkeit", arabisch *hudan wa-raḥma.* Mit diesen beiden Begriffen wird im Koran sonst allein die koranische Offenbarung charakterisiert: „Dies sind die Verse der weisen Schrift – eine Rechtleitung und Barmherzigkeit für die Frommen" (Sure 31, Vers 2–3).
2) In Vers 156 passiert ein eigenartiger Wechsel. Dieser Vers „bildet den Übergang von dem Bericht über die Zeitgeschichte Moses zu der Bezugnahme auf Mohammeds eigene Zeit."[4] Nahtlos geht dieser Vers von Moses auf Muhammad über. Nach dem Ende der Rede Moses und seiner Bitte an Gott, spricht dieser von seiner Barmherzigkeit denen gegenüber, die seinen Zeichen glauben, gottesfürchtig sind und (Vers 157) „dem Gesandten, dem heidnischen Propheten folgen". Die Bitte des Moses an Gott beantwortet dieser mit einer Aufforderung, seinem Gesandten Muhammad zu folgen. Muhammad hat Moses Erbfolge angetreten, ihn gewissermaßen überboten, ihn ersetzt.
3) Muhammad wird bezeichnet als „Gesandter, der heidnische Prophet", arabisch: *ar-rasūla n-nabīya l-ummīya.* Das ist eine höchst merkwürdige Wendung. *rasūl* (Gesandter) und *nabīy* (Prophet) bedarf keiner Erklärung, wohl aber das Adjektiv *ummī,* das abgeleitet ist von *umma,* Volk, Nation. Die Koran-Kommentatoren vermuten, dass das arabische Wort *umma* abgeleitet worden ist aus der hebräischen Bezeichnung *ummōt ha-ʿolam,* „die Völker der Welt" im Gegensatz zum Volk Israel. Gott verweist in seiner Rede an Moses in Sure 7 also auf den Gesandten und Propheten Muhammad, der nicht in Israel entstand, „wohl aber unter den anderen Nationen", außerhalb Israels. Muhammad wird in Sure 7 gegenüber den Juden also als genau der bezeichnet, von dem die Rabbinen vermutet hatten (im

---

4 Rudi Paret, *Der Koran. Kommentar und Konkordanz* (Stuttgart: Kohlhammer, 1971), S. 171.

Anschluss an Deuteronomium 34:10), dass solch ein Prophet einmal erstehen könne: „in Israel nicht, aber wohl unter den anderen Nationen." Moses wurde im Koran als „Gesandter und Prophet" bezeichnet, Muhammad nun als „Gesandter und Prophet, der nach Moses erstand in den Völkern der Welt". Das ist eine Katastrophe – und Maimonides antwortet *hierauf* in Kapitel 35 des *Führers der Unschlüssigen*: Moses unterscheide sich nicht nur von allen seinen Nachfolgern in Israel, sondern auch von seinen möglichen Nachfolgern „unter den übrigen Völkern". Maimonides benutzt in seinem arabischen Text dieses koranisch-arabische Wort: *umma,* Plural: *umam.* (Das ist das hebräische Wort *ummōt* der *Mišneh Torah.*) Und darum liest Maimonides Deuteronomium 34 futurisch: „und es *wird* kein Prophet auftreten wie Moses." Die schon erwähnte rabbinische Stelle sei hier nochmals und zwar ganz zitiert: „Es stand hinfort kein Prophet auf in Israel, der Moses geglichen hätte. In Israel stand keiner auf, aber unter den Völkern der Welt stand einer auf, damit sie keine Ausrede hätten und nicht von sich sagen sollten: Hätten wir einen Propheten gehabt, wie Moses einer war, wir hätten gleichfalls Gott gedient." Sure 5 („Der Tisch") scheint auf diese Überlegung der Rabbinen zu antworten: „Unser Gesandter ist nunmehr zu euch gekommen, um euch während einer Zwischenzeit (in der Reihe) der Gesandten Klarheit zu geben, damit ihr (nicht etwa) sagt: ‚Zu uns ist kein Verkünder froher Botschaft und kein Warner gekommen.' Nun ist ja ein Verkünder froher Botschaft und ein Warner zu euch gekommen. Gott hat zu allem die Macht." *Musste* Maimonides solche und ähnliche Koran-Verse nicht auf die Moses-Berichte in der jüdischen Tradition beziehen? Kannte Maimonides vielleicht folgenden Ausspruch Muhammads: „Wenn Moses bis zu meiner Zeit lebte, so wäre ihm nichts anderes möglich, als mir zu folgen." (Maimonides hätte diesen Satz bei Averroes lesen können.) Darum musste Maimonides den rabbinischen Text abändern in: „Es *wird* kein Prophet mehr aufstehen […], auch unter den Völkern der Welt nicht!". Das heißt: Kapitel 35 ist, was bis jetzt noch kein Forscher erkannt hat, eine direkte Antwort und Entgegnung des Anspruches Muhammads in Sure 7, er sei der Nachfolger Moses unter den Völkern der Welt (*be-ummōt ha-ʿolam*).

Im Koran ist Moses als der Prophet vorgestellt worden, der die meisten und größten Wunder vollbrachte. Maimonides musste darum seine früher geschriebenen vier Charakteristika der Sonderstellung Moses' um ein weiteres vermehren: Auch die Wunder, die Moses getan hat, haben eine Sonderstellung, weshalb Muhammad nicht sein „Nachfolger unter den Völkern" sein kann. Da Muhammad selbst kein einziges Wunder vollbracht hat, ist er damit widerlegt, und sein Anspruch in Sure 7, er sei der Nachfolger Moses', ist hinfällig. Muhammad ist das, als was Maimonides ihn schon in seinem „Brief an den Jemen" bezeichnet hatte: ein Betrüger.

Der „heidnische" Prophet im Koran ist nach muslimischer Auslegung ein Prophet, der – so Ibn Sīnā – die Fähigkeit zur *unmittelbaren* Erkenntnis besitzt, das heißt, dass er nicht auf Unterricht angewiesen ist. Noch deutlicher formuliert dies Ibn Rušd: „Man weiß, dass der Prophet [nämlich Muhammed] Illiterat war in einem illiteraten, gemeinen, nomadischen Volke, das sich nie mit Wissenschaften abgegeben und dem man nie ein Wissen zugeschrieben, das sich nie mit Untersuchungen über die existierenden Dinge beschäftigt hat, wie die Griechen und andere Völker, bei denen die Philosophie in langen Zeiträumen vollendet wurde." Ibn Rušd beruft sich zur Bekräftigung seiner Ansicht auf drei Koranstellen. Diese Ansicht ist tatsächlich die orthodoxe Lehre des Islam. Maimonides' nachdrückliche Hervorhebung der Notwendigkeit des Unterrichts für den Propheten zur Erlangung eines vollkommenen Verstandes (*Moreh Nevukhim* II.32, 36, 38, 42) dürfte also als Polemik gegen den Islam zu verstehen sein: Er akzeptiert die islamische Tatsachenbehauptung, dass Muhammed keinerlei Unterricht gehabt habe, findet aber durch sie bereits anerkannt, dass Muhammeds Anspruch, Prophet zu sein, unberechtigt ist. Es bleibt dabei: Muhammad kann nichts anderes als ein Betrüger sein.

Torah

Nach der 7. der *Ikkarīm*, worin Maimonides die Sonderstellung des Moses begründet hatte, lässt er noch die Grundlehre folgen, „dass die Torah vom Himmel ist" (Nr. 8). Das heißt: Die Torah ist göttlich. Das begründet Maimonides ausführlich, nicht ohne den Hinweis auf Psalm 119:18: „Öffne mir die Augen, dass ich schaue Wunder aus deiner Torah." Die Torah selbst ist das Wunder – wenn Maimonides diesen Vers zitiert, tut er das sicher auch im Hinblick auf den Islam, dem der Koran als das einzige und eigentliche Wunder gilt (*iʿǧāz*). Doch nicht genug damit: Maimonides fügt noch eine weitere Grundlehre hinzu, die von der Unabänderlichkeit der Torah (Nr. 9):

> Die neunte Grundlehre betrifft die Aufhebung. Sie bedeutet, dass dieses Gesetz nicht aufgehoben wird und dass keine andere Torah außer ihr von Gott her ist und man ihr nichts hinzufügen und von ihr nichts fortlassen darf, weder im Text [der „schriftlichen Torah"] noch in der Erklärung [der „mündlichen Torah"], denn es heißt: „Du sollst dazu nichts hinzufügen und nichts davon weglassen".

Nach der Sonderstellung Moses' unter den Propheten und nach der Göttlichkeit der Torah wird nun auch noch deren Unabänderlichkeit als Grundsatz erhoben. Aber ist dieser 9. *Ikkar* wirklich notwendig? Josef Albo weist zu Recht darauf hin, dass sich für die Grundlehre von der Unabänderlichkeit der Torah in der Torah selbst „kein Beweis" findet. Albo sagt: „Die von Maimonides angeführten Beweisgründe [für die Unabänderlichkeit der Torah] haben für mich durchaus keine Kraft, auch sehe ich sonst die Notwendigkeit nicht ein, warum es ein besonderer Grundsatz der göttlichen Lehre überhaupt, oder der Mosaischen ins Besondere sein müsse, dass an der Lehre Nichts modificirt und sie nicht verändert werden würde [dürfe]".[5] Albo hat Maimonides nicht verstanden, beziehungsweise nicht verstanden, warum Maimonides diesen *Ikkar* hinzufügen musste. Albo nämlich lebte unter Christen in Spanien, Maimonides jedoch unter Muslimen in Ägypten. Er hielt den *Ikkar* von der Unabänderlichkeit für notwendig, weil die Gefahr bestand, dass ein neuer Prophet die Gültigkeit der Torah in Frage stellen könnte – nicht ein Irgendwer, sondern ein Prophet von der Qualität eines Moses, ein Prophet, der seine eigene Sendung als Fortführung und Vollendung der Sendung Moses' verstand: Muhammad.

Maimonides musste zu den Grundlehren von der Sonderstellung des Moses und der Göttlichkeit der Torah noch die Grundlehre von der Unabänderlichkeit der Torah aufstellen, weil Muhammad

a) sich als Vollender der Sendung Moses und als dessen Nachfolger ansah,
b) der Koran auch als „vom Himmel" und göttlich interpretiert wurde (nicht als Schrift des Muhammad).

Der letzte „Rettungsanker" vor dem Propheten der *ummōt* war also das Insistieren auf der Unabänderlichkeit der Torah.

Albo

Meine These von der Abhängigkeit der jüdischen „Dogmen" (*Ikkarīm*) von dem Auftreten und der Botschaft Muhammads wird bestätigt durch einen längeren Passus bei Albo:

> Immer aber bleibt es zu verwundern, warum Maimonides, da er die Prophetengabe Mosis als Grundsatz aufstellte, und die Differenzpunkte zwischen Mosis und Anderer Prophetie angebend, ausspricht, daß alle vor- und nachmosaische Propheten eine niedrigere Stufe einnehmen, dann auch noch die Unabänderlichkeit und Unwandelbarkeit des Gesetzes als besondern Grundsatz aufstellt? Augenscheinlich that er dies, von der Ansicht ausgehend, daß ohne diesen Grundsatz man wohl geneigt seyn könnte, *einem andern Propheten zu der Abschaffung*

5 Albo wird nach der folgenden Übersetzung wiedergegeben: Josef Albo, *Buch Ikkarim. Grund- und Glaubenslehren der Mosaischen Religion*. Nach den ältesten und correctesten Ausgaben in's Deutsche übertragen von Wolf Schlessinger, eingeleitet von Ludwig Schlesinger. Frankfurt am Main 1844 = 2. Auflage Berlin: Lamm, 1922 (Die religionsphilosophischen Werke des Judentums 8).

> *des Mosaischen Gesetzes Gehör zu geben.* Ist aber, wie er selbst schreibt, Moses größer als alle nachfolgende Propheten, so wäre es gewiß höchst sonderbar, wenn wir einen andern ihm vorziehen könnten! [...] Weil jedoch ein Spitzfindiger sophistisch demonstriren dürfte, *dass unter den übrigen Völkern später wohl ein Moses ähnlicher oder größerer Prophet aufstehen könnte,* haben wir Mosis Prophetie nicht zum Folgesatz sondern als einen Zweig zum Berufe des Gesandten aufgestellt, um damit zu sagen, daß man unmöglich Mosis Gesetz auf die Dauer aboliren kann, wenn die Sendung *des spätern Propheten* sich uns nicht zuvor auf eben die unzweideutige Weise bewährt hat, wie die Mosis. Und somit hätten wir uns der Verlegenheit enthoben, mit Maimonides die Unabänderlichkeit des Gesetzes zum Grund- oder Folgesatz zu erheben.[6]

Dies ist ein ganz erstaunlicher Text, denn trotz des Unverständnisses Albos macht er aufmerksam auf die Gefahr, die Maimonides vom Islam befürchtete; dieser Text wirft ein neues Licht auf die Moses-Interpretation des Maimonides. Albo sagt hier, die Aussagen des Maimonides seien nur verständlich, wenn dieser angenommen habe, ohne die zusätzliche Grundlehre von der Unabänderlichkeit der Torah bestünde die Gefahr, einem anderen Propheten Gehör zu schenken. Und genau das hat Maimonides befürchtet: Er sah in Muhammad einen ernst zu nehmenden Konkurrenten des Moses. Wegen Muhammad hat Maimonides von den Wundern des Moses geredet (die eigentlich gar nicht in das Konzept des Maimonides von der Sonderstellung des Moses passen); weil Muhammad sich mit Schielen auf die Juden als „Prophet unter den Völkern" (*ummōt*) bezeichnet hatte, muss Maimonides ihm im *Führer der Unschlüssigen* entgegentreten. Albo lebte im christlichen Spanien, die akute Gefahr, die von Muhammad für die Juden unter dem Islam ausging, war ihm fremd. Doch gerade sein Unverständnis für die Situation des Maimonides und seine Vermutung über die Motive für Maimonides' Grundlehre von der Unabänderlichkeit der Torah bestätigen meine Vermutungen über die Moses-Interpretation des Maimonides im Schatten Muhammads. Albo kann sich gar nicht vorstellen, dass einmal ein späterer Prophet „unter den Völkern" (*be-ummōt*) auftreten könne, der wie Moses oder noch größer als dieser sei. Darum braucht er auch keinen *Ikkar* (Grundlehre) von der Sonderstellung des Moses, wie Maimonides ihn formulierte, darum braucht er nicht von den Wundern des Moses zu sprechen, darum braucht er keine Grundlehre von der Unabänderlichkeit der Torah.

Der 7. und 9. der *Ikkarīm* sowie das 35. Kapitel des II. Teils des *Führers,* unverständlich für Albo, werden verständlich, wenn man weiß, wie gut Maimonides den Islam und den Propheten und Gesandten Muhammad kannte, der sich angeschickt hatte, die Nachfolge des Moses anzutreten.

6 Ibid., S. 316–317 (Hervorhebung durch den Autor).

Saʿadya

Vor Maimonides hatte es schon einmal den Versuch gegeben, das ethische Judentum zu einem dogmatischen umzuinterpretieren: Saʿadya ben Josef Gaʾon (882–942) hat dieses in seinem religionsphilosophischen Werk *Kitāb al-amānāt wa-l-iʿtiqādāt* (*Sefer ha-Emunōt we ha-Deʿōt*) in ersten Ansätzen versucht („Buch über Glaubensmeinungen und Überzeugungen"). Saʿadya möchte die Zugehörigkeit zur Gemeinde von der Annahme theologischer Lehrsätze abhängig machen. Diese Lehrsätze entsprechen den zehn Kapiteln seines Buches – von der Prophetie des Moses und seiner Sonderstellung unter den Propheten wird *nicht* geredet.

Als Saʿadya 933 das Buch in Sura in Babylonien schrieb, ging dort von Muhammad keine Gefahr für die jüdische Gemeinde aus. Erst Maimonides war es, der auf Grund seiner Kenntnisse des Islam (und des Koran) Muhammads Anspruch auf die Nachfolge Moses erkannte und darauf mit seinen *Ikkarīm* reagierte.

Das Zittern

Moses hatte am Sinai mit Gott „wachend" und „von Mund zu Mund" geredet, das zeichnet ihn vor allen anderen Propheten aus. Man kann aber auch zeigen, dass auch das 3. und 4. Charakteristikum der Sonderstellung Moses' (er zitterte nie und prophezeite zu jeder Zeit, da er wollte) im Schatten Muhammads formuliert worden sind. Muhammad hatte es nämlich nicht in seiner Gewalt, seine Verkündigung „nach Belieben oder planmäßig auszudenken" oder eine Offenbarung bewusst eintreten zu lassen; er wird von ihr überwältigt und kann sie allenfalls passiv erwarten. Der Koran selbst belehrt den Propheten in Sure 28:86: „Du hofftest nicht, dass dir zuteil wurde die Schrift, es geschah allein durch die Barmherzigkeit des Herrn."

Die Überlieferung hält fest, wie Muhammad einmal Gabriel fragte, warum dieser ihm denn nicht öfters Offenbarungen zuteil werden lasse. Da wurde ihm eingegeben, dass die Engel nur auf Geheiß ihres Herrn herabkommen. Die muslimische Überlieferung kennt das vergebliche und qualvolle Warten auf eine Inspiration als *fatra*, das „Ausbleiben": Damit wird die verhältnismäßig lange Zeit zwischen der ersten und zweiten Offenbarung bezeichnet, in der Muhammad, ohne zu wissen, ob Gott jemals wieder zu ihm sprechen würde, voller Unruhe auf eine Eingebung wartete, „bis es ihm unerträglich wurde und ihn mit Trauer erfüllte", wie es bei Ibn Hišām heißt. Auch im weiteren Verlauf seiner Gesandtschaft blieb die Offenbarung oft aus, obwohl er sie erwartete, oder kam sie umgekehrt völlig überraschend. Facettenreich beschreibt die Überlieferung, wie die Eingebungen Muhammad über die

Grenzen seiner Kräfte hinaus beanspruchten. Oft begann er zu zittern, obwohl es glühend warm, oder zu schwitzen, obwohl es eisig kalt war. „Ich habe gesehen, wie auf ihn die Offenbarung an einem sehr kalten Tag herabkam", berichtet ʿĀʾiša. „Dann wich sie von ihm, und seine Stirn troff von Schweiß." Moses jedoch konnte jederzeit, wann er wollte, und ohne Furcht und Zittern prophezeien.

Maimonides sagt im *Führer der Unschlüssigen*, man müsse nicht nur die Lehre und Verkündigung eines Propheten prüfen, sondern auch, „ob derjenige, der sie verkündet, der Vollkommene ist, dem sie durch prophetische Eingebung mitgeteilt wurde, oder jene Person, welche sich dieser Ansprüche rühmt, sie aber einem anderen entwendet hat. Dies kann man aber nur in der Weise untersuchen, dass man die Vollkommenheit dieser Person betrachtet". Die Person (der Prophet), die ihre Ansprüche jemand anderem gestohlen hat, ist für Maimonides Muhammad und sein Insistieren, der Nachfolger des Moses zu sein. Auch wenn der Name Muhammad an dieser Stelle nicht fällt, so ist doch eindeutig dieser gemeint, wie schon J. Albo bemerkt hat. Er sagt nämlich in seiner Besprechung dieses Kapitels des Maimonides, dieser habe mit seiner Forderung, nicht nur die Lehre, sondern auch die Person zu prüfen, „auf jenen Mann angespielt, der sich bei den Arabern der Prophetengabe rühmte" – Muhammad also. Moses muss stark gemacht werden, damit er Muhammad übertreffen kann.

Der Jemen

Im Jahr 1165 lässt Maimonides sich in Ägypten nieder, 1172 schreibt er einen öffentlichen „Brief an den Jemen". Dort drängte der Schiite ʿAbd an-Nabī ibn Mahdī alle Juden zur Konversion. Die Not war groß, zumal die Muslime mit den Juden „disputierten" und der Torah den Koran entgegenstellten, dem Moses den Muhammad. Maimonides schreibt den Bedrängten:

> Meine Freunde in der Diaspora, ihr müsst euch gegenseitig unterstützen, die Älteren sollen die Jugend leiten und die Führer die Massen. Gewinnt die Zustimmung eurer Gemeinschaft zu der Wahrheit, die unumstößlich und unabänderlich ist, [und findet die Zustimmung] zu folgenden Postulaten des wahren Glaubens, die niemals falsch sind: „Gott ist einer in einem einzigartigen Sinne, und Moses ist sein Prophet und sein Sprecher, er ist der größte und vollkommenste aller Propheten".

Das ist ein eigenartiges Glaubensbekenntnis: Nach dem Bekenntnis zur Einheit Gottes folgt sofort der Hinweis auf das Prophetentum des Moses. Dieser Doppelgrundsatz ist genau dem islamischen Glaubensbekenntnis, der *šahāda,* nachempfunden, die auch zweigliedrig ist: 1. Glied: „Es ist kein Gott außer Gott" – *lā ilāh illā Allāh;* 2. Glied: „Und Muhammad ist der Gesandte Gottes" – *wa-Muḥammad rasūl Allāh.* Der *Ikkar* des Maimonides soll also so verstanden werden: „Es ist kein Gott außer Gott, und Moses ist sein Gesandter" (vgl. Sure 4:136: „Glaubet an Gott und seinen Gesandten!"). Doch dann fügt Maimonides noch etwas hinzu: Moses ist „der Sprecher Gottes, er ist der größte und vollkommenste aller Propheten". Für „Sprecher Gottes" wählt Maimonides im arabischen Text *kalīm Allāh,* was eigentlich heißt: „der von Gott Angesprochene" – es ist der in der *islamischen* Tradition gebräuchliche Beiname des Moses im Anschluss an Sure 7:144. Und wenn Maimonides auch noch hinzufügt, Moses sei „der größte und vollkommenste aller Propheten", dann will das sagen: Nicht Muhammad, sondern Moses ist das Siegel der Propheten. Maimonides bezieht sich hier auf den Koran, und er wollte genau so, wie ich dargelegt habe, verstanden werden, denn die nächsten Sätze lauten: „Moses ist die Kenntnis von Gott gewährt worden, welche niemals einem anderen Propheten vor ihm gewährt worden ist, noch wird sie *in der Zukunft* (einem Propheten) gewährt werden. [...] Die Torah wird niemals überflüssig und überholt sein, niemals vergrößert oder verkürzt werden."

Das Glaubensbekenntnis, das Maimonides den Juden empfiehlt, ist also genau genommen dreigliedrig. Es wird gefordert der Glaube (1) an einen Gott, (2) an Moses, Gottes Gesandten, (3) an die Torah.

Dieses Glaubensbekenntnis entspricht in seiner Einfachheit exakt dem islamischen Glaubensbekenntnis in Sure 4 Vers 136: „Glaubet an Gott und an seinen Gesandten, und an das Buch, das er auf ihn herabgesandt hat."

Wenn die Muslime im Jemen die Juden mit Sure 4:136 auffordern, zum Islam überzutreten, können diese in der Disputation gelassen antworten, auch sie glaubten an Gott – er wird in diesem Text als *al-ḥaqq* bezeichnet, „der Wahre"; es ist einer der 99 „schönen Namen" für Allah, wie sie Muhammad al-Ġazālī beschrieben hat –, seinen Gesandten und die ihm geoffenbarte Schrift – nur sei diese viel älter als der Koran, und es wäre ihnen ja auch zusätzlich mitgeteilt worden, nach Moses könne auch *in Zukunft* kein Prophet wie Moses, auch *nicht unter den Völkern,* erstehen.

Die Betrüger

Eine Untersuchung über „Muhammad und Moses" gibt es bis jetzt noch nicht. Doch dieses Thema klingt an bei den radikalen Früh-Aufklärern des 17. Jahrhunderts – bei den Denkern also, die die Sonderstellung von Moses und Muhammad zwar nicht als *Propheten* hervorheben, wohl aber als *Betrüger* (*impostores*). Johann Joachim Müller verfasste 1688 das Buch *Von den drei*

Betrügern (*De tribus impostoribus*). Darin heißt es: „Du führst die Schriften des Moses, der Propheten und Apostel an. Der Koran stellt sich Dir entgegen, der das auf Grund einer neuen Offenbarung als eine Fälschung bezeichnet und dessen Verfasser sich auf göttliche Weisung durch Wunder beruft." Hier wird deutlich gesagt, dass sich jedem, der sich auf die Torah oder die Evangelien beruft, der Koran entgegenstellt, das heißt: Die Tatsache, dass es Muhammad und den Koran gibt, zwingt die „alten" Religionen zu einer erneuten Begründung ihrer eigenen Legitimität. Auch Moses bedurfte einer neuen Rechtfertigung. Die 13 *Ikkarīm* des Maimonides, der erste Versuch einer Art dogmatischen Festlegung der jüdischen Glaubensinhalte, sind solch eine Rechtfertigung. Die *Ikkarīm* des Maimonides sind seit 1578 in jedem *sidur* zu finden, das so genannte „Jigdal"-Lied am Anfang des Morgengottesdienstes in der Bearbeitung des Daniel Ben Jehuda Dajjan aus Rom (um 1300). Die Spuren Muhammads sind in dieser Fassung verwischt. Doch an diese zu erinnern ist das Ziel dieses Beitrags.

Nachspiel

Der Dichter Ibn Sahl (ca. 1212–1261) begründet seine Konversion vom Judentum zum Islam mit folgenden Zeilen:

Von Moses zu Muhammad
„Muhammads Liebe lenkte mich von Moses ab,
Ich lasse mich allein vom Allerbarmer leiten.
Nicht aus Verachtung hab ich mich von ihm getrennt,
Muhammad hat Moses außer Kraft gesetzt."

„Ein Zerstörer des Judentums …?"

Mose ben Maimon über den historischen Jesus

von

Stefan Schreiner

Universität Tübingen

Dreimal in seinem umfangreichen Werk kommt Mose b. Maimon (Maimonides) explizite auf Jesus zu sprechen. Während er an der ersten Stelle nicht mehr tut, als gerade einmal dessen Namen zu erwähnen, weiß er an den beiden anderen Stellen durchaus etwas mehr von ihm zu berichten, wenn auch der Bericht beide Male vergleichsweise kurz ausfällt.

Das, in chronologischer Hinsicht, erste Mal erwähnt Maimonides den Namen Jesu in der *Abhandlung über die Logik*, die er 1158, im Alter von nur 20 Jahren,[1] bald nach Ankunft der Familie Maimon im marokkanischen Fes verfasst hat.[2] Dort begegnet man dem Namen Jesus im Kapitel 12, und zwar in der Erklärung der fünf verschiedenen Bedeutungen von „früher und später" (*anna š-šay'a aqdamu mina š-šay'i al-'āḫar*). Als Beispiel für „früher und später"

1 Das früher angenommene Geburtsdatum 14. Nissan 4895 (= 30. März 1135) ist vor Jahren schon durch Shlomo D. Goitein („Mose Maimonides. ‚Man of Action': A Revision of the Master's Biography in Light of the Geniza Documents", in *Hommage à Georges Vajda: Études d'histoire et de pensée juives*, ed. Gérard Nahon und Charles Touati [Collection de la Revue des Études Juives 1; Louvain: Peeters, 1980], S. 155–167, hier S. 155) korrigiert worden. Zudem sagt Maimonides am Ende seines *Kommentars zur Mischna* selber: „Ich – Mose, Sohn des R. Maimon des Richters […], habe diesen Kommentar zu schreiben begonnen, als ich 23 Jahre alt war, und ihn im Alter von 30 Jahren in Kairo im Jahre 1479 nach den Dokumenten [= 1167/1168] beendet", was eindeutig auf den 14. Nissan 4898 (= 1138) als Geburtsdatum hinweist.

2 Maimonides, *Treatise on Logic: The Original Arabic and Three Hebrew Translations*, ed. Israel Efros (New York: American Academy for Jewish Research, 1938) [= arabischer Text und die drei hebräischen Übersetzungen von Mose b. Samuel ibn Tibbon, Aḥituv b. Isaak und Josef b. Josua b. Vives de Lorca]; Israel Efros, „Maimonides' Arabic ‚Treatise on Logic' – Introduction", in *Proceedings of the American Academy for Jewish Research* 34 (1966), S. 155–160 (judaeo-arabischer Text: S. 10-42 [hebräische Paginierung]); Maïmonide, *Traité de logique. Traduction, présentation et notes* par Rémi Brague (Paris: Desclée de Brouwer, 1996), S. 12.

im Sinne einer zeitlichen Abfolge (*at-taqaddum bi-z-zamān*) führt Maimonides darin an: *Mūsā aqdam min ʿĪsā* („Mose ist früher als Jesus").[3]

Diese Erwähnung Jesu gibt für unser Thema freilich nichts her; es sei denn, man unterstellt, Maimonides habe diesen Beispielsatz, demzufolge Mose Jesus vorausgeht, in bewusst polemischer Absicht formuliert. Davon kann jedoch keine Rede sein. Allerdings findet sich dieser Satz nur im arabischen Originaltext des Werkes. Dagegen spricht auch nicht, dass Mose b. Samuel ibn Tibbon (um 1200–1283), der das Werk 1254 im „christlichen" Marseille ins Hebräische übersetzt hat, an die Stelle der arabischen beziehungsweise koranischen Namen *Mūsā* und *ʿĪsā* stillschweigend Noah und Abraham (*Noaḥ yoter qodem me-Avraham ba-zman*) gesetzt hat.[4] Dass er dies wirklich nicht getan hat, um eine vermeintliche Polemik zu entschärfen, ist daraus zu ersehen, dass er auch an anderer Stelle Namen ausgetauscht und die arabischen Allerweltsnamen *Zayd* und *ʿAmr* durch die jüdischen Allerweltsnamen *Ruben* (*Reʾuven*) und *Simeon* (*Šimʿon*) ersetzt hat.[5]

Aussagekräftig im Sinne unseres Themas hingegen sind die beiden anderen Texte, in denen uns Jesus bei Maimonides begegnet, zum einen in seinem 1172 geschriebenen *Iggeret Teman*,[6] und hier an zwei Stellen,[7] und zum anderen in

3 Maïmonide, *Traité de logique* (wie Anm. 2), S. 25,8 (arabisch) und S. 84 (französisch).

4 Maïmonide, *Makala fi sanaʿat al-mantik – millot ha-higgayon – Terminologie logique*, ed. [hebräisch mit paralleler französischer Übersetzung] Moïse Ventura (Paris: Vrin, 1982), S. 103.

5 Siehe dazu R. Brague, in Maïmonide, *Traité de logique* (wie Anm. 2), S. 17.

6 Vom *Iggeret Teman* liegen mehrere Ausgaben sowohl des arabischen Textes als auch seiner hebräischen Übersetzungen vor. Benutzt werden hier: (1) Moses Maimonides, *Epistle to Yemen. The Arabic Original and the three Hebrew Versions*, ed. Abraham S. Halkin with an English translation by Boaz Cohen (New York: American Academy for Jewish Research, 1952) (im Folgenden zitiert: Halkin, *Iggeret*, mit Angabe der Seite), (2) Moše b. Maimon, *Iggeret Teman – ar-risāla al-yamanīya*, in R. Moše b. Maimon, *Iggerot – maqor we-tirgum*, ed. Joseph Kafaḥ [= Y. D. Qāfiḥ] (Jerusalem: Mosad Harav Kook, ²5747/1987), S. 15–60 (im Folgenden zitiert: Qāfiḥ, *Iggeret*, mit Angabe der Seite), (3) Samuel ibn Tibbons Übersetzung in: *Iggerot ha-Rambam – maqor we-tirgum*, ed. Isaac Shailat (2 Bände; Jerusalem: Mosad Harav Kook, ²5747/²1987–1988), Band I, S. 82–112 (arabisch) und S. 113–168 (hebräisch), und (4) Naḥum ha-Maʿaravis Übersetzung *Iggeret Teman o petaḥ tiqwa*, in Moše b. Maimon, *Iggerot*, ed. Mordecai Dov Rabinowitz (Jerusalem: Mosad Harav Kook, ²5747/1987), S. 101–193 (im Folgenden zitiert: Rabinowitz, *Iggeret*, mit Angabe der Seite). Zitiert beziehungsweise übersetzt wird im Folgenden stets, wenn nicht anders angegeben, nach dem arabischen Text nach der Ausgabe Halkins. – Zur Textüberlieferung und den drei hebräischen Übersetzungen von Samuel b. Jehuda ibn Tibbon (1160–1230), Abraham b. Samuel ha-Lewi ibn Ḥasdai (13. Jahrhundert) und Naḥum ha-Maʿaravi siehe A. S. Halkin, ibid., S. XXXI–XXXVI. – Deutsche Übersetzung: Moses Maimonides, *Der Brief in den Jemen. Texte zum Messias*, herausgegeben, übersetzt und kommentiert von Sylvia Powels-Niami (Jüdische Geistesgeschichte 1; Berlin: Parerga, 2002).

7 Halkin, *Iggeret* (wie Anm. 6), S. 12,7–14,4 und 92,7–13 (arabisch/hebräisch), S. III–IV und XVII–XVIII (englisch); Qāfiḥ, *Iggeret* (wie Anm. 6), S. 21,20–22,9 und 53,3–11;

seinem zwischen 1170 und 1180 entstandenen halakhischen Kodex *Mišneh Torah*,[8] im *Sefer šofṭim* am Ende von „Hilkhot Melakhim“, Kapitel 11. Allerdings ist sogleich hinzuzufügen, dass dieser Abschnitt, von den älteren Ausgaben Rom 1469, Toledo 1480, Soncino 1490, Spanien (?) 1491 und Konstantinopel 1509 sowie Amsterdam 1702 abgesehen,[9] in späteren beziehungsweise jüngeren Drucken der Zensur zum Opfer gefallen und nur in jemenitischer handschriftlicher Überlieferung beziehungsweise darauf fußenden Ausgaben zu finden ist.[10]

Auf den ersten Blick erscheinen die Aussagen, die Maimonides in den erwähnten Texten über – den historischen – Jesus macht, ebenso fragmentarisch wie inkonsistent, jedenfalls lassen sie sich nicht nur nicht ohne weiteres auf einen Nenner bringen, sondern ergeben auch in der Summe kein geschlossenes Bild. Vielleicht kann dies auch anders nicht sein; denn sowenig Maimonides eine zusammenhängende Darstellung seiner Sicht des Christentums (und des Islams) vorgelegt hat, obwohl er sich immer wieder veranlasst sah, beiden Religionen gegenüber Stellung zu beziehen, so wenig hat er das, was er über Jesus zu sagen hat, an einer Stelle zusammengefasst und systematisch dargelegt. Zudem interessiert ihn Jesus nicht als Person, als – der historische – Jesus. Kommt er auf ihn zu sprechen, geschieht es nicht um seiner selbst willen. Vielmehr dient ihm Jesus als ein Exempel, an dessen Person und Geschichte er wesentliche Gedanken über den Messias und die messianische Zeit einerseits und seine Sicht des Christentums andererseits veranschaulichen kann. Was also von Jesus gesagt wird, richtet sich stets nach dem Kontext, in dem er als Exempel figuriert; und so verschieden die Kontexte sind, so verschieden, ja, zwiespältig oder widersprüchlich können daher die Aussagen über ihn sein, ganz so wie die, die er über das Christentum insgesamt gemacht hat. Bevor wir also auf Maimonides' Aussagen über Jesus zu sprechen kommen, ist ein kurzer Blick auf Maimonides' zwiespältige Aussagen über das Christentum angebracht.[11]

Rabinowitz, *Iggeret* (wie Anm. 6), S. 119,1–120,7 und 182,7–13; deutsch: *Der Brief in den Jemen* (wie Anm. 6), S. 35–36 und 77–78.

8 Mose b. Maimon, *Mišneh Torah hu᾽ ha-yad ha-ḥazaqa*, ed. Mordecai Dov Rabinowitz, Shmuel T. Rubinstein et al. (17 Bände; Jerusalem: Mosad Harav Kook, [6.7]5741–5745/1981–1985) (im Folgenden zitiert: „Hilkhot ...“ mit Angabe von Kapitel und Paragraph/*Mišneh Torah* mit Band und Seite dieser Edition).

9 Siehe dazu die bibliographischen Angaben bei Yeshayahu Vinograd, *Oṣar ha-sefer ha-ʿivri* (2 Bände; Jerusalem: Ha-Makhon l-Bibliyographya Memuhshevet, 5753–5755/1993–1995), Band II, S. 659 Nr. 3; S. 337 Nr. 6–7; S. 687 Nr. 39; S. 496 Nr. 9, und S. 603 Nr. 16, sowie S. 48 Nr. 744.

10 Mose b. Maimon, *Mišneh Torah* (wie Anm. 8), Band XVII (1962 [[6]1985]): *Sefer šofṭim*, ed. Rubinstein, S. 415–417; deutsche Übersetzung: Mose b. Maimon, „Über den König Messias und das messianische Zeitalter“, deutsch: Martin Cunz, in *Judaica* 42 (1986), S. 74–79, hier S. 75–76.

11 Zum Ganzen siehe unter anderem Joseph Sarachek, *The Doctrine of the Messiah in Medieval Jewish Literature* (New York: Jewish Theological Seminary of America, 1932

1. Maimonides' zwiespältige Aussagen über das Christentum

Gleich den anderen jüdischen Apologeten des Mittelalters sieht auch Maimonides allein im Judentum nicht nur die „wahre Religion" (*dīn al-ḥaqq, dat ha-emet*),[12] sondern die „Religion Gottes, Lob sei Ihm" (*dīn Allāh subḥānahu*).[13] Entsprechend unzweideutig und nachgerade selbstverständlich definiert er daher das Christentum als *'avodah zarah* („Götzendienst") und die Christen als *'ovde 'avodah zarah* („Götzendiener"):

> Die Edomiter [= Christen][14] sind Götzendiener (*'ovde 'avodah zarah*). Der Sonntag ist ihr Feiertag (*yom eydam*)[15]]; deshalb ist es verboten, mit ihnen am Donnerstag und Freitag und erst recht am Schabbat in Eretz Israel Handel zu treiben. Vom Sonntag gar nicht zu reden, denn [an ihm] ist es überall verboten; ebenso soll man mit ihnen an allen ihren Feiertagen verfahren („Hilkhot 'Avodat kokhavim" 9.4/*Mišneh Torah* II, S. 181).

Ebenso hatte er zuvor schon in seinem *Kommentar zur Mischna, Avodah Zarah* 1:3 geschrieben: „Wisse, dass die Christen, die in allen ihren Gruppen behaupten, dass der Messias [bereits] gekommen ist, sämtlich Götzendiener sind, und ihre Feiertage sind alle verboten [für Handel etc. mit ihnen], und man verfährt mit ihnen gemäß der Tora, wie man mit sonstigen Götzendienern verfährt." Und in Ergänzung dazu heißt es im *Kommentar zur Mischna, Avodah Zarah* 1:4:

[New York: Hermon Press, ²1968]), S. 126–161; G. Tchernowitz, *Ha-yaḥas ben Yisra'el la-goyim lefi ha-RaMBaM* (New York, 1950); Jacob Posen, „Die Einstellung des Maimonides zum Islam und zum Christentum", in *Judaica* 42 (1986), S. 66–73; David Novak, *Jewish-Christian Dialogue* (New York etc.: Oxford University Press, 1989), besonders Kapitel 3: „Maimonides' View of Christianity"; idem, *Maimonides on Judaism and Other Religions. The Samuel H. Goldenson Lecture, 23 February 1997* (Hebrew Union College – Jewish Institute of Religion, Cincinnati, Oh. [http://www.icjs.org/what/njsp/maimonides.html]).

12 Siehe dazu Jerusalemer Talmud, *Pea* II,6/17°; Mose b. Maimon, *Sefer ha-miṣwot*. Edited and translated into Hebrew by Joseph Kafaḥ [= Y. Qāfiḥ] (Jerusalem: Mosad Harav Kook, 1971 [²1994]), S. 63 (= *miṣwot 'aseh* Nr. 9), und „Hilkhot Melakhim" 12.1/*Mišneh Torah* XVII, S. 417.

13 Halkin, *Iggeret* (wie Anm. 6), S. 14,7–8; Qāfiḥ, *Iggeret* (wie Anm. 6), S. 23,1.

14 Zu dieser Typologie siehe Abraham b. Esra, *Peruš 'al ha-torah*, in *Torat Ḥayyim – Ḥamiša Ḥumše Torah*, ed. Mordechai L. Katzenellenbogen (7 Bände; Jerusalem: Mosad Harav Kook, 1986–1993), Band II, S. 34b zu Genesis 27:40; dazu ferner Solomon Zeitlin, „The Origin of the Term *Edom* for Rome and the Roman Church", in *Jewish Quarterly Review* 60 (1969–1970), S. 262–263; ferner Gerson D. Cohen, „Esau as Symbol in Early Medieval Thought", in *Jewish Medieval and Renaissance Studies*, ed. Alexander Altmann (Studies and Texts 4; Cambridge, Mass.: Harvard University Press, 1967), S. 19–48; Johann Maier, *Geschichte der jüdischen Religion* (Freiburg etc.: Herder, ²1992), S. 140ff.

15 Wörtlich „ihr Unglückstag"; der Begriff stammt aus Deuteronomium 32:35: „denn nahe ist der Tag ihres Unglücks".

„Man muss wissen, dass jede Stadt, in der Christen wohnen und in der eine *bamah* („Kirche“)[16] steht, ohne Zweifel ein Ort des Götzendienstes ist etc.“[17]

Die Charakterisierung des Christentums als „Götzendienst“ und die Einstufung der Christen als „Götzendiener“ sind allerdings erst die eine Seite der maimonideischen Ansicht; denn auf der anderen scheint Maimonides weder alle Christen als „Götzendiener“ noch das Christentum als „Götzendienst“ zu betrachten. Erlaubte er doch, dass man die Christen – im Gegensatz zu den Muslimen – die Torah lehrt, was er Nichtjuden gegenüber für verboten erklärt hat. Mit Bezug auf Babylonischer Talmud, *Sanhedrin* 59a[18] „*Torah hat uns Mose als Erbe anvertraut* (Deuteronomium 33:4) – uns als Erbe, nicht ihnen“, dekretiert er in „Hilkhot Melakhim“ 9.9 (*Mišneh Torah* XVII, S. 410): „Ein Nichtjude, der sich mit der Torah befasst, verdient die Todesstrafe (*goy še-ʿasaq ba-torah – ḥayyav mita*). Er soll sich allein mit ihren [das heißt den Nichtjuden gegebenen] sieben Geboten [der Kinder Noahs] (*ševaʿ miṣwot bene noaḥ*) befassen. Ebenso ein Nichtjude, der den Schabbat feiert (*goy še-šavat*), selbst wenn an einem anderen Wochentag: wenn er ihn für sich als Schabbat begeht, verdient er die Todesstrafe[19] etc.“ Hingegen nennt Maimonides einen Nichtjuden, der sich mit den sieben Geboten der Kinder Noahs befasst und nach ihnen handelt, „einen der Frommen der Völker der Welt“, der ebenso Anteil an der kommenden Welt hat wie ein Jude, der die 613 *miṣwot* der Torah beachtet („Hilkhot Melakhim“ 8.11/*Mišneh Torah* XVII, S. 398).

Diese Regelung gilt aber für Christen offenbar nicht. Denn Christen darf man die Torah lehren, wie Maimonides in einem Responsum ausdrücklich festgestellt hat: „Erlaubt (*muttar*) ist, die Christen (*noṣrim*) die Gebote und die Kommentare zu lehren entsprechend unserer Religion (*lefi ha-din*). Es ist aber nicht erlaubt, die Muslime etwas davon zu lehren, denn ihr wisst, dass sie glauben, dass diese Torah nicht vom Himmel ist; und wenn man sie etwas davon lehrt, befindet man sich im Widerspruch zu ihrer Lehre (*yimmaṣʾu mitnagged le-qabbalatam*) [...].“[20] Den Christen jedoch hält Maimonides darüber

16 Der in der Bibel zur Bezeichnung des bis zur Errichtung des Zentralheiligtums (zunächst in Schilo, dann in Jerusalem) legitimen und nach der Errichtung dieses Zentralheiligtums illegitimen „temporären Altars“ (vgl. Mischna, *Megillah* 1:10; *Zevaḥim* 14:4–8 und Tosefta, *Zevaḥim* 13:17–18) ist in der hebräischen apologetisch-polemischen Literatur des Mittelalters die übliche Bezeichnung für eine Kirche; siehe Eliezer Ben-Yehuda, *Millon ha-lašon ha-ʿivrit ha-yešana weha-ḥadaša* (17 Bände; Jerusalem: Yehuda, ²1948–1959), Band II, Sp. 557b–559a, hier Sp. 559a.

17 *Commentary on the Mishnah: ʿAvodah zarah* 1:3, ed. Josef Kafaḥ [= Yosef D. Qāfiḥ] (Jerusalem: Mosad Harav Kook, 1965), Band II, S. 225; vgl. ibid., S. 226 zu Mischna, *ʿAvodah Zarah* 1:4; *Mišneh Torah*, „Hilkhot ʿAvodah zarah“ 9.4.

18 Vgl. dazu Babylonischer Talmud, *Sanhedrin* 57a.

19 Vgl. ibid., 58b.

20 *Tešuvot ha-Rambam*, ed. Joshua Blau (4 Bände; Jerusalem: Magnes, 5718–5746/1957–1986), Band I, S. 284–285, Nr. 149. In etwas anderem Wortlaut ist dieses *Responsum* abgedruckt im Anhang zu: Mose b. Maimon, *Mišneh Torah*, Band XVII (wie Anm. 10), S. 427.

hinaus zugute, dass sie die Torah nicht nur kennen, sondern „anerkennen, dass der Text der Torah in ihrer Gesamtheit so ist, wie er sich in unserer Hand befindet, wenn sie sie in manchen Kommentaren auch falsch auslegen und in ihr Hinweise finden, die nur ihnen verständlich sind. Wenn man sie aber von der richtigen Auslegung [der Tora] überzeugt, ist es möglich (*efšar*), dass sie zu dem zurückkehren, was gut ist (*še-yaḥzoru la-muṭav*). Und wenn sie nicht zurückkehren, ist es für Israel [die Juden] auch kein Problem, denn man findet in ihrer Torah nicht das Gegenteil von unserer Torah (*lo' yimṣe'u be-toratam hefekh toratenu*)".[21]

Dies ist bei den Muslimen eindeutig nicht der Fall; denn nach dem Koran ist die Torah abrogiert, und zwar gleich auf doppelte Weise: zum einen durch das Evangelium (*inǧīl*) und zum anderen, und dies endgültig, durch den Koran (Sure 5:44–49).[22]

Gegen diese muslimische Position hatte sich übrigens Maimonides bereits mit der achten und neunten seiner dreizehn Grundlehren (*'iqqarīm*) gewandt: (VIII) „Die achte Grundlehre lautet: die Torah ist vom Himmel (*Torah min ha-šamayim*). Das heißt, es ist zu glauben, dass diese ganze, in unseren Händen heute befindliche Torah die auf Mose herabgesandte ist (*al-munazzala*) und dass sie ganz aus dem Mund der Allmacht (*mippi ha-gevurah*) stammt, das heißt, dass sie als ganze von Gott zu ihm kam in einer Weise, die in übertragenem Sinne Rede (*kalām 'alā sabīl al-maǧāz*) genannt wird, man aber nicht weiß, *wie* sie zu ihm gekommen ist, nur, dass er, Friede über ihn, derjenige ist, zu dem sie gekommen ist, und dass er einem Schreiber glich, dem man vortrug und der nachschrieb alle Ereignisse der Zeiten, die Berichte und die Gebote, und deshalb Gesetzgeber (*meḥoqeq*) genannt wird. [...]" (IX) „Die neunte Grundlehre betrifft die Abrogation (*an-nasḫ*). Das heißt, dass die Torah des Mose (*šarī'at Mošeh*) nicht abrogiert und keine andere Torah (*šarī'a*) von Gott außer ihr ausgehen wird. Weder wird zu ihr hinzugefügt noch von ihr weggestrichen werden, weder hinsichtlich des Wortlautes (*lā fī n-naṣṣ*) noch hinsichtlich der Auslegung (*lā fī t-tafsīr*), wie gesagt ist (Deuteronomium 13:1): ‚Alle Rede, die Ich euch gebiete, wahrt im Tun/ füge nichts hinzu/ streiche nichts davon'."[23]

---

21 *Tešuvot ha-Rambam*, ed. Blau (wie Anm. 20), Band I, S. 285. Dagegen werden in „Hilkhot Tešuvah" 3.8/*Mišneh Torah* I, S. 224, die „Jesuaner" (*ha-yešu'im*), das ist die Christen, und die „Hagarianer" (*ha-hagarim*), das sind die Muslime, gleichermaßen als *koferim ba-torah*, als „Leugner der Torah", bezeichnet.

22 Vgl. dazu „Hilkhot Yesode torah" 7.6, 9.2, 10.4/*Mišneh Torah* I, S. 37–38, 42–43, 47–48, und „Hilkhot Tešuvah" 3.8/ibid., S. 223–224.

23 Den arabischen Text mit der hebräischen Übersetzung des Salomo ibn Ya'qūb aus Saragossa edierte Joseph Holzer, *Zur Geschichte der Dogmenlehre in der jüdischen Religionsphilosophie des Mittelalters. Mose Maimûni's Einleitung zu Chelek* ... (Berlin: M. Poppelauer, 1901), S. 1–30, hier S. 26–27. Die hebräische Übersetzung auch in Mose b. Maimon, *Haqdamot le-feruš ha-mišnah*, ed. Mordecai Dov Rabinowitz (Jerusalem: Mosad Harav Kook, [8]1980) (= Mose b. Maimon, *Mišneh Torah* [wie Anm. 8], Band XVIII,

Allerdings ist Maimonides auch gegenüber dem Islam zwiespältig; denn an anderer Stelle sagt er: „Die Muslime sind keineswegs Götzendiener. Alle Spuren von Götzendienst haben sie in ihren Reihen ausgerottet." Vielmehr bescheinigt er ihnen: „Sie sind wahre und reine Bekenner der Einheit und Ausschließlichkeit Gottes (*muwaḥḥidūn/meyaḥadim*). Selbst wenn sie die Lehre des Judentums entstellen und uns falschen Glauben vorwerfen, dürfen wir ihnen gegenüber dennoch nicht dasselbe tun und sie des Götzendienstes bezichtigen. Im Übrigen warnt uns unsere Schrift vor lügenhafter und verächtlicher Rede. Denn was soll's, dass die Muslime vor langer Zeit einmal Götzendiener gewesen sind und ‚heidnische' Kulte praktizierten? Heute, wenn sie in ihren Moscheen und heiligen Stätten beten, sind ihre Herzen auf den einen wahren Gott im Himmel gerichtet."[24]

Am Ende hat ihn seine zwiespältige Haltung auch nicht gehindert, beiden, Christen und Muslimen, dem Christentum und dem Islam, gleichermaßen zuzugestehen, nicht nur irgendeinen Platz in der Geschichte Gottes mit den Menschen zu haben, sondern darin sogar eine positive Rolle zu spielen. In beiden nämlich, im Christentum wie im Islam, erkennt Maimonides eine Art *praeparatio messianica*:

> Die Gedanken des Schöpfers der Welt – der Mensch hat nicht die Kraft, sie zu begreifen, denn unsere Wege sind nicht Seine Wege, und unsere Gedanken sind nicht Seine Gedanken.[25] So alle diese Dinge, die von Jesus dem Nazarener und diesem Ismaeliten [= Muḥammad], der nach ihm aufgetreten ist, dienen allein dazu, dem König Messias den Weg zu ebnen (*le-yaššer derekh le-melekh ha-mašiaḥ*) und die ganze Welt auszurichten (*le-taqqen ha-ʿolam kullo*), gemeinsam dem Ewigen zu dienen (*la-ʿavod et H' be-yaḥad*), wie es heißt: *Dann werde Ich mich einem jeden Volk mit klarer Stimme zuwenden, dass sie alle den Namen des Ewigen anrufen und Ihm in Eintracht dienen* (Zephanja 3:9). Wie das? Schon jetzt ist die ganze Welt voll von Dingen, die den Messias betreffen, von Dingen, die die Torah betreffen, und von Dingen, die die Gebote betreffen, und man verhandelt (*pašṭu*) diese Dinge auf entfernten Inseln und unter vielen Völkern unbeschnittenen Herzens,[26] und sie diskutieren über diese Dinge und über die Gebote der Torah. Die einen sagen: Diese Gebote waren Wahrheit, aber sie haben bereits jetzt ihre Gültigkeit verloren und sind nicht länger verbindlich. Die anderen sagen: Verborgene Dinge enthalten sie und sind nicht in ihrem Literalsinn (*ki-fšuṭan*) zu nehmen, aber

S. 109–150, hier S. 144–146). – Zur Sache siehe Marc B. Shapiro, *The Limits of Orthodox Theology. Maimonides' Thirteen Principles Reappraised* (Oxford und Portland, Or.: Littmann Library of Jewish Civilization, 2004), S. 91–131.

24 Zitiert nach Gilbert S. Rosenthal (Ed.), *Maimonides: His Wisdom for our Time. Selected from his twelfth-century classics* (New York: Funk & Wagnalls, 1969), S. 43.

25 Anlehnung an Jesaja 55:8.

26 Vgl. Ezechiel 44:7.

> ein Messias[27] ist bereits gekommen und hat ihre Geheimnisse enthüllt. Wenn jedoch der wahre König Messias auftreten, *Erfolg haben, erhöht und erhaben sein wird,*[28] werden sie alle sofort umkehren und erkennen, dass *Lüge ihre Väter vererbt*[29] und ihre Propheten und ihre Väter sie in die Irre geführt[30] haben" („Hilkhot Melakhim" 9.4 Ende/*Mišneh Torah* XVII, S. 416–417).[31]

Neu ist das, was Maimonides hier geschrieben hat, freilich nicht. Ähnliche Worte hatte vor ihm bereits Jehuda (Abū l-Ḥasan) b. Samuel ha-Lewi (um 1070/1075–1141) in seinem *Sefer ha-Kuzari* dem jüdischen Gelehrten in den Mund gelegt und ihn sagen lassen: „Diese Völker (*hāḏihi l-milal*) [= Christen und Muslime] sind eine Vorbereitung und Einleitung für den erwarteten Messias (*tawṭiʾa wa-muqaddima li-l-masīḥ* [*li-l-mašiaḥ*] *al-muntaẓar*), der die Frucht ist, und sie alle werden seine Frucht; wenn sie ihn aber anerkennen, dann wird alles ein Baum (*wa-taṣīru šaǧara wāḥida*). Dann werden sie die Wurzel (*al-aṣl*) verehren, die sie vordem gering geachtet hatten" (*Kuzari* IV,23).[32]

Aufgefallen ist die Ähnlichkeit zwischen Maimonides und Jehuda ha-Lewi, darauf haben bereits Moritz Steinschneider und nach ihm Abraham S. Halkin hingewiesen,[33] übrigens schon Jakob b. Ḥayyim in seinem Kommentar zum *Kuzari*. Maimonides' Worte wiederum zitieren andere (mittelalterliche) Autoren, so beispielsweise Mose b. Naḥman (Nachmanides) (1194–um 1270) in seiner Abhandlung *Torat YHWH temima*[34] und Netanʾel b. Yešaʿyā

---

27 Wie aus einem *Responsum* des Maimonides zu *Mišneh Torah*, „Hilkhot Melakhim" 10.9 hervorgeht (abgedruckt im Anhang zu: Mose b. Maimon, *Mišneh Torah*, Band XVII [wie Anm. 10], S. 427), ist damit Muḥammad gemeint.

28 Anlehnung an Jesaja 52:13.

29 Anlehnung an Jeremia 16:19.

30 Vgl. Ezechiel 13:10.

31 Siehe dazu auch Aviezer Ravitzky, „'To the Utmost of Human Capacity': Maimonides on the Days of the Messiah", in *Perspectives on Maimonides. Philosophical and Historical Studies*, ed. Joel L. Kraemer (Oxford: Oxford University Press, 1991), S. 221–256, hier S. 228–230.

32 Jehuda ha-Lewi, *Kitāb ar-radd wa-d-dalīl fī d-dīn aḏ-ḏalīl (al-kitāb al-ḫazarī)*, ed. David Zvi Baneth und Haggai Ben-Shammai (Jerusalem: Magnes Press, 1977), S. 172,15–16; idem, *Sefer ha-Kuzari – maqor we-tirgum*, ed. Yosef D. Qāfiḥ (Qiryat Ono: Mekhon Mishnat ha-Rambam, 5757/1997, S. 173 (deutsche Übersetzung: *Das Buch al-Chazarī: aus dem Arabischen des Abu-l-Hasan Yehuda Hallewi*. Übersetzt von Hartwig Hirschfeld [Breslau: Wilhelm Koebner, 1885], S. 214). – An anderer Stelle (*Kuzari* III,9) lässt Jehuda ha-Lewi den jüdischen Gelehrten Christentum und Islam „Abbildungen" (*tašbīhāt*) des Judentums nennen (ed. Baneth, S. 96,17–20; Qāfiḥ, *Iggeret* [wie Anm. 6], S. 97,11–16; deutsch: Hirschfeld, ibid., S. 120).

33 Moritz Steinschneider, *Polemische und apologetische Literatur in arabischer Sprache zwischen Muslimen, Christen und Juden* (Leipzig: Brockhaus, 1877 [Nachdruck Hildesheim: Olms, 1966]), S. 351–352; A. S. Halkin in idem, *Iggeret* (wie Anm. 6), S. XIV, Anm. 91.

34 In *Kitve Mošeh b. Naḥman*, ed. Charles Ber Shawel (2 Bände; Jerusalem: Mosad Harav Kook, [10]5748/1988), Band I, S. 139–175, hier S. 143.

(14./15. Jahrhundert) in seinem 1392 abgeschlossenen Kommentar zur Torah *Nūr aẓ-ẓalām* (zu Deuteronomium 33:2).[35] Ganz andere Töne hingegen schlägt Maimonides in seinem *Iggeret Teman*, seinem „Brief an die Juden Jemens“ an.

2. Der Brief an die Juden Jemens

Zum ersten Mal erscheint darin der Name Jesu im Zusammenhang einer Auflistung derer, die das Judentum zerstört haben beziehungsweise zerstören wollten. Nach Maimonides hat es im Laufe der Geschichte der Juden zwei Arten (*nawʿ* beziehungsweise *anwāʿ*)[36] von Zerstörern Israels und dementsprechend auch zwei Arten beziehungsweise Methoden seiner Zerstörung gegeben: eine Zerstörung mit Gewalt, durchs Schwert, und eine Zerstörung mit den Mitteln des Geistes, der geistigen Auseinandersetzung beziehungsweise religiösen antijüdischen Polemik (*al-ġalaba wa-l-muḥāǧaǧa wa-l-munāẓara*) (*Iggeret*, ed. Halkin [wie Anm. 6], S. 10,16–17/ed. Qāfiḥ [wie Anm. 6], S. 21,8–9).

Für die erste Art der Zerstörung stehen die Namen und Taten von ʿAmaleq,[37] Sisera,[38] Sanherib,[39] Nebukadnezar,[40] Titus,[41] Hadrian[42] und anderer.[43] Als Beispiele für die zweite Art beziehungsweise Methode, das Judentum zu zerstören, nennt Maimonides „die Klugen der Völker und ihre Gelehrten (*ḥuḏḏāq al-milal wa-ʿulamāʾuhum*) wie die Syrer, die Perser und die Griechen“, die „mit frei ersonnenen Argumenten“ (*bi-ḥuǧaǧin yūhimūna bihā*) und „polemischen Auseinandersetzungen“ (*muǧādalāt yuʾallifūnahā*) ebenso wie mit administrativen Maßnahmen „die Abschaffung der Torah“ (*naqḍ aš-šarīʿa*) und „ihre Außerkraftsetzung beziehungsweise Annullierung“ (*fasḫuhā*) bewerkstelligen wollten (*Iggeret*, ed. Halkin, S. 8,16–18/ed. Qāfiḥ, S. 20,9–11).

Während im Hinblick auf die Namen der ersten Reihe unschwer erkennbar ist, warum Maimonides sie zu den Zerstörern Israels rechnet, ist unklar, an wen er bei den „Syrern, Persern und Griechen“ gedacht hat.[44] Bei den „Syrern“ (*as-*

35 *Nūr aẓ-ẓalām* (*meʾor ha-afela*), ed. Josef Kafaḥ [= Yosef D. Qāfiḥ] (Jerusalem: Mosad Harav Kook, 5717/1957), S. 570–571.

36 Naḥum ha-Maʿaravi macht daraus den hebräischen Arabismus *ha-noaʿ*, Plural *ha-noʿim* (Halkin, *Iggeret* [wie Anm. 6], S. 116,6).

37 Exodus 17:8–13.

38 Richter 4–5.

39 2. Könige 18:13–19:37.

40 2. Könige 24–25.

41 Babylonischer Talmud, *Gittin* 56b–57a.

42 *Berešit Rabbah* 63:7 (ed. Mose A. Mirkin, *Midrash Rabbah* [11 Bände; Tel Aviv: Yavneh, 1956–1967], Band III, S. 14).

43 Halkin, *Iggeret* (wie Anm. 6), S. 8,11–12; Qāfiḥ, *Iggeret* (wie Anm. 6), S. 20,2–4.

44 Siehe die Bemerkungen dazu in Qāfiḥ, *Iggeret* (wie Anm. 6), S. 20, Anm. 9, und Rabinowitz, *Iggeret* (wie Anm. 6), S. 116, Anm. 10.

suryān) hatten offenbar schon Maimonides' mittelalterliche Übersetzer ihre Schwierigkeiten. Samuel b. Tibbon liest *ha-suryanim* („Syrer"), Ibn Ḥasdai übersetzt *ha-ašurim* („Assyrer"). Naḥum ha-Maʿaravi hingegen hat nach *Iggeret*, ed. Halkin (S. 9,19) *ha-aramiyyim* („Aramäer") und nach *Iggeret*, ed. Rabinowitz (S. 116,9): *ha-edomim*, mit denen hier jedoch nicht die „Christen", sondern das antike Edom beziehungsweise die Idumäer gemeint sein dürften, die in der Bibel und im frühjüdischen Schrifttum bereits vielfach als *die* Gegner Israels und der Juden beziehungsweise als *Feindbild* schlechthin figurieren.[45] Ebenso unklar ist, auf wen Maimonides anspielt, wenn er von „Persern" spricht. Nach Y. Qāfiḥ (mit Bezug auf *Sefer ʿarugat ha-bosem, haqdama*) wären damit Ḥīwī al-Balḫī und Ibn Sāqawaih gemeint, die beide persischer Herkunft waren.[46] Ḥīwī al-Balḫī (9. Jahrhundert), den man einen „jüdischen Marcion" (M. Stein) genannt hat, ist Verfasser eines – nicht erhaltenen und nur aus Zitaten Anderer bekannten – *Šeʾelot* oder *Ṭaʿanot* genannten Buches, in dem er die Autorität der Torah in Zweifel gezogen hat.[47] Der Karäer Ibn Sāqawayh (10. Jahrhundert) hingegen, neben Anan b. Dawid und Ben Asher einer der Adressaten von Saadja Gaons *Kitāb ar-radd* („Buch der Zurückweisung"), soll ein – gleichfalls nicht erhaltenes – antirabbanitisches „Buch der schandbaren Dinge" verfasst haben.[48] Unklar ist schließlich auch, wen Maimonides mit den „Griechen" meint. Da er auf die Christen erst später zu sprechen kommt, darf man annehmen, dass mit den „Griechen" hier kaum christliche griechische Gelehrte gemeint sein können. Sollte indessen Maimonides von der so genannten heidnisch-antiken griechischen (und römischen) antijüdischen Polemik gewusst haben, gegen die sich nicht zuletzt Josephus Flavius in seinem *Contra Apionem* zur Wehr setzt?[49] Oder sind mit den Griechen die syrischen Seleukiden und

45 Vgl. Jesaja 63:1–6; Jeremia 49:7–22; Obadja 1; Maleachi 1:2–5 etc.; siehe dazu Bert Dicou, *Edom, Israel's brother and antagonist. The role of Edom in biblical prophecy and story* (Journal for the Study of the Old Testament. Supplement Series 169; Sheffield: Sheffield Academic Press, 1994); ferner Aryeh Kasher, *Jews, Idumaeans, and Ancient Arabs* (Texte und Studien zum Antiken Judentum 18; Tübingen: J.C.B. Mohr [Paul Siebeck], 1988).

46 Qāfiḥ, *Iggeret* (wie Anm. 6), S. 20, Anm. 9*.

47 Salo W. Baron, *A Social and Religious History of the Jews* (18 Bände; New York etc.: Columbia University Press, 1952–1983), Band VI, S. 299–306 und S. 478–484, Anm. 88–100.

48 Ibid., Band V, S. 253–254 und S. 406, Anm. 53; Nathan Schur, *The Karaite Encyclopedia* (Beiträge zur Erforschung des Alten Testaments und des antiken Judentums 38; Frankfurt am Main etc.: Peter Lang, 1995), S. 140.

49 Siehe dazu Emil Schürer, *The History of the Jewish People in the Age of Jesus Christ*. Edited and revised by Geza Vermes, Fergus Millar and Martin Goodman (3 Bände [in 4]; Edinburgh: T.&T. Clark, 1973–1987), Band I, S. 54–55 und Band III, S. 610–616; ferner Samuel Krauss, *The Jewish-Christian Controversy from the Earliest Times to 1789*, ed. William Horbury, Band I (Texte und Studien zum Antiken Judentum 56; Tübingen: J.C.B. Mohr [Paul Siebeck], 1996), S. 1–3 und die dort genannte Literatur. – Zur antiken

ihre auch mit administrativen Mitteln durchgesetzten Hellenisierungsbestrebungen gemeint, auf die die Juden am Ende mit dem Aufstand unter Judas Makkabäus reagierten?[50]

Wie dem auch sei, schließlich sind – so Maimonides – beide Arten der Zerstörung des Judentums miteinander verbunden worden, und zwar im Christentum ebenso wie in dem ihm folgenden Islam, mit denen die Geschichte der versuchten Zerstörungen des Judentums ihren unbestrittenen Höhepunkt erreicht hat:

> Der erste, der die Absicht und den festen Willen hatte, die Zerstörung des Judentums auf beide Weisen in die Tat umzusetzen, ist nach Maimonides Jesus gewesen. Kurz und bündig sagt er daher von ihm: „Der erste, der darauf aus war (*fa-awwalu man ʿamada ʿalā hāḏā r-raʾyi*), war Jesus der Nazarener (*Yešuaʿ ha-noṣri*) – seine Knochen mögen zu Staub zermahlen sein! (*šeḥiq ʿaṣamot*)“ (*Iggeret*, ed. Halkin, S. 12,7/ed. Qāfiḥ, S. 21,20–21).

Dem Anlass des Briefes und seinem Zweck geschuldet,[51] ist Maimonides im Folgenden zwar mehr an Jesus und seinem Lehren und Tun als Messiasprätendent interessiert; gleichwohl fällt auf, dass er sich, bevor er darauf zu sprechen kommt, mit einem anderen Thema beschäftigt, nämlich mit dessen Herkunft beziehungsweise Abstammung (2.1.). Erst danach geht er auf (2.2.) Jesu Worte und Taten und schließlich (2.3.) die Wirkungen ein, die sein Auftreten in der Geschichte gehabt hat. Wenn sich Maimonides bei alledem auch größtmöglicher Kürze befleißigt, enthält seine Darstellung dennoch eine Reihe interessanter Aussagen, deren Klarheit und Deutlichkeit nichts zu wünschen übrig lassen.

(paganen) Judenfeindschaft insgesamt siehe unter anderem John G. Gager, *The Origins of Anti-semitism. Attitudes toward Judaism in Pagan and Christian Antiquity* (New York: Oxford University Press, 1983); Zvi Yavetz, *Judenfeindschaft in der Antike. Die Münchener Vorträge*. Eingeleitet von Christian Meier (Beck'sche Reihe 1222; München: Beck, 1997); Peter Schäfer, *Judeophobia. Attitudes toward the Jews in the Ancient World* (Cambridge, Mass.: Harvard University Press, 1997).

50 Vgl. unter anderem 2. Makkabäer 4–7; zur Sache siehe Peter Schäfer, *Geschichte der Juden in der Antike* (Stuttgart, Neukirchen: Verlag Katholisches Bibelwerk, 1983), besonders S. 43–95; idem, *The History of the Jews in the Greco-Roman World* (London: Routledge, 2003).

51 Siehe dazu M. D. Rabinowitz' Einleitung zu seiner Edition des *Iggeret* (wie Anm. 6), S. 77–96; Halkin, *Iggeret* (wie Anm. 6), S. V–IX; Moshe Ṣadoq, *Yehude Teman. Toldotehem we-orḥot ḥayyehem* (Tel Aviv: Am Oved, 1967), S. 34ff.; Friedrich Niewöhner, „‚Terror in die Herzen aller Könige.‘ Der Messias und das Ende der weltlichen Welt im Jahre 1210 nach Maimonides“, in *Der Brief in den Jemen* (wie Anm. 6), S. 9–29, hier S. 13ff.

2.1. Maimonides über die Herkunft beziehungsweise Abstammung Jesu

Seine Aussagen über Jesu Herkunft beziehungsweise Abstammung beginnt Maimonides nachgerade unvermittelt mit der Feststellung, dass „er ein Jude ist" (*wa-huwa min Yisrā'ēl*) (*Iggeret*, ed. Halkin, S. 12,7–8/ed. Qāfiḥ, S. 21,20–21), und setzt sie ebenso unvermittelt fort mit der Erörterung der an entsprechende talmudische Überlieferungen anknüpfenden Frage, ob Jesus ein *mamzer*, das heißt ein „Bastard" beziehungsweise „illegitimer Sprössling", oder ein „legitimes Kind" gewesen ist. Dies ist insofern bemerkenswert, als eine Erörterung dieser Frage mit dem eigentlichen Thema des *Iggeret Teman* ebenso wenig zu tun hat wie mit Maimonides' Interesse an Jesus.

Geschuldet zu sein scheint diese Erörterung wohl den volkstümlichen *Toldot Jeschu*, von denen Maimonides, wenn auch gewiss nicht unmittelbar beeinflusst, so doch zumindest angeregt worden ist. Während nämlich die Frage, ob Jesus ein legitimes oder ein illegitimes Kind gewesen ist, die seit frühjüdischer Zeit Gegenstand der Polemik zwischen Juden und Christen gewesen ist,[52] in der gelehrten jüdisch-christlichen beziehungsweise christlich-jüdischen Auseinandersetzung des Mittelalters kaum mehr von Belang ist, schon gar nicht, wenn es – wie hier – um die Messianität Jesu beziehungsweise um Jesus als den gekommenen Messias und das Problem der Christologie geht,[53] steht sie in den volkstümlichen *Toldot Jeschu* stets am Anfang und spielt in ihnen eine entscheidende Rolle. Für die Versionen der *Toldot Jeschu*, die im islamischen

---

52 Das gesamte einschlägige Material ist ausgewertet von Johann Maier, *Jesus von Nazareth in der talmudischen Überlieferung* (Erträge der Forschung 82; Darmstadt: Wissenschaftliche Buchgesellschaft, 1978), und idem, *Jüdische Auseinandersetzung mit dem Christentum in der Antike* (Erträge der Forschung 177; Darmstadt: Wissenschaftliche Buchgesellschaft, 1982). Wie wenig eindeutig die Texte jedoch oft sind, zeigen deren zum Teil anderslautende Interpretationen unter anderem von Kurt Hruby, „Die Stellung der jüdischen Gesetzeslehrer zur werdenden Kirche", in idem, *Aufsätze zum nachbiblischen Judentum und zum jüdischen Erbe der frühen Kirche*, ed. Peter von der Osten-Sacken und Thomas Willi (Arbeiten zur neutestamentlichen Theologie und Zeitgeschichte 5; Berlin: Institut Kirche und Judentum, 1996), S. 349–414. Zur Sache siehe auch Krauss, *The Jewish-Christian Controversy* (wie Anm. 49), besonders S. 1–51.

53 Siehe dazu unter anderem Amos Funkenstein, „Basic Types of Christian anti-Jewish Polemics in the Later Middle Ages", in *Viator* 2 (1971), S. 373–382; Jeremy Cohen, „Towards a Functional Classification of Jewish anti-Christian Polemic in the High Middle Ages", in *Religionsgespräche im Mittelalter*, ed. Bernard Lewis und Friedrich Niewöhner (Wolfenbütteler Mittelalter-Studien 4; Wiesbaden: Harrassowitz, 1992), S. 93–114; ferner *Judaism on Trial. Jewish-Christian Disputations in the Middle Ages.* Edited and translated by Hyam Maccoby (Rutherford: Fairleigh Dickinson University Press, und London: Associated University Presses, 1982), und Maier, *Geschichte der jüdischen Religion* (wie Anm. 14), S. 424–436.

Raum kursierten, gilt dies noch mehr als für die im christlichen Europa in Umlauf befindlichen.[54]

Hier, in den *Toldot Jeschu*, in ihren verschiedenen Versionen – einschließlich der judaeo-arabischen Version, von der allerdings nur eine einzige, bislang unveröffentlichte Handschrift bekannt ist (Ms. Krupp) –, wird von Jesus immer wieder als einem *mamzer* („Bastard“) gesprochen und dies damit begründet, dass er nicht nur ein außereheliches Kind, sondern ein *ben ha-nidda* („während der Menstruation gezeugtes Kind“) gewesen ist. Jedenfalls werden in den *Toldot Jeschu* die beiden Begriffe *mamzer* und *ben ha-nidda* (beziehungsweise *bar de-zanyeta* = *ben ha-zenut*) nicht nur mit konstanter Regelmäßigkeit wiederholt und stets nebeneinander gebraucht, sondern der erste (*mamzer*) wird gleichsam mit dem zweiten begründet: Weil Jesus ein *ben ha-nidda* ist, ist er *eo ipso* ein *mamzer*.[55]

Dieser Argumentation schließt sich Maimonides nicht an. Im Gegenteil. Zwar kennt auch er die auf talmudische Überlieferung zurückgehende polemische Aussage von Jesus als einem *mamzer* und zitiert sie auch; doch er weist sie sofort zurück und sagt: Wenn „wir Jesus einen *mamzer* nennen“, ist dies nicht nur halakhisch nicht korrekt, sondern allein der antichristlichen Polemik geschuldet und „im Sinne einer Übertreibung“ (*ʿalā ǧihati l-mubālaġa*) zu verstehen (*Iggeret*, ed. Halkin, S. 12,10/ed. Qāfiḥ, S. 21,25),[56] nämlich – wie Samuel ibn Tibbon die Stelle übersetzt hat – „um ihn noch mehr zu verunglimpfen“ (*le-haflig be-ḥerpato*) (*Iggeret*, ed. Halkin, S. 13,10–11). Seine Zurückweisung des polemischen Satzes begründet Maimonides mit der geltenden rabbinischen Halakhah, wie er sie nicht zuletzt selber in seinem *Mišneh Torah* zusammengefasst hat.

Nach der geltenden rabbinischen Halakhah ist zunächst festzuhalten, dass ein *šetuqi* (feminin *šetuqit*), ein „un- oder außereheliches Kind“ (Mischna, *Qiddušin* 4:2; Babylonischer Talmud, *Yevamot* 100b) kein *mamzer* ist. Wird das Kind zudem während des Bestehens einer gültig geschlossenen Ehe geboren, wird darüber hinaus im Allgemeinen dessen „Ehelichkeit“ unterstellt (Babylonischer

---

54 Zu den *Toldot Jeschu* insgesamt siehe Samuel Krauss, *Das Leben Jesu nach jüdischen Quellen* (Berlin: Calvary, ²1902 [Nachdruck Hildesheim etc.: Olms, 1994]) und die darin abgedruckten hebräischen und deutschen Texte. Weitere Textausgaben: Günter Schlichting, *Ein jüdisches Leben Jesu. Die verschollene Toledot-Jeschu-Fassung Tam ū-mūʿād. Einleitung, Text, Übersetzung, Kommentar etc.* (Wissenschaftliche Untersuchungen zum Neuen Testament 24; Tübingen: J.C.B. Mohr [Paul Siebeck], 1982); *Vom Leben und Sterben des Juden Jeschu und wie die Rabbanim wieder Frieden zwischen Christen und Juden stifteten: Eine jüdische Erzählung. Sefer Toldos Jeschu – Liber Toldos Jeschu*, herausgegeben und mit einer deutschen Einleitung und Übersetzung versehen von Michael Krupp (Jerusalem: Lee Achim Sefarim, 2001); *Tam u-Muʿad. A Jewish Life of Jesus*, ed. Michael Krupp (Jerusalem: Lee Achim Sefarim, 2001).

55 Maier, *Jesus von Nazareth* (wie Anm. 52), S. 244–248.

56 Wie auch Qāfiḥ, *Iggeret* (wie Anm. 6) übersetzt hat: *ʿal derekh ha-haflagah*.

Talmud, *Sota* 27a). Vielmehr gilt aufgrund der Mischna (*Yevamot* 4:13 und Babylonischer Talmud, *Yevamot* 49aff.) und des tannaitischen Kommentars *Sifre Devarim* (§ 248) als *mamzer* (feminin *mamzeret*) ein Kind nur dann, wenn es aus einer von der Torah verbotenen Verbindung (Auflistung in Leviticus 18; Deuteronomium 23,3) hervorgegangen ist,[57] sei es aus einer Verbindung, auf die die göttliche „Strafe der Ausrottung" (*'ones karet*) steht, sei es aus einem Ehebruch, das heißt aus der Verbindung mit einer verheirateten Frau, der mit Todesstrafe sanktioniert war (Jerusalemer Talmud, *Yevamot* IV,15/6b; Babylonischer Talmud, *Yevamot* 49a–b; 80b).

Demgegenüber erklärt nun Maimonides, dass ein Kind allein dann als *mamzer* zu betrachten ist, wenn entweder seine Mutter bereits eine *mamzeret* ist („Hilkhot Issure bi'a" 15.3/*Mišneh Torah* VII, S. 95; vgl. Babylonischer Talmud, *Qiddušin* 66) oder aber das Kind „aus *'erwa* („Unzucht") oder *'arayot* („Inzest") hervorgegangen ist" („Hilkhot Issure bi'a" 15.1/ibid., S. 94), das heißt, aus den unerlaubten Verbindungen, die – wie bereits erwähnt – nach der Torah mit der göttlichen „Strafe der Ausrottung" bedroht sind („Hilkhot Išut" 1.5/*Mišneh Torah* VI, S. 3), und zwar völlig unabhängig davon, „ob [die Zeugung] durch Vergewaltigung (*be-ones*) oder durch [beiderseitigen] Willen (*be-rașon*), ob vorsätzlich (*be-zadon*) oder fahrlässig (*bi-šgaga*) erfolgt ist" („Hilkhot Issure bi'a" 15.1/*Mišneh Torah* VII, S. 94). Und nicht nur das; denn nach Maimonides ist nicht nur die Frage, „ob [die Zeugung] durch Vergewaltigung oder durch [beiderseitigen] Willen erfolgt ist", in diesem Zusammenhang irrelevant, sondern ebenso auch die Frage, „ob [die Frau] eine unverheiratete (*p^enuya*) oder eine verheiratete Frau (*ešet iš*) ist" („Hilkhot Issure bi'a" 15.3/ibid., S. 95).

Darüber hinaus zählt er auch den Beischlaf während der Menstruation nicht nur nicht zu den unerlaubten Verbindungen, sondern schließt ihn ausdrücklich aus deren Reihe aus (*ḥuș min ha-nidda*). Damit ist ein mit einer Menstruierenden gezeugtes Kind zwar *pagum*, das heißt ein „mit einem Makel behaftetes" Kind, aber es ist dennoch kein *mamzer* (*we-eno mamzer*) („Hilkhot Issure bi'a" 15.1/ibid., S. 94).

Mit dieser Feststellung widerspricht Maimonides den *Toldot Jeschu* in gleich dreifacher Hinsicht; denn: (1) auch nach den *Toldot Jeschu* ist die Mutter Jesu keine *mamzeret*, sondern gilt als rechtschaffene Frau. (2) Selbst wenn Jesus in den *Toldot Jeschu* ein *ben ha-nidda*, ein während der Menstruation gezeugtes Kind genannt wird, ist seine Einstufung als *mamzer* dennoch ebenso wenig gerechtfertigt wie die dafür angegebene Begründung stichhaltig, denn nach Maimonides zählt auch Beischlaf während der Menstruation nicht zu den unerlaubten Verbindungen. Auch ein *ben ha-nidda* ist danach kein *mamzer*. (3) Schließlich ist auch die in den *Toldot Jeschu* immer wieder geschilderte Gewalt-

57 Maier, *Jesus von Nazareth* (wie Anm. 52), S. 49–50.101–103; Calum M. Carmichael, *Law, Legend and Incest in the Bible – Leviticus 18–20* (Ithaca, N.Y.: Cornell University Press, 1997).

tätigkeit, mit der die Mutter Jesu zum Beischlaf gezwungen worden ist, kein Argument gegen Jesus. Denn ob der Beischlaf eine Vergewaltigung war oder im beiderseitigen Einverständnis geschehen ist, hatte Maimonides im Blick auf den Status des gezeugten Kindes für ebenso belanglos erklärt wie die Frage, ob die Frau verheiratet war oder nicht. Folglich gilt für Maimonides, dass Jesus – trotz allem – ein Jude (*wa-huwa min Yisraʾel*) war, und dies ganz im Sinne der geltenden Halakhah (vgl. Babylonischer Talmud, *Yevamot* 45a; *Qiddušin* 68b):

> Was ihn betrifft – wenngleich sein Vater ein Nichtjude (*goy*) und seine Mutter eine Jüdin (*yisraʾelit*) war, war er folglich ein Jude (*fa-huwa min Yisraʾel*). Denn hinsichtlich der Abstammung (*al-aṣl*) gilt bei uns: „Zeugen ein Nichtjude oder ein Sklave [ein Kind] mit einer Jüdin (*bat Yisraʾel*), dann ist das Kind legitim (*ha-walad kašer*)“ [also ebenfalls Jude beziehungsweise Jüdin] (*Iggeret*, ed. Halkin, S. 12,8–10/ed. Qāfiḥ, S. 21,22–24).

Dass Maimonides dabei noch einen Hinweis auf die nichtjüdische Herkunft des Vaters Jesu unterbringt, ist wiederum der auf talmudischen Quellen basierenden antichristlichen Polemik der *Toldot Jeschu* zu verdanken, genannt seien hier dafür nur die so genannten *Ben-Pandera*-Texte,[58] die im vorliegenden Zusammenhang jedoch nicht weiter zu vertiefen sind, und beweist einmal mehr, dass es wohl eben diese *Toldot Jeschu* gewesen sind, aus denen Maimonides die Anregung zu seinen Aussagen über die Person Jesu bezogen hat.

2.2. Lehre und Taten Jesu

Im Hinblick auf die Lehre und Taten Jesu bringt Maimonides drei Gesichtspunkte ins Spiel, die er als dessen Absicht und angestrebtes Ziel (*ʿalā mā qaṣada wa-aġraḍa*) beschreibt, und zwar:

> (1) Er [Jesus] gab vor (*fa-awhama*), dass er von Gott gesandt ist (*mabʿūṯ min allāh*), die Probleme der Torah zu lösen (*li-yubayyina muškilāti t-tōrā*), und (2) dass er der von jedem Propheten angekündigte Messias ist (*wa-annahu l-mašīaḥ al-mawʿūdu bihi ʿalā yaday kulli nabīyin*). (3) Dann legte er aber die Torah in einer Weise aus (*fa-taʾawwala t-tōrā taʾwīlan*), die darauf hinausläuft, das ganze Gesetz abzuschaffen (*yuʾaddī li-ibṭāli ǧumlati š-šarīʿa*) und alle seine Gebote aufzuheben (*wa-taʿṭīli ǧamīʿi awāmirihā*), alle seine Verbote hingegen zu tun (*wa-rtikābi ǧamīʿi manāhīhā*) (*Iggeret*, ed. Halkin, S. 12,10–14/ed. Qāfiḥ, S. 21,25–30).

Dass es sich bei diesen drei Themen um die üblichen Gegenstände der christlich-jüdischen/jüdisch-christlichen Auseinandersetzung handelt, ist nicht schwer zu erkennen. Nicht zu übersehen ist dabei allerdings zugleich auch,

58 Maier, *Jesus von Nazareth* (wie Anm. 52), S. 238–243.264–273.

dass sich Maimonides in seiner Rezeption dieser drei Themen, vor allem in ihrer Darlegung, von manchen anderen Polemikern seiner Zeit unterscheidet. Wenn auch nach christlicher Überlieferung Jesus *der Christus*, und das heißt: *der gottgesandte Messias* ist, so wird Jesus in der jüdischen polemisch-apologetischen Literatur, jedenfalls des Mittelalters, doch immer wieder gegen diese Identifikation in Schutz genommen und entsprechend verteidigt. Denn danach ist es nicht er gewesen, der ihn als Messias ausgegeben hat, vielmehr waren es seine Anhänger, die von seiner Messianität überzeugt waren und in ihm den in der hebräischen Bibel angekündigten Messias sahen, dies aber erst nach seiner Auferstehung (und Himmelfahrt) erkannt haben. Noch in einer arabischen Version des so genannten *Testimonium Flavianum*,[59] die der christlich-arabische Historiker Agapius (10. Jahrhundert) in seinem *Kitāb al-ʿunwān* überliefert hat,[60] wird erzählt, „dass zu jener Zeit ein weiser Mann (*ḥakīm*) war, der Ješuaʿ genannt wurde, einen guten Lebenswandel aufwies und als tugendhaft (oder: gelehrt) bekannt war und viele Leute von den Juden und von anderen Völkern als Jünger hatte. Pilatus hatte ihn zur Kreuzigung und zum Tode verurteilt, aber diejenigen, die seine Jünger geworden waren, gaben seine Jüngerschaft (oder: Lehre) nicht auf und erzählten, dass er ihnen drei Tage nach der Kreuzigung erschienen sei und lebe und daher *vielleicht der Messias sei*, in bezug auf den die Propheten Wunderbares gesagt haben".[61]

Die unendlich oft verhandelte Frage nach dem Messiasbewusstsein Jesu, das heißt die Frage, ob er selbst sich als Messias verstanden hat oder ob es erst seine Jünger und Nachfolger waren, die in ihm den Messias erkannt haben, mag hier dahingestellt bleiben. Für Maimonides steht fest, dass sich Jesus selber als Messias gesehen, als solcher ausgegeben und durch entsprechende Taten, vergeblich freilich, auszuweisen versucht hat.

Was dies für Taten waren, sagt Maimonides zunächst zwar nicht. Nur summarisch spricht er davon, dass „er [Jesus] die Gabe der Prophetie zu haben und gewaltige Dinge zu tun vorgegeben habe" (*bi-ddiʿāʾihi n-nubūwa wa-taʿāṭīhi l-umūra l-ʿaẓīma*) (*Iggeret*, ed. Halkin, S. 12,16–18/ed. Qāfiḥ, S. 22,6–7). Erst am Ende seines *Iggeret Teman* lässt er „die Christen" (*an-naṣārā*) diese „gewaltigen Dinge" als „Wiederbelebung der Toten" (*iḥyāʾ al-mawtā*) und „jene [anderen] Wunder" (*tilka l-ʿaǧāʾib*) erklären, fügt allerdings gleich hinzu, dass es sich dabei nur um Taten handelt, die die Christen Jesus nachträglich „zugeschrieben" (*mā nasabat ilayhi n-naṣārā*) beziehungsweise „die sie erlogen haben" (*yakḏibūnahā*) (*Iggeret*, ed. Halkin, S. 92,7–9/ed. Qāfiḥ, S. 53,3–6). Interessant ist gleichwohl,

59 Gemeint sind damit die beiden Texte in Josephus, *Antiquitates* XVIII,3,3 und XX,9,1, in denen von Jesus die Rede ist. Ihre Echtheit ist allerdings mehr als zweifelhaft. Siehe dazu Schürer, *The History of the Jewish People* (wie Anm. 49), Band I, S. 428–441; Maier, *Jesus von Nazareth* (wie Anm. 52), S. 42–45.

60 Shlomo Pines, *An Arabic Version of the Testimonium Flavianum and its Implications* (Jerusalem: Israel Academy of Sciences and Humanities, 1971).

61 Zitiert nach der Übersetzung von Maier, *Jesus von Nazareth* (wie Anm. 52), S. 42–43.

dass Maimonides die „Wiederbelebung der Toten“ und „sonstigen Wunder“ hier erwähnt; denn damit nennt er jene beiden Geschehen, die der rabbinischen Überlieferung nach zu den „Beglaubigungswundern des Messias“ zählen und nicht nur die messianische Zeit von dieser Zeit unterscheiden, sondern Zeichen der messianischen Zeit sind.[62] Wie jedoch *Mišneh Torah*, „Hilkhot Melakhim“ 11 und 12 zu entnehmen ist, lehnt Maimonides diese überlieferte Ansicht entschieden ab: „Es falle dir nicht ein, dass der König Messias Zeichen und Wunder (*otot u-moftim*)[63] tun muss, eine Neuerung in der Welt einführt (*meḥaddeš devarim ba-ʿolam*), Tote wiederbelebt (*meḥayyeh metim*)[64] und dergleichen Dinge mehr – dem ist nicht so!“ (11.3/*Mišneh Torah* XVII, S. 414). Vielmehr insistiert er mit allem Nachdruck daher darauf, dass auch in der messianischen Zeit „die Weltordnung bleibt, wie sie ist“ (*ʿolam ke-minhago noheg*). Der einzige Unterschied zwischen dieser Welt und der messianischen Zeit besteht darin, dass es in ihr „keinen Hunger und keinen Krieg, keinen Zank und keinen Streit“ mehr gibt, sondern „die ganze Welt voll der Erkenntnis Gottes ist“ (12.1, 4/*Mišneh Torah* XVII, S. 417, 419–420).

Wenn nun Maimonides des Weiteren gegen Jesus vorbringt, dass er sich zum einen die Lösung aller Probleme der Torah angemaßt und zum anderen zugleich deren Abschaffung angestrebt habe, liegt dies ganz auf seiner Argumentationslinie. Während jedoch die erste Aussage dem entspricht, was Maimonides an anderer Stelle als Kennzeichen der messianischen Zeit ansieht, nämlich nicht nur die universale Kenntnis der Torah, sondern auch die Lösung aller ihrer Schwierigkeiten und Probleme (*Mišneh Torah*, „Hilkhot Melakhim“ 12.4/B. XVII, S. 419–420), so widerspricht er mit dem zweiten Argument einer traditionellen jüdischen Ansicht, der zufolge die Torah vom Sinai in der messianischen Zeit keine Gültigkeit mehr hat, sondern durch eine andere Torah beziehungsweise eine andere Auslegung der Torah ersetzt werden wird.[65] Überliefert sind die beiden diesbezüglichen *loci classici* zum einen im Namen R. Josefs: „Die *miṣwot* [das heißt die Torah vom Sinai] werden in der zukünfti-

---

62 Vgl. Mischna, *Sanhedrin* 10:1; Babylonischer Talmud, *Ketubbot* 111a–b und öfter; vgl. dazu „Hilkhot Melakhim“ 12.3/*Mišneh Torah* XVII, S. 414; siehe dazu auch die Belege in Schürer, *The History of the Jewish People* (wie Anm. 49), Band II, S. 539–544.

63 Nach *Sifre Devarim* § 83 und R. Schelomo b. Isaak (Raschi), *Peruš ʿal ha-torah*, in *Tora Ḥayyim – Ḥamiša Ḥumše Torah* (wie Anm. 14), Band VI, S. 114b zu Deuteronomium 13:2, geschehen *otot* „im Himmel“ und *moftim* „auf der Erde“.

64 Nach „Hilkhot Yesode ha-torah“ 10.1/*Mišneh Torah* II, S. 45, wäre dies eine „Änderung der Weltordnung“ (*šinnuy minhago šel ha-ʿolam*), die es nach Maimonides jedoch auch in der messianischen Zeit nicht geben wird.

65 Zur rabbinischen Diskussion um die Frage einer Torah der messianischen Zeit und das Problem ihrer Abrogation siehe unter anderem Abraham Joshua Heschel, *Tora min ha-šamayim be-aspeqlarya šel ha-dorot* (3 Bände; London, Jerusalem: The Soncino Press, 1962–1990), Band III, S. 49–81; William David Davies, *The Setting of the Sermon on the Mount* (Cambridge: Cambridge University Press, 1964), S. 156–190; Shapiro, *The Limits of Orthodox Theology* (wie Anm. 23), S. 122–131.

gen Welt abgeschafft" (Babylonischer Talmud, *Niddah* 61b), und zum anderen im Namen R. Abin b. Kahanas, der mit Bezug auf Jesaja 51:4 lehrte: „Der Heilige, gepriesen sei Er, sagte: ‚Neue Torah (*Torah ḥadaša*)[66] wird von Mir ausgehen', [das meint,] eine Erneuerung [Novellierung] der Torah (*ḥidduš torah*) wird von Mir ausgehen" (*Wayiqra Rabbah* 13:3/ed. Mirkin, Band VII, S. 140–141).[67]

Gegen eine solche Anschauung hatte Maimonides bereits in der neunten seiner dreizehn Glaubenslehren ebenso eindrücklich wie unmissverständlich Stellung bezogen und erklärt, (IX) „[...] dass die Torah des Mose (*šarīʿat Mošeh*) nicht abrogiert und keine andere Torah (*šarīʿa*) von Gott außer ihr ausgehen wird. Weder wird zu ihr hinzugefügt noch von ihr weggestrichen werden, weder hinsichtlich des Wortlautes (*lā fī n-naṣṣ*) noch hinsichtlich der Auslegung (*lā fī t-tafsīr*)".[68]

Wenn Maimonides nun Jesus unterstellt, die Abschaffung der Torah angestrebt zu haben, begibt er sich wiederum in Widerspruch zu manchen seiner Zeitgenossen, früherer oder späterer Generation, die Jesus gegen eben diesen Vorwurf in Schutz genommen haben, wie dies beispielsweise Saʿd b. Manṣūr Ibn Kammūna (um 1215–um 1285) in seinem *Kitāb tanqīḥ al-abḥāṯ li-l-milal aṯ-ṯalāṯ* („Buch der Kritik der Untersuchungen der drei Religionen") getan hat.[69] In Aufnahme einer Aussage Yaʿqūb al-Qirqisānīs (10. Jahrhundert) aus dessen *Kitāb al-anwār wa-l-marāqib* („Buch der Lichter und Leuchttürme")[70] hat er mit

66 In Jesaja 51:4 fehlt das Adjektiv *ḥadaša*, dort heißt es nur: *torah me'itti teṣe'* („Torah wird von Mir ausgehen").

67 Ähnlich heißt es in *Yalquṭ Shim'oni* II § 429 (zu Jesaja): „Eine neue Torah wird durch den Messias gegeben werden".

68 Arabischer und hebräischer Text: Holzer, *Zur Geschichte der Dogmenlehre* (wie Anm. 23), S. 27. Ebenso auch in „Hilkhot Yesode ha-torah" 10.1/*Mišneh Torah* II, S. 42; „Hilkhot Tešuva" 3.8/ibid., S. 223–224; „Hilkhot Megilla" 2.18/*Mišneh Torah* V, S. 655; „Hilkhot Melakhim" 11.1, 3/*Mišneh Torah* XVII, S. 412–414.

69 Arabischer Text: *Sa'd b. Manṣūr Ibn Kammūna's Examination of the Inquiries into Three Faiths. A Thirteenth-Century Essay in Comparative Religion*, ed. Moshe Perlmann (University of California Publications, Near Eastern Studies 6; Berkeley, Los Angeles: University of California Press, 1967), englische Übersetzung: Moshe Perlmann, *Ibn Kammūna's Examination of the Three Faiths. A Thirteenth-Century Essay in the Comparative Study of Religion* (Berkeley etc.: University of California Press, 1971). – Siehe dazu Stefan Schreiner, „Ibn Kammûna's Verteidigung des historischen Jesus gegen den paulinischen Christus", in *Geschichte – Tradition – Reflexion. Festschrift für Martin Hengel zum 70. Geburtstag*, ed. Hubert Cancik, Hermann Lichtenberger und Peter Schäfer (3 Bände; Tübingen: J.C.B. Mohr [Paul Siebeck], 1997), Band I, S. 453–479; ferner auch Simone Rosenkranz, „Judentum, Christentum und Islam in der Sicht des Ibn Kammūna", in *Judaica* 52 (1996), S. 4–22.

70 Ed. Leon Nemoy (5 Bände; New York: Alexander Kohut Memorial Foundation, 1939–1943). In Buch I, Kapitel 8 hat er sich ausführlich mit Jesus und den Anfängen des Christentums befasst; siehe dazu Bruno Chiesa und Wilfrid Lockwood, *Ya'qūb al-Qirqisānī on Jewish Sects and Christianity. A Translation of* Kitāb al-anwār *Book I, with two introductory essays* (Judentum und Umwelt 10; Frankfurt am Main etc.: Peter Lang, 1984).

allem Nachdruck nicht nur Jesu Judesein, sondern ebenso auch seine unbedingte Treue zur Torah betont. Nicht zufällig zitiert er den Satz aus Matthäus 5:17 „Ich bin nicht gekommen, sie [die Torah] zu zerstören, sondern zu erfüllen" gleich dreimal[71] und macht ihn zum Schlüsselsatz für das Verstehen Jesu und seiner Sendung. Selbst dort, wo in den Evangelien von einem tatsächlichen oder vermeintlichen Verstoß Jesu gegen ein Gebot der Torah erzählt wird, geht es, wie Ibn Kammūna zu erklären weiß, im Grunde um nichts anderes als um Halakhah, um legitime Auslegung und Anwendung des Gebotes der Torah unter veränderten Bedingungen. So schreibt er: „Als sie [die Juden] ihm, wie es ihnen schien, Missachtung einiger ihrer [der Tora] Gesetze vorwarfen (*ankarū ʿalayhi mā tawahhamūhu tafrīṭan fī baʿḍi aḥkāmihā*), erklärte er ihnen, dass es nicht Missachtung ist, und erläuterte ihnen dies entsprechend dem, was ihre Rechtsauslegung und ihr Gesetz verlangen (*wa-awḍaḥa lahum ḏālika mimmā yaqtaḍīhi fiqhuhum wa-šarʿuhum*), wie es im Evangelium erwähnt ist".[72]

Und ganz im Gegensatz zu Maimonides hält Ibn Kammūna in seinem Schlussplädoyer für den historischen Jesus fest: „Der Herr Christus hat keines der Gesetze der Torah verletzt (*lam yanquḍ šayʾan min aḥkāmi t-tawrāt*), sondern er hat nach allen ihren Geboten gehandelt bis zum letzten Ende (*bal ʿamila bi-ǧamīʿi farāʾiḍihā ilā āḫiri waqtin*), wie wir erläutert haben, und in diesem Sinne ist er auch ihr Vollender (*fa-huwa mutammimun lahā min hāḏā l-waǧhi ayḍan*)."[73]

Es ist dies übrigens zugleich auch Ibn Kammūnas Antwort an alle diejenigen unter den Christen, die der Ansicht sind, dass der Vers Matthäus 5:17 von Römer 10:4 („Christus ist das Ende der Tora") her zu interpretieren sei, und zwar in dem Sinne, „dass in der Torah die Ankunft des Christus verheißen ist, für die Gesetze, die in ihr enthalten sind (*aš-šarāʾiʿ allatī fīhā*), daher [gilt], dass sie alle zu tun verpflichtend ist bis zu seinem Erscheinen (*innamā yalzamu l-ʿamalu bi-ǧamīʿihā ilā ḥīni ẓuhūrihi*), nicht aber für immer oder bis zum Tag der Auferstehung (*lā ilā l-abadi aw ilā yawmi l-qiyāma*). Denn seit er [Jesus] erschienen ist, ist sie zum Ende gekommen (*fa-qad kamulat*), erstens durch Erfüllung seiner Verheißung (*bi-naǧāzi l-waʿdi bihi awwalan*) und zweitens durch Vollendung ihrer Verbindlichkeit (*bi-kamāli t-taklīfi bihā ṯāniyan*)."[74]

Nach Ibn Kammūna, der diesbezüglich in guter karäischer Tradition steht,[75] hat indessen nicht nur Jesus allein der Torah und damit der jüdischen Tradition

---

71 *Ibn Kammūna's Examination of the Inquiries into Three Faiths*, ed. Perlmann (wie Anm. 69), S. 54 (arabisch)/S. 83 (englisch); S. 58/S. 88; S. 63/S. 95.

72 Ibid., S. 54/S. 83.

73 Ibid., S. 63/S. 95.

74 Ibid.

75 Leon Nemoy, „The Attitude of the Early Karaites Towards Christianity", in Saul Lieberman (Ed.), *Salo Wittmayer Baron Jubilee Volume on the Occasion of his Eightieth Birthday* (3 Bände; Jerusalem: American Academy for Jewish Research, 1975), Band II, S. 697–715; Daniel J. Lasker, *Jewish Philosophical Polemics Against Christianity in the Middle Ages* (New York: Ktav, 1977), S. 52.57–61.191–192.194.196–200.210.

die Treue gehalten, auch seine Jünger (und Nachfolger) haben es getan, jedenfalls bis zu einem bestimmten Zeitpunkt: „Nach langer Zeit" jedoch haben die Anhänger der Lehre Jesu angefangen, die Gebote der Torah nicht mehr zu befolgen, und dies damit begründet, dass die Torah ihrer Meinung nach nur bis zur Ankunft des Messias, bis zum Auftreten des Christus also, Gültigkeit gehabt hätten, nicht aber über diesen Zeitpunkt hinaus. Den entscheidenden Anteil an dieser Veränderung – und damit an der Begründung des Christentums – schreibt Ibn Kammūna ebenso, wie es vor ihm Yaʿqūb al-Qirqisānī getan hatte,[76] Paulus zu:

> Veränderungen der Gesetze der Torah (*taġyīr aḥkāmi t-tawrāt*), wie die Erlaubnis [zum Genuss] des Schweinefleisches und das Unterlassen der Beschneidung und der [rituellen] Waschungen, sind von den Jüngern berichtet, nicht aber vom Herrn Christus; denn er hat an ihren [der Torah] Gesetzen festgehalten (*fa-innahu lam yazal mutamassikan bi-aḥkāmihā*), bis ihn die Juden gefangen genommen haben. [...] Seine [Jesu] Gefährten hielten lange Zeit an der Treue zu ihr [der Torah] fest, bevor sie gegen sie zu verstoßen begannen und ihre Abrogierung verkündeten, [indem sie sagten,] dass sie zu befolgen nur bis zur Erscheinung des Herrn Christus verbindlich gewesen war, nicht länger. Das meiste davon geht auf die Meinung des Gesandten Paulus zurück (*akṯar ḏālika ʿan raʾyi Fūlūs ar-rasūl*).[77]

Zwar nimmt auch Maimonides (wie andere noch nach ihm) einen längeren Zeitraum zwischen dem Auftreten Jesu und dem Aufkommen beziehungsweise der Ausbreitung des Christentums an,[78] anders als Ibn Kammūna hindert ihn das jedoch nicht, in Jesus den Initiator des Christentums, also Urheber der Abschaffung der Torah und *eo ipso* der versuchten Zerstörung des Judentums zu sehen, um allerdings sogleich hinzuzufügen, dass ihm, Jesus, dies freilich nicht gelungen ist:

> Lange Zeit nach ihm (*wa-min baʿdihi bi-muddatin ṭawīla*) breitete sich eine Religion aus, die die Kinder Esaus auf ihn zurückführen. Obwohl dies sein Ziel gewesen war (*wa-maʿa kāna ḏālika ġaraḍahu*), das er erhofft hatte (*allaḏī kāna yuʾammilu*), schadete er dennoch Israel nicht (*fa-mā ḏālika*

---

76 „The Christian religion as practiced now was invented and proclaimed by Pūlus: it was he who ascribed divinity to Jesus and claimed to be himself the prophet of Jesus his Lord. He introduced no duties and imposed nothing at all. He asserted that religion is nothing but humility. They say that the fasting and prayers which they observe are not compulsory duties but purely voluntary. They forbid no form of food but allow all animals, from the gnat to the elephant" (*Kitāb al-anwār*, Buch I, Kapitel 8, § 2/ed. Nemoy [wie Anm. 70], Band I, S. 43/englisch [zitiert nach W. Lockwoods Übersetzung (wie Anm. 70)] S. 135–136).

77 Ed. Perlmann (wie Anm. 69), S. 54/S. 82–83. Während der Name bei Ibn Kammūna *fūlūs* lautet, schreibt ihn Yaʿqūb al-Qirqisānī *fūlūṣ*.

78 Siehe dazu die Belege in Halkin, *Iggeret* (wie Anm. 6), S. 14, Anm. 15.

> *ḍarra Yisra'el*), und sie gerieten nicht in Zweifel seinetwegen, weder alle noch Einzelne (*lā ǧam' wa-lā furād*), denn klar war ihnen, dass er unterlegen (*ḫusruhu*) und besiegt (*ġalabatuhu*) und in unsere Hände gefallen war (*inqiṭā'uhu fī aydīnā*), bis mit ihm geschehen ist, was geschehen ist (*ilā an tamma 'alayhi mā tamma*) (*Iggeret*, ed. Halkin, S. 14,1–4/ed. Qāfiḥ, S. 22,10–15).

Dass Maimonides an dieser Stelle eine gewisse Schönfärberei betreibt, liegt auf der Hand. Denn davon, dass „er, Jesus, Israel nicht schadete“, kann im Hinblick auf die von seiner Lehre und seinem Tun ausgegangene Wirkungsgeschichte, um die Maimonides durchaus wusste, wohl ebenso wenig die Rede sein wie davon, dass seinetwegen niemand in Zweifel geraten ist. Geschuldet ist diese Schönfärberei freilich dem pädagogischen Anliegen, das Maimonides mit seinem Brief verfolgte. Dies zeigt sich unmissverständlich schließlich an seinen Äußerungen über das Ende Jesu.

2.3. Das Ende Jesu

Dass es trotz Jesu Lehre und Wirken nicht zum Ende, das heißt zur Zerstörung des Judentums gekommen ist, also Jesus als Messias(prätendent) gescheitert ist, ist nach Maimonides der Aufmerksamkeit und Wachsamkeit der jüdischen Gelehrten zu verdanken:

> Doch die Weisen, ihr Andenken zum Segen, haben seine Absicht verspürt, bevor sich sein Ansehen im Volk verbreitet hatte (*fa-ša'ara [...] li-ġaraḍihi qabla an tatamakkana šuhratuhu fī l-milla*), und sie machten mit ihm, was er verdient hat (*fa-fa'alū bihi mā kāna ahlan lahu*). Vorausgegangen war an uns bereits die diesbezügliche Warnung (*wa-qad kāna taqaddama lanā l-inḏāru bi-ḏālika*) durch Daniel, der gesagt hatte, dass einer von den Ruchlosen Israels und seinen Abtrünnigen (*raǧul min wuqaḥā'i Yisra'el wa-ḫawāriǧihim*) danach streben werde, die Religion zu zerstören (*sa-yarūmu ifsāda d-dīn*), indem er die Gabe der Prophetie zu haben behauptet (*bi-ddi'ā'ihi n-nubūwa*) und gewaltige Dinge tut (*wa-ta'āṭīhi l-umūra l-'aẓīma*), das heißt, dass er der Messias ist, dass aber Gott ihn [Jesus] zu Fall bringen werde, wie er [ihn] zu Fall gebracht hat (*wa-inna llāha yu'aṯṯiruhu ka-mā 'aṯṯara*). Und das ist seine [Daniels] Rede: „Und Ruchlose deines Volkes werden sich erheben, damit sich die Weissagung erfüllt, aber sie werden zu Fall kommen“ (Daniel 11:14b) (*Iggeret*, ed. Halkin, S. 12,14–20/ed. Qāfiḥ, S. 21,30–22,9).[79]

Bemerkenswert ist bei dieser Begründung, dass Maimonides in der Erklärung des Todes Jesu auf ein Zitat aus dem Propheten Daniel zurückgreift. Ebenso

79 Das gleiche – mit demselben Danielzitat belegt – sagt Maimonides noch einmal in „Hilkhot Melakhim“ 11.4/*Mišneh Torah* XVII, S. 416.

hatte es vor ihm auch schon Saadja Gaon (892–942) in seiner antichristlichen Polemik getan.[80] War es doch gerade das Buch Daniel, aus dem in der christlichen Überlieferung seit alters die *loci probantes* für die Sendung Jesu und seine Messianität bezogen worden sind. Es spricht für Maimonides' Vertrautheit mit dieser Problematik, wenn er jetzt dasselbe Danielbuch zitiert, um das Gegenteil zu beweisen.[81]

Das Ende Jesu ist freilich nicht allein das gerechte Ende eines selbsternannten Messiasprätendenten; es ist zugleich im Sinne eines Gottesurteils der Beweis dafür, dass er nicht der Messias war. Wie wahre und falsche Prophetie an ihrem Erfolg oder Misserfolg erkennbar sind, ein wahrer Prophet allein der ist, dessen Wort eintrifft, ein erfolgloser Prophet sich *eo ipso* als ein falscher Prophet erweist (Deuteronomium 18:20–22), so sind auch im Falle des Messias Erfolg oder Misserfolg entscheidend. Ein Messias, der scheitert und dazu noch getötet wird, ist kein Messias, wie Maimonides am Beispiel des von R. Aqiva, dem „großen Gelehrten unter den Gelehrten der Mischna" (*ḥakham gadol me-ḥakhme mišna*), zum Messias proklamierten und von „allen Gelehrten seiner Generation (*kol ḥakhme doro*) als König Messias anerkannten" Bar Kochba aufzeigt: „Als [weil] er getötet wurde, wurde [war] ihnen klar, dass er es nicht ist" (*kewan še-neherag noda' lahem še-eno*) („Hilkhot Melakhim" 12.3/*Mišneh Torah* XVIII, S. 414).

3. Schluss

Verfasst hatte Maimonides seinen *Iggeret Teman* in pädagogischer Absicht.[82] Ihm war es darum zu tun, die Juden Jemens vor der Gefahr zu bewahren, einem falschen Messias auf den Leim zu gehen. Am Beispiel der Geschichte Jesu, seines Lehrens und Wirkens, vor allem aber seines schmählichen Endes kann er überzeugend darlegen, wohin ein selbsterhobener Messiasanspruch führt. Am Schluss seines Briefes ruft er daher noch einmal in Erinnerung:

---

80 Siehe dazu Eliezer Schlossberg, „*Pulmuso šel Rav Se'adya Ga'on neged ha-naṣrut*", in *Heritage and Innovation in Medieval Judaeo-Arabic Culture* (hebräisch), ed. Joshua Blau und David Doron (Ramat-Gan: Bar-Ilan University Press, 2000), S. 243–262, hier besonders S. 252–262.

81 Vgl. dazu auch das Beispiel in Stefan Schreiner, „‚Und nach 62 Wochen wird umgebracht ein Gesalbter …' – Isaak Troki's Kritik an der christlichen Auslegung von Dan 9,24–27", in *Hören und Lernen in der Schule des NAMENS. Mit der Tradition zum Aufbruch. Festschrift für Bertold Klappert zum 60. Geburtstag*, ed. Jochen Denker, Jonas Marquardt und Borgi Winkler-Rohlfing (Neukirchen-Vluyn: Neukirchener Verlag, 1999), S. 134–145.

82 Niewöhner, „‚Terror in die Herzen aller Könige'" (wie Anm. 51), S. 21ff.

> Ihr wisst, dass [im Hinblick auf] Jesus den Nazarener – seine Knochen mögen zu Staub zermahlen sein! – trotz allem, was die Christen (*an-naṣārā*) ihm zugeschrieben haben, dass er [es] getan habe, angefangen von der Wiederbelebung der Toten, wie sie behaupten, bis zu jenen Wundern, die sie erlogen haben (*wa-min tilka l-ʿaǧāʾibi llatī yakḏibūnahā*), selbst wenn wir sie ihnen im Sinne einer Diskussionsgrundlage zugestehen (*ḥattā iḏā sallamnāhā lahum ʿalā ǧihati taqdīri l-ḥuǧǧa*), sie bei uns nicht entbunden sind, [den Beweis] für ihre Annahme [zu erbringen] (*mā yataḫallaṣū maʿanā fī daʿwāhum*), nämlich dass Jesus der Messias ist. Denn wir können ihnen in den Texten etwa an die tausend Belege (*alf ʿalāma aw qurbahā*) zeigen, die nicht auf Jesus bezogen sind, selbst nach ihrer Annahme (*wa-law ʿalā daʿwāhum*) (*Iggeret*, ed. Halkin, S. 92,7–12/ed. Qāfiḥ, S. 53,3–11).

Auch um den Preis, dass – historisch gesehen – nicht alles stimmt, was Maimonides hier geschrieben hat, seinen pädagogischen Zweck hat er erreicht. Das Bild, das Maimonides vom historischen Jesus entwirft, ist begrenzt auf dessen Bedeutung als abschreckendes Beispiel eines selbsternannten Messiasprätendenten und seines schmählichen Endes. Was immer im Widerspruch zu diesem Bild steht, wird ausgeklammert oder nachgerade ins Gegenteil verkehrt. Auch wenn Maimonides' Jesus im Zusammenhang mit den Jesusbildern der Zeit steht, den Jesusbildern der volkstümlich-polemischen *Toldot Jeschu* ebenso wie denen der karäischen und rabbanitischen Gelehrten, so war sein Interesse am historischen Jesus doch nur begrenzt.

Die antike Welt

"Life is Short, the Art is Long": Maimonides' Comments on Hippocrates' First Aphorism

by

Samuel Kottek

The Hebrew University, Jerusalem

"Life is short, the Art is long": This famous beginning of Hippocrates' first Aphorism is most probably the most widely known of the statements of the Hippocratic Corpus. Jones remarked that "the Greek manuscripts (of the Aphorisms) are more numerous than those containing any other work (of the Hippocratic Corpus)."[1] We shall not consider in this essay the Aphorisms in detail. "The tradition is that Hippocrates composed this work in his old age as a summary of his vast experience."[2] The most comprehensive ancient commentaries of the Aphorisms are those of Galen and Theophilus, to whom may be added those of Stephanus and Meletius. Among the numerous medieval commentaries, Maimonides' work, written in Arabic (as were all his medical treatises) is of no minor interest, particularly his comments on the first aphorism to which this essay refers. We have used the Hebrew edition of Suessman Muntner[3] and the English translation of Ariel Bar-Sela and Hebbel E. Hoff.[4]

---

1 Jones counted 140 Greek manuscripts, 232 Latin, 70 Arabic, 40 Hebrew and 1 Syriac. See Hippocrates, *Works*, ed. and trans. William Henry Samuel Jones, vol. IV (Loeb Classical Library; Cambridge, Mass. and London: Heinemann, 1931), p. XXXIII, n. 1.

2 Ibid., p. XXXIV.

3 Suessman Muntner (Ed.), *Commentary on the Aphorisms of Hippocrates* (Jerusalem: Mosad Harav Kook, 1961) [Hebrew; Brief introduction in English (pp. VII–XIV)]. The work was written by Maimonides around 1195.

4 Ariel Bar-Sela and Hebbel E. Hoff, "Maimonides' Interpretation of the First Aphorism of Hippocrates", in *Bulletin of the History of Medicine* 37 (1963), pp. 347–354. Their translation was made from the Arabic (Ms. Hunt 427 of the Bodleian Library in Oxford).

Hippocrates' First Aphorism

> Life is short, the Art is long, the occasion (καιρός) fleeting, the experiment (πεῖρα) deceptive; and judgement (κρίσις) uncertain. The physician must be prepared, not only to do his own duty, but also to secure the cooperation of the patient, of the attendants and of externals.[5]

Before turning to Maimonides' commentary, I would like to refer to Galen's detailed discussion, which has been accurately epitomized in Daremberg's edition of the Aphorisms of Hippocrates.[6]

The "art" is considered as "a formulation of a number of particular data into general principles."[7]

There are two ways of achieving knowledge (of an art): one is empiricism,[8] based on trials and errors, but this is dangerous in the case of medicine, for two reasons. One, there is no time ("occasion fleeting"); second, man is not a subject for experiments[9] ("experiment deceiving") like inanimate objects. But what is the aim of the dictum "Life is short..."? Maybe, this observation will deter those who are not serious from studying the Art of Medicine, and stimulate the others to learn unceasingly. The real reason might be a justification of the aphorismatic literary genre. Indeed, such formulae, very briefly expounded and easily memorized, stimulating afterthought and comment, constitute a didactic way of learning a lot in few words. This epitomization of the Art was pursued in the Middle Ages, explaining the vogue of the *Articella* throughout that period. Regarding the second part of the first aphorism, it stresses the foremost importance of the authority of the healer, who should invest ardour and energy in gaining the confidence of the patient and of his environment. All these aspects will be considered and developed in Maimonides' commentary.

---

5 My own translation.

6 *Les Aphorismes d'Hippocrate: Suivis des Aphorismes de l'École de Salerne*. Préface et notes du Dr. Daremberg (Paris: L'Enseigne du Pot Cassé, 1945), See n. 1, pp. 159–161. My translation from the French. But see also Galen, *Hippocratis Aphorismi et Galeni in eos Commentarii,* ed. Carl Gottlob Kühn (*Claudii Galeni Opera Omnia* [20 volumes; Leipzig: Knobloch, 1821–1833]), vol. XVIIb (1829), pp. 345–356.

7 "L'art consiste à formuler en principes généraux les faits particuliers" (*Les Aphorismes d'Hippocrate* [see above n. 6], p. 159).

8 Galen was sympathetic to the doctrine of the Empiricists (cf. *De Locis Affectis* 3.3); he relied on experience rather than theory and speculation. However experience should be based on rational thinking, for positive results may also be based on chance.

9 I chose to translate πεῖρα "experiment" (rather than "experience"), for it has the connotation of 'trial'. I say 'experiment', not experimentation.

Maimonides' Preface

In his introduction to this work, Maimonides writes that he considers the *Aphorisms* as Hippocrates' most useful work.[10] He praises Galen's commentary, while nevertheless remarking that it is often disconnected from the Hippocratic statement. Maimonides readily acknowledges that he will use Galen's commentary, while aiming at brevity and succinctness. For the first aphorism, however, he will be somewhat more discursive. In this preface, Maimonides gives us a general statement on the importance of brevity: if one can expose clearly his thought in one thousand words he should not do so with one thousand and one words.[11]

Life is Short, the Art is Long

What Hippocrates wanted to stress, according to Maimonides, was that the Art of Medicine is only mastered after a much longer training than other crafts or skills. Therefore life will be (too) short to achieve perfection in Medicine. This being accurately asserted, Maimonides quotes al-Fārābī[12] who divided the Art of Medicine, theoretical and practical, into seven parts. This will not be detailed here; the components include anatomy and physiology, diagnosis, regimen of health, sick-care and the use of instruments. *Materia Medica* is also part of the requested knowledge, even the names of the plants in various languages, for the physician should be able to identify them wherever he will be living.[13] Once this extensive bulk of knowledge has been learned and memorized from books and teachers, the budding physician has to acquire practical experience.

> [He will then attend] to individuals in the state of health and in the state of illness, acquire [the skill of] discriminating between significant symptoms, […] know to appreciate the constitution[14] of each individual and of his organs.

---

10 "I decided to comment [on the Aphorisms], for they should be known by heart by any physician. I even witnessed their being taught by heart to the young in the frame of non-medical studies."

11 A similar statement was made by Maimonides in his *Dissertation on Resurrection*.

12 Abū Naṣr al-Fārābī (870–950), perhaps through commentaries of Avicenna.

13 Accordingly, Maimonides wrote a treatise on the *Explanation of the Names of Drugs*, discovered and first published by Max Meyerhof in 1940.

14 Hebrew *mezeg*. I prefer 'constitution' to 'temperament' (cf. Bar-Sela and Hoff, "Maimonides' Interpretation" [see above n. 4]). Galen indeed used the Latin *temperamentum*, however the Greek κατάστασις is better rendered by 'constitution'.

Maimonides even differentiates between various "kinds" of health and of diseases, which means that there are various levels in the state of health and various degrees (of severity?) in a given disease. Likewise, the amount of damage to each organ should be evaluated. The observation in depth of a great number of patients will obviously take a long time. Moreover, to become an expert in choosing the right drug or the adequate diet, in choosing a simple drug, or a combined formula with the fitting dosis of each drug, all this will necessitate a long period as well. "In truth it was said that this Art takes longer (to be mastered) than all the others, for whoever aims at perfection."

Maimonides' detailed delineation of the Art of Medicine is based on al-Fārābī and on his follower Avicenna,[15] but obviously also on his own personal curriculum. Before considering further Maimonides' commentary on the first aphorism, let us turn to the relevant statements on the Art of Medicine in his *Book on Asthma.*

The Art of Medicine in the *Book on Asthma*

Chapter 13, the last chapter of the *Book on Asthma,*[16] defines Medicine more briefly and somewhat differently.

> You should know that Medicine is a knowledge [or science, Hebrew *ḥokhmah*] which is quite necessary to man in any time and any place, not only in the time of disease, but also in a state of health (ed. Muntner, p. 38,20–22).

"It is known to all who take interest in the Art [Hebrew *melakhah*] of medicine and to most people, that it is an Art that necessitates experience [Hebrew *nisayon*]." Here Maimonides has an interesting development on the way he considers the concept of experience. It is not, he says, the experience of one individual, but the result of procedures that have been tested through many generations and remained valid. Moreover, Maimonides asserts that there can be no expertise (Hebrew *beqi'ut*) without knowledge (*ḥokhmah*). "Medicine cannot be mastered like other crafts such as carpentry or weaving which can be learned by mere practice [...]" (ed. Muntner, p. 40,10–11, 18–22, 30–31). And here comes one of these aphorismatic statements that illustrate Maimonides' excellence:

15 Avicenna (Ibn Sīnā), 980–1037, whose *Canon* had a major influence on medieval medicine, was on the whole faithful to Galenic medicine.

16 Suessman Muntner (Ed.), *The Book on Asthma* (Jerusalem: Rubin Mass, 1940) [Hebrew, Foreword and Contents in English]. References are to Muntner's edition with page number and lines. My translation.

> Every sick person necessitates a renewed deliberation, and one should never say "This disease is like that other one". [...] For a physician does not (or should not) cure a disease, he cures a sick person (ed. Muntner, p. 40,1–3).

The keywords of this section are the following: The Art of Medicine is based on knowledge and (real) experience. The cure of the sick must be individualized. Judging through analogy is problematic, for there are too many parameters that have to be considered. The parameters are those that have been discussed in the commentary on the First Aphorism, but the patient as a specific individual is particularly pointed out in the *Book on Asthma*.

Perfection in Medicine

In the Commentary, Maimonides writes that Galen stated, in his Commentary to Plato's *Timaeus*, that nobody can attain perfection in the Art of Medicine.[17] To which Maimonides retorts that a physician who is not accomplished may do more harm than good and that it is more advisable to have recourse to no physician at all than to one who is liable to commit an error. This is why Maimonides urges the physician to aim at being accomplished, for "the Art is long, while life is short". This topic is mentioned and developed in the *Book on Asthma*. A patient should not confide, says Maimonides, on a physician who is not accomplished (Hebrew *shalem*), as are most of them. He should rather confide in Nature. On the other hand if the physician is quick (in his judgements) and accomplished[18] in his Art, he will know and remember the principles that will lead him to decide whether Nature will be effective, or whether the disease needs to be curbed and assuaged before it flares up and cannot anymore be subdued (ed. Muntner, pp. 38,24–25, 28–31; 39,1–2).

Moreover, Maimonides adds two important parameters. The physician should be aware of "the place of fear and anxiety", i.e., he should take into account the patient's anxiety and "carefully relieve him". Moreover, he should "know the place of doubt", i.e., whenever in doubt (about diagnosis or treatment) he should refrain from any action and wait, while letting Nature[19] work (ed. Muntner, p. 39,2–4).

17 On this topic see Samuel S. Kottek, "Maimonides on the Perfect Physician", in *Moses Maimonides, Physician, Scientist, and Philosopher*, ed. Fred Rosner and Samuel S. Kottek (Northvale, N.J.: Aronson, 1993), pp. 25–32.

18 The ideal physician is quick and accomplished. But if he is too quick and not accomplished, he is obviously rather dangerous.

19 On Nature's quasi-divine power, see Owsei Temkin, *Galenism: Rise and Decline of a Medical Power* (Ithaca and London: Cornell University Press, 1973), pp. 25–26 and

Thus the accomplished physician should not be irresolute, however he should not act whenever in doubt. Moreover psychology of the patient should not be neglected.

Judgement is Uncertain

Having briefly stated that there is no time to experiment, i.e., to try one treatment, then another, for the disease is pressing, thus linking together the two Hippocratic phrases: "occasion is fleeting" and "experiment is deceptive" (or dangerous – Greek σφαλερή, Hebrew *sakana*), Maimonides turns to "judgement". This phrase is steered toward prognosis,[20] which is uncertain, "because the elements do not persist in the same state." It happens quite often that there seems to be little hope, but the patient recovers, and vice versa. Therefore there is a need for long personal experience and careful management of the disease's evolution.

Maimonides at this point adds a rather long development on the difficulties and dangers of experiments, due to the constant changes in "form" and in "matter"[21] that may occur to the sick person. The frequent side-effects of the drugs are another problematic factor, even nutrients may have undesirable effects. These notions are developed in the pure Galenic tradition and will not be detailed here. I would like rather to stress the last paragraph of Hippocrates' aphorism and Maimonides' comments that are of social and ethical content.

The Cooperation of the Patient and his Environment

Hippocrates here extends the duties of the physician beyond the mere application of the Art of Medicine. He prescribes that the physician should also secure the cooperation of the patient and his attendants, and even of strangers (or

---

idem, *Hippocrates in a World of Pagans and Christians* (Baltimore, Md.: Johns Hopkins University Press, 1991), pp. 189–196.

20 Prognosis was a major element in Hippocratic lore. An exact prognosis characterizes the able physician and wins him respect from the patient and his family. See Hippocrates, *Prognostic* I, in idem, *Works* (ed. and trans. Jones [see above n. 1]), vol. II (1923), pp. 7–9.

21 "Form" (Hebrew *ṣurah*) and "matter" (Hebrew *ḥomer*) are philosophical terms, current in Aristotelian literature and through the Middle Ages.

"externals", Greek ἔξωθεν).[22] Maimonides' comment will in this case be quoted more at length.

> In accordance with his remarkable ethical standards, Hippocrates prescribes that the physician should not constrain his activity to what is proper only [...], for this is not sufficient to bring forward health to the patient. Indeed this target will only be attained [...] if the patient himself and all the attendants will do what has to be done and if the external factors that are troublesome [...] will be cast aside.[23]

Maimonides (and of course Hippocrates) knew that the success of a disease's management is conditioned by the exact and adequate application of the treatment. The patient (or his attendants) might well oppose the application of painful or disturbing procedures (clysters, surgery and cautery are mentioned) or the intake of bitter potions. Thus one of these "external factors" might be the surgeon (or the medical attendant) who is due to perform clysters, surgery or cautery, at least in Maimonides' times.[24] The patient and the attendants must be properly warned from doing mistakes or allowing laxity in the treatment when the physician is absent. Then Maimonides details some of the "external factors" that should not be neglected.

> In case the sick person is poor and lives in a place that is harmful for his disease, and has no other place [to go], he [the physician] should remove him to another place [where he will recover more easily].[25] He should also provide [to his patient, befitting] nourishment and drugs if he cannot afford them.[26] Such things, and others of the kind, are the "external factors" to which the physician is liable[27] as befits his Art.

Such a course of conduct, says Maimonides, is indeed indispensable in order to attain the goal, i.e., the health of his patient.

---

22 ἔξωθεν may also be understood as "external factors", such was seemingly Maimonides' reading (Hebrew *ha-devarim asher mi-huṣ*).

23 My translation. The "troublesome factors" (Hebrew *me'iqim*), meaning disturbing, or deranging, or painful factors that are related to the management of the illness, will be further considered in detail.

24 In Hippocratic times there was apparently no clear-cut differentiation between medicine and surgery, as was the case in the Middle Ages.

25 Cf. the Hippocratic treatise *Airs, Waters and Places*, in Hippocrates, *Works* (ed. and trans. Jones [see above n. 1]), vol. I, pp. 70–137.

26 Literally "he does not have them", which may include a patient who has the money, but there is nobody to help him. This is actually real sick care.

27 The Hebrew version may also be understood as follows: "These 'external' factors are outside the things for which the physician is responsible according to the Art." They would thus be considered as a necessary *addition* to the principles of the Art.

> Only to say what should be done and then to depart, this he should not do, for this may sometimes jeopardize the result of his undertaking.

In the brief treatise entitled *The Art*, which is part of the Hippocratic Collection, though not written by Hippocrates himself,[28] it says that failure is not to be imputed automatically to the physician. "It is much more likely that the physician has given proper orders, which the patient [...] is unable to follow; and not following them, he meets with death."[29]

Here (in the First Aphorism) Hippocrates does not have in mind to vindicate the physician's expertise in front of the criticism of laymen, on the contrary he adds to the duty of curing the category of caring.[30] However Hippocrates merely hints at such 'external' factors, whereas Maimonides brings factual evidence of caritative action (Hebrew *ṣedaqah*, Latin *caritas*).

The Confidence of the Patient

When Hippocrates requires that the physician secure the cooperation of the patient, the condition is obviously that the patient's full confidence and trust has to be acquired. Neither Hippocrates nor Maimonides explain how to attain this goal. One may imagine that the physician should give evidence of authority, of expertise, of experience.[31] But I guess that Maimonides would put forward the psychological approach of the patient. In his *Regimen Sanitatis*, Maimonides stressed the foremost importance of studying "the movements of the soul" of the patient, even in state of health, and to restore equilibrium whenever necessary: "This should precede any medical treatment".[32] Once the physician has gained full knowledge of his patient's psychology, he may find the best way of gaining full cooperation. But why should this be considered as an "external factor"? Maimonides answers this question when he remarks: "The physician, as such, should not put forward his Art and knowledge [in order] to reject this psychological [function]".[33] He would argue that such

28 The author could have been, according to Jones, a sophist from the end of the fifth century B.C.E.

29 *The Art*, cf. Hippocrates, *Works* (ed. and trans. Jones [see above n. 1]), vol. II, p. 203.

30 On religious aspects of caring, see Ronald L. Numbers and Darrell W. Amundsen (Eds.), *Caring and Curing: Health and Medicine in the Western Religious Traditions* (New York, London: Macmillan, 1986).

31 See the treatise *On Decorum*, in Hippocrates, *Works* (ed. and trans. Jones [see above n. 1]), vol. II, pp. 278–301. Also *The Physician*, ibid., pp. 310–313.

32 See *Regimen Sanitatis*, ed. Suessman Muntner (Jerusalem: Geniza, 1957) [Hebrew, with English Introduction], III, 13, p. 59.

33 Ibid., III, 14, p. 59. This is my own understanding of this somewhat elliptic statement. Muntner has a similar approach (cf. n. 140).

action pertains "to philosophy and to biblical moralists".[34] It thus appears that average physicians would then consider psychology as extra-medical. Even for Galen himself, the soul must be treated only when it is diseased, while Maimonides holds that any patient should be taken into account in his whole, body and soul, or rather, soul and body.

The Art is Long-winded, the Physician is Short-lived

We have seen that for Maimonides medicine is an indispensable science, anywhere and at any time. Quoting al-Fārābī, he argues that the physician should exercise his Art as suitable, with utmost excellence, and be on the watch that there occur no oversight, neither on the side of the physician, nor on that of the patient.[35] The two qualities required are knowledge and conscientiousness, or responsibility. Again the notion of excellence, or accomplishment, is stressed. However, the physician being short-lived, excellence remains utopian, or say, idealistic. Maimonides readily acknowledges that he has not reached full accomplishment.[36] As I have argued elsewhere, his idea was that the physician should throughout his life-span *strive* toward perfection, through constant rehearsal and study.[37] The Art is long-winded: Maimonides, leaning on Galen, divides practical medicine into three sections. First, the management of the healthy (i.e., *regimen sanitatis*); second, the management of the sick (generally considered medical practice); and third, the management of those who are neither fully healthy nor really sick (which includes the management of old people).[38] The physician is thus in charge of his patient, as it were, throughout his life, he is his constant adviser. Even his psychological problems, as we have seen, are taken into account by the physician, in health and disease.

Now we may be able to understand the strange way in which Maimonides defines the accomplished physician. The Art of Medicine should only be sought when an accomplished physician can be found,

> who has attained such standard (of competence) that the patient will (readily) entrust him his mind and body, and steer them according to his directions.[39]

---

34 Ibid., p. 60.

35 *Book on Asthma* (see above n. 16), pp. 34–35.

36 Ibid., pp. 39,30–31; 40,1–9.

37 See my essay "On the Perfect Physician" (see above n. 17), pp. 30–31.

38 See *Regimen Sanitatis* (see above n. 32), II, 1, p. 43.

39 Cf. *Book on Asthma* (see above n. 16), p. 38,23–24.

Conclusion

Let us first epitomize what we culled from the *Book on Asthma* regarding Maimonides' remarks on the Art of Medicine.

Medicine is an Art based on knowledge, and necessitates knowledgeable experience.[40] The Art of Medicine includes the management of the sick, of the healthy and of intermediate situations. Each patient should be considered as a special entity whose soul and body are taken into account in the treatment.

Turning now to the central object of this essay, i.e., Maimonides' Commentary of Hippocrates' first Aphorism, I would like to stress the following details. *Time* is a central factor: a whole life is not enough to fully master the Medical Art; moreover, whenever treating a patient, there is no time to make experiments, the time to act is "fleeting" (i.e., fading away, or fluctuating), no time to hesitate. *Judgement* is uncertain: prognosis is problematic and there are no certain means of judging how the disease will develop.[41]

But the most remarkable aspect of Maimonides' comments lies in the last segment of the Aphorism, dealing with the cooperation of the patient and his caretakers. Hippocrates briefly mentions that the physician should see to it that nobody and nothing hinder or resist the implementation of the treatment. This concern is beyond "his own duty", however it conditions efficiency. Maimonides asserts straightforwardly that this is a necessity in order to bring the patient back to health, and for him it is indeed part of the physician's duty. In other words, for Maimonides the physician's duty is to heal – not to treat. Any negative interference has to be taken into consideration. The psychology of the patient and of the caretakers, the local environment (climate, conditions of accommodation),[42] the patient's ability to obtain the appropriate diet and/or the drugs – all these factors "and others of the kind" are included in the physician's necessary care for his patient. The physician's duty is curing, and caring for appropriate implementation of the cure.

I would like to conclude with a reflection on the fact that the Art is long – longer than man's life-time. In a Hebrew medieval paraphrase of the Hippocratic Oath[43] that was published for the first time in 1978, the conclusion,

---

40 I mean, of course, experience based on knowledge and understanding.

41 Isaac Israeli, in his *Ethical Aphorisms* (no. 28), thus addresses the physician: "Restrain your mouth from prophetizing, […] most of your statements should be on the conditional mode." See M. Levey, "Medical Ethics of Medieval Islam", in *Transactions of the American Philosophical Society* n.s. 57(3) (Philadelphia, 1967), pp. 95–97.

42 Incidentally, Galen in his Commentary mentions the dwelling conditions among the "externals".

43 See Samuel S. Kottek, Joshua O. Leibowitz and Benjamin Richler, "A Hebrew Paraphrase of the Hippocratic Oath (from a 15th century manuscript)", in *Medical History* 22 (1978), pp. 438–445. I have slightly amended my own previous translation from the Hebrew. The text was no doubt composed much earlier than the fifteenth

which takes the place of the adjuration of the Greek original text, enhances the necessity of constant learning.

> Above all, he [the physician] should acquire a habit of constant learning on [the ways that] restore the body to health, and he should never weary of studying from books.

Maimonides, the "Eagle of the Synagogue" would not have rejected such a conclusion to a Jewish version of the ethical admonitions of the "Father of Medicine".

---

century (probably late twelfth century), and may thus have been contemporary to Maimonides' medical writings.

Maimonides als Galenleser

von

Gotthard Strohmaier

Berlin-Brandenburgische Akademie der Wissenschaften, Berlin

Der aus Bagdad gebürtige muslimische Arzt und Philosoph ʿAbd al-Laṭīf al-Baġdādī (1162–1231) wurde schon früh in der europäischen Forschung mit seiner lebendigen Schilderung eines Ägyptenaufenthaltes bekannt. Er berichtet darin von Seuchen und einer katastrophalen Hungersnot, welche die Menschen bis zum Kannibalismus trieb. In der Medizingeschichte hat er einen großen Namen, weil er durch eigene Skelettuntersuchungen gegen die Autorität Galens, der in Rom im zweiten nachchristlichen Jahrhundert nur Tieranatomie betreiben konnte, nachwies, dass der menschliche Unterkiefer nur aus einem Knochen besteht, was auch für das Kreuzbein zu gelten habe, jedenfalls in den allermeisten Fällen.[1] Er vertraute diese Erkenntnis seiner Reisebeschreibung an und unterstrich sie mit dem markanten Bekenntnis, dass der Wahrnehmung mehr zu trauen sei als der Autorität Galens (*fa-inna l-ḥissa aṣdaqu minhu*).[2]

Einen kritischen Geist zeigte er auch, als er in Kairo Moses Maimonides bei sich empfing, wovon er in seiner Autobiographie, von der Ibn abī Uṣaibiʿa Auszüge mitteilt, Folgendes erzählt: „Zu mir kam Mūsā. Ich fand ihn nicht über die Maßen gelehrt, er war eingenommen von der Liebe zur Herrschaft und vom Dienst bei den Mächtigen dieser Welt."[3] Auch in einer etwas anderen Version der

1 Zu Galens Vorstellungen vgl. Galen, *On the Usefulness of the Parts of the Body*, übersetzt von Margaret Tallmadge May (Ithaca, N.Y.: Cornell University Press, 1968), Band 2, S. 574, Anm. 46.

2 ʿAbd al-Laṭīf al-Baġdādī, *Kitāb al-ifāda wa-l-iʿtibār fī l-umūri l-mušāhada wa-l-ḥawādiṯi l-muʿāyana bi-arḍi Miṣr*, ed. Salāma Mūsā unter dem Titel *Fī Miṣr* (Kairo, o.J.), S. 73–74; Edition von Kamal Hafuth Zand, John A. und Ivy E. Videan unter dem Titel *The Eastern Key* (London: Allen and Unwin, 1965), S. 273–277.

3 „*wa-ǧāʾanī Mūsā fa-waǧadtuhu fāḍilan lā fī l-ġāya qad ġalaba ʿalayhi ḥubbu r-riyāsa wa-ḫidmatu arbābi d-dunyā*" (Ibn abī Uṣaibiʿa, *ʿUyūn al-anbāʾ fī ṭabaqāti l-aṭibbāʾ*, ed. August Müller, Band 2 [Kairo/Königsberg, 1882; Nachdruck in einem Band: Westmead, Farnborough, Hants.: Gregg, 1972], S. 205,29). Zu verschiedenen Übersetzungen, in denen die Negation *lā* übergangen ist, vgl. Gerrit Bos (Ed.), *Maimonides, On Asthma* (The Complete Medical Works of Moses Maimonides 1; Provo, Ut.: Brigham Young University Press, 2002), Einleitung, S. XXX, Anm. 31; die Handschriften, die August Müller im Nachtragsband (Königsberg, 1884, S. 55, Zeile 11) verzeichnet, geben dafür keinen Anhalt.

Autobiographie, die in der Handschrift Bursa, Hüseyin Çelebi 823 vorliegt, ist die Aussage nach dem Referat Albert Dietrichs in gleicher Weise negativ.[4] ʿAbd al-Laṭīf berichtet weiter: „Für die Juden hat er ein Buch verfasst, das er *Buch der Wegleitung* (*Kitāb ad-dalāla*) nannte, und er hat diejenigen verflucht, die es mit einer anderen Schrift als der hebräischen abschreiben. Ich habe es gelesen und fand, dass es ein schlechtes Buch ist, das die Grundlagen der Religionsgesetze und der Glaubenslehren untergräbt, indem er meint, sie zu befestigen."[5] ʿAbd al-Laṭīf ist auch sonst als scharfer Polemiker bekannt, von ihm stammt zum Beispiel eine vernichtende Invektive gegen das Treiben der Alchemisten.[6] Trotzdem erscheint es merkwürdig, dass der philosophisch gebildete Muslim genauso urteilt wie die jüdischen Gegner des Maimonides. Die Art der Beurteilung des Maimonides ist auch auf dem Hintergrund zu verstehen, dass ʿAbd al-Laṭīf aus dem Osten der islamischen Welt stammt, wo die Juden ein geringeres Ansehen genossen als in den westlichen Regionen.[7] So ist auch ein spöttischer Unterton in einem anderen Satz nicht zu überhören: „Er hat ein medizinisches Buch verfasst, in dem er von den sechzehn Büchern Galens[8] und von fünf anderen eine Sammlung veranstaltet hat, wobei er lediglich ausgewählte Abschnitte übertragen hat und es sich dabei zur Pflicht machte, keinen Buchstaben zu verändern außer den Konjunktionen *wa* und *fa*."[9] Bei diesem Buch handelt es sich um die *Muḫtaṣarāt*, die *Exzerpte*,[10] zu

---

4 Albert Dietrich, „Die arabische Version einer unbekannten Schrift des Alexander von Aphrodisias über die Differentia specifica", in *Nachrichten der Akademie der Wissenschaften in Göttingen. I. Philosophisch-historische Klasse*, 1964, Nr. 2 (Göttingen, 1964), S. 109.

5 *„wa-ʿamila kitāban li-l-yahūd sammāhu kitāba d-dalāla wa-laʿana man yaktubuhu bi-ġayri l-qalami l-ʿibrānīyi wa-waqaftu ʿalayhi fa-waǧadtuhu kitāba sauʾin yufsidu uṣūla š-šarāʾiʿi wa-l-ʿaqāʾidi bi-mā yaẓunnu annahu yuṣliḥuhā"* (Ibn abī Uṣaibiʿa [wie Anm. 3], Band 2, S. 205,31–206,1).

6 Vgl. das Referat bei Johann Christoph Bürgel, *Allmacht und Mächtigkeit. Religion und Welt im Islam* (München: Beck, 1991), S. 205–206; die Textquelle ist die in Anm. 4 genannte Handschrift, siehe ibid., S. 106.

7 Gotthard Strohmaier, „Juden, Christen und Muslime als Förderer mittelalterlicher Wissenschaft", in Johannes Irmscher (Ed.), *Rapports entre juifs, chrétiens et musulmans. Eine Sammlung von Forschungsbeiträgen* (Amsterdam: Hakkert, 1995), S. 59–63 (Nachdruck in Strohmaier, *Hellas im Islam. Interdisziplinäre Studien zur Ikonographie, Wissenschaft und Religionsgeschichte* [Diskurse der Arabistik, ed. Hartmut Bobzin und Angelika Neuwirth, 6; Wiesbaden: Harrassowitz, 2003], S. 177–179).

8 Gemeint sind die des alexandrinischen Kanons, siehe Gotthard Strohmaier, „Die christlichen Schulen in Bagdad und der alexandrinische Kanon der Galenschriften. Eine Korrektur in Ḥunains Sendschreiben an ʿAlī ibn Yaḥyā", in *Oriens* 36 (2001), S. 268–275 (Nachdruck in Strohmaier, *Hellas im Islam* [wie Anm. 7], S. 180–185).

9 *„wa-ʿamila kitāban fī ṭ-ṭibbi ǧamaʿahu mina s-sittata ʿašara li-Ǧālīnūs wa-min ḫamsati kutubin uḫrā wa-šaraṭa an lā yuġayyira fīhi ḥarfan illā an yakūna wāw ʿaṭfin aw fā waṣlin wa-innamā yanqulu fuṣūlan yaḫtāruhā"* (Ibn abī Uṣaibiʿa [wie Anm. 3], Band 2, S. 205,30–31).

10 Manfred Ullmann, *Die Medizin im Islam* (Leiden, Köln: Brill, 1970), S. 169; übersetzt sind die *Exzerpte* aus der *Methodus medendi* in *The Art of Cure. Extracts from Galen*, übersetzt von Uriel S. Barzel (Haifa: Maimonides Research Institute, 1992), siehe dazu die kritischen Bemerkungen von Elinor Lieber, „Maimonides the medical humanist", in Arthur Hyman

denen Maimonides selber betont hat, dass er nichts anderes als eine Komprimierung in Form von wörtlichen Exzerpten im Sinn hatte.[11]

Aber ʿAbd al-Laṭīf hatte keinen Grund, sich gegenüber Maimonides überlegen zu dünken. Er war kein Vorläufer Vesals. Er berichtet selber, dass er nur auf die Idee zu seinen Untersuchungen kam, weil Teilnehmer seines Medizinunterrichts bei der Lektüre von Galens *Kitāb at-tašrīḥ*, nämlich *De anatomicis administrationibus*, Schwierigkeiten hatten, sich den darin beschriebenen Knochenbau konkret vorzustellen, woraufhin man beschloss, gemeinsam einen Ausflug zu der nahe gelegenen Ortschaft al-Maqs zu unternehmen. Dort lagen nach der Beschreibung ʿAbd al-Laṭīfs über 20.000 Opfer der Seuche und der Hungersnot unbestattet auf einem Hügel, einige auch schon skelettiert. Er untersuchte nach seinen Worten über zweitausend Schädel und bat andere, ohne sein Beisein ein Gleiches zu tun, weil er es zunächst nicht glauben mochte, dass sich Galen geirrt haben könnte, denn alle Anatomen sagten dasselbe wie er, wobei ʿAbd al-Laṭīf bezeichnenderweise hinzufügt: „wenn wir ‚alle' sagen, so meinen wir damit hier allein Galen, denn er war derjenige, der die Anatomie selbst ausgeführt hat [...]"[12].

Dies soll genügen, um die überragende Autorität Galens zu illustrieren. Sie war durch die Iatrosophisten der alten alexandrinischen Schule und in ihrem Gefolge durch den Fleiß der Bagdader Übersetzer im neunten Jahrhundert[13] fest eingeführt. Ibn abī Uṣaibiʿa stellt an den Anfang seiner umfänglichen und sehr ordentlich gearbeiteten Galenbiographie die Feststellung, dass er bei Gebildeten und Ungebildeten (*al-ḫāṣṣ wa-l-ʿāmm*) als „das Siegel der großen lehrenden Ärzte (*ḫātam al-aṭibbāʾi l-kibāri l-muʿallimīna*)" angesehen werde.[14] Das steht in fataler Nähe zur muslimischen Lehre, der zufolge Mohammed laut Sure 33:40 „das Siegel der Propheten" ist, dem bis zum Tag des Gerichts kein weiterer zu folgen hat.

Auch als Philosoph wurde Galen zwar nicht von allen ernst genommen, aber doch von vielen Intellektuellen, auch Nichtmedizinern, eifrig studiert. Maimonides erörtert im *Führer der Verirrten* die These der *mutakallimūn*, der muslimischen philosophierenden Theologen, dass unsere Sinneswahrnehmungen allesamt unzuverlässig seien. Das halten sie für eine Neuerung, die sie zuerst eingeführt hätten,

---

(Ed.), *Maimonidean Studies*, Band 4 (New York: The Michael Scharf Publication Trust of Yeshiva University Press, 2000), S. 49.

11 Vgl. Maimonides, *Medical Aphorisms. Treatises 1–5*, ed. Gerrit Bos (Provo, Ut. 2004), arabisch S. 2,15–16 (Übersetzung S. 2,24–26); Moritz Steinschneider, „Die Vorrede des Maimonides zu seinem Commentar über die Aphorismen des Hippokrates", in *Zeitschrift der Deutschen Morgenländischen Gesellschaft* 48 (1894), arabisch S. 222 (Übersetzung S. 234).

12 „*wa-qawlunā al-kullu innamā naʿnī bihi hāhunā Ǧālīnūsa waḥdahu fa-innahu huwa llaḏī bāšara t-tašrīḥa bi-nafsihi*" (ʿAbd al-Laṭīf al-Baġdādī, *Kitāb al-ifāda* [wie Anm. 2]).

13 Gotthard Strohmaier, „Der syrische und der arabische Galen", in *Aufstieg und Niedergang der Römischen Welt*, ed. Wolfgang Haase und Hildegard Temporini, Teil II, Band 37,2 (Berlin, New York: de Gruyter, 1994), S. 1987–2017 (Nachdruck in Strohmaier, *Hellas im Islam* [wie Anm. 7], S. 85–106).

14 Ibn abī Uṣaibiʿa (wie Anm. 3), Band 1, S. 71,10–11.

aber Maimonides verweist auf die alten griechischen Sophisten und auf „Galen in seinem Werk über die Naturkräfte, worin er über diejenigen, die die Sinneswahrnehmung leugnen, die dir bekannten Dinge erzählt" (I.73). Das steht in *De facultatibus naturalibus*,[15] und Maimonides fühlte sich nicht bemüßigt, dazu nähere Angaben zu machen, er konnte die Stellen bei seinem Leser als bekannt voraussetzen. Für den heutigen Editor arabischer philosophischer oder wissenschaftlicher Texte kann die Identifizierung von Galenzitaten mit ihrer Originalfassung manchmal zum Problem werden, und dies selbst dann, wenn er des Griechischen mächtig ist. Das liegt daran, dass das umfängliche Lebenswerk Galens nur ungenügend erschlossen ist, und die mit Übersetzungen und Indizes versehenen Ausgaben des Berliner „Corpus Medicorum Graecorum" sollen voraussichtlich erst im Jahre 2050 abgeschlossen sein. Immer ist auch damit zu rechnen, dass arabische Autoren und darunter auch Maimonides aus verlorenen Schriften zitieren und damit die Funktion einer fragmentarischen Quelle haben.

Die Rezeption Galens im Islam wurde auch dadurch befördert, dass er den sinnreich konstruierten animalischen Körperbau als Werk einer übermenschlichen Intelligenz begriff, die er manchmal Natur, manchmal auch einen Demiurgen nannte. Das harmonierte mit dem Schöpfungsglauben aller drei monotheistischen Religionen. Maimonides beruft sich in diesem Zusammenhang im *Führer der Verirrten* (III.32) auf die in *De usu partium* beschriebene Konstruktion von Nerven, Sehnen und Muskeln.[16] Den Umstand, dass der wunderbar eingerichtete menschliche Körper nichtsdestoweniger sterblich ist, erklärt Maimonides nicht mit der Sünde des Urelternpaares oder schlicht mit dem Willen Gottes, sondern er zitiert wörtlich aus dem dritten Buch von *De usu partium*: „Gib dich darüber keiner Täuschung hin, dass es möglich sei, dass aus dem Blute der Menstruation und aus dem männlichen Samen ein Lebewesen entstehe, welches nicht stirbt und keinen Schmerz empfindet oder welches sich immer bewegt und klar wie die Sonne ist" (III.12).[17]

Im Rahmen von Galens Weltanschauung ergab sich dies daraus, dass die Natur oder der Demiurg nicht unbeschränkt allmächtig ist, sondern nur materielle Gegebenheiten manipulieren kann. Und hier fühlte sich Galen herausgefordert, sich deutlich vom Glauben der Juden und Christen zu distanzieren, die im zweiten nachchristlichen Jahrhundert in Rom in seinen Gesichtskreis getreten sein müssen, was dann wiederum eine Antwort von Maimonides provoziert hat. Galen

15 Galen, *De facultatibus naturalibus* I,2, in *Scripta minora*, Band 3, ed. Georg Helmreich (Leipzig: Teubner, 1893), S. 101,16–106,3 = idem, *Opera omnia*, ed. Carl Gottlob Kühn (Leipzig: Knobloch, 1821–1833; Nachdruck Hildesheim: Olms, 1965), Band 2, S. 2,6–9,6.

16 Galen, *De usu partium* II,1–7, ed. Georg Helmreich (Leipzig: Teubner, 1907–1909), Band 1, S. 64,10–88,3 = *Opera omnia*, ed. Kühn (wie Anm. 15), Band 3, S. 88,4–120,8; Übersetzung von May (wie Anm. 1), Band 1, S. 113–130.

17 Vgl. Galen, *De usu partium* III,10, ed. Helmreich (wie Anm. 16), Band 1, S. 175,3–7 = *Opera omnia*, ed. Kühn (wie Anm. 15), Band 3, S. 238,11–14; Übersetzung von May (wie Anm. 1), Band 1, S. 189.

äußert sich in *De usu partium* zu dem Problem, warum die Augenwimpern in eine knorpelige Unterlage eingepflanzt sind. Die Begründung läuft darauf hinaus, dass sie über den Augen nicht so ungehemmt wachsen sollen wie die anderen Haare. Die Natur richtet sich nach den materiellen Gegebenheiten. Moses, den auch er für den Verfasser der Torah hält, aber meine, dass Gott alles möglich sei, dass er etwa aus Asche eine Kuh oder ein Pferd oder aus einem Felsen einen Menschen schaffen könne. Würde aber Gott, und Galen verwendet hier auch einmal die Vokabel ὁ θεός, die Wimpern in weiches Fleisch einpflanzen, so wäre er noch dümmer als Moses oder als ein unfähiger Feldherr, der einen Palisadenzaun in einen morastigen Untergrund rammen lässt.[18]

Im Alten Testament würden wir freilich nach den von Galen genannten Beispielen für die göttliche Allmacht vergebens suchen. Es ist meines Erachtens anzunehmen, dass Galen nur sehr flüchtige Kontakte zu Juden und Christen hatte und dass die unmotiviert erscheinende Assoziation von Asche und Kuh durch zeitgenössische jüdische Diskussionen um den Reinigungsritus mit der Asche der roten Kuh von Numeri 19:2–10a angeregt wurde, wovon der Mischnatraktat *Para* Zeugnis gibt. Auf der gleichen Linie liegt es, wenn die Rede des Täufers Johannes im Neuen Testament, dass Gott dem Abraham aus Steinen Kinder erwecken könne (Matthäus 3:9 und Lukas 3:8), der jüdischen Tradition zugerechnet wird.[19] Der Täufer wiederum hatte sich vermutlich ein aramäisches Wortspiel geleistet, *abnayyā* sind „Steine", *benayyā* „Söhne".[20]

Maimonides fühlte sich herausgefordert und antwortete im fünfundzwanzigsten Kapitel seiner medizinischen *Aphorismen*.[21] Er knüpft an den von ihm hochgeschätzten al-Fārābī an, der Galen wegen der Vernachlässigung der hypothetischen Schlussformen und wegen seiner von Aristoteles abweichenden und dabei richtigeren Auffassungen von der Funktion des Herzens und des Gehirns die philosophische Kompetenz abgesprochen hatte.[22] Des weiteren wirft ihm Maimonides

---

18 Galen, *De usu partium* XI,14, ed. Helmreich (wie Anm. 16), Band 2, S. 156,21–159,21 = *Opera omnia*, ed. Kühn (wie Anm. 15), Band 3, S. 903,7–907,8; Übersetzung von May (wie Anm. 1), Band 2, S. 532–534.

19 Gotthard Strohmaier, „Galen als Vertreter der Gebildetenreligion seiner Zeit", in *Neue Beiträge zur Geschichte der Alten Welt*, ed. Elisabeth Charlotte Welskopf, Band 2 (Berlin: Akademie-Verlag, 1965), S. 377–378 (Nachdruck in G. Strohmaier, *Von Demokrit bis Dante. Die Bewahrung antiken Erbes in der arabischen Kultur* [Olms Studien 43; Hildesheim etc.: Olms, 1996], S. 96–97).

20 Walter Grundmann, *Das Evangelium nach Lukas* (Theologischer Handkommentar zum Neuen Testament 3; Berlin: Evangelische Verlagsanstalt, ²1961), S. 103.

21 Joseph Schacht und Max Meyerhof, „Maimonides against Galen on philosophy and cosmogony", in *Bulletin of the Faculty of Arts of the University of Cairo* 5,1 (1937, gedruckt 1939), S. 53–88.

22 Johann Christoph Bürgel, „Averroes ‚contra Galenum'", in *Nachrichten der Akademie der Wissenschaften in Göttingen, I. Philologisch-historische Klasse*, 1967, Nr. 9 (Göttingen, 1968), S. 286–290; Friedrich W. Zimmermann, „Al-Farabi und die philosophische Kritik an Galen von Alexander zu Averroes", in *Akten des VII. Kongresses für Arabistik und Islamwissen-*

vor, dass er sich den Rang eines Propheten anmaße, indem er behaupte, dass zu ihm ein gottgesandter Engel gekommen sei, der ihn dies und jenes gelehrt und befohlen habe (*iddaʿā n-nubūwa wa-qāla an ǧāʾahu malakun min ʿindi llāh wa-ʿallamahu kaḏā wa-amarahu bi-kaḏā*). Wie kann er sich dann erlauben, über einen anderen Propheten schlecht zu reden?[23] Hier haben die christlichen Übersetzer in Bagdad für Missverständnisse gesorgt, die bei aller sonstigen philologischen Gewissenhaftigkeit pagane Aussagen auf eine oft unberechenbare Weise ins Monotheistische umgebogen haben.[24] Maimonides könnte hier auf einschlägige Stellen in *De usu partium*[25] und in *De curandi ratione per venae sectionem*[26] anspielen, wo Galen durch „einen Gott (θεὸς δέ τις)" im Traum angewiesen wurde, etwas über die Funktion des Auges zu schreiben oder an sich selbst einen Aderlass zwischen Daumen und Zeigefinger der rechten Hand vorzunehmen. Von einem Engel ist dabei nicht die Rede; leider liegen die arabischen Übersetzungen nicht mehr vor, so dass wir nicht wissen, was der arabische Übersetzer mit diesen Stellen gemacht hat.

Maimonides erkennt, dass die unbeschränkte göttliche Allmacht, die er grundsätzlich verteidigt, eng mit der Frage nach der zeitlichen Erschaffung der Welt zusammenhängt. Al-Fārābī hatte an Galen gerügt, dass er in der Frage der Weltewigkeit unsicher sei, wovon er seinerseits als Neuplatoniker fest überzeugt war. Damit bezog er sich auf *De placitis Hippocratis et Platonis*[27] und auf das heute nur lückenhaft erhaltene Spätwerk *De propriis placitis*, das jetzt Vivian Nutton im „Corpus Medicorum Graecorum" vorgelegt hat.[28] Maimonides kennt die beiden Schriften und Galens Schwanken in dieser Frage auch,[29] und im *Führer der Verirrten* erwähnt er bei der Unsicherheit der Philosophen in der Frage, ob die Welt ewig ist oder in der Zeit geschaffen wurde, den auf ihn gemünzten Spott al-Fārābīs

---

schaft, Göttingen, 15. bis 22. August 1974, ed. Albert Dietrich (Abhandlungen der Akademie der Wissenschaften in Göttingen, Philologisch-historische Klasse, 3. Folge, Nr. 98; Göttingen: Vandenhoeck & Ruprecht, 1976), S. 401–414; die ebenfalls ablehnende Stellungnahme von Maimonides in seinen *Aphorismen* 25,69–72, ed. Muntner (wie Anm. 33), S. 390–394; Rosner/Muntner (wie Anm. 33), Band 2, S. 218–222.

23 Schacht/Meyerhof (wie Anm. 21), arabisch S. 82,2 (Übersetzung S. 69).

24 Gotthard Strohmaier, „Ḥunayn ibn Isḥāq et le serment hippocratique", in *Arabica* 21 (1974), S. 321–323 (Nachdruck in Strohmaier, *Von Demokrit bis Dante* [wie Anm. 19], S. 219–221).

25 Galen, *De usu partium* X,12–14, ed. Helmreich (wie Anm. 16), Band 2, S. 93,5–110,8 = *Opera omnia*, ed. Kühn (wie Anm. 15), Band 3, S. 812,14–837,5; Übersetzung von May (wie Anm. 1), S. 490–502.

26 Galen, *De curandi ratione per venae sectionem* 23, in *Opera omnia*, ed. Kühn (wie Anm. 15), Band 11, S. 314,18–315,4.

27 Galen, *De placitis Hippocratis et Platonis* IX,9–12, ed. Phillip De Lacy, Band 2 (Corpus Medicorum Graecorum V 4,1,2; Berlin: Akademie-Verlag, [2]1984), S. 588–589.

28 Galen, *De propriis placitis* 2, ed. Vivian Nutton (Corpus Medicorum Graecorum V 3,2; Berlin: Akademie-Verlag, 1999), S. 56–57, vgl. den Kommentar S. 131–134, der auch auf die muslimischen Reaktionen eingeht.

29 Schacht/Meyerhof (wie Anm. 21), arabisch S. 79 ult. und 88,4 (Übersetzung S. 66 und 76).

(II.15–16). Dabei hat sich Maimonides mit seinem Festhalten an der biblischen Lehre noch weiter von al-Fārābī entfernt als Galen, der mit seiner gesunden Skepsis die Dinge in der Schwebe ließ. Aber damit war dieser als Philosoph hoffnungslos zwischen die Fronten geraten und konnte es niemandem recht machen.

In seinem philosophischen Frühwerk *De demonstratione*, das nur in Bruchstücken erhalten ist, hatte er übrigens noch mit großer Sicherheit die Welt für ewig gehalten,[30] und dagegen hatte sich unter dem programmatischen Titel *Zweifel an Galen* der persische Arzt und notorische Ketzer Rhazes gewandt, der sich seinerseits einen gnostischen Weltentstehungsmythos zurechtgelegt hatte. Dieser wusste auch von dem späteren Schwanken Galens in dem Alterswerk *De propriis placitis*.[31] Im Zusammenhang mit der Frage nach der Weltewigkeit hatte Galen auch nach dem Wesen der Zeit gefragt; bei Maimonides heißt es dazu im *Führer der Verirrten*: „so dass sogar Galen sagt, die Zeit sei ein göttliches Ding, deren wahres Wesen nicht begriffen werden kann" (I.73), wovon sich aber in den erhaltenen Werken meines Wissens nichts findet. Jedoch hat Rhazes in seinen *Zweifeln an Galen* auf entsprechende Ausführungen in *De demonstratione* Bezug genommen. Rhazes zitiert in der erwähnten Schrift einen Satz: „Der leere Raum ist nicht wahrnehmbar", und erläutert dazu: „Er erklärt nicht, ob er überhaupt existiert oder nicht. Was die Zeit anlangt, so existiert sie unbedingt, die Quantität ist ja von ihr nicht abzutrennen, obwohl sie kein Körper ist. Er verkündet, daß die Zeit nach seiner Auffassung eine Substanz ist, weil sie Träger der Quantität ist."[32] Wir sehen also nur so viel, dass Galen in *De demonstratione* ausführlich auf das Problem der Zeit eingegangen war.

In den medizinischen *Aphorismen* hat Maimonides in den ersten vierundzwanzig Kapiteln interessante Stücke hauptsächlich aus Galen mit genauen Quellenangaben teils wörtlich, teils sinngemäß wiedergegeben. Die textkritische Edition hat nunmehr Gerrit Bos in Angriff genommen.[33] Neben Galen zitiert Maimonides

30 Iwan von Müller, „Über Galens Werk vom wissenschaftlichen Beweis", in *Abhandlungen der königlichen bayerischen Akademie der Wissenschaften*, I. Klasse, Band 20, 2. Abteilung (München, 1895), S. 461–463.

31 *Kitāb aš-šukūk ʿalā Ǧālīnūs*, ed. Mehdi Mohaghegh (Teheran: International Institute of Islamic Thought and Civilization, 1993), S. 3,17–6,11, vgl. S. 7,23–8,6 und 14,3–10; Gotthard Strohmaier, „Bekannte und unbekannte Zitate in den *Zweifeln an Galen* des Rhazes", in *Text and Tradition. Studies in Ancient Medicine and its Transmission Presented to Jutta Kollesch*, ed. Klaus-Dietrich Fischer, Diethard Nickel und Paul Potter (Studies in Ancient Medicine 18; Leiden etc.: Brill, 1998), S. 271–274.

32 *Kitāb aš-šukūk*, S. 8,7–9; Strohmaier, „Bekannte und unbekannte Zitate" (wie Anm. 31), S. 272.

33 Maimonides, *Medical Aphorisms. Treatises 1–5* (wie Anm. 11); die Fortsetzung ist geplant im Rahmen der von der Brigham Young University in Provo betreuten Reihe der „Medical Works of Moses Maimonides"; Edition der hebräischen Übersetzung von R. Nathan Hameati in Moshe ben Maimon, *(Medical) Aphorisms of Moses in Twenty Five Treatises*, ed. Suessman Muntner (Jerusalem: Mosad Harav Kook, 1959); darauf beruhend die Übersetzung von Fred Rosner und Suessman Muntner, *The Medical Aphorisms of Moses Maimonides* (2 Bände; New York: Yeshiva University Press, 1970–1971; Nachdruck 1973);

noch einen Kommentar zu Hippokrates, *De fracturis*, von einem sonst wenig bekannten Asklepios,[34] und einige muslimische Ärzte, so at-Tamīmī (gest. 980),[35] Ibn Wāfid von Toledo (11. Jahrhundert),[36] Abū l-ʿAlāʾ Zuhr (gest. 1131)[37] und dessen Sohn Abū Marwān ibn Zuhr (gest. 1161), der einer seiner Lehrer in Spanien war.[38]

Interessant ist auch, inwieweit sich Maimonides in das Gebiet der so genannten höheren Kritik vorgewagt hat, nämlich in der Frage nach der Echtheit bestimmter Schriften. Hinsichtlich zweier pseudaristotelischer Schriften, dem *Apfelbuch* und dem *Brief über das Goldene Haus*, hat er in seinem Brief an Samuel ibn Tibbon ein klares Urteil bewiesen, indem er sie als „Faseleien und leere Einfälle" abqualifiziert.[39] Umsichtig verhält er sich zu einer pseudogalenischen Schrift über die Gefahr des Lebendigbegrabenwerdens, hält aber den Inhalt doch für erwähnenswert und meint, dass der Verfasser ein anderer Arzt namens Galen gewesen sein könnte.[40] Hingegen akzeptiert er *De theriaca ad Pisonem* mit seinen unwahrscheinlichen Wundergeschichten, darunter auch der, dass Hippokrates die Griechen durch das Abbrennen wohlriechender Substanzen vor einer Seuche rettete.[41] Auch einen wohl erst im syrischen oder arabischen Milieu entstandenen Kommentar zu Hippokrates' *De septimanis* hält er für ein Werk Galens, was ihm in der Einleitung zu seinem Kommentar zu den hippokratischen *Aphorismen* Gelegenheit zu sarkastischer Kritik gibt, wenn der Verfasser zu dem Satz, dass die Erde das Wasser umgibt, die einfältige Bemerkung anfügt, Hippokrates habe wohl gemeint, dass das Wasser

---

Gerrit Bos, „The Reception of Galen in Maimonides' *Medical Aphorisms*", in Vivian Nutton (Ed.), *The Unknown Galen* (Bulletin of the Institute of Classical Studies. Supplement 77; London: Institute of Classical Studies, 2002), S. 139–152.

34 Ibid., S. 145–146; vgl. Friedrich Reinhold Dietz (Ed.), *Apollonii Citiensis, Stephani, Palladii, Theophili, Meletii, Damascii, Ioannis, aliorum scholia in Hippocratem et Galenum*, Band 2 (Königsberg: Borntraeger, 1834; Nachdruck Amsterdam: Hakkert, 1966), S. 478.

35 Bos, „The Reception" (wie Anm. 33), S. 147; vgl. Jutta Schönfeld, *Über die Steine. Das 14. Kapitel aus dem „Kitāb al-muršid" des Muḥammad ibn Aḥmad at-Tamīmī*, nach dem Pariser Manuskript herausgegeben, übersetzt und kommentiert (Islamkundliche Untersuchungen 38; Freiburg: Alber, 1976).

36 Bos, „The Reception" (wie Anm. 33), S. 146.

37 Ibid.; vgl. jetzt sein *Kitāb al-muǧarrabāt*, ed. Cristina Álvarez Millán (Madrid: Consejo superior de investigaciones científicas, 1994).

38 Bos, „The Reception" (wie Anm. 33), S. 146.

39 Zitiert nach Moritz Steinschneider, *Die hebräischen Übersetzungen des Mittelalters und die Juden als Dolmetscher* (Berlin: Bibliographisches Bureau, 1893; Nachdruck Graz: Akademische Druck- und Verlagsanstalt, 1956), S. 41; vgl. Francis Edward Peters, *Aristoteles Arabus. The Oriental Translations and Commentaries on the Aristotelian Corpus* (Leiden: Brill 1968), S. 61–62 und 65–66; vgl. auch die im *Führer der Verirrten* (III.29) erwähnten Pseudepigraphen der Sabier.

40 Maimonides, *Aphorismen* 24,44 (ed. Muntner [wie Anm. 33], S. 311; Rosner/ Muntner [wie Anm. 33], Band 2, S. 165, Nr. 44); vgl. Ullmann, *Medizin im Islam* (wie Anm. 10), S. 59, Nr. 95.

41 Maimonides, *Aphorismen* 24,25–28 (ed. Muntner [wie Anm. 33], S. 307; Rosner/Muntner [wie Anm. 33], Band 2, S. 159–161).

die Erde umgibt.[42] Aber der Vorwurf, dass er Hippokrates immer und unter allen Umständen zu rechtfertigen suche, ist ungerecht, er stimmt vor allem nicht im Hinblick auf den neuentdeckten Kommentar zu *De aere, aquis, locis,* den ich als Band V im „Supplementum Orientale" des „Corpus Medicorum Graecorum" herausgebe. Maimonides kannte ihn sehr wohl, denn er hat Stücke daraus in seine *Aphorismen* aufgenommen.

Von dem fünfundzwanzigsten Kapitel der *Aphorismen* wurde schon die grundsätzliche Antwort auf Galens Polemik gegen Moses besprochen. Es ist ganz der Auseinandersetzung mit Galen gewidmet, wobei er sich darauf beschränkt, widersprüchliche Aussagen in dem umfänglichen Lebenswerk des Pergameners einander gegenüberzustellen. Die eigene ärztliche Erfahrung spielt bei ihm, anders als bei Rhazes, dessen *Zweifel an Galen*[43] er sehr wohl kennt, keine Rolle. Hingegen fühlt er sich hier genötigt, Galen gegen Rhazes in Schutz zu nehmen, und das ausgerechnet bei einer Stelle, wo dieser die in *De pulsuum differentiis* geäußerte Behauptung zurückweist, dass das Griechische die allein menschliche Sprache sei.[44] Das findet Maimonides nicht völlig verkehrt,[45] er führt die Klimatheorie ins Feld, die ein fester Bestandteil gräko-arabischer Bildung war und auch die Theorie einschloss, dass den Bewohnern der extremen nördlichen und südlichen Zonen das Menschsein abgesprochen werden müsse,[46] was Maimonides im *Führer der Verirrten* übernimmt (III.51). Er kommt Galen insoweit entgegen, dass dieser nach seiner Meinung sagen wollte, dass alle Sprachen in den mittleren Zonen von dem spezifisch menschlichen Charakter ihrer Bewohner abhängig seien. Er bezieht jedoch anders als Galen das Hebräische, Arabische, Persische und Syrische mit ein, was schwerlich mit dem hellenischen Selbstbewusstsein Galens übereinstimmt.[47]

Auf einen anderen unausgeglichenen Widerspruch hat Elinor Lieber aufmerksam gemacht, wenn Maimonides in der Frage des vom Gesetz verbotenen

---

42 Steinschneider, „Die Vorrede ..." (wie Anm. 11), arabisch S. 220 (Übersetzung 232); vgl. *Pseudogaleni in Hippocratis De septimanis commentarius 13*, ed. Gotthelf Bergsträßer (Corpus Medicorum Graecorum XI 2,1; Leipzig, Berlin; Teubner, 1914), S. 18–19.

43 Siehe oben Anm. 31.

44 Galen, *De pulsuum differentiis* II 5, in *Opera omnia*, ed. Kühn (wie Anm. 15), Band 8, S. 585,19–586,6; vgl. bei Rhazes, *Kitāb aš-šukūk*, S. 87,4–12; dazu Strohmaier, „Bekannte und unbekannte Zitate" (wie Anm. 31), S. 269.

45 Maimonides, *Aphorismen* 25,56–58 (ed. Muntner [wie Anm. 33], S. 360–362; Rosner/Muntner, Band 2, S. 201–203); vgl. Shalom Rosenberg und Charles H. Manekin, „Philosophical Observations on Maimonides' Critique of Galen", in *Koroth* 9 (Special Issue) (1988), S. 253.

46 Gotthard Strohmaier, „Arabische Autoren des Mittelalters über die Nordvölker", in Elisabeth Piltz (Ed.), *Byzantium and Islam in Scandinavia. Acts of a Symposium at Uppsala University, June 15–16, 1996* (Studies in Mediterranean Archaeology 126; Jonsered: Åström, 1998), S. 61–62 (Nachdruck in Strohmaier, *Hellas im Islam* [wie Anm. 7], S. 17–19).

47 Maimonides, *Aphorismen* 25,56–58 (ed. Muntner [wie Anm. 33], S. 360–362; Rosner/Muntner [wie Anm. 33], Band 2, S. 201–203); vgl. auch in der Einleitung zu den *Aphorismen* die Hervorhebung der „vollkommenen Sprachen" (*al-luġāt al-kāmila*), ed. Bos (wie Anm. 33), S. 1,7 und den Kommentar S. 96.

Schweinefleisches, das Galen als gesund und nahrhaft angepriesen hatte, dennoch irgendeinen Ausgleich sucht.[48] Alles in allem gewinnt man anhand seiner Haltung zu Galen den Eindruck, dass er wegen der widerstreitenden Traditionen, in denen er stand, manche Probleme nicht bis zum Ende durchdenken konnte und weil er vor allem ausgleichend wirken wollte. Auf alle Fälle ist er aber ein herausragender Repräsentant der arabisch-islamischen Medizingeschichte und damit Zeuge einer zu seiner Zeit noch sehr lebendigen Rezeption antiker Wissenschaft.

48 Lieber, „Maimonides the medical humanist" (wie Anm. 10), S. 56–58.

Christliche Rezeption / Wirkungsgeschichte

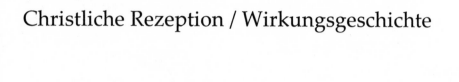

Natur und Übernatur

Moses Maimonides und Thomas von Aquin über Glauben und Wissen*

von

Maximilian Forschner

Universität Erlangen-Nürnberg

I.

Moses Maimonides' überragende Reputation zu seinen Lebzeiten ist die eines rabbinischen Gesetzesgelehrten. Er dient auch einem Thomas von Aquin als Autorität, wenn es diesem, wie etwa in seinem „Lex"-Traktat der *Summa theologiae,* um das Verständnis der jüdischen Gesetzesreligion geht.[1] Seine große Wirkung auf die Formierung der hochmittelalterlichen Gedankenwelt des lateinischen Westens verdankt sich allerdings nicht dem einen seiner Hauptwerke, der *Mišneh Torah,* sondern dem anderen, dem *Moreh Nevukhim,* dem *Führer der Unschlüssigen,* einem Werk, dessen Charakter eigenartig ist und dessen disziplinäre Einordnung nach wie vor Schwierigkeiten bereitet. Haben wir es mit einem philosophischen oder mit einem theologischen Werk zu tun? Colette Sirat etwa schreibt in einer neuen großen Geschichte der Philosophie des Mittelalters,[2] Moses Maimonides sei ein Philosoph in all seinen Werken, den juridischen ebenso wie den philosophischen, den Texten, die er für ein breites Publikum ebenso wie jenen, die er für Studierende der Philosophie geschrieben hat. Rémi Brague hingegen äußert in einem neuen Sammelwerk über Philosophen des Mittelalters die Ansicht, Maimonides könne schwerlich als Philosoph gelten; er habe, mit Ausnahme eines schmalen Traktats über Logik, kein philosophisches Buch geschrieben.[3]

Nun ist die Unsicherheit, die sich bis heute in diesen unterschiedlichen Urteilen bekundet, nicht singulär, sondern betrifft nahezu alle großen Köpfe des Hochmittelalters, die sich selbst als Theologen betrachten und die pagane

---

* Leicht veränderte Fassung von Kap. 6.2 meines Buches *Thomas von Aquin* (München: Beck, 2005), S. 164–184.

1 *Summa theologiae,* I–II, qu. 91–108, insbesondere qu. 98–105.

2 *Routledge History of Philosophy,* Band III: „Medieval Philosophy", ed. John Marenbon (London, New York: Routledge, 1998), S. 77.

3 Rémi Brague, „Maimonides. Bibel als Philosophie", in Theo Kobusch (Ed.), *Philosophen des Mittelalters* (Darmstadt: Primus-Verlag, 2000), S. 96–110, hier S. 97.

Philosophie der Antike für die theoretische Formulierung ihres religiös geprägten Weltbildes in Anspruch nehmen. Die entscheidende Frage ist, welche Rolle die Philosophie bei diesem Unternehmen spielt. Bei Maimonides, so meine These, besteht das für uns Merkwürdige gerade darin, dass sich das meiste seines jüdischen Glaubens in Philosophie auflöst und auflösen kann, ohne letztlich unorthodox zu sein, während aus christlicher Perspektive zwischen Glaubenswahrheit und philosophischer Erkenntnis eine präzise Grenze besteht und bestehen muss, soll der Boden des wahren Glaubens nicht verlassen werden.

Als ernsthaftes Problem wurde die Rolle der Philosophie allerdings im Rahmen aller drei großen Offenbarungsreligionen empfunden, als im Hochmittelalter über die Begegnung mit der Kultur und Wissenschaft des Islam die Rezeption der avanciertesten Philosophie anstand: des Werks des Aristoteles, seiner antiken Kommentatoren und seiner Fortbildung durch arabischsprachige Denker. Im Unterschied zum antiken (Neu-)Platonismus ließ sich die aristotelische Philosophie nur schwer in das Weltbild der drei großen Offenbarungsreligionen integrieren. Papst Gregor IX. verbot 1131 das Studium der naturwissenschaftlichen Werke des Aristoteles, weil sie mit Kerndogmen des biblischen Christentums unvereinbar schienen: mit dem Schöpfungsgedanken, der Lehre von der individuellen göttlichen Providenz, der Wunder, der übernatürlichen Offenbarung.[4] 1233 versuchten südfranzösische Rabbiner (vergeblich) die Verbrennung von Moses Maimonides' *Führer der Unschlüssigen* bei der von den Dominikanern wahrgenommenen Inquisition zu erwirken, weil seine Art der Aristotelesrezeption ihrer Überzeugung nach gegen den biblischen Glauben verstoße.[5] Das Christentum teilte mit dem Judentum das Schicksal der Herausforderung durch die aristotelische Philosophie; und die von Beginn virulent gewordenen Schwierigkeiten des Islam mit den Aristotelikern in seinen Reihen waren notorisch; sie erreichten mit dem Lebenswerk des Averroes ihren Höhepunkt.

Moses Maimonides, in islamischen Ländern lebend, begegnet dieser Herausforderung früher als die christlichen Denker. Er schätzt, wie unter Logikern, Naturforschern und Ärzten seiner Zeit üblich, das aristotelische Œuvre als Gipfel profaner Philosophie und Wissenschaft. Albertus Magnus und Thomas von Aquin werden diese Ansicht teilen und sich durch päpstliche Verbote nicht in ihrer Forschung und Rezeption beeinträchtigen lassen. Durch sie vor allem findet die lateinische Scholastik im Werk des Moses Maimonides ein

4 Vgl. Kurt Schubert, „Die Bedeutung des Maimonides für die Hochscholastik", in *Kairos* 10 (1968), S. 2–18, hier S. 2.

5 Vgl. Wolfgang Kluxen, „Maimonides und die philosophische Orientierung seiner lateinischen Leser. Eine interpretatorische Reflexion", in *Prudentia und Contemplatio. Ethik und Metaphysik im Mittelalter. Festschrift für Georg Wieland zum 65. Geburtstag*, ed. Johannes Brachtendorf (Paderborn etc.: Schöningh, 2002), S. 107–119, hier S. 108–109.

Paradigma kritischer Aufnahme des Aristotelismus auf der Basis eines zum Teil gemeinsamen biblischen Glaubens.

Albert und Thomas lesen den *Führer der Unschlüssigen* in lateinischer Übersetzung. Den Forschungen von Jacob Guttmann[6] und Wolfgang Kluxen[7] verdanken wir die Erhebung der fassbaren Tatsachen, die die Literargeschichte zum lateinischen Moses Maimonides betreffen. Die lateinische Übersetzung des vollständigen *Führers der Unschlüssigen,* den der Autor auf arabisch verfasst und dessen Übersetzung ins Hebräische (durch Ibn Tibbon) er noch zu seinen Lebzeiten betreut hat, liegt kurz nach 1230 vor. Sie entstand (allerdings aus der hebräischen Version des Al Charisi) vermutlich in Italien oder in Frankreich, veranlasst wahrscheinlich von christlichen und wohl in Zusammenarbeit mit jüdischen Gelehrten und Theologen. Albertus Magnus hat das Werk in den vierziger Jahren in Paris studiert. Über ihn lernt es Thomas kennen. Der lateinische Titel lautet in den Handschriften: *Dux neutrorum vel dubiorum.* Um die Jahrhundertmitte ist der Text in Paris und Oxford den Gelehrten allgemein zugänglich.[8]

Im *Führer der Unschlüssigen* stellt Maimonides sich die Aufgabe, „demjenigen eine Anleitung zu geben, welcher der Religion kundig und mit dem Gesetze vertraut ist, der an die Wahrheit der Tora glaubt und in seinem Glauben und Charakter untadelig ist, der aber Philosophie studiert hat und ihre Probleme kennt, und den die menschliche Vernunft angezogen hat, um ihn in ihrem Bereiche wohnen zu lassen."[9] Maimonides möchte also mit seinem Werk den Torah-Glauben mit der Philosophie, gemeint ist die von der arabischen Kultur getragene aristotelische Philosophie, in ein passendes Verhältnis setzen. Und

---

6 Vgl. Jacob Guttmann, *Das Verhältnis des Thomas von Aquino zum Judenthum und zur jüdischen Literatur* (Göttingen: Vandenhoeck & Ruprecht, 1891); idem, „Der Einfluß der maimonidischen Philosophie auf das christliche Abendland", in *Moses ben Maimon. Sein Leben, seine Werke und sein Einfluß,* ed. Wilhelm Bacher, Marcus Brann, David Jacob Simonsen (2 Bände; Leipzig: Fock, 1908–1914; Reprint beider Bände in einem Band: Hildesheim, New York: Olms, 1971), Band I, S. 135–230.

7 Vgl. Wolfgang Kluxen, „Literargeschichtliches zum lateinischen Moses Maimonides", in *Recherches de théologie ancienne et médiévale* 21 (1954), S. 23–50; idem, „Maimonides und die Hochscholastik", in *Philosophisches Jahrbuch* 63 (1955), S. 151–165; idem, „Maimonides and Latin scholasticism", in *Maimonides and Philosophy,* ed. Shlomo Pines and Yirmiyahu Yovel (Dordrecht: Nijhoff, 1986), S. 224–232.

8 Vgl. dazu jetzt auch Görge K. Hasselhoff, „Rabbi Moyses – zur Wirkungsgeschichte von Moses Maimonides im christlichen Mittelalter", in *Judaica* 60/1 (2004), S. 1–20, hier S. 3ff.

9 Mose ben Maimon, *Führer der Unschlüssigen,* „Einleitung", S. 4. Ich zitiere nach der deutschen Übersetzung: *Mose ben Maimon, Führer der Unschlüssigen.* Übersetzung und Kommentar von Adolf Weiß. Mit einer Einleitung von Johann Maier (Hamburg: Meiner, ^{2}1995). Die vorliegende Abhandlung steht unter dem Vorbehalt meiner Unkenntnis des Arabischen und des Vertrauens auf die Stimmigkeit der benutzten Übersetzung.

das Ergebnis dieses Verhältnisaufbaus soll so sein, dass der durch sein Werk Angeleitete sowohl im Torah-Glauben als auch im Bereich der menschlichen Vernunft zu leben (und richtig zu leben) vermag.

Thomas von Aquin hat die Beschäftigung mit dem neu zugänglichen aristotelischen Œuvre zu einer präzisen Abgrenzung und Verhältnisbestimmung von religiösem Glauben und profanem Wissen, von Philosophie und Offenbarungstheologie motiviert. Wie seine hierfür einschlägigen Texte belegen, war der *Führer der Unschlüssigen* des Rabbi Moyses dabei für ihn ein wichtiger Bezugstext. Er hat ihn genau studiert und seine Gedanken und Argumente zum Teil übernommen, aber stets in einen wissens- und glaubenstheoretischen Rahmen integriert, der sich von dem des Rabbi wesentlich unterscheidet. Thomas nämlich zieht eine eindeutige Grenze zwischen Natur und Übernatur, zwischen Wissen und Offenbarungsglauben, zwischen dem diesseitigen *status viae* und dem jenseitigen *status perfectionis* des Menschen. Der Rabbi Moyses dagegen zieht zwar eine präzise Grenze zwischen dem transzendenten Gott und seinem uns zugänglichen Werk, aber er unterscheidet in Gottes Werk und seinem Verhältnis zu seinem Werk nicht zwischen Natur und Übernatur, zwischen Natur und Gnade und hebt den für alle notwendigen und verbindlichen Glauben für die wenigen Fähigen, Tüchtigen und Berufenen nach dem Modell der aristotelischen Theoria weitgehend in Wissen auf. Diese These soll im Folgenden anhand von Vergleichsthemen, die das Verhältnis von Glauben und Wissen betreffen, beispielhaft erläutert und begründet werden.

II.

Die christliche Religion ist von ihrer Frühzeit an stark mit heils- und unheilsgeschichtlichen Dogmen befasst, die schrittweise in philosophischer Sprache ausformuliert werden. Ihre Mitte bildet, an diesen gemeinschaftsstiftenden Dogmen orientiert, das sakramentale Leben mit seinen Symbolen. Die jüdische Religion ist, ähnlich dem Islam, weit weniger an offenbarungstheologischen Glaubenswahrheiten ausgerichtet. Ihre Mitte bildet der praktische Gehorsam gegenüber dem mosaischen Gesetz.[10] So gesehen dürfte nicht überraschen, dass die Verhältnisbestimmung von Glauben und Wissen bei einem jüdischen und einem christlichen Denker des Mittelalters merklich differiert. Gleichwohl ergibt sich für das mittelalterliche Judentum in einer islamischen und christlichen Umwelt das Bedürfnis nach einer Vergewisserung der eigenen theologisch-religiösen Verbindlichkeiten. Dieses Bedürfnis wird umso drängender, als sich, unter dem Einfluss des Aristotelismus, in der intellektuellen Elite gewisse Verunsicherungen und Lösungstendenzen von der überlieferten Religion

10 Vgl. Johann Maier, Einleitung (wie Anm. 9), S. XXXIV*.

abzeichnen. Maimonides stellt sich diesem Bedürfnis. Er ist von der Wahrheit der ererbten Religion überzeugt. Sie allein bietet ihm den Weg zum Heil. Die Wahrheit der Religion ist in einer Heiligen Schrift formuliert, die die Sprache des einfachen Volkes spricht. Am Glauben der Sprache des Volkes kann der philosophisch Gebildete in Zweifel geraten, verwirrt und irre werden. Um dieser Gefahr zu begegnen, will Maimonides dem Philosophierenden den Weg zeigen, wie man die Heilige Schrift mit Hilfe wissenschaftlich-philosophischen, am Aristotelismus orientierten Denkens, auf dem Weg der Ersetzung von Bildern durch Wesensbegriffe, zuallererst adäquat zu verstehen vermag. Bei dieser von philosophisch-wissenschaftlichem Wissen getragenen Interpretation leitet ihn allerdings eine Kanonik, die ihm die Zugehörigkeit zur Glaubensgemeinschaft definiert und die für ihn auch im Falle einer Differenz niemals zugunsten einer aristotelischen Lehre zu verlassen ist.

In seinem Mischnakommentar formuliert Maimonides 13 verbindliche Glaubenslehren der jüdischen Religion, die auch im *Führer der Unschlüssigen* leitend sind und nicht in Frage gestellt werden, vielmehr hier zum Teil ihre adäquate philosophische Interpretation erfahren. Es sind dies:[11] die Existenz des Weltschöpfers, die Einzigkeit Gottes, seine Unkörperlichkeit und Ewigkeit; die Verehrungs-, Dienst- und Gehorsamsverpflichtung des Menschen; die Möglichkeit und Wirklichkeit von Prophetie; die herausragende Stellung des Moses; die Torah als von Gott gegebenes, von Moses übermitteltes, unaufhebbares Gesetz; Gottes Kenntnis der Taten jedes Menschen, ihre Belohnung und Bestrafung; das Kommen des Messias und die Auferstehung der Toten.

III.

Im Kapitel I, 34 des *Führers der Unschlüssigen* gibt Maimonides fünf Gründe, „die es verbieten, den Unterricht mit der Metaphysik zu beginnen und die Laien über das aufzuklären und ihnen das zu zeigen, worauf man sie eigentlich aufmerksam machen müßte".[12]

Am Beginn und für alle zum Glauben und Heil Erwählten muss eine für alle verständliche Offenbarung und Überlieferung stehen. Wäre dem nicht so, so würden die meisten Menschen sterben, ohne zu wissen, ob es für die Welt einen Gott gibt oder nicht, ob ihm die Herrschaft zuzusprechen ist oder nicht[13] und wie sie sich entsprechend zu verhalten haben. Diese Offenbarung und Überlieferung, die der Heiligen Schrift, erfolgt in der Sprache von Kindern und

---

11 Der Text in deutscher Übersetzung bei Maier in seiner oben (Anm. 9) zitierten Einleitung, S. XLIV*ff.

12 *Führer der Unschlüssigen* (wie Anm. 9), S. 98–99.

13 Vgl. ibid., S. 103.

Laien, enthält indessen eine Tiefendimension, die nur für Auserwählte, und auch für sie erst nach entsprechend geordneter Vorbereitung des Charakters und des Geistes, verstehbar wird. Die fünf Gründe rechtfertigen die Notwendigkeit eines allgemeinen Volksglaubens, die Notwendigkeit eines geordneten Bildungsgangs zum esoterischen (das heißt der Verständnismöglichkeit Weniger vorbehaltenen) Gehalt des „wahren Glaubens" und die Notwendigkeit einer an der Fassungskraft der Menschen ausgerichteten Aufklärung. Maimonides beschließt das Kapitel im Blick auf die Interpretation des Glaubensguts mit Mitteln aristotelischer Philosophie mit dem Satz: „Aus all diesen Gründen eignen sich diese Dinge ausschließlich für einzelne Auserwählte, nicht aber für die große Menge, und deshalb müssen sie dem Anfänger vorenthalten und der dazu nicht Geeignete gehindert werden, wie man kleinen Kindern untersagt, schwere Speisen zu essen oder schwere Lasten zu tragen".[14] Das anschließende Kapitel I, 35 handelt dann von einer adressatenbezogenen, wohldosierten und graduierten Aufklärungspflicht der Verstehenden gegenüber dem einfachen Volk.

Thomas von Aquin benützt die Argumente des Kapitels I, 34 des *Dux neutrorum* sämtlich für ein eigenes Argumentationsziel: Er möchte mit ihnen, wie das 1. Buch der *Summa contra Gentiles* in zwei prägnanten Kapiteln erklärt, zum einen begründen, warum die Wahrheit von göttlichen Dingen, die prinzipiell der natürlichen Vernunft zugänglich sind, den Menschen gleichwohl passenderweise (*convenienter*) zu glauben vorgelegt werden.[15] Er möchte mit ihnen aber auch begründen, warum dem Menschen passenderweise Wahrheiten zum Glauben vorgelegt werden, die mit natürlicher Vernunft nicht erforschbar sind.[16] Die beiden Kapitel I, 4 und I, 5 der *Summa contra Gentiles* stehen beispielhaft für die Art, in der Thomas Gedanken des Maimonides aufnimmt und in ein von diesem wesentlich verschiedenes Gesamtkonzept integriert.[17]

Thomas unterscheidet in dem, was wir von Gott bekennen, einen zweifachen Wahrheitsmodus.[18] Einiges von Gott, so Thomas, ist wahr, was jede Fähigkeit der menschlichen Vernunft übersteigt; anderes ist wahr, zu dem auch die natürliche Vernunft gelangen kann. Zu Ersterem gehören die Glaubensgeheimnisse etwa der Trinität oder der Inkarnation oder der Auferstehung des Fleisches. Zu Letzterem gehören Erkenntnisse etwa, dass Gott ist und dass er einer ist.

---

14 Ibid., S. 108.

15 *Summa contra Gentiles*, I, 4.

16 *Summa contra Gentiles*, I, 5.

17 Vgl. dazu die wichtige Studie von Paul Synave, „La révélation des vérités divines naturelles d'après saint Thomas d'Aquin", in *Mélanges Mandonnet: Etudes d'histoire littéraire et doctrinale du moyen âge*, Band I (Bibliothèque thomiste; Paris: Vrin, 1930), S. 327–370; Nachdruck in Jacob I. Dienstag (Ed.), *Studies in Maimonides and St. Thomas* (New York: Ktav, 1975), S. 290–333.

18 *Summa contra Gentiles*, I, 3.

Dass die strikten Glaubensgeheimnisse einer besonderen Offenbarung bedürfen, um dem Menschen in diesem Leben zur Kenntnis zu gelangen, versteht sich von selbst. Dass Gott dem Menschen solche Wahrheiten auf übernatürliche Weise als etwas im Glauben zu Ergreifendes geoffenbart hat, hat mit dem Ziel des Menschen zu tun. Der Mensch, so Thomas, ist durch die Gnade Gottes auf ein übernatürliches Ziel ausgerichtet, auf eine von Gott frei gewährte ewige Erkenntnis- und Liebesgemeinschaft mit ihm. Dieses Ziel ist vom Menschen mit seinen natürlichen Kräften weder erkennbar noch erstrebbar und realisierbar. Um nach diesem Ziel sinnvollerweise streben und entsprechend handeln zu können, muss der Mensch es in wenn auch noch so unklarer und rätselhafter Weise vorwegnehmen können. Dies wird ihm, was sein Endziel betrifft, durch die übernatürliche Offenbarung ermöglicht. „Da nun die Menschen durch die göttliche Vorsehung auf ein höheres Gut hingeordnet sind, als es die menschliche Gebrechlichkeit im gegenwärtigen Leben erfahren kann [...], musste der Geist zu etwas Höherem aufgerufen werden, als unsere Vernunft im gegenwärtigen Leben erreichen kann, damit er so lerne, nach etwas zu verlangen und sich strebend auf etwas hin auszurichten, was über den ganzen Stand des gegenwärtigen Lebens hinausgeht."[19]

Warum aber, so Thomas, werden dem Menschen durch übernatürliche Offenbarung nicht nur strikte Glaubensgeheimnisse, sondern auch Sachverhalte zu glauben vorgelegt, die der natürlichen Vernunft zugänglich sind? Vor allem für die Beantwortung dieser Frage nimmt Thomas die Autorität von Maimonides in Anspruch, in den *Quaestiones disputatae de veritate* XIV, 10 in explizitem Verweis, in der *Summa contra Gentiles* I, 4 dann nicht mehr mit Nennung seines Namens. Ich zitiere zunächst den Passus von *De veritate*:

> [Auch was sich von Gott demonstrative aufweisen lässt,] „müssen wir gleichwohl anfangs glauben, aus fünf Gründen, die Rabbi Moyses aufstellt. Der eine ist die Tiefe und Feinheit dieser Erkenntnisgegenstände, die von den Sinnen sehr weit entfernt liegen; darum ist der Mensch nicht dazu geeignet, sie anfangs vollkommen zu erkennen. Der zweite Grund ist die Schwäche des menschlichen Verstandes in seinem Beginn. Der dritte ist die große Zahl von Tatsachen, die für den Beweis jener Wahrheiten im Voraus benötigt werden und deren Kenntnis der Mensch nur in sehr langer Zeit (hinzu)erwerben kann. Der vierte ist die Indisponiertheit zum beweisenden Erkennen, die manchen wegen der Insuffizienz ihrer Körperverfassung eigen ist. Die fünfte ist die Notwendigkeit von (von der Gotteserkenntnis abhaltenden) Beschäftigungen zur Beschaffung der lebensnotwendigen Dinge. Aus all diesen Gründen geht hervor, dass zu dem, was man notwendig von Gott erkennen muss, wenn man es nur auf dem Weg des Beweises erreichen könnte, nur sehr wenige gelangen würden, und auch die erst nach langer Zeit. Deshalb ist den Menschen offenbar auf heilsame Weise der Weg des

19 *Summa contra Gentiles*, I, 5.

> Glaubens geboten, durch den für alle zu jeder beliebigen Zeit ein leichter Weg zum Heil offen steht.[20]

Der entsprechende Text der *Summa contra Gentiles* ist vollständiger, ausführlicher, systematisch prägnanter und für das Verständnis des Textes von *De veritate* von einigem Erklärungswert. Er notiert drei Nachteile für das Heil der Menschen, die sich ergäben, wenn Wahrheiten über Göttliches, die prinzipiell der natürlichen Vernunft zugänglich sind, allein der Vernunft zu erforschen überlassen blieben. Der eine ist, dass nur wenige Menschen eine Gotteserkenntnis besäßen, teils weil sie aufgrund ihrer physischen Verfassung dazu nicht in der Lage wären, teils weil die Sorge um das Lebensnotwendige sie von der Muße spekulativer Forschung abhielte, teils weil sie nicht bereit sind, aus Liebe zum Wissen die große Anstrengung des Studiums auf sich zu nehmen. Der zweite Nachteil ist, dass die wenigen zu dieser Erkenntnis kaum anders denn erst nach langer Zeit gelangten: wegen der Tiefe der Wahrheit, die einen langen Weg der Einübung des Geistes erfordert, wegen der sinnlichen Affektbestimmtheit der Jugendphase, die für derartige Erkenntnis ungeeignet ist. Der dritte Nachteil ist, dass wegen der Schwäche und Irrtumsanfälligkeit der menschlichen Vernunft selbst unter den Weisen vieles zweifelhaft und mit Falschem vermischt bliebe, was durch die Offenbarung nun leicht, zweifels- und irrtumsfrei dargelegt ist.

In dieser Allgemeinheit und Schärfe fehlt der letzte Gedanke bei Maimonides; und bei Thomas findet sich signifikanterweise nichts, was im Sinne von Weisungen für einen geordneten Bildungsgang zu esoterischem Wissen verstanden werden könnte; und es findet sich bei ihm auch nichts, was als Weisung zur dosierten Aufklärung der Kinder und Laien zu gelten hätte. Thomas benützt vielmehr die bei Maimonides nicht vorhandene Unterscheidung von Offenbarungswahrheit und Vernunftwahrheit, um zu betonen, dass der

20 *Quaestiones disputatae de veritate*, qu. 14 a. 10 co.: „Quaedam vero sunt ad quae etiam in hac vita perfecte cognoscenda possumus pervenire, sicut illa quae de Deo demonstrative probari possunt, quae tamen a principio necesse est credere, propter quinque rationes quas Rabbi Moyses ponit: quarum prima est profunditas et subtilitas istorum cognoscibilium quae sunt remotissima a sensibus, unde homo non est idoneus in principio perfecte ea cognoscere; secunda causa est debilitas humani intellectus in suo principio; tertia vero est multitudo eorum, quae praeexiguntur ad istorum demonstrationem, quae homo nonnisi in longissimo tempore addiscere potest; quarta est indispositio ad sciendum, quae inest quibusdam propter pravitatem complexionis; quinta est necessitas occupationum ad providendum necessaria vitae. Ex quibus omnibus apparet quod, si oporteret per demonstrationem solummodo accipere ea, quae necessarium est cognoscere de Deo, paucissimi ad hoc pervenire possent et hi etiam nonnisi post longum tempus; unde patet quod salubriter est via fidei hominibus provisa per quam patet omnibus facilis aditus ad salutem secundum quodcumque tempus."

menschliche Geist zum Heil des Menschen zu etwas Höherem aufgerufen werden musste, als unsere Vernunft in diesem Leben je zu erreichen vermag.[21] Er hält dies gerade für ein Privileg der christlichen Religion, die einzigartig geistliche und ewige Güter in Aussicht stelle, während das Alte Gesetz, das für seine Befolgung zeitliche Güter versprach, nur weniges vorstellte, was die Erforschung der menschlichen Vernunft übersteigt.[22] Und ganz wesentlich ist ihm der Gedanke, dass durch die Offenbarung übernatürlicher Wahrheiten, die mit natürlicher Vernunft prinzipiell nicht erfassbar sind, der Tendenz zur Überheblichkeit des menschlichen Geistes heilsamer Abbruch widerfährt. „Ein weiterer Nutzen besteht in der Unterdrückung der Vermessenheit *(praesumptionis repressio)*, die die Mutter des Irrtums ist. Es gibt nämlich Menschen, die sich so viel auf ihr Ingenium einbilden, dass sie die gesamte göttliche Natur mit ihrem Intellekt vermessen zu können sich rühmen, in der Überzeugung, das Ganze sei wahr, was ihnen scheint, und falsch, was ihnen nicht scheint. Damit also von dieser Überheblichkeit der menschliche Geist befreit zur bescheidenen Erforschung der Wahrheit gelange, war es notwendig, dass dem Menschen etwas von göttlicher Seite vorgelegt wird, was gänzlich seinen Intellekt übersteigt."[23]

IV.

Maimonides versteht den Menschen im Sinne der Heiligen Schrift als Ebenbild Gottes. Ebenbild Gottes ist er ihm durch seinen Verstand. Entsprechend sieht er das Ziel des menschlichen Lebens in der vollendeten Erkenntnis Gottes. Das mosaische Gesetz dient dem Erreichen dieses Ziels; es hat zwei (unentbehrliche) Funktionen für die Vervollkommnung des Menschen. Die erste besteht in der individuellen und gemeinschaftlichen Sicherung von sozial relevanten Verhaltensweisen, die eine geordnete Befriedigung der leiblichen Bedürfnisse ermöglichen. Diese erste Vervollkommnung ist Voraussetzung einer zweiten – und diese ist Voraussetzung des ewigen Lebens.

Maimonides ordnet die Zeit des Messias der ersten Funktion zu. Gedacht ist an eine irdische Wiederherstellung des Reiches Israel, in dem die politische und gesellschaftliche Ordnung eine optimale Erfüllung des Gesetzes ermöglicht und damit die Basis bietet für Tätigkeiten zur Vervollkommnung der

21 *Summa contra Gentiles*, I, 5: „[...] oportuit mentem evocari in aliquid altius quam ratio nostra in praesenti possit pertingere."

22 Ibid.: „Et hoc praecipue christianae religioni competit, quae singulariter bona spiritualia et aeterna promittit. [...] Lex autem vetus, quae temporalia promissa habebat, pauca proponit, quae humanae rationis inquisitionem excederent."

23 Ibid.

Seele. Diese besteht zunächst in gläubig-autoritätsbestimmter Annahme der Überlieferung, dann im wissenschaftlichen Erwerb und kontemplativen Vollzug der Gotteserkenntnis, von Maimonides ganz so gedacht, wie Aristoteles in seiner *Nikomachischen Ethik* die dem Menschen mögliche höchste Lebensform der Theoria skizziert. Sie fällt für Maimonides mit der Verwirklichung des wahren Glaubens zusammen. Der wahre Glaube ist die auf die Erkenntnis Gottes zentrierte optimale Aktualisierung des menschlichen Geistes. Und diese Aktualisierung des Geistes bildet den Grund seiner Unsterblichkeit, indem Gott den ewigen Bund der Seele und ihre Seligkeit sichert in dem Maße, in dem sie ihn auf Erden erkannt und geliebt hat. Dies besagt: Die vollkommene Gottesverehrung ist ohne metaphysische Gotteserkenntnis nicht möglich.[24] Es ist die philosophische Theoria, die den Menschen vollendet und deretwegen er eines ewigen Fortbestandes würdig ist.[25]

> Seine letzte Vollkommenheit aber ist, daß er in Wirklichkeit denke und dass er die Vernunft wirklich besitze, nämlich daß er alles wisse, was dem Menschen seiner letzten Vollkommenheit gemäß von den seienden Dingen zu wissen möglich ist, und es ist klar, daß diese letzte Vollkommenheit nicht in Handlungen oder Charaktereigenschaften, sondern nur in Kenntnissen besteht, und zwar führt zu diesen das Studium und sie sind ein notwendiges Ergebnis der Forschung. Es ist aber auch klar, daß diese letzte erhabene Vollkommenheit nur nach der Erlangung der ersten Vollkommenheit erreichbar ist […]. Aber nach Erreichung der ersten Vollkommenheit ist es ihm möglich, zur letzten, die ohne Zweifel die höhere ist, zu gelangen, da diese und nichts anderes die Ursache des ewigen Lebens ist.[26]

Zwei Punkte sind es, die hier besondere Beachtung verdienen: einmal die Bestimmung des wahren Glaubens und zum anderen die Bestimmung des wahren Glaubens als „Ursache des ewigen Lebens".

Maimonides kennt Stufen des Glaubens, jenen, der etwas für wahr hält und als verbindlich tut, weil es so überliefert ist, und jenen Glauben, der etwas für wahr hält, weil es bewiesen und unwiderlegbar oder wohl begründet ist. Nur der Letztere ist „wahrer Glaube": „Wenn nun mit diesem Glauben die Gewißheit verbunden ist, daß das Gegenteil des Geglaubten in keiner Weise möglich ist, wenn im Denken kein Raum zur Widerlegung dieses Glaubens vorhanden ist und man sich die Möglichkeit des Gegenteils nicht vorstellen kann, dann ist es ein wahrer Glaube".[27]

24 Vgl. *Führer der Unschlüssigen* (wie Anm. 9), III, 51, S. 345.

25 Vgl. ibid., III, 54, S. 365.

26 Vgl. ibid., III, 27, S. 174–175.

27 Ibid., I, 50, S. 154.

Nun sind Gewissheit und Unwiderlegbarkeit auch Bestimmungen des religiösen Glaubens, wie Thomas von Aquin ihn verstehen wird.[28] Doch Maimonides geht entschieden weiter. Wahrer Glaube ist für ihn durch Forschung erwiesener Glaube. Er unterscheidet unter den Gläubigen einmal „die große Mehrzahl der Gesetzesgläubigen, nämlich der Unwissenden, die die Gebote ausüben"; ferner „die Talmudkundigen, die zwar auf dem Wege der Überlieferung die wahren Glaubenslehren angenommen und die praktische Gottesverehrung erlernt haben, aber mit dem Studium der Grundlehren des Gesetzes nicht bekannt sind und überhaupt nicht danach fragen, ob man die Wahrheit einer Glaubenslehre auch erweisen kann"; dann „diejenigen, die sich darauf eingelassen haben, über die Grundlehren des Glaubens nachzudenken"; und schließlich jenen, der „dahin gelangt ist, den Beweis für alles das zu kennen, wofür es einen Beweis gibt, und der hinsichtlich der göttlichen Dinge das Wesen von allem kennt, dessen Wesen zu erkennen möglich ist, und der der Erkenntnis des wahren Wesens desjenigen nahegekommen ist, bei dem es möglich ist, der Erkenntnis seines wahren Wesens nahezukommen."[29]

Der Erwerb dieser höchsten Stufe des Glaubens führt über die Logik und mathematischen Wissenschaften, die Naturwissenschaft, die Metaphysik bis hin zur Stufe der Prophetie. Der wahre Prophet ist schließlich derjenige, der „nach seiner Vervollkommnung sein ganzes Denken auf das Göttliche richtet, ganz Gott ergeben ist, sein Denken von allem anderen abkehrt und alle Tätigkeiten seiner Vernunft hinsichtlich der existierenden Dinge darein setzt, aus ihnen die Erkenntnis Gottes abzuleiten und zu erkennen, in welcher Weise die Weltregierung Gottes möglich sein kann."[30]

Maimonides beschließt den *Führer der Unschlüssigen* mit einem Gleichnis von der königlichen Stadt und dem Königshof,[31] das die eschatologischen Perspektiven der verschiedenen Stufen des Glaubens bekundet. Die Ungläubigen befinden sich außerhalb der Stadt. Die Menge der Gläubigen ist zwar in der Stadt; aber sie haben den Königshof noch gar nicht zu Gesicht bekommen. Die Talmudkundigen sind bis zum königlichen Palast gelangt. Diejenigen, die über die Glaubenslehren nachdenken, befinden sich im Vorhof beziehungsweise in den Vorräumen, und nur die Wissenden sind bereits beim König. „Anteil an der kommenden Welt" beziehungsweise „ewiges Leben" werden die Gläubigen nach Maßgabe ihrer Gotteserkenntnis haben.

Alle praktisch Gläubigen werden in messianischer Zeit wieder von den Toten auferstehen.[32] Sie erhalten eine Chance zur Reflexion und Kontemplation

28 Zum Folgenden vgl. den Traktat „De fide" bei Thomas in *Quaestiones disputatae de veritate*, qu. 14; *Summa theologiae*, II–II, qu. 1–16.

29 *Führer der Unschlüssigen* (wie Anm. 9), III, 51, S. 342–343.

30 Ibid., III, 51, S. 343.

31 Ibid., III, 51, S. 340ff.

32 Maimonides unterscheidet zwischen „kommender Welt" als transzendentem Heilsziel der vom Leib befreiten Geistseele und „messianischer Zeit" als eschatologischem

und damit zum Glück ewigen Lebens, während jene, die sich praktisch von Gott trennen und nicht um die Erkenntnis Gottes bemühen, den Tieren gleich dem Tod überantwortet sind.[33] Der „Anteil an der kommenden Welt" wird dem Gläubigen gewährt nach dem Maß seiner in dieser Welt erworbenen Gotteserkenntnis. „Der Bestand der Seele bis in Ewigkeit ist [...] im Bestande des Schöpfers, gepriesen sei er, begründet, der die Ursache für ihren Bestand ist, entsprechend dem, wie sie ihn erfaßt hat [...] und das vollkommene Übel und die große Rache bestehen darin, daß die Seele ausgerottet wird und zugrunde geht und nicht lebendig und beständig bleibt."[34]

Auf Gemeinsamkeit und Unterschiede in den entsprechenden Auffassungen des Thomas von Aquin kann ich hier nicht vollständig und nicht im Detail, sondern nur zum Teil und dies nur im Umriss eingehen. Wie für Maimonides besteht auch für Thomas die Auszeichnung des Menschen in der Gottebenbildlichkeit. Wie dieser bestimmt er das Endziel des Menschen als *visio beatifica,* als erfüllende Verbindung mit Gott in Erkenntnis und Liebe, allerdings nicht nur, wie Maimonides, als Verbindung der vom Leib befreiten Geistseele, sondern des ganzen verklärten Menschen mit Gott.

Wie der Prolog zur „pars prima secundae" der *Summa theologiae* eindrucksvoll belegt, will Thomas allerdings mit der Gottebenbildlichkeit des Menschen nicht nur seinen Intellekt, sondern auch die Freiheit seines Willens und die Selbstverantwortlichkeit seines Tuns hervorgehoben wissen.[35] Entsprechend spielt für ihn, jedenfalls in dieser Welt, nicht die Vervollkommnung des Intellekts die fraglos dominante Rolle, wenn es darum geht, wer sich des „Anteils an der kommenden Welt" als würdig erweist.

---

irdischem Heilsziel. Die Auferstehung von den Toten bezieht sich auf Letztere. In der messianischen Zeit leben die gläubigen Juden nicht mehr unter Diasporaverhältnissen, ist Israel nicht mehr der Fremdherrschaft unterworfen und bietet so den Gläubigen die Möglichkeit einer besseren Erfüllung der Torah, einer besseren Gotteserkenntnis und damit eines vollkommeneren „Anteils an der kommenden Welt". Letzterer besteht in der definitiven (und graduierten) Verbindung des aktualisierten (erworbenen) menschlichen Intellekts mit dem aktiven Intellekt. Vgl. Maier, „Einleitung" (wie Anm. 9), S. LVI*–LVII*; Joshua Finkel, „Maimonides' Treatise on Resurrection", in Salo W. Baron (Ed.), *Essays on Maimonides* (New York: Columbia University Press, 1941; Nachdruck New York: AMS Press, 1966), S. 93–121.

33 Vgl. *Führer der Unschlüssigen* (wie Anm. 9), III, 51, S. 352.

34 Mischnakommentar zu *Sanhedrin* 10 (*ḥeleq*), zitiert nach Schubert, „Die Bedeutung des Maimonides" (wie Anm. 4), 4.

35 „[...] homo factus ad imaginem Dei dicitur, secundum quod per imaginem significatur *intellectuale et arbitrio liberum et per se potestativum;* [...] restat ut consideremus de eius imagine, idest de homine, secundum quod et ipse est suorum operum principium, quasi liberum arbitrium habens et suorum operum potestatem" (Hervorhebung im Original. Thomas von Aquin zitiert hier aus *De fide orthodoxa* von Johannes von Damaskus.).

Diesem Unterschied entspricht die Differenz im Begriff des Glaubens. Zwar betont Thomas, wie wir sahen, in expliziter Übernahme von Argumenten des Rabbi Moyses, dass es angebracht ist, wenn auch natürliche Vernunftwahrheiten geoffenbart werden. Konsens besteht auch darüber, dass mit Mitteln der Logik, Wissenschaft und Philosophie Glaubenswahrheiten verständlicher gemacht und gegen Angriffe verteidigt werden können. Einig ist man sich nicht zuletzt darin, dass der Akt des Glaubens ein Akt des Intellekts ist dahingehend, dass man sich im Glauben einen Sachverhalt vorstellt und ihn als wahr annimmt. Worin Thomas jedoch Maimonides nicht zu folgen vermag, ist die weitgehende Aufhebung des wahren Glaubens in metaphysisches beziehungsweise prophetisches Wissen. Im Glauben, so Thomas, kommt der Verstand nicht an das ihm eigene Ziel der Einsicht. Man glaubt jemandem etwas, weil man ihm vertraut und weil man es für gut hält, ihm zu glauben, was er sagt. Aber man glaubt etwas und kann es nur glauben, insofern man es nicht weiß; es ist nicht möglich, dass ein und dasselbe von ein und demselben gewusst und geglaubt wird. Glauben und Wissen beziehen sich bei derselben Person unter den gleichen Umständen auf Verschiedenes.[36] Und der Kernbestand des religiösen Glaubens geht auf Erden niemals in Wissen auf.

Ein teils nur in Nuancen bemerkbarer, gleichwohl signifikanter Unterschied bekundet sich auch in der Auffassung und Wertung diesseitiger *contemplatio* und der Verhältnisbestimmung von aktivem und kontemplativem Leben. Wie Maimonides betont auch Thomas die sittlichen Voraussetzungen, die eine Konzentration auf das Studium und die Betrachtung der göttlichen Dinge erst freisetzen. Wie für diesen führt auch für Thomas der Weg zur Erkenntnis Gottes nur über die Betrachtung seiner Wirkungen. Doch Thomas unterscheidet bezüglich der Wirkungen Gottes zwischen Natur und Übernatur, und er unterscheidet zwischen einem natürlichen erkennenden Zugriff und einer Form der Betrachtung aus der Perspektive und in der Einstellung des religiösen Glaubens.

Wie für Maimonides besteht für Thomas die letzte und vollendete Stufe der Erkenntnis in der Betrachtung der göttlichen Wahrheit selbst. Maimonides spricht sie (auf Erden) der Prophetie, in Vollendung der Person des Moses zu und erklärt sie, in Anlehnung an die islamisch-aristotelische Intellekttheorie seiner Zeit, in Begriffen des Einflusses des tätigen auf den passiven Intellekt.[37] Was ihr Inhalt ist, wird nicht ganz klar. Die Kennzeichnung ihrer Höhe als Zuwendung des gesamten Denkens auf das erste der intelligiblen Dinge entspricht

36 Vgl. *Summa theologiae*, II–II, qu. 1 a. 5 co.: „Non autem est possibile quod idem ab eodem sit visum et creditum, sicut supra dictum est. Unde etiam impossibile est quod ab eodem idem sit scitum et creditum [...]. Et ideo fides et scientia non sunt de eodem." Vgl. Schubert, „Die Bedeutung des Maimonides" (wie Anm. 4), S. 5.

37 Vgl. *Führer der Unschlüssigen* (wie Anm. 9), III, 51, S. 345, 349, 352.

ganz offensichtlich dem aristotelischen Konzept von Theoria,[38] allerdings eingeschränkt durch Wendungen, die auch die prinzipielle Unerkennbarkeit des Wesens Gottes für den Menschen betonen, jedenfalls solange seine Seele im Leibe ist. Die Kenntnis der Himmel, ihrer Zahl und Beschaffenheit, die Kenntnis dessen, was darinnen ist, das Wissen, was die Engel sind, wie die Welt erschaffen wurde, wie ihre Teile zweckmäßig aufeinander hingeordnet sind, was die Seele ist, wie sie im Leib entstanden ist und ob sie sich von ihm trennen kann, und wie, wodurch und wozu dies geschehe – dies alles sind Dinge, die Maimonides eindeutig zu den Vorstudien rechnet.[39] Die Endstufe wird gekennzeichnet als Gottesliebe „mittels der Erkenntnis des ganzen Seienden, wie es ist, und der Betrachtung der göttlichen Weisheit in ihm."[40] Gedacht ist an eine Vollkommenheit des Menschen, in der er „alle Tätigkeiten seiner Vernunft hinsichtlich der existierenden Dinge darein setzt, aus ihnen die Erkenntnis Gottes abzuleiten und zu erkennen, in welcher Weise die Weltregierung Gottes möglich sein kann."[41] Maimonides bleibt auch auf der Höhe der auf Gott zentrierten Theoria auf der Ebene der Natur und der Erkenntnis Gottes (nur) über sein erkennbares Werk.

Thomas ist dagegen geneigt, im Ausgang von den für ihn heilsrelevanten übernatürlichen Glaubenswahrheiten, die Vollendung des von der aristotelischen Theoria Angezielten ganz ins Jenseits zu verlegen. Diese letzte Stufe der Betrachtung der göttlichen Wahrheit selbst ist in diesem Leben nicht auf natürlich-wissenschaftliche Weise, sondern nur als anfanghafter Vorschein im Glauben und auf indirekte, gebrochene Weise in Bildern, Gleichnissen und Rätseln möglich: „Jetzt aber kommt uns die Betrachtung der göttlichen Wahrheit unvollkommen zu, nämlich ‚durch den Spiegel und im Rätsel': deshalb wird uns durch sie eine Art Anfang der Seligkeit zuteil, der hier beginnt, um in Zukunft vollendet zu sein. Deshalb setzt auch der Philosoph, im 10. Buch der Ethik, das äußerste Glück des Menschen in die Betrachtung des besten Erkennbaren".[42]

Bei Thomas bleiben, in welch kindlich-laienhafter oder hochphilosophischer Sprache auch immer formuliert und verständlich gemacht, die strikten Glaubenswahrheiten, weil übernatürlich, in diesem Leben weitgehend „Bilder, Gleichnisse und Rätsel", während für Maimonides und seine Glaubenswahrheiten derjenige, der „den Glauben an diese Wahrheiten nach den Methoden

38 Vgl. *Führer der Unschlüssigen* (wie Anm. 9), III, 51, S. 245.

39 So ibid., I, 34, S. 100.

40 Ibid., III, 28, S. 177.

41 Ibid., III, 51, S. 343.

42 *Summa theologiae*, II–II, qu. 180 a. 4 co.: „Nunc autem contemplatio divinae veritatis competit nobis imperfecte, videlicet ‚per speculum et in aenigmati': unde per eam fit nobis quaedam inchoatio beatitudinis, quae hic incipit, ut in futuro terminetur. Unde et Philosophus, in 10 Ethicorum, in contemplatione optimi intelligibilis ponit ultimam felicitatem hominis."

des wahren Glaubens besitzt, […] diese Dinge, die ihm bisher Gleichnisse und Bilder waren, nach ihrem wahren Sinne vorstellen und ihre wahre Wesenheit verstehen" kann.[43]

Maimonides empfiehlt deshalb auch ganz ungebrochen den für die Theoria Geeigneten die kontemplative Lebensform, die sich am besten in Isolation von den Geschäften des praktischen Alltags realisieren lasse: „Es ist also einleuchtend, daß das Endziel darin besteht, sich, wenn man Gott erkannt hat, ihm zu widmen und das vernünftige Denken stets auf die Sehnsucht nach ihm zu richten. Dies wird aber zumeist durch Einsamkeit und Zurückgezogenheit erreicht, und deshalb soll sich jeder Fromme meist einsam und zurückgezogen halten und sich anderen Menschen nur im notwendigen Bedarfsfall zugesellen".[44]

Auch Thomas betont mit Aristoteles grundsätzlich die Vorzüge der theoretischen gegenüber der praktischen Lebensform. Gleichwohl räumt er die Möglichkeit ein, „dass etwas für sich genommen hervorragender ist, was dennoch in bestimmtem Kontext von einem anderen übertroffen wird"[45], nämlich das theoretische vom praktischen Leben. „In gewisser Hinsicht jedoch und je nach Sachlage ist das tätige Leben wegen der Notwendigkeit des gegenwärtigen Lebens vorzuziehen."[46] Thomas will, im Sinne einer Verbindung von *vita contemplativa* und *vita activa*, den Freiraum der „heiligen Muße" in einem aktiven Leben gewahrt wissen. Unter dieser Bedingung, wenn jemanden die Notwendigkeit der Liebe zum äußeren Wirken in der Welt zwingt, gilt sogar der Satz: „Wenn jemand vom beschaulichen Leben weggerufen wird zum tätigen, dann erfolgt dies nicht im Sinne einer Verminderung, sondern einer Vermehrung."[47]

V.

„Die Tora spricht in der Sprache der Menschen".[48] Maimonides zitiert diesen Spruch der Rabbiner häufig. Er will ihn im Sinne einer allegorischen Interpretation der Heiligen Schrift, im Sinne der Ersetzung der Bilder durch Wesensbegriffe verstanden wissen.

---

43 *Führer der Unschlüssigen* (wie Anm. 9), I, 33, S. 98.

44 Ibid., III, 51, S. 345.

45 *Summa theologiae*, II–II, qu. 182 a. 1 co.: „[…] nihil prohibet aliquid secundum se esse excellentius quod tamen secundum aliquid ab alio superatur."

46 Ibid.: „Secundum quid tamen, et in casu, est magis eligenda vita activa, propter necessitatem praesentis vitae".

47 *Summa theologiae*, II–II, qu. 182 a. 1 ad 3: „Et sic patet quod, cum aliquis a contemplativa vita ad activam vocatur, non hoc fit per modum subtractionis, sed per modum additionis."

48 *Führer der Unschlüssigen* (wie Anm. 9), I, 26, S. 74.

(1) Dieser Devise folgend deutet er den ersten Schöpfungsbericht (Genesis 1) im Sinne der philosophisch-wissenschaftlichen Lehre von den vier Elementen[49] und die Ezechielvision (Ezechiel 1) von den vier geflügelten Wesen, dem Wagen und seiner Bewegung im Sinne der aristotelisch-ptolemäischen Theorie des Sphärengefüges.[50] Was die Heilige Schrift in der Sprache der Menschen über die Natur der Schöpfung sagt, ist nichts anderes als die Lehre der avanciertesten philosophisch-wissenschaftlichen Kosmologie.

(2) Analoges gilt für ethische Fragen und Gedanken der Vorsehung. Die biblische Geschichte Hiobs, gleichgültig ob historisch oder nicht, habe Gleichnischarakter. Sie beziehe sich auf das Wissen Gottes und seine Vorsehung, auf das Unglück und Leiden eines Rechtschaffenen und den wahren Glauben.[51] Bemerkenswert an dieser Geschichte sei dies, „daß die H. Schrift Ijob [zunächst, M. F.] keinerlei Wissenschaft zuschreibt. Sie sagt nicht, er sei ein verständiger oder weiser oder ein denkender Mensch gewesen, sondern schildert ihn mit vorzüglichen Charakterzügen und rechtschaffener Handlungsweise. Denn, wäre er weise gewesen, so hätte er […] über seine Lage nicht im Ungewissen sein können."[52] Hiob klage, solange sein Glaube der der Überlieferung ist und dem der großen Menge der Gesetzesgläubigen gleicht.[53] Der Mangel an Einsicht sei der Grund seines Unglücks.[54] Sobald er Weisheit erlangt beziehungsweise einer prophetischen Offenbarung zuteil wird,[55] deren Inhalt identisch sei mit der Meinung des Aristoteles[56] und wahrhaft Gott erkennt, verstumme seine Klage und müsse er bekennen, dass nicht Gesundheit, Reichtum und Kindersegen das Ziel des Daseins sind, sondern „daß das wahre Glück, welches die Gotteserkenntnis ist, ohne Zweifel für jeden vorbehalten ist, und daß keine von allen diesen Bedrängnissen dieses Glück dem Menschen zerstören kann."[57] In der Tat, ganz so hat zwar nicht Aristoteles, aber so haben Philosophen des Hellenismus und des Neuplatonismus gesprochen.

(3) Philosophie und Prophetie rücken hier in erstaunliche Nähe. Moses verkörpert für Maimonides die höchste Form von Weisheit und Prophetie. Was Prophetie in Wahrheit ist, decke sich nicht mit der Ansicht der unwissenden

---

49 *Führer der Unschlüssigen* (wie Anm. 9), II, 30.

50 Ibid., III, 1–7.

51 Ibid., III, 22, S. 129ff.

52 Ibid., III, 22, S. 133.

53 Ibid., III, 22, S. 143.

54 Vgl. Daniel H. Frank, „Maimonides and medieval Jewish Aristotelianism", in *The Cambridge Companion to Medieval Jewish Philosophy*, ed. Daniel H. Frank and Oliver Leaman (Cambridge: Cambridge University Press, 2003), S. 136–156, hier S. 151.

55 *Führer der Unschlüssigen* (wie Anm. 9), III, 22, S. 149.

56 Ibid., III, 22, S. 146.

57 Ibid., III, 22, S. 143.

Menge, sondern weitgehend mit der Ansicht der Philosophen.[58] Prophetie, so Maimonides, ist eine gewisse Vollkommenheit der menschlichen Natur, die die Macht Gottes zur prophetischen Schau, Rede und Tat gelangen lässt, soweit sie dies nicht verhindert.[59] Diese Vollkommenheit kann nicht bei allen Einzelwesen der menschlichen Species vorkommen,[60] sondern nur bei Individuen, deren Einbildungskraft und Charakter exzellent und die unter diesen Voraussetzungen zu den höchsten Vernunfterkenntnissen gelangt sind. Sie gipfeln in der dem Menschen möglichen Erkenntnis Gottes. „Diese wird aber durch die Metaphysik erreicht, zu der man jedoch nur mittels der Naturwissenschaft gelangt, die ihr benachbart ist [...]".[61] Prophet wird man also nur, wenn man in Naturwissenschaft und Metaphysik gebildet ist. Die wissenschaftlich-philosophische Ausbildung ist zwar nicht zureichende, sehr wohl aber notwendige Voraussetzung der Prophetie.

Was Prophetie ihrem Wesen nach ist, lasse sich in Begriffen der Physik und Seelenlehre erklären. Das körperliche Organ, das als Träger der Einbildungskraft fungiert, müsse die denkbar beste Mischung im denkbar besten Maß mit den denkbar besten Säften besitzen.[62] Ähnliches gilt für die physische Disposition des Charakters. Der göttliche Geist, so Maimonides im Anschluss an islamische Aristoteliker, breitet sich über die Intelligenzen der Himmelssphären bis zur zehnten und letzten Sphäre, der des Mondes, aus. Die Intelligenz der Mondsphäre ist der tätige Verstand, der den sublunaren Bereich bestimmt. Der Prophet, so Maimonides, ist derjenige, in dessen möglichem Geist das Einströmen des tätigen Intellekts zur umfassendsten Wirkung gelangt. Er erfasst nicht nur Göttliches wie der Gelehrte, sondern vermag es auch der Menge in ihrer Sprache situationsgerecht mitzuteilen. Voraussetzung sei neben optimaler physischer Prädisposition eine harte Bildung des Charakters und des Geistes. In der Charakterbildung stehen Mut und Askese im Vordergrund. Ein Mensch wird nur dann zum Propheten, „wenn sein Verlangen ganz auf die Erkenntnis dieses Seienden und seiner Ursachen geht, seine Gedanken immer auf erhabene Dinge hinzielen und sein Augenmerk auf die Erkenntnis Gottes, auf die Betrachtung seiner Werke und dessen, was man von ihm glauben muß, gerichtet sind und er zu denjenigen gehört, deren Denken und Verlangen nach den tierischen Dingen bereits überwunden ist, nämlich das Verlangen nach Ergötzung an Speise und Trank und Beischlaf und insbesondere der Tastsinn, von dem Aristoteles in seiner Ethik ausdrücklich sagt, daß dieser für uns eine Schande ist."[63]

58 Ibid., II, 32, S. 220ff.
59 Ibid., II, 32, S. 223ff.
60 Ibid., II, 32, S. 222.
61 Ibid., „Einleitung", S. 9.
62 Ibid., II, 36, S. 239.
63 Ibid., II, 36, S. 243.

Thomas von Aquins Abhandlungen über Prophetie, die *quaestio* XII der *Quaestiones disputatae de veritate* und die *quaestiones* 171–174 der II–IIae der *Summa theologiae*, bezeugen eine intime Kenntnis der Lehre des Maimonides. Ebenso deutlich ist allerdings auch das Bemühen um inhaltliche Abgrenzung und Distanz. Für Thomas ist wahre Prophetie eine besondere Gnadengabe; er will sie von Fähigkeiten und Akten natürlicher Vollkommenheit des Menschen streng unterschieden wissen. Die Prophetie, so Thomas, gehört zu einer Erkenntnis, die jenseits des Bereichs natürlicher Vernunft liegt.[64] Ihr Ursprung ist nicht das natürliche Licht des tätigen Verstandes, durch das wir die Prinzipien aller Dinge erfassen, die wir auf natürliche Weise verstehen, sondern ein übernatürliches Licht, das den Propheten nicht habituell, sondern in einer episodischen Widerfahrnis erleuchtet.[65] Inhalt der Prophetie ist das, was unserer Erkenntnis fern ist, insbesondere *contingentia futura,* deren Wahrheit im Zeitrahmen noch nicht festliegt[66] und aus zeitgebundener menschlicher Erklärungs- und Prognoseperspektive nicht vorweggenommen werden können. Ausgangspunkt der Sachverhalte, die der Prophet erfasst, ist demnach nicht Geschaffenes, sondern Gott selbst.

Die prophetische Schau ist indessen im Allgemeinen nicht die Schau des göttlichen Wesens selbst; und der Prophet sieht nicht in der Schau des göttlichen Wesens das, was er sieht, so wie das die Seligen im Himmel tun.[67] Er sieht es über unkörperliche, intelligible Bilder, die ihn zum Göttlichen führen, wie in einem Spiegel.[68] Seine Erkenntnis ist deshalb noch unvollkommen.

Eine alles überragende Ausnahme stelle allerdings die Prophetie des Moses dar; sie wiederhole sich beim Apostel Paulus; und dies angemessenerweise, weil Moses der erste Lehrer der Juden und Paulus der erste Lehrer der Heiden gewesen sei.[69] Die Ausnahmestellung sei darin begründet, dass Moses und Paulus ihre Schau nicht auf natürlich-menschliche Weise, sondern in einer Entrückung hatten (*in raptu*).[70] In einer Entrückung, so Thomas, liegt der Grund

---

64 *Summa theologiae,* II–II, qu. 171 a. 2 co.

65 Thomas unterscheidet, im Unterschied zu Maimonides, zwischen natürlichem Licht (*lumen naturale*), Gnadenlicht (*lumen gratiae*) und Glorienlicht (*lumen gloriae*). Vgl. *Summa theologiae,* I, qu. 106 a. 1 ad 2; I, qu. 12 a. 13 co.; I–II, qu. 109 a. 1 co.

66 *Summa theologiae,* II–II, qu. 171 a. 3 co.; vgl. qu. 171, a. 6 ad 1.

67 *Summa theologiae,* II–II, qu. 171 a. 4 co.

68 *Summa theologiae,* II–II, qu. 173 a. 1 co.

69 *Summa theologiae,* II–II, qu. 175 a. 3 ad 1.

70 Der Text bei Thomas, *Summa theologiae,* II–II, qu. 174 a. 4 co., lautet: „Moyses ergo fuit aliis excellentior, primo quidem, quantum ad visionem intellectualem: eo quod vidit ipsam Dei essentiam, sicut Paulus in raptu; sicut Augustinus dicit, 12 super Genesim ad Litteram. Unde dicitur Num. 12, quod ‚palam, non per aenigmate Deum videt'." Der Text schließt dem Wortlaut nach nicht aus und legt systematisch nahe, dass auch die Vision des Moses, wie die des Paulus, den Begriff des *raptus* erfüllt. Avital Wohlman, *Thomas d'Aquin et Maïmonide. Un dialogue exemplaire* (Paris: Cerf, 1988), S. 298

der Bewegung des menschlichen Geistes ganz außerhalb; sie erfolgt so gesehen gewaltsam;[71] und das Ziel einer Entrückung liegt außerhalb der Natur des Bewegten.[72] Ausgeschaltet wird das, wodurch der Mensch in diesem Leben sich der Wirklichkeit des Erfassten versichert, nämlich die Wahrnehmung und Empfindung der Sinne. In der Entrückung wird also jemand durch den göttlichen Geist unter Ausschaltung seiner derzeitigen Bindung an die Leiblichkeit zu Übernatürlichem erhoben.[73] Was er hier erfasst, geht über die Fassungskraft der menschlichen Natur hinaus.[74] Er schaut Gott selbst, von Angesicht zu Angesicht, er schaut Gott selbst, nicht im natürlichen Verstandeslicht, sondern im Glorienlicht, allerdings nicht kraft einer dauerhaft verliehenen Form, wie die Heiligen im Himmel, sondern episodisch, aufgrund einer vorübergehenden Widerfahrnis (*passio*)[75], in der der Akt des Glaubens, durch den wir in diesem Leben Übernatürliches vergegenwärtigen, von einem Akt übernatürlichen Wissens überholt wird.[76] So gesehen ist auch das in Entrückung Geschaute von der Art, dass es sich nicht systematisch verorten lässt.

Die Vision des Moses repräsentiert für Maimonides die Vollendung der menschlichen Natur, für Thomas einen episodisch-gnadenhaften Einbruch der Übernatur. Wie sehr sich Thomas hier von Maimonides distanziert, mag ein entsprechender Passus beim Rabbi belegen: „Es gibt aber nun Leute, denen der Blitz einmal nach dem anderen mit geringer Unterbrechung aufleuchtet, so daß sie fast in einem beständigen ununterbrochenen Lichte weilen und ihnen die Nacht zum Tage wird. Dies ist die Stufe des größten der Propheten, zu dem Gott sprach: ‚Du aber bleibe hier bei mir' (Deut. 5:33)".[77]

Maimonides differenziert nicht zwischen einer Natur- und Gnadenordnung; für ihn ist alle menschliche Erkenntnis durch das Licht des aktiven Intellekts vermittelt. Für Thomas ist zur Gnadengabe der Prophetie keinerlei natürliche Eignung erforderlich. Der spekulative Akt der Wissenschaft ist davon völlig verschieden; er erfolgt aus natürlichem Grund und setzt eine entsprechende Disposition voraus.[78] Was die Prophetie betrifft, so könne Gott zugleich mit der geistigen Wirkung auch die passende Disposition herbeiführen, wie sie nach der Naturordnung erforderlich wäre. Prophetie ist für Thomas konsequenterweise auch ohne Liebe, ohne den Stand der Gnade und infolgedessen

---

übersetzt: „Il a contemplé l'essence même de Dieu, comme Saint Paul, sans le ravissement." Das *„sans"* ist offensichtlich durch ein *„dans"* zu ersetzen.

71 *Summa theologiae*, II–II, qu. 175 a. 1 co.

72 Ibid.

73 *Summa theologiae*, II–II, qu. 175 a. 5 co.

74 Ibid., ad 2.

75 *Summa theologiae*, II–II, qu. 175 a. 3 ad 2.

76 Ibid., ad 3.

77 *Führer der Unschlüssigen* (wie Anm. 9), „Einleitung", S. 7.

78 *Summa theologiae*, II–II, qu. 172 a. 3 ad 1.

ohne Güte des Charakters möglich.[79] Nur darin gibt Thomas Maimonides explizit Recht: Wenn jemand den (sinnlichen) Leidenschaften ausgeliefert und in äußere weltliche Geschäfte verstrickt ist, so hindert dies die Prophetie, da sie die höchste Erhebung des Geistes zur Betrachtung von Geistlichem (*summa spiritualitas mentis*) erfordert,[80] weshalb Propheten eine Art einsames Leben führen.

Maimonides kennt keine Unterscheidung zwischen Natur und Übernatur, zwischen Natur und Gnade. Er lässt den Glauben in prophetischem beziehungsweise philosophischem Wissen gipfeln. Dies ist es, was ihn entscheidend von Thomas trennt.[81] Für Thomas muss dem Menschen die freie Selbstmitteilung übernatürlicher Gnade Gottes zu Hilfe kommen, damit er in diesem Leben die göttliche Wirklichkeit anfanghaft, in Bildern, Gleichnissen und Rätseln vorwegnehmen und im anderen Leben im Anblick von Gottes Wesen erkennen kann. Thomas unterscheidet genau zwischen natürlichem Wissen, religiösem Glauben und jenseitiger beseligender Gotteserkenntnis. Religiöser Glaube gipfelt für ihn nicht in philosophischer Erkenntnis. Die heilsrelevante Rolle der Philosophie wird von ihm gegenüber der Auffassung von Rabbi Moyses entscheidend herabgestuft. Philosophie hat gegenüber dem Glauben nur eine dienende Funktion, den Glauben auf natürliche Weise vorbereitend und verteidigend. Sie ist zum Heil, gar zum Gipfel des Heils nicht unbedingt erforderlich. Im Glauben an Jesus, den Christus, so Thomas, ist das schlichteste Gemüt eines alten Weibleins dem größten paganen Philosophen überlegen.[82]

Den Gipfel der Wissenschaft kann in diesem Leben nur die Glaubenswissenschaft, die *sacra doctrina* beanspruchen. Sie geht im Unterschied zur Philosophie von den übernatürlichen Wahrheiten aus, die Gott von sich selbst außerhalb der Naturordnung dem Menschen in der Sprache der Menschen mitgeteilt hat. Sie versucht, soweit möglich, diese der natürlichen Vernunft unzugänglichen, heilsrelevanten Wahrheiten nach der Methodik strenger analysierender, definierender und deduzierender aristotelischer Wissenschaft zu durchdringen und zu ordnen. Der Weise ist demnach nicht der Philosoph, der auf natürlich Erkennbares bezogen ist, sondern der Meister der *sacra doctrina*. Doch diesen Titel kann auch er nur beanspruchen, wenn seine Disziplin der Entwicklung und Stärkung des Glaubens des Volkes dient.[83]

---

79 *Summa theologiae*, II–II, qu. 172 a. 4 co.

80 Ibid.; *de veritate*, qu. 12 a. 5; deutsch S. 311.

81 Vgl. Wohlman, *Thomas d'Aquin* (wie Anm. 70), S. 198.

82 „Nullus philosophorum ante adventum Christi cum toto conatu suo potuit tantum scire de deo, et de necessariis ad vitam aeternam, quantum post adventum Christi scit vetula per fidem" (Thomas von Aquin, *Expositio super Symbolum apostolicum*, in idem, *Opuscula omnia*, ed. Pierre Mandonnet [Paris: Lethellieux, 1927], S. 349; zitiert nach Wohlman, *Thomas d'Aquin* [wie Anm. 70], S. 374 Anm. 113).

83 Zur Verwendung der aristotelischen Philosophie vgl. beispielhaft: *Summa theologiae*, I–II, qu. 94 a. 2 co.; zum Verständnis christlicher Weisheit und Führungsaufgabe (bei

Thomas hat Sinn für Übernatürlich-Gnadenhaftes, aber keinen Sinn für Esoterik. Er hat zugegebenermaßen viel vom Rabbi Moyses gelernt. Er zitiert ihn freilich nur in seinen früheren Werken, und zwar (auch) positiv, beim Namen. Später, in seinen beiden *Summen*, sind die Gedanken des Rabbi nach wie vor präsent; aber die Distanz wird deutlicher und schärfer in den Texten, in denen es um das Verhältnis von Glauben und Wissen geht. Er schien ihm da wohl zu nahe am Averroismus zu sein, dessen Intellektlehre (oder das, was Thomas dafür hielt) er in späten Jahren explizit und heftig bekämpft hat.[84]

Thomas) vgl. *Summa theologiae*, I–II, qu. 100 a. 1 co.; II–II, qu. 2 a. 6 co. und ad 1; II–II, qu. 16 a. 2 ad 2; Wohlman, *Thomas d'Aquin* (wie Anm. 70), S. 193.

84 Wenn Görge K. Hasselhoff in seiner Studie „Anmerkungen zur Rezeption des Maimonides in den Schriften des Thomas von Aquino", in Wolfram Kinzig, Cornelia Kück (Eds.), *Judentum und Christentum zwischen Konfrontation und Faszination* (Stuttgart: Kohlhammer, 2002), S. 55–73, resümierend glaubt feststellen zu können: „Das bleibende Bild von Maimonides [sc. in den Texten bei Thomas von Aquin, M. F.] ist das eines Juden, das besser zurückgewiesen wird" (S. 72–73), so scheint mir dies gerade nicht auf die (wichtigen) Texte zuzutreffen, in denen es um die Verhältnisbestimmung von Glauben und Wissen geht. Thomas distanziert sich von Maimonides nicht etwa, weil dieser von der jüdischen Offenbarungsreligion her denkt, sondern weil er den Inhalt der Offenbarungsreligion und die Einstellung des religiösen Glaubens zu weitgehend in (neuplatonisch überformte und dem Averroismus nahe) aristotelische Philosophie auflöst.

The Translations and the Reception of the Medical Doctor Maimonides in the Christian Medicine of the Fourteenth and Fifteenth Centuries*

by

Görge K. Hasselhoff

Friedrich-Wilhelms-Universität Bonn

In medieval Christian readers' eyes Maimonides not only was seen as the philosopher who wrote the *Dux Neutrorum* (or: *Dux Dubitancium*), i.e. the Latin translation of the *Dalālat al-ḥāʾirīn* or *Moreh Nevukhim*, but he was also seen as a Jew who provided some information on a Jewish understanding of Jesus as the Messiah and as a medical doctor who wrote on the use of antidotes and who criticised the ancient authority Galen.

In this paper I shall proceed in two major steps. First, I shall give some summarising remarks on the Latin translations of the – not only – medical oeuvre of Moses Maimonides. Second, I shall give two examples of the reading of Maimonides in the fourteenth and fifteenth century respectively. The first example will be William of Brescia who is closely linked with some of the translations. The second example will be taken from the literature which was written in the times of the plague.

I. Medieval Latin translations of the Maimonidean (medical) oeuvre

Since the Latin scholars normally were not able to read Hebrew they needed translations. (Latin itself usually was the first foreign language medieval people had to learn to communicate in university.) First Maimonides' philosophical work *Moreh Nevukhim* was translated into Latin: one short version is entitled

* I am indebted to Georges Tamer for the opportunity to present an earlier version of this paper at the conference "Die Trias des Maimonides: Jüdische, arabische und antike Wissenskultur", Erlangen July 7th–11th, 2004; and to the participants of the conference, especially Gad Freudenthal, for the vivid discussion; and to Michael McVaugh, Chapel Hill, N.C., as well as Samuel S. Kottek, Jerusalem, who commented on an earlier draft of this article.

Liber de Uno Deo Benedicto (*Book of the One Blessed God*) and one more or less complete translation is called *Dux Neutrorum* (*Guide of the Indifferent*). My thesis concerning the two translations – as recently published in my book *Dicit Rabbi Moyses* – is that they were made shortly after the burning of the Talmud in Paris in 1242–1244. The reason that Maimonides was translated is to provide a new image of a non-Jewish Jew, i.e. a Jew who – from a Christian point of view – was not a "Halakhic man" but a philosopher in the Aristotelian tradition. Although we do not know who the translator (or translators) were we have to search them in the Dominican order. There are at least two figures who were in one way or other acquainted with Jewish traditions. First, Nicolaus (Niklas) Donin who initiated the Talmud trials, and second, Theobaldus de Saxonia (Thibaud of Sézanne) who in 1248 signed the Talmud condemnation and who wrote the famous but still unedited *Extracciones ex Talmud*.[1] To me it seems quite likely that there is a connection between the translations and the two men mentioned.[2]

Half a century later a new interest in translating Maimonidean works arose, now related to Maimonides' medical writings. Towards the end of the thirteenth century, at a time when a new discussion on philosophy in Christian thought arose,[3] some medical treatises were translated for the first time. It is quite remarkable that within a period of two decades two translators whose names we know translated in one or two cases the same treatises. Both translators were medical doctors at the Papal court.

The first translator is John of Capua who in his *Proemium Interpretis* to his translations identifies himself. The preface is included in at least six manuscripts.[4]

---

1 Gilbert Dahan, "Rashi, sujet de la controverse de 1240: Edition partielle du ms. Paris, BN lat. 16558", in *Archives juives: revue d'histoire des Juifs de France* 14 (1978), pp. 43–54; idem, *Les intellectuels chrétiens et les juifs au moyen âge* (Paris: Cerf, 1990 [reprint 1999]), pp. 218, 250, 258–259, 355–356, 461–464; idem, "Les traductions latines de Thibaud de Sézanne", in idem (Ed.), *Le brûlement du Talmud à Paris 1242–1244* (Paris: Cerf, 1999), pp. 95–120.

2 Görge Hasselhoff, *Dicit Rabbi Moyses: Studien zum Bild von Moses Maimonides im lateinischen Westen vom 13. bis zum 15. Jahrhundert* (Würzburg: Königshausen & Neumann, 2004, 2nd ed. 2005), pp. 126–129; the book deepens the discussion which I initiated with my article "The Reception of Maimonides in the Latin World: The Evidence of the Latin translations in the 13th to 15th Century", in *Materia Giudaica* 6 (Firenze, 2001), pp. 258–280. – The following descriptions of manuscripts are based on personal examinations made on various travels to European and Israeli libraries since 1999. For reasons of space I do not repeat the manuscript catalogues used; they are listed in *Dicit Rabbi Moyses*, pp. 345–351.

3 See, for example, Alain de Libera, *Penser au moyen Âge* (Paris: Éditions du Seuil, 1991); *Nach der Verurteilung von 1277: Philosophie und Theologie an der Universität von Paris im letzten Viertel des 13. Jahrhunderts. Studien und Texte*, ed. Jan A. Aertsen et al. (Miscellanea Mediaevalia 28; Berlin, New York: de Gruyter, 2001).

4 For the manuscripts known see below, p. 408, Appendix II/0.

John says that he is a Jewish-born *converso* who learned Hebrew as well as Latin to be able to translate some useful but Hebrew-written tracts into Latin. He does so to keep away from dangers and to introduce health to the honour of God and the pope's soul.

John made – so he says – his translations by request of William of Brescia (Guglielmo de' Corvi; Guilelmus de Brixia)[5] who was one of Pope Bonifacius VIII's physicians. From these two names we may conclude that John translated between 1298 and 1303.

As said before, John writes that he learned Hebrew to be able to translate and then again: *opus ab hebrayca lingua in latinam transferre.* John seems to tell the truth. In most places the Latin text corresponds to the translation by Moshe Ibn Tibbon although in some cases the translation follows the Arabic original.[6]

What then did John of Capua translate and how do we know he did? As I have stated elsewhere[7] it seems quite likely that he translated the *Regimen Sanitatis* together with the tract *De Causis Accidencium* as a fifth chapter.[8] In this *Regimen Sanitatis* Maimonides gives some dietetical advice to the wezir of Kairo. In the first chapter Maimonides discusses and criticises Hippocrates and Galen. In the second chapter he lists various diets. In the third chapter he gives a philosophical explanation of the hygiene of the soul. In the final fourth chapter a list of seventeen practical cures is listed. The treatise *De Causis Accidencium* is originally a separate *Regimen on Health* which was made a fifth chapter of the *Regimen Sanitatis* by John of Capua. This translation is preserved in nine manuscripts of which six mention John as the translator.[9] Of these manuscripts two have an abbreviated text which in 1477 served as the basis for the first printed edition.[10] John of Capua seems to have translated two further treatises, namely

---

5 On William see below II.1.

6 Cf. Moses Maimonides' Two Treatises on the Regimen of Health: *Fī Tadbir al-Ṣiḥḥah* and *Maqālah fī Bayān Baʿḍ al-Aʿrāḍ wa-al-Ǧawāb ʿanhā*, translated from the Arabic and edited in accordance with the Hebrew and Latin versions by Ariel Bar-Sela et al. (Transactions of the American Philosophical Society, N.S. 54; Philadelphia: The American Philosophical Society, 1964), 12.

7 See my article "The Reception" (see above n. 2), pp. 270–274.

8 Although Joshua O. Leibowitz with a team of scholars edited the latter treatise separately we have to treat the two *Regimina* as one single tract for the time in focus of this essay (*Moses Maimonides on the Causes of Symptoms: Maqālah fī Bayān Baʿḍ al-Arāḍ wa-al-Ǧawāb ʿanhā. Maʾamar ha-haḫraʿah. De causis accidentium,* ed. Joshua O. Leibowitz and Shlomo Marcus. In collaboration with Malachi Beit-Arié et al. [Berkeley, Los Angeles, London: University of California Press, 1974]).

9 The manuscript München, Bayerische Staatsbibliothek, Clm 77, which leaves out the *Proemium Interpretis* does not mention any translator; the same is true for the two manuscripts mentioned in the next note.

10 There is something quite interesting to note concerning two manuscripts in London, Wellcome Library MS 466, fol. 1r–54v, and Bamberg, Staatsbibliothek, C Med. 12, fol. 89r–104r. Both manuscripts were written in the fifteenth century and both differ from

De Venenis and *De Hemorhoidibus*. In the treatise *De Venenis* Maimonides – in the typical manner of an Arabic medical doctor – describes several poisons and collects several antidotes, some of these seem to be of Maimonidean origin. This particular translation of *De Venenis* is preserved in seven manuscripts. Five of these copies are submitted together with the afore-mentioned *Regimen Sanitatis;*[11] two further manuscripts with a rather unclear attribution to a translator.[12] The same is true for the translation of *De Hemorhoidibus* mentioned which is transmitted in four manuscripts with the name of the translator[13] and in three further manuscripts without any reference to a translator.[14] A different problem is treated by Maimonides in *De Hemorhoidibus*. This treatise, too, shows the philosophical character of Maimonides' medicine, i.e. before using surgical medicine for hemorrhoids all sorts of healthy dietetics should be employed.[15]

The second translator who is known by name is Armengaud Blaise (or Blasius). Armengaud was a nephew of the famous physician Arnau (Arnald) of Villanova (c. 1240–1311).[16] Armengaud was body physician of the French King

---

the other tracts in two regards: They have a different beginning and a different end: preface and first chapter are just the same as the first print in 1477 or 1481 had and the second part of the tract *De causis Accidentium* is left out – again in accordance with the *editio princeps* (cf. Bar-Sela, *Moses Maimonides' Two Treatises* [see above n. 6], p. 12 [without mentioning the manuscripts]).

11 The codices are: Todi, Biblioteca comunale "Lorenzo Leonj", Ms. 53; Città del Vaticano, Biblioteca Apostolica Vaticana (= BAV), Pal. Lat. 1,298; Jerusalem, National and University Library (= JNUL), 2° FR. R 571/576 MS; München, Bayerische Staatsbibliothek, Clm 77; Wien, Österreichische Nationalbibliothek, Ms. lat. 2,280.

12 The codices are: Wien, Österreichische Nationalbibliothek, Ms. lat. 5,306 and the fragmentary manuscript Wrocław, Biblioteka Uniwersitecka, Ms. III F 10.

For the moment the status of the manuscript Torino, Biblioteca nazionale di Torino, Ms. I.III.35, fol. 37ra–40ra remains uncertain. The manuscript was described by Piero Giacosa, *Magistri Salernitani nondum editi: Catalogo ragionato della Esposizione di Storia della Medicina aperta in Torino nel 1898* (Torino etc.: Fratelli Bocca, 1901), pp. 503–505. Unfortunately, in 1904 the library burned down and what is left over are only fragments of the manuscript which on the film I ordered in 2000 are only partially readable. It is not unlikely that the translation is Armengaud's (see below).

13 Città del Vaticano, BAV, Pal. Lat., Ms. 1,298; ibid., Pal. Lat., Ms. 1,147; Todi, Biblioteca comunale, Ms. 53; Wien, Österreichische Nationalbibliothek, Ms. lat. 2,280.

14 München, Bayerische Staatsbibliothek, Clm 77; Jerusalem, JNUL, 2° FR. R 571/576 MS; Wrocław, Biblioteka Uniwersitecka, Ms. III F 10.

15 Two further translations which sometimes are attributed to John of Capua (those of *De coitu* and of the *Aphorismi*) must have been made by someone else. On the *Aphorisms* see below; on *De coitu* see my discussion in "The Reception" (see above n. 2), p. 273.

16 Cf. Miguel Batllori, "La documentacion de Marsella sobre Arnau de Vilanova y Joan Blasi", in *Analecta Sacra Tarraconensia* 21 (1948), pp. 75–119, here p. 75; Michael McVaugh, "Theriac at Montpellier 1285–1325: (with an edition of the '*Questiones de tyriaca*' of William of Brescia)", in *Sudhoffs Archiv: Zeitschrift für Wissenschaftsgeschichte* 56 (1972), pp. 113–144, here p. 122. – On his life and works cf. Ernest Renan, "Armengaud, Fils de Blaise, Médicin", in *Histoire Littéraire de la France.* Ouvrage commencé

Philippe IV le Bel (1268–1314) and taught medicine at the university of Montpellier. Already in 1284 he was translating treatises by Avicenna. About the turn of the century, we find him doing the same with Maimonidean tracts. According to the *subscripta,* these translations seem to have been made in Barcelona and in Montpellier in c. 1302–1310. Armengaud seems to have died in 1312.[17]

Armengaud translated at least two Maimonidean treatises, first *De Venenis,* second *De Asmate.* Both treatises have their own explicits in which Armengaud states where and why he made the translations. The treatise *On Poisons* was translated in 1305 or 1307 either in Barcelona or in Montpellier. The treatise is dedicated to Clement V who was elected Pope in 1305. Until today, four manuscripts containing the translation have survived, three of them including the translator's *subscriptum.*[18] The treatise *On Asthma* was translated before the one on poisons. According to a manuscript kept in Cambridge Armengaud translated it for his own purpose in 1294 and published it in 1302. There are three surviving manuscripts of this treatise.[19] Only one contains a note on the translator. Whether he is also responsible for a third translation carrying his name as a translator, namely the translation of the treatise *De Hemorhoidibus,* remains uncertain. There is only one fifteenth-century manuscript containing this translation. This manuscript is heavily damaged.[20] It is possible that Armengaud is responsible for that particular translation as is indicated by a note in the *subscriptum.* If Armengaud is responsible for the translation, then he made it in 1310.

---

par des religieux bénédictins de la congrégation de Saint-Maur et continué par des membres de l'institut, Tome XXVIII: *Suite du quatorzième siècle* (Paris: Imprimerie Nationale, 1881), pp. 127–138, 490; Michael McVaugh, Lola Ferre, *The* Tabula Antidotarii *of Armengaud Blaise and Its Hebrew Translation* (Transactions of the American Philosophical Society 90/6; Philadelphia: American Philosophical Society, 2000), pp. 1–3, 170–195. – On Arnau cf. Michael McVaugh, "Moments of Inflection: The Careers of Arnau de Vilanova", in Peter Biller and Joseph Ziegler (Eds.), *Religion and Medicine in the Middle Ages* (York Studies in Medieval Theology 3; York: York Medieval Press, 2001), pp. 47–67.

17 Cf. McVaugh, Ferre, *The Tabula Antidotarii* (see above n. 16), p. 190 (no. 29).

18 Cf. the uncritical transcription by McVaugh, "Theriac at Montpellier" (see above n. 16), p. 122 n. 33. The treatise is to be found in: Cambridge, Peterhouse College, MS 101; Paris, Bibliothèque de la Sorbonne, Ms. 1,031; Oxford, Corpus Christi College, MS C. C. C. 125. McVaugh transcribed only the text of the Oxford manuscript. – The manuscript Krakov, Biblioteka Jagiellonska, Cod. 839, leaves out the preface but indicates translator and addressee of the translation in the *subscriptum.*

19 Cambridge, Peterhouse College, MS 101, fol. 158ra–168rb; Cambridge, Gonville and Caius College, MS 178, fol. 130–165. – Michael McVaugh pointed out to me that there is a third manuscript of the treatise preserved in Torino, Biblioteca Nazionale, Ms. I.III.35. On this manuscript see above n. 12.

20 Torino, Biblioteca Nazionale di Torino, Ms. I.III.35, fol. 78vb–81ra; cf. above n. 12.

In all three *subscripta* Armengaud states that he made the translations from the Arabic. In one case (*De Asmate*) he adds that he had a helper, presumably Jacob ben Makhir, a grandson of Shmuel Ibn Tibbon.[21]

Apart from the translations provided by John and Armengaud we find quite a number of further translations being made throughout the fourteenth century. All of them are done anonymously. Among these translations are a third translation of *De Venenis*, a translation of *De Coitu*, a second translation of *De Asmate*, a second translation of the *Regimen Sanitatis*, and a translation of the *Aphorismi*. This latter translation deserves a closer look, namely the medical chef d'oeuvre *Pirke Mosheh*, or in the Latin form *Aphorismi*.

This translation is sometimes attributed to John of Capua[22] but there is no proof that John could have translated the treatise. On the contrary, there are several reasons indicating that the translation was provided much later. First, there is no manuscript indicating John as the translator. Second, the first author to quote from the *Pirke Mosheh* is Guy de Chauliac in the middle of the fourteenth century.[23] His scarce use of the treatise and the way it is quoted, namely in a manner far from being accurate different from the other quotations from the Maimonidean oeuvre, made me suggest that the translation was made after Guy's lifetime. Third, the oldest manuscript of the translation extant was written and decorated towards the end of the fourteenth century or the beginning of the fifteenth century in Paris.[24] This manuscript is richly ornamented. Since at that time only few and normally "modern" treatises, or to be more precise, Latin manuscripts containing new and modern treatises, were ornamented this way

---

21 It is remarkable that Armengaud's *Tabula Antidotarii* was translated into Hebrew by Estori ha-Parhi; see McVaugh, Ferre, *The Tabula Antidotarii* (see above n. 16), pp. 23–157.

22 Most recently Gerrit Bos, "Maimonides' Medical Aphorisms: Towards a Critical Edition and Revised English Translation", in *Qorot: The Israel Journal of the History of Medicine and Science* 12 (1996–97), pp. 35–79, here p. 45.

23 On Guy's use of the *Aphorismi* see my *Dicit Rabbi Moyses* (see above n. 2), pp. 306–308. A similar spurious reference to the *Aphorismi* is made by Gentile da Foligno, see Danielle Jacquart, "Moses, Galen and Jacques Despars: Religious Orthodoxy as a Path to Unorthodox Medical Views", in Biller, Ziegler, *Religion and Medicine* (see above n. 16), pp. 35–45, here p. 43.

24 The manuscript is kept in Paris, Bibliothèque nationale de France, Ms. fonds latin 7,067 (cf. *Catalogus Codicum Manuscriptorum Bibliothecæ Regiæ*. Pars III, Tom. IV [Paris: Typographia Regia], 1744, p. 310). – To this description it should be added that the codex contains III + 128 + III leaves and measures c. 130 x 190 mm with a written space of 26 lines measuring 78 x 110 mm. The book paintings and ornaments hint to Paris as the place of copying. The codex seems to be part of a two-volume copy since it contains the chapters 13–25, ending *Explicit xxv^a p(ar)ticula amphor(ismor)um / raby moysi Et in hoc completur / totus liber Deo gratias.*). – Further manuscripts are Lüneburg, Ratsbücherei, Ms. Miscell. D 2° 5; London, British Library, Add. MS 22,313; Città del Vaticano, BAV, Palatina Latina 1,298; Florence, Biblioteca Nazionale Centrale, II, IV, 31; Città del Vaticano, BAV, Palatina Latina, 1,147.

it seems to be a further hint that the translation was quite recent at that time. Finally, John, as we have seen, was unable to speak or read Arabic. But the translation is made from the Arabic, as Professor Gerrit Bos assured me some years ago.[25]

So to sum up, in the end of the thirteenth century or the beginning of the fourteenth century two translators can be singled out who translated some Maimonidean medical treatises. The first is John of Capua who did so somewhere in Italy on the basis of one of the Hebrew translations. The Latin translations were used in the Italian medical schools.[26] The second translator is Armengaud Blaise who translated in Catalonia or Southern France. His translations which were made from the Arabic were used at the university of Montpellier and by medical doctors connected with this school. Later further treatises became translated for a second or even for a third time but we cannot give more precise information on the translators or the places where they translated. Towards the end of the fifteenth century two Maimonidean medical treatises were being printed. The first tract was his *Regimen Sanitatis* in 1477 or 1481. It was reprinted five times until 1535.[27] The second tract to be printed was the collection of aphorisms in 1489. It was reprinted three times until 1518.[28]

Nonetheless, all these translations were used in one way or other. I pick two examples. The first exemplary user is William of Brescia.

---

25 This was already supposed by Moritz Steinschneider, *Die Hebräischen Übersetzungen des Mittelalters und die Juden als Dolmetscher* (Berlin: Kommissionsverlag des Bibliographischen Bureaus, 1893 [reprint Graz: Akademische Druck- und Verlagsanstalt, 1956]), p. 766; idem, *Die arabische Literatur der Juden: ein Beitrag zur Literaturgeschichte der Araber, grossenteils aus handschriftlichen Quellen* (Frankfurt am Main: Verlag von J. Kauffmann, 1902), p. 215.

26 See Graziella Federici Vescovini, *"Arti" e filosofia nel secolo XIV: Studi sulla tradizione aristotelica e i "moderni"* (Firenze: Vallecchi, 1983), pp. 236–238.

27 Printed by Jacopo di Ripoli without date; reprinted: *Regimen Sanitatis des Maimonides für den Sultan el-Malik al-Afdhal*. Faksimile der Ausgabe Florenz nach dem Exemplar der Bayerischen Staatsbibliothek mit einem Vorwort von A. Freimann (Heidelberg: Grossberger, 1931); for further prints cf. Joshua O. Leibowitz, "Introduction", in *Moses Maimonides on the Causes of Symptoms* (see above n. 8), pp. 9–17, here p. 9; Hasselhoff, *Dicit Rabbi Moyses* (see above n. 2), pp. 287, 289–290.

28 Leibowitz ("The Latin Translations of Maimonides' Aphorisms", in *Koroth: The Israel Journal of the History of Medicine and Science* 6 [1973], pp. 273–281 [Hebrew]; pp. XCIII–XCIX [English]) lists four editions, too, but leaves out a Venetian 1500 print. Instead he writes on a (further) edition in Basle, 1579, which offers a new translation.

II. Examples

1. Example 1: William of Brescia[29]

William of Brescia is mentioned in the medieval sources with his Italian name Guglielmo de' Corvi or with his Latin name Guilelmus de Brixia. "Brixia" can mean both today's Brixen in Southern Tyrol or Brescia south of the Lago di Garda. The scholarly consensus places him in Brescia since it is quite likely that he was born in Canneto near Brescia in 1250. In 1274–1279 William taught logic as a *baccalaureus* (bachelor) at the university of Padova. He then moved to Bologna where he studied medicine with Taddeo Alderotti. In 1298 he became one of Bonifacius VIII's court physicians. When in 1303 the Pope died William stayed at the Holy See and later became one of Clement V's body physicians. Clement moved the Holy See to Avignon. So William also moved to Avignon. On September 8th, 1308 Clement signed a Papal bull sending William to Montpellier as a Bachelor of Medicine. Nonetheless William remained court physician to Clement V and to his successor John XXII. In 1313 William was made Archdeacon of Bologna but he still stayed in Avignon. In 1326 (May 7th) William is mentioned for the last time in a written document when he donated some money to a students' house in Bologna.

William's importance does not rest on being a pope's physician, but the job gave the basis for some of his other achievements. William wrote some medical treatises on his own and he was financially able to let other people translate modern Arabic literature into Latin. As I said before John of Capua states that he translated the *Regimen Sanitatis* on behalf of William of Brescia. I am not sure – and John does not tell us – whether he translated without any payment. But since it means to spend some strength (and time) on a translation he should have received some payment for it; presumably from William.

William wrote several *Consilia*, i.e. short letters in which he gave medical advice.[30] In addition he wrote a standard work called *Practica in Chirurgia*, and as a bachelor in Montpellier he disputed some questions, namely the *Questiones*

---

29 On William see McVaugh, "Theriac at Montpellier" (see above n. 16), pp. 115–116, 124–129; Erich Walter Georg Schmidt, *Die Bedeutung Wilhelms von Brescia als Verfasser von Konsilien: Untersuchung über einen medizinischen Schriftsteller des XIII.–XIV. Jahrhunderts* (Diss. Leipzig; Leipzig: Emil Lehmann, 1922), pp. 10–11; Nancy G. Siraisi, *Taddeo Alderotti and his Pupils: Two Generations of Italian Medical Learning* (Princeton, N.J.: Princeton University Press, 1981), pp. 49–54; Gundolf Keil, Thomas Holste, "Randnotizen zu Wilhelm von Brescia", in *Opuscula Silesiaca: Festschrift Josef Joachim Menzel = Jahrbuch der Schlesischen Friedrich-Wilhelms-Universität zu Breslau* 38–39 (1997–98), pp. 181–184.

30 These *consilia* are for the most part unedited. Professor McVaugh was so kind to give me some insight into his transcription of Ms. München, Bayerische Staatsbibliothek, Clm 77, see below n. 34.

de Tyriaca. Since I have no copy of the *Practica in Chirurgia* at hand I only refer to the *Questiones* which some years ago were edited by Michael McVaugh.

Within these *Questions* there is only one reference to Maimonides, but this reference is really interesting and revealing. William quotes a small story that Maimonides tells in the end of the treatise on asthma. To illustrate what he says about the doses for the theriac William introduces a story which is told by Maimonides (*sicud narrat Raby Moyses*). The story is about the ruler (or "king", *rex*) of Morocco who fell ill from an unknown illness. When he recovered the doctors disputed what they should do now with the no longer ill but weak king. They decided to give him some theriac for his general well-being. (To explain the importance of the matter: Theriac is a drug which is mixed from several poisons taken from animals and vegetables and herbs. There were several theories which herbs and poisons should be mixed in the theriac.) So in the third hour of the night the king received a dose of half a dram of theriac and was told not to eat until the early morning. While the doctors discussed what the king now was allowed to eat the king died. As things go the doctors went on debating; now they asked *why* the king died. Some doctors said because half a dram of theriac was too much for the weak king and the king could have tolerated only a quarter of a dram of theriac. Others said the king died because he received too little theriac and the right measure would have been half an *aureus*. So, Maimonides remarks, as a consequence a strong drug such as theriac might only be given by a well-trained medical doctor who could estimate the state of the ill person and the right measurement of the drug. This was already stated by Galen and even by Hippocrates.

So far Maimonides in William's words,[31] which I now would like to comment on. First, the way Maimonides is introduced. As I said before the

31 Guilelmus de Brixia, *Quaestio de tyriaca* (ed. McVaugh, "Theriac at Montpellier" [see above n. 16], pp. 136,267–137,295): Quia vero exempla positus ut sentiat qui addiscit, ponenda est quedam historia de casu quodam mirabili exhibitionis tyriace qui accidit regi maroci, sicud narrat Raby Moyses. Ecce enim cum ipse rex ex quadam egritudine convaluisset et non bene resumeretur, cum tamen corpus eius esset mundificatum, concordaverunt medici propter debilitatem digestionis et caloris innati exhibere tyriacam, que calorem innatum et digestionem et omnes operationes nature confortare habet. In hora igitur tercia noctis ʒ semis ministraverunt; illa autem hora exhibuerunt ut usque ad horam terciam diei in qua solitus erat comedere <non> posset cibari, quia in tanto tempore potuisset tyriaca operationem suam exercuisse et de stomaco exivisse, ne scilicet adhuc existens in stomaco cum cibo corrumperetur et ipsum corrumperet propter mixtionem secum; et tunc cum ordinarent de cibo eius mortuus est. Cuius rei causam estimaverunt quidam superfluam dosim tyriace propter debilitatem virtutis eius, que non poterat sustinere nisi quartam partem dragme aut aurei; alii vero econtra estimaverunt propter paucitatem hoc fuisse, dicentes quod conveniens dosis erat medius aureus. Quia igitur propter superfluam quantitatem tyriace aut diminutam accidunt nocumenta magna que predicta sunt, sicud universaliter accidit in exhibitione cuiuscumque medicine fortis, que si debite exhibeatur iuvat multum et si

reference is the only one to Maimonides within this *questio*. This one reference is of the kind, 'well I am going to tell you a story which is reported by this Jewish doctor Moyses who happens to be a rabbi'. Second, the story itself could be reported by anybody and it is not original for that particular doctor. Third, most interesting is what William does not tell. He does not say, *where* in the Maimonidean oeuvre he found that story although at that time Rabbi Moyses was quite famous for both his philosophical (or theological) writings and for his medical writings. Since William had the *Regimen of Health* translated by John of Capua the story should be found in that particular treatise. But Maimonides does not tell the story there. It can be found in the treatise *On Asthma*. That fact is known to Maimonides-specialists only. Now the question arises whether William had further treatises at hand when he disputed the question on the theriac. A second question is, who translated the other treatise for him. In my book *Dicit Rabbi Moyses* I suggested that William used Armengaud's translation.[32] But now it seems to me more likely that it was the anonymous translation, which is preserved in two mansucripts, that was used by William.[33]

Leaving this philological and historical question aside something else is worth being mentioned concerning the reference to Maimonides. William does not only tell the reader that Maimonides told "funny" stories to illustrate the problems to find the right dose for theriac, but that he also made a contribution to the discussion on the dose of theriac itself. (We know from other medical texts of the time that this was common.) William himself introduced the solutions of other medical doctors on the dose of the theriac.

This might be sufficient to illustrate the use of Maimonidean works in William's writings.[34] I now might turn to a second, much shorter example.

---

indebite sive ex parte quantitatis superflue sive temporis aut ordinis multum nocet (sicud patet per Galienem in primo regiminis acutorum), manifestum [est, McVaugh] quod non nisi cum magna consideratione et deliberatione periti medici et experti sumi oportet tyriaca aut alia medicina fortis, quia licet si recte datur considerando omnia particularia requirenda magnum sequatur iuvamentum, tamen si error contigat qui sepe accidit maximum sequitur nocumentum et aliquando mors. Et ideo nullus medicus presumat dare tyriacam et alias medicinas fortes (de numero quorum est flebotomia, sicud ponit Galienus super 1° afforismo) inchoantibus morbis, nisi prius habita magna consideratione".

32 See Hasselhoff, *Dicit Rabbi Moyses* (see above n. 2), pp. 293–294.

33 The manuscripts are Jerusalem, JNUL, 2° FR. R 571–576 MS, fol. 30va with a peculiar *explicit*, and München, Bayerische Staatsbibliothek, Clm 77, fol. 71rb–76vb missing chapter 13 of the translation. – I am indebted to Michael McVaugh that he shared his ideas concerning the translations in an e-mail correspondence throughout the summer 2004 which made me change my point of view in this matter.

34 Professor McVaugh pointed to me that there are several further references to Maimonides in William's *consilia* which are still unedited. The examples from Ms. München,

2. Example 2: The Plague Literature

In the first quarter of the twentieth century the pioneer of the history of medicine, Karl Sudhoff, published a series of articles on c. 300 medieval treatises which were in one way or other connected with the literary production connected with the fighting of the plague. This series of articles contains some descriptions of printed books or of medieval manuscripts as well as transcriptions of medical treatises. In a few of these treatises Sudhoff says Maimonides is quoted. As far as I see Maimonides is mentioned in three of these works related to the plague. One treatise is the French version of Thomas le Forestier's *Regimen Against the Plague.*[35] A second work is Giacopo Soldi's *Opus on the Plague.*[36] Here I focus on the third collection which is an anonymous writing called *Collectum de Peste.* According to Sudhoff this collection was written by an unknown physician. The treatise belonged to a physician from Lübeck called Heinrich Lamme who possibly was the author himself. The treatise was finished in Lübeck in the last week of March 1411 and is preserved in two manuscripts kept in Lübeck.[37] In this treatise the author gives several descriptions of the plague in Europe and the different forms of the disease. In the middle of the treatise the author comes to talk on a remedy against the plague on which, among others, Galen, Rhazes, and Avicenna have written. It is quite clear from the description of the remedy that the author means the theriac which we already met in the other example. After a lengthy description of how the medicine should be produced we find a single reference to Maimonides which reads:

Bayerische Staatsbibliothek, Clm 77, he sent me show a pattern similar to the example demonstrated above.

35 Thomas le Forestier, *Le regime contre epidemie et pestilence* (Rouen: Jacques Le Forestier, 1495). In the Latin version *Tractatus Contra Pestilentiam, Tenasmonem et Dissenteriam* (Rouen: Guillaume Le Talleur, 1490; reprint: *Traité de la peste.* Publié avec introduction, analyse et notes par Gustave Panel [Société des Bibliophiles Normands 73; Rouen: Léon Gy, 1909]) Maimonides is not referred to, see Panel, "Introduction", in ibid., pp. vii–lxxxiv, here pp. x and lxxxiv. Both prints are described by Arnold C. Klebs, "Geschichtliche und bibliographische Untersuchungen", in idem, Karl Sudhoff, *Die ersten gedruckten Pestschriften* (München: Münchner Drucke, 1926), pp. 1–167, here pp. 36–37 (nos. 67–68).

36 Giacopo Soldi [Jacobus Soldus], *Opus Insigne de Peste* (Bologna: Johannes Schriber de Annunciata for Thomas de Bononia, 1478); idem, *Insigne Opus de Epidemia* (Antwerpen: Gerard Leeu[w], 1490). See also the translation: *Antidotario per il tempo di Peste,* tradotto da Dionigi Bussoti Servita (Firenze 1630). For a description of these prints see Klebs, "Geschichtliche und bibliographische Untersuchungen" (see above n. 35), pp. 48–49 (nos. 98–99) and ibid., p. 130 on the history of the first print.

37 Lübeck, Stadtbibliothek, Ms. med. 4° 8, fol. 150r–159r; Ms. med. 4° 10, fol. 288v–301v.

> In the usage (*amministratione*) of this medicine the doctor must be extremely (*maxime*) solicitous and cautious, for that he must know the exact time, when he must give the medicine (*amministrari*), so that he makes no mistake, which was made by [some] doctors, about whom Galen writes to Epigenes about the cure of the quartan fever, that one illness becomes two and that not a sudden death occurs, as Rabbi Moyses says in the end of *De Asmate*.[38]

It is obvious that the anonymous writer might refer to the same passage as does William of Brescia. But there are two characteristic differences. First, he mentions the writing in which Maimonides wrote about the theriac. Second, other than William, the anonymous doctor clearly indicates that the idea reported originates from Maimonides.

Both ways to quote from Maimonides are typical of the way Maimonides is referred to in medieval medical treatises. William quoted a lengthy story including some Maimonidean advice which could also have been written by someone else. The anonymous writer gives a short but relatively exact reference to Maimonides which might be traced back to a reading by the author himself or might be taken from another medical treatise.

III. Conclusion

To draw a conclusion: Until the middle of the fifth decade of the thirteenth century the knowledge of Maimonides was rather scarce. With the translation of the *Liber de Uno Deo Benedicto* Maimonides served as one of the Aristotelians who provided additional "modern" philosophical knowledge. With the translation of the *Dux Neutrorum* which followed soon after the situation changed radically. The broader reception of Maimonidean ideas began with Albert the Great and Thomas Aquinas. With the condemnation of some of Meister Eck-

38 *Collectum de Peste* (Lübeck, c. 1411): *In huius medicine* [i.e. *tiriaca*] *amministracione oportet medicum esse maxime sollicitum et cautum, ut sciat tempus certum, quando huiusmodi debet amministrari, ne contingat <error>, qui contingebat medicis, de quibus scribit Galienus ad Epigenem de cura quartane, ne de vna egritudine fiant due et ne subitam mortem inferant, ut dicit Rabi Moyses in vltimo de asmate* (Karl Sudhoff, "Pestschriften aus den ersten 150 Jahren nach der Epidemie des 'schwarzen Todes' 1348. XII. Ausarbeitungen über die Pest vor der Mitte des 15. Jahrhunderts, entstanden im niederen Deutschland", in *Archiv für Geschichte der Medizin* 11 [1919], pp. 121–176, here pp. 155, 462–468). – On Sudhoff's library see now Andreas Frewer, *Bibliotheca Sudhoffiana: Medizin und Wissenschaftsgeschichte in der Gelehrtenbibliothek von Karl Sudhoff* (Sudhoffs Archiv: Beihefte 52 = Schriftenreihe der Bayerischen Staatsbibliothek München 2; Stuttgart: Steiner, 2003).

hart's theological sentences in 1329 the development came to an abrupt end.[39] The last years of the philosophical and theological reception overlapped with the first translations of Maimonides' medical treatises. Here we can see an interesting development. The first treatises were related to the philosophical cure of the soul and afterwards of the body, e.g. *Regimen Sanitatis* and *De Asmate*.[40] (By the way, that means to categorise the *Regimen Sanitatis* and *De Causis Accidencium* among the philosophical tracts!) These translations were accompanied by "dissertations" (S. Kottek) on special problems such as *De Venenis* and *De Hemorhoidibus*. These tracts remained valuable as the ongoing production of new translations proves. The final step of the translation activities was reached with the translation of the aphorisms. With this collection Maimonides was no longer seen as an authority for only one or two special medical problems but his authority now comprises the whole of the medical science. At the same time this collection functions as a source book for the knowledge of ancient medical authorities such as Hippocrates and Galen.

Among the readers of these translations are some illustrious and famous medical doctors of the Middle Ages. Apart from the authors presented who either were immediate users of the translations such as William of Brescia or "normal" users like the anonymous presented we find references to Maimonides in the writings of the two greatest authorities of medieval medicine. Guy de Chauliac and Henry of Mondeville[41] more than once quoted from Maimonidean works. Other users of the Maimonidean oeuvre were Arnold of Bamberg and Hartmann Schedel,[42] not to mention all those anonymous doctors who copied Maimonidean works and made excerpts or inserted recipes from Maimonidean treatises into their own lists of recipes. The reception of Maimonides as a medical doctor ended only after Paracelsus introduced new categories into the medical discourse.

---

39 See Hasselhoff, *Dicit Rabbi Moyses* (see above n. 2), pp. 37–221; on Meister Eckhart see in addition Yossef Schwartz, "Meister Eckharts Schriftauslegung als maimonidisches Projekt", in *Moses Maimonides (1138–1204): His Religious, Scientific, and Philosophical* Wirkungsgeschichte *in Different Cultural Contexts*, ed. Görge K. Hasselhoff and Otfried Fraisse (Ex Oriente Lux: Rezeptionen und Exegesen als Traditionskritik; Würzburg: Ergon, 2004), pp. 173–208; on Thomas Aquinas, cf. Maximilian Forschner's article in this volume (see above pp. 373–393).

40 Cf. Samuel S. Kottek, "Maimonides on the Perfect Physician", in Fred Rosner, idem (Eds.), *Moses Maimonides: Physician, Scientist, and Philosopher* (Northvale, N.J., London: Aronson, 1993), pp. 25–32, 237–239; idem, "The Philosophic Medicine of Maimonides", in Hasselhoff, Fraisse, *Moses Maimonides* (see above n. 39), pp. 65–81; idem, "'Life is short, the Art is long': Maimonides Comments on Hippocrates' First Aphorism", in this volume pp. 349–359.

41 Hasselhoff, *Dicit Rabbi Moyses* (see above n. 2), pp. 303–309 (on Guy) and pp. 295–298 (on Henry).

42 Ibid., pp. 298–302 (on Arnold) and pp. 311–312 (on Schedel).

Appendix:
Latin Manuscripts Containing Maimonidean Medical Works

I. Translations by Armengaud Blaise

1. *De Asmate*
   - Cambridge, Gonville and Caius College, MS 178, fol. 130r–165r
   - Cambridge, Peterhouse College, MS 101, fol. 158ra–168rb
   - Torino, Biblioteca nazionale di Torino, Ms. I.III.35, fol. 67rb–75ra
2. *De Venenis*
   - Cambridge, Peterhouse College, MS 101, fol. 152ra–156ra
   - Krakov, Biblioteka Jagiellonska, Cod. 839, fol. 1r–10r
   - Oxford, Corpus Christi College, MS C. C. C. 125, fol. 1r–13v
   - Paris, Bibliothèque de la Sorbonne, Ms. lat. 1,031, fol. 171vb–182vb
   - (?) Torino, Biblioteca nazionale di Torino, Ms. I.III.35, fol. 37ra–40ra
3. *De Hemorhoidibus*
   - Torino, Biblioteca nazionale di Torino, Ms. I.III.35, fol. 78vb–81ra

II. Translations by Giovanni da Capua (John of Capua)

0. *Proemium Interpretis*
   - Wien, Österreichische Nationalbibliothek, Ms. lat. 2,280, fol. 89ra
   - Jerusalem, Jewish National and University Library, 2° FR. R 571–576 MS, fol. 7ra (186ra)
   - Todi, Biblioteca comunale "Lorenzo Leonj", Ms. 53, fol. 23ra
   - Città del Vaticano, Biblioteca Apostolica Vaticana, Palatina latina, Ms. 1,298, fol. 189ra
   - Wien, Österreichische Nationalbibliothek, Ms. lat. 5,306, fol. 1ra–b
   - Città del Vaticano, Biblioteca Apostolica Vaticana, Palatina latina, Ms. 1,147, fol. 99v
1. *Regimen Sanitatis*
   - Wien, Österreichische Nationalbibliothek, Ms. lat. 2,280, fol. 89ra–95rb
   - München, Bayerische Staatsbibliothek, Clm 77, fol. 60ra–66vb
   - Jerusalem, Jewish National and University Library, 2° FR. R 571–576 MS, fol. 7rb–20ra (186rb–199ra)
   - Todi, Biblioteca comunale "Lorenzo Leonj", Ms. 53, fol. 23rb–34rb
   - Città del Vaticano, Biblioteca Apostolica Vaticana, Palatina latina, Ms. 1,298, fol. 189ra–199ra
   - Wien, Österreichische Nationalbibliothek, Ms. lat. 5,306, fol. 1rb–17ra
   - Città del Vaticano, Biblioteca Apostolica Vaticana, Palatina latina, Ms. 1,147, fol. 99v–117r

1a. *Regimen Sanitatis* (abbreviated form used for the print editions)
   - Bamberg, Staatsbibliothek, Ms. C Med. 12, fol. 89r–104r
   - London, Wellcome Historical Medical Library, MS 466, fol. 1r–54v

2. *De Venenis*
   - Wien, Österreichische Nationalbibliothek, Ms. lat. 2,280, fol. 95rb–98rb
   - München, Bayerische Staatsbibliothek, Clm 77, fol. 66vb–69vb

- Jerusalem, Jewish National and University Library, 2° FR. R 571–576 MS, fol. 20ra–26rb (199ra–205rb)
- Todi, Biblioteca comunale "Lorenzo Leonj", Ms. 53, fol. 34rb–39vb
- Città del Vaticano, Biblioteca Apostolica Vaticana, Palatina latina, Ms. 1,298, fol. 199ra–204ra
- Wien, Österreichische Nationalbibliothek, Ms. lat. 5,306, fol. 17ra–25va
- Wrocław, Biblioteka Uniwersitecka, Ms. III F 10, fol. 16rb–27ra (fragment)

3. *De Hemorhoidibus*
   - Wien, Österreichische Nationalbibliothek, Ms. lat. 2,280, fol. 98rb–99va
   - München, Bayerische Staatsbibliothek, Clm 77, fol. 69vb–71ra
   - Jerusalem, Jewish National and University Library, 2° FR. R 571–576 MS, fol. 26va–28vb (205va–207vb)
   - Todi, Biblioteca comunale "Lorenzo Leonj", Ms. 53, fol. 39vb–42rb
   - Città del Vaticano, Biblioteca Apostolica Vaticana, Palatina latina, Ms. 1,298, fol. 204ra–206ra
   - Città del Vaticano, Biblioteca Apostolica Vaticana, Palatina latina, Ms. 1,147, fol. 117v–121r
   - Wrocław, Biblioteka Uniwersitecka, Ms. III F 10, fol. 44ra–48ra

III. Further Anonymous Translations

1. *De Venenis*
   - Città del Vaticano, Biblioteca Apostolica Vaticana, Palatina latina, Ms. 1,146, fol. 83va–86va
2. *De Coitu*
   - Wien, Österreichische Nationalbibliothek, Ms. lat. 2,280, fol. 99va–100va
   - Jerusalem, Jewish National and University Library, 2° FR. R 571–576 MS, fol. 28vb–30va (207vb–209va)
   - Venezia, Biblioteca Nazionale Marciana, Cod. Marcianus 2,613 (Lat. 7. 3), fol. 35va–36va
   - Città del Vaticano, Biblioteca Apostolica Vaticana, Palatina latina, Ms. 1,205, fol. 25r–28v
   - Wrocław, Biblioteka Uniwersitecka, Ms. III F 10, fol. 27rb (fragment)
3. *De Asmate*[43]
   - München, Bayerische Staatsbibliothek, Clm 77, fol. 71rb–76vb
   - Jerusalem, Jewish National and University Library, 2° FR. R 571–576 MS, fol. 30va–44vb (209va–223vb)
4. *Aphorismi*
   - Paris, Bibliothèque nationale de France, Ms. fonds latin 7,067 (only *particulas* XIII–XXV)
   - Lüneburg, Ratsbücherei, Ms. Miscell. D 2° 5, fol. 17ra–99va
   - Firenze, Biblioteca Nazionale Centrale, II, IV, 31

---

43 Professor McVaugh in an e-mail dated August 27th, 2004 emphasised that this translation shows similarities to John of Capua's translation of the *Regimen Sanitatis*. This might be true but we have no indication in the manuscripts that John actually made the translation.

- London, British Library, Add. MS 22,313, fol. 249ra–338rb
- Città del Vaticano, Biblioteca Apostolica Vaticana, Palatina latina, Ms. 1,298, fol. 109ra–164rb
- Città del Vaticano, Biblioteca Apostolica Vaticana, Palatina latina, Ms. 1,147, fol. 1r–99r
- Krakov, Biblioteka Jagiellonska, Cod. 519, fol. Vr–v (fragments)
- London, Wellcome Historical Medical Library, MS 560, fol. 38r–86v (excerpts)

5. *Regimen Sanitatis*
   - Torino, Biblioteca nazionale di Torino, Ms. I.III.35, fol. 81ra–88ra

Johannes Reuchlin – Der erste christliche Leser des hebräischen *Moreh Nevukhim*

von

Reimund Leicht

Universität Potsdam

1. Einleitung

Johannes Reuchlin, der in den bewegten Jahren des erwachenden Humanismus und der beginnenden Reformation von 1455–1522 lebte, hat sich neben dem Ansehen als Gräzist auch bleibenden Ruhm als vielleicht nicht erster, aber doch wichtigster christlicher Hebraist und Mitbegründer der christlichen Kabbalah erworben. Unter seinen Werken befindet sich die erste vollständige hebräische Grammatik in lateinischer Sprache, die unter dem Titel *De Rudimentis Hebraicis Libri III* im Jahre 1506 erschien, und seine beiden philosophischen, „christlich-kabbalistischen" Bücher: das frühe *De Verbo Mirifico* (1494) und später das sicher bekannteste *De Arte Cabalistica* (1517). Ebenso berühmt wie verfemt wurde Reuchlin aber auch durch den so genannten „Bücherstreit", in dem er – ein Liebhaber hebräischer Bücher – zu deren öffentlichem Verteidiger wurde und damit selbst in die Schusslinie antijüdischer Polemik geriet.[1]

Weniger bekannt ist jedoch, dass Reuchlin auch ein eifriger Leser des Maimonides war. Mehr noch: Reuchlin war der erste christliche Denker überhaupt, der den *Moreh Nevukhim* in seiner hebräischen Fassung rezipiert hat, und er war zugleich für etwa hundert Jahre der letzte, wenn man Johannes Buxtorfs lateinische Übersetzung des *Moreh Nevukhim* aus dem Jahre 1629 als nächste Station christlich-hebraistischer Maimonides-Lektüre ansieht. Dennoch ist in der bisherigen Forschung über Maimonides und Reuchlin gleichermaßen diese Rolle des Pforzheimer Hebraisten kaum thematisiert worden. Zwar nennt Ludwig Geiger Maimonides unter den Quellen Reuchlins,[2] aber noch Jacob Guttmann fand nur wenig schmeichelhafte Worte für dessen Maimonides-Kenntnisse: „Wie sehr die Vorliebe für die Kabbalah, an deren dunklen und geheimnis-

1 Zur Biographie Johannes Reuchlins vgl. Ludwig Geiger, *Johann Reuchlin. Sein Leben und seine Werke* (Leipzig: Duncker & Humblot, 1871; Nachdruck Nieuwkoop: de Graaf, 1964).

2 Ibid., S. 119, Anm. 2 und S. 173, Anm. 2.

vollen Lehren die Geister sich berauschten, weil sie in ihnen eine Bestätigung für die Mysterien des Christentums zu finden glaubten, das Interesse für die anderen Erzeugnisse der jüdischen Literatur in den Hintergrund drängte, das zeigt sich am deutlichsten bei Johann Reuchlin (1455–1522). [...] Allein im Vergleich mit der umfassenden Verwertung der kabbalistischen Literatur, die er in ihren älteren wie jüngeren Autoren, in ihren echten wie in ihren apokryphen Erzeugnissen auf das Genaueste kennt, kommen doch die vereinzelten Citate aus anderen Schriftwerken kaum in Betracht. So wird auch der Führer des Maimonides, den er einmal auch in der hebräischen Übersetzung des Ibn Tibbon citiert, nur an wenigen Stellen benützt, die von keiner besonderen Wertschätzung des Werkes Zeugnis ablegen."[3]

Das Paradigma einer kabbalistisch gefärbten Lektüre des Maimonides durch Reuchlin wurde viele Jahre später durch Moshe Idel unter anderen Vorzeichen erneuert. Er geht davon aus, dass Reuchlin in seinem Verständnis der Kabbalah maßgeblich von den Lehren des Abraham Abulafia geprägt sei, mit dessen Lehren er durch den philosophierenden italienischen Grafen Pico della Mirandola vertraut gemacht worden war. Abulafia und der gesamte Zweig der so genannten „ekstatischen Kabbalah" sind ihrerseits in so vielen Punkten von Maimonides inspiriert, dass auch Reuchlins Verständnis der Lehre des Maimonides durch die Kabbalah geprägt gewesen sei.[4] Dieser Sicht folgt im Wesentlichen auch Karl Erich Grözinger in seiner Darstellung der kabbalistischen Lehren Reuchlins.[5]

Gegen die Annahme, dass Reuchlins Interesse an Maimonides ausschließlich kabbalistisch motiviert und zudem überhaupt nur durch die Begegnung mit Pico entstanden sei, sprechen jedoch gewichtige, bisher kaum gewürdigte Indizien. So ist auffällig, dass Reuchlin Maimonides in seinem kabbalistischen Erstlingswerk *De Verbo Mirifico* (1494), das noch ganz unter dem Eindruck der Begegnung mit Pico auf seiner zweiten Italienreise (1490) steht, überhaupt nicht erwähnt. Zudem muss man bedenken, dass die Begegnung mit Pico ohnehin nicht so intensiv gewesen ist, wie es manche Hinweise Reuchlins in seinen

---

3 Jacob Guttmann, „Der Einfluß der maimonidischen Philosophie auf das christliche Abendland", in *Moses ben Maimon. Sein Leben, seine Werke und sein Einfluß*, ed. Wilhelm Bacher, Marcus Brann, David Jacob Simonsen (2 Bände; Leipzig: Fock, 1908/1914; Reprint beider Bände in einem Band: Hildesheim, New York: Olms, 1971), S. 214.

4 Moshe Idel, *Maïmonide et la mystique juive* (Paris: Cerf, 1991), S. 51: „Il n'est donc pas étonnant que l'un des premiers successeurs de Pic, Johann Reuchlin, cite fréquemment le *Guide* comme si c'était une œuvre de la cabale. Ce furent ces auteurs qui diffusèrent une version ‚cabalisante' des einseignements de Maïmonide dans la culture européenne"; vgl. auch idem, *The Mystical Experience in Abraham Abulafia* (New York: State University of New York Press, 1988), S. 10 (deutsch: *Abraham Abulafia und die mystische Erfahrung* [Frankfurt am Main: Jüdischer Verlag, 1994]).

5 Karl Erich Grözinger, „Reuchlin und die Kabbala", in Arno Herzig, Julius H. Schoeps, Saskia Rohde (Eds.), *Reuchlin und die Juden* (Sigmaringen: Thorbecke, 1993), S. 175–187.

späteren Werken anzudeuten scheinen und auch manche neuere Forscher behaupten.[6] Es fehlen beispielsweise sichere Hinweise darauf, dass Reuchlin Abschriften der lateinischen Übersetzungen abulafianischer Werke in Picos Bibliothek gesehen oder gar abgeschrieben hat.[7] Nur Picos bereits 1486 veröffentlichte *Conclusiones* werden von Reuchlin wiederholt zitiert.[8] Damit wird die oft behauptete vorrangige Abhängigkeit Reuchlins von Abulafia ebenso zweifelhaft wie die Annahme, er habe Maimonides durch Pico kennen gelernt. Hinzu kommt, dass abgesehen von dem abulafianisch geprägten Frühwerk Joseph Gikatillas unter dem Titel *Ginnat Egoz* weder der Besitz noch die Lektüre abulafianischer Werke für Reuchlin nachweisbar ist.[9] Schließlich erweist auch eine Analyse der Maimonides-Zitate bei Reuchlin, dass ein spezifisch abulafianischer Kontext in keinem Fall eindeutig feststellbar ist.

Reuchlins Kenntnis des Maimonides, die sich wie ein roter Faden durch sein hebraistisches Schaffen zieht, erweist sich bei genauerer Analyse als vielschichtig. Vieles spricht dafür, dass sie auf eigenem, intensivem Studium des *Moreh Nevukhim* beruht. Leider ist nicht mehr genau bestimmbar, wann Reuchlin erstmals mit dem hebräischen Text des *Moreh Nevukhim* in Berührung gekommen ist, da in dem ansonsten noch weitgehend erhaltenen Hebraica-Nachlass aus seiner Bibliothek gerade dieses Werk verloren ist.[10] Der Zeitpunkt der ersten Lektüre muss jedoch vor dem Jahre 1505 gelegen haben, da Reuchlin in diesem Jahr erstmals ein hebräisches Zitat aus Maimonides' philosophischem Hauptwerk anführt. Es kann daher als wahrscheinlich gelten, dass Reuchlin es wie einen großen Teil seiner hebraistischen Bibliothek auf der dritten Italien-

---

6 Vgl. dazu Geiger, *Reuchlin* (wie Anm. 1), S. 34. Der von Geiger zitierte Brief ist neu ediert in Matthias Dall'Asta, Gerald Dörner (Eds.), *J. Reuchlin – Briefwechsel* (Stuttgart-Bad Cannstatt: Frommann-Holzboog, 1999ff.), Band I, S. 143–146.

7 Zum Umfang von Reuchlins hebraistischer Bibliothek vgl. Wolfgang von Abel, Reimund Leicht, *Verzeichnis der Hebraica in der Bibliothek Johannes Reuchlins* (Pforzheimer Reuchlinschriften; Ostfildern: Thorbecke [im Druck]).

8 Schon im Jahre 1506 in *De Rudimentis Hebraicis Libri III* (Pforzheim: Anshelm, 1506; Nachdruck Hildesheim: Olms, 1974), S. 124. Der Einfluss von Picos *Conclusiones* auf Reuchlins Verständnis der Kabbalah ist bedeutend und bedarf einer eigenen detaillierten Untersuchung, die hier nicht geleistet werden kann. Es sei an dieser Stelle daher nur angemerkt, dass gerade in der Art des Umgangs mit Picos Aussagen deutlich wird, dass Reuchlin dahinter ein korrektes Verständnis dessen, was Kabbalah ist, vermutet, er aber keine genaueren Informationen hatte, wie die teilweise sehr änigmatisch formulierten Thesen im Einzelnen zu verstehen seien. Ein wesentlicher Teil von Reuchlins kabbalistischen Studien scheint daher im Versuch bestanden zu haben, den fehlenden Kontext für Picos die Kabbalah betreffenden *Conclusiones* zu rekonstruieren.

9 Spuren der Rezeption abulafianischer Gedanken lassen sich allenfalls noch in einer weiteren, kurzen Schrift nachweisen, die Reuchlin unter dem Titel *Hacdama* zitiert; vgl. dazu Moshe Idel, *Studies in Ecstatic Kabbalah* (Albany: State University of New York Press, 1988), S. 54.

10 Vgl. zum Folgenden von Abel/Leicht, *Verzeichnis* (wie Anm. 7), Kapitel 1.3.8.

reise erworben hat (1498). Vermutlich handelte es sich um den vor 1480 erschienenen Erstdruck des *Moreh Nevukhim*, auch wenn dies nicht endgültig beweisbar ist.[11] Ob er daneben auch die lateinische Fassung des Werkes kannte und benutzte, und ob die Intensität, mit der Reuchlin gerade Maimonides verwendet, auch darauf beruht, dass ihm der Text auch in Übersetzung zugänglich war, ist bislang nicht mit Sicherheit rekonstruierbar.[12] Seit den letzten Jahren des ausgehenden 15. Jahrhunderts jedenfalls las und zitierte Reuchlin den *Moreh Nevukhim* in verschiedenen – und zwar durchaus nicht nur kabbalistischen – Kontexten regelmäßig und eigenständig, wie bereits die Analyse der Werke *vor* der Veröffentlichung des kabbalistischen Hauptwerks *De Arte Cabalistica* im Jahre 1517 zeigen wird.

2. Maimonides in Reuchlins Werken vor 1517

2.1 Die *Tütsch Missive* (1505)

Das erste Zitat aus dem *Moreh Nevukhim* – und damit auch der erste Hinweis auf Reuchlins Kenntnis dieses Werkes überhaupt – findet sich, wie bereits angemerkt, nicht in dem kabbalistischen Erstlingswerk *De Verbo Mirifico*, sondern erst in einer kurzen Schrift, die er im Jahre 1505 als Antwort auf die Frage eines namentlich nicht genannten Junkers *„Warumb die Juden so lang im ellend sind"* verfasst hat.[13] Es ist hier nicht der Ort, die ausführliche theologisch-kirchenrechtliche Argumentation der Schrift im Detail nachzuzeichnen, in der Reuchlin daran gelegen ist, den Juden eine konkrete Schuld nachzuweisen, die der göttlichen Strafe ihres langen Exils zugrunde liegt. Es ist dabei kaum zufällig, dass sich Reuchlin hierfür nur auf die hebräische Bibel und ihre mittelalterlichen jüdischen Ausleger stützt, denn so hofft er, einen Schuldspruch gegen die Juden ganz auf deren eigene Aussagen gründen zu können. Ihre eigenen Worte sollen sie von ihrer Schuld überzeugen.

In Reuchlins Argumentation ist auffällig, dass er sich zwar des verbreiteten Argumentes bewusst ist, die Tötung Jesu sei Grund für die Strafe des Exils,

---

11 Vgl. Moritz Steinschneider, *Catalogus Librorum Hebraeorum in Bibliotheca Bodleiana* (Berlin: Friedlaender, 1852–1860; Nachdruck Hildesheim: Olms, 1964), Sp. 1894–1895. Ein bedeutendes Indiz für die Annahme, Reuchlin habe diesen Druck des *Moreh Nevukhim* verwendet, ist das Zitat aus dem 44. Kapitel des II. Buches, das von Reuchlin in *De Arte Cabalistica*, fol. LVIIb, unvollständig wiedergegeben wird. Dabei entspricht das Ende des Zitats bei Reuchlin genau dem Textende auf fol. 134a des Erstdrucks.

12 Vgl. dazu von Abel/Leicht, *Verzeichnis* (wie Anm. 7).

13 Johannes Reuchlin, *Sämtliche Werke* (Stuttgart-Bad Cannstatt: Frommann-Holzboog), Band IV.1, S. 5–12. Alle Zitate aus Reuchlins Werken werden, soweit nicht anders angegeben, nach der neuen Werkausgabe zitiert, die seit 1999 durch Widu-Wolfgang Ehlers, Hans-Gert Roloff und Peter Schäfer herausgegeben wird.

dies aber nicht als einzige Ursache der gegenwärtigen Strafe gelten lassen will. Vielmehr kann es nur das andauernde Verharren in der Sünde sein, das ihr Judesein an und für sich bedeutet, das eine derart harte Strafe bedingt. Um diese Ansicht zu stützen, beruft sich Reuchlin am Ende und Höhepunkt des *Tütsch Missive* nun auf Maimonides und zitiert zweimal aus dem 23. Kapitel des dritten Buches des *Moreh Nevukhim*, in dem die biblische Hiob-Geschichte einer eingehenden Auslegung unterworfen wird.

Reuchlins erstes Zitat besteht in der prägnanten Aussage, dass „Wer boeß tuot der muoß verdammnus liden“ (כל עשה רע יענש וגו). Nach der Darstellung des Maimonides sind sich die Freunde Hiobs in diesem Punkt einig, was Reuchlin in der Form deutet, dass „ir eigen meister schriben“, dass die göttliche Strafe des Exils so lange andauern werde, wie sie in der Sünde – also ihrem Judentum – verharren. Diese Aussage wird durch ein zweites Zitat aus demselben Kapitel des *Moreh Nevukhim* ergänzt, in dem Maimonides die Ansicht des Eliphaz in der Form zusammenfasst, dass dieser glaube, dass „alles, was dem Menschen widerfährt, nach Gerechtigkeit geschieht, daß uns aber die Kenntnis aller unserer Mängel abgeht, um deren willen wir gestraft werden“.[14] Dies wertet Reuchlin als offenes Eingeständnis jüdischer Unwissenheit schlechthin, woraufhin er als guter Christ nur noch mit der frommen Bitte antworten kann: „Jch bit gott er woell sye erlüchten vnd bekern zuo dem rechten gluoben, das sye von der gefencknüs des düfels erledigt werden, als die gemeinschafft der Christenlichen kirchen an dem karfritag andechtlich für sye bitt. Vnnd wann sye Jhesuh den rechten Messiah erkennen so würdt all ir sach guot hie in diser wellt, vnd dort ewiglichen amen.“[15]

Die Frage, in welchem Maße Reuchlin in der Geschichte des christlichen Antijudaismus mit diesem Text eine positive oder negative Rolle zukommt, soll hier auf sich beruhen, da an dieser Stelle nur die Maimonides-Rezeption interessiert. Zunächst kann als sicher gelten, dass Reuchlin das Werk des Maimonides mit der Zielsetzung instrumentalisiert hat, die Juden mit ihren eigenen Waffen zu schlagen, das heißt aus ihren eigenen Werken und Autoritäten zu belegen, dass sie an Jesus Christus glauben müssten, wenn sie nicht so *„verstopt“* wären.[16] Die christliche Vorstellung, dass die Bibel die Wahrheit des Christentums belege und nur die Hartnäckigkeit der Juden diese von der Bekehrung fernhalte und daher Judenmission in erster Linie in dem Versuch bestehen muss, den Juden ihre eigene Tradition zu erklären, wird von Reuchlin hier also auf Maimonides ausgedehnt.

---

14 Reuchlin, ibid., zitiert: חסרונותינו כלם אשר נחייב בעבורם העונש תעלם ממנו השבתם und übersetzt: *„Vnsere gebrechenheitten alle, daruff die verdammnus gesetzt Jst verborgen vor uns ir missetat“* (korrigiere zu: השגתם).

15 Ibid.

16 Ibid.

Reuchlin hat Maimonides zu diesem Zeitpunkt offenbar zunächst als Theologen gelesen, aber gerade vor dem Hintergrund der antijüdischen Tendenz der Reuchlin'schen Schrift stellt sich die Frage, ob die Auswahl der Zitate völlig willkürlich dem Argumentationsinteresse Reuchlins oder aber zumindest einer ansatzweise echten Lektüre des *Moreh Nevukhim* entspringt. Das Ergebnis ist hierbei zwiespältig: Wie bekannt, teilt Maimonides die vier Freunde Hiobs und Hiob selber im 23. Kapitel auf die fünf Ansichten hinsichtlich der Vorsehung auf, die er im 17. Kapitel des Buches dargelegt hatte. Die Ansicht des Eliphaz, aus der Reuchlin die These von der Unwissenheit der Juden über den Grund ihrer Strafe zitiert, ist dabei diejenige, die im 17. Kapitel als „die unsrige, nämlich die Meinung unseres Gesetzes" bezeichnet wird. Reuchlin folgt also in seiner Argumentation einerseits dem allgemeinen Konsens, dass jeder, der Böses tut, Verdammnis leiden muss, andererseits der als „jüdisch" deklarierten Auffassung von der Unergründlichkeit der göttlichen Gerechtigkeit, die er jedoch recht willkürlich in ein Unwissenheitseingeständnis der Juden umformt. Was Reuchlin in seiner Maimonides-Lektüre an dieser Stelle jedoch völlig ignoriert, ist die Aussage im 23. Kapitel, dass nicht die Ansicht des Eliphaz, sondern die des Elihu die „an edler Denkungsart und Weisheit größte war". Der subtilen Argumentation des Maimonides konnte oder wollte Reuchlin an dieser Stelle offenbar nicht folgen.

2.2 *De Rudimentis Hebraicis* (1506)

Diese nicht sehr genaue (und bei Lichte betrachtet infame) Art der Maimonides-Lektüre ist für den Reuchlin dieser Jahre aber nur bedingt charakteristisch. Chronologisch an zweiter Stelle zu behandeln ist Reuchlins Grammatik der hebräischen Sprache, an der er nachweislich schon vor der Jahrhundertwende gearbeitet hat,[17] die aber erst 1506 erscheinen konnte.

Die Grammatik *De Rudimentis Hebraicis* teilt sich in einen lexikographischen und einen grammatischen Teil, wobei sich alle sieben Zitate im ersten, also dem lexikographischen Teil finden. Allerdings ist Reuchlin weit davon entfernt, nur die lexikographischen Daten aus den dafür vielleicht besonders geeignet erscheinenden „lexikographischen Kapiteln", wie Shlomo Pines die ersten Kapitel des *Moreh Nevukhim* genannt hat,[18] auszuwerten. Vielmehr lässt sich Reuchlin durch Maimonides an vielen Stellen zu theologisch-philosophischen Hinweisen verleiten, die er im Rahmen seines Wörterbuches jedoch nicht weiter ausführt.

---

17 Vgl. Brief an Frater Crisman vom 13. April 1501; ediert und kommentiert in *J. Reuchlin – Briefwechsel* (wie Anm. 6), Band I, S. 350–353.

18 Shlomo Pines, „Translator's Introduction", in idem (Übersetzer), *Moses Maimonides. The Guide of the Perplexed* (Chicago, London: Chicago University Press, 1963), S. xxiv.

Am ehesten noch lexikographisch ausgerichtet ist Reuchlins zweifacher Verweis auf Maimonides bei der Homonymität des Wortes *elohim*,[19] wobei er das 2. Kapitel des I. Buches nennt, aber auch auf eine weitere Passage im 61. Kapitel anspielt.[20] Als reiner Beispielgeber für die Verwendung des Wortes *mi* als Relativum dient der *Moreh* jedoch auch.[21] Demgegenüber verraten einige andere Lemmata eindeutig ein philosophisches Interesse am *Moreh Nevukhim*: So verweist Reuchlin zum Wort *gešem* auf das Kapitel über die Unkörperlichkeit der Engel (I. Buch, 49. Kapitel),[22] zu *teva'*[23] auf die naturphilosophischen Ausführungen im Kapitel 72 des I. Buches, und er gibt als Beleg für die philosophische Bedeutung des Wortes *ṣurah* das erste Kapitel des II. Buches des *Moreh Nevukhim* an. Einem spezifischen philosophischen Interesse der Renaissance dürfte auch der Verweis entspringen, dass Maimonides im 30. Kapitel des III. Buches Ausführlicheres über die „Landwirtschaft der Chaldäer", also die so genannte *Nabatäische Landwirtschaft*, zu berichten weiß.[24]

In ihrer Zielsetzung unterscheidet sich Reuchlins Grammatik grundlegend von der *Tütsch Missive*, und entsprechend unterschiedlich ist auch die Verwendung des *Moreh Nevukhim*. Er dient hier nicht als Fundgrube für antijüdische Argumente, sondern als philosophisch-theologisches Werk, das dem Nutzer der Grammatik zugänglich gemacht werden soll. Mehr noch, Reuchlin betont durch die Verweise auf den *Moreh Nevukhim* und andere philosophische Werke wie die Schrift *Sefer ha-Kuzari* von Jehuda ha-Levi, dass es überhaupt eine philosophische Seite des Judentums gibt. Der Hebraist und Philosoph Reuchlin spricht also mit deutlich anderer Zunge als der Jurist und Theologe, auch wenn die Kürze der Zitate und Verweise nur wenig Auskunft darüber geben, wie er die entsprechenden Kapitel interpretiert hat.

2.3 *Augenspiegel* (1511), *In Septem Psalmos Poinitentiales* (1512) und Briefe

Die Jahre von 1509 an sind für Reuchlin durch den so genannten „Bücherstreit" gekennzeichnet, der ihn bis zu seinem Lebensende verfolgen sollte. Ursache des Konfliktes war die judenfeindliche Agitation des Konvertiten Pfefferkorn, die schließlich dazu führte, dass Kaiser Maximilian Reuchlin neben anderen Gelehrten der Zeit um einen Ratschlag bat, „ob man den Juden alle ihre Bücher nehmen, abtun und verbrennen solle". Der schriftlich ergangene Ratschlag

19 Reuchlin, *De Rudimentis Hebraicis* (wie Anm. 8), S. 55 und 425.

20 Das in *De Rudimentis Hebraicis* (wie Anm. 8), S. 425, erwähnte ausschließliche Zukommen des Namens YHWH zu Gott findet sich nicht im 2. Kapitel, sondern nur im 61. Kapitel des ersten Buches.

21 Ibid., S. 283.

22 Ibid., S. 114–115.

23 Ibid., S. 201–202.

24 Ibid., S. 42–43.

Reuchlins wurde von Pfefferkorn scharf kritisiert, da Reuchlin als einziger der Gutachter ein vergleichsweise ausgewogenes Bild von der jüdischen Literatur zu zeichnen wagte und von einer pauschalen Verurteilung abriet. Dieser Angriff durch Pfefferkorn provozierte Reuchlin zu vehementer Gegenwehr, da nun er selbst in die Fänge der kirchlichen Inquisition zu geraten drohte.[25]

Auch in dieser für Reuchlin schwierigen Zeit finden sich Hinweise auf das Werk des Maimonides: So wird deutlich, dass er von der *Mišneh Torah* wusste, sie ihm aber nicht zur Verfügung stand, da er nur indirekt durch Paulus von Burgos berichten kann, dass dort ein Bericht über die Entstehung des Talmuds enthalten sei.[26] Zudem nimmt er Maimonides und Raschi gegen die Angriffe des Paulus von Burgos in Schutz und sagt, er kenne keine Äußerungen, in denen diese beiden jüdischen Schriftsteller die *malkhut zadon* (sündhaftes Königreich, Imperium) mit dem Römischen Reich oder die *minim* mit den Aposteln identifizierten.[27]

Am interessantesten ist jedoch ein Zitat aus Wilhelm von Auvergnes *De Legibus*: „Später dann, zur Zeit des Kommentators Averroes aus Cordoba, begannen die Juden Philosophie zu treiben; der erste, sagt man, war Rabbi Moses aus Ägypten. Wilhelm von Paris sagt: ‚Daher schließen sie sich infolge des engen Kontakts auch mit arabischen Philosophen in vielerlei Hinsicht deren Auffassung an. Unfähig, das Bekenntnis zu ihrem Gesetz und den Glauben Abrahams zu verteidigen, sind sie im Gesetz zu Irrenden und im Glauben Abrahams zu Ketzern geworden'. So Wilhelm von Paris."[28]

Bemerkenswert an diesem Zitat, das Reuchlin wegen erheblicher Abweichungen vom Wortlaut des Originals vielleicht nur indirekt kannte,[29] ist nun, dass Maimonides eindeutig in einen philosophischen Kontext gestellt wird. Reuchlin präsentiert Maimonides historisch als den ersten jüdischen Philosophen und zeigt sich zugleich mit der ambivalenten Haltung der christlichen Scholastik gegenüber diesem Denker vertraut. Letzteres ist umso erstaunlicher, als Wilhelm von Auvergne Maimonides gar nicht namentlich nennt.[30] An dieser Stelle zeichnet sich also eine weitere Dimension des Reuchlin'schen Maimonides-Verständnisses ab, das maßgeblich durch die scholastische Denktradition geprägt zu sein scheint.

---

25 Vgl. dazu die ausführliche Darstellung bei Geiger, *Reuchlin* (wie Anm. 1), S. 205–454.

26 Reuchlin, *Werke* (wie Anm. 13), Band IV.1, S. 40.

27 Ibid., S. 153.

28 Ibid., S. 115.

29 Vgl. zu diesem Zitat Jacob Guttmann, *Die Scholastik des dreizehnten Jahrhunderts in ihren Beziehungen zum Judenthum und zur jüdischen Literatur* (Breslau: Marcus, 1902), S. 24–25, und idem, „Der Einfluß der maimonidischen Philosophie" (wie Anm. 3), S. 146.

30 Die Kenntnis des Maimonides durch Wilhelm von Auvergne wird neuerdings bezweifelt durch Görge K. Hasselhoff, *Dicit Rabbi Moyses. Studien zum Bild von Moses Maimonides im lateinischen Westen vom 13. bis zum 15. Jahrhundert* (Würzburg: Königshausen & Neumann, 2004), S. 72.

In derselben Epoche ist Reuchlin aber noch ein weiterer Aspekt des Maimonides bekannt: In einem Brief an den Mediziner Johannes Stocker aus dem Jahr 1512 verweist er explizit auf ihn, als er von dem besonderen medizinischen Wissen spricht, das zuerst den Juden zugekommen sei. Sie hätten noch vor den Ägyptern solches Wissen besessen, worin das für Reuchlin typische Motiv der hebräischen Urweisheit zum Ausdruck kommt. Um dies zu begründen, beruft er sich auf den *Rabi Moyses Aegyptius*, der im 48. Kapitel des III. Buches sage, dass das Gesetz medizinisch ungeeignete Speisen verbiete.[31] Die maimonidische Argumentation über die Gründe der Gesetze erfährt hier also eine überraschende Umdeutung, die dennoch etwas von dem Ruhm erkennen lässt, den Maimonides auch als Mediziner in der christlichen Umwelt genoss.[32]

Eher sprachlich orientiert ist Reuchlins kurze Bemerkung über die Schönheit und Reinheit der hebräischen Sprache, die sich mit Hinweis auf das achte Kapitel des III. Buches des *Moreh Nevukhim* in einem Brief an den Theologen und Juristen Jakob Lemp findet, der dem Kommentar *In Septem Psalmos Poinitentiales* (1512) vorangestellt ist.[33]

2.4 Maimonides in der Interpretation Reuchlins vor 1517

Fasst man Reuchlins Zitate und Anspielungen auf Maimonides, insbesondere den *Moreh Nevukhim*, in der Dekade von 1505 bis ca. 1515 zusammen, so ist festzuhalten, dass er ihn an ganz unerwarteten Stellen teils wörtlich, teils indirekt, meist aber mit direktem Verweis auf die Autorschaft des Maimonides zitiert, und zwar ohne erkennbare Vorliebe für bestimmte Themen. Die Verwendung und Interpretation der Zitate orientiert sich dabei in der Regel nicht am Kontext der maimonidischen Argumentation, ja, Maimonides als systematischer Denker bleibt verschwommen, weil das systematische Gerüst, in das die Zitate eingefügt wurden, aus anderen Kontexten stammt: So im Falle der *Tütsch Missive* aus dem Repertoire der christlichen Missionstheologie und im Fall des Briefes an den Mediziner Stocker aus der renaissancistischen Vorstellung einer den Juden geoffenbarten Urweisheit, die auch die Medizin umfasst. An kaum einer Stelle zeigt sich ein spezifisch kabbalistisches Interesse am Werk des Maimonides, während andere Rezeptionskontexte wie die scholastische Auseinandersetzung mit der jüdischen Philosophie zumindest eine Rolle gespielt zu haben scheinen.[34]

---

31 *J. Reuchlin – Briefwechsel* (wie Anm. 6), Band II, S. 251.

32 Vgl. dazu Hasselhoff, *Dicit Rabbi Moyses* (wie Anm. 30), S. 280–316.

33 *J. Reuchlin – Briefwechsel* (wie Anm. 6), Band II, S. 325.

34 Einzige Ausnahme scheint ein Brief vom 1. Juli 1515 an Pietro Galatino zu sein, in dem Reuchlin mit Verweis auf das 22. Kapitel des III. Buches des *Moreh Nevukhim* auf den Gottesnamen zu sprechen kommt; vgl. *J. Reuchlin – Briefwechsel* (wie Anm. 6), Band IV, Nr. 270 (in Vorbereitung). Ich danke den Herausgebern des *Briefwechsels*, dass sie mir eine Abschrift dieses Briefes mit Kommentar zur Verfügung gestellt haben.

3. *De Arte Cabalistica* (1517)

Die Bedeutung der zahlreichen Zitate aus dem *Moreh Nevukhim* in Reuchlins Schriften vor dem Jahre 1517 ist vor dem Hintergrund der Frage, aus welcher Perspektive Reuchlin Maimonides zunächst betrachtet und kennen gelernt hat, kaum zu überschätzen. Dennoch ist unzweifelhaft, dass Maimonides in Reuchlins kabbalistischem Hauptwerk *De Arte Cabalistica* die größte Rolle spielt. Es ist hier nicht der Rahmen, die Gedankenführung dieses Werkes im Detail nachzuzeichnen, zumal es sich dabei insgesamt ohne Zweifel um ein Buch handelt, das in vielen Punkten vom Denken des Maimonides kaum weiter entfernt sein könnte: Reuchlin entwickelt in den drei Büchern von *De Arte Cabalistica,* die aus einem mehrteiligen Dialog zwischen dem kabbalistisch versierten Juden Simon, einem zwischen Judentum, Christentum und Islam stehenden Marranus und dem Pythagoräer Philolaos besteht, das, was er als die „symbolische Philosophie" (*symbolica philosophia*)[35] der Kabbalah betrachtet. Das Werk ist tief verwurzelt im Renaissance-Denken und weist Kennzeichen des Renaissance-Platonismus auf. Es übernimmt die Vorstellung einer *philosophia perennis,* ein alles durchdringendes Analogie-Denken und Emanationsmotive in der Epistemologie und Kosmologie. Mehr noch, es ist ein kabbalistisches Werk, das die *Sefirot*-Lehre ebenso darstellt wie die Lehre von Buchstabenkombinationen und messianische Spekulationen, also ein Kontext, in dem Maimonides sich kaum zu Hause gefühlt hätte.[36] Dennoch spielt maimonidische Philosophie eine überraschend große Rolle in *De Arte Cabalistica,* auch wenn Reuchlin Maimonides nicht immer namentlich nennt, sondern ihn – wie weiter unten zu diskutieren sein wird – mehrfach nur als kabbalistischen Meister bezeichnet.

Das erste Buch von *De Arte Cabalistica* bemüht sich um eine Bestimmung dessen, was Kabbalah überhaupt sei, und an erster Stelle versucht Reuchlin, sich dieser Frage aus epistemologischer Perspektive zu nähern. Ausgehend von der Annahme, dass alles Seiende aufwärts strebe und nur durch die Materie zurückgehalten werde, entwickelt Reuchlin zunächst ein Schema des stufenweisen Aufstiegs der Erkenntnis[37]:

---

35 Reuchlin, *De Arte Cabalistica,* fol. b. Alle Zitate aus *De Arte Cabalistica* werden nach den Folioangaben der Erstausgabe zitiert. Der Text ist mehrfach nachgedruckt worden, zuletzt mit einer französischen Übersetzung von François Secret, *La Kabbale* (Milano: Archè, 1995), und Martin und Sarah Goodman (Übersetzer), *On the Art of the Kabbalah: De arte cabalistica* (Lincoln, London: Nebraska Press, 1993).

36 Zu einer neuen philosophiegeschichtlichen Interpretation Reuchlins vgl. Wilhelm Schmidt-Biggemann, *Philosophia Perennis. Historische Umrisse abendländischer Spiritualität in Antike, Mittelalter und Früher Neuzeit* (Frankfurt am Main: Suhrkamp, 1998), S. 148–188 und öfter, sowie idem, „Johannes Reuchlin und die Anfänge der christlichen Kabbalah", in idem (Ed.), *Christliche Kabbala* (Pforzheimer Reuchlinschriften 10; Ostfildern: Thorbecke, 2003), S. 9–48.

37 Reuchlin, *De Arte Cabalistica* (wie Anm. 34), fol. IIIa.

1. *obiectum/diaphanon/sensus exterior*
2. *sensus interior/phantasia/iudicium brutum*
3. *iudicium humanum/ratio/intellectus*
4. *mens*

Die *mens* ist ihrerseits aber auf die Erleuchtung durch das Licht des aktiven Intellekts angewiesen, so dass als Ziel der Erkenntnis – ganz im Sinne klassischer Intellektmystik – die Vereinigung mit dem aktiven Intellekt erscheint (עד השכל והמשכיל והמושכל אחד – „bis das Denken, der Denkende und das Gedachte eins sind"),[38] oder doch zumindest in maimonidischer Begrifflichkeit die Erleuchtung durch ihn (כי בשפע השכל אשר שפע ממך נשכיל ונתישר – „denn durch die Emanation deines Denkens, das aus dir hervorgeht, denken wir und erlangen rechte Erkenntnis"; *Moreh Nevukhim*, II. Buch, 12. Kapitel).[39]

Gefahr droht diesem Erkenntnisaufstieg jedoch von zwei Seiten: Zunächst durch moralische Unvollkommenheit, wie Reuchlin mit einem Zitat aus dem III. Buch des *Moreh Nevukhim* Kapitel 33 belegt (כי בהמשך אחר התאוה לבד כמו הסכלים יבטלו התשוקות העיוניות – „denn durch das Befolgen einzig der Begierde, wie es die Toren tun, werden die spekulativen Begierden zunichte gemacht"). Auch dies wird wie alles vorhergehende als allgemeine Lehre der Kabbalisten ausgegeben (*tradunt Cabalistae*).[40]

Daneben ist der Erfolg auf dem Weg zur Erkenntnis auch aufgrund der Größe der Aufgabe gefährdet: Die Kosmologie ist prinzipiell nicht verstehbar, ein Motiv, das erneut mit zwei Zitaten aus dem II. Buch des *Moreh Nevukhim* Kapitel 24 untermauert wird, in dem Maimonides tatsächlich die inneren Aporien der philosophischen kosmologischen Systeme beschreibt.[41] Auch diese Zitate schreibt er jedoch wieder nicht Maimonides persönlich, sondern den *Cabalistae* allgemein zu, obwohl er kurz vorher darauf verweist, nach Meinung des *Rambam* sei Abraham ein *insignis astrologus* gewesen, womit Reuchlin vermutlich auf den Beginn des 29. Kapitels im III. Buch des *Moreh Nevukhim* anspielt.[42]

Demgegenüber hebt Reuchlin die Erhabenheit der Kabbalah als Metaphysik (*mercava*) unter anderem durch ein Diktum aus dem talmudischen Traktat

---

38 Ibid., fol. IIIb; Reuchlin zitiert dies nach einem bisher nicht identifizierbaren *Commentator arboris decem Sephiroth*.

39 Ibid., fol. IIIb; zitiert als Auslegung der *magistri* zu Psalm 36:10.

40 Ibid., fol. IIIIa.

41 Reuchlin zitiert ibid., fol. IIIIb, die Sätze כל מה שבשמים לא ידע האדם דבר אלא בזה השעור הלמודי המעט („und über alles im Himmel weiß der Mensch nicht mehr als dieses kleine mathematische Maß") sowie כי הלמודים לא נשלמו בזמנו („denn die [mathematischen] Wissenschaften waren zu dieser Zeit noch unvollkommen").

42 An dieser Stelle kommt vermutlich ein spezielles Übersetzungsverständnis Reuchlins zum Ausdruck, da er die Formulierung ידוע אברהם אבינו ע"ה גדל באמונת הצאבה als „er war groß (*insignis*) im Glauben der Sabier" und nicht „er wuchs auf" übersetzt.

Chagiga hervor, das ebenso aus dem *Moreh Nevukhim* stammt[43] wie das Maimonides-Zitat, nach dem die Physik (wie auch die Metaphysik) menschlichen Wesen nicht erklärbar sei.[44]

Der zweite Argumentationskomplex, in dem Maimonides eine noch wichtigere Rolle spielt, findet sich am Ende des ersten Buches von *De Arte Cabalistica* und kann als groß angelegte Gegenüberstellung der „Talmudisten" und der „Kabbalisten" angesehen werden.[45] Diese Gegenüberstellung beginnt mit der berühmten Gleichsetzung von *Maʿaseh Berešit* und *Maʿaseh Merkavah* mit Physik und Metaphysik aus der Einleitung des *Moreh Nevukhim,* obwohl Reuchlin auch hier wieder von den Kabbalisten schlechthin spricht.[46] In deutlich renaissancistischer Analogie-Liebe setzt Reuchlin damit auch die Begriffe *ʿOlam ha-ze* und *ʿOlam ha-bah* („diese Welt" und „die kommende Welt") gleich, wozu er ein indirekt aus dem 62. Kapitel des I. Buches des *Moreh Nevukhim* zitiertes talmudisches Diktum anführt (Babylonischer Talmud, *Qiddushin* 71a): אהוב למעלה ונחמד למטה ונוחל שני עולמים העולם הזה והעולם הבא – „Geliebt oben und angesehen unten, und er wird die beiden Welten erben, diese Welt und die kommende Welt".[47]

Reuchlin treibt diese Antithese von „Physikern" und „Metaphysikern" – Talmudisten und Kabbalisten – aber noch weiter: Er beschreibt, wie die Talmudisten auf die wörtliche Erklärung der 613 Gebote und Verbote (תרי"ג) ausgerichtet seien, während die Kabbalisten das Gesetz zwar alle hingebungsvoll erfüllen, aber die אנשי עיון מבעלי התורה – „die spekulativen Denker unter den Anhängern der Tora" – sind (III. Buch, Kapitel 26).[48] Sie zögen sich daher vom öffentlichen Geschäft so weit als möglich zurück, denn (hier zitiert Reuchlin wieder Maimonides aus dem III. Buch, Kapitel 27, im Namen der Kabbalisten) כוונת כל התורה שני דברים והם תקון הנפש ותקון הגוף – „die Absicht der gesamten Tora besteht in zwei Dingen: die Vervollkommnung der Seele und die Vervollkommnung des Körpers".[49]

Weiter stellt Reuchlin die grundlegenden Unterschiede zwischen Talmudisten und Kabbalisten in der Auslegung des Schöpfungsberichtes dar, die stark an die Ausführungen von Maimonides im 29. Kapitel des II. Buches des *Moreh Nevukhim* über den Wortsinn des biblischen Berichts erinnern, und kommt schließlich auf den Messianismus in kabbalistischer und talmudistischer

---

43 Reuchlin, ibid., fol. Vb; vgl. Babylonischer Talmud, *Chagigah* 13a, zitiert nach *Moreh Nevukhim,* I. Buch, Kapitel 34.

44 Reuchlin zitiert ibid., fol. VIa, aus *Moreh Nevukhim,* Einleitung: כי להגיד כח מעשה בראשית לבשר ודם אי איפשר.

45 Vgl. dazu auch Moshe Idels Einleitung zu Goodman und Goodman, *On the Art of the Kabbalah* (wie Anm. 34), S. xxi–xxiii.

46 Reuchlin, *De Arte Cabalistica* (wie Anm. 34), fol. XIIIIb; vgl. *Moreh Nevukhim,* Einleitung: שמעשה בראשית הוא חכמת הטבע ומעשה מרכבה הוא חכמת האלהות.

47 Reuchlin, *De Arte Cabalistica* (wie Anm. 34), fol. XVa.

48 Ibid., fol. XVa.

49 Ibid., fol. XVb.

Deutung zu sprechen. Hiermit erreicht Reuchlin gewissermaßen die Klimax seiner Darstellung: Mit Verweis auf Maimonides' *Mišneh Torah* hebt Reuchlin deutlich den nicht politisch-nationalen Charakter des Messianismus hervor, sondern ganz im maimonidischen Sinn die spirituelle, geistige Dimension des messianischen Erlösung.[50]

Der Argumentationsgang dieser Passage macht deutlich, wie stark Reuchlin seine Definition der Kabbalah auf maimonidische Gedanken gründet. Zugespitzt kann man formulieren, dass sich hier nicht eine kabbalistische Lesart des Maimonides, sondern eine maimonidische Lesart der Kabbalah abzeichnet. Dabei ist besonders hervorzuheben, dass Reuchlin in der Frage des jüdischen Gesetzes Talmudisten und Kabbalisten durchaus nicht gegeneinander ausspielt, sondern betont, dass die Kabbalisten die Gebote hingebungsvoll befolgten (*teste veritate viri sint legem pie observantes*).[51] Nach Auffassung Reuchlins führen also Kabbalah und „Metaphysik" nicht zur automatischen Abrogation des Gesetzes, womit er sich auf eine – insbesondere für einen Christen – erstaunlich positive und mit Maimonides verwandte Position hinsichtlich der Funktion des Gesetzes für den „Metaphysiker" festlegt. An kaum einer Stelle wird so deutlich wie hier, dass es Reuchlin in *De Arte Cabalistica* keinesfalls nur um eine christliche Deutung der Kabbalah gegangen ist, sondern durchaus ein ausgewogenes Gesamtbild gezeichnet werden sollte.[52]

Der dritte Argumentationskomplex, in dem Maimonides eine Rolle spielt, ist aus originär maimonidischer Sicht vielleicht besonders problematisch. Er behandelt die kabbalistische Schöpfungstheologie im dritten Buch von *De Arte Cabalistica* und verbindet Kabbalistisches mit Elementen aus mehreren Kapiteln des *Moreh Nevukhim* (I. Buch, Kapitel 61; II. Buch, Kapitel 26 und 29–30). Dabei setzt Reuchlin mit einer ganz unproblematisch postulierten Schöpfung der Welt aus Gottes Lichtgewand ein, wofür er auf das Diktum מאור לבושו לקח („vom Licht seines Gewandes nahm Er", das heißt Gott) aus dem dritten Kapitel der *Pirqe de-Rabbi Eliezer* verweist, das Reuchlin sowohl aus dem 26. Kapitel des II. Buches des *Moreh Nevukhim* als auch aus dem kabbalistischen Werk *Ginnat Egoz* des Joseph Gikatilla kannte.[53] Dieses Gewand setzt Reuchlin nun mit dem

50 Ibid., fol. XVIIa–b. Reuchlins direkte Quelle für dieses Zitat ist bislang noch nicht identifiziert, da Reuchlin den Text der *Mišneh Torah* nicht selber besaß.

51 Ibid., fol. XVa.

52 Zwei weitere Maimonides-Zitate im ersten Buch von *De Arte Cabalistica* finden sich in der schöpfungstheologischen Passage fol. XVIa (aus *Moreh Nevukhim*, II. Buch, Kapitel 30: התחלה ברא השם העליונים והתחתונים) und fol. XVIIa, wo Reuchlin ein Zitat aus dem Babylonischen Talmud, *Berakhot* 18a, aus dem *Moreh Nevukhim*, I. Buch, Kapitel 42, wiedergibt.

53 Ibid., fol. LIIIa. Vgl. Gikatilla, *Sefer Ginnat Egoz*, ed. M. Attiah (Jerusalem: Yešivat ha-Ḥayyim we-ha-Šalom, 1989), S. 166 und S. 191, der sich ebenfalls auf Maimonides beruft. Hierbei handelt es sich um die einzige Stelle, an der Reuchlin Maimonides neben einem kabbalistischen Werk zitiert. Dennoch scheint sich der Diskussionsfaden Reuchlins eher an Maimonides als an Gikatilla zu orientieren.

Reich der Ideen (*mundus idearum*) gleich, also der *vorletzten* Stufe der Erkenntnis vor der Erkenntnis Gottes selbst.[54] Die höchste Stufe der Erkenntnis besteht aber in der Erkenntnis Gottes, die Reuchlin im Sinne der Ausführungen des Maimonides im 61. Kapitel des I. Buches des *Moreh Nevukhim* mit dem Tetragramm identifiziert, worin unzweifelhaft Reuchlins kabbalistisches Interesse zum Tragen kommt. Vor der Schöpfung, so fährt Reuchlin mit einem aus demselben Kapitel im *Moreh Nevukhim* übernommenen Zitat aus den *Pirqe de-Rabbi Eliezer* fort, „existierte nur Gott und sein Name" (עד שלא נברא העולם היה הקב"ה ושמו בלבד).[55] Dies wiederum setzt Reuchlin in Analogie zu einem anderen Maimonides-Zitat, dass „am Anfang nichts war als der Name und seine Weisheit" (תחילה שלא היה שום דבר נמצא כלל אלא השם וחכמתו, II. Buch, Kapitel 29), und führt dies noch weiter bis hin zur Schaffung der Elemente aus, wobei er nochmals auf den schöpfungstheologischen Komplex im 30. Kapitel des II. Buches des *Moreh Nevukhim* verweist.[56]

Diese Art von emanationistischer Schöpfungstheologie, die mit Maimonides freilich nur noch wenig zu tun hat (selbst wenn sie durch eine Lektüre des vierten Kapitels im II. Buch möglich erscheinen mag), nimmt Reuchlin an anderer Stelle[57] mit Verweis auf das Zitat aus den *Pirqe de-Rabbi Eliezer* erneut auf, und zwar mit dem Hinweis darauf, dass Maimonides den Aktiven Intellekt mit einem Engel identifiziere.[58]

Im Gegensatz zu den vorangegangenen Argumentationen zur Typologie der Kabbalisten versus Talmudisten wird hier deutlich, wie weit sich Reuchlin – scheinbar *mit* Maimonides – von Maimonides entfernen konnte. Dabei lässt sich kaum noch feststellen, ob er sich der so entstandenen Differenzen überhaupt bewusst war. Es ist aber auffällig, dass Reuchlin paradoxerweise gerade hier, wo er Maimonides' Gedanken besonders stark kabbalistisch umformte, den *Moreh Nevukhim* ausdrücklich und nicht mehr als Worte der *Cabalistae* zitiert. Darauf wird zurückzukommen sein.

Der letzte Argumentationskomplex in *De Arte Cabalistica*, in dem sich Reuchlin an zentraler Stelle auf Maimonides beruft, ist seine Kritik an der Theurgie und Magie. Grundsätzlich wäre von einem kabbalistisch inspirierten Geist, der auch noch von Abulafia beeinflusst worden sein soll, zu erwarten, dass er eine positive Einstellung zur Theurgie, also der praktischen Anwendung der mystischen Spekulationen, haben müsste. Dies umso mehr, wenn man bedenkt, dass die Renaissance-Kultur insgesamt besonderes Interesse am Thema Magie hatte. Gleichwohl ist das Gegenteil der Fall: An zwei Stellen im dritten Buch von *De Arte Cabalistica* übt Reuchlin explizit Kritik an einem ritualistisch-magischen

54 Ibid., fol. LIIIa.

55 Ibid., fol. LIIIb.

56 Reuchlin, ibid., fol. LIIIb, nennt fälschlich das 26. Kapitel.

57 Ibid., fol. LXXVIIa.

58 Vgl. *Moreh Nevukhim*, I. Buch, Kapitel 4.

beziehungsweise theurgischen Verständnis seiner metaphysisch-kabbalistischen Spekulationen.

In diesem Sinne sagt Reuchlin in einer längeren Passage über Buchstabenpermutationen und die Möglichkeit, durch sie Engel dienstbar machen zu können: „Alle diese Dinge sind für uns gemacht, damit wir aufwachen und angeregt werden, uns hinzuwenden, uns umzuwenden von den sichtbaren zu den unsichtbaren Dingen und den Glauben zu stärken", und fügt anschließend als Begründung das Maimonides-Zitat aus dem 44. Kapitel des II. Buches hinzu: „denn die Zielsetzung dieser Taten ist die ständige Erinnerung an den Namen, seine Furcht, seine Liebe und die Bewahrung aller Gebote, damit man an Gott, gepriesen sei er, glaubt, was alle glauben müssen" (שכונת העבודות ההם זכרון השם תמיד ויראתו ואהבתו ושמירת המצוות כולן שיאמין בשם יתברך מה שהוא הכרחי לכל).[59]

Noch an einer zweiten Stelle kritisiert Reuchlin die magisch-theurgische Verwendung der kabbalistischen Spekulationen und sagt, dass die Kabbalisten diejenigen „dumme Lügner" (*mendaces et stultos*) nennen, die Figuren, Schriften oder Sprüchen wundertätige Kraft zuschreiben, wie Maimonides im 62. Kapitel des ersten Buches des *More Nevukhim* darlegt – also in dem bereits mehrfach zitierten Kapitel über den Gottesnamen.[60]

Fasst man diese Beobachtungen zur Verwendung des *Moreh Nevukhim* in *De Arte Cabalistica* zusammen, so wird wiederum deutlich, dass Reuchlin weit davon entfernt ist, Maimonides ausschließlich „kabbalistisch" zu lesen. In gewisser Weise verwendet Reuchlin Maimonides zuweilen gerade in umgekehrter Richtung im Sinne einer „maimonidischen" Zähmung und Domestizierung der Kabbalah als Form einer intellektuellen Erkenntnis, die zu ethischer Reinigung und Festigung des Glaubens führt. Eben dies ist, was Reuchlin an einer Stelle unter Verweis auf Maimonides als Kabbalah על דרך האמת – „in der wahren Methode" bezeichnet.[61]

Vor diesem Hintergrund ist auch die Anonymisierung des Maimonides im ersten Buch von *De Arte Cabalistica* neu zu interpretieren, wo anders als im dritten Buch alle wörtlichen Zitate aus dem *Moreh Nevukhim* als Lehre der Kabbalisten schlechthin dargestellt werden. Dieses Phänomen ist stets als Hinweis gewertet worden, dass Reuchlin Maimonides kabbalistisch interpretiere,[62] eine Vermutung, die durch die Nennung des „*liber perplexorum Rambam*" unter den kabbalistischen Büchern in der so genannten „kabbalistischen Bibliothek" in *De Arte Cabalistica* gestützt zu werden scheint.[63] Richtig ist daran sicher, dass Reuchlin ein weiteres Verständnis von „Kabbalah" hatte, als es heute üblich

59 Reuchlin, *De Arte Cabalistica* (wie Anm. 34), fol. LVIIb.

60 Reuchlin, ibid., fol. LXXVIIIb, schreibt versehentlich 72. Kapitel.

61 Ibid., fol. LXIIIIa; vgl. *Moreh Nevukhim*, Einleitung.

62 Vgl. Idel, *Maïmonide* (wie Anm. 4), S. 51.

63 Reuchlin, *De Arte Cabalistica* (wie Anm. 34), fol. XIIIIa.

ist, und somit Maimonides mit eingeschlossen werden konnte. Andererseits erklärt dies immer noch nicht, warum der „Kabbalist" Maimonides nicht namentlich genannt wird, so dass man vermuten könnte, Reuchlin habe die Zitate aus einer kabbalistischen Quelle übernommen und selbst gar nicht als maimonidisch erkannt. Bislang ist aber kein kabbalistisches Werk bekannt, das gerade die von Reuchlin zitierten Passagen enthielte, geschweige denn, dass es unter seinen auch sonst bekannten Quellen nachgewiesen wäre.[64] Man wird daher davon auszugehen haben, dass die Tilgung von Maimonides' Namen bei den Zitaten im ersten Buch von *De Arte Cabalistica* ein von Reuchlin bewusst gewähltes Stilmittel ist, das er im dritten Buch aus nicht erklärlichen Gründen aufgab. So kann das Maimonides-Bild in *De Arte Cabalistica* als Versuch bezeichnet werden, Maimonides als „Kabbalisten" zu präsentieren, ohne dass es zuträfe, Reuchlin deute ihn einseitig „kabbalistisch" um.

5. Zusammenfassung

Reuchlin war der erste christliche Leser des hebräischen *Moreh Nevukhim*. Dieses Buch hat ihn vermutlich seit seiner dritten Italienreise (1498) begleitet, und er zitiert es wiederholt in unterschiedlichen Kontexten, so dass kein Zweifel daran bestehen kann, dass er das Buch intensiv gelesen hat. Die These, Reuchlin habe Maimonides nur durch Pico della Mirandola und durch dessen abulafianische Sichtweise wahrgenommen, trägt im Hinblick auf Reuchlins Werk nicht. Vielmehr lässt sich beobachten, dass sich Reuchlin schnell von der polemischen

64 Von den kabbalistischen Handschriften aus Reuchlins Besitz hat sich nur eine erhalten, die das *Sefer Ginnat Egoz* und eine lateinische Übersetzung des *Sefer Yeṣirah* enthält. Besonders umstritten ist die Frage der Identität einer kabbalistischen Sammelhandschrift, die vermutlich dem Typ der Handschrift *Halberstam 444* (heute New York, JTSL 1887) entsprach. Ein Text, der als Quelle für die Maimonides-Zitate in Frage kommt, findet sich dort jedoch nicht. Hinzuweisen ist auch auf einen anonymen Kommentar zu dem Baum der *Sefirot* (*commentator arboris decem Sephiroth*), den Reuchlin mehrfach zitiert (zum Beispiel *De Rudimentis Hebraicis* [wie Anm. 8], S. 80 und 123, *De Arte Cabalistica* [wie Anm. 34], fol. IIIb), der aber bisher nicht identifiziert werden konnte. Er war vermutlich weder Bestandteil der oben genannten Sammelhandschrift, noch ist er mit dem von M. Idel als Teil des *Midraš ha-Ne'elam* identifizierten Textes identisch, den Reuchlin als *Sefirot*-Kommentar einem *Rabi Tedacus* zuschreibt; vgl. zu Letzterem Moshe Idel, „An Unknown Text from *Midrash Hane'elam*" (hebräisch), in Josef Dan (Ed.), *The Age of the Zohar* (Jerusalem Studies in Jewish Thought 8; Jerusalem: Magnes, 1989), S. 73–87. Zumindest im Falle des Zitats in *De Arte Cabalistica*, fol. IIIb, ist auffällig, dass Maimonides in ganz engem Kontext mit dem anonymen *Sefirot*-Kommentar zitiert wird. Ob dies aber für die Vermutung ausreicht, dass dieser Text weitere relevante Zitate aus Maimonides enthielt, bleibt zweifelhaft; vgl. zu diesem Text auch von Abel/Leicht, *Verzeichnis* (wie Anm. 7), Kap. 1.3.1.

Verwendung des *Moreh Nevukhim* in der *Tütsch Missive* hin zu einem Maimonides-Verständnis entwickelt hat, das den Subtilitäten der maimonidischen Argumentationen zwar nicht immer folgt und Maimonides' Werk als komplexes Denksystem nicht wahrnimmt. Dennoch war Reuchlin durchaus bereit, sich von Maimonides an verschiedenen Stellen leiten zu lassen: Dies zeigt sich nicht nur in der Darstellung des „Kabbalisten", der manche Kennzeichen von Maimonides' Philosophen trägt, sondern vielleicht noch deutlicher an solchen Punkten, an denen Reuchlin klar gegen den Erwartungshorizont seiner Leser verstößt: Hier ist die strikte Ablehnung der Theurgie ebenso zu nennen wie die Auffassung, dass die intellektuelle Erkenntnis nicht die Abrogation des jüdischen Gesetzes impliziere.

Verbindet man diese Punkte mit dem, was als Anleihen aus Maimonides in der Epistemologie und der Messianologie angesehen werden kann, so entsteht nicht so sehr das Bild einer kabbalistischen oder gar abulafianischen Maimonides-Lektüre durch Reuchlin als das einer maimonidischen Lesart der Kabbalah als intellektueller Erkenntnis hin zum Glauben. Maimonides war für Reuchlin einer der wichtigsten Zugänge zu dem, was er als die Urweisheit der Juden ansah, er war ihm eine Art *praeparatio cabalistica*, die in manchen Punkten für Reuchlins Verständnis der Kabbalah prägend blieb. Auch wenn vieles von dem, was in *De Arte Cabalistica* gesagt wird, den philosophischen und religiösen Ideen der christlichen Kultur seiner Zeit entspringt, zeigt sich somit dennoch, dass Reuchlin Maimonides trotz aller Beschränkungen durchaus eigenständig und mit Erfolg gelesen hat. Dies macht ihn selbst vielleicht nicht zu einem großen Philosophen und auch kaum zu einem besonders scharfsinnigen Maimonides-Interpreten, aber doch zu einer einzigartigen und höchst bemerkenswerten Persönlichkeit.

Index of Names and Subjects

Index of Modern Authors